D0906359

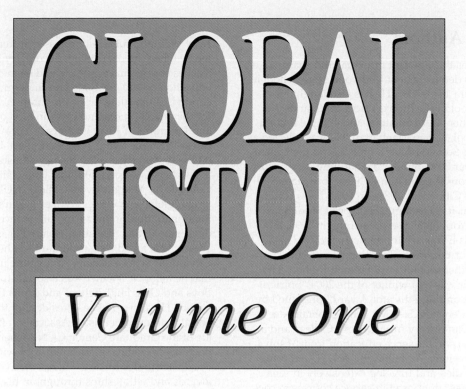

GLOBAL HISTORY

Volume One

The Ancient World to the Age of Revolution

Mark Willner, M.S.
Adjunct Faculty, Brooklyn College
Former Assistant Principal and Chairman of the Social Studies Department,
Midwood High School at Brooklyn College, Brooklyn, NY

George Hero, M.A.
Director of Social Science Research, Midwood High School
at Brooklyn College, Brooklyn, NY

Jerry Weiner, Ph.D.
Professor, Kean University, NJ
Former Social Studies Supervisor at Boys and Girls High School
and Louis D. Brandeis High School

About the Authors

Mark Willner was the assistant principal and chairman of the social studies department at Midwood High School in Brooklyn, NY from 1973–2005. He has also taught at Morris High School in the Bronx, Wadleigh (Harlem) Evening High School in Manhattan, and Temple Emanu-El Religious School, also in Manhattan. He was selected as the "Outstanding Social Studies Supervisor in the United States" for the year 2000. Similar outstanding supervisory honors were bestowed upon him in New York State (1991) and in New York City (1984, 1988). In 1997, New York State chose him as its "Distinguished Social Studies Educator." New York State also chose him, in 1995, to receive the "Louis E. Yavner Teaching Award for Outstanding Contributions to Teaching About The Holocaust and Other Violations of Human Rights." His most recent honor was as a winner of the 2004 "Spirit of Anne Frank Outstanding Educator Award" presented by The Anne Frank Center, U.S.A. Mr. Willner obtained a bachelor's degree in history from Queens College and a master's degree in social science education from Yeshiva University. As a recipient of Fulbright, N.E.H. and other grants, he has studied and traveled extensively in Asia and Europe. He has supervised in-service courses in conjunction with consulates, museums, and universities in New York City on China, India, Japan, Korea, the Middle East, and the Holocaust.

He is a past President of the New York City Social Studies Supervisors Association (SSSA), and has sat on the Executive Boards of the New York State SSSA and the New York City Association of Teachers of Social Studies/United Federation of Teachers (ATSS/UFT). He is currently one of the twelve members on the Executive Board of the NSSSA (National Social Studies Supervisors Association). Mr. Willner is the lead author of Barron's *Let's Review: Global History and Geography*. He has also contributed to Barron's *Regents Exams and Answers: Global History and Geography, Regents Exams and Answers: U.S. History and Government*, and *CLEP (How to Prepare for the College Level Exam Program)*. He has been a frequent presenter at social studies conferences on the national, state, and local levels.

George Hero has taught in the social studies department of Midwood High School at Brooklyn College in New York City since 1984. He is also the founder and director of the Social Science Research program at Midwood. A specialist in Eastern European History, he has also taught at Brooklyn College and Long Island University. Mr. Hero serves as the co-Chairperson of the Human Rights Committee of the World Federation for Mental Health. He is a co-author of Barron's *Global Studies, Volume II*. In recent years, he has worked on a new edition of American diplomat George Horton's account of the persecution of Christians in Turkey, *The Blight of Asia*. In 2003, he won an award for the "Outstanding Teacher of Social Studies" in New York City. Currently, he is an adjunct faculty member at Brooklyn College, and a concultant/education coordinator with the Gilder Lehman Institute of American History.

Jerry Weiner, Ph.D. is a professor at Kean University in New Jersey where he coordinates Secondary Education Programs, teaches courses in secondary and elementary social studies education on the graduate and undergraduate levels, and supervises graduate thesis preparation. He is also responsible for the development and coordination of European Studies and Programs at Kean University. Dr. Weiner has had a long career in public and private education. He has taught classes on the university level in history and social studies education at Teachers College, Columbia University, and Hunter College and Medgar Evers College, CUNY. He has also taught global economics courses in Europe at the Ecole Superieure de Commerce in Pau, France and the Universidad de Deusto in San Sebastian, Spain. For many years, Dr. Weiner was an administrator and teacher in the New York City public school system. Among the numerous positions that he held, Dr. Weiner was a social studies supervisor at Boys and Girls High School and Louis D. Brandeis High School. He also served as President of the New York City Social Studies Supervisors Association (SSSA). He is a graduate of the Graduate Center, CUNY where he was awarded his doctorate in Latin American History with a specialization in Brazilian Studies in 1980. He has received a number of awards and fellowships throughout his academic career and as an educator. Among these honors were a Fulbright Fellowship for Study in Brazil in 1976–1977 and the John Brunzel award for outstanding social studies supervision in 1987. Dr. Weiner is the author of many books and articles dealing with history and social studies education. Among these works, he has participated in the writing of all Barron's "Let's Review World and Global History" editions.

Unless otherwise specified, all photos have been supplied by The Granger Collection, New York.

Photos on front cover: Piazzadella Rotonda, Rome; Great Wall of China; Stonehenge; Chichen Itza; Person riding camel near Taj Mahal.

Photos on back cover: Pyramids in Egypt; Ruined castle; Machu Picchu; The Potala; Columns & statues in Madrid.

All inquiries should be addressed to:
Barron's Educational Series, Inc.
250 Wireless Boulevard
Hauppauge, New York 11788
http://www.barronseduc.com

ISBN-13: 978-0-7641-5811-7
ISBN-10: 0-7641-5811-2

Library of Congress Catalog No. 2004057490

Library of Congress Cataloging-in-Publication Data
Willner, Mark.
    Global history / by Mark Willner, George Hero, Jerry Weiner.
        p. cm.
    Includes biographical references and index.
    ISBN 0-7641-5811-2
    1. World history. I. Hero, George. II. Weiner, Jerry III. Title.
D21.W735 2005
909—dc22   2004057490

Printed in China
9 8 7 6 5 4 3 2 1

Contents

Preface   vi

Introduction to the Social Sciences   ix

ERA I

THE ANCIENT WORLD: CIVILIZATIONS AND RELIGION (4,000 B.C.E.–500 C.E.)

Introduction   1

Chapter 1   **Ancient Middle East and Africa**   2

Chapter 2   **Ancient Southern and Eastern Asia**   28

Section 1: Ancient India   29
Section 2: Ancient China   42
Section 3: Ancient Southeast Asia   49
Section 4: Ancient Japan   51
Section 5: Ancient Korea   55

Chapter 3   **The Greco-Roman World**   64

Section 1: Ancient Greece   65
Section 2: The Hellenistic World   83
Section 3: Ancient Rome   91

Chapter 4   **Ancient America and the Caribbean**   130

ERA II

EXPANDING ZONES OF EXCHANGE AND ENCOUNTER (500–1200)

Introduction   151

Chapter 5   **The Byzantine Empire and the Rise of Eastern European Nations**   152

Chapter 6   **Medieval Europe**   174

Chapter 7   **The Rise and Spread of Islam**   208

Chapter 8   **Asia**   226

    Section 1: Southern Asia   227
    Section 2: China   228

Chapter 9   **Changing Times in the Americas**   236

ERA III

GLOBAL INTERACTIONS (1200–1650)

Introduction   253

Chapter 10   **The Renaissance**   254

Chapter 11   **The Reformation**   276

Chapter 12   **The Commercial Revolution**   296

Chapter 13   **Global Interactions in Asia**   316

    Section 1: The Mongols   317
    Section 2: The Yuan Dynasty   319
    Section 3: Japan and Korea   321

Chapter 14   **Empires in the Americas**   334

ERA IV   **THE FIRST GLOBAL AGE (1450–1770)**

Introduction   **355**

Chapter 15   **The Rise of Nation-States**   **356**

     Section 1: England   357
     Section 2: France   363
     Section 3: Spain   370
     Section 4: Austria   374
     Section 5: Prussia   376

Chapter 16   **The Growth of Democracy in England**   **384**

Chapter 17   **The Age of Exploration**   **406**

Chapter 18   **Civilizations in Africa**   **428**

Chapter 19   **Additional Globalism in the Middle East and Asia**   **442**

     Section 1: The Middle East and Eastern
                Europe Under Ottoman Rule   443
     Section 2: The Muslims in India   447
     Section 3: The Ming Dynasty in China   451

ERA V   **AN AGE OF REVOLUTIONS (1750–1826)**

Introduction   **461**

Chapter 20   **The Enlightenment and the Scientific Revolution**   **462**

Chapter 21   **The French Revolution**   **484**

Chapter 22   **Revolution and War in the Age of Napoleon**   **504**

     Indexes
     General Index 529   Event Index 542   Maps Index 544
     Names Index 545   Era I Index 548   Era II Index 553
     Era III Index 557   Era IV Index 560   Era V Index 563

Preface

FOR WHICH COURSE WAS THIS BOOK DESIGNED?

This book was designed to be used as the first volume of a basic two-volume high school text for a two-year, four-term study of the world—its history and its people. It can also be used in a one-year, two-term study. The material is presented in a manner that is appropriate for an introductory survey course. This volume covers the regions of Africa, Asia, Europe, and Latin America, from ancient times to the early nineteenth century.

WHAT ARE THE SPECIAL FEATURES OF THIS BOOK?

The information included here is mainly historical. It is a global history book. We begin with a general introduction to the social sciences. We then embark on a "trip through time" as we "travel" from ancient civilizations onward. Additional features of the book that you should know about include:

1. **A great deal of attention, more than is usual in a textbook, is given to the history of Eastern Europe and the former Soviet Union.** These areas of Europe have undergone crucial changes during your lifetime. A background historical knowledge is needed to understand these changes. Even with the publication of this book, historic events are occurring there that will have an impact in this century. Americans of your general need to be well-informed about these areas and how they have changed.

2. **All the authors of this book are high school social studies teachers.** This is very rarely the case with high school history textbooks. The authors have, combined, more than eighty years of successful experience in teaching global history classes. Much of this book is based upon that experience and therefore contains information that students such as you need to know. The authors also have traveled in the regions described, can speak several foreign languages, and have earned fine reputations for writing other instructional material on global issues.

3. **This book also explains, and has references to, various concepts and issues described in the global history and geography part of the social studies**

syllabus of New York State and that of other states. The fifteen key history concepts are change, choice, citizenship, culture, diversity, empathy, environment, human rights, identity, interdependence, justice, political systems, power, scarcity, and technology. The five key geography concepts are the world in spatial terms (places and regions), physical systems, human systems, environment and society, and the uses of geography. The eleven major world issues are population, war and peace, terrorism, energy resources and allocations, human rights, hunger and poverty, world trade and finance, environmental concerns, political and economic refugees, economic growth and development, and determination of political and economic systems.

4. **Each historical era in the book is broken into chapters and sections.** Enriching the text chapters are questions, maps, timelines, and charts.

5. **Significant attention is focused on Africa, Asia, and Latin America.** These are the areas where most of the world's people live and where the earliest known civilizations began.

SPECIAL MESSAGE TO HIGH SCHOOL STUDENTS OF THE TWENTY-FIRST CENTURY

In this book and in volume II, you will learn much about the past history of the four major world regions outside the United States—Africa, Asia, Europe, and Latin America. As a result, you will be able to understand the world that exists now and the world that will exist in the future years of the twenty-first century. The world of the 1990s and 2000s—during your lifetime—is different from the world of the twentieth century prior to your birth. During those earlier years, there were many changes on the world map, as well as crucial global events. There were, for example, two "hot" wars, a "cold" war, and several revolutions— some bloody and some peaceful. This was the world that your teachers, parents, and grandparents knew and studied about.

The present-day world is a different place, for reasons that you will learn about in this book and in the next volume. In addition, your generation probably knows more about the world than any earlier generation of American high school students. This knowledge has been acquired mainly from outside of school and may stem from one or more of the following reasons:

1. You or someone you know may have already traveled somewhere overseas, in Europe, Africa, Asia, or Latin America.

2. You may know somebody who works for a global company or someone who does business with people from around the world.

3. Television, movies, and advertising carry much information about people in other countries.

4. You may have something in your home that was made in a foreign nation.

5. Through the process of cultural diffusion and education, you may already be familiar with one or more languages other than English. You probably know something about music, sports, clothes, cosmetics, and food that are originated elsewhere.

6. The United States is a multicultural society. Throughout our nation, and probably right in your own community, are people who can trace their ancestry to different parts of the globe.

7. In each year of your lifetime, thousands of foreign tourists have traveled to the United States. Perhaps you have met some of them in your community.

SUMMARY

Although citizens of the United States, you, your family, and your friends are also "citizens of a global community." To understand this community, you are about to begin a study of it. Africa, Asia, Europe, and Latin America have strongly influenced our own nation's history. And of ironic historical interest, it is the United States that has greatly influenced the global community during the past two centuries. What will be the nature of the United States' relations with that community in the twenty-first century? Your generation's actions may well furnish the answer to this question. Upon reading this textbook, you will be well informed and well equipped to take your place as a citizen of the United States and of the world.

Good luck with this book. It will help you in your travels through the world—past, present, and future.

Mark Willner

Introduction to the Social Sciences

Social science is the term used for all or any of the branches of study that deal with humans in their social, economic, and political relations. These studies are referred to as the social sciences. Modern social sciences use the scientific method. The use of this organized and systematic way of research dates from the eighteenth century. Social sciences use quantitative methods and statistical techniques to analyze humans and their behavior with each other.

The social sciences are sometimes called the people sciences. Social sciences help us to understand how people lived and acted in the past as well as the present. The social sciences are anthropology, geography, history, political science, economics, sociology, and psychology. In all of these subject areas, scientists have their special interests and areas of expertise. The information that social scientists collect and analyze helps us to interpret how people behave and the reasons why events occurred.

History in its broadest sense is the story of all people and their past. History is closely related to the social sciences when it is studied and written about in a systematic and scientific way. History is the record of human accomplishments and failures. It is the story of how people have lived on our planet since the beginning of recorded events. Historians are people who study and write about human beings, events, and places in the world since the beginning of recorded civilization. To write about history, they use different records that tell them about our past. Historical records help the historian to analyze and explain how and why things happened the way they did so that we can learn from the past. Historians look for all kinds of evidence about why events happened. For this reason, the other areas of the social sciences are important to historians if they want to get a complete story. Sometimes historians write about situations in the hope that the same type of event will not happen again. This is particularly true of wars and situations in parts of the world where acts of genocide occurred.

THE METHODS AND SKILLS OF HISTORICAL ANALYSIS

Various methods can be used to study and analyze history. These methods of historical analysis and study require different types of skills.

- Interpretations of historical events are investigated. Developing perspectives or pictures and perceptions or understandings are the key skills in this type of analysis and study of history.

- Hypotheses about interpretations of historical events are investigated. The skill of constructing hypotheses that work is essential in this method of study and analysis.

- Examination of primary historical evidence leads to explanation and analysis. Finding differences and classifying types of evidence are crucial in this method.

- Concepts or ideas and themes are studied over a period of time. The skills in developing a conceptual or thematic framework are important in this method.

- Comparisons and contrasts are made concerning similar types of historical events. The skill to make proper comparisons and contrasts is essential in this method of analysis and study.

Economics is the study of how human beings use resources to produce various goods and how these goods are distributed for consumption among people in society. Throughout human history, people have lived and worked in different economic systems. These economic systems include barter, capitalism, fascism, socialism, and communism. Economists use complex mathematical techniques and statistical data in economic forecasting and analysis and management of resources.

Sociology is the scientific study of human behavior. As the study of humans in their collective or group aspect, sociology is concerned with all group activities—economic, social, political, and religious. Sociology tries to determine the laws governing human behavior in social contexts. Sociologists investigate a selected group of social facts or relations.

Psychology is the science or study of living things and their interactions with the environment. Psychologists study processes of how people sense other people, things, and their own feelings. They concentrate on the development of learning, motivations, personality, and the interactions of the individual and the group. Psychology is concerned with human behavior and its physiological and psychological basis.

Anthropology is the study, classification, and analysis of humans and their society—descriptively, historically, and physically. Its unique contribution to studying the links of human social relations has been the special concept of culture. Its emphasis is on data from nonliterate peoples and archaeological remains explorations. Anthropologists study the characteristics, customs, and cultures of people.

Political science is the study of government, political processes, institutions, and political behavior. Political scientists study and comment on fields such as political theory, national and local government, comparative government, and international relations. Political scientists are often called upon to make predictions about politics such as elections and people's reactions to different events.

GEOGRAPHY—THE PHYSICAL WORLD

Human beings and societies in all regions of the earth share a common global environment. This environment is a closed system consisting of a variety of physical features—land forms, bodies of water, vegetation and animal species, and climatic regions. These physical features are the result of several natural processes including the rotation and revolution of the earth, geological activity, the water cycle, and biological interactions.

The environment provides humans with a variety of renewable and non-renewable resources, which can be used to meet the needs of both individuals and societies. Though these needs are basic to all humans, the different ways in which these are met are determined by the differences in environments that exist from one part of the earth to another.

The land surface of the earth is generally divided into seven large land masses, called continents—North America, South America, Asia, Africa, Europe, Australia, and Antarctica. Large bodies of water, called oceans—Atlantic, Pacific, Indian, and Arctic—and smaller ones called seas cover about 70 percent of the earth's surface. The bodies of water separate some of the continents from one another.

In recent centuries, humans have improved their abilities to use more of the earth's limited resources, and technology has created closer contacts among peoples of different cultures. This global interdependence has made it increasingly important to understand the similarities and differences among cultures. Hopefully, such understanding will aid in solving shared problems and resolving disputes between peoples of different cultures.

MAPS AND THEIR USES

We can illustrate much information about the world with maps, but we must be aware of their limitations and distortions. Projecting the features of a sphere (the globe) on a flat surface (a map) can distort sizes and distances, especially when we attempt to show the entire world.

Attempting to illustrate the shapes of land masses correctly can distort the sizes of the land masses. On the other hand, trying to show size can distort shape, as in the Gall-Peters projection. Thus, maps can convey inaccurate impressions of the importance and influence of certain areas of the world.

Placement or location can give false impressions of the relationships among regions or the relative importance of an area. For example, in the Mercator projection, with the Atlantic Ocean in the middle, North America and Europe are located top center. This seems to illustrate both the importance and the closeness of their relationship. Compare the Mercator projection and the Japan Airlines map. The Japan Airlines map centers on the Pacific Ocean and therefore islands in the Pacific become important. If you look at the Macarthur Corrective Map, which was created by Australians, you will see a different story and emphasis in which land areas in the South Pacific are prominent.

Reading maps requires an understanding of their language. The scale provides a tool for determining distances. A map's legend or key provides information about the meanings of lines, symbols, colors, and other markings found on the map itself.

Modern technology has changed how we think about the size of the world. Actual (or absolute) distance has become less important than relative distance—how quickly communication and transportation can move ideas and people from one part of the world to another. Culture regions once separated by thousands of miles or formidable physical barriers now interact with one another.

Maps can present information in many ways. A topographical map attempts to show physical features, a political map focuses on the way humans divide up the world (the boundaries of nations), and economic maps illustrate the ways in which people use the environment and resources. Comparing specific maps, such as rainfall patterns and population distribution, can be useful in understanding ways of life and the relationships between humans and the world in which they live.

ERA I

THE ANCIENT WORLD: CIVILIZATIONS AND RELIGION

(4000 B.C.E.–500 C.E.)

INTRODUCTION

History is the result of actions taken by people. We learn about these actions from various sources. The sources can be written records, as well as buildings, artwork, fossils, and various artifacts. Who were the earliest humans and what have we learned about them? How did their civilizations and empires emerge? What were their political, economic, and religious belief systems? Our attempts to answer these questions for the time era from 4000 B.C.E. to 500 C.E. will concern us in this part of the book. To do this, we will travel around the globe to four areas: Africa, Europe, Asia, and Latin America.

Each early civilization in these areas has much to teach us. We will be introduced, for example, to ancient Egyptians, Greeks, Chinese, and Latin American Indians. Are there links between their cultures and our own? Were their leaders the kind of people whom we should admire? You will find the answers in the following pages. Welcome aboard as we travel through time to distant lands.

CHAPTER I

Ancient Middle East and Africa

TIMELINE OF EVENTS

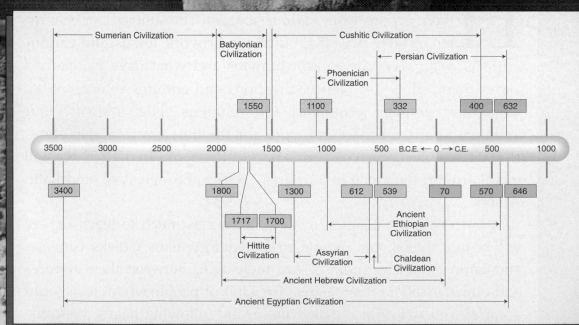

Sumerian Civilization

Babylonian Civilization

Cushitic Civilization

Persian Civilization

Phoenician Civilization

| 1550 | 1100 | 332 | 400 | 632 |

| 3500 | 3000 | 2500 | 2000 | 1500 | 1000 | 500 | B.C.E. ← 0 → C.E. | 500 | 1000 |

| 3400 | 1800 | 1300 | 612 | 539 | 70 | 570 | 646 |

| 1717 | 1700 |

Hittite Civilization

Ancient Ethiopian Civilization

Assyrian Civilization

Chaldean Civilization

Ancient Hebrew Civilization

Ancient Egyptian Civilization

Two of the earliest civilizations began in Africa and the Middle East. These were the *Egyptian* and the *Mesopotamian*. Each would have an enormous influence on its neighbors and lead to the creation of new and more technologically advanced societies.

MIDDLE EAST

Mesopotamian Civilization

Hammurabi was Babylon's most famous king. (See the top of page 5.)

In the Middle East, several civilizations developed in **Mesopotamia**, beginning around 4000 B.C.E. The area was part of a region known as the **Fertile Crescent**, which was a large arc of land. It began in the eastern part of the **Mediterranean Sea**, going northward and then southward along the **Tigris** and **Euphrates Rivers**, and ending at the *Persian Gulf*. The Tigris and Euphrates provided an excellent means of communication and transportation for trade as well as fish and waterfowl for food. The area between them was known as Mesopotamia, which means "between the two rivers." The distance between the two rivers was only between 20 and 45 miles at any point. Because the surrounding country was desert, populations were kept from spreading over too large an

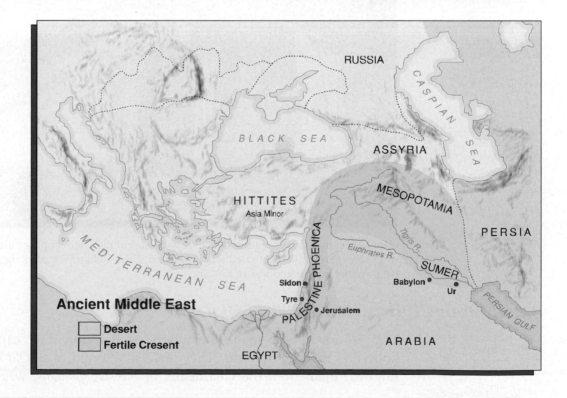

area. These factors encouraged the development of cities and governments, which would regulate trade and create laws to maintain order and encourage cooperation between large numbers of people.

Despite the yearly floods of the rivers, which made the land fertile, the intense heat and limited rainfall in Mesopotamia forced its inhabitants to become creative. The civilizations of the region, beginning with the **Sumerian**, developed irrigation systems and dams. This made large-scale agriculture possible. Due to a limited amount of resources and constant invasions from foreigners, the Mesopotamian cultures became aggressive and warlike. Their religious beliefs showed a greater concern for the present life than the one after death. Their interest in this world influenced the development of science, technology, and mathematics. As was the practice of most ancient civilizations, the Mesopotamians conquered and often enslaved neighboring peoples. Yet, they also developed the concept of social justice, gradually creating laws and a legal system.

Sumerian Civilization (3500–2000 B.C.E.)

The first of the Mesopotamian civilizations, the Sumerians, began in the lower **Tigris-Euphrates valley** around 3500 B.C.E. Between 2800 and 2340 B.C.E., a number of independent Sumerian cities developed. The most important of these were **Ur** and **Lagash**, which became centers of trade and learning. The frequent civil wars between the Sumerian cities ended temporarily under **Sargon I**, who unified them in 2360 B.C.E. After his death, new fighting between the cities began. This led to their decline and conquest around 2000 B.C.E. by the **Amorites**, a **Semitic** tribe from northern **Syria**. The Semites are a branch of the Afro-Asiatic peoples and languages.

The largest buildings in Sumerian cities were ziggurats. Their sloping sides had wide steps, that were sometimes decorated with trees and shrubs. On top of each ziggurat stood a shrine to the chief god or goddess of the city.

Babylonian Civilization (2000–1550 B.C.E.)

The Amorites, who made the village of **Babylon** their capital city, are also known as the **Babylonians**. They are also referred to as *Old Babylonians* to distinguish them from the **Chaldeans** or *Neo-Babylonians*, who later dominated

Mesopotamia. They adopted Sumerian culture but established an *autocracy* or rule by one individual. Their most famous king, **Hammurabi**, who reigned from 1792 to 1750 B.C.E., expanded the empire. He also created one of the first known systems of written laws. Although harsh in its punishments, the **Hammurabi Law Code** did provide order and justice in Babylonia. After his death, the Babylonian state declined and was conquered by the **Kassites** around 1550 B.C.E.

The Kassites were considered to be **barbarians** or uncivilized by the Mesopotamians. They had no interest in continuing the culture of the Sumerians and Babylonians. Their only cultural contribution was the introduction of the horse into the region. Mesopotamian culture almost died out during this period but was saved by the conquest of the region by the **Assyrians**.

Assyrian Civilization (1300–612 B.C.E.)

The Assyrians, another Semitic people, developed a kingdom around 3000 B.C.E. on the **Plateau of Assure** in modern Syria, on the upper part of the Tigris River. Because the region had no natural barriers to protect it, the Assyrians became skillful warriors who were able to drive out invaders. By 1300 B.C.E., the Assyrians began to conquer neighboring lands, developing a large empire that extended to **Asia Minor** (now Modern Turkey) in the west, Egypt in the south, Syria in the north, and **Persia** (present day Iran) in the east. They introduced new military tactics that transformed warfare. This included the use of iron weapons, armor, and techniques for destroying enemy defenses.

The Assyrians developed an efficient central government that ruled the empire from their capital city of **Nineveh**. They valued and adopted the knowledge and cultures gained from their conquered peoples. A library in Nineveh contained clay tablets that preserved the literature of the Mesopotamian civilizations.

> **Main Idea:**
> The Assyrians developed an efficient central government. They valued and adopted the knowledge and cultures gained from their conquered peoples.

By the tenth century B.C.E., the Assyrians conquered Babylonia. Under **Sargon II**, who ruled from 722 to 705 B.C.E., and **Sennacherib**, the king from 705 to 681 B.C.E. who rebuilt Nineveh as a new capital city on the Tigris, Assyrian power reached its height. They grew too large, however, and overextended their military power. By 612 B.C.E., the Assyrians had lost their empire to the Chaldeans, another Semitic people from the southeast.

Chaldean Civilization (612–539 B.C.E.)

Under the Chaldeans or Neo-Babylonians, Babylon was restored as the capital city and Mesopotamian civilization continued. King **Nebuchadnezzar**, who ruled

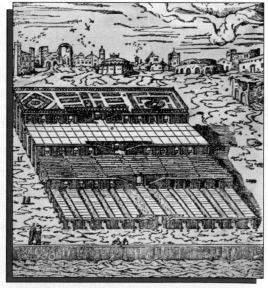

Nebuchadnezzar ordered the construction of the "Hanging Gardens of Babylon," destined to become one of the Seven Wonders of the ancient world. He supposedly built the gardens for his queen to remind her of the mountains and trees of her Median homeland.

from 605 to 562 B.C.E., further expanded the empire by conquering **Judah**. This was the site of modern-day Israel and was the holy land of the *Jewish* people. Many Jews were taken away to Babylon. Their forced slavery there is known as the *Babylonian Captivity*. Anger at the harsh treatment under the Chaldeans led the Jews and other subject peoples to assist the Persians in overthrowing Chaldean rule in 539 B.C.E. Mesopotamia then became part of the Persian Empire.

Mesopotamian Culture and Religion

This clay tablet has *The Epic of Gilgamesh* written on it.

Beginning with the Sumerians, the Mesopotamian civilizations developed a writing system called **cuneiform**, in which symbols stood for names, ideas, and later sounds. The Mesopotamians developed this system into an efficient way of communication. It was used for keeping records, business contracts, and literature. The most famous example of this is the Babylonian poem, **The Epic of Gilgamesh** (composed c. 2000 B.C.E). It describes a great flood, which many scholars believe was the basis of a similar account in the story of **Noah** in the Hebrew **Old Testament**.

The Mesopotamians were also responsible for many advances in science and technology. The Sumerians first developed the use of *bronze* (a mixture of copper and tin). They were also the first to use the wheel for both pottery and transportation.

Babylonian astronomers developed the *lunar calendar* (based on the phases of the moon), which created the 24-hour day, 7-day week, and 12-month year. They also were responsible for the development of the 60-minute hour and the 360-degree circle.

The Assyrians advanced Mesopotamian architecture and engineering. They built larger and more elaborate buildings, decorating them with stone slabs covered with carved depictions of battles and hunts. The Chaldeans further developed Mesopotamian astronomy, but only for astrology and predicting the future.

Mesopotamian religion taught that humans existed to serve the gods and would be punished if they failed. Every natural phenomenon had its own god. Religious belief was unconcerned with immortality, focusing on life in the present world. In the Sumerian period, a powerful priesthood ran society. They even controlled the king, who was seen as an agent of the gods, but not one himself. Under the Babylonians, Assyrians, and Chaldeans, Mesopotamian monarchy gradually took back political power and influence from the priesthood.

A statue of a Sumerian deity, circa 2130 B.C.

Persian Civilization (539 B.C.E.–632 C.E.)

The Persians are an **Indo-European** people about whom little is known before the sixth century B.C.E. In 550 B.C.E., King **Cyrus**, who ruled from 559 to 529 B.C.E., conquered and unified all the Persian tribes. By his death in 329 B.C.E., he had built a larger empire than any that had previously existed. This included Asia Minor, the Chaldean Empire, and the nations on the Syria–Palestine coast. Cyrus created a strong central government, supported by an effective military and an efficient bureaucracy. He built roads to link the empire, a policy continued by succeeding kings. His son **Cambyses**, king from 529 to 522 B.C.E., conquered Egypt. Under **Darius I**, who ruled from 522 to 486 B.C.E., the Persian Empire was extended to the borders of *India*. He divided it into **satrapies** or provinces, establishing a standard currency and system of weights and measures throughout the empire.

Even though the Persians collected tribute from their conquered peoples, they generally allowed them to keep their own customs, laws, and religion. Persian rule resulted in *cultural diffusion* or the mixing of cultures, throughout the Near East. One example of this was the Persian adaptation of various architectural styles in developing their own. The great differences between *Hellenic* (**Greek**) culture and that of Persians led, however, to conflict with the Greek cities in Asia Minor. Darius' increased oppression of the Hellenes led to open rebellion by the Greek cities. The rebels were assisted by **Athens** in mainland Greece. Both Darius and his son **Xerxes**, king from 486 to 478 B.C.E., unsuccessfully tried to conquer Greece and punish Athens (see Era I, Chapter 3, Section 1).

Persia's conquest by **Alexander the Great** (r. 336–323 B.C.E.) was temporary. It resulted in limited cultural diffusion with Hellenic civilization (see Era I Chapter 3, Section 2). Later Persian attempts to conquer Roman territory were also unsuccessful (see Era I, Chapter 3, Section 3).

A statue of a Persian King.

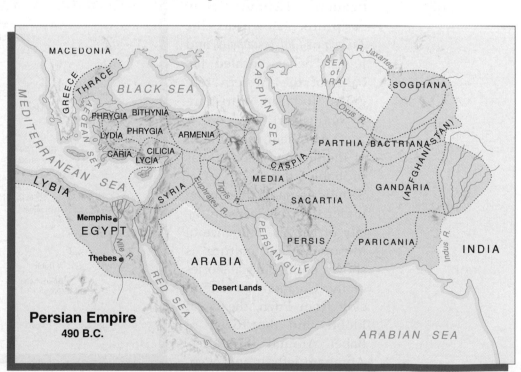

Persian Empire
490 B.C.

Persian Culture and Religion

Persian civilization was a combination of the cultures of their subject peoples, in particular those of Mesopotamia and Egypt. Persian writing was originally cuneiform, but later an alphabet system was adopted. The Egyptian solar calendar was modified and used. Babylonian art, with its emphasis on battles and hunting, was imitated in Persian artwork. The Persians combined aspects of Babylonian, Assyrian, Egyptian, and Greek architecture to produce their own style of building.

Main Idea:
Persian civilization was a combination of many cultures, including the Egyptians, Babylonians, and Greeks.

The most unique aspect of Persian culture was its emphasis on the *secular* or nonreligious. They did not glorify the gods, but rather their ruler, who was called the *King of Kings*. The most magnificent Persian buildings were not temples, but royal palaces. The most famous were those of Darius and Xerxes in the Persian capital city of **Persepolis**.

The Persian religion, known as **Zoroastrianism**, was highly influential throughout western Asia and the Mediterranean. Founded around 600 B.C.E. by the Persian theologian **Zarathustra** or **Zoroaster** in Greek, it emphasized the struggle between good and evil. It was the first religion to create the concept of evil as a separate force and the necessity of choosing good as a means of salvation of the soul after death. It influenced the development of both Judaism and Christianity.

Ancient Hebrew Civilization (1800 B.C.E.–70 C.E.)

Of all the Middle Eastern civilizations, the *Hebrew* or *Jewish* was most directly influential on Western civilization. Hebrew Holy Scripture, known as the *Tanach* or *Old Testament*, and Jewish beliefs formed the basis of the Western religions (Judaism, Christianity, and Islam).

Abraham, the founder of the Hebrew people, was probably the head of a Semitic nomadic tribe living under the Chaldeans in the city of Ur. The influence of Mesopotamian culture is shown in the Biblical stories of the Creation, the expulsion from Eden, the Great Flood, and the Tower of Babel. Around 1800 B.C.E., Abraham left Ur and even-

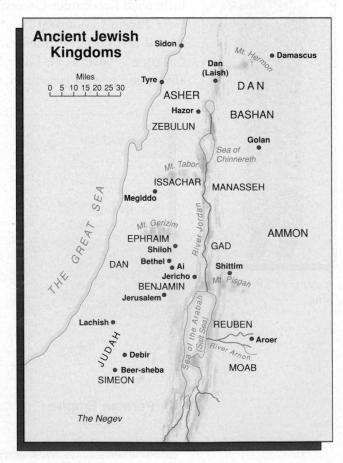

Ancient Jewish Kingdoms

The Western Wall is a retaining wall from the time of the Jewish Second Temple. Jews still come to pray at the wall.

tually settled in **Canaan**, which became *Palestine* (modern Israel). According to Jewish belief, Abraham had made a *covenant* or agreement with God, or **Yahweh** as the Hebrews called him. His descendants, known as the **Israelites**, became, in their view, God's "chosen people," forming a nation in Canaan. In return for protection, they would worship the one God and follow a new way of life. This belief, which can be labeled *ethical monotheism*, was an important development in world history.

Around 1700 B.C.E., a group of Israelites led by Abraham's grandson **Jacob** went to Egypt. They initially prospered but were eventually enslaved. Under *Ramses II*, who ruled from 1279 to 1213 B.C.E., a new leader named **Moses** led them out of Egypt. After a forty-year period of wandering, the Israelites resettled in Canaan. They organized into twelve tribes, each led by judges who interpreted the Hebrew legal code on which all decisions were based.

By the twelfth century B.C.E., the **Philistines**, a sea-faring commercial people who had settled along the coast of southern Canaan, began to push out the Israelites. The *autonomous* or self-ruling Jewish tribes unified to form the nation of Israel under a monarchy and central government.

Under the reigns of **Saul**, who ruled from 1020 to 1000 B.C.E., and **David**, king from 1000 to 960 B.C.E., the Israelites defeated the Philistines. David later created Israel's first capital city at **Jerusalem** and developed a professional army. Under **Solomon**, who ruled from 960 to 922 B.C.E., Israel developed into a powerful state. Despite a growth of the arts, and many large-scale building projects (including the *Temple of Solomon* at Jerusalem), the kingdom divided after Solomon's death into two countries: **Israel** in the north and **Judah** in the south.

In 721 B.C.E., the Assyrians conquered Israel. By 586 B.C.E. the Chaldeans captured Judah. During the period of Mesopotamian control or the Babylonian Captivity (586 to 538 B.C.E.), many Jews were enslaved or exiled to parts of Egypt and Babylonia. Others remained in Palestine.

After the conquest of Mesopotamia by the Persians and defeat of the Babylonians in 538 B.C.E., the Jews returned to Palestine. They rebuilt the Temple of Solomon in Jerusalem and enjoyed much autonomy under Persian rule (539 to 332 B.C.E.). This was known as the *Period of the Second Temple.*

In 332 B.C.E., Alexander the Great conquered Palestine (see Chapter 2, Section 2). The Hellenistic and Jewish civilizations experienced cultural diffusion, in which they influenced each other greatly. The Jews adopted the Greek alphabet system for Hebrew, writing out the entire Bible for the first time. The adoption of Greek as a second language exposed them to the ideas and knowledge of the Hellenistic world, as well as allowed them to share Jewish belief and thought with the Hellenized peoples of the Mediterranean area. After Alexander's death in 323 B.C.E., his empire was divided between his most powerful generals. Palestine became part of the **Seleucid Empire**. The repressive rule of the later Syrian kings of *Antioch* led to a successful revolution in 167 B.C.E. under *Judas Maccabaeus.* He and his family, the Maccabees, created an independent Jewish Hellenistic Kingdom. In 63 B.C.E., Palestine was conquered by the Romans and became a *protectorate*. The Jews were given much autonomy especially in religious worship. Internal conflicts between the Hellenized upper classes, including the religious leadership, and Jewish nationalist/religious fanatics, known as the **Zealots**, led to public disorders and rebellions. In 70 C.E., after an unsuccessful revolt in which the Romans punished them by destroying the temple of Solomon and making Palestine a province, most of the Jewish populations were exiled throughout the Empire. This became known as the **Diaspora** or "dispersion" of the Jews from their homeland. Palestine would not be the Jewish homeland until the creation of the modern state of Israel in 1948.

> **Main Idea:** Palestine experienced many changes, which ultimately led to the dispersion of Jews from their homeland in 70 C.E.

Ancient Hebrew Culture and Religion

Unlike their polytheistic neighbors, the Jews worshipped one God, who was a supreme being and the creator of the universe. Israel's God was an energy that could not be seen or touched. This was a great change from the idol worship of the other ancient religions.

Hebrew culture focused on the personal relationship of God with humans in general, and the Jews, the "chosen people," in particular. A culture of interpretation, debate, and study developed from the Jewish tradition of basing decisions on law. A huge body of Hebrew literature consists of commentaries on Jewish law known as the *Talmud*, which was developed over many centuries.

A page from the Babylonian Talmud.

Hittite Civilization (1700–717 B.C.E.)

The **Hittites** were an Indo-European people who settled in Asia Minor about 2000 B.C.E. By 1700 B.C.E. they had formed a unified kingdom. Between 1400 and 1200 B.C.E., the Hittites established a powerful empire in Asia Minor. Hittite power reached its height under King **Suppiluliumas**, who ruled from 1380 to 1340 B.C.E. and who extended the empire's control over northern Syria. The Hittite Empire declined between 1200 and 800 B.C.E. By 717 B.C.E., the last Hittite territories became part of the Assyrian Empire.

Hittite Culture and Religion

Hittite culture was heavily influenced by Mesopotamian civilization. Their government developed from a ruling class of warrior-nobles to a hereditary absolute monarchy after 1500 B.C.E. The Hittite nobles ruled over a native population.

The Hittites worshipped different gods taken from the religions of Egypt, Mesopotamia, and Asia Minor as well as their own Indo-European culture. Women, as well as men, took an active role in religious ceremonies. The Hittites wrote in cuneiform adopted from the Sumerians. Their literature consisted mostly of records and official histories.

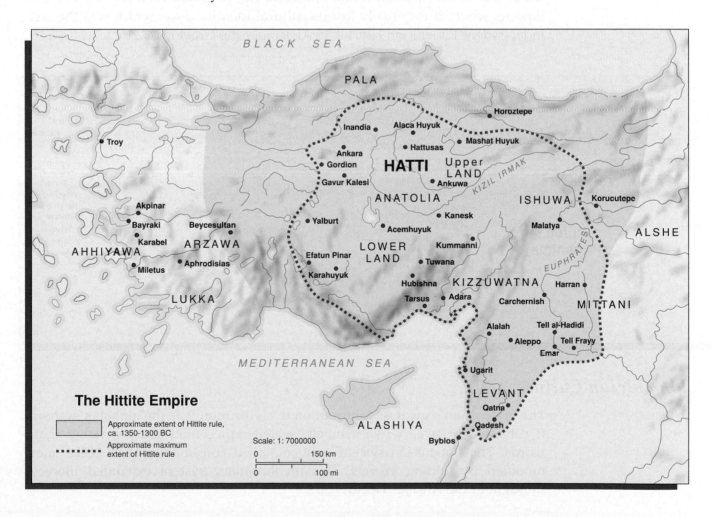

The Hittite Empire

Approximate extent of Hittite rule, ca. 1350-1300 BC

Approximate maximum extent of Hittite rule

Scale: 1: 7000000

0   150 km

0   100 mi

The Hittites were the first people to produce iron weapons and tools. They also worked with copper and bronze. Hittite art consisted of carving stone reliefs and decorating metal objects, such as shields, armor, and plates. Their architecture focused on the construction of military fortifications and huge gateways.

Phoenician Civilization (1100–332 B.C.E.)

The **Phoenicians** were a mixed Semitic people who first settled along the Mediterranean coast in an area called Phoenicia, which is now modern-day *Lebanon*. They were expert sailors who developed a confederation of city-states with great commercial power by 1100 B.C.E. The most important of these were **Tyre** and **Sidon**. The Phoenicians established trading colonies throughout the Mediterranean. The most famous of these was **Carthage** in North Africa, which was founded around 800 B.C.E. Carthage later became an independent commercial and military empire, which was a rival to both the Greeks and the Romans (see Chapter 3, Section 3).

The Phoenician city-states were too small to be a political or military power. By the sixth century B.C.E., the Greeks surpassed them as the dominant sea power in the Mediterranean. Phoenicia was later absorbed into the Persian Empire, where it eventually lost its cultural identity. Tyre, which was the last independent Phoenician city, fell to Alexander the Great in 332 B.C.E.

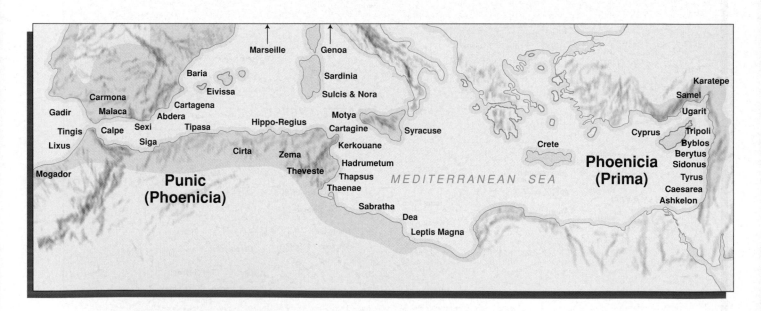

Phoenician Culture

The Phoenician's greatest contribution to civilization was the alphabet system. It consisted of twenty-two symbols, which represented sounds, rather than words. The Phoenician system only contained consonants. The Greeks later modified by adding vowels. This revolutionary system expanded literacy throughout the Ancient World.

AFRICA
Ancient Egypt (3400 B.C.E.–646 C.E.)

The **Nile River** played a great role in the development of Ancient Egyptian civilization. Its regular flooding gave the Egyptians extremely fertile soil, which produced great agricultural wealth. This also gave them a belief that nature was both predictable and favorable. Egypt was also fortunate to be surrounded by deserts and seas, which protected them from invading forces. The Nile provided easy transportation within the kingdom. These conditions helped to create a flourishing civilization that would last over three thousand years. It is for this reason that Egypt has often been called the *Gift of the Nile*.

Egyptian civilization emerged during the fourth millenium. Around 3400 B.C.E., two distinct kingdoms were created, *Upper Egypt* and *Lower Egypt*. During this time, which is known as the *Predynastic Period* (c. 3400–3100 B.C.E.), the Egyptians began irrigation projects and developed a system of writing.

In 3100 B.C.E., **King Menes** of Upper Egypt unified the two kingdoms and founded Egypt's first dynasty. Egypt developed rapidly during this time, which is known as the *Archaic Period* (c. 3100–2700 B.C.E.). Among its many accomplishments was the invention of the earliest known solar calendar of 365 days.

During the following period, known as the **Old Kingdom** (c. 2700–2200 B.C.E.), Egyptian civilization developed its major institutions. The monarchy became absolute in its power and an efficient central government was created. Egyptian culture was also developed at this time. By the end of this period, however, the king's centralized power

Map: Ancient Egypt

MEDITERRANEAN SEA

Dead Sea

Rosetta
Alexandria
NILE DELTA
Bitter Lakes
LOWER EGYPT

N
W — E
S

Gixa
Saqqara
Memphis
Lake Moens
SINAI

UPPER EGYPT
Sinai Peninsula

LIBYAN
Akhetaton

DESERT
ARABIAN DESERT
RED SEA

Valley of the Kings
Thebes
Karnak
Luxor

Ancient Egypt

☐ Fertile land
◈ Pyramids
★ Temples

Syene (Aswan)

Nile River

0   Miles   100
0   Kilometers   200

Abu Simbel ★

Statue of Egyptian deities Isis, Osirus, and Horus.

Egyptian mummy.
See page 16.

See page 16.

Main Idea:
Until the reign of Amenhotep IV, and incompetent Pharaoh, Egypt grew and prospered.

began to decline. This was due to corruption within the government that resulted from the growing power of the high priests and provincial governors. This led to the collapse of the Old Kingdom.

A time of disorder followed, known as the **First Intermediate Period** (2200–2050 B.C.E.). The lack of governmental authority resulted in civil wars and invasions. This finally ended with the establishment of a new dynasty based in the city of *Thebes*.

The kings of the **Middle Kingdom** (2050–1800 B.C.E.) restored central government and absolute monarchy. Provisional governors were directly controlled by the monarchy, and the high priests lost much of their influence. During this time, Egypt expanded its empire to the south. New irrigation and drainage projects expanded agricultural output as well. Toward the end of this period, the rule of a series of incompetent kings resulted in Semitic nomads, known as the *Hyksos*, conquering Egypt.

Under the rule of the Hyksos, known as the **Second Intermediate Period** (1800–1570 B.C.E.), the horse and chariot were introduced to Egypt. The Egyptians hated their conquerors who would not honor native religion and customs. The Hyksos were finally overthrown in 1570 B.C.E.

Ahmose I, who had led the expulsion of the Hyksos, restored a strong central government and efficient bureaucracy. The reign of this **pharaoh**, as Egyptian kings were now called, began a period known as the **New Kingdom** (1570–1085 B.C.E.). **Thutmose III**, who ruled from 1482 to 1450 B.C.E., and who was Ancient Egypt's greatest military leader, expanded Egypt's borders to include Syria, Palestine, and northern Mesopotamia. During the reign of **Amenhotep III**, who reigned from 1417–1379 B.C.E., Egypt experienced a *Golden Age*. This was a period of great commercial prosperity and artistic creativity.

The reign of incompetent Pharaoh **Amenhotep IV**, who ruled from 1379 to 1362 B.C.E., resulted in the decline of the monar-

Tomb decorations of an Egyptian Pharaoh.

chy and the loss of most of Egypt's empire. *Ramseses II*, who was pharaoh from 1304–1237 B.C.E., attempted to restore Egypt's empire but was only able to reconquer Palestine. By the end of the thirteenth Century B.C.E., Egypt had been invaded several times by groups of raiders known as the **sea peoples**. These attacks greatly weakened the kingdom, resulting in the loss of the remaining parts of its empire. Priests and provincial governors once again undermined royal authority. By 1085 B.C.E., Egypt was once more divided into northern and southern kingdoms.

Carving of Cleopatra VII.

From 940 to 332 B.C.E., Egypt came under the control of the **Libyans**, Assyrians, **Nubians**, and Persians. In 332 B.C.E., Alexander the Great conquered Egypt. This led to a period of cultural diffusion and the creation of a Hellenistic Egyptian state. Alexander built a new capital city for his empire, named **Alexandria**, on the Egyptian coast of the Mediterranean Sea. It became a center of trade and learning in the Hellenistic world. It was also the site of one of the greatest libraries of the Ancient World.

After Alexander's death in 323 B.C.E., Egypt became an independent Hellenistic kingdom (see Chapter 3, Section 2). *Ptolemaic Egypt* (323–31 B.C.E.) created a unique society that combined Egyptian and Greek cultures. It eventually came under the control of the Romans after the defeat of its last independent Ptolemaic ruler **Cleopatra VII**, who ruled from 46 to 31 B.C.E.

As a Roman province, Egypt was extremely important. Its enormous agricultural output gave it the title of the "Breadbasket" of the Roman Empire. It also continued to serve as one of Rome's most important commercial cities. The Egyptians became Christians with the rest of the Empire in 395 C.E. (see Chapter 3, Section 3).

After the fall of Rome and its Western Empire in 476, Egypt remained part of the **Byzantine** or Eastern Roman Empire. In 646, Arab armies conquered Egypt, making *Islam* the official faith. Egypt became an Arab nation and the Christian Egyptians, also known by this time as *Copts*, became a minority.

Ancient Egyptian village located on the banks of the River Nile, north of Luxor. Karnak stood as a beacon of intellectual illumination. See map on page 13.

Ancient Egyptian Culture and Religion

Ancient Egyptian culture revolved around its religion. Egyptian kings and pharaohs were considered to be gods. They owned all land, made laws, raised taxes, and were the final authority in all matters. Provincial governors were appointed to run the kingdom on behalf of the monarchy. Their highest advisors were priests who had enormous influence over their decisions.

The Ancient Egyptians also worshiped many gods who represented the forces of nature. The gods were often depicted as having both human and animal physical features. The Egyptians were also the first civilization to believe in an afterlife. It was for this reason that they practiced **mummification**. This was the process of embalming and wrapping a corpse in order to preserve the body so that the soul, which was released by death, would have a place to return when it revisited the world. Originally the belief in the afterlife and mummification were reserved only for the king. By the period of the New Kingdom, it had become a common Egyptian practice.

The Old Kingdom was also known as the *Pyramid Age*. During this period, huge **pyramids** or tombs were built for the mummified bodies of the king and royal family. The Egyptians believed that the immortality of the king would guarantee the survival of their civilization. They believed that life

Egyptian tomb painting.

Huge pyramids or tombs were built for the mummified bodies of the king and royal family.

The Rosetta Stone has writing on it in two languages, Egyptian and Greek, using three scripts, Hieroglyphic, Demotic Egyptian, and Greek. Because Greek was well known, the stone was the key to deciphering the hieroglyphs.

after death would be similar to earthly life, and therefore included needed material possessions in these tombs. The building of pyramids was abandoned after the Old Kingdom ended.

Egyptian society was divided into a class system, which had a good deal of social mobility. The vast majority of the free population were either farmers or laborers. There were also large groups of craftsmen and merchants. Slaves, however, among whom were the Israelites, provided most of Egyptian labor. In Egyptian society, women enjoyed an unusual amount of independence when compared to other ancient civilizations. They could buy, sell, and inherit property. Inheritance depended on both the mother and the father. Kings and pharaohs often married their sisters in order to maintain their dynastic lines.

The Egyptians developed writing, which was known as **hieroglyphics**. At first the hieroglyphs or "sacred signs" were pictures representing objects or words. Later on, the signs became representations of consonant sounds that could be read phonetically. After the conquest of Egypt by Alexander the Great, the Egyptians adopted the Greek alphabet system for the Egyptian language, using Phoenician and Greek letters. This writing became known as **Coptic**. The Egyptians wrote on **papyri**, which were rolls of writing material made from the papyrus plant. Education and literacy were limited to the priests and upper classes.

Ancient Egyptian art focused on religion. Statues and wall paintings were mainly of the gods, kings, and pharaohs. Statues were often massive in size. An example of this is the gigantic statue of the sphinx at Giza. Egyptian architecture was highly advanced, consisting of decorative temples, palaces, and **obelisks** (tall four-sided stone shafts). The pyramids are another example of the Egyptians' ability to build on a large scale.

The Great Sphinx of Giza is a large statue in Egypt. It is one of the largest single-stone statues on Earth.

Cushitic Civilization
(1500 B.C.E.–400 C.E.)

Cushitic Civilization developed in the upper Nile region known to the Egyptians as *Cush* (modern *Sudan*). This area was also referred to as **Nubia**. Beginning around 1500 B.C.E., the Negroid people who inhabited the region developed an independent kingdom. They traded with Egypt and were highly influenced by Egyptian culture. The Cushites established a capital city at **Napata**. It became a major religious center for the worship of the Egyptian sun god *Amon-Re*.

Main Idea:
The Cushites were greatly influenced by other cultures through trading and war.

The Cushites developed an absolute monarchy, which expanded their kingdom into an empire. Under King **Kashta**, the Cushites conquered Egypt in 750 B.C.E. Kashta's son **Piankhy** became pharaoh and established the *Nubian Dynasty* (745–671 B.C.E.). Hellenism later influenced the Cushites through trade with Egypt during the Ptolomaic and Roman Periods. Cushite civilization declined in the fourth century C.E. after the fall of the Roman Empire in the West. This was due to raids by barbarians and the rise of the neighboring *Axhumite* (later *Ethiopian*) *Kingdom*. The Cushites were later Christianized by Ethiopian missionaries.

Ancient Ethiopian Civilization (1000 B.C.E.–570 C.E.)

Ancient Ethiopian civilization began around 1000 B.C.E. with the development of the Axumite Kingdom. The Axumites were a mixture of Black Africans and migrating Semitic Arabs in the *Ethiopian highlands*. Unlike the landlocked Cush, the kingdom of **Axum** was able to profit from trade with Ptolomaic Egypt and the Arabs of southern Arabia. Its ports provided opportunities for trade and products from around the Mediterranean world. Axum, located in the mountainous highlands, was secure from invasion. This produced an advanced civilization. The Axumites were able to work with great precision in stone, producing objects such as huge religious obelisks. The development of the plow and use of stone terracing created agricultural wealth.

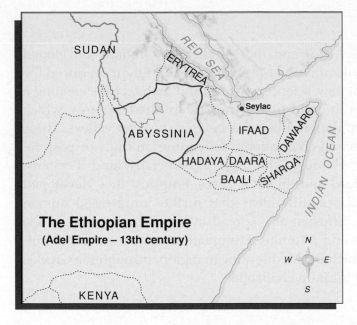

The Ethiopian Empire
(Adel Empire – 13th century)

According to tradition, the emperors of Ethiopia were descended from the Queen of Sheba and King Solomon of Israel. Their son, **Melinik I**, became the ruler of Ethiopia and founded its royal dynasty. Based on this tradition, the Ethiopian emperors used the title of the **Lion of Judah**.

In 330 C.E., **King Ezena** converted to Christianity and made it the national religion. Axum was one of the first ancient kingdoms to become Christian. Christianity created cultural and political as well as religious unity. The Axumite chieftains accepted a central government as Axum became the Kingdom of *Ethiopia* or *Abyssinia*. The Church provided legitimacy for the new absolute authority of the monarchy. Monasteries developed as centers of learning throughout the kingdom. Ethiopian monks translated the Bible church services, and works of theology from Greek and Coptic into **Ge'ez** (the Ethiopian language). Church and state funded missionary work to neighboring kingdoms led to the conversion of those peoples. The *Ethiopian Orthodox Church* and the autocracy became stable institutions that made the nation unified and orderly. Ethiopia continued under this system until the mid-twentieth century.

Ethiopia became an empire as it extended its control over its neighbors. The Abyssinian conquest of southern Arabia (modern *Yemen*) in 543 was short-lived. Military overextension forced them to withdraw in 570. Ethiopia remained dominant in eastern Africa until it became surrounded by Islamic states in the next century.

LINK TO TODAY
The Tradition of Babylonian Law

Many Americans consider the execution of individuals who are guilty of extreme crimes, such as premeditated murder, a proper punishment. Others oppose capital punishment, no matter what the crime. This is a controversy that continues to create debate in the United States.

The basis of capital punishment can be found in Ancient Babylonian law. The legal code of Hammurabi, one of the oldest in the world, specifically calls for penalties that match the crimes. Murderers would be executed, while thieves would lose their hands, and builders guilty of cheating would be forced to pay for the damage their inferior work created. This concept of an eye-for-an-eye justice has had its supporters and detractors throughout history. Each civilization has had to decide how harshly punishment would be dispensed.

CHAPTER SUMMARY

The ancient civilizations of Africa and the Middle East initially developed around river valleys. The civilizations of Mesopotamia and Egypt produced the earliest forms of government, law, science, writing, and architecture, creating a foundation for later peoples to build upon. They established empires, which expanded both trade and populations into areas beyond the river valleys. These developed into new cultures and civilizations, depending on trade or pastoral pursuits, and include the Hebrews, Hittites, Phoenicians, and Persians. Becoming independent nations and, in some cases, empires, they developed religions, philosophical, and scientific ideas that further progressed human advancement. This cultural diffusion also spread into Africa, resulting in the development of the Cushite and Axumite (Ethiopian) civilizations. These cultures were the basis upon which the Mediterranean region, through the Greeks, developed into the cradle of Western civilization.

IMPORTANT
PEOPLE,
PLACES,
AND TERMS

KEY TERMS	PEOPLE	PLACES
Sumerian	King Sargon I	Mesopotamia
Semite	King Hammurabi	Fertile Crescent
Indo-European	King Sargon II	Mediterranean Sea
Amorite	King Sennacherib	Tigris River
Kassite	King Nebuchadnezzar	Euphrates River
Assyrian	King Cyrus	Persian Gulf
Chaldean	King Cambyses	Nile River
cuneiform	King Darius I	Tigris-Euphrates valley
hieroglyphs	King Xerxes	Ur
Babylonian	Alexander the Great	Lagash
Hammurabi Law Code	Zaroaster/Zarathustra	Syria
barbarians	Abraham	Babylon
Epic of Gilgamesh	Jacob	Selucid Empire
Philistines	Moses	Plateau of Assure
Israelite	King Saul	Persia
Diaspora	King David	Asia Minor
Zealot	King Soloman	Nineveh
Hittite	Judah	Alexandria
Phoenician	Yahweh	Persopolis
Old Kingdom	Maccabees	Jerusalem
Middle Kingdom	King Suppiluliumas	Judah
New Kingdom	King Menes	Israel
Intermediate Period	Pharaoh Ahmose I	Canaan
pharoah	Pharaoh Thutmose III	Tyre
Lybian	Pharaoh Amenhotep III	Sidon
Nubian	Pharaoh Amenhotep IV	Carthage
sea peoples	Queen Cleopatra VII	Egypt
Byzantine	King Kashta	Cush
mummification	King Piankhy	Nubia

KEY TERMS	PEOPLE	PLACES
Coptic	King Ezena	Axum
papyrus	King Melinik I	Ethiopia
obelisks		
pyramid		
Ge'ez		
Lion of Judah		

EXERCISES FOR CHAPTER 1

MULTIPLE CHOICE

Select the letter of the correct answer.

1. The river valleys of the Tigris-Euphrates and the Nile were centers of civilization because they

   a. had rich deposits of iron ore and coal.
   b. were isolated from other cultural influences.
   c. were easily defended from invasion.
   d. provided a means of transportation and irrigation.

2. What geographic factor had the greatest influence on Mesopotamian civilization?

   a. The surrounding deserts protected it from invasions.
   b. Limited resources and constant invasions made it warlike.
   c. Access to the sea made it prosperous through trade.
   d. The mountainous terrain made it isolationist.

3. Mesopotamian religious belief

   a. showed a greater concern for the present life.
   b. showed a greater concern for the next world.
   c. was monotheistic.
   d. focused on the worship of the king.

4. The most important cities in Mesopotamian history were

   a. Ur, Lagash, Babylon, Jerusalem
   b. Babylon, Nineveh, Tire, Sidon
   c. Ur, Lagash, Babylon, Nineveh
   d. Axum, Babylon, Napata, Persepolis

5. The Code of Hammurabi was a major contribution to the development of civilization because it

   a. treated citizens and slaves equally.
   b. ended all physical punishment.
   c. recorded existing laws for all to see.
   d. rejected the principle of filial piety.

6. The *Epic of Gilgamesh* was written during the period of

   a. Sumerian civilization.
   b. Babylonian civilization.
   c. Assyrian civilization.
   d. Chaldean civilization.

7. Cuneiform writing was developed by the

   a. Sumerians.
   b. Babylonians.
   c. Assyrians.
   d. Chaldeans.

8. Hieroglyphics were developed by the

   a. Hebrews.
   b. Greeks.
   c. Egyptians.
   d. Persians.

9. Unsuccessful invasions of Greece were attempted under which Persian rulers?

   a. Cyrus and Darius I
   b. Cambyses and Darius I
   c. Cyrus and Xerxes
   d. Darius I and Xerxes

10. The title "King of Kings" referred to the ruler of

    a. Babylon.
    b. Persia.
    c. Egypt.
    d. Ethiopia.

11. The title "Lion of Judah" referred to the ruler of

    a. Babylon.
    b. Persia.
    c. Egypt.
    d. Ethiopia.

12. The founder of the Ancient Hebrew civilization was

    a. Abraham.
    b. Moses.
    c. David.
    d. Solomon.

13. Israel's first capital city was

    a. Judah.
    b. Babylon.
    c. Nineveh.
    d. Jerusalem.

14. The exile of Rome's Jewish population in 70 C.E. was known as the

    a. exodus.
    b. Babylonian Captivity.
    c. diaspora.
    d. wandering.

15. Who were the first people to produce iron weapons and tools?

    a. Assyrians.
    b. Egyptians.
    c. Persians.
    d. Hittites.

16. The alphabet system was created by the

    a. Sumerians.
    b. Phoenicians.
    c. Egyptians.
    d. Greeks.

17. Which of the following was true of the Nile River?

    a. It flooded irregularly and couldn't be depended upon.
    b. It was too shallow for transportation.
    c. It enabled the Egyptians to trade with the Greeks.
    d. It provided the Egyptians with easy internal transportation.

18. The building of the pyramids was during the

    a. Predynastic Period.
    b. Old Kingdom.
    c. Middle Kingdom.
    d. New Kingdom.

19. The major result of the development of civilization in ancient Egypt was the

    a. conquest and settlement of Western Europe by the Egyptian Empire.
    b. establishment of a democratic system of government in Egypt.
    c. establishment of trade routes between Egypt and other kingdoms.
    d. decline in agriculture as an important occupation in Egypt.

20. Ancient Ethiopian civilization began with the development of the

    a. Egyptian kingdom.
    b. Nubian kingdom.
    c. Cushite kingdom
    d. Axumite kingdom.

1. How was geography responsible for the development of the Mesopotamian civilizations? Describe three ways in which the land influenced the creation of the civilizations of the Fertile Crescent.
2. Was Hebrew civilization the most directly influential on Western thought? Give three reasons why this statement is true or untrue.
3. What is meant by the statement, "Egypt was the gift of the Nile?" Give three examples to show how the Nile shaped Egyptian civilization.
4. Many would agree that leaders decide history. Select three rulers of Ancient African or Middle Eastern civilization and show one way each influenced the development of that society.
5. Imagine that you are a merchant in the Ancient World. You wish to tell your family about the many places you have been. Select two different civilizations and write a letter describing two aspects of their culture for each.

DOCUMENT-BASED QUESTIONS

This task is based on the accompanying documents. Some of these documents have been edited for the purposes of this task. This task is designed to test your ability to work with historical documents. As you analyze the documents, take into account both the source of each document and the author's point of view.

Directions: Read the following documents and answer the questions after each document. Use the information in the reading and this chapter in writing your answers.

Document #1

CODE OF HAMMURABI

I established law and justice in the language of the land and promoted the welfare of the people. At that time [I decreed]:

—If a man accuses another man, charging him with murder, but cannot prove it, the accuser shall be put to death.

—If he bear [false] witness concerning grain or money, he shall himself bear the penalty imposed in that case.

—If a judge pronounced a judgment, rendered a decision, delivered a verdict duly signed and sealed, and afterward altered his judgment, they shall call that judge to account for the alteration of the judgment which he has pronounced, and he shall pay twelvefold the penalty in that judgment; and, in the assembly, they shall expel him from his seat of judgment, and with the judges in a case he shall not take his seat.

—If a man practices robbery and is captured, that man shall be put to death.

—If the robber is not captured, the man who has been robbed shall, in the presence of god, make an itemized statement of his loss, and the city and the governor in whose province and jurisdiction the robbery was committed shall compensate him for whatever was lost.

—If a man opens his canal for irrigation and neglects it and the water carries away an adjacent field, he shall pay out grain on the basis of the adjacent field.

—If a man takes a wife and does not arrange a contract for her, that woman is not a wife.

—If the wife of a man is caught lying with another man, they shall bind them and throw them into the water.

—If a son strikes his father, they shall cut off his hand.

—If a man destroys the eye of another man, they shall destroy his eye.

—If he breaks another man's bone, they shall break his bone.

—If a builder builds a house for a man and does not make its construction sound, and the house which he has built collapses and causes the death of the owner of the house, that builder shall be put to death.

—If a builder builds a house for a man and does not make its construction sound, and a wall cracks, that builder shall strengthen that wall at his own expense.

From *The Law Code of Hammurabi*
Translated by Robert F. Harper

Questions

1. What is the significance of a set of laws? What effects, both positive and negative, does a legal code have on a society?

2. From examining the Code of Hammurabi, what aspects of daily life did Babylonian society find most important? Why do the laws distinguish class differences in their punishments?

3. In Hammurabi's legal code, the punishments are extremely severe. Why are these laws so harsh? What might this severity indicate about the nature of Mesopotamian civilization?

Document #2   *THE EPIC OF GILGAMESH*

So the gods agreed to exterminate mankind. . . . Ea [Mesopotamian god] because of his oath warned me in a dream. "O man of Shurrupak, son of Ubara-Tutu; tear down your house and build a boat, abandon possessions and look for life, despise worldly goods and save your soul alive. Tear down your house, I say, and build a boat. These are the measurements of the barque as you shall build her: Let her be of equal her length, let her deck be roofed like the vault that covers the abyss; then take up into the boat the seed of all living creatures.

I loaded into her all that I had of gold and of living things, my family, my kin, the beast of the field both wild and tame, and all the craftsmen. The time was fulfilled, the evening came, the rider of the storm sent down the rain. I looked out at the weather and it was terrible, so I too boarded the boat and battened her down. All was now complete, the battening and the caulking; so I handed the tiller to Puzur-Amurri the steersman, with the navigation and the care of the whole boat.

With the first light of dawn a black cloud came from the horizon; it thundered within where Adad, lord of the storm was riding. In front over hill and plain Shullat and Hanish, heralds of the storm, led on. Then the gods of the abyss rose up; Nergal pulled out the dams of the Nether Waters. A stupor of despair went up to the heavens when the god of the storm turned daylight to darkness, when he smashed the land like a cup. One whole day the tempest raged, gathering fury as it went. It poured over the people like the tides of battle; a man could not see his brother nor the people to be seen from heaven.

For six days and six nights the winds blew, torrent and tempest and flood raged together like warring hosts. When the seventh day dawned the storm from the south subsided, the sea grew calm, the flood was stilled; I looked at the face of the world and there was silence, all mankind was turned to clay. The surface of the sea stretched as flat as a rooftop; I opened a hatch and the light fell on my face. Then I bowed low, I sat down and wept, the tears streamed down my face, for on every side was the waste of water. I looked for land in vain, but fourteen leagues distant there appeared a mountain, and there the boat grounded; on the mountain Nisir the boat held fast, she held fast and did not budge. When the seventh day dawned I loosed a dove and let her go. She flew away, but finding no resting-place she returned. I made a sacrifice . . . I heaped up the wood and cane and setter and myrtle. When the gods smelled the sweet savor, they gathered like flies over the sacrifice.

From *The Epic of Gilgamesh*
Translated by N. K. Sandars

Questions	1. What can the reader learn about Mesopotamian civilization from reading *The Epic of Gilgamesh*? How does the story show everyday life in Mesopotamian society?
	2. In what ways does the story of the flood in *The Epic of Gilgamesh* show the way in which Mesopotamian civilization imagined their gods and their relationship with them?
	3. Compare the story of the flood in *The Epic of Gilgamesh* with that of Noah in the Old Testament. What are the similarities and differences between the two accounts?

Document #3   *BOOK OF THE DEAD*

What is said on reaching the Broad-Hall of the Two Justices [gateway to afterlife], absolving X [the individual] of every sin, which he has committed, and seeing the faces of the gods:

Hail to thee O great god . . . I have come to thee:
I have not committed evil against men.
I have not mistreated cattle.
I have not blasphemed a god.
I have not done violence to a poor man.
I have not defamed a slave to his superior.
I have not made [anyone] sick.
I have not made [anyone] weep.
I have not killed.
I have given no order to a killer.
I have not caused anyone suffering.
I have not cut down on the food [income] in the temples.
I have not damaged the bread of the gods.
I have not taken the loaves of the blessed [dead].

I have neither increased or diminished the grain-measure.
I have not taken milk from the mouths of children.
I have not driven cattle away from their pasturage.
I have not held up the water in its season.
I have not built a dam against running water.
I have not stopped a god on his procession.
I am pure.

O Wide-of-Stride, who comes forth from Heliopolis, I have not committed sin.

[This is] to be done in conformance with what takes place in this Hall-Hall of the Two Justices. This spell is to be reflected when one is clean and pure, clothed in [fresh] garments, shod with white sandals, painted with stibium, and anointed with myrrh, to whom cattle, foul, incense, bread, beer, and vegetables have been offered. Then make thou this text in writing on a clean pavement with ochre smeared with earth upon which pigs and small cattle have not trodden. As for him on whose behalf this book is made, he shall be prosperous and his children shall be prosperous, without greed, because he shall be a trusted man of the king and his courtiers. Loaves, jars, bread, and joints of meat shall be given to him from the alter of the great god. He cannot be held back by any door of the west, [but] he shall be ushered in with the Kings of Upper and Lower Egypt, and he shall be in the retinue of Osiris.

Right and true a million times.

From the Egyptian *Book of the Dead*
Translated by James Pritchard

Questions

1. According to the Egyptian *Book of the Dead*, what sins should a righteous individual avoid and what actions should he take in order to enter the afterlife successfully?

2. Based on the *Book of the Dead*, in what ways is the Egyptian moral code both similar and different from that of modern Western society?

3. In what ways was the *Book of the Dead* also a guide for the living? What type of behavior does the work encourage in everyday life?

Document #4   **MOSES AT MOUNT SINAI**

And Moses led the people forth out of the camp to meet God . . . The mount of Sinai was covered in smoke, because God had descended on it in fire . . . and the people were exceedingly amazed . . . Moses spoke, and God answered him in a voice . . .

And the Lord spoke all these words saying: "I am the Lord thy God, who brought thee out of the land of Egypt, out of the house of bondage. Thou shalt have no other gods beside me. Thou shalt not make to thyself an idol, nor any likeness of anything . . . in the heaven above, nor . . . in the earth beneath, nor . . . in the waters under the earth . . . for I am the Lord thy God, a jealous God, recompensing the sins of the fathers on the sons, . . . and bestowing mercy on them that love me and . . . keep my commandments. Thou shalt not take the name of the Lord thy God in vain . . . Remember the sabbath day to keep it holy. Six days thou shalt labor...But on the seventh day . . . thou shalt do no work . . . Honor thy father and mother . . . Thou shalt not commit adultery. Thou shalt not steal. Thou shalt not bear false witness against thy neighbor. Thou shalt not covet thy neighbor's wife; Thou shalt not covet thy neighbor's house . . . nor whatever belongs to thy neighbor."

And all the people . . . feared and stood afar off . . . and Moses said to them, "Be of good courage, for God is come to try you, that fear of Him may be among you, and that ye sin not."

From *The Bible: The Septuagint Version*
(Zondervan Publishing House)

Questions

1. According to the *Book of Exodus*, what does God expect of the Hebrews (Jews)?
2. What practical purpose do the commandments imposed on the Hebrews by God serve in organizing Jewish society?
3. In what ways are these rules similar or different from those of other Middle Eastern and African civilizations at that time?

Document #5   PRAYER TO ST. MOSES THE ETHIOPIAN

Thou did forsake [abandon] riches, earthly fame, and fleshly pleasure and did freely choose a life of poverty and deprivation [living with no comfort] to become rich in spirit. Having tasted the momentary sweetness of sin, thou did foresee the bitter end that awaits a life of self-indulgence. Having stained thy hands with the blood of thy brother, thou did foretaste the anguish [pain and suffering] of Hell . . . By following the path of the Cross, thy soul was empowered by the might of the Holy Spirit, thy mind was illumined with the understanding of things divine, and thy heart was with the burning love of God for thy fellow man . . . Pray that we be strengthened to live uprightly . . . ever seeking to do the will of God. And on the dreadful day of judgment, pray that we may be received by God with His Son and His most holy and life creating Spirit, to Whom belongs all honor and worship, now and forever and o the ages of ages. Amen.

From *An Unbroken Circle: Linking Ancient African*
Christianity to the African-American Experience
Fr. Paisius Altschul, ed.

Questions

1. According to the Prayer to St. Moses the Ethiopian, what type of behavior was admired by the Abyssinians (Ethiopians) after their conversion to Orthodox Christianity?
2. Based on the text, what kind of life did St. Moses the Ethiopian lead before adopting Christianity?
3. What does the Prayer reveal about the values of Abyssinian (Ethiopian) civilization?

CHAPTER 2

Ancient Southern and Eastern Asia

Section 1—Ancient India 29

Section 2—Ancient China 42

Section 3—Ancient Southeast Asia 49

Section 4—Ancient Japan 51

Section 5—Ancient Korea 55

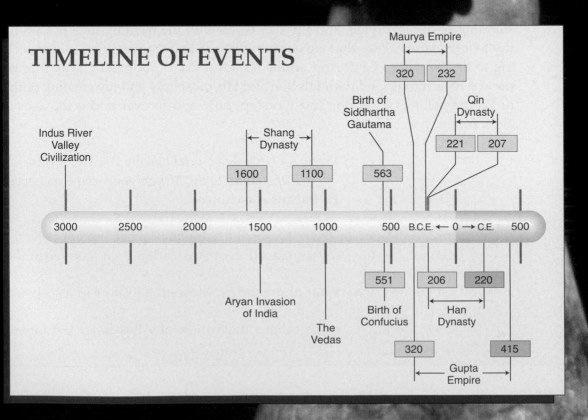

TIMELINE OF EVENTS

Maurya Empire

320   232

Birth of Siddhartha Gautama

Qin Dynasty

221   207

Indus River Valley Civilization

Shang Dynasty

1600   1100   563

3000   2500   2000   1500   1000   500   B.C.E. ← 0 → C.E.   500

551   206   220

Aryan Invasion of India

Birth of Confucius

Han Dynasty

The Vedas

320   415

Gupta Empire

28

The two most populated nations in today's world are China and India. Was this always so? We cannot say, as we have no census nor population records for the earliest inhabitants who settled in those areas. Yet, we do know that these people formed some of the world's earliest civilizations. They lived mostly near river valleys, as was true of the other early civilizations you have read about. Our trip back in time to the regions known as southern Asia (including India) and eastern Asia (including China) will start with the Indian subcontinent and then move eastward.

Ancient India

Mohenjo-Daro seals.

The Indus River lies in present day Pakistan. It seems to have been the site of the earliest known civilization in southern Asia. In fact, over 100 settled areas have been discovered on and near the Indus River. The largest of these were at **Harrapa** and **Mohenjo-Daro**. Archaeologists thus decided to label the Indus River valley civilization as Harappan civilization. The inhabitants along the Indus built cities that were carefully planned. These cities had streets that ran both north and south, intersected by others that ran east and west. Buildings were made of mud bricks that had been baked in ovens. There is also evidence of sewage and drainage systems, features that must have made the cities suitable for habitation. Harappan society was marked by an economy that was primarily agricultural. Floods from the Indus River enriched the soil, leading to the growth of such crops as barley, wheat, and peas. Trade was carried on with many parts of Mesopotamia. Sumer, for example, sent textiles to Harappan people in exchange for copper and precious stones. The quality and amount of trade, along with the sophisticated urban environments show that a strong central government had ruled in the Indus River valley. It apparently was well-organized and powerful.

> **Main Idea:**
> More than 100 settled areas have been discovered on and near the Indus River.

The End of the Indus River Valley Culture

If the inhabitants of the Indus River valley area had left written records and had successfully met the challenges faced by them around the year 1750 B.C.E., we would certainly know much more about them, for it was in that time period when a general and severe decline set in. The society that existed here came to an end. Why did this happen? We do not know for sure, but the reasons could have been natural as well as human. Natural reasons could have been any or all of the following: earthquakes, changes in the flow of the Indus River, floods. A human factor may have rested with the movement into the area of a group of people from outside. These outsiders, the **Aryans**, came from central Asia. They were a nomadic people of Indo-European background. Even though historians believe that the Aryans began to appear in southern Asia around 1500 B.C.E., they do not know why the Aryans left their original homelands. They defeated the remaining Harappans and built an entirely new society. As was true of many nomadic people, the Aryans were skilled warriors. Gradually, over a period of perhaps 300 years, they moved from the Indus River valley eastward into what is now India. Their invasion of southern Asia occurred over many years and did not take place all at once. The changes and transformations they made in the subcontinent had important consequences that last up to the present day. Indeed, Aryan society laid the roots for what we can call Indian society. Therefore, we must now examine the Aryan way of life to understand the beginnings of modern India.

Aryan Culture

The Aryans were herders, hoping to find good land for grazing their sheep and livestock. They led a nomadic lifestyle, moving from one place to another. The land in India appealed to them, and they eventually settled there and became farmers. Yet, their settlement came at a cost to the people who originally lived there. These were darker skinned people, know as Dravidians. The Dravidians were forced to move southward, as the Aryan conquest was complete over north and central India.

Much of what we know about the Aryans can be found in their sacred writings. These writings were the **Vedas**. As religious literature, the Vedas may well be the very first set of writings in India. They contain prayers, hymns, and rules for conducting rituals, written in the ancient language of *Sanskrit*. There are four Vedas: Rig-Veda, Sama-Veda, Yajur-Veda, and Atharva-Veda. The Rig-Veda, dating from about 800 B.C.E., is considered to be the earliest known religious literature in the world. The Rig-Veda contains over 100 hymns, describing many Aryan gods. There were, for example, gods of the wind, sun, and rain. Rig is a word that means hymn. One of the hymns in the Rig-Veda has a creation story that is very similar to the creation story found in the Bible. The Sama-Veda also contains hymns, while the Yajur-Veda has instructions for priests concerning their responsibilities in conducting religious rituals. The Atharva-Veda consists of several magical spells. For hundreds of years, the Vedas were passed down orally from one generation to another. Ultimately, they were written down and became the basis for the religion that came to be known as Hinduism.

Main Idea:
The religious literature of the Aryans eventually became the basis for the religion that came to be known as Hinduism.

The Religion of Hinduism

Before we move on with our historical exploration of people and history in ancient India, we need to explain some basic ideas of Hinduism. The religion we call Hinduism is an enormous collection of religious beliefs that have grown over many centuries, beyond simply the Aryan era. Our approach will be to look at these various items:

- The caste system
- Fundamental ideas and beliefs
- Gods and goddesses
- Holy literature

THE CASTE SYSTEM

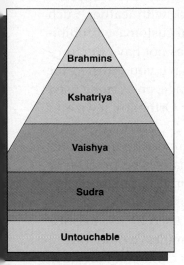

The Hindu way of living had very specific political, economic, and social patterns, with people divided into different castes.

Main Idea: A person born into a particular caste, would stay in that group for life and be obligated to follow all the rules for that caste.

The people who today call themselves Hindus did not originally use this word for the religion. The word ("indoos," taken from the Indus River) was used by foreigners to describe the people practicing this religion. India itself is named for the Indus River and was once referred to as Hindustan. The actual name that Indians use for their nation, however, is Bharata. In a similar way, the word **caste** is actually taken from a foreign word, *casta*. This is a Portuguese word used by Portuguese explorers when they came to southern Asia in the 1400s and saw the way in which Indians were living. That way of life had very specific political, economic, and social patterns, with people divided into different **castas**, groups or classes. The four basic classes were not equal, as some had more power, privilege, and prestige than other ones. These classes came to be identified as **varnas**. The varnas in order of rank and importance were the following: Brahmins, Kshatriyas, Vaishyas, and Shudras. Within each varna, over time, many subdivisions grew. These were known as **jatis** or subcastes. Therefore, a much better name for the caste system would be the varna/jati system.

How did this system begin? No one knows for sure. The following theories have been considered by scholars:

1. The Aryans had such a system of group ranking that they brought with them and imposed on the native Dravidians.

2. Varna is connected to skin color. As the Aryans were lighter-skinned than the Dravidians, the Aryans set up a system with themselves at the top.

3. Every society needs to have some kind of division of labor. Thus, the Aryans created a system where different groups would have different assigned tasks to perform.

4. According to the Code of Manu, a religious writing, the four varnas came from the body of the first human being. The Brahmins, who were priests, came from the first human's mouth. The Kshatriyas, rulers and warriors, came from the arms. The Vaishya, peasants and traders, came from the legs. The Shudras, laborers, came from the feet.

A fifth and lowest group were the untouchables. They were considered to be outside of the caste system because they engaged in ritually unclean or impure occupations. An example would be making and working with leather items. (The impurity attached to this activity is due to the sacred attitude held toward cows.) Other examples of unclean occupations would be gravediggers, butchers, and sweepers. Every society needs such people. Yet, such jobs were looked down upon by the other castes. The people who performed these tasks were thus outcastes, a word that developed into our own standard English word *outcast*. Traditionally, untouchables were treated miserably by other Hindus and suffered severe discrimination. Even their touch was thought to be impure.

A person born into a particular caste, as well as into untouchability, would stay in that group for life, responsible for all rules, duties, responsibilities, and obligations. Caste membership would determine correct behavior in regard to

Mahatma Gandhi attempted to improve the status of untouchables by calling them "children of God."

many activities with other people: eating, drinking, residing, marrying, and working. If a person did what he/she was supposed to do, following caste rules or dharma, the person would live a ritually pure life and thus have a chance of being reincarnated or born into a higher caste in a future life. The "glue" that kept this system intact for centuries, as well as in many rural parts of India today, is the fear of pollution or becoming impure. This term is used in a spiritual or religious sense, not a biological or environmental sense. For example, a Brahmin is not supposed to eat beef from a cow, nor work with leather. Such restrictions are called **taboos**. A taboo is an unwritten social customary prohibition. It is something you are not supposed to do, but it does not have the force of law behind it; that is, the law cannot punish you nor have you arrested for breaking a taboo. The word is from Hindi, an Indian language, and can be used as an adjective or a noun. For example, a taboo action for Orthodox Jews and Muslims is eating pork. Eating pork for them is a taboo.

As a matter of tradition and custom, it is taboo for Hindus to marry outside of their castes, or more specifically, outside of their jatis. The practice of marrying within one's own ethnic group is called **endogamy**. Throughout history, many societies have been endogamous. The custom of endogamy ensures preservation of the group; thus, it is a powerful argument used by its supporters for its continuance. In maintaining this practice, families would hire a matchmaker in order to have marriages arranged for their children at an early age. Even today, some families will place marriage advertisements in newspapers and on Web sites asking for a marriage partner from their own caste.

Although such ads can be found in major newspapers as placed by well-educated and modern urban families, there nevertheless have been significant changes affecting the caste system in the last hundred years. Among these are the following:

1. In an attempt to improve the status of untouchables by having people view them differently, Mahatma Gandhi, the great Indian independence leader, suggested that they be called *harijans* or "children of God." Gandhi claimed that the "curse of untouchability" did much to "disfigure Hinduism" and struggled "to rid Hinduism of its greatest blot."

2. The Indian Constitution of 1947 prohibits caste discrimination. This means that it is illegal to use a person's caste as a reason for denial of a job, school admission, a home, civil and political rights, and so on.

3. The government has created an *affirmative action* policy. This is designed to reserve a certain percentage of government jobs and university admissions for members of *scheduled castes*. This term refers to members of lower castes, untouchables, and tribal groups.

4. Some lower status jatis have tried to move up in a ranking system and hoped to have other people look upon them with more respect. This process is called *sanskritization*. It occurs when a given jati takes on a feature of a group higher than itself. The feature can be cultural or religious, such as performing certain rituals or changing eating habits. It can also be economic, such as making occupational changes.

5. Dr. Bhimrao Ramji Ambedkar was an untouchable who became a renowned intellectual and politician. He was the head of the committee that wrote India's Constitution. Another famous untouchable was Dr. Kocheri R. Narayanan. He was president of India from 1997 to 2002, a position however that is not as important as that of prime minister.

6. There are some marriages that do take place between members of different castes. In fact, some marriage advertisements will say "caste no bar."

These descriptions do not signify that abuses of the caste system have been completely eliminated in India. Certain traditions built up over centuries are not easily changed. Yet, as economic, political, and social conditions undergo transition, there is hope that the worst features of caste will subside. Our discussion of caste in India has similarities with the history of race in the United States. The caste system will not end. Caste provides a sense of identity, of helping you know who you are in a particular ethnic group.

FUNDAMENTAL IDEAS AND BELIEFS

A statue of the deity Shiva.

As with all the world's great religions, Hinduism is a system of beliefs that provide answers to some of the perennial questions humans have asked. These questions concern the origins and meaning of life and proper conduct toward others. Over 80 percent of the people of India consider themselves Hindus, while Hindus make up 13 percent of the world's population. Even though there are differences in some beliefs and practices among Hindus, certain basic ideas are accepted.

Each human being occupies a place on the wheel of life, or **mandala**, and has within him/her a soul. The wheel of life is constantly turning. A person's position on the mandala is determined by the law of **karma**. Karma can be compared to an action and reaction, to a cause-and-effect relationship. If you do well now, the future will be good. This means that where the person is now on the mandala, with his soul, depends on a previous life of another person who had that soul. According to this law, what happened to a person's soul in the previous life, or incarnation, will affect the person's current status. The soul undergoes a process of rebirth, or reincarnation to a higher or lower caste. This is called **samsara**. Whether reincarnation results in the soul's moving "up" or "down" depends on how a person performed his or her **dharma**. Dharma refers to the specific obligations and behavior based on a person's family and caste. Therefore, if a Shudra performs his/her dharma correctly, then he/she will perhaps be reincarnated as a Brahmin. However, the ultimate goal of a Hindu is to escape from or be released from the cycle of endless birth and rebirth on the mandala. This release is called **moksha**.

GODS AND GODDESSES

There are many gods and goddesses in Hinduism. However, it could be said that each of these deities is but one form or manifestation of a single God. Therefore, the issue of whether Hinduism can be considered a monotheistic or a polytheistic religion is not a major problem for Hindus. From about 3000 B.C.E., and for many years thereafter, the three chief Hindu deities were **Brahma** (associated with creation), **Vishnu** (associated with preservation), and **Shiva** (associated with destruction). The most popularly worshiped today however are

Vishnu and Shiva, either in their own form or in the different male and female forms they take. The different forms they take needs some explanation.

A dualism exists in regard to the two major deities. This means that each god has both male and female qualities as well as powers over good and evil, and birth and death. These dual characteristics can be seen in different forms of the deity. Shiva, for example, is associated with destruction and thus may take the form of the female *Durga* (a many clawed tiger with the head of a woman) or *Kali*. And yet, you cannot have destruction without creation. Therefore, a Shiva temple may have a lingam structure that represents male fertility. To worship either Durga or the lingam is to worship Shiva as well as to worship God. Durga and lingam images can be seen in temples, for example, in a city holy to Shiva. The city is Benares (Varanasi) and lies along the Ganges River. Its holiness is based on the belief that it lies at a point on the Ganges where Shiva is thought to have redirected its flow. Because water from the Ganges is considered holy, many Hindus believe that if their bodies are cremated in Benares and their ashes placed in the river, their souls will escape from the wheel of life and they will achieve moksha. In addition, devout Hindus will carry Ganges water to their homes in order to perform certain rituals and ceremonies.

Vishnu also has special features. In his role as preserver, Vishnu has come down to earth over time and taken a human form. In each of these forms or avatars or incarnations, Vishnu has come to correct a problem, to seek a balance between good and evil, and to instruct about dharma. Vishnu has had nine avatars, the most well known being *Rama* and *Krishna*. These two avatars, unknown as Vishnu upon coming to earth, spoke and acted in ways to teach and preserve dharma. Their activities are described, respectively, in two great Hindu epic pieces of literature, **The Ramayana** and **The Mahabharata**. Those Hindus who worship Rama, such as Gandhi did, are worshippers of Vishnu and are also worshiping God. The same is true for devotees of Krishna. Furthermore, Hindus see no problem or contradiction between whom they wor-

Main Idea:
A dualism exists in regard to the two major deities. Each god has both male and female qualities as well as powers over good and evil.

A view of Madras, India (also known as Chennai). Madras' oldest temple is Kapaleeswarar Temple, which is dedicated to Shiva.

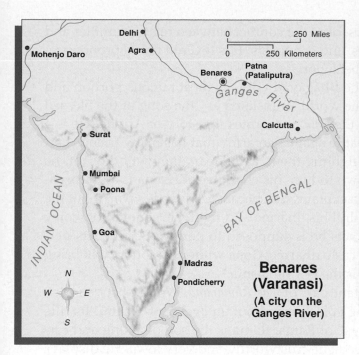

A cremation near the Ganges River.

Benares
(Varanasi)

(A city on the
Ganges River)

A stupa in Benares. A stupa is a spiritual monument that represents the Buddha's body, his speech, and his mind. Every part shows the path to Enlightenment.

ship. In other words, those who are devoted to Rama have no anger or ill will toward those devoted to Krishna, or to Shiva. This tolerant aspect of Hinduism is remarkable in light of the fact that the religion has never suffered the kind of religious warfare and divisions that have been true, on occasion, in Christianity and Islam.

HOLY LITERATURE

There is no one specific holy text, bible, or set of scriptures in Hinduism. Rather, there are several writings that are looked to for guidance and inspiration. The Vedas were written somewhere between 1500 and 800 B.C.E., and they contain hymns dealing with creation and reverence for nature. The Upanishads were written about 500 B.C.E. and 800 B.C.E., and they include discussions about the origins of the universe and appropriate ways of behavior. They consist of conversations between a teacher and a student.

While the Vedas and Upanishads make for very profound, abstract, and, at times, difficult reading, two other literary works have much more popular appeal. They are *The Mahabharata* and *The Ramayana*. Originally written as far back as 500 B.C.E., *The Mahabharata* is the longest poem in the world, containing over 200,000 lines. *Maha* can be translated as "great," while *Bharata* stands for the ancient name for India. It describes the conflict between related families and kingdoms, involving exile, wars, and conquests. It is revered for its pronouncements on morality and proper behavior.

There is a section called the **Bhagavad Gita**, its most famous portion and known throughout India and the world. Translated as "the song of the blessed one" and referred to simply as the *Gita*, it narrates the story of Arjuna. He is a warrior who is about to go to battle against an army that has many friends and relatives. He is worried about fighting them, as he fears they will die. Yet, he wants to obtain victory. Unknown to him, his charioteer Krishna is an incarnation or avatar of Vishnu. Krishna explains that because Arjuna is a warrior of the Kshatriya caste, Arjuna must fulfill his dharma and fight. He should not worry about the consequences of the acts he is supposed to perform. Good acts performed according to a person's caste dharma, done without emotion, will bring good results for the doer. Such is the law of karma.

Dharma also is an important part of *The Ramayana*. Written between 400 and 100 B.C.E., this is also a long epic poem about an avatar of Vishnu. Its title may be translated as the "goings" of Rama. Rama is the son of a king and carries out his dharma by being obedient, trustworthy, and very loyal. He displays proper loyalty to his father, even when banished to the forest from the royal palace. He is also loyal to his eventual wife Sita and his brother Lakshman. Along the lines of a classic love story, Sita is captured by the demon Ravana but is rescued by Rama with the aid of Hanuman (the general of a monkey army). Rama and Sita then return to the palace as king and queen. None of the characters realize that Rama is actually Vishnu. Although there are slightly different versions of the story as it evolved over the centuries, particularly with regard to the ending, the characters have remained the same.

Both *The Mahabharata* and *The Ramayana* are dramatized frequently as stage, dance, and reading performances in India and much of Southeast Asia. The main characters have been portrayed by endless numbers of artists and sculptors. Via a process of culture diffusion, these portrayals as well as the performances have become very popular in such places as the Buddhist nations of Myanmar (Burma), Cambodia, and Thailand and the largest Muslim nation in the world—Indonesia.

> **Main Idea:**
> There is no one specific holy text in Hinduism. Rather, there are several writings that are looked to for guidance and inspiration.

The Religion of Buddhism

It would be appropriate for us now to explore the religion described as **Buddhism**. Although there are very few Buddhists today in India, the religion has its origins in India. Buddhists make up approximately 6 percent of the

An image of Buddha in the lotus position.

world's population. Our approach will be to look at these various items:

- The life of Siddhartha Gautama
- Fundamental ideas and beliefs
- Holy literature
- Spread of Buddhism in Asia

THE LIFE OF SIDDHARTHA GAUTAMA

The founder of Buddhism, **Siddhartha Gautama**, was born as a Hindu in northern India in 563 B.C.E. As the son of a king, enjoying wealth and comfort, he was a member of the Kshatriya caste. Nevertheless, he was upset over the differences between his lifestyle and that of others who were poor and suffering. He left his palace to search for wisdom and the meaning of existence. After six years of wandering, living simply, fasting at times, and denying himself many comforts, he meditated under a large bo or fig tree for forty-nine days. This site, now holy, is in

Siddhartha was upset over the differences between his lifestyle and that of others who were poor and suffering. This is illustrated in this painting of Siddhartha encountering an old man.

Gaya, a small town on the Ganges, several miles east of Benares. It is here that he gained complete wisdom or *enlightenment* and became a *Buddha* (an enlightened one). He then went to Sarnath, just outside of Benares, and preached his first sermon. Buddhism was now born.

FUNDAMENTAL IDEAS AND BELIEFS

This sermon was of great importance as it contained Gautama's thoughts about the meaning of life and the problem of suffering. These thoughts are known as the **Four Noble Truths**. They are as follows:

1. Life contains and is full of suffering.

2. The cause of suffering is selfish desire.

3. The best way to end suffering is to end or extinguish desire.

4. In order to end or extinguish desire, a person has to follow the *Eightfold Path of Conduct* and take *the middle way*.

> **Main Idea:**
> Guatama's ideal was that a person should avoid extremes of pleasure or denial. To do this, a person should follow the Eightfold Path.

Gautama's ideal was to follow *the middle way*. This meant that a person should avoid extremes of pleasure and denial. To do this, according to the Eightfold Path, a person should pursue these goals: right views, right speech, right effort, right conduct, right mindfulness, right livelihood, right intentions, and right concentration. Ultimately, a person would be able to escape the wheel of life, avoid reincarnation, and thus achieve **nirvana**. Nirvana is similar to the Hindu idea of moksha. It is important to remember that Gautama was a Hindu and accepted such Hindu beliefs as the mandala and the idea of **ahimsa**. The latter refers to nonviolence. Buddhism obviously grew out of Hinduism. However, Gautama rejected the caste system as well as the power of Brahman priests.

Even though he did not intend to start a new religion, and never wrote down any thoughts himself, these thoughts over time did cause a new religion to emerge. One factor was the role played by his followers. Another factor was the appeal that Buddhism had to poor people, such as Shudras and untouchables. In addition, the growth of Buddhism in India was greatly helped when its ideas were accepted and promoted by King Asoka (274–232 B.C.E.). (We will meet him in a few pages.)

HOLY LITERATURE

The five people who were the first to hear Gautama's first sermon became monks and therefore were the initial members of the Buddhist order known as the *sangha*. Soon after his death, they and others began to write down the Buddha's teachings, ways to meditate, and commentaries on his life. No single holy book like the Bible was produced, however. The best known writings are the *Jatakas*, the *Ttipitaka*, and various *sutras*. Besides literature, painting and other expressive forms about Buddhism have grown. Many statues and sculptures of the Buddha show him sitting in a *lotus* and *yoga* position, a carryover from Hinduism. His feet are crossed, with his hands in different configurations. These configurations, called *mudras*, are meant to convey messages of hope, courage, faith, and so on. Other sculptures show him standing or reclining. **Stupas** are mounds of earth as well as buildings that are said to contain relics of the Buddha. Buddhists believe that hair and teeth were cast by winds over Asia after Gautama was created. *The Temple of the Tooth* in China is thus a holy site. A *pagoda* is usually a structure serving as a Buddhist educational and social center. Most pagodas today are found outside of India, as are most of the world's Buddhists. How can we explain this?

A rendering of the Buddha statue in Kamakura, Japan.

SPREAD OF BUDDHISM IN ASIA

As we have seen, Buddhism had several similarities with Hinduism. Over time, Hinduism actually recognized Gautama, although it did not accept all of his teachings. Hindus, however, in a broad and tolerant manner, did view Gautama as an incarnation of Vishnu. Buddhism was regarded by some people as part of Hinduism. A sharp blow to Buddhism's existence in India came with the Muslim thrust into South Asia starting in the eighth century C.E. The invaders destroyed many pagodas, statues, and libraries, while killing scores of monks.

If the seed that was Buddhism did not flower much in India, it certainly blossomed in other areas of Asia. For reasons we will soon explain, a Buddhist monastery was established in China as early as 65 C.E. From China, Buddhism came to Southeast Asia by 200 C.E., to Korea by 300 C.E., and from Korea to Japan by 550 C.E. The reasons for these migrations were several:

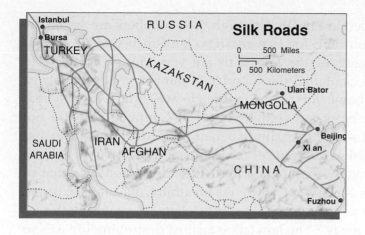

1. Traders and missionaries along the **Silk Road** through Central Asia and through the Bay of Bengal were both indirect and direct carriers of information about Buddhism.

2. Buddhists were not upset with the fact that people who accepted the new faith still practiced native systems of belief. They did not attempt to wipe out earlier systems of belief. Because Buddhism does not claim to have a belief in gods or goddesses, it has not come in conflict with any religions that do have such beliefs.

3. There was much admiration by other societies of the cultures of India and China, with a willingness to adopt some of their elements.

4. Buddhism offered a means of salvation from the toils and hardships of life on earth. This proved to be very appealing to masses of people. Some of the stricter features of the original Buddhist teachings were loosened, thereby making the religion easy to practice. Nirvana was something open to all people.

> **Main Idea:**
> Religions that have expanded from their birthplaces have undergone changes, been reinterpreted, and blended with customs of new areas.

This last point was very critical in explaining the success of Buddhism as it spread eastward from India. For those religions that have expanded from their birthplaces, they have undergone changes, been reinterpreted and blended with customs of new areas. This has been true of Judaism, Christianity, and Islam. Buddhism is no different. The Buddhism that began in India, the original Buddhism, now exists in India, Myanmar (Burma), Cambodia, Sri Lanka, and Thailand and is referred to as *Theravada*. This form is also called *Hinayana, Southern School*, and *"Little Vehicle."* It is more rigid and strict in beliefs and practices when contrasted with the later form, referred to as *Mahayana*. This form is also known as *Northern School* and *"Greater Vehicle."* It is found mainly in China, Vietnam, Korea, and Japan. In the Theravada areas, nirvana is considered very difficult to achieve and is only open to a select few. These select few follow very strict lives, refrain from most daily economic and social activities, beg for food and generally live a very isolated, monastic existence. Mahayana Buddhism is different in that anyone can achieve nirvana, and can engage in ordinary commercial and social activities. The path to nirvana is much easier and may be helped by a *bodhisattva*. A bodhisattva is someone who has achieved Buddhahood and enlightenment, but has returned to earth to help others. Found only in Mahayana Buddhism, this belief made Buddhism very popular and stirred much artistic activity.

Other Religions in India

The percentage breakdown of the largest religions among India's population today is as follows: Hindu—80, Muslim—14, Christian—2.4, and Sikh—2. There are also small communities of Jains, Jews, and Parsees. In addition to Hinduism, both Sikhism and Jainism are native to India. Sikhism developed in the fifteenth

A symbol for Jainism

century and will be discussed in Era III. Although their numbers are small, the Jains deserve some mention here for two reasons. Jainism began in ancient times. In addition, the origins of the Jain faith are very similar to those of Buddhism. As was true of Gautama, the founder of Jainism was a Kshatriya who wandered from his home for many years. He was Mahavira ("Great Hero"). Born in 540 B.C.E., he was a contemporary of Gautama and did not accept the caste system and some other Hindu beliefs. Indeed, both Jainism and Buddhism have been labeled as "renouncer traditions of India." However one Hindu belief that Jains strongly maintained and expanded upon was that of ahimsa, or nonviolence. For Mahavira, "all things breathing, all things existing, all things living, all beings whatever, should not be slain, or treated with violence, or insulted or driven away." The Jain taboo against destroying life was so extreme that followers will wear masks over their mouths lest they inhale a fly. They will not eat meat nor do farm work as they are against killing animals and fear that working the soil may destroy plant life. Thanks to Jainism, the concept of ahimsa was to assume more of a key feature of Hinduism in later years. Furthermore, it was the basis of Mahatma Gandhi's struggle for independence from the British in the twentieth century.

Early Empires in India

Throughout its long history, India has seen many empires on its land. Some have come from far away, such as the British. Others have sprung from within India itself. Of those from within, the two most important in ancient times were the *Maurya* and *Gupta Empires.*

For several centuries after the Aryan invasions, the Indian subcontinent was filled with many small kingdoms. There was little unity among them. The Persians took over part of the northern area along the Indus River from 529 to 522 B.C.E. Many Persian words were then mixed into Sanskrit, the ancient language of India. In 326 B.C.E., Greek armies under Alexander the Great came to the region that is now Pakistan. Although they left shortly afterward, due to weariness and a desire to return home, one of Alexander's generals kept the northern part of the subcontinent. As Seleucus I, he faced opposition from the native Magadha kingdom. Its ruler, Chandragupta Maurya, was able to fight and acquire land from Seleucus I in 303 B.C.E. Thus was born the Maurya Empire, thereby achieving the first political unification in the north of the subcontinent.

Chandragupta established a stable and popular government. One of his advisers, Kautilya, wrote a handbook that was used to rule the empire. It was called the Arthashastra. It laid out, for example, regulations for the selection and supervision of government officials. This may have been one reason for the successful creation of a postal system, irrigation works, and tax procedures. Although a renowned ruler, Chandragupta's fame was overshadowed by that of his grandson, **Asoka**. Ascending to the throne in 274 B.C.E., Asoka expanded the empire into the south. In spite of his military successes, he was very disturbed by the huge loss of life in battles. Upon studying Buddhism, he became impressed with its teaching about the middle way and nonviolence. He consequently decided to rule by Buddhist principles. He had stone pillars erected that described his policies and goals. Religious toleration, improved transportation and communication, and construction of wells were some of the highlights of his rule. He was known for caring for the needs and well-being of those he governed. For many reasons, he is thus considered the greatest king ever to rule in India. A set of three lions on one of his pillars is now used as a symbol of India.

Shortly after his death in 232 B.C.E., the Maurya Empire began to crumble. Several kingdoms that had been under Mauryan rule broke away. Different central Asian peoples began to flood into northern India, blending in with the native population. Three kingdoms in the far south, an area never conquered by the Mauryas, frequently fought among themselves. They were Dravidian people, who spoke mainly Tamil. For about 500 years, these patterns of immigration and internal disorder characterized the subcontinent. A change came about in 320 C.E. with the rise of the **Gupta** family. Its head was Chandragupta I, no relation to Chandragupta Maurya.

The Gupta empire came into being in northern India when Chandragupta I married the daughter of another royal family and became emperor. His son, Samudra, expanded the empire, but did not become as famous as his son, Chandragupta II. His reign, 375–415 C.E., was notable for its unification efforts, stable, organized government, and outstanding cultural accomplishments.

> **Main Idea:** Chandragupta II's reign was notable for its unification efforts, stable, organized government, and outstanding cultural accomplishments.

1. **Medicine**—Indian doctors were far advanced for their times, especially in the field of surgery. They were able to diagnose and treat many illnesses and clearly established the value of cleanliness in preventing infections.

2. **Mathematics**—The numerals we use today were invented in Gupta India. We call them Arabic numbers only because it was the Arabs who transmitted them from India to the Western world. The concepts of zero, infinity, and the decimal system also originated in India. The mathematician Aryabhata calculated the value of pi as 3.1416 and also estimated the duration of the solar year as 365.3586805 days.

3. **Literature**—Poetry was a very popular form of writing. The greatest poet of the period was Kalidasa, the author of "Shakuntala." This love story about a king and his beautiful bride is still read today in India.

4. **Art and architecture**—The Guptas were instrumental in providing funds for temple buildings. They encouraged painting and sculpture featuring Hindu religious themes. Because Buddhism had declined by this time, Hinduism became a strong, unifying force in the empire.

5. **The economy**—a tax system was created whereby farmers would make payments on a percentage of the crops they raised.

6. **Village life**—Under the Guptas, village councils were set up to rule in local areas. Each council had five members and was called the *panchayat* (*pancha* meant "five"). This system is still in existence today.

7. **Trade and commerce**—A banking system began to emerge. Loans were given to merchants, particularly to engage in overseas trade. Trade developed between Gupta India and such areas as present day Sri Lanka, Cambodia,

Thailand, and Indonesia. These commercial ties were also a factor in the spread of Hinduism and Indian culture to these areas.

During the sixth century C.E., well after the death of Chandragupta II, the empire started to dissolve. Invasions by Huns, Turks, and Mongols led to disunity. Such was the situation in India for the next 500 years.

SECTION 2

Ancient China

It is believed that human beings have lived in China for almost one million years. A skeleton known as Peking Man found in northern China was dated as far back as 500,000 years ago. It should not surprise us that such a fossil was located in this part of China, as a major river valley exists here. It is formed by the Huang He River, or **Yellow River**. As we have previously seen, other river valley civilizations formed along, for example, the Tigris, Euphrates, Nile, and Indus Rivers. Legend has it that the first Chinese ruling dynasty was the Xia (Hsia) and was near the Huang He. Supposedly, its leader was an engineer named Yu. He was alleged to have devised ways to control the river's flood waters and to build irrigation projects. Although archaeologists have found little evidence about the Xia, the need for China's population to adapt to river patterns and other geographic conditions still exists today. The next four dynasties, whose given dates here are approximate, are the ancient ones that did leave many items as proof of their existence. They are the Shang, Zhou, Qin, and Han dynasties.

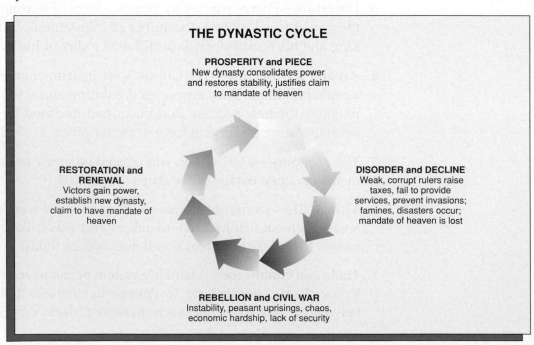

THE DYNASTIC CYCLE

PROSPERITY and PIECE
New dynasty consolidates power and restores stability, justifies claim to mandate of heaven

DISORDER and DECLINE
Weak, corrupt rulers raise taxes, fail to provide services, prevent invasions; famines, disasters occur; mandate of heaven is lost

RESTORATION and RENEWAL
Victors gain power, establish new dynasty, claim to have mandate of heaven

REBELLION and CIVIL WAR
Instability, peasant uprisings, chaos, economic hardship, lack of security

An illustration of the dynastic cycle.

The Shang Dynasty

The symbol for the yin and yang.

The first dynasty for which archaeological evidence such as written records exists is the Shang (1600–1100 B.C.E.). With the discovery of the ruins of Anyang, a city in the northern China plain, we have learned about the great wealth of Shang kings. They built large palaces and encouraged bronze working. Objects made of bronze were often used in religious ceremonies but were also symbols of royal power. Silk production was also carried on under the Shang. However, from a cultural standpoint, the most significant feature of this early dynasty was development of a writing system. The oldest form of Chinese writing ever found was on cattle bones and tortoise shells. These have been called "oracle bones" because they were utilized by Shang kings to consult with their gods. Examples would be a tree and the moon. Over succeeding years, the Chinese developed a system of ideographs. These became symbols used for the expression of ideas and thoughts.

Another set of symbols developed stood for a sense of balance and harmony. These were the *yin and yang*. These two intertwined U-shaped symbols in a circle divided in half, represented natural rhythm patterns. Yin stood for female forces, passivity, and earth. Yang symbolized male forces, action, and heaven. It was thought that pain was brought on by an imbalance in the body between yin and yang forces. Herbal medicines and acupuncture would supposedly help to restore the proper balance of forces.

The Zhou Dynasty

Main Idea:
The Zhou dynasty was the longest in Chinese history, lasting from 1100 –256 B.C.E.

The Shang dynasty was overthrown by the Zhou (pronounced "joh") people, who established their own ruling dynasty. This new dynasty proved to be the longest in Chinese history, lasting from 1100 to 256 B.C.E. It was marked by economic and cultural advances as well as by political weakness. The economy was stimulated with improved iron and bronze production, jade carving, money coining, and road and canal construction. For one of the few times in China's cultural history, a limited amount of freedom of thought and expression was permitted. During the last three centuries of the Zhou emperors, scholars and philosophers were referred to as the *Hundred Schools*. These intellectual figures would debate, discuss political and spiritual matters, and frequently travel to different areas of the country. They were thus called *wandering scholars* and included the sage Confucius among them. It was during this dynasty that the *Great Wall of China* began to be built. The early sections were designed for protection from invasions of non-Chinese people in the north, beyond the upper part of the Huang He River. To the east and south of this point was what can be called China Proper, an area smaller than the size of current China. Several emperors after the Zhou reign added sections to the wall until it extended for over 2000 miles.

The weakness of the Zhou dynasty was the lack of strong, effective rulers. In an effort to gain the loyalty of the many Chinese states under them, the Zhou emperors gave some control to local nobles and lords. This political arrangement, called *feudalism*, would also arise later in Japan and western Europe. It is an arrangement whereby a ruler grants land and some power to nobles and lords who then promise loyalty and military support to the ruler. During its first three centuries in power, the Zhou emperors were to dominate the local lords, especially since many lords fought among themselves. After these times, Zhou rulers lost power and influence. Invaders started to come in from the north. As local states gained power, with conflict among them increasing, the last 400 years of Zhou rule became known as "the time of the warring states."

These years witnessed political unrest, civil wars, and general instability. Traditional Chinese values of harmony, order, and respect for authority appeared to be forgotten. In an attempt to bring back these values, provide stability for society, and offer new solutions for peaceful living, philosophers and scholars put forth ideas that were to affect China's people. As these grew during the Zhou dynasty, we will stop here to examine them before we move on to other dynasties. These ideas were contained in three philosophies: *Confucianism*, *Daoism*, and *Legalism*. These are labeled philosophies and not religions because they were not concerned with God and gods, nor the soul, nor the meaning of birth and of death.

Confucianism

Confucianism is based on the thoughts and teaching of **Confucius**, or Kung Futzu (551– 479 B.C.E.). His teachings were destined to become the basis of Chinese society and were mainly an ethical set of ideas about human nature and proper conduct. This means that he was concerned with correct and appropriate behavior by people toward one another and toward their government. He felt that there existed a set pattern in the world and that people must live in ways that can help them contribute to and help society. Every person has a specific place in society, with certain moral duties to fulfill. If everyone behaved well, according to place and duties, then society would achieve harmony and peace. As a guide to this achievement, Confucius taught *five basic relationships*. These were as follows:

Confucius (551–479 B.C.E.)

1. Ruler and subject

2. Father and son

3. Husband and wife

4. Older brother and younger brother

5. Friend and friend

All the relationships were based on the notion of reciprocity. In the first four relationships, there is a superior and an inferior. The superior exhibits respect and responsibility for the inferior. The inferior shows loyalty and obedience to the superior. In the fifth relationship, friends are to honor and respect each other.

The family would be the foundation and core of society and was the basis for three of the five relationships. Indeed, a vital value was *filial piety*. This could be described as love and devotion to family and respect and obedience to parents. Children had a lifelong, caring obligation to their parents. Indeed, ancestor worship was maintained and passed on to succeeding generations of Chinese families. Family members were to live near the graves of their ancestors and conduct proper ceremonies to honor the ancestors and the spirits that supposedly watched over them. Family life was viewed as preparing young people for life in society.

Main Idea: Knowledge and mastery of Confucious' teachings was absolutely necessary for becoming a government official.

The government was seen as an extension of the family. The dynastic rulers had responsibilities and obligations toward their subjects, just as parents had toward their children. Accordingly, subjects owed obedience and loyalty to their rulers just as children did to their elders. However, a ruler had a special responsibility, given his power over society. He was to be an example of virtue, a righteous, moral, and wise person who would be an example for his subjects. If he possessed and governed with these characteristics, then he had the *Mandate of Heaven*. This meant that he had the right to rule. If the emperor acted badly, however, by being harsh toward his subjects, then he was said to have lost the Mandate of Heaven. This doctrine, formulated even before Confucius, was adopted by him and further expounded upon by his disciple **Mencius** (327–289 B.C.E.). Accordingly, people had the right to rebel against the dynasty. The leader of the rebellion would then be entitled to be the head of a new dynasty.

Mencius and other students of Confucius wrote down and spread his teachings. Chief among these was a book titled *The Analects*. Knowledge and mastery of these teachings was absolutely necessary for becoming a government official. A person would have to pass a challenging examination based on Confucianism to become a member of what could be called the Chinese civil service. In the ancient Chinese social system, scholars thus held the highest position of the four main social classes. They were the only ones who could take the civil service examinations and serve in government. The second highest class was the peasants. This was due to their providing the grains and textiles necessary for food and clothing. Artisans and craftspeople were the third group, consisting of skilled workers. The lowest social class was the businessmen and merchants. They had this rank, though very wealthy, because they profited from the labor of others. The nobility was considered to be above the class system, while soldiers were below the system.

Daoism (Taoism)

Another Chinese philosophy arising about the same time as Confucianism was Daoism. The name comes from Dao (Tao), the Chinese word for "the way." Its beliefs were mainly the work of the philosopher Lao Tzu. Scholars are unsure as to whether such a person ever existed or whether he was simply a representative of a school or group of philosophers. Nevertheless, as contrasted with

Confucianists, Daoists are primarily interested in nature and the natural order of things in the universe. Recall that Confucius was most concerned with family, social relationships, and government. The Daoist wants government to do little and let people alone to freely express themselves. People would live peacefully, in harmony with nature and themselves, and would find the Dao or way of the universe.

To clearly define the Dao is difficult. Daoists never gave a definition because they felt that language could not give clear meaning to the idea. At best, the Dao could be thought of as an unseen power and force in nature. It is the force or nature of a fish to live in water, of a man to breathe, of a bird to fly. Daoism has had a significant affect on Chinese culture, particularly in art and literature.

Legalism

Legalism is a philosophy that became prominent during the period of the "warring states," 475–221 B.C.E. As with Confucianism and Taoism, this belief system wanted to find a way to end warfare, strife, and chaos and to establish an improved society. Yet, unlike these two older philosophies, Legalism held that humans were evil by nature. People had to be restrained by laws and government. Harmony can be restored to Chinese society only by a strong and powerful ruler. Government cannot let individuals act freely and therefore must control their ideas and thoughts. This notion went against Daoist ideas. In addition, it opposed the Confucian idea of the ruler as a wise and virtuous model person. The Legalists claimed that an effective ruler was one who was dictatorial, strict, and quick to use punishment to keep order. The Legalist school could trace most of its teachings to Hsun-tzu (298–238 B.C.E.). Its impact was felt for a limited time, when it became the policy of the Qin (Chin) dynasty. We turn now to that period of Chinese history.

> **Main Idea:**
> Legalism wanted to find a way to end warfare, strife, and chaos and to establish an improved society.

The Qin Dynasty

The warring states period ended when the most powerful of these states, that of **Qin**, defeated all the others. The Qin ruler took the name **Shi Huangdi**, "the first emperor," and used Legalist ideas during his reign (221– 206 B.C.E.). To his credit, he expanded Chinese territory beyond the Zhou dynasty borders and unified his country. He thus could be called an imperial ruler, the head of imperial China. To further strengthen the country's defenses, he added fortifications to the walls built by the Zhou rulers. The result was a 1400-mile barrier, part of what we know today

Statue of a Qin infantryman.

The Great Wall of China is 1400 miles long.

as the Great Wall of China. Later emperors added even more to the wall built by Shi Huangdi. However, true to his nature and personality, he had the wall constructed in a harsh and costly way. An untold number of peasants, perhaps in the hundreds of thousands, worked to build the wall. They were treated badly, were not paid, and frequently suffered injuries and death.

Additional harshness could be seen in his treatment of the rest of China's population. He severely limited free expression of ideas, particularly any attempt to speak out against him. With the advice of his Legalist prime minister, Li Su, he murdered hundreds of Confucian scholars and teachers. Many were supposedly buried alive. Book burnings were ordered for Confucian and other texts that disagreed with Legalist philosophy. His self-glorification and distorted sense of values was also shown in the construction of a huge underground palace that would be near his tomb. This mausoleum would reflect his life and power. It would take 700,000 convicts, working for ten years, to finish the job. Buried and untouched for centuries, part of this underground complex was discovered by accident in 1974 near the present day city of Xi'an (formerly the capital city of Chang'an). While excavating for a factory in an open field, a peasant and some workers came upon an astonishing caved-in area. This proved to be a vast hall containing almost 7000 life-sized figures made from terra cotta materials. The figures were bodyguards and members of the army of Shi Huangdi. Placed in battle formation, next to figures of life-sized horses, these stunning figures were less than a mile from the actual tomb of the emperor. Although the tomb itself has not yet been opened, the area containing the terra-cotta soldiers has been carefully preserved by the Chinese government and is currently a major tourist attraction.

The mausoleum and the Great Wall stand as magnificent legacies of his rule, but the same cannot be said of the ruling philosophy of Shi Huangdi. His brutal treatment of the population and his costly extravagances provoked displeasure and led to several peasant revolts. Led by a peasant from the land of Han, troops finally overthrew the Qin dynasty only fifteen years after it began. Thus was born the Han dynasty. One other legacy however remains from the Qin reign. The name China comes from Qin.

The Han Dynasty

For many good reasons, the Han dynasty (206–220 B.C.E.) lasted much longer than did the Qin. The first Han emperor, Liu Bang, for example, refused to follow Legalist ideas. He also lowered taxes, did not build grandiose monuments, and lessened punishment for criminal acts. His rule was characterized by a strong centralized government that strengthened national unity. In other words, local lords and rulers accepted his authority. Future emperors, some of whom were as successful, were able to maintain Han control over 400 years. This dynasty was so influential that in modern China today most people describe themselves as "Han people" or "Han Chinese" or "sons of Han."

Han China has been admired for accomplishments both within and outside of its area. The early emperors, particularly Wudi, had Confucian scholars as court advisers. He was very partial toward Confucianism and felt that government officials should possess Confucian values. In addition, he established a productive civil service system that required passing a difficult examination. It was during the Han reign that the Chinese invented paper and porcelain. The latter was much desired by people outside of China, and thus became a major item for trade along the **Silk Roads**. These trade routes extended from China, through Xi'an, across central Asia, to the Middle East. From ports in this region, ships carried Chinese products to Rome. The product most in demand was silk. In return, many Roman and Middle Eastern items made their way to China.

> **Main Idea:**
> Han China has been admired for accomplishments both within and outside of its area.

Trading routes such as the Silk Roads also brought about contact between different cultures. A good example of cultural diffusion was the bringing of Buddhism to China. Two Indian Buddhist scholars brought sacred sutras and images and founded the first Buddhist monastery in China in 67 C.E., east of Xi'an, in Loyang. The new religion, however, was of interest primarily to small numbers of Han officials and some Chinese scholars. Intellectual life was still dominated by Confucianism. Buddhism did not affect the masses of people. This situation was to change, however, after the fall of the Han dynasty. For reasons that will be discussed in Chapter 8, Buddhism became very popular and presented a challenge to Confucianism.

The Han rule collapsed for both economic and political reasons. Farmers were taxed heavily by later Han leaders, frequently went into debt, and lost their lands. Political stability began to crack as government officials and powerful rival families competed and clashed as they tried to influence policies made by the emperors. Early in the third century C.E., the Han dynasty was replaced by three different smaller kingdoms.

Ancient Southeast Asia

The early history of Southeast Asia is not very well known. Its population was a mix of native inhabitants plus people who had migrated from China and India. These two countries had long-lasting influence on the history and culture of both the mainland and island areas of Southeast Asia. Therefore, it is not surprising that the one of the two peninsulas that makes up the mainland portion of this region is called **Indo-China**. Commercial ties between India and Southeast Asia occurred as early as 100 C.E. Boats would sail, for example, across the Bay of Bengal, between India and the Malay Peninsula, making use of monsoon winds. During the Han dynasty, in 111 C.E., China seized most of what is now northern Vietnam and controlled it for 1000 years. The main empires in ancient Southeast Asia were those of Funan, Srivijaya, and the Khmer.

Main Idea:
China and India had long-lasting influence on the history and culture of both the mainland and island areas of Southeast Asia.

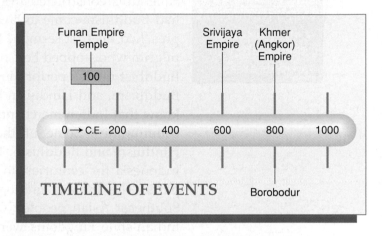

TIMELINE OF EVENTS

Funan and Srivijaya

From approximately 100–500 C.E., Funan grew in importance because of its location. Situated on the southern tip of the Indo-China Peninsula, the site of present-day southern Cambodia and Vietnam, it was involved in trade between India and China that went through the Isthmus of Kra on the Malay Peninsula. However, with improved seafaring ships and the increased use of the China Sea and the **Strait of Malacca**, Funan began to decline in

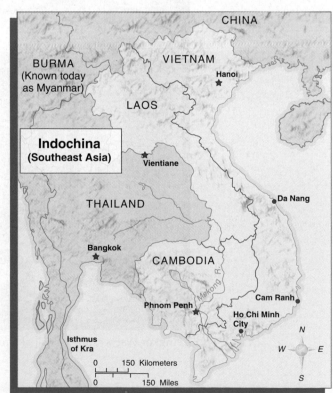

importance. Its place was taken by the island empire of Srivijaya. This powerful empire controlled the Strait of Malacca and ruled the areas that are present-day southern Malaysia, Singapore, and most of Indonesia. Both Srivijaya and Funan owed their wealth and prominence more to trade than to agriculture. Furthermore, as trading societies, they became exposed to cultural diffusion and new ideas from other lands.

A striking example of culture spread and absorption can be seen in an empire that existed with and was then taken over by Srivijaya. This was the Sailendra dynasty, on the island of Java in present-day **Indonesia**. The Sailendras constructed the magnificent Buddhist temple of Borobodur. How had Buddhism come to Java, hundreds of miles to the east of where Gautama preached his first sermon? In fact, we have the account of a Chinese Buddhist pilgrim who stopped here on his way to India in 671 C.E. He observed over 1000 Buddhist monks performing ceremonies similar to those in India. Apparently, Buddhism, and Hinduism before it, had existed here for quite some time. We know that Indian merchants, as noted previously, traded with Southeast Asian communities. Some of them even settled there, bringing their beliefs in Hinduism and Buddhism. The Ramayana, for example, has been performed in Indonesia for centuries. In addition, Buddhist missionaries traveled to these parts. The Indians gradually gained the respect and admiration of many Southeast Asian peoples. Consequently, in addition to Indian culture, many Indian-style kingdoms were created by people who were not Indians themselves. Sailendra and Srivijaya are examples of some of the first powerful mainland Southeast Asian empires. This was the empire of the Khmers.

Angkor Wat was the principal temple in the capital city of Angkor.

Khmer (Angkor) Empire

The **Khmer** people grew to prominence in what is now Cambodia. Their empire gradually expanded to include parts of present-day Vietnam, Laos, and Thailand. Scholars, however, are unsure of their origin. The Khmers, according to some accounts, were one of many tribal groups that originated in southern China. Among these groups were those peoples who migrated southward, a pattern of migration that has been true for centuries in East Asia. These groups included Khmers Thais, Viet, and Malays, among others. Khmer society became wealthy, thanks mainly to the rich fertile soil that it controlled. Unlike the trading societies of Funan and Srivijaya, Khmer wealth was due to its success as an agricultural society. Political advance reached a high point in 802 C.E. when an eminent and powerful figure name Jayavarman united the Khmer people into a kingdom. With the capital at the city of Angkor Thom, the Khmer or Angkor Empire came into existence. It was to become the most powerful mainland Southeast Asian empire until the fourteenth century.

SECTION 4

Ancient Japan

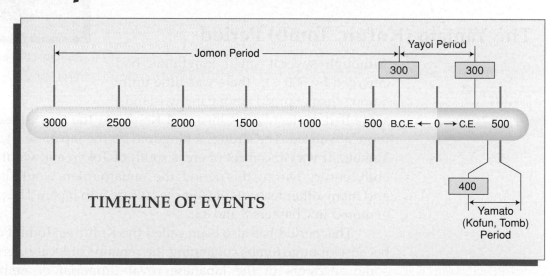

TIMELINE OF EVENTS

People have lived in Japan for almost 100,000 years, according to archaeological findings. Japan, or we could say, the Japanese islands, was once connected to the Asian mainland via a land bridge. The first written mention of Japan is in Chinese writings in about 300 C.E. It was not very flattering and did not refer specifically to a place called Japan. Indeed, there was not at that time a united nation but rather hundreds of scattered clans. The name Japan is actually a Western pronunciation, jih-pen, of the Chinese name for the islands: *ri ben*. The Japanese call their nation *nihon* ("land of the rising sun" or "origin of the sun").

The earliest period of Japanese history is the Jomon, beginning in about 3,000 B.C., followed by the Yayoi Period in about 300 B.C.E. Shortly thereafter arose the Yamato Kingdom, the most powerful of many kingdoms at the time.

Jomon and Yayoi Periods

The use of stone tools dating as far back as 16,000 years ago is proof of some civilization in Japan at the time. At about 3,000 B.C.E., a type of pottery called jomon was produced. At this time, people inhabited houses made from thatch. Pottery production was also the criterion used for labeling the second period of Japanese history, the Yayoi Period (300 B.C.E.—300 C.E.) The name was adopted from the Yayoi section of modern-day Tokyo. It was here that segments of a reddish pottery were discovered. Besides pottery, figures of warriors and horses were found. Food production was plentiful, thanks to the development of wet rice agriculture. Bronze and iron handiwork was evident, as a result of contact with China.

A sample of a jomon figurine.

The Yamato (Kofun, Tomb) Period

Although several small kingdoms had emerged by 500 C.E., there was little unity among them. Spread among many islands, some had contact with China and Korea. At the time, these civilizations were more advanced. The strongest kingdom on the Japanese islands was that of the Yamato. It was in control of areas south of Tokyo and would last until the seventh century. During this period, the Yamato rulers would introduce Buddhism and many other features of Chinese culture into Japan. These items will be fully explored in Chapters 8 and 13.

This period has also been called the Kofun or Tomb Period. The reason is because of huge tombs containing the remains of local rulers and perhaps even some ancestors of the Japanese royal (imperial or emperor's) household. Beginning around 200 C.E., Korean influence became very evident in Japan. Industrial processes such as metalworking, weaving, tanning, and shipbuilding were introduced from Korea, having been developed in China during the Han dynasty. In addition, over the next three centuries, many large burial mounds were constructed throughout the western two thirds of the main island of Honshu. Some of these have been excavated, revealing human remains as well as mirrors, swords, bracelets, shoes, and **haniwa**. Haniwa are delicately designed small terra-cotta figurines. They represented animals, furniture, and humans.

A Chinese terra-cotta horse.

A more intriguing aspect revolving around the unopened tombs is whether the human remains therein are those of Koreans. Scholars are unsure as to the origins of the Japanese royal household. The Japanese royal or imperial line of emperors is the oldest in the world going back over 2000 years. Did this unbroken line originate with Koreans who came to Japan in early times? The issue is very controversial. For many Japanese, it would be embarrassing if there was a Korean connection to the royal family. Because many burial mounds have still not been opened, the issue remains unresolved.

Shintoism

Whatever may be the historical and archaeological explanations for Japan's origins, there is also a mythical and legendary account. This can be called the *Shinto Creation Myth*. It was first described in a book written in 720 C.E. titled the *Nihon-shoki* or *Nihongi*. This may be translated as *Chronicles of Japan*. Along with another book called the *Kojiki (Records of Ancient Matters)*, written in 712 C.E., it was compiled at the command of the emperor. He was a descendent of the Yamato clan and wanted an official history prepared that would justify his claim to rule Japan. Both books can be thought of as the closest texts that could possibly be considered the "bibles" of Japan. However, they do not command the deep religious and spiritual reverence among Japanese that the Bible has for Jews and Christians. Nevertheless it is necessary for us to understand the creation myth, its link to Shintoism, and basic features of Shintoism itself.

Followers of Shintoism believe in kamis (spirits, forces, gods) that can be found in natural things such as mountains, birds, rocks, etc. This is a picture of Mount Fuji.

Two deities or god-like heavenly forces, Izanagi and Izanami, created the "Great Eight-Island Country." As husband and wife, they then produced many gods and goddesses. Among these was the sun goddess, Amaterasu. She had a grandson, a god, who was sent from heaven to possess and rule the Japanese islands with his descendents forever. A great-grandson of this god, called Jimmu, was ultimately enthroned as the first emperor of Japan. The seventh-century C.E. Yamato rulers could now say that they were emperors of divine origin. This divinity claim was strongly in force in Japan in the late nineteenth and early twentieth centuries, as Shintoism became the state religion. Under "State Shinto," the emperor was a god-like figure to whom obedience would be unquestioned. This belief was done away with, as a result of the 1945 defeat of Japan in World War II. The great majority of Japanese people today would not accept the divine origin theory of their emperor, but they do look upon him with profound respect and deep admiration. Nevertheless, they do accept several Shinto beliefs as part of their spiritual traditions. We turn now to examine some of those beliefs.

Shintoism means "the way of the kami or gods." It was first used in the sixth century C.E. to describe the earliest religious practices of the Japanese people. Even though those practices go back over thousands of years, there was no name given to them. The reason for naming in the sixth century was done to distinguish these ancient, traditional practices from a new foreign religion. The "imported" belief system was Buddhism, having been adopted from China. Over time, and up until the present, Japan's population saw no serious conflicts between these faiths. In the twenty-first century, a Japanese family, for example, would ask a Shinto priest to preside at a birth ceremony or the opening of a new business, but would have a Buddhist priest officiate at a funeral.

The beginnings of Shintoism are obscure. There was no one founder or group of founders, nor is there any set of sacred scriptures. It seemed to be chiefly a form of nature worship. There are **kami** (spirits, forces, gods), thousands of them, who are everywhere. They can be found in natural things such as mountains, birds, rocks, winds, trees, and waterfalls, and they live in shrines. Shintoism can thus be considered an example of an animistic religion. **Animism** is a category of religion that emphasizes great admiration of and close links with the forces of nature. Examples, besides Shintoism, would be native American and African religions.

Ancient Korea

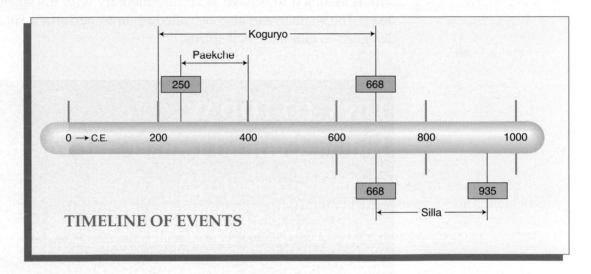

TIMELINE OF EVENTS

As a peninsula off the east coast of the Asian mainland, Korea has a history that goes back for at least 30,000 years. This was the result of archaeological finds during the 1960s C.E. Scholars believe that migrations of people took place from northern China and Manchuria. Stone artifacts left by these early dwellers have been discovered. Yet, we know little about them. Two legends concern the origins of Korea, on that is Korean and one that is Chinese.

The Korean story is that a state called Choson was founded by a leader named Tan'gun. He was the product of a union between a god, his father, and a bear, his mother. In the Chinese story, he ruled until 1122 B.C.E., until he was displaced by Kija. Kija was a descendent of the Shang dynasty in China. As a matter of proven history, however, in 108 B.C.E. the Han dynasty of China took over the northern half of the Korean peninsula. As a result, the conquered Korean natives learned about ideas such as Confucianism, Buddhism, Chinese writing, and iron production. With the collapse of the Han dynasty, however, a Korean tribal state was ultimately able to seize control of this territory by the fourth century C.E. This was the first real Korean kingdom. In the southern half of the peninsula, meanwhile, during the third and fourth centuries, two other kingdoms arose. These were Paekche and Silla. Thus began the Three Kingdoms Period. This did not usher in a time of peace however. In several wars that followed, the "Struggle of the Three kingdoms," Silla emerged victorious over the other two. By the end of the seventh century, Silla controlled the entire peninsula.

The unification of the peninsula by Silla was to continue until the tenth century. Even with Silla's defeat by another dynasty, some form of unity of the Korean people was to be maintained until the Korean War (1950–1953). The break-up caused by that conflict, into a communist North Korea and a democratic South Korea, was a new and unusual phenomenon in the peninsula's long history.

One feature of modern Korea, mostly in South Korea, that is not new is the practice and belief in **shamanism**. This is the oldest belief system in Korea. As a religion with some nature worship similarities to Shintoism, it can be categorized as an animistic religion. A central figure is the shaman. This is a person who is assumed to behave as an intermediary with the spiritual world and the dead. The shaman can also be called upon to perform a *kut*, a ritual ceremony designed to eliminate evil spirits.

Main Idea:
Despite the many changes in Korea over the centuries, the belief in shamanism still exists.

LINK TO TODAY

India—Cultural Impact and Vocabulary

Do Americans realize how much we have borrowed from Indian cultures and mixed them into our own culture? Examples certainly can be found. Do you know someone who does *yoga*? This is an ancient Indian method of seeking relaxation of the mind and body. It helps to achieve a condition of meditation and to remove materialist thoughts from one's mind. Images and sculptures of Buddha are often in a sitting yoga position. If someone is no longer liked by a group of friends and is shunned by them because the person violated a social rule of the group and engaged in bad and embarrassing behavior, the situation could be summed up as follows: The person became an *outcast* because of breaking a *taboo*.

The Reverend Martin Luther King, Jr., won worldwide fame for his fight against racial discrimination and his promotion of equal rights for all people. Yet, he did not fight with weapons that killed. His weapon was nonviolence. He had admiration for Mahatma Gandhi, who employed a similar strategy in his fight for Indian independence from the British. Gandhi looked for inspiration to the ancient Hindu and Jain doctrine of *ahimsa*.

China—Places and Philosophy

Have you ever been to Chinatown? Well, if you live in a big city in the United States, chances are that you went there or at least have heard of it. There are many Chinatowns in our nation, created by Chinese immigrants. The migration from their original homeland is not surprising. It has been going on for centuries, starting in ancient times as we have seen in this chapter. The reason has usually been economic. In addition, we can understand why, in New York City's Chinatown, there is an address known as Confucius Plaza.

However, this site is not the only impact of Confucius in New York City, nor in the rest of the United States for that matter. Let us look at education and our schools. Given the high regard Confucius himself had for scholars and education, and the traditional concern for education found in most Chinese families, it is not surprising to observe so many Chinese students, in proportion to their total numbers, doing so well in their studies. The Confucian admiration for education and teachers, as well as his emphasis on showing respect toward one's parents and superiors, has even another consequence. You can see this with regard to the relationship between recently arrived immigrant children and their new American teachers. These children, when talking to a teacher, will generally not look the teacher in the face. To do so would be considered disrespectful. Ironically, this would not be so from the teacher's point of view. The teacher would think the child would be disrespectful by *not facing* the teacher! Such a culture clash is not surprising, given different traditions and philosophies from different societies.

There is one more irony we should note concerning ancient China and the modern-day world. It is about one of the most famous places in the world and clearly the most famous place in China—the Great Wall of China. As we have learned from this chapter, the Great Wall was built to keep foreigners from invading China. Yet, in the current century, China welcomes foreigners to the Great Wall! The Wall has become a prime tourist attraction. Foreigners "invade" China today with money, not weapons.

CHAPTER SUMMARY

The book you are now reading is called *Global History*. It could also be called a *World History* textbook. In fact, a book like this one would have been called World History several years ago. In those books, a chapter such as the one on the ancient world that you have just finished would have been included. Yet, there would have been one major difference. The World History textbooks would have emphasized the Middle East as the "cradle of civilization" with a corresponding focus on European history. Such an emphasis and focus is neither fair nor historically accurate. Even though the Middle East has played an enormous role in the history of our planet, as has Europe, it is not the only cradle. Indeed, as we have seen in this chapter, there have been many cradles of civilization. The history as well the richness of culture that grew, for example in Asia, warrants our study and appreciation. Awareness and knowledge of *who we are* as humans and *what we are* begins with an understanding of the global past.

Another item about this chapter, and connected to the preceding discussion, concerns cultural diffusion. We have seen how ideas and thoughts beginning in one area have spread and affected other areas. Even though this spreading may take place peacefully or forcefully, and may indeed change from the original ideas and thoughts, it is an ongoing theme in world history. It certainly has been true in China and Southeast Asia and, as we will see, even in our own nation.

IMPORTANT PEOPLE, PLACES, AND TERMS

KEY TERMS

Buddhism	*The Mahabharata*	stupa
Nihon-shoki	*Bhagavad Gita*	endogamy
haniwa	Brahma	Varna
Shintoism	Vishnu	Shamanism
Kojiki	Shiva	Four Noble Truths
kami	taboo	mandala
animism	caste	Koguryo
Aryan	jati	ahimsa
Vedas	nirvana	dharma
The Ramayana	moksha	karma

PEOPLE

Siddhartha Gautama	Shui Huangdi	Khmer
Confucius	Gupta	Han
Mencius	Asoka	Qin

PLACES

Great Wall of China	Yamato	Indochina
Silk Roads	Benares	Strait of Malacca
Ganges River	Yangtze River	Indonesia
Yellow River	Harappa	

EXERCISES FOR CHAPTER 2

MULTIPLE CHOICE

Select the letter of the correct answer.

1. The practice of endogamy results in married couples who

   a. will have many children.
   b. have come from village communities.
   c. have come from the same jati.
   d. will live in cities.

2. Which does not belong with the others?

   a. Krishna
   b. Vishnu
   c. Shiva
   d. Mandala

3. Which of the following did Asoka most admire?

   a. Chandragupta Maurya
   b. Siddhartha Gautama
   c. Chandragupta II
   d. Mahatma Gandhi

4. "I must burn those books I do not like, as I do not want them read by my people." This statement was most likely made by

   a. Confucius.
   b. Shi Huangdi.
   c. Lao Tzu.
   d. Liu Bang.

5. A common goal of Confucianism, Daoism, and Buddhism was to

   a. promote artistic activity.
   b. increase the power of emperors.
   c. expand China's borders.
   d. establish peace and harmony.

6. The control of vital water ways as routes for commerce and trade added to the power of the

   a. Han Dynasty.
   b. Koguryo Kingdom.
   c. Gupta Empire.
   d. Srivijaya Empire.

7. Which would be a good example of cultural diffusion?

   a. A Vishnu temple is erected in India.
   b. The Ramayana is performed in Indonesia.
   c. Confucianism is taught in Chinese schools.
   d. A Shaman priest officiates at a ritual in Korea.

8. Which of the following share the greatest emphasis with admiration for the natural world?

   a. Jainism and Buddhism
   b. Legalism and Hinduism
   c. Daoism and Shintoism
   d. Confucianism and Shamanism

9. The river valleys of the Tigris-Euphrates, the Nile, and the Indus were centers of civilizations because they

   a. had rich deposits of iron and coal.
   b. were isolated from other cultural influences.
   c. were easily defended from invasion.
   d. provided a means of transportation and irrigation.

10. Which statement best explains a reason for the Golden Ages of the Gupta Empire of India and the Han Dynasty of China?

    a. The winning of a war often inspires scientific and artistic achievement.
    b. A combination of wealth and a time of relative peace often leads to cultural achievement.
    c. A dictatorship usually encourages cultural growth and development.
    d. Periods of censorship are needed for a nation to achieve cultural and scientific greatness.

11. Which of the following most greatly influenced the establishment of civil servants in China?

a. Distrust of the nobility by the emperor
b. The absence of the emperor's relatives to help in ruling territories
c. The need for administrators to govern territories as the empire grew
d. The demands of the military forces

12. Reference to the idea of the Mandate of Heaven was made in China in order to explain why

a. an emperor died.
b. a revolt occurred and a new ruler took over.
c. soldiers went out to sea to do battle.
d. people accepted Buddhism.

13. Which of the following statements about Confucianism is true?

a. It focuses on the salvation of the soul.
b. It emphasizes a belief in monotheism.
c. It is mainly concerned with life after death.
d. It is centered on achieving a proper life on earth.

14. Which of the following is not an accomplishment of the Han?

a. The Han made the ideas of Confucius the law of the land.
b. The Han destroyed the power of the Mongols.
c. The Han invented paper and porcelain.
d. The Han developed trade with the Roman Empire.

15. The Hindu religion in India was developed by the

a. Sikhs.
b. Muslims.
c. Jains.
d. Aryans.

16. The Maurya Dynasty fell because of

a. repeated invasions by Muslims.
b. the revolt by untouchables.
c. the lack of a stable government to defend the kingdom from invaders.
d. the failure of the monsoons to bring rain for a ten-year period.

17. The main difference between the Chinese philosophies of Confucius and Lao-tzu were their views on

a. the need to live modestly.
b. the way to treat and respect other human beings.
c. the importance of practicing self-control.
d. the individual's relationship to the government.

18. The Japanese practice both Shintoism and Buddhism. Koreans practice both Shamanism and Buddhism. These are examples of

a. interdependence.
b. cultural diffusion.
c. diversity.
d. nationalism.

19. The Vedas, Bhagavad Gita, Kojiki, and Nihongi were developed by different societies. To read these books would help us learn about these societies'

a. belief systems.
b. technological developments.
c. political systems.
d. movement of people and goods.

20. The reforms made by Gautama that affected Hinduism and the reforms made by the Zhou Dynasty over the Shang Dynasty are examples of the concept of

a. urbanization.
b. change.
c. power.
d. scarcity.

ESSAYS FOR CHAPTER 2

1. Confucius and the Confucianists said that people are basically good and can be led by good models and examples. Hanfeizi and the Legalists claimed that people are basically evil and have to be controlled by laws. Select one of these philosophies and write three arguments to defend it.

2. In many parts of Asia, religious and historical writings have included great messages and ideas. Listed here are several such written works: *The Ramayana, The Bhagavad Gita, The Nihon-shoki, The Code of Manu,* and The Five Relationships of Confucius as described in *The Analects*. Select any three of these works and do the following for each one:
   a. Name the country where it was written.
   b. State one belief or message or idea in the work.
   c. Pose a question that this belief or message or idea tried to answer.

3. Hinduism and Buddhism have similarities and differences. Describe two similarities and two differences.

4. Civilizations develop where geography and climate present humans with conditions in which they can live together in large cooperative groups.
   a. Define the term civilization.
   b. Select two different early civilizations and demonstrate how each developed in a way that was based on geography and climate.

DOCUMENT–BASED QUESTIONS

This task is based on the accompanying documents. Some of these documents have been edited for the purposes of this task. This task is designed to test your ability to work with historical documents. As you analyze the documents, take into account both the source of each document and the author's point of view.

Directions: Read the following documents and answer the questions after each document. Use the information in the reading and this chapter in writing your answers.

Document #1

Heaven, unpitying, has sent down ruin on the Shang. Shang has lost the mandate, and we Zhou have received it. I dare not say that our fortune would continue to prosper, even though I believe that heaven favors those who are sincere in their intentions. I dare not say, either that it would end in certain disaster . . .

The Mandate of Heaven is not easy to gain. It will be lost when men fail to live up to the reverent and illustrious virtues of their forefathers.

The Duke of Shao, from *The Chinese Heritage*

Questions

1. What happened to the Shang?
2. What is the Mandate of Heaven?
3. What is required to gain the Mandate of Heaven?

Document #2
He who thinks this Self and eternal spirit to be a slayer, and he who thinks this Self to be slain, are both without discernment; the Soul slays not, neither is it slain. . . . But if you will not wage this lawful battle, then you will fail your own caste and incur sin. . . . The people will name you with dishonor; and to a man of fame dishonor is worse than death.

Krishna talking to Arjuna, from *The Mahabharata*

Questions
1. What does Krishna want Arjuna to do?
2. Why does Krishna speak like this?

Document #3
Kalinga [a state in India] was conquered by his Sacred and Gracious Majesty when he had been consecrated [in power] eight years. 150,000 persons were thence carried away captive, 100,000 were slain, and many time[s] that number died. . . . Thus arose his Sacred Majesty's remorse for having conquered the Kalingas, because the conquest of a country previously unconquered involves the slaughter, death, and carrying away captive of the people.

Asoka, from P. Spear, *A History of Modern India*

Questions
1. Explain whether Asoka won or lost when he fought Kalinga.
2. Why was Asoka sad?
3. Would Asoka now be willing to accept or reject Buddhism? Explain.

Document #4

CLAY SEAL, A PRODUCT OF INDUS VALLEY CULTURE, CA. 2600–1900 B.C.E.

Questions

1. What conclusions can you draw or inferences can you make about the Indus River valley culture from examining this seal?
2. Who do you think is the figure on the seal?

Document #5

MAP OF THE SILK ROAD

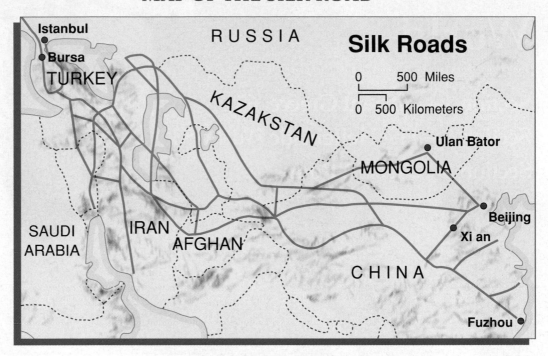

Questions

1. In what country was the eastern end of the Silk Road?
2. Discuss the importance of the Silk Road in promoting commerce and communication in the Ancient World.

CHAPTER 3

The Greco-Roman World

Section 1—Ancient Greece 65
Section 2—The Hellenistic World 83
Section 3—Ancient Rome 91

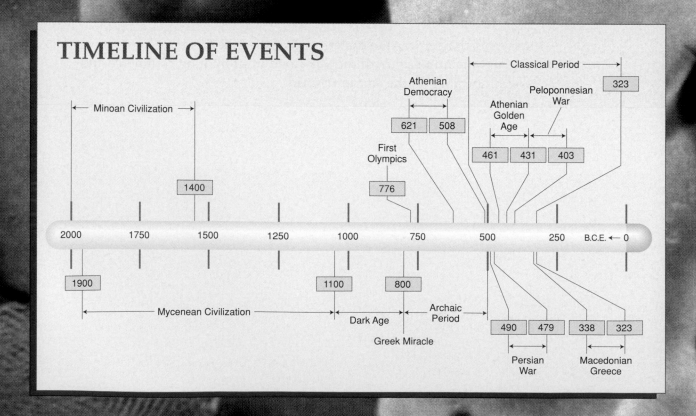

TIMELINE OF EVENTS

Minoan Civilization

Athenian Democracy

Classical Period

Athenian Golden Age

Peloponnesian War

First Olympics

323

621   508

461   431   403

776

1400

| 2000 | 1750 | 1500 | 1250 | 1000 | 750 | 500 | 250 | B.C.E. ← 0 |

1900

1100   800

490   479   338   323

Mycenean Civilization

Dark Age

Archaic Period

Greek Miracle

Persian War

Macedonian Greece

Ancient Greece

Ancient Greece is known as the cradle of Western civilization. Its ideas influenced the development of the cultures of Europe and the peoples who lived around the Mediterranean Sea. The Ancient Greeks or *Hellenes* (*Hellas* is the Greek term for Greece) created their unique civilization in the southeastern part of the Mediterranean beginning in the ninth century B.C.E. Many Greek ideas and institutions were so different from those of other civilizations in the Mediterranean and Middle East that those countries and areas influenced by the Greeks became known as Western society. The religions of the Middle East (Judaism, Christianity, and Islam) are regarded as Western faiths due to the connections with Greek philosophical ideas in the beliefs of all three.

Characteristics of Greek Civilization

Hominocentrism

The Greeks changed the way human beings looked at both themselves and the world. This new idea, **hominocentrism**, saw human beings at the center of the universe. To the Hellenes, their gods were superhumans or stronger and greater versions of themselves. The Ancient Greek gods also shared human weaknesses and could become jealous or angry. In Greek mythology, they often fell in love or fought with human beings.

Geography

Geography greatly influenced the development of Greek culture. The mountainous land made Greece unlike the early civilizations of the Middle East. Greek civilization did not develop in a river valley. The lack of natural resources forced the Greeks to be creative and to overcome limitations created by nature rather than to see themselves as a harmonious part of it.

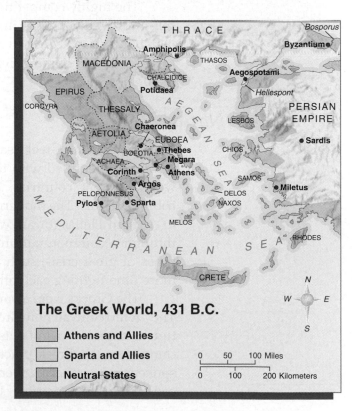

The Greek World, 431 B.C.

Athens and Allies
Sparta and Allies
Neutral States

0   50   100 Miles
0   100   200 Kilometers

Because Greece was not fertile enough to support a large population, its people were forced to turn to the sea to find other sources of food. This led to the development of Greek sea power, trade with other peoples, and colonization. The Greeks became skilled merchants as well as expert sailors. The irregular coastline created excellent harbors. Greece's close location to areas inhabited by the *Egyptians* (northeast Africa), *Hittites* (eastern Asia Minor), and *Phoenicians* (northwest Africa) led to cultural diffusion and economic dependence on trade (for example, many letters used in the Greek alphabet were Phoenician).

The mountainous landscape made farming very difficult. This forced the Greeks to become shepherds and raise livestock. The various problems nature placed on the Greeks actually helped them to become resourceful and develop skills that eventually made them powerful.

The rugged land had an effect on the psychology of the Greek people. They developed a strong sense of individualism, which had both positive and negative results. While this emphasis on the individual made them imaginative, daring, and constantly looking for improvement, it also led to disunity and civil wars. These characteristics were responsible for both their greatest achievements and their eventual downfall. Greek creations, such as democracy, the Olympics, and philosophy, coexisted with constant fighting between Greek cities as well as the ancient evil of slavery.

The challenge of everyday living made the Ancient Greeks both creative and strong. The Greek belief in developing both the physical and mental side of the individual ("A sound mind in a sound body") and achieving a balance ("Everything in moderation" or "The middle is the best") were seen as the main goals of each person. The lack of luxuries also helped to toughen the Greeks and make them fully use the few resources they possessed.

The highly competitive nature of the Greeks led to a constant struggle for self-improvement. This made them powerful soldiers in war and aggressive merchants in peace. The Greek determination to achieve all-around excellence raised the level of their civilization and made their many outstanding achievements possible.

> **Main Idea:**
> The various problems nature placed on the Greeks actually helped them to become resourceful and develop skills that eventually made them powerful.

The Greek Nation

Even though the Greeks saw themselves as one *ethnos* (nation) or people, they primarily identified with their local city. The Greek city-states acted as if they were different countries. The mountainous geography of Greece also contributed to this. The modern concept of nationhood and nationality did not exist in Ancient Hellas (or anywhere else in the Ancient World). A sense of identity through a common culture, language, and religion could unite the Greeks in times of great crisis, such as the Persian War. Generally, however, they spent more time fighting each other than any foreign enemy.

The Greeks were aware of their achievements and took great pride in them. They referred to all non-Greek peoples as *barbaroi*, or barbarians, seeing their culture as superior to any outside of Greece. In fact, the term *barbaros*, or barbarian came from the Greek practice of making fun of the way other languages were spoken and comparing them with the sounds sheep and goats made. Despite the constant internal warfare, the Greeks were very ethnocentric and did not consider anyone outside of their nation to be civilized. This attitude was similar to that of the Chinese, who viewed all non-Chinese as barbarians.

The definition of exactly who was a Hellene kept changing throughout Ancient Greek history. The term itself originally referred only to the inhabitants of the southern and central parts of the Greek peninsula, but it came to include those of the Greek islands, the western coast of Asia Minor, and northern Greece (**Macedonia**). As Greek power and influence spread, through colonization by Athens and conquest under the Macedonians, the term eventually came to mean anyone who spoke Greek and adopted Hellenic culture.

The Proto-Greeks (2000–800 B.C.E.)

Minoan Civilization (2000–1400 B.C.E.)

The term *Minoan* refers to the unique civilization that developed on the island of Crete from 2000 to 1400 B.C.E. This society is named after the mythical Greek ruler of the island, King Minos. He was punished for refusing to make his promised sacrifice to the gods by having his wife give birth to the *Minotaur* (a monster that was half-human, half-bull). The name *Minoan* was given to this civilization by **Sir Arthur Evans**, a British archaeologist who discovered the first Minoan ruins at Knossos on Crete at the beginning of the twentieth century C.E. He based the name on the art he found, which seemed to depict the King Minos myth. In fact, the Minoans had been lost to human memory since 1400 B.C.E., when their civilization was destroyed. Although they may have been the source of the myth of the "lost city" of *Atlantis*, later Greek Civilization was completely unaware that the Minoans had ever existed. Yet, they had an important influence on the *Myceneans*, the direct ancestors of the Greeks.

Minoan civilization was unlike any that came before or after it. The rich and fertile land of **Crete** at that time produced a wealthy society that worshipped nature and practiced *hedonism*, or the pursuit of pleasure. Unlike their later Mycenean and Greek descendants, the Minoans saw themselves as a part of the natural world. They prayed to fertility goddesses and glorified natural phenomena. Their magnificent art and architecture reflect this love and respect for the natural world around them.

Although they were excellent sailors who developed trade and commerce throughout the eastern Mediterranean region, the Minoans do not seem to have been very aggressive or warlike. They influenced the cultural development on neighboring islands, probably through trade rather than aggression.

Minoan Crete had a central government under a priest-king, probably known as the Minos (a term which may have been the equivalent to the Egyptian pharaoh). A well-organized bureaucracy or civil service from a series of palaces located throughout the island administrated it.

An example of Minoan pottery.

These magnificent buildings served as the centers of local production and trade as well as government. The most impressive aspect of this "Palace civilization," however, was its remarkable technology. Luxurious palace apartments were equipped with running water and the equivalent of flushing toilets. An advanced system of writing, known today as *Linear A*, allowed the Minoan bureaucracy to keep records and efficiently administer Crete.

As the Minoans developed trade relations with the Greek mainland, they influenced the development of Mycenean civilization, which adopted their art, writing system, and sailing expertise. This relationship ended in disaster for the Minoans when the aggressive Myceneans invaded and dominated Crete (c. 1450–1400 B.C.E.). Soon after, Minoan civilization disappeared.

Mycenean Civilization (1900–1100 *B.C.E.*)

The most direct ancestors of the Ancient Hellenes appeared on the Greek peninsula and Asia Minor around 1900 B.C.E. Speaking an Indo-European language, which made them the first true "Greeks" to settle in the area, the Myceneans were given their name by a German archaeologist, **Heinrich Schleimann**, who first discovered the ruins of their world in the late nineteenth century C.E.

Mycenean Greece was a collection of independent city-kingdoms governed by local rulers. Unlike Minoan Crete with its central government, in Mycenean Greece each warrior-king ruled his own area and often fought with his neighbors. It was this disunity that led to a civil war among the city-kingdoms from 1200 to 1100 B.C.E. This resulted in the decline of Mycenean

Mycenean
beehive tomb.

civilization. The legendary attack on the city of Troy (in Western Asia Minor), which was later made famous in **Homer's** epic poem *Iliad*, probably took place around 1250 B.C.E. and marked the beginning of the civil wars.

The Myceneans developed a strong economy based on a combination of "trading and raiding" (commercial relations backed up by force and aggression). They became expert sailors and built strong navies capable of conducting business and war with equal effectiveness. As trade increased, Mycenean art and craftwork showed the influence of other civilizations, particularly that of the Minoans.

Unlike most civilizations of the time, the Myceneans worshipped male sky gods. Their religion clearly influenced the development of the later Greek hominocentric concept of the gods. It was well suited to the feudal warrior society of the Myceneans.

A palace bureaucracy of scribes who kept records, wrote treaties, and sent messages supported the Mycenean warlords. Their writing is known as *Linear B*. Its characters are borrowed from the Minoan Linear A, which has so far remained a mystery to scholars. In 1956, the Greek scholar Michael Ventris was able to decipher Linear B when he discovered that it was actually an early form of Greek. His work proved that the Myceneans were truly the direct ancestors of the Ancient Greeks.

Mycenean culture and power reached its peak around 1300 B.C.E. The cultural diffusion that resulted from trade contacts with the Hittite Empire and Egypt started to break down around 1250 B.C.E. The fall of Troy, which took place about that time, was probably brought about by an economic crisis that seized the entire eastern Mediterranean area. The loss of Minoan Crete as a trading partner, combined with droughts and overpopulation, had probably created the conditions that led to this crisis. The destruction of Troy and records of attacks on both the Hittites and Egyptians are further evidence that this economic depression led to pirating on the part of the Myceneans. In 1200 B.C.E., wars between city-kingdoms began which resulted in the decline of the Mycenean states by 1100 B.C.E. As these cities disappeared, so did Mycenean culture and society. A wave of northern invaders called the *Dorians*, possibly led by exiled warlords, moved into the Greek peninsula. The Mycenean World came to an end, and with it, the first chapter of Ancient Greek history.

The Dark Age of the Aegean World (1100–800 B.C.E.)

Following the fall of Mycenean civilization, a time of poverty and backwardness took place in the *Aegean World*. This period (1100–800 B.C.E.) is known as the *Dark Age*. With the disappearance of the city-kingdoms and their palace bureaucracies, literacy and art vanished as well. Technical skills declined, and trade was replaced by *subsistence farming* (producing enough to survive). A decrease in population, despite the Dorian invasions, led to an abandonment of the remaining Mycenean settlements and a return to a more primitive existence. Small farming communities became the basic units of Dark Age Greek society, but many basic skills were carried over from the Mycenean World. The lack of traditional leadership allowed the Greeks to reorganize their society in new and different ways.

During the Dark Age, the Ancient Greek World was formed. The mixture of peoples in the Greek peninsula, Aegean islands, and western Asia Minor due to migration formed the ethnic, cultural, and linguistic basis that would result in the brilliant Hellenic civilization. As these peoples interacted, they developed common traits. In this way, the future foundation of Ancient Greek society was established.

The Archaic Period (800–500 B.C.E.)

The Greek Miracle

By 800 B.C.E., the various peoples who had mixed together during the Dark Age shared a common language, culture, and religion. This development became known as the **Greek Miracle**. A new and revolutionary writing system was created. Using Phoenician letters, the *Greek alphabet* was based on sound value and allowed greater expression in writing than ever before. Art reflected the creativity of the new culture being formed. Pottery with *geometric designs* and the gradual reappearance of luxury items signaled the revival of a more sophisticated society. This was expanded by the development of *Iron Age* technology (use of iron for making tools and weapons).

The Development of Democracy

As the Dark Age progressed, the small farming communities developed into tribal kingdoms. Unlike the feudal warrior kings of the Mycenean period, chieftains were limited in power by their nobles. The ruler met with his nobility to discuss problems and make decisions. Peasants and artisans (craftsmen) often voiced opinions in tribal assemblies as well. This development of **oligarchies**, or small elite ruling groups, as opposed to strong monarchies, sowed the seeds of Ancient Greek **democracy** (citizens running government).

The Development of the Polis

As the Dark Age came to a close, the tribal groups grew into larger communities. Even though they shared a common ethnic identity that would be known as Hellenic or Greek by 800 B.C.E., local tribes maintained rivalries that prevented the creation of a unified Greek nation. These communities would form a new unit, the **polis** or **city-state**, which would be the basis of Greek life. This concept would later expand through the Greek-speaking world in the Hellenistic Period, the Roman World, the Byzantine Empire, and the Christian Church in the Middle Ages.

Archaic Greece

The creation of *poleis* (the plural for polis) throughout Ancient Greece was the beginning of the **Archaic Period** (800–500 B.C.E.). While each city developed at its own pace in its own way, the polis created strong bonds between the individual and the community. The concept of *citizenship* was created, as some members of a polis felt personally responsible for helping their city to run efficiently and prosper. The Greeks developed a **direct democracy**. This is a system in which all citizens participate in the running of the government. In Ancient Greece, only members of the *aristocracy* or wealthy males over 18 were allowed to be citizens since they had the education, money, and time to participate. Even though each city-state did not necessarily develop into a democracy as Athens did, individual citizens saw themselves as a vital part of their community. Even rural dwellers associated themselves with their polis. The old bonds of family and tribe were replaced by new ones to the local city.

Archaic Greek Society

Physically and psychologically the polis became the center of Greek life. Each city revolved around two sites, the **acropolis** and the *aghora*. Built on the highest point of each community, the acropolis was originally a fortress, which was the ruler's residence and the center of government as well as a place where the population could find safety during an invasion. Temples to the gods were built there as well. Eventually it also became the center of religious life in each polis, containing the treasury and armory (storehouse for weapons) for its community.

The aghora or marketplace was the site of a city's economic and social life. It was there that both urban and rural dwellers met. As some city-states developed democratic forms of government, the aghora was divided into two parts and became the center of political life as well. In Athens, for example, while merchants and farmers bargained on one side of the marketplace, the Athenian citizens debated and voted on the other.

As civic life developed further, many city-states established courts of justice. The development of a legal system led to both *written constitutions* and *trial by jury*. Many democracies established an **areopagus** or courthouse where retired citizens served as judges to hear cases regularly. These important inno-

> **Main Idea:**
> Each city revolved around two sites: the acropolis and the aghora.

This scene depicts a nobleman and hoplite leaving for combat (see page 72).

vations further strengthened the bonds that held the individual and community together.

Participation on the part of the citizens also extended to military service. Unlike previous centuries, when nobles dominated warfare, military organization was based on the **phalanx** (roughly equivalent to a regiment) made up of **hoplites**, or infantrymen, chiefly citizen volunteers. This system increased the loyalty of the soldiers, as each had a real stake in the effectiveness of the military. This made Greek armies very powerful. The improvements in military organization and the development of strong navies by many of the city-states resulted in many colonies outside of Greece itself. This expansion was also a response to pressures created by an increased need for food supplies due to population growth in the eighth century B.C.E. The new Greek settlements became independent poleis. They expanded Hellenic civilization further into Asia Minor as well as into the Crimea, southern France, southern Spain, northern Africa, and southern Italy and Sicily, which were known as "Greater Greece."

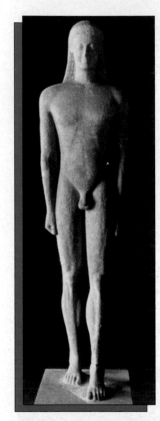

The Kouros statues dominate the Archaic period of Greek Art.

Archaic Greek Art and Architecture

Culturally Archaic Greece developed new expressions of creativity as well as expand on older ones. Greek religion was responsible for much of this. The hominocentric beliefs of Hellenic religion resulted in revolutionary changes in art. Sculptures were far more realistic than ever before. This was due to the Greek view that the human body was beautiful. The *kouros* (statue of a nude young man) became an example of the Greek glorification of the human being. The *koura* (statue of a young woman) and sculptures of the gods were further examples of this.

Archaic architects developed a basic style for temples and public buildings (rectangular form with surrounding columns and a low-pitched roof) that applied mathematical principles and the Greek concept of *symmetry* (balance or proportion). Citizens of Greek city-states were very interested in beautifying their polis with statues, temples, and decorative public buildings.

The Development of Theater and the Olympics

Greek religious practice also led to the development of two unique and important institutions, the *Olympics* and *theater*. Held locally every summer and nationally at Olympia every fourth year, the Olympics were an athletic competition between city-states in which every adult male citizen participated. The contests included footraces (chariot races were later added), field events (discus, javelin), and combat competitions (wrestling, boxing, and a brutal mixture of the two called *pancration*). The event was so important to the Greeks that their calendar was based on *Olympiads* (years when the Olympics were held), starting in 776 B.C.E., the traditional year of the first Olympic Games. The Olympics were one of the few examples of widespread cooperation, with warring city-states even signing temporary truces to participate in the competition.

The feast of *Dionysius*, the god of wine and hedonism, was celebrated by the wearing of costumes and masks. Poems and songs were composed to honor the gods, while myths were retold and acted out. These customs eventually

A depiction of the Greek wrestlers. Wrestling was one of the competitions in the Olympics.

developed into full theatrical productions. Contests were held annually in which playwrights competed for awards. Greek drama was divided into **tragedy** and **comedy**, performed on alternating evenings during festivals. The most famous Ancient Greek playwrights were **Aeschylus**, **Sophocles** and **Euripides** (tragedy) and **Aristophanes** (comedy).

Archaic Literature

Literature was born during the Archaic period. The *Iliad* and *Odyssey* of Homer were *epic poems* that glorified the legendary figures of Mycenean Greece. These first pieces of Western literature, written between 800 and 750 B.C.E., preserved the oral poetry of professional *bards* or traveling singers during the Dark Age. The literary genius of the Greeks came out fully in the writings of the farmer-poet **Hesiod**, who wrote around 700 B.C.E. In *Works and Days*, Hesiod objected to the injustice of contemporary society, especially the inequality between the wealthy and the poor. It is, in fact, the first work of protest ever written. The development of *lyric poetry* gave literary expression to personal reactions and emotions for the first time. The works of **Pindar** (c. 418–438 B.C.E.), who praised the accomplishments of athletes, and **Sappho** (c. 600 B.C.E.), the poetess who examined life from a woman's point of view, are the best examples of the early development of literature.

The Development of Science and Philosophy

Science and philosophy also began in the Archaic Period. Initially, the two were considered to be part of the same pursuit. Archaic thought centered around explaining and understanding the fundamental forces behind the universe as well as observing the natural world around mankind. This led to a rejection of the traditional myths and attempts to find rational explanations.

One group of thinkers, the *Materialists*, concluded that natural elements (fire, water, and air) were the basic substances of all things. The Materialist tradition was best represented by **Democritus** (c. 460 B.C.E.), who first developed the theory that the universe is composed of tiny particles called atoms (**atomic theory**). Rejecting the Materialist school of thought, the mathematician

Pythagoras (c. 580 B.C.E.) believed that the key to the universe lay in a numerical relationship among its parts. The philosopher **Heraclitus** (c. 500 B.C.E.) founded a group of thinkers who maintained that a being with perfect intelligence provided the creative force of order in the universe.

By the end of the Archaic Period, philosophical and scientific inquiry had separated. Philosophers began to speculate about human nature, and scientists continued their investigation of the natural world.

Classical Greece (500–323 B.C.E.)

The Development of Classical Greece

Classical Greece marked both the height of Hellenic civilization and its downfall. Although the Greeks had some of their greatest achievements during this period, the independent city-states almost destroyed each other. The later domination of Macedonia not only preserved Hellas and its civilization but spread Greek learning across the known world.

By 500 B.C.E., most Greek city-states, with the notable exception of **Sparta**, had developed governments that allowed at least some form of citizen participation. Many others followed the example of the city-state of Athens and established democracies.

The Persian War (490–479 B.C.E.)

Many Greek cities in Asia Minor came under *Persian* rule by 500 B.C.E. The Persian system of *autocracy*, or rule by one king, was forced on the Greeks. This system was completely opposed to Greek ideas. In addition, the Persians made the Greeks pay tribute. This made Persian rule unbearable. The clash of these two opposing cultures led to the *Persian War* (490–479 B.C.E.).

THE PERSIAN INVASION UNDER DARIUS

Some mainland Greek poleis supported unsuccessful revolts by the dominated cities in Asia Minor. **King Darius I** used this support as an excuse to invade the Greek peninsula. In 490 B.C.E., a Persian army attacked **Attica** (central Greece where Athens is located) and was defeated by the Athenian army under the brilliant general Miltiades at the Battle of Marathon. The Spartans did send an army to help, but it arrived too late. This created further tension between the two city-states.

Fearing a Persian attack for the humiliating defeat at Marathon, the cities of the Greek mainland formed a military alliance, the *Greek League*, which brought together all their armies and navies for a mutual defense of Greece. Due to the efforts of two far-sighted leaders, **Themistocles** of Athens and **King Leonidas** of Sparta, the two hostile city-states cooperated in this alliance.

THE PERSIAN INVASION UNDER XERXES

In 480 B.C.E., King Darius's son **Xerxes** invaded the Greek peninsula. This time the Persians brought a huge army that left no doubt of the need for unity on the part of most central and southern Greek city-states. Xerxes marched around the northern Aegean coast and first engaged the Greek army at a narrow pass at **Thermopolaye**. With the assistance of the Athenian navy, the smaller Greek forces were able to stop Xerxes' advance. When a local traitor showed the

Persians a trail around the pass, the Greek forces were trapped. The Greek commander at Thermopolaye, King Leonidas, managed to evacuate the bulk of his forces and remained with his personal bodyguard of 300 Spartans to fight to the death, delaying the Persian advance. The Persians finally invaded Attica and destroyed Athens, but Leonidas's sacrifice allowed the population to evacuate and gave the Greek forces time to regroup.

In autumn of 480 B.C.E., the Athenian navy maneuvered the Persians into the narrow strait between Attica and the island of **Salamis**. Unable to use their numerical superiority, the Persian fleet was completely beaten. Their defeat in the Battle of Salamis forced the Persians to retreat to Asia Minor for the winter.

Xerxes renewed his campaign in the spring of 479 B.C.E., attacking from bases in northern Greece. The Persians were crushed at **Platea** by the combined forces of the Greek League under the command of a Spartan general and led by the Spartan Army. The Athenian navy sailed across the Aegean and destroyed the Persian fleet at *Mycale*. The secret escape of Xerxes back to Persia signaled the end of the Persian War.

ATHENIAN IMPERIALISM

Even though Xerxes' forces had been driven out of mainland Greece, the Persians were still a powerful threat. This danger kept the spirit of unity alive in the Greek World. The Athenians took the lead against Persia because Sparta was no longer willing to remain involved in a project that was so distant from

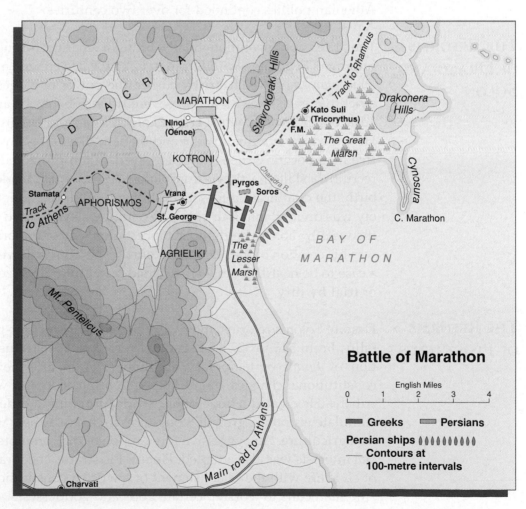

Battle of Marathon

English Miles
0   1   2   3   4

■ Greeks   ▭ Persians
Persian ships ◊◊◊◊◊◊◊◊◊◊
— Contours at 100-metre intervals

The Battle of Marathon was important because it was indicative of the Greeks' refusal to submit to Persian power despite great odds.

the **Peloponnese** (southern Greece where Sparta is located). In 478 B.C.E., under Athens' direction, the **Delian League** began a campaign to drive the Persians out of the Mediterranean area. By 465 B.C.E., all the Greek city-states in Asia Minor had been liberated from Persian rule. The Delian League's fleet, which was almost completely Athenian, cleared both the Aegean and Mediterranean of Persian naval power.

The success of the Delian League in ending the Persian threat resulted in a desire by many smaller members to withdraw. Athens, which had benefited economically from its participation, converted the voluntary alliance into an empire to serve its own commercial interests. Using intimidation and military power, the Athenians forced the other Greek city-states in its sphere of influence to continue their participation in the Delian League.

THE DEVELOPMENT OF ATHENIAN DEMOCRACY

The rise of Athenian imperialism occurred at the same time that democracy was most fully developed in that city. Athens began the creation of democratic government about 750 B.C.E., when absolute monarchy was abolished and replaced with a king elected in an assembly of the **archons**, or leaders of the city-states. These archons, who were originally the heads of tribal clans, soon shared power with the archon-king. Archons were also elected to head the military and to a nine-member body of chief magistrates who carried out Athenian law. Despite growing resentment from the lower classes, the aristocratic domination of Athenian politics continued for over two centuries.

THE REFORMS OF DRACO AND SOLON

The threat of revolution finally brought change through the work of four reformers beginning with **Draco** in 621 B.C.E. He created a legal code, known as *Draconian Laws*, which strictly curbed the power of judges. These laws were so strict that ever since the use of severe rules of behavior are often referred to as "draconian." **Solon**, who became known as a great lawgiver, continued reform. He ended slavery due to debt and made it illegal for any Athenian, meaning a free man born in Athens, to be enslaved. Solon promoted economic growth by recruiting skilled artisans from outside Athens. He made wealth, rather than birth, the qualification for citizenship and holding public office. Athenian society was divided into four classes, excluding slaves, based on income, with only the wealthy able to hold public office. Solon's most important reform, however, was his creation of the "People's Court." This court allowed any citizen to bring a case to be heard. Cases were decided by a group of citizens selected by lottery or **trial by jury**.

THE REFORMS OF PISISTRATUS

Despite Solon's reforms, the rivalry between aristocratic groups prevented stability. From 546 to 527 B.C.E. another reformer, **Pisistratus,** was given the position of *tyrant* or temporary absolute ruler in an emergency. He made no constitutional changes, but he helped to bring economic wealth and stability to Athens. He created a huge public works program in order to provide jobs and stimulate economic growth. Long-term loans to farmers were added to revitalize agriculture. An aggressive foreign policy that promoted Athenian commercial interests was also adopted. Finally, Pisistratus encouraged the development of civic life with the establishment of a written constitution and the creation of Athenian cults to worship certain gods and goddesses.

THE REFORMS OF CLEISTHENES

In 510 B.C.E., the sons of Pisistratus, who succeeded their father as tyrants, were overthrown by aristocrats who wished to reestablish the old order. They were forced out of power in 508 B.C.E. by the reformer *Cleisthenes*, who finally established democracy in Athens. He divided Attica into territorial units, allowing each to elect its own local officials. This helped to expand civic participation. A *Council of 500* was established, consisting of fifty representatives from each unit, selected by lot for one-year terms, to decide on policy issues to be voted on by the citizenry. All male citizens over 18 years of age voted in the Athenian Assembly. Since women, *metics* (foreigners), and slaves could not vote, final authority in the Athenian state rested with roughly 40,000 males. Even though they were a minority of the population, the Athenian Assembly was a first-time experiment in power sharing.

THE SPARTAN SYSTEM

Although many Greek cities followed a pattern similar to that of Athens, the Spartans developed in a very different way. Spartan society took the form of a militaristic state. One reason was to protect itself against revolt by the peoples it ruled over. The Spartan system also led to *xenophobia*, or a fear of foreigners. A legendary lawgiver, **Lycurgus**, supposedly created the Spartan way of life. These changes took over a century to develop, but ultimately they created a unique society.

Three hereditary classes were created by the *Lycurgan Reforms*: the Spartans, or **citizens**, who ran the polis; the **perioeci**, or merchants and artisans; and the **helots**, or slaves, who farmed for the benefit of Sparta. All Spartan males were trained as soldiers from early childhood. They were separated from their parents when 7 years old and lived in military barracks until the age of 20. Spartan boys were given rigorous military training and an education that stressed physical fitness, discipline, obedience, patriotism, and simplicity. Spartan girls were trained at home by their mothers, developing household skills and keeping physically fit. At 20, the Spartan male became a regular soldier who trained every day. He was assigned a piece of public land and helots in order to support him. He could marry, but a Spartan could not live with his wife until he reached 30, at which time he became an "equal," with full rights to participate in political life. While Spartans were *isolationists*, meaning they did not bother with anyone outside their society and did not provoke conflict, they were constantly prepared for war. This preparation resulted in their developing the finest army of their day. Religious to the point of superstition, the Spartans rejected all luxuries and decorative arts. Today a plain and comfortless way of living is still referred to as a "Spartan existence." They regarded foreigners, especially the Athenians, as sinful people who had a corrupting influence.

F. Bonneville del et Sculp

Lycurgus is said to have created the Spartan way of life.

The Peloponnesian War (431–403 B.C.E.)

With such great differences and suspicion between them, it was inevitable that the Athenian policy of imperialism under **Pericles**, who led Athens from 461 to 429 B.C.E., would lead to another Athenian-Spartan conflict. Athens continued to

A bust of Pericles, who led Athens from 461–429 B.C.E.

force member city-states to stay in the Delian League, which existed only to enrich Athens further. When it tried to impose membership on independent Peloponnesian cities, Sparta responded by creating the **Peloponnesian League**. Unlike its Athenian-dominated counterpart, this was a voluntary alliance of southern Greek city-states that did not want to be controlled by Athens. In 454 B.C.E., the member cities of the Delian League unsuccessfully revolted against Athens and were assisted by the Spartans, who had become alarmed at the growth of the Athenian Empire. Fearing that Athens would be overwhelmed, Pericles made peace with Sparta in 449 B.C.E. Athens and Sparta agreed not to interfere in each other's *sphere of influence*, or area of domination.

In 431 B.C.E., the peace was broken when the city of **Corinth**, a member of the Peloponnesian League, convinced Sparta that Athens' attempt to dominate the island of *Corcyra*, which is modern-day Corfu in the Adriatic Sea off the central Greek coast, was a violation of the peace agreement. Arrogant and over-confident, the Athenians plunged into the *Peloponnesian War* (431–403 B.C.E.). Fearing a land war with the Spartan army, Pericles convinced the Athenian population to withdraw behind Athens' walls rather than fight. This left the Spartans free to ravage Attica's countryside in annual raids. A plague behind the city walls in 429 B.C.E. decimated the Athenian population and claimed the life of Pericles. The Spartan commander, *Brasidas*, ended the attacks on Attica and encouraged the subject cities to revolt against Athens. The new Athenian leader, *Cleon*, finally led the army outside the walls and counterattacked. After a period of indecisive fighting, both Brasidas and Cleon were killed in 422 B.C.E. In 421 B.C.E., the two sides signed a truce, which lasted until 415 B.C.E., when Athens attacked the powerful Greek city-state of *Syracuse* on the island of Sicily. The ill-fated and foolish *Sicilian Expedition* (415-413 B.C.E.) was conceived by the ambitious politician *Alcibiades*. He wrongly thought that capturing Sicily, which he considered an easy target, would build up his reputation.

The disastrous defeat of Athens encouraged Sparta and her allies to renew the war and encourage revolt by the members of the Delian League. Led by the brilliant general *Lysander*, the Spartans destroyed the Athenian navy and defeated Athens' armies in a series of battles. Sparta also made an alliance with Persia, which supplied money and ships in return for being allowed to reoccupy Asia Minor. By 404 B.C.E., the Athenians surrendered.

Athens was forced to tear down its walls and destroy all but twelve of its ships. A government consisting of fifteen Spartan generals and fifteen exiled Athenian aristocrats, known as **The Thirty**, was set up in Athens, guarded by a Spartan army. The Thirty were ousted in 403 B.C.E., and democratic government was restored. Athens, however, never recovered its former power.

THE UNIFICATION OF GREECE UNDER MACEDONIA

Sparta tried to dominate the Greek city-states from 403 to 371 B.C.E., but limited resources and shortage of labor made such control impractical. The city-state of **Thebes** dominated Greece briefly from 371 to 362 B.C.E., but an Athenian-led coalition of cities ended Theban domination in 362 B.C.E. The constant warfare between the city-states weakened the Greek World considerably and made it an easy target for the Persians, who, back in Asia Minor, were once again a great threat.

Realizing the danger and a need for unity, **Philip II** of Macedonia, who ruled from 359 to 336 B.C.E., began a conquest of Greece in order to create one

Philip's conquest of Greece unified the Hellenes for the first time in their history and saved Greek civilization from furthur decline due to disunity.

Hellenic state. Athens tried to lead a coalition to oppose the Macedonians but was unsuccessful. Despite massive propaganda, especially by the Athenian leader *Demosthenes*, Philip found much support among the city-states of Greece, who were tired of the Athenian-Spartan conflict. In 338 B.C.E., the Macedonians defeated the forces of the Athenians at the *Battle of Chaeronea*. A meeting of all the Greek city-states was called later that year at which a new alliance was created, the **Hellenic League**. Although the new union was controlled by Macedonia, Philip did allow each city-state much freedom in domestic affairs. A national Greek army and navy were created, and regular meetings were held at which representatives could discuss and debate league policy. Philip had planned a war against Persia to free the Greek cities of Asia Minor but was assassinated in 336 B.C.E. The full potential of a unified Greece was realized by his son and successor, **Alexander III**, who reigned from 336 to 323 B.C.E. and was known as "the Great." (See Section 2.)

CULTURE OF THE CLASSICAL PERIOD

Culturally, the Classical period was one of the most creative in Greek history. The Greeks tried to depict the human being in an idealized way, stressing human potential rather than criticizing human weaknesses. This became known as the *Classical Ideal*. By the fifth century B.C.E., Athens had become the center for the arts. Under *Pericles*, Athens was called the *School of Hellas* because it attracted artists, sculptors, architects, poets, and philosophers from all over Greece. The arts, culture, and intellectual life flourished during this period, which came to be known as the *Golden Age of Athens* (461–431 B.C.E.).

Sculpture reached new levels of excellence during the Classical Period.

Classical Sculpture and Architecture

Sculpture reached new levels of excellence. Statues portrayed idealized human beauty and physical perfection. Sculptors like *Phidias, Polyclitus*, and *Praxiteles* created idealized figures of gods and goddesses. Architecture surpassed anything done before in its realism and perfection of form. Even functional pieces, such as columns, became highly decorative as the Greeks developed three types—*Ionic, Doric*, and *Corinthian*—which are still used today. The greatest examples of Greek Classical building were the temples of the **Athenian Acropolis**, especially the **Parthenon**, which was dedicated to the Virgin Athena; the *Erectheum*, dedicated to three different gods; and the *Nike*, dedicated to the Victorious Athena. The architects of these achieved harmony, balance, and proportion, making buildings works of art.

The Parthenon, or Temple of the Virgin Athena, is considered to be a masterpiece of Classical Greek architecture.

Architecture surpassed anything done before in its realism and perfection of form, as can be seen here in the ruins of Delphi.

The Development of Historical Writing

In addition to poetry and drama, the first historical works were written during this period. **Herodotus** (c. 480–425 B.C.E.), known as the "Father of History," first began the study with his book *Historia*. The term *historia* literally means "investigation." He examined the political, social, and economic causes of the Persian War. Unlike the chronicles of past civilizations, which merely kept records, Herodotus's purpose was to examine objectively why hostility existed between the Greeks and Persians and how that led to war. This type of writing was continued by **Thucydides** (c. 460–400 B.C.E.) in his work *The Peloponnesian War*, in which the causes and results of the Peloponnesian War were examined. Despite his being an Athenian, Thucydides objectively concluded that Athens was primarily responsible for the conflict.

Philosophy in the Classical Period

Philosophy became a separate study from science in the Classical period. Shifting from speculation about the nature of the universe to that of human nature, philosophers concentrated on the development of reason and a search for knowledge. This new attitude was reflected in the writings of *Protagoras* (fifth century B.C.E.), who believed that thinkers should search for useful knowledge that would make life better. These ideas were adopted by philosophers who became known as **Sophists**, or "wise ones." They were primarily teachers who taught the sons of wealthy citizens the subject of *rhetoric*, or the art of speaking persuasively in public. This was done in order to prepare them for success in political life.

Known as the "father of history," Herodotus' "investigation" of the causes and results of the Persian War laid the foundations of the social sciences.

Socrates

The Sophists came under attack around 400 B.C.E. from a revolutionary thinker, **Socrates** (469–399 B.C.E.), who felt that they had betrayed their duty as philosophers and were more concerned with gaining wealth than with searching for truth. He felt that human ignorance was responsible for this. He developed a system for discovering truth, the **Socratic method**, which used questioning with precise definition and exact logic. Socrates would often use this method and embarrass influential citizens in the aghora in order to expose hypocrisy or illogical arguments in Athenian political life. As he developed a following, especially among the younger men, Socrates became a threat to Athenian politicians. He was arrested on charges of "corrupting the youth," found guilty in a prearranged trial, and executed by being forced to drink poison in 399 B.C.E.

Socrates became a great threat to Athenian politicians.

Plato

Socrates' work was continued by his student **Plato** (428–347 B.C.E.), who wrote down his teacher's ideas. He established a school, *the Academy*, in which he taught both Socrates' ideas and his own. Plato developed his own ideas about metaphysics, or the nonphysical world. He argued that all physical reality that humans experience are really only reflections of a perfect world that exists elsewhere in the universe. For example, if someone looks into a mirror, the reflection he sees is close to, but not exactly, what the person looks like. This is because light refraction distorts the image. Plato believed that human beings in this world were like the imperfect reflection in the mirror. The material world that human beings inhabit is an imperfect reflection of a perfect world that exists elsewhere in the universe. Plato also struggled with the questions of justice and political institutions in a series of works on these problems, *The Republic*, *The Politician*, and *The Laws*. Plato concluded that wise laws, created by statesmen with philosophical guidance, were the surest way to provide for justice and good government.

Plato opened a school in which he taught both Socrates' ideas and his own.

Aristotle

Plato's most brilliant student, **Aristotle** (384–322 B.C.E.), rejected his teacher's ideas and developed his own school of philosophy based on *empiricism* (knowledge based on the observable and on experiment). He believed that reality was a combination of form or ideas and physical matter. Aristotle argued that, without matter, form has no reality. He thought that every object in the universe has a *telos*, a purpose or end, including human beings, which was to be "happy" by achieving a balance between the physical and spiritual. Through his school, the *Lyceum*, Aristotle and his students copied and cataloged all existing works of human knowledge, which they divided and organized into subject areas. Aristotle was also a tutor to Alexander the Great and was very influential in developing a love of Greek culture and learning in his pupil.

Aristotle was Plato's most brilliant student.

Science in the Classical Period

Finally, science made great strides in the Classical period, especially medicine. The work of **Hippocrates** greatly advanced medical care. Hippocrates argued that the traditional belief that sickness was caused by evil spirits was irrational. He also believed that nothing could be learned about illness without observation. Since disease was due to natural causes, the cure for a sickness had to be a natural process. He collected information on the curative powers of drugs and the effects of diet on health. An oath taken by all physicians to the present day is attributed to him. It is called the *Hippocratic Oath*.

The Classical period marked the end of the Greek World. The hominocentrism and rationalism of this brilliant civilization led to great changes in the way human beings viewed themselves and the world. The Classical Greek spirit of curiosity influenced Western civilization in many ways, namely to experiment and progress in the fields of knowledge that the Greeks had discovered and developed. The values and ideas they created influenced the direction future generations would take. The Classical Period would pave the way for the Hellenistic Age, a time when Hellenic culture would expand throughout the Mediterranean region and beyond.

LINK TO TODAY
The Greeks Had a Word for It

Many words and expressions used commonly today have their origin in Ancient Greece. The character of Gus Protokalis in the popular film *My Big Fat Greek Wedding* (2002) may have exaggerated this, but he was not totally wrong. These are some examples:

1. The expression *O.K.* is actually an abbreviation for the Greek term *Ola kala* or "All is well."

2. A person with a good personality is said to have *charisma*, which is a Greek word that really means "gifted."
3. The term *sophomore*, taken from the Greek term *sopho* or "wise" and *moro* or "child," is a good description of many tenth graders.
4. The word *phobia* is actually a Greek term meaning "fear of." It is used in such English words as *agoraphobia* (fear of being in an open place), *arachnophobia* (fear of spiders), *acrophobia* (fear of heights), and *claustrophobia* (fear of small or closed-in spaces).
5. The word *philia*, which means "love of," is used in many English words such as *philanthropy* (love of fellow human beings), *philosophy* (love of wisdom), and *philharmonic* (love of serious music).
6. The word *auto*, meaning "self," has become part of many words in English. Some examples are *automobile* (self-moving), *automatic* (self-acting), *autobiography* (writing about oneself), and *autonomy* (self-governing).

SECTION 1 SUMMARY

When we look back at the accomplishments of the brilliant Greek civilization, it is difficult to believe that all of this happened so long ago. This truly was one of those "golden ages" that happen once in a great while in history. Our debt to these ancients can never be repaid. The values and ideas raised influenced the direction future generations would take. Their spirit of curiosity to experiment and progress in the fields of knowledge remain with us today. In political forms, in law, in architecture, in philosophy, and in medicine, they are with us. The Classical Period paved the way to the Hellenistic Age, a time when Greek culture expanded throughout the Mediterranean region and beyond.

SECTION 2

The Hellenistic World

Do great leaders make history? Or does history make great leaders? These questions are not easy ones for us to answer. Nevertheless, in this section we will meet one such leader. This was Alexander the Great. He was the son of Philip II, who brought about the Macedonian conquest of Greece. Alexander inherited leadership of the Greeks. During and after his lifetime, Greek civilization spread into many areas beyond Greece. The Greek language and culture gradually unified the Mediterranean region with the Near East. The conquests of Alexander brought about enormous **cultural diffusion**, or the mixing of cultures. This policy, known as *Hellenism*, combined the dominant Greek culture with those of the other civilizations it came into contact with. We thus refer to this time as the *Hellenistic period*. Despite political divisions and constant warfare, the Hellenistic era witnessed many important achievements in the arts, sciences, and technology.

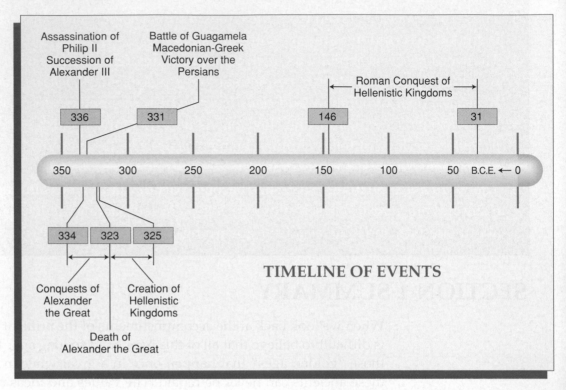

TIMELINE OF EVENTS

Alexander the Great (336–323 B.C.E.)

Alexander's Conquests

When **Philip II** was assassinated in 336 B.C.E., he was succeeded by his 20-year-old son, **Alexander III**. The young king, who had been raised at Philip's court in the capital city of Pella, and tutored by the philosopher **Aristotle**, shared his father's love of Greek civilization and desire to destroy the Persian threat to the Greek World. In 334 B.C.E., Alexander led a combined Macedonian-Greek army into Asia Minor and defeated the occupying Persian forces. From 333 to 332 B.C.E., he took control of Asia Minor, Syria, Palestine, and Egypt. Because of its great wealth and central location, Alexander greatly favored Egypt, founding the city of **Alexandria** on its northern coast. He did not live long enough to retire to it, but his body was entombed there after his death.

Alexander's death left a huge empire without any single individual capable of leading it.

In 331 B.C.E., Alexander invaded Persia, decisively defeating its forces in the *Battle of Gaugamela* and capturing the capital city of **Persepolis**. Alexander then continued eastward, conquering the regions of **Parthia**, in modern-day Iraq and Iran, and **Bactria**, in modern-day Afghanistan. Pushing across the *Hindu Kush Mountains*, the Greeks came into contact with *Indian civilization*. According to tradition, upon reaching the ***Indus Valley*** Alexander's troops, sick with unknown diseases and exhausted from five years of constant marching and fighting, refused to go any further. He was forced to return through southern Persia into *Mesopotamia*, where he fell ill and died in June of 323 B.C.E. His death left a huge empire without any single individual capable of leading it.

Alexander's Goals

Alexander had planned to create a single unified Hellenistic Empire that would bring all the Near Eastern peoples together with the Greeks to share and expand Hellenic civilization. To encourage this, in 323 B.C.E. he held a mass marriage ceremony in the city of **Susa** in modern Iraq, in which Greek soldiers took local brides. Alexander himself married a Bactrian princess, **Roxanne,** in the hopes of creating a new dynasty to rule this multicultural state. Opposition from his Macedonian and Greek commanders, however, prevented him from placing any non-Greeks in important positions. According to some historians, Alexander had developed *megalomania*. This is an exaggerated sense of importance in oneself.

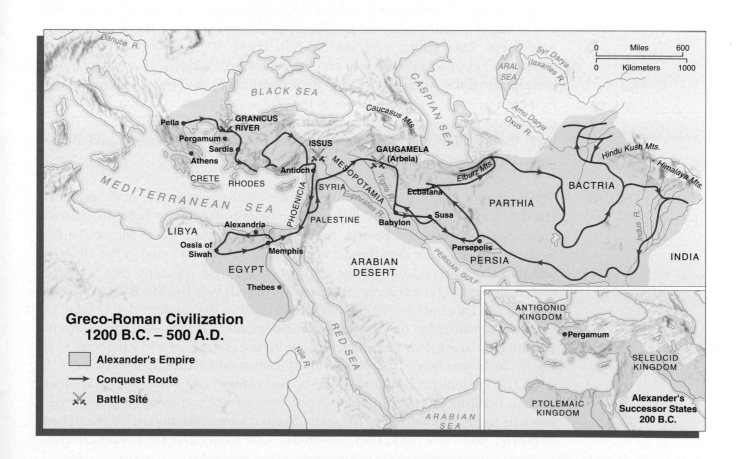

**Greco-Roman Civilization
1200 B.C. – 500 A.D.**

- Alexander's Empire
- → Conquest Route
- ⚔ Battle Site

Unfortunately, this affected his judgment and made him unpopular with many of his officers. For example, his practice of dressing like a Persian monarch at official ceremonies greatly offended his Greek troops and commanders.

The Hellenistic Kingdoms (323–31 B.C.E.)

The Foundation of the Hellenistic Kingdoms

Finding a successor for a leader who was seen by many as a god was exceptionally difficult. Soon after Alexander's death, three of his generals began fighting with each other. By 275 B.C.E., they had carved up Alexander's vast empire and established independent Hellenistic kingdoms: **Ptolemaios** in Egypt, **Antigonus** in Macedonia and the Aegean World, and **Seleucus** in Asia Minor and the former Persian Empire.

THE ANTIGONID KINGDOM

The *Antigonid dynasty* ran Macedonia very effectively. It faced problems, however, in keeping out barbarian tribes and controlling the Greek city-states. Around 200 B.C.E., the city-states appealed to the Romans to assist them in regaining their independence. This resulted in a series of wars that led in turn to Roman domination over Macedonia, Greece, and the Aegean by 129 B.C.E.

THE PTOLEMAIC KINGDOM

Ptolemaic Egypt was the most stable Hellenistic kingdom created. Under the Ptolemies, a traditional Egyptian autocracy was established. It combined the Greek and Egyptian cultures and developed a prosperous economy. Its wealth and political stability allowed the Ptolemaic kingdom to influence and dominate Syria, Asia Minor, and the Aegean. Proof of the economic power of Ptolemaic Egypt was the growth and splendor of Alexandria. It was the largest metropolis of the Ancient World, with a population of about 1 million by the first century B.C.E. As the influence of the Ptolemies began to decline because of internal unrest, they became dependent on the Romans, who had come to dominate the Mediterranean. They eventually overthrew the dynasty, and Rome made Egypt part of its empire in 30 B.C.E.

THE SELEUCID EMPIRE

The huge size and mixture of nations within the *Seleucid Empire* made political stability and unity extremely difficult to maintain. Unable to hold the eastern provinces of Parthia and Bactria, the Seleucid state consisted of Mesopotamia, Syria, and Asia Minor. Small independent kingdoms developed in the western and northern parts of Asia Minor, some of which were unhappy with Seleucid rule. Among several uprisings, the most successful was the **Maccabean Revolt** in 167 B.C.E. This uprising by the Jews, celebrated in the modern-day holiday of Chanukah, resulted in the creation of an independent Jewish state in the area of present-day Israel. This kingdom, along with the entire Seleucid Kingdom, was finally destroyed in 63 B.C.E. as a result of Roman and Parthian expansion.

The Hellenistic kingdoms were a combination of Greek ideas and Near Eastern institutions. Even though strong rulers were common, they nevertheless had to prove themselves through effective administration or be swept out of power. No longer could they rely on the Near Eastern concept of kingship as something sacred. The wealth and power of these kingdoms gave the Greeks great political influence. The cultural influence of Greece upon these kingdowns can be seen in many aspects.

Hellenistic Society

Hellenistic society was in some ways different from the Greek World that had inspired it. Greek language and culture provided a common basis; yet, the traditions, beliefs, and practices of Near Eastern civilizations soon became incorporated within it. The result was a multicultural and cosmopolitan society that, despite political tension and wars, both expanded and enriched Greek culture.

THE HELLENISTIC STATES

The Greeks, who had been divided into small warring city-states, were spread throughout the Mediterranean and Middle East. The knowledge, techniques, and ideas of the various peoples with whom they came into contact added a new dimension to their civilization. The term *Greek* took on a new meaning, coming to include all "Hellenized" or "educated" (in the new Hellenistic style) peoples. Anyone who did not adopt this new international learning was considered a **barbarian**. The polis still remained the center of cultural life. The old Greek cities continued to flourish, and new ones developed throughout the Hellenistic World, most notably **Alexandria** in Egypt, **Antioch** in Syria, and **Pergamum** in Asia Minor.

Because citizen participation in most Hellenistic city-states was limited by the autocratic rulers, a new concern with the arts and private luxury developed. As in Classical poleis, new buildings and public decorations, such as temples and statues, were built to beautify each city. Unlike the attitudes of the previous period, however, there was new interest in the decoration of private homes as

A depiction of the Alexandria lighthouse.

well. Wealthy citizens competed with each other to acquire art and to commission works by artists. This greatly encouraged the growth of the arts. *Libraries* and *museums* were created by monarchs who were anxious to show their support of culture and education. This preoccupation with the attainment of wealth and culture also weakened civic participation among citizens, creating the need for large bureaucracies to run each city. The decline of the older concepts also allowed women greater mobility in society.

ART AND ARCHITECTURE

For Hellenistic artists and architects, the artistic works of Ancient Greece served as models. Hellenistic sculptors, however, preferred to show their subjects in a far more realistic way. Unlike the Classical Greeks, who believed that art should idealize human beings by depicting only physically perfect specimens, they sculpted people as they actually looked, with all their flaws and imperfections. Classical artists presented their subjects only at their physical prime of life, but the Hellenistic sculptors chose children and old people as well. The greater social freedom of women was reflected in sculpture as the female nude made its appearance in the Hellenistic Period. The most famous example of which was the *Aphrodite of Melos*, better known as the *Venus de Milo*. Hellenistic relief carvings and painting reflect a similar development toward realism. Architecture continued to develop, combining Classical Greek models with those of Near Eastern building.

LITERATURE

Literature in the Hellenistic period grew as well. A simpler form of Greek, known as **Koine**, was adopted by the Hellenistic World for use in government, business, and learning. This resulted in a growing literacy in a common language that made communication and the sharing of knowledge easier. With the exception of the *novel*, the Classical forms of Greek literature were continued in the Hellenistic period. These included epic and lyric poetry, tragic and comic plays, and histories. There were also scholars who devoted themselves to the study of earlier Greek literature, writing commentaries on their meaning, style, and grammar as well as establishing and preserving copies of these *classics*. Other scholars developed rules for grammar, rhetoric, and literary form. They

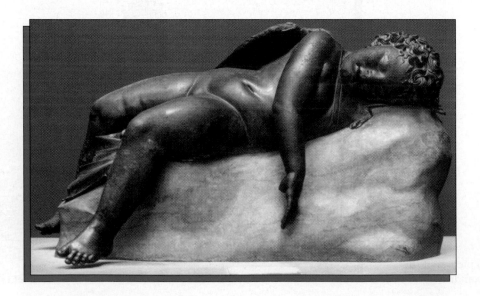

Hellenistic artists sculpted people as they actually looked, with all their flaws and imperfections, as can be seen in this statue of Sleeping Eros. Eros was the great Greek god of love and is represented as a sleeping child, complete with pudgy limbs and tousled hair.

further worked on methods of education and preparation for the ruling elite. Near Eastern works were also translated into Greek, expanding the general body of knowledge and inspiring new ideas. Many translated works became highly influential, most notably the **Septuagint** or **Hebrew Tanach (Old Testament)**. This was put into Greek by Jewish scholars in Alexandria in the third and second centuries B.C.E.

PHILOSOPHY

The philosophers of the Hellenistic period were not as interested in finding the "absolute truth" about things as their Classical predecessors. They were concerned instead with the problems of human conduct or **ethics**. Ethics is concerned with principles by which people should live. Several schools of philosophical thought developed in this era. The **Skeptics** doubted everything and argued that there should be no concern with values or truth because neither really existed, and both were only the creation and interpretation of humans. The **Cynics** mocked society and believed that it should abandon all civilized practices in order to return to nature. They wore rags and preached openly against the established authorities and social structure. The **Epicureans** argued that humans should be concerned only with material happiness, as death was final and there was no evidence of a future existence. Achieving happiness for most Epicureans meant a balance between physical and spiritual development as well as avoiding excessive involvement with the world. The most influential Hellenistic school of philosophy was the **Stoic**. It was founded by **Zeno** (c. 300 B.C.E.). He earned the name "the Stoic" because he taught on his front porch or *stoa*. The Stoics believed that humans had to learn to understand and adapt to the unchanging laws of nature and the universal order. Both good and misfortune had to be accepted because they were the work of a supreme intelligence that ordered the universe. Concern for the material world had to be overcome in order for the soul to reach the "perfect state" of *apatheia*, or **apathy**. This is an absence of feeling and would protect the individual from much of the pain that life could bring. The Stoics also stressed the need for community among humans and involvement in public life in order to maintain balance in society.

THE SCIENCES

Science made great progress in the Hellenistic era. A vast body of scientific information was compiled, based on all the knowledge accumulated by both the Greeks and the Middle Eastern civilizations in the previous centuries. With the advent of the common language of Greek in the Hellenistic World and the greater accessibility of information, Hellenistic scientists had a large base to build upon. Geographic knowledge was expanded by **Eratosthenes**, who calculated the circumference of the earth as well as developed lines of longitude and latitude dividing the earth into zones. This is still used by geographers. In the field of astronomy, **Aristarchus** and **Hipparchus** made important contributions. Aristarchus argued that the earth revolved around the sun. This was known as the **heliocentric theory**. However, his ideas were overshadowed by those of Hipparchus, who believed that the earth was the center of the universe. This was the geocentric theory. Hipparchus misled Western society on the orbit of the planets for centuries, but his work in compiling an atlas of the stars and their movements as well as an accurate calculation of the solar year were very valuable contributions.

MATHEMATICS   In the field of mathematics, Hipparchus developed trigonometry. Another Hellenistic mathematician, **Euclid**, compiled a textbook for geometry that was used for centuries. The scientist **Archimedes** calculated the value of *pi* (the ratio between the circumference and the diameter of a circle), devised a system for expressing large numbers, and laid the foundations of calculus. These subjects are still studied in schools throughout the modern world. In physics, Archimedes discovered the laws governing floating. According to tradition, he made this discovery while in his bath and cried out, *"Eureka!"* ("I found it!"). It is not uncommon today for someone who has made a new discovery to use this expression.

ENCYCLOPEDIAS   Most students today would be lost without a set of encyclopedias to refer to. The concept of collecting information in series of books to make its knowledge accessible to the average person was first created during the Hellenistic Period. Scientific encyclopedias compiled all the knowledge accumulated during this time: in geography by **Strabo**, in astronomy and geography by **Ptolemy**, and in medicine by **Galen**. These works served as resources for later generations to learn from and build on.

LINK TO TODAY
The Creation of Libraries

One of the most familiar sites for any student is a library. It is a source of knowledge and often a quiet place to study. Most Americans have at one time or another borrowed books from a library as well. The origins of this institution date back to the empire of Alexander the Great.

Following the example of his former tutor, Aristotle, Alexander collected works in many languages from the various countries that he had conquered. They were copied and Greek translations were created. The copies in both their original language and the Greek translations were then distributed to libraries throughout his empire. This made it possible for both scholars and educated individuals to share ideas and knowledge.

Libraries helped the process of cultural diffusion, spreading Hellenic culture to the non-Greek world as well as acquainting the Hellenized peoples with the culture and learning of Africa and the Near East. Books, which consisted of papyrus rolls, were available in cities throughout the Mediterranean world in the Hellenistic period and after. The greatest of these libraries, not surprisingly, was in Alexander's capital city of Alexandria. Unfortunately, this great collection of knowledge from the Ancient World was accidentally destroyed in a fire during the Roman takeover of the city in 46 B.C.E.

SECTION 2 SUMMARY

The Hellenistic period preserved and expanded the culture of the Greeks. The combination of Ancient Greek and Near Eastern learning made great progress possible in the arts, sciences, and technology. The creation of a common culture that used the best of the Greek and Near Eastern civilizations provided the structure for an empire in which the entire Mediterranean World would eventually be united. It would be, however, the Romans, not the Hellenistic Greeks, who would finally achieve this. For all their creative genius and brilliance, the Greeks lacked the political and economic stability to bring this about. Yet they provided the foundation on which the imitative Romans would build their empire. This empire, as we will see in the next section, would act as both a unifying and civilizing agent for the continent of Europe.

SECTION 3

Ancient Rome

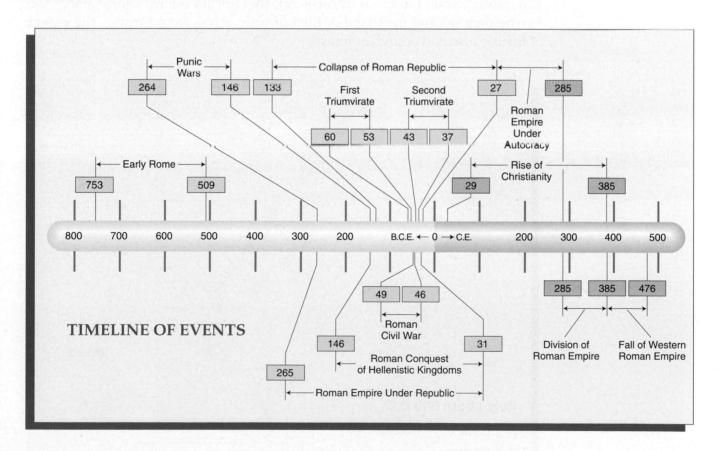

TIMELINE OF EVENTS

One of our greatest debts to Ancient Greece is the development of philosophy. The debt we owe to Ancient Rome is mainly in politics and law. The Romans themselves, however, owed much to Greece. Although not as original or creative as the Greeks, the Romans were masters of imitation and organization. Preserving and improving upon Hellenic and Hellenistic accomplishments, they spread the civilization of Greece throughout western Europe, northern Africa and the eastern Mediterranean. Acting as **civilizing agents** and transmitters of established culture to the many tribes they conquered, the Romans transformed western Europe and built foundations on which nations would be formed in the centuries to come. The dream of Alexander the Great to form one united and Hellenized world was finally achieved by Rome.

Geography

As with the Greeks, geography also influenced the development of Roman culture. When compared with its Hellenic neighbor, the Italian peninsula was relatively rich in the Ancient Period. The **Po valley** in the north, the **Campania** region to the south, and the regions of **Apulia** and **Calabria** on the eastern coast of the peninsula along the **Adriatic Sea** were very fertile. The island of **Sicily**, south of the Italian peninsula, was agriculturally productive as well, especially in grain. In addition, Italy was rich in raw materials. In particular, iron, tin, gold, and silver were found in **Etruria** on the northwestern shore along the **Tyrrhenian Sea** and the island of **Elba** directly across from Etruria. The region of Etruria also had abundant forests.

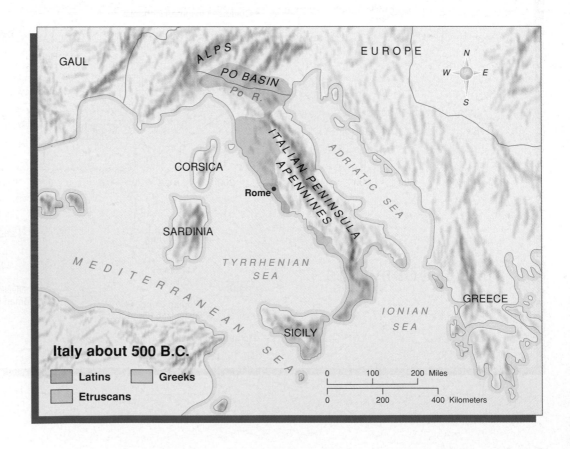

The city of Rome is located in an area called **Latium**, in the center of Italy, which was limitedly productive, but relatively poor when compared to these other regions. Rome is situated inland, with the **Tiber River** connecting it to the Tyrrhenian Sea. It is cut off from these wealthy areas, except for Etruria, by the **Apennine** mountain range, which extends through the Italian peninsula and connects with the **Alps** in the northwest. Unlike the mountains of Greece, however, the Apennines did not completely divide the country. If one state could dominate the peninsula, it would control fairly wealthy agricultural and natural resources as well as some excellent harbors. Being in the center of Italy, Rome had many natural land routes, as well as the Tiber, which were used for trade throughout the country. This is probably the origin of the later proverb, "All roads lead to Rome." Its central location, accessibility, and relative poverty made Rome's conquest of its neighbors a logical goal.

In addition to encouraging the Romans to be conquerors, the limited agriculture and resources of Latium taught the Romans to be organized and disciplined. A sense of unity and cooperation as well as determination and persistence were developed. The Romans were a mixed population of *Etruscans* and *Latins*, who were the ancient peoples that lived in the Italian peninsula. They showed a willingness to learn from others, especially the Greeks. This enabled the Romans to create a political organization that could conquer and administer an empire.

The Mythological Origins of the Romans

The two legendary stories of how Rome was created reveal the mind of the Roman people and the way they viewed themselves. According to the first, the Romans were descended from the Trojans. The Trojan hero *Aeneas* was ordered by the gods to lead the survivors of Troy to Rome and establish a new polis that would rule the world. This story both tied the Romans to the Greeks in their origins and justified their expansionist policy.

A statue of Romulus and Remus being nursed by a she-wolf.

The second story explained the actual founding of the city. The god of war, *Mars*, fathered twin sons, **Romulus** and **Remus**, by the Etruscan princess *Rhea Silvia*. Their mother was however, forced to throw the infants into the Tiber. The gods interfered and washed the children ashore. The brothers were protected and fed by a she-wolf, considered a sacred animal by the Latin tribes. Eventually, Romulus and Remus founded a new settlement at the place where they were saved as infants. They quarreled over who would rule, despite a divine sign that Romulus should be king. The resentful Remus was finally killed by his brother and the new city, *Roma*, was founded in honor of Romulus.

Early Rome (753–509 B.C.E.)

The Foundation of Rome

Founded, according to tradition, in 753 B.C.E., the city of Roma or **Rome** did not seem particularly suited to possess a huge empire. It was a series of tiny villages built on a group of seven hills on the south bank of the Tiber River in an area known as Latium. Originally a settlement of farmers and herdsmen, it was conquered between 800 and 700 B.C.E. by the Etruscans, a people who probably migrated from Asia Minor and established a series of cities along the western coast of Italy north of the Tiber River. The Etruscans had a highly advanced civilization, which had been greatly influenced by the Greeks in the regions of southern Italy and Sicily, known as *Magna Graecia*. Divided into independent city-states like the Greeks, they came to dominate north and central western Italy between 800 and 650 B.C.E. After 500 B.C.E., Etruscan power declined under pressure from the Greeks, *Carthaginians* from northwestern Africa, and native resistance. While they controlled Latium, however, the Etruscans transformed Rome into a single city-state with a central government under a king.

The Establishment of the Republic

According to tradition, Rome had seven kings. They ruled from the foundation of the city (753 B.C.E.) until the establishment of the **Republic** (509 B.C.E.). Each king was advised by a council of elders called the **Senate**, which consisted of about 300 wealthy men who headed powerful families. All Roman citizens, who were free males, belonged to two assemblies, the **Curiae** and the **Centuries**. Membership in the Curiae was based on tribe or clan; the Centuries divided the citizenry into military units. Both bodies, however, were severely limited in power and did little more than approve the decisions of the king. The wealthier citizens, from whom the *senators* were chosen, were known as **Patricians**; the rest, who made up the bulk of the population, were called **Plebians**. At this time, women and slaves had no place politically and had the same legal status as children. Custom prohibited intermarriage between the two classes; however, Patricians were often *patrons* (providers and protectors) for Plebian *clients* (political supporters). In this way, the Patrician class dominated early Rome.

> **Main Idea:**
> The Patricians led a revolt that overthrew Estruscan rule and established a republic.

Early Roman religion, art, and architecture was influenced by the Greeks. Greek religious practices and temples served as models for the Romans. Commerce and trade advanced as Rome was transformed into a commercial city. Finally, the creation of an alphabet and a written Latin language brought Roman society a new sophistication and self-awareness.

The development of a new sense of identity for the Romans led to great resentment at Etruscan domination. In 509 B.C.E., the Patricians led a revolt that overthrew Etruscan rule and established a **republic**, which is a representative or indirect democracy. The king was replaced by two annually elected **consuls**, or presidents, who held the *imperium*, which was executive authority. They were, however, selected by and from the Senate, keeping the control of the Republic within the Patrician class.

The Early Republic (509–265 B.C.E.)

The Conquest of Italy

At first, the newly liberated Romans allied themselves with other Latin tribes in the *Latin League* to defend themselves against the Etruscans and mountain peoples of northern Italy. Invasions by the *Gauls*, a Celtic people who settled in northwestern Europe, beginning around 400 B.C.E., further threatened the survival of the Roman state. These dangers forced the Romans to develop a strong and disciplined army. By 350 B.C.E., the success of the Latin League in defeating the northern invaders left the Romans free to begin dominating their allies. By 338 B.C.E., Rome controlled Latium. From 326 to 290 B.C.E., they conquered the *Samnites*, a mountain people living to the southeast. During these conflicts, the Romans also defeated the Etruscans and Gauls, occupying northern Italy as well. Finally, Rome captured Magna Graecia, putting the Greek colonies of southern Italy and Sicily under their control. By 265 B.C.E., the Romans were masters of the entire Italian peninsula.

The key to the success of the Romans in unifying Italy was their military organization and political stability. Unlike the Greeks, they were able to develop a successful citizen army and adjust the political system to create loyalty among the conquered peoples. The peoples of Latium received Roman citizenship, and others were given a more limited political status. Many cities were made **Socii**, or Italian allies. They were allowed local self-government provided they met certain military and economic obligations. Colonies of Roman citizens were planted throughout Italy to further the process of *Romanization*. This was the spread of Roman culture. The Greeks were given the special status of teachers because the Romans became obsessed with adopting and imitating Hellenic culture. By giving each conquered people a stake in the new order, the Romans were able to maintain the loose confederation that gave them control of the Italian peninsula.

The Struggle of the Orders

The true genius of Roman organization was shown in the development of the legal system. The *Roman constitution*, which was constantly modified during the Early Republic, promoted both allegiance and loyalty among the citizens. After the overthrow of Etruscan rule, the Patrician aristocrats controlled the Senate as well as the two assemblies, Curiae and Centuries. During the following 250 years, however, a conflict between the ruling aristocracy and the Plebians developed, which resulted in a gradual, if limited, sharing of power. This was known as the *Struggle of the Orders*. The need for the Plebians as soldiers gave them a strong bargaining position. By 494 B.C.E., they gained the right to elect special Plebian officials, known as **Tribunes.** They had the power to veto any law that they thought threatened the interests of their class. A Plebian representative body, the **Assembly of Tribes**, was elected to direct the Tribunes and pass Plebian laws, which later were recognized by all Roman citizens.

The Twelve Tables

In 450 B.C.E., the Plebians pressured the Patricians into writing down and creating a system of Roman law known as the **Twelve Tables**. Law had previously been kept by oral tradition. Once written down, the Twelve Tables made the law known to everyone and protected the Plebians from Patrician judges. By 367 B.C.E., as a result of gradual legal reform and the opening of the major elected offices to all citizens, a law was created requiring that one consul be a Plebian. This eventually created a growing number of Plebians in the Senate and a threat to Patrician power. The aristocrats maintained their control by absorbing these powerful Plebians, through economic alliances or marriage, into their own ranks. Although Rome was in theory a fully representative democracy by 265 B.C.E., a small group of wealthy families, known as the **Nobilis** or ruling nobility, actually held power. Yet the flexibility of the Roman constitution, and the ability of the system to provide for its citizens, at least maintained the illusion of political equality, which made the Early Republic successful.

The Roman Empire Under the Republic (265–31 B.C.E.)

The First Punic War (264–241 B.C.E.)

Rome's conquest of Italy had made it a major power and pushed it into the world of Mediterranean politics. Rome soon came into conflict with the *Carthaginians* over the island of **Sicily**. **Carthage**, which had been a northwest African colony of the *Phoenicians*, became independent about 800 B.C.E. and proceeded to create an empire of its own. By 300 B.C.E., the Carthaginians controlled the western Mediterranean and had become serious commercial rivals of the Greeks. In 265 B.C.E., Carthage attempted to expand its hold on the western part of Sicily. By 264 B.C.E., the Romans answered the call for assistance from their Greek allies and became involved in a series of conflicts with Carthage known as the *Punic Wars* (264–146 B.C.E.).

With no navy, Rome was unsuccessful against Carthage at first. Turning to their traditional teachers, the Greeks, the Romans soon developed an impressive fleet and were able to defeat the Carthaginians decisively at sea in 241 B.C.E. Victory in the *First Punic War* gave Rome the islands of Sicily, **Corsica**, and **Sardinia**, as well as prestige in the

First Punic War battle, 256 B.C.

Mediterranean World. The Carthaginians began to rebuild their military strength in order to get revenge on the Romans and reestablish their dominance in the western Mediterranean.

The Second Punic War (218–201 B.C.E.)

In 218 B.C.E., the brilliant Carthaginian general **Hannibal** led his army on a thousand mile march from its base in Spain through southern Gaul, part of modern-day France, into the Alps, and down into northern Italy. This attack surprised the Romans, who had been preparing to attack the Carthaginians in Spain. Despite many defeats and fifteen years' occupation of much Roman territory by Carthaginian armies, the Romans were able to defend Rome itself and prevent Hannibal from controlling the peninsula. The key to Rome's survival was that Hannibal was unable to persuade the Italian allies to turn against Rome. In 203 B.C.E., under the leadership of the Consul **Cornelius Scipio**, Rome began a counteroffensive. Launching attacks on Carthaginian bases in Spain and on Carthage itself, Scipio cut off Carthaginian reinforcements in Italy and forced Hannibal to return to North Africa to save his city. Because his forces were divided and tired from years of campaigning, Hannibal was completely defeated by the Romans in North Africa at the *Battle of Zama* in 203 B.C.E. Carthage surrendered in 201 B.C.E. to Scipio, who was given the title "Africanus" (Conqueror of Africa) by the Senate. As a result of the *Second Punic War* (218–201 B.C.E.) Rome gained all of Spain and forced the Carthaginians to destroy their fleet.

The Third Punic War (149–146 B.C.E.)

The Romans attacked Carthage one last time in the *Third Punic War*, which lasted from 149 to 146 B.C.E. They feared a future threat from another revival of Carthaginian power. They destroyed the city and, according to tradition, poured salt on the site where the city had stood so that nothing could ever grow or be built there. This act marked a turning point in Roman conquest. Thereafter, the Romans followed an aggressive and sometimes brutal policy of conquest. Northwest Africa became part of the Roman Empire, which now completely controlled the western Mediterranean.

The Conquest of the Hellenistic Kingdoms (146–31 B.C.E.)

The economic benefits and commercial growth that resulted from the Punic Wars encouraged Rome to expand its empire further. At first occupying territory only to restore peace and prevent conflict, Rome gradually annexed the Hellenistic kingdoms in Greece, Asia Minor, Syria, Palestine, and Egypt between 146 and 30 B.C.E. This made Rome the master of the Mediterranean, which became known in Latin as *Mare Noster* or "Our Sea." The conquered areas were divided into provinces, and Roman administrators were appointed by the Senate to rule them. Larger provinces, such as Egypt, had *governors*; smaller areas, such as Palestine, were ruled by *procurators*. Military forces were needed throughout the Empire in order to keep peace and discourage rebellion as well as to defend its frontiers from barbarian tribes.

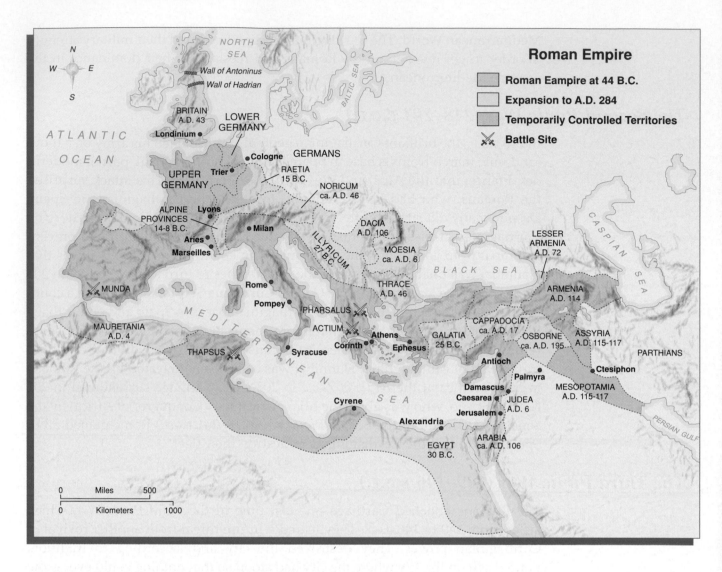

Roman Empire

- Roman Eampire at 44 B.C.
- Expansion to A.D. 284
- Temporarily Controlled Territories
- Battle Site

The Collapse of the Republic (133–27 B.C.E.)

Expansion from Civitas to Empire

The expansion of Rome into an empire created new problems and needs as well as luxuries and wealth. The military forces required to protect the Empire's new borders put a great strain on Rome's monetary resources. Political change was also called for, particularly by the Italian allies, who still made up the bulk of the Roman army. The unfulfilled promise of citizenship for the majority of Socii and the domination of the Patricians in government created great resentment. The wealth generated by Rome's expansion chiefly benefited the Nobilis. Many Romans became part of the **proletariat** (poor laborers), who often turned to crime in order to survive in the city slums. Wealthy Romans, ambitious for political power, began to use the proletariat in planned mob violence to put pressure on rivals and opponents. Another social group, the *Equites*, was made up of Patricians who had lost their wealth and were therefore excluded from political power. This group also included wealthy businessmen who lacked the family background to be part of the ruling class. The Equites, also struggling for a share of political power, further complicated the situation.

The Reforms of the Gracchi and Marius

Main Idea:
The inability of the Roman system to adjust to the changes that expansion had brought led to a struggle between the Optimates and the Populares.

The inability of the Roman system to adjust to the changes that expansion had brought led to a struggle between two factions for control of the government. The **Optimates,** which means "the best suited to hold power" or aristocrats, represented the ruling Nobilis. The **Populares,** or "the People," was led by reform-minded Patricians but consisted mainly of Equites and poor urban citizens. The Optimates favored the continuation of an **oligarchy,** or rule of the few in government, arguing that the Nobilis were the best qualified to rule, while the Populares demanded that the political decision-making process be shared by a wider range of classes and that citizenship be given to the Italian allies. Between 133 and 121 B.C.E., the brothers **Tiberius** and **Gaius Gracchus,** grandsons of Scipio, became champions of the Populares and tried to implement reforms (the *Gracchi Reforms*). These included

- A redistribution of land in order to reestablish independent farms in Italy
- The establishment of new colonies to resettle impoverished Romans
- The provision of cheaper grain to feed the poor
- The granting of full citizenship to the Socii

The Optimates, who controlled the Senate, blocked the reforms by provoking violence in Rome and proclaiming a state of crisis for which martial law was needed. They used these "crises" as reasons to execute the Gracchi as well. Tiberius was killed in 133 B.C.E. and Gaius in 121 B.C.E. The leadership of the Populares was taken up in 108 B.C.E. by **Marius,** a soldier of common background who had advanced to be elected consul (r. 107–86 B.C.E.) through his association with a Patrician family and his outstanding military record. Marius's victories over rebels in North Africa and in campaigns against the Germanic tribes made him extremely popular and powerful. He adopted a reform program similar to that of the Gracchi, but his poor ability as a politician prevented him from overcoming senatorial opposition and implementing it.

The Social War and the Dictatorship of Sulla

The failure of the Populares to bring about reform led to great frustration and anger among the Italian allies. In 90 B.C.E., the Socii revolted, threatening the existence of the Roman state. The *Social War* (90–85 B.C.E.), as the revolt was later known, was finally ended when the Senate granted the allies citizenship in 85 B.C.E. The Optimate **Sulla,** an impoverished aristocrat who had also advanced through connections and military ability during the Socii Revolt, seized power in 83 B.C.E., establishing a military dictatorship. Under Sulla, complete power was restored to the Patrician-controlled Senate, and the Populares were removed from public office. The powers of the Tribunes and Assembly of Tribes were also severely limited. Even though the Senate was enlarged to include the Equites and some very wealthy Socii, it once again became a highly unrepresentative body. More importantly, it had set a precedent for powerful military commanders seizing control and imposing their personal rule on the Empire.

The First Triumvirate (60–53 B.C.E.)

Gaius Julius Caesar was one of the military commanders who made up the First Triumvirate.

Main Idea:
Using a combination of intimidation and popular support, the Triumvirate took control of the government.

As the resentment to aristocratic domination grew, the Senate became increasingly dependent on military leaders to preserve its power. A succession of revolts in Italy, Spain, and Asia Minor, as well as an uprising of slaves, led by the slave rebel **Spartacus**, from 79 to 70 B.C.E. frightened the Senate into granting extraordinary powers to three military commanders: **Marcus Licinius Crassus, Cneius Pompey**, and **Gaius Julius Caesar**. Crassus was a wealthy and ambitious businessman who became famous for putting down the slave revolt of Spartacus. Lacking nobility and popularity, however, Crassus allied himself with Caesar, an impoverished young commander who had both Patrician background and public appeal. Caesar had distinguished himself in the *Gallic Wars* (58–55 B.C.E.), a series of military campaigns in which rebellions in **Gaul** were successfully put down and Roman control in that region was expanded. Pompey was a general who won acclaim for putting down the revolts in Italy and Spain as well as expanding Roman control over Asia Minor and the East.

The Senate soon began to regret the power it had given these military leaders. Influenced by the lawyer and orator **Cicero**, as well as other critics of the decision, the Senate began to oppose them. This resulted in an alliance of the three generals, the *First Triumvirate* or "rule by three people" (60–53 B.C.E.).

Using a combination of intimidation and popular support, the Triumvirate took control of the government. Alternating as consuls, they pushed through reforms, won great military victories, and spent huge sums of money in order to build popular support. After Crassus's death during a military campaign in 53 B.C.E., the Triumvirate disintegrated. Pompey, jealous of the popular Caesar, allied himself with the Senate, who gave Pompey dictatorial powers. In 49 B.C.E., the Senate declared that Caesar was no longer a consul and was to face criminal charges, authorizing Pompey to use the military to enforce this decision. Rome went into civil war.

The Civil War (49–46 B.C.E.)

Caesar, who was in Gaul at the time of Pompey's alliance with the Senate, responded by invading Italy. His decision to attack Rome, despite the fact that it was a violation of Roman tradition and would make him a rebel, was symbolized by his crossing of the **Rubicon**. This was the river separating Italy from Gaul. The expression "crossing the Rubicon" has come to mean someone making an irreversible decision. Caesar's veterans easily defeated Pompey's forces, first on the Italian peninsula and then in Spain and Greece. In 48 B.C.E., Pompey fled to Egypt to gather a new army but was murdered by the Egyptians. They sent his head to Caesar in the hopes that it would prevent Roman forces from crossing their borders. Seizing the opportunity, Caesar used Pompey's death as an excuse to become involved in the affairs of the only Hellenistic kingdom that had not come under Roman domination. Supporting the claim of **Cleopatra VII** over that of her brother, Caesar made her queen of Egypt in return for strong Roman influence in Egyptian affairs.

The Dictatorship of Caesar (46–44 B.C.E.)

When Caesar returned to Rome in 46 B.C.E., he enlarged the Senate with his supporters and used his popularity with the masses to intimidate the Nobilis. From 45 to 44 B.C.E., Caesar ruled as dictator, a title the Senate had been giving him annually since 49 B.C.E. when he drove Pompey out of Italy. His mistrust and dislike of both the senators and the republican system grew stronger. The Senate increasingly saw Caesar as power hungry and a threat to the survival of Roman democracy. The vast majority of Romans, disillusioned with the unrepresentative nature of the Republic, supported Caesar, who used his power to address some of the major problems of

An image of Mark Antony.

> **Main Idea:**
> The vast majority of Romans supported Caesar, who used his power to address some of the major problems of the time.

the time. Among these were financial debt, crime, the decline of small independent farms, and the extension of citizenship. It was rumored that Caesar was not satisfied with the title of dictator and wanted to have the Senate officially declare him king. Convinced they were saving the Republic, a group of senators, including two of Caesar's former supporters, **Marcus Brutus** and **Gaius Cassius**, assassinated Caesar in the Senate on March 15, 44 B.C.E. This day is known as the *Ides of March*. Caesar's murder was followed by outrage and riots that forced the senatorial conspirators to flee Rome. An alliance, the *Second Triumvirate*, was formed in 43 B.C.E. between the two main candidates to succeed Caesar. They were the military commanders **Mark Antony** and **Octavian Caesar.** Octavian was a grandnephew whom Caesar adopted as his legal son and heir. *Lepidus*, a loyal general who was dedicated to punishing Caesar's assassins, also joined the Triumvirate.

The Second Triumvirate (43–37 B.C.E.)

The *Second Triumvirate* marched on Rome and forced the frightened Senate to give it temporary absolute power. By 42 B.C.E., the armies of the senatorial conspirators had been defeated and all political opposition to the Triumvirate, including Cicero, were eliminated. While they might initially have intended to rule the Empire jointly, the members of the Triumvirate in fact prepared to remove one another from power. Lepidus, who was given the northwestern African provinces, was exiled by Octavian in 37 B.C.E. in a struggle for command of Sicily. Antony, who had taken the eastern provinces, became romantically involved with the ambitious Cleopatra VII. After marrying the Egyptian queen, Antony tried to establish *Caesarion*, supposedly Cleopatra's son by Caesar, as the rightful heir to rule the Empire. This gave Octavian who was, under Roman law, Caesar's only heir, an excuse to remove Antony. He declared war on his rivals and defeated the Egyptian forces of Antony and Cleopatra in Greece at the *Battle of Actium* in 31 B.C.E. In 30 B.C.E., Octavian invaded Egypt. This resulted in the suicides of the defeated Antony and Cleopatra. Octavian had Caesarion killed and established Egypt as a Roman province.

The Roman Empire Under the Autocracy (27 B.C.E.–285 C.E.)

The Establishment of the Autocracy

With the removal of Antony, Octavian became the sole ruler of the Roman Empire. While claiming to restore the Republic, he set up an **autocracy**, or system of one-man rule, that was basically a restoration of monarchy. The Senate was slowly stripped of any real power by Octavian and his successors. Unlike his uncle Julius Caesar, Octavian realized that the title of king was offensive to most Romans and that maintaining the illusion that Rome was still ruled by the Senate would make the transition easier. Having control of the army and chief magistrates as well as inheriting popularity from his uncle, Octavian forced the Senate to make him "First Consul for life." In 27 B.C.E., he was declared *princeps* or "First Citizen," which amounted to being made absolute ruler. Changing his name to **Augustus**, or "Revered One," he took on the titles of *Pater Patriae* ("Father of His Country") and *Imperator* or Emperor ("One Who Holds the Supreme Power"). Armed with these titles and the power they represented, he became **semi-divine** as kings in the Hellenistic East had been and therefore a new symbol with which all in the Empire could identify.

The Reign of Augustus (27 B.C.E.–14 C.E.)

Augustus's reign (27 B.C.E.–14 C.E.) restored order in the Roman Empire. This in itself won him enormous support. Trade and commerce were allowed to grow, easing the economic problems and food shortages that had plagued the Roman World during the Civil War. The army was brought under control and reassigned to guarding the frontier borders. The navy kept the seas clear of pirates and protected commercial shipping. The government was made into an efficient bureaucracy that offered opportunities for advancement for citizens throughout the Empire. *Romanization*, which was the adoption of Roman culture and the Latin language, was encouraged, especially outside Italy. Citizenship was likewise extended, which once again gave the population a stake in maintaining the Empire. Augustus pacified the Nobilis by giving them important positions within the government and continuing the pretense that Rome was still a republic. In fact most of the population, which had never had any political power in the Republic to begin with, did not seem to care that Rome was no longer a democracy. The urban poor were given welfare, cheap grain was available for the proletariat, and the reestablishment of independent farmers throughout Italy was encouraged and assisted. Most importantly, Rome began a period of relative peace known as the **Pax Romana,** or "Roman Peace" (27 B.C.E.–180 C.E.). This improved the standard of living for the majority of the Empire's inhabitants. Augustus also improved Roman morale and patriotism by developing a pride in the past. He led a revival of the Ancient Roman religion. This included worshiping Julius Caesar as a god and establishing the Emperor as the semi-divine ruler of the Empire. The idea that Rome's conquests were its historical destiny was also developed. The poems of **Vergil** and the histories of **Livy**, both of whom were supported by Augustus, reflect this. The emperor greatly supported and encouraged those Roman writers, poets, playwrights, historians, architects and artists whose works praised the greatness of Rome and its people. He also encouraged traditional Roman morals and family values, enacting strict laws to punish individuals who did not follow them (see "Roman Society" in this chapter). These policies also inspired citizens, especially in Italy, to join the army and defend the Empire.

> **Main Idea:**
> Augustus won enormous support for many reasons—most notably for the period of relative peace that began under his rule.

A statue of Augustus.

The Julio-Claudian Dynasty (27 B.C.E.–68 C.E.)

Augustus himself did much to revitalize and strengthen the Empire, but his successors were not always as capable or conscientious as he was. Hoping to create a hereditary system, Augustus established the **Julio-Claudian dynasty** by deciding that all emperors who followed would be from his family. He chose his adopted son-in-law **Tiberius**, a capable military man, to succeed him as emperor. In Tiberius's reign (14–37 C.E.), the policies of Augustus were continued. There was, however, a struggle within the family for the succession. This resulted in the madman **Gaius**, nicknamed **Caligula** or "Little Boots" because of his small size as a boy, murdering Tiberius and succeeding him as emperor. Caligula's incompetent and bloody rule (37–41 C.E.) hurt the prestige of the autocracy and ended only when the *Praetorian Guard* (personal troops of the emperor) killed him and made his uncle **Claudius** emperor. Claudius, a handicapped scholar, was a dedicated ruler, but his reign (41–54 C.E.) was hurt by poor advisors. Claudius was poisoned by his fourth wife and her son by a previous marriage, **Nero**, who succeeded him as emperor. Nero later had his mother and two wives killed as well. During the reign of Nero (54–68 C.E.), the last of the Julio-Claudians, the image of the emperor sank to its lowest level. Nero provoked the resentment of many groups in Roman society by

- Wasting Rome's treasury on personal luxuries and projects
- Posing as an artist despite an obvious lack of any talent
- Humiliating and killing many important senators
- Persecuting **Christians** (See section on Christianity later in chapter.)
- Forcibly rebuilt the city of Rome after chasing out the whole population and burning down the existing buildings

Nero followed a policy of "bread and circuses," in which the government fed the poor and gave the population free shows to prevent them from noticing the poor quality of leadership. He grew extremely unpopular and was overthrown in 68 C.E. by a group of generals. This established the practice that all Roman emperors were to be military men and that the army controlled their selection. The Empire, which had grown large and difficult to maintain, could not afford to support incompetent or wasteful rulers. When they appeared, the efficient Roman military machine removed them.

The Flavians and "Good Emperors" (69–180 C.E.)

Beginning with the *Flavian dynasty*, which consisted of *Vespasian* (r. 69–79 C.E.) and his sons *Titus* (r. 79–81 C.E.) and *Domitian* (r. 81–96 C.E.), the emperors efficiently ruled the Empire, completely ignoring the Senate. The Flavians were succeeded by a group of gifted and brilliant rulers who became known as the "Good Emperors" (r. 96–180 C.E.). They were *Nerva* (r. 96–98 C.E.), *Trajan* (r. 98–117 C.E.), *Hadrian* (r.117–138 C.E.), *Antoninus* (r. 138–161 C.E.), and **Marcus Aurelius** (r.161–180 C.E.), who was also a noted Stoic philosopher. Under the "Good Emperors," Roman law became universal for the entire Empire, and many humanitarian projects were undertaken to assist the poor. By 180 C.E. however, the army had become

In addition to being an emperor, Marcus Aurelius was also a Stoic philosopher.

overextended guarding the vast frontiers of the Empire. The Romans were finally forced to use paid foreign armies, which were usually unreliable. Money, not patriotism, had become the important factor. Defending Rome's borders became an increasing problem for its emperors.

Roman Society

The Greek Model

Main Idea:
The four basic forces that shaped the early Roman World were agriculture, family life, war, and religion.

The Romans admired the Greeks greatly. Their society was, to a large degree, an imitation of the Hellenic. The four basic forces that shaped the early Roman World were agriculture, family life, war, and religion. Interest in culture developed only after 250 B.C.E., when Rome was transformed into an empire and came into greater contact with the Hellenistic World. Although the Romans may have physically conquered Greece, they were highly influenced by Hellenic learning and culture. They went to great lengths to become as "Greek" as possible. As a later poet put it, "Captive Greece held Rome captive." This was especially true of the upper classes, who competed to bring Greek slaves, scholars, artists, literature, and art to Rome. One of the earliest and greatest champions of Hellenization was Cornelius Scipio, the conqueror of Carthage. He was patron to a group of imported Greek poets, scholars, and artists. This included the historian *Polybius* (c. 202–120 B.C.E.), who wrote the first account of Roman history, *The Rise of the Roman Republic,* in Greek. As they learned from their Hellenic teachers, the Romans developed their own literature in Latin as well as art and architecture. Not known for their originality, the Romans nonetheless expanded on the Greek models and showed a great talent for imitation.

Roman Architecture

Architecture was one of Rome's two great contributions to world civilization. The Romans perfected both the **arch** and the **dome**. These advances allowed them to build larger buildings and expand upon the Greek forms they studied.

The Romans perfected both the arch and the dome, as can be seen in this picture of the Pantheon.

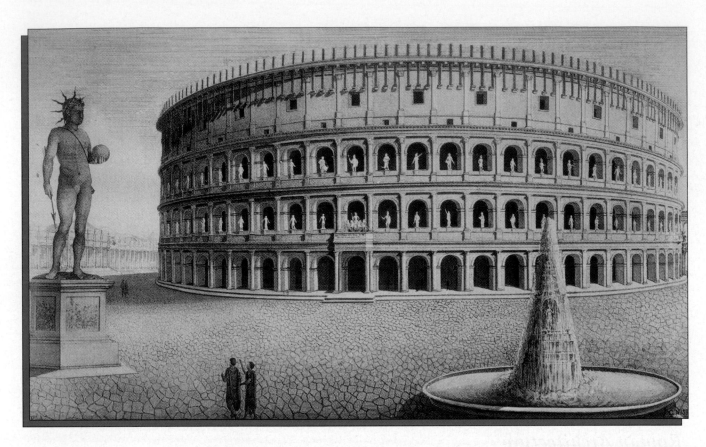

Although the Romans were not known for their temples, they built the greatest round temple of the Ancient World, the *Pantheon* or Temple to All the Gods, noted for its huge dome with an opening in the center. They excelled at secular public buildings such as baths, palaces, meeting halls or *basilicas*, amphitheaters, aqueducts, bridges, and ceremonial arches. The huge complex of public meeting halls and marketplaces in Rome, known as the *Forum*, and the massive sports facility called the *Colosseum* were especially impressive examples of the Roman genius for architecture. Roman basilicas and temples later served as models for Christian churches.

Roman Art

Even more than architecture, Roman art was imitative of the Greek, emphasizing the realistic aspect, especially in sculpture. It was, however, in *bas-relief*, which are sculptures that project slightly from a background, and painting that the Romans excelled. Their excellent *mosaics*, pictures made of small colored pieces of inlaid stone or glass, served as models for early Christian artwork in churches. In public buildings, the Romans preferred historical or natural rather than mythological and religious scenes, which were limited to temples. They also avoided the excessive idealization of Classical Greek art.

Roman Literature

Roman literature produced its own distinctive qualities of realism. The Latin language also developed, especially through poetry. The greatest of Roman poets was **Vergil** (90–70 B.C.E.), whose epic poem *Aeneid* gave the Romans a sense of identity, claiming they were descendants of the Trojans. A national saga, it both inspired patriotism and justified Rome's expansion as a matter of destiny. The Roman love of nature and agricultural life was emphasized in Vergil's work *Georgics*, which reinforced many traditional values. **Catullus** (c. 85–54 B.C.E.) wrote lyric poetry about the subject of love and the pain it often causes. **Horace** (65–8 B.C.E.), also a lyric poet, presented a picture of reason, intelligence, education, and wit, which was the Roman ideal of a civilized person. **Lucretius** (c. 95–55 B.C.E.), in his work *On the Nature of the Universe*, used poetry to instruct his readers to seek fulfillment in philosophy. **Ovid** (43 B.C.E.–17 C.E.) translated Greek mythology into Latin poetry in his *Metamorphoses* and amused his readers with his humorous work on seduction, *The Art of Love*. The poetry of **Martial** (c. 38–102 C.E.) and **Juvenal** (c. 55–140 C.E.) revealed the flaws of Roman society in satires.

Political Philosophy and Historical Writing

Rome's greatest writer of prose was the lawyer and statesman **Cicero** (106–43 B.C.E.). He developed the art of rhetoric in his speeches, which were written down and studied by others. His essays, such as "The Republic" and "The Laws," defended the republican system of government but argued that a "First Citizen" was needed to lead it.

The Romans excelled most in historical writing. Some of Rome's greatest historians were Greeks, such as Polybius and later **Plutarch** (c. 46–120 C.E.), who wrote biographies of famous Greeks and Romans in his work *Parallel Lives*. The majority, however, were Romans, writing in Latin. The most influential was **Livy** (59 B.C.E.–17 C.E.), whose huge *History of Rome* covered events from Rome's foundation until his own time. **Tacitus** (c. 55–117 C.E.) wrote about the century

The Roman artists' excellent mosaics served as models for early Christian artwork in churches.

following Augustus in his *Histories* and *Annals* as well as providing detailed information about the German barbarians in his *Germania*. **Suetonius** (c. 75–150 C.E.) portrayed the Roman rulers from Julius Caesar to Domitian in his history *The Twelve Caesars*. Prominent Romans also produced personal histories, as did Julius Caesar, whose commentaries *On the Gallic War* and *On the Civil War* were standard reading on military strategy, and the emperor Marcus Aurelius, whose *Meditations* was a brilliant explanation of Stoic philosophy.

Roman Philosophers

Roman philosophers were not original in their thought, but they adopted Greek philosophies and expanded on them. Lucretius, who had studied under the Hellenistic philosopher Epicurus, started a Roman school of Epicureanism. Many other Roman Epicureans, however, misinterpreted these ideas and used them as an excuse for a life of sexual pleasure. Stoicism was a far more popular philosophy among the Romans. Its two greatest champions were **Seneca** (c. 4 B.C.E.–65 C.E.) and later Marcus Aurelius.

Roman Science

Science also made great progress during the Roman period. Scholars such as **Pliny the Elder** (c. 32–79 C.E.), **Galen** (131–201 C.E.), and **Ptolemy** (c. 121–151 C.E.) compiled great encyclopedias of scientific knowledge. This store of information was practically used in all areas, especially engineering.

Christianity

Religion was an important part of Roman society. Initially, the pagan Roman religion shaped the society's values. As contact with the East grew through conquest, Hellenistic mystery religions became popular and weakened the authority of the family. During the periods of civil war and crisis in the second and third centuries C.E., Christianity began to attract Romans who were searching for a new, spiritual meaning in their lives.

A mosaic of Jesus of Nazareth.

Originally a radical sect that broke away from Judaism, Christianity is based on the teachings of **Jesus of Nazareth** (c. 4 B.C.E.–29 C.E.). The traditional year of Jesus' birth, 1 C.E., was a miscalculation when the Christian system of annual dating was later developed. Born Jewish, under Roman rule, Jesus taught his followers to pursue peace, love people, seek spiritual development over material gain, avoid becoming too ritualistic in religious practice, and respect the equality of all human beings. His teachings were firmly based on Judaic tradition. Many

Later known in the Christian tradition as St. Paul, Saul of Tarsus provided much needed leadership to the early Christian movement, opening it up to non-Jews.

Jews saw Jesus as a reformer who wanted to make certain changes in religious practices. Others believed he was the **Messiah**, or "Anointed One," which is *Christos* (or Christ) in Greek. The Messiah was the Jewish leader whose coming was predicted in the Old Testament. Jesus also proclaimed that he was the Son of God or God in a human form. He had come to prepare humanity for the kingdom of Heaven, which was spiritual, rather than material, through repentance and spiritual renewal. This created much controversy in the Jewish community. Many Jews feared that the Romans would see Jesus as a potential rebel and thus harm the Jewish community by creating Roman displeasure. Perceived as a threat to the established order, the leadership of the Jewish community arrested Jesus and put him on trial. He was found guilty of *blasphemy*, or disrespectful teaching about God, and given to the Roman authorities. The Romans approved the decision and ordered execution by crucifixion. After Jesus' death, his followers claimed that he had risen from the dead, proving that he was both the Messiah and God. This series of events was described in the New Testament, which were written years after.

Jesus' original followers consisted of a group of men called **Apostles** or disciples, led by a fisherman named **Peter**. They preached Jesus' beliefs and gained a small following among the Jews. The Christian *Church*, or body of followers, soon came under the leadership of a Hellenized Jew, **Paul of Tarsus**, who influenced the movement to accept non-Jews. As a result of this decision, Christianity grew in its appeal, especially among slaves and the poor. The new religion spread rapidly throughout the Mediterranean region, even to Rome itself. By the reign of Nero, Christians were a large enough minority to be viewed as a threat and were openly persecuted. Despite a great misunderstanding of Christian teaching and frequent, violent persecution of them by the Roman government, the Christians won many converts. By the reign of Constantine, they were a fairly powerful and influential minority.

The Divided Empire (285–476 C.E.)

The Division of the Empire (285-385 C.E.)

While Christianity was spreading, the military commander **Diocletian** became Emperor. Diocletian (r. 284–305 C.E.) restored order after a period of civil war between rival generals, know as the **Barrack Emperors**, fighting for power (193–284 C.E.). Through the revival of a central government, trade and commerce were protected and encouraged in an effort to restore the economy. The losses, however, both of land and people, during the civil war had changed the overall needs of the Empire. Diocletian felt that the Empire was far too large and its borders too vast for one individual to rule alone. In 285 C.E., he divided the Empire into two parts: the *East*, including **Greece**, **Asia Minor**, **Egypt**, **Syria** and **Palestine** and the *West*, including Italy, **Northwest Africa**, **Gaul**, **Iberia** (modern Spain and Portugal), **Germania** (modern Austria and Germany), and **Britain**. Each part had an **Augustus**, or emperor, and a **Caesar**, or co-emperor, who would assist him. Diocletian believed the administration of the Empire and the defense of its borders would be far more efficient if it were divided among four leaders. Despite very careful preparation and many determined attempts to assure a peaceful and orderly succession, conflict between the augusti and caesars broke out soon after Diocletian's retirement in 305 C.E.

THE REIGN OF CONSTANTINE I (312–337 C.E.)

Following a series of struggles (306–311 C.E.), the Emperor **Constantine** (312–337 C.E.) again unified the Empire. In 313 C.E., he issued the *Edict of Milan* (in Italy), which allowed Christianity to exist freely alongside the official pagan Roman religion. This new freedom encouraged the growth of Christianity, the faith to which Constantine himself converted on his deathbed (His mother Helen was a Christian and may have had a great influence on him). He built churches, encouraged Christian clergymen to join state councils, and even presided over the first Christian conference, the **Council of Nicaea** in 325 C.E. Constantine probably had political motivations as well as religious ones. The borders of the Empire were greatly threatened by this time, especially in the West. Recognizing that the lack of patriotism and religion was in great part responsible for this disintegration, Constantine hoped that the Christian Church would become an institution that would unify the Romans. Christianity did not oppose the existence of the autocracy and might encourage a revival of the Empire.

Constantine issued the *Edict of Milan*, which allowed Christianity to exist freely alongside the official pagan Roman religion.

Recognizing political realities, Constantine erected a new capital city, **Constantinople**, formerly known as **Byzantium**, in Asia Minor. It had become clear that Rome was no longer in the center of its own Empire and was exposed to barbarian invasion. More importantly, it was a recognition that the East was the heart of the Roman World and that the West, outside of Italy and North Africa, was a shrinking frontier full of barbarians.

THE RISE OF THE CHRISTIAN CHURCH

After the Edict of Milan granted them toleration, the Christians encountered new problems, such as attempts by emperors to dominate the Church, corruption among the clergy, and a lack of devotion on the part of many members. Rules for proper Christian behavior were created (*canon law*) as were courts to judge and discipline the clergy. Many Christians moved to isolated places, such as deserts and mountains, in order to pray and worship away from the distractions of everyday life. These **ascetics** (people who deny all physical pleasure in order to develop spiritually) were called *monastic* or *monks* (those who live alone). Living by themselves or in small communities, monastics became heroes for Christians in the Late Roman Period. **Anthony of Egypt** (c. 251–356 C.E.) founded the Christian monastic movement when he went to live alone in the desert. Monasticism grew very popular. By 400 C.E., rules had been established for monastic communities. The Christian Church soon became an enormously powerful institution throughout Europe and the Middle East.

THE FALL OF THE WESTERN ROMAN EMPIRE (385–476 C.E.)

Christianity was not able to prevent the collapse of the West, but it did unify the East. By 395 C.E., Emperor **Theodosius I** (r. 385–397 C.E.), Constantine's nephew, felt the Christian population had grown substantially enough for him to make it the official religion of the Roman Empire. After Theodosius's reign, however, the Empire was again divided into two parts. In the West, where the erosion of Roman authority was too great, the Empire was overrun by Germanic barbarians. Ironically, these Germanic tribes had initially been given Roman borderlands in order to protect the frontier of the Empire as *Foederati*, or "Federates." By 450 C.E., they had taken most of Italy. In 476 C.E., the Germanic general

Odoacer deposed the last Western Roman Emperor, Romulus Augustulus, and occupied the city of Rome. The Eastern Emperor in Constantinople became the sole ruler of the Roman Empire. This marked the beginning of the Byzantine or Eastern Roman Period. There were many reasons for the fall of the Western Roman Empire. No one factor can be given total blame. These include

- The peaceful penetration of Germanic barbarians into the Empire as foedorati or mercenaries in the army

- The violent penetration of Germanic tribes through invasion

- The economic burden of maintaining a large army to protect the borders

- The many civil wars between ambitious generals to become emperor

- A decrease in the population due to plague and civil war

- A greater degree of dependency on barbarians for both labor and military service as a result of the population decrease

- Overdependency on slave labor

- The decline of Roman cities due to the poor economy

- Corruption and inefficiency in the government bureaucracy

Romulus Augustulus is deposed by Odoacer.

LINK TO TODAY
The Influence of Roman Law

One of the most important Roman contributions to Western society is the concept of law. The Romans greatly valued their laws and legal system. They maintained the order and stability of the Roman system.

In front of most American courthouses, there is always some reference to Roman law. Often one will see a statue of a blindfolded woman holding a scale, symbolizing the Roman belief that justice is blind. Inscribed underneath is usually the Latin word *lex*, which means "law."

The tradition of lawyers defending clients is also of Roman origin. The Roman writer, Cicero, was in fact a great trial lawyer, whose eloquence often resulted in a successful defense. The Roman concept of law as the protector of the individual in society is a vital part of the American tradition. This inheritance is greatly valued.

SECTION 3 SUMMARY

The Romans adopted Greek civilization and improved on it. They created a large Hellenized empire, which not only preserved Greco-Roman culture and learning but spread it. Roman contact with the peoples of western Europe had a lasting influence. For many tribes and nations, the Empire was the transmitter of civilization. The Christian Church, which the last Western Roman Emperors established, was the only Roman institution to survive the Germanic invasions. It both preserved Greco-Roman learning and later shaped the new society that was formed in western Europe. While it collapsed in the West, the Eastern Roman Empire continued to thrive for another 1000 years. Rome would later serve as a model and measure for European leaders to judge their own accomplishments.

CHAPTER SUMMARY

We can never fully repay our debt to Greco-Roman civilizations, which had created, accomplished, and transmitted so much. It had great influence on the latter civilizations of Europe, the Middle East, and northern Africa. While we may remember the battles and names of the famous leaders, we should not forget that these civilizations built beautiful buildings, wrote poetry, recorded history, created philosophy, and promoted science. Although the Roman Empire collapsed in the west, the Eastern Roman Empire, or Byzantium, continued to thrive for another one thousand years. The Roman Catholic Church would preserve Greco-Roman culture throughout the Middle Ages in western Europe. In northern Africa, the Coptic and Ethiopian Orthodox Churches would maintain much of Greco-Roman civilization. The influence of Greco-Roman learning would also be evident in the Islamic faith, which would spread throughout the Middle East as well. Arabic civilization would also benefit from Greco-Roman philosophy and science. Most importantly, Greco-Roman civilization continues to be the basis for modern learning and values.

SECTION 1: IMPORTANT PEOPLE, PLACES, AND TERMS

KEY TERMS	PEOPLE	PLACES
city-state/polis	Sir Arthur Evans	Crete
hominocentrism	Heinrich Schleimann	Peloponnese
myth	Homer	Attica
Greek Miracle	Hesiod	Macedonia
history	Pindar	Asia Minor
constitutional monarchy	Sappho	"Greater Greece"
oligarchy	Pythagoras	Knossos
aristocracy	Democritus	Troy
democracy	Heraclitus	Mycenae
direct democracy	Aeschylus	Sparta
tyranny	Sophocles	Athens
archon	Euripides	Thebes
helot	Aristophanes	Corinth
citizen	Themistocles	Mediterranean Sea
hoplite	King Leonidas	Aegean Sea
phalanx	Darius I	Marathon
drama	Xerxes	Thermopolaye
tragedy	Pericles	Platea
comedy	The Thirty	Salamis
satire	Philip II	Athenian Acropolis
philosophy	Alexander III	Parthenon
Sophist	Socrates	
trial by jury	Plato	
areopagus	Aristotle	
acropolis	Draco	
Delian League	Solon	
Peloponnesian League	Pisistratus	
Hellenic League	Lycurgus	
Socratic method	Hippocrates	
	Herodotus	
	Thucydides	

EXERCISES FOR SECTION 1

MULTIPLE CHOICE

Select the letter of the correct answer.

1. Greek Civilization was
   a. monotheistic.
   b. hominocentric.
   c. theocentric.
   d. atheistic.

2. How did geography influence the development of Ancient Greece?
   a. Rich farm land led to dependence on agriculture.
   b. Excellent harbors encouraged seafaring trade
   c. Flat plains made centralized rule possible.
   d. Tropical climate discouraged urban development.

3. What was one cause of the development of many small independent city-states in Ancient Greece?

   a. Greece and Rome were often at war.
   b. The moutainous terrain of Greece resulted in widely scattered settlements.
   c. Military leaders found small Greek settlements easy to control.
   d. The Greek people had many different languages and religions.

4. The Greeks became very creative because

   a. they were inspired by the natural beauty of the land.
   b. they had to overcome a difficult environment.
   c. they had a surplus of crops.
   d. they were more intelligent than the Persians.

5. The Greeks imagined their gods to be

   a. spirits.
   b. half-animal, half-human.
   c. strange creatures.
   d. superhumans.

6. Which statement is true of Ancient Greek beliefs?

   a. Physical strength is all one needs for success.
   b. Only the development of one's spirit can save the soul.
   c. A sound mind in a sound body.
   d. Eat, drink, and be merry, for tomorrow we die.

7. All of the following are true of Mycenean civilization **EXCEPT**

   a. The Myceneans were expert sailors.
   b. The Myceneans worshiped male sky gods.
   c. The Mycenean economy was based on trading and raiding.
   d. The Myceneans had a strong central government.

8. The Greek Miracle was a unity of

   a. language, religion, and government.
   b. language, culture, and government.
   c. language, religion, and culture.
   d. religion, culture, and government.

9. The life of a Greek city-state revolved around the

   a. acropolis and areopagus.
   b. gymnasium and areopagus.
   c. gymnasium and aghora.
   d. acropolis and aghora.

10. Base your answer on the following quote:

    "For the administration is in the hands of the many and not of the few . . . an Athenian citizen does not neglect the state because he takes care of his own household. . . . We alone regard a man who takes no interest in public affairs, not as a harmless but as a useless character."   Pericles, 431 B.C.E.

    Which type of political system does the quotation suggest that people of ancient Athens valued?

    a. Monarchy   c. Democracy
    b. Aristocracy   d. Autocracy

11. The alliance that the Athenians used to create a commercial empire was

    a. the Delian League.
    b. the Hellenic League.
    c. the Greek League.
    d. the Peloponnesian League.

12. Which is the correct chronological order of the following events?

    1. Peloponnesian War
    2. Greek Miracle
    3. Formation of the Delian League
    4. Persian Wars

    a. 1 → 2 → 3 → 4
    b. 1 → 4 → 2 → 3
    c. 2 → 4 → 3 → 1
    d. 3 → 2 → 4 → 1

13. The Heliea ("People's Court") created the practice of

   a. trial by jury.
   b. being tried by a judge.
   c. deciding the constitutionality of a law.
   d. defendants being represented by a lawyer.

14. Athenian citizenship was limited to

   a. wealthy males over 21 years of age.
   b. wealthy males over 18 years of age.
   c. wealthy males and females over 18 years of age.
   d. any freeborn male over 21 years of age.

15. Under Pericles, all of the following occurred in Athens **EXCEPT**

   a. an extensive public works program.
   b. prosperity based on the imperialism of smaller city-states.
   c. a flourishing of the arts and culture.
   d. the establishment of a new political system.

16. The "Father of History" was

   a. Hippocrates.
   b. Herodotus.
   c. Thucydides.
   d. Protagoras.

17. The Socratic method is used by

   a. engineers.
   b. philosophers.
   c. architects.
   d. artists.

18. Which title best completes the outline?

   I. Creation of archons
   II. Creation of People's Court and trial by jury
   III. Establishment of a written constitution
   IV. _____

   a. Establishment of the Mycenean feudalism.
   b. Establishment of united Greek state.
   c. Establishment of Athenian democracy
   d. Establishment of Spartan system

19. What inferences can be made about the values of Ancient Greek culture based on the illustration of the statue below?

   a. The Ancient Greeks were great warriors.
   b. Humans and the human body were celebrated in art.
   c. The Greek gods were superhumans.
   d. Ancient Greek art focused on the gods.

20. Ancient Greek Civilization's chief features were its

   a. hominocentrism and isolationism.
   b. rationalism and isolationism.
   c. rationalism and legalism.
   d. rationalism and hominocentrism.

1. What is meant by the statement, "Ancient Greece is the cradle of Western Civilization?" Give three examples of how Greek civilization shaped Western society.
2. How was the geography of Greece responsible for the great accomplishments of its civilization? Describe two ways in which the land and its location shaped the Ancient Greek national character.
3. What was the Classical Greek ideal? Give three examples of how this concept was reflected in the art, architecture, and philosophy of Classical Greek society.
4. Imagine that you are an Ancient Greek historian writing a history of the Peloponnesian War. Remembering that you must follow the Western tradition of unbiased investigation and analysis, give two causes for the Athenian-Spartan conflict as well as two effects it had on Ancient Greece.
5. Was unity between Sparta and Athens possible? Citing four specific examples, compare and contrast the life of a citizen of Athens with that of a Spartan.

**DOCUMENT-
BASED
QUESTIONS**

This task is based on the accompanying documents. Some of these documents have been edited for the purposes of this task. This task is designed to test your ability to work with historical documents. As you analyze the documents, take into account both the source of each document and the author's point of view.

Directions: Read the following documents and answer the questions after each document. Use the information in the reading and this chapter in writing your answers.

Document #1

THE POEMS OF SAPPHO

WHEN I SEE YOU

When I even see you,
my voice stops,
my tongue is broken,
a thin flame runs beneath all my skin,
my eyes are blinded,
there is thunder in my ears,
the sweat pours from me,
I tremble through and through,
I am paler than grass,
And I seem almost like one dead.

From *The Portable Greek Reader*
Translated by John Addington Symonds

THE MOON IS SET

The silver moon is set;
The Pleiades are gone;
Half the long night is spent, and yet
I lie alone

From *The Portable Greek Reader*
Translated by J. H. Merivale

Document #2

THE ATHENIAN CONSTITUTION

For our (Athenian) government is not copied from those of our neighbors: we are an example to them rather than they to us. Our constitution is named a democracy, because it is in the hands not of the few, but of the many. But our laws secure equal justice for all in their private disputes, and our public opinion welcomes and honors talent in every branch of achievement . . . on the grounds of excellence alone. . . . We decide or debate, carefully and in person, all matters of policy, holding, . . . that acts are foredoomed to failure when undertaken undiscussed.

Pericles' Funeral Oration from Thucydides, *History of the Peloponnesian War*
Translated by Alfred Zimmern
The Greek Commonwealth: Politics and Economics in Fifth Century Athens (4th ed.)

As for the constitution of the Athenians . . . they chose that rascals should fare better than good citizens. . . . Among the best elements (aristocrats) there is very little license and injustice . . . while among the commons there is very great ignorance, disorderliness, and rascality. . . . As it is, anyone who wants . . . gets up and makes a speech, and devises what is to the advantage of himself and those like him. . . . From such a procedure then a city would not attain the ideal. . . . For it is the wish of the commons not that the state should be well ordered . . . but that the commons should have its freedom and be in control. . . . If on the other hand you investigate good order . . . you will see the most capable make laws . . . then the good citizens will keep the rascals in check and will deliberate on matters of state, refusing to allow madmen to sit on the Council or make speeches or attend the general assemblies.

From *The Old Oligarch, Being the Constitution of the Athenians Ascribed to Xenophon*
Translated by James A. Petch

SECTION 2: IMPORTANT PEOPLE, PLACES, AND TERMS

KEY TERMS	PEOPLE	PLACES
Hellenistic	Alexander III	Greece
cultural diffusion	Philip II	Macedonia
Kione	Antigonis	Egypt
ethics	Ptolomaios	Syria
apathy	Seleucus	Palestine
Cynic	Antiochus	Persia
Stoic	Epicurus	Asia Minor
Skeptic	Zeno	Parthia
Epicurean	Galen	Bactria
heliocentric theory	Eratosthenes	Pella
Septuagint	Hipparchus	Alexandria
Maccabean Revolt	Aristotle	Antioch
barbarian	Ptolomy	Persepolis
Tanach	Aristarchus	Susa
	Roxanne	Pergamum
	Euclid	Gaugamela
	Archimedes	
	Strabo	

EXERCISES FOR SECTION 2

MULTIPLE CHOICE

Select the **letter** of the **correct** answer.

1. Hellenism was based on

  a. democracy.
  b. cultural diffusion.
  c. autocracy.
  d. rationalism.

2. Alexander's empire included all of the following **EXCEPT**

  a. northern Europe.
  b. the Greek peninsula.
  c. Asia Minor.
  d. Mesopotamia.

3. The term *Hellenized* referred to someone who

  a. was educated in the *Hellenistic* Greek culture.
  b. had married a Greek.
  c. was fully or partly Greek by birth.
  d. lived in a place where the majority was Greek.

4. Which title best completes the outline?

  I. Alexander the Great's conquest of Mediterranean
  II. Death of Alexander
  III. Division of Alexander's empire by head generals
  IV. _____

a. Greek civil war
b. Development of Hellenistic states
c. Conquest of Greece by Persia
d. Creation of new empire under Alexander's nephew

5. Which beliefs did both the Ancient Greeks and the people of Hellenistic states share?

a. Humans must strive to be like the gods.
b. All people who are not born Greek are barbarians.
c. Culture should be shared.
d. Humans are the center of the universe.

6. The Ptolemaic kingdom consisted of

a. Macedonia and the Aegean World.
b. Asia Minor and the old Persian Empire.
c. Egypt.
d. Syria, Palestine, and Mesopotamia.

7. The Seleucid kingdom consisted of

a. Macedonia and the Aegean World.
b. Asia Minor and the old Persian Empire.
c. Egypt.
d. Syria, Palestine, and Mesopotamia.

8. Which statement best describes the reason for the collapse of the Hellenistic states?

a. There were conflicts between them.
b. There was a lack of internal stability.
c. There was a common language and culture.
d. They were a large mixture of nations within the states.

9. The new and simpler form of Greek used in the Hellenistic Period was

a. Macedonian.
b. Koine.
c. Maccabean.
d. Attic.

10. The Hellenistic philosophers were primarily concerned with

a. ethics and metaphysics.
b. ethics and politics.
c. the search for absolute truth.
d. the search for absolute beauty.

11. The main result of Alexander's policy of Hellenism was

a. hominocentrism.
b. cultural diffusion.
c. religious uniformity.
d. cultural unity.

12. Which of the following is a Hellenistic institution?

a. Library
b. Olympics
c. People's Courts
d. Theater

13. Which of the following groups of philosophical schools were created in the Hellenistic period?

a. Skeptics, Cynics, Sophists
b. Skeptics, Cynics, Stoics
c. Skeptics, Sophists, Platonists
d. Cynics, Stoics, Empiricists

14. How did Epicurean philosophy differ from the other Hellenistic schools of thought?

a. Humans should obey authority blindly.
b. Humans should try to return to nature.
c. A balance between the material and spiritual should be obtained.
d. Material happiness should be rejected and spiritual development pursued.

15. Which belief was true of Hellenistic art only?

a. Art should focus on humans.
b. Art must be realistic.
c. Humans and children should not be subjects of art.
d. The human body should be idealized.

16. Eratosthenes is famous for his contributions to

  a. astronomy.
  b. mathematics.
  c. physics.
  d. geography.

17. The mathematician Euclid is best known for his contributions to

  a. geometry.
  b. algebra.
  c. trigonometry.
  d. calculus.

18. What fact relating to the Hellenistic World was the result of the other three?

  a. Many Hellenistic nations worshiped gods from other countries.
  b. The Hellenistic states traded extensively with each other.
  c. Alexander's generals established independent kingdoms.
  d. Greek became the international language promoting cultural exchange.

19. Archimedes made all of the following contributions to mathematics **EXCEPT**

  a. calculating the value of pi.
  b. developing trigonometry.
  c. devising a system for expressing larger numbers.
  d. laying the foundations of calculus.

20. Which pairs of compilers and encyclopedias are **correct**?

  a. Strabo/geography, Galen/medicine, Ptolemy/astronomy
  b. Strabo/medicine, Galen/geography, Ptolemy/astronomy
  c. Strabo/astronomy, Galen/medicine, Ptolemy/geography
  d. Strabo/geography, Galen/astronomy, Ptolemy/medicine

ESSAYS FOR
SECTION 2

1. To what extent did Alexander the Great Hellenize the Mediterranean? Give three examples of how Greek culture was mixed with those of earlier civilizations during and after Alexander's conquests.
2. Greek Civilization improved during the Hellenistic period.
   a. List three Hellenistic achievements and show how they benefited society.
   b. Explain why they were an improvement over the Classical period.
3. Why were the Hellenistic kingdoms unsuccessful in realizing Alexander's dream? Was his goal of one unified Hellenized world practical? Give three reasons to support your opinion.
4. Imagine that you are a Macedonian soldier in Alexander's army who has married a non-Greek and is residing in some part of the Hellenistic World. In a letter to your family, describe two differences between Greece and the place in which you are living. Show two ways in which the country you have moved to has become Hellenized.

This task is based on the accompanying documents. Some of these documents have been edited for the purposes of this task. This task is designed to test your ability to work with historical documents. As you analyze the documents, take into account both the source of each document and the author's point of view.

Directions: Read the following documents and answer the questions after each document. Use the information in the reading and this chapter in writing your answers.

Document #1

THE YOUNG ALEXANDER

Philonicus the Thessalian brought the horse Bucephalus to Philip, offering to sell him for thirteen talents; but when they went into the field to try him, they found him so very vicious and unmanageable, that he reared up when they endeavored to mount him, and would not so much as endure the voice of any of Philip's attendants. Upon which as they were leading him away as wholly useless and intractable, Alexander, who stood by, said, "What an excellent horse do they lose, for want of skill and boldness to manage him!" Philip at first took no notice of what he said; but when he heard him repeat the same thing several times, and saw he was very frustrated to see the horse sent away, "Do you criticize," said Philip, "those who are older than yourself, as if you knew more, and were better able to manage him than they?" "I could manage this horse," replied Alexander, "better than others do." "And if you do not," said Philip, "what will you forfeit for your rashness?" "I will pay," answered Alexander, "the whole price of the horse." At this the whole company fell laughing; and as soon as the wager was settled among them, he immediately ran to the horse, and, taking hold of the bridle, turned him directly toward the sun, having, it seems, observed that he was disturbed at and afraid of the motion of his own shadow; then letting him go forward a little, still keeping the reins in his hand, and stroking him gently when he began to grow eager and fiery, . . . with one nimble leap, Alexander securely mounted him, and when he was seated, by little and little drew in the bridle, and curbed him without either striking or spurring him. Presently, when he found him free from all rebelliousness, and with a commanding voice, and urging him also with his heel. Philip and his friends looked on at first in silence and anxiety for the result, [but when he came] back rejoicing the triumphing for what he had performed they all burst out into acclamations of applause; and his father, shedding tears, it is said, for joy, kissed him as he came down from his horse, and in his transport said "O my son, carve out a kingdom equal to and worthy of yourself, for Macedonia is too small for you.

From Plutarch, *Lives of Famous Greeks*
Translated by Ian Scott-Kilvert

Questions	1. What does Plutarch's account reveal about the character of Alexander the Great?
	2. Since Plutarch wrote this account after Alexander's death, in what ways might this story have served as propaganda for Alexander?
	3. Why would Plutarch, a Roman historian, be interested in creating stories that built up Alexander the Great's image?

Document #2

ALEXANDER'S CAMPAIGNS

The army was crossing a desert of sand; the sun was already blazing down upon them, but they were struggling on under the necessity of reaching water, which was still far away. Alexander, like everyone else, was tormented by thirst, but he was nonetheless marching on foot at the head of his men. It was all he could do to keep going, but he did so, and the result (as always) was that the men were the better able to endure their misery when they saw that it was equally shared. As they toiled on, a party of light infantry, which had gone off looking for water, found some—just a wretched little trickle collected in a shallow gully. They scooped up with difficulty what they could and hurried back, with their priceless treasure, to Alexander; then, just before they reached him, they tipped the water into a helmet and gave it to him. Alexander, with a word of thanks for the gift, took the helmet, and, in full view of his troops, poured the water on the ground. So extraordinary was the effect of this action that the water wasted by Alexander was as good as a drink for every man in the army. I cannot praise this act too highly; it was a proof, if anything was, not only of his power of endurance but also of his genius for leadership.

From *The Campaigns of Alexander*, by Arrian
Translated by Aubrey de Sélincourt

Questions	1. Why does Arrian believe that Alexander the Great's actions prove that he is a great leader?
	2. How does Arrian's story help to explain the enormous support Alexander had from his troops?
	3. To what extent might Arrian, as a Greek soldier, be biased toward Alexander?

SECTION 3: IMPORTANT PEOPLE, PLACES, AND TERMS

KEY TERMS	PEOPLE	PLACES
civilizing agent	Romulus and Remus	Italy
Senate	Cornelius Scipio	Rome
Republic	Hannibal	Sicily
consuls	Gracci Brothers	Mediterranean Sea
Patrician	Marcus Crassus	Adriatic Sea
Plebian	Gaius Julius Caesar	Tyrrhenian Sea

KEY TERMS	PEOPLE	PLACES
Curiae	Cneius Pompey	Sardinia
Centuries	Marius	Apennine
citizen	Sulla	Mountains
Nobilis	Marcus Brutus	Alps
proletariat	Gaius Cassius	Rubicon
Socii	Cleopatra VII	Carthage
Assembly of Tribes	Octavian Caesar	Tiber River
Tribunes	Emperor Augustus	Iberia
Twelve Tables	Mark Antony	Gaul
Optimates	Emperor Tiberius	Germania
Populares	Emperor Caligula	Britain
oligarchy	Emperor Claudius	Asia Minor
autocracy	Emperor Nero	Syria
dictatorship	Emperor Marcus Aurelius	Egypt
emperor	Tacitus	Alexandria
Punic	Livy	Constantinople
basilica	Plutarch	Byzantium
aqueduct	Vergil	Milan
arch	Jesus of Nazareth	Po valley
Pax Romana	Paul of Tarsus	Campania
Messiah	Emperor Diocletian	Apulia
Apostles	Emperor Constantine	Calabria
Christians	Emperor Theodosius	Latium
Ascetics	Cicero	Elba
dome	Suetonius	Corsica
	Seneca	

EXERCISES FOR SECTION 3

MULTIPLE CHOICE

Select the **letter** of the **correct** answer.

1. Etruscan civilization was greatly influenced by the

   a. Greeks.
   b. Egyptians.
   c. Phoenicians.
   d. Carthaginians.

2. According to one tradition that linked it to Greece, Rome was first settled by

   a. Numitor.
   b. Aeneas.
   c. Romulus and Remus.
   d. Faustulus

3. The Romans traditionally believed that their city was founded by

    a. Numitor.
    b. Aeneas.
    c. Romulus and Remus.
    d. Faustulus.

4. Unlike the Greeks, Roman government was

    a. a direct democracy.
    b. an autocracy.
    c. a republic.
    d. a dictatorship.

5. In the ancient kingdom of Babylon and in the Roman Republic, an important feature of life was the development of

    a. codified laws.
    b. social and political equality.
    c. a monotheistic religion.
    d. agricultural communes.

6. The conflicts between Rome and Carthage were known as the

    a. Social Wars.
    b. Numidian Wars.
    c. Samnite Wars.
    d. Punic Wars.

7. Which of the following groups were the members of the First Triumvirate?

    a. Pompey, Octavian, Lepidus
    b. Julius Caesar, Octavian, Crassus
    c. Mark Antony, Octavian, Lepidus
    d. Pompey, Julius Caesar, Crassus

8. Julius Caesar was assassinated for all of the following reasons EXCEPT

    a. he wanted the Senate to proclaim him king.
    b. the Senate viewed him as a threat to the republican system.
    c. the Senate was convinced that his policies had damaged the economy.
    d. the Senate feared losing its power.

9. Which of the following groups did the Second Triumvirate consist of?

    a. Pompey, Julius Caesar, and Lepidus
    b. Pompey, Julius Caesar, and Crassus
    c. Octavian, Marc Antony, and Lepidus
    d. Octavian, Marc Antony, and Crassus

10. Which set of Roman conquest is in the correct chronological order?

    a. Greece → Carthage → Egypt → Gaul
    b. Carthage → Egypt → Greece → Gaul
    c. Carthage → Greece → Gaul → Egypt
    d. Egypt → Carthage → Gaul → Greece

11. The period of relative peace in the Empire from 27 B.C. to 180 C.E. was known as the

    a. Imperium.
    b. Noster Mare.
    c. Pater Patriae.
    d. Pax Romana.

12. The "Barrack Emperors"

    a. divided the Empire up into parts.
    b. neglected the Empire's borders.
    c. expanded the Empire's borders.
    d. restored peace and order to the Empire.

13. Based on the map on page 125, which geographic areas were the chief inheritors of the Greco-Roman legacy?

    a. Europe, the Middle East, and the Indian subcontinent
    b. Europe, the Middle East, and northern Africa
    c. Europe, northern Africa, and the Indian subcontinent
    d. The Middle East, northern Africa, and the Indian subcontinent

14. The Edict of Milan

    a. outlawed the old pagan Roman religion.
    b. outlawed Christianity.
    c. tolerated Christianity.
    d. made Christianity the official religion of the Roman Empire.

15. Which of the following best completes the chronological order of events?

   I. Edict of Milan
   II. Foundation of Constantinople
   III. Council of Nicaea
   IV. _____

   a. Great Fire of Rome
   b. Division of Roman Empire
   c. Christianity made official religion of Roman Empire
   d. Fall of the Western Roman Empire

16. Constantine founded a new capital city in the East for all of the following EXCEPT

   a. Rome was no longer in the center of the Empire.
   b. Rome was constantly in danger from barbarian attacks.
   c. the "heart" of the Empire was in the East.
   d. Rome had become economically unimportant.

17. The barbarian tribes that were given Roman borderlands to protect were

   a. Praetorians.   c. Socii.
   b. Foedoratai.   d. Centuries.

18. The four basic forces that shaped Roman society were

   a. agriculture, family life, law, and religion.
   b. agriculture, family life, war, and religion.
   c. agriculture, war, law, and religion.
   d. family life, war, law, and religion.

19. Which of the following pairs were the two aspects of architecture that the Romans perfected?

   a. The arch and the dome
   b. The arch and the column
   c. The stadium and aqueduct
   d. Roads and bridges

20. The lifestyle that BEST describes Christian monasticism is

   a. stoic.
   b. epicurean.
   c. ascetic.
   d. hedonistic.

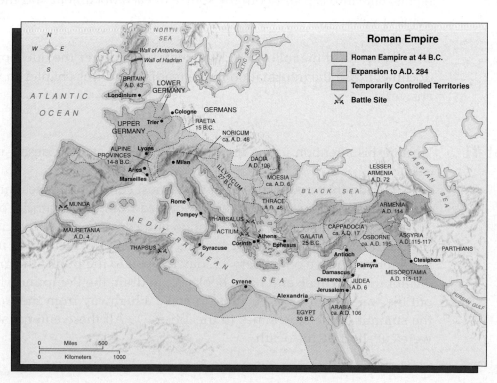

1. Explain the statement, "Captive Greece held Rome captive."
   a. Describe two ways in which the Greeks influenced Roman society.
   b. Give two examples of how Rome's relationship with the Greeks were different from that with other conquered peoples.
2. Compare the story of Aeneas with that of Romulus and Remus.
   a. What purpose does each tale serve?
   b. Give two Roman ideals or values that each story emphasizes.
3. Many historians view Augustus as the successor to Alexander the Great.
   a. Give two examples of how the Romans fulfilled the dream of the Macedonian conqueror.
   b. List two ways in which the Roman Empire was different from the empire of Alexander.
4. Rome made the transition from a city-state to an empire.
   a. Did this make the collapse of Roman democracy inevitable?
   b. List three problems created by Roman imperialism and why the republican system was able or unable to deal with each.
5. Imagine you are a Roman in 476 looking back at what had happened to the Empire. In your diary, discuss those factors that led to the decline of the Western Empire. Give three reasons for the decline of Roman dominance in Western Europe.

DOCUMENT-BASED QUESTIONS

This task is based on the accompanying documents. Some of these documents have been edited for the purposes of this task. This task is designed to test your ability to work with historical documents. As you analyze the documents, take into account both the source of each document and the author's point of view.

Directions: Read the following documents and answer the questions after each document. Use the information in the reading and this chapter in writing your answers.

Document #1

Turning his attention to the reorganization of the state, [Caesar] reformed the calendar . . .

He administered justice with the utmost conscientiousness and strictness, those convicted of extortion he even expelled from the senatorial order.

In particular, for the beautification and convenience of the city, as well as for guarding and extending the bounds of the empire, he formed more projects and more extensive ones every . . . day to open to the public the greatest possible libraries of Greek and Latin books . . . to drain the Pomptine Marshes; to let out the water from Lake Fucinus; to make a highway from the Adriatic across the summit of the Apennines to the Tiber. . . . All these enterprises and plans were cut short by his death.

Yet after all, his other actions and words so turn the scale that it is thought that he abused his power and was justly slain. For not only did he accept excessive honors, such as an uninterrupted consulship, the dictator for life . . . he also allowed honors to be bestowed on him which were too great for mortal men; a golden throne in the House on the judgment seat . . . temples, altars, and statues beside those of the gods . . . and the calling of one of the months by his name. . . .

No less arrogance were his public utterances . . . that the Republic was nothing, a mere name without body or form . . . that men ought now to be more circumspect [cautious and wise] in addressing him, and to regard his word as law. . . .

From *The Twelve Caesars* by Suetonius
Translated by J. C. Rolfe

Questions	
	1. According to Suetonius, what were the positive and negative aspects of Julius Caesar's dictatorship? Give one example of each.
	2. Is Suetonius's assessment of Caesar fair and balanced?

Document #2   THE AUGUSTAN AUTOCRACY

In this way the power of both people and Senate passed entirely into the hands of Augustus, and from this time there was, strictly speaking, a monarchy; for monarchy would be the truest name for it. . . . Now, the Romans so detested the title "monarch" that they called their emperors neither dictators nor kings nor anything of this sort. . . . In order to preserve the appearance of having this authority not through their power but by virtue of the laws, the emperors have taken themselves all the offices (including the titles) which under the Republic possessed great power with the consent of the people. By virtue of the titles named, they secure the right to make levies, collect funds, declare war, make peace, and rule foreigners and citizens alike everyone and always. . . .

Thus by virtue of these Republican titles they have clothed themselves with all the powers of the government, so that they actually possess all the prerogatives of the kings without the usual title. For the appellation "Caesar" or "Augustus" confers upon them no actual power but merely shows in the one case that they are the successors of their family line, and in the other the splendours of their rank. . . .

Augustus did not enact all laws on his sole responsibility, but some of them he brought before the popular assembly in advance, in order that, if any features caused displeasure, he might learn it in time and correct them; for he encourages everybody whatsoever to give him advice, in case anyone could think of any improvement in them, and he accorded them great freedom of speech; and he actually changed some provisions. . . . For although he brought some matters before the whole senate, he generally followed this course, considering it better to take under preliminary advisement in a leisurely fashion most matters, and especially the most important ones on consultation with a few. . . . The senate as a body . . . continued to sit in judgment as before, and in certain cases transacted business with embassies and envoys from both peoples and kings; and the people and the plebs, moreover, continued to come together for the election but nothing was actually done that did not please Caesar. . . . In the case of those who were to hold office, he himself selected and nominated some; and though he left the election of others in the hands of the people and the plebs, in accordance with the ancient practice, yet he took care that no persons should hold office who were unfit or elected as the result of factious combinations or bribery.

From *History* by Dio Cassius
Translated by Earnest Cary

Questions
1. According to Dio Cassius, how did Augustus change Rome's government from a democracy to an autocracy?
2. Was Augustus's method of quietly and gradually taking power an effective means of transforming the political system of the Roman Empire?

Document #3   THE PERSECUTION OF THE CHRISTIANS

All human efforts, all the lavish gifts of the emperor, and the propitiations of the gods, did not banish the sinister belief that the fire was the result of an order. Consequently, to get rid of the report, Nero fastened the guilt and inflicted the most exquisite tortures on a class hated for their abominations, called Christians by the populace. Christus, from whom the name had its origin, suffered the death penalty during the reign of Tiberius at the hands of one of our procurators, Pontius Pilate, and a most mischievous superstition, thus checked for the moment, again broke out not only in Judea, the first source of the evil, but even in Rome, where all things hideous and shameful from every part of the world find their centre and become popular. Accordingly, an arrest was first made of all who placed guilty; then, upon their information, an immense multitude was convicted, not so much of the crime offering the city, as of hatred against mankind. Mockery of every sort was added to their deaths. Covered with the skins of beasts, they were torn by dogs and perished, or were nailed to crosses, or were doomed to the flames and burnt, to serve as a nightly illumination, when daylight had expired. . . . Even for criminals who deserved extreme and exemplary punishment, there arose a feeling of compassion; for it was not, as it seemed, for the public good, but no glut one man's cruelty that they were being destroyed.

From *The Annals of Rome* by Tacitus
Translated by Alfred Church and William Brodribb

Questions   1. According to Tacitus, why did Emperor Nero persecute the Christians?
2. Why were Christians the object of suspicion, hatred, and persecution in the Roman Empire?

Document #4   ## THE DECLINE OF THE WESTERN ROMAN EMPIRE

Innumerable and most ferocious people have overrun the whole of Gaul. The entire area bounded by the Alps, the Pyrenees, the ocean and the Rhine of occupied . . . oh weep for the empire. . . . Mainz, once a noble city, is captured and razed and thousands have been massacred in the church. . . . The provinces of Acquitane . . . of Lyons and Narbonne are completely occupied and devastated either by the sword from without or famine from within. . . .

Who would believe that Rome, victor over all the world, would fall, that she would be to her people both the womb and the tomb. Once all the East, Egypt and Africa acknowledged her sway and were counted among her men servants and her maidservants. Who would believe that holy Bethlehem would receive as beggars, nobles, both men and women, once abounding in riches? . . . There is not an hour not even a moment, when we are not occupied with crowds of refugees. . . .

From *The Epistles of St. Jerome*
Translated by Roland H. Bainton

Questions   1. According to Jerome's account, how had the invasions of barbarian peoples affected the cities of the Roman Empire?
2. What does Jerome's description reveal about the attitudes of the Romans about their empire during this period?

CHAPTER 4

Ancient America and the Caribbean

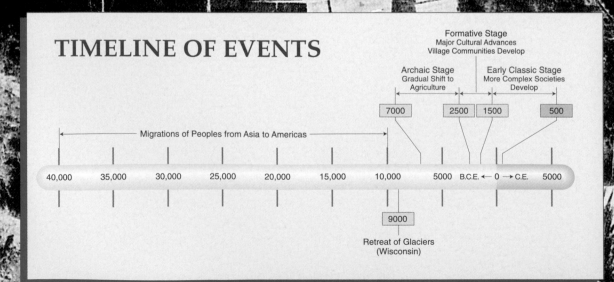

TIMELINE OF EVENTS

Formative Stage
Major Cultural Advances
Village Communities Develop

Archaic Stage
Gradual Shift to
Agriculture

Early Classic Stage
More Complex Societies
Develop

7000   2500   1500   500

Migrations of Peoples from Asia to Americas

40,000   35,000   30,000   25,000   20,000   15,000   10,000   5000   B.C.E. ← 0 → C.E.   5000

9000

Retreat of Glaciers
(Wisconsin)

A   t the time of Columbus' arrival in 1492, the Americas were populated by
        a large number of peoples who originally came from Asia. These Native
        American groups spoke many languages and had different ways of life.
The European explorers and conquerors called the Americas the **New World**.
For at least ten thousand years, the Americas existed in isolation from the **Old
World**. There was no cultural diffusion between the Old World and the
Americas. The lack of contacts prevented the early American civilizations
from learning about technological advances made in Asia, Europe, and Africa.
There probably were a number of previous contacts between the Americas and
the rest of the known world before 1492. However, these earlier voyages did
not fundamentally change the way the Native American cultures developed or
peoples lived.

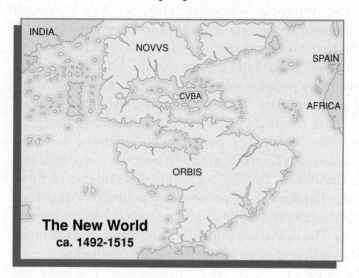

The New World
ca. 1492-1515

The Bering Strait

Early European
impression of the
New World after its
discovery.

The Americas were a home to peoples who
had come from the Asian continent in the
period of the last **Ice Age**. For thousands of
years, the peoples who first came to the
Americas remained culturally isolated from
human events and influences taking place on
other continents. This was a time period of
great climatic changes. Blankets of ice, *glaciers*,
covered large areas of the Old and New
Worlds. The periods of ice alternated with periods of thaw or melting. The peoples crossed
over into the American continents from Asia
across the **Bering Sea**, which served as a frozen
bridge that connected the two continents. In
addition to the huge areas of ice blanketing the
land and frozen sea, there was increased *precipitation*, or rainfall. This led to the growth of lush
pastures and woodlands that supported a wide
variety of plants and animals, which could be
gathered, hunted, and eaten. These conditions
attracted some of the migrating Asian peoples
to the Americas.

There is controversy about when the first
waves of migrating peoples crossed over into
what is today Alaska and spread out over the
continents until they reached as far as **Tierra
del Fuego** at the bottom of South America.
Some archaeologists believe that the first inhabitants came over as early as 40,000 years ago
and that the migration of peoples continued to
about 10,000 B.C.E. The Ice Age ended about this
time, and the Bering Sea once again became a
body of water. Other archaeologists argue that there is no firm historical evidence to support the claim for such an early date. Today, arguments for an earlier migration and occupation of the lands of the Americas are considered to be
stronger. There are two reasons to support the theory of the earlier date. One

reason is the finding of stone artifacts, called the *Folsom projectile points*. The second reason is based on language evidence. A very long time was needed for the development of the many languages that were spoken in Ancient America.

THE CULTURE AND ENVIRONMENT OF ANCIENT AMERICA

The First Peoples

The first inhabitants of **Ancient America** were mixtures of several Asiatic physical types. They had dark eyes, straight or wavy hair, and copper or yellowish skin. Today we know that there is a blood type relationship among the peoples of northern Asia and the Native-American peoples. Two waves of migration seem to have taken place over the thousands of years of the last Ice Age. The first waves brought very primitive peoples who lived by gathering wild fruit, fishing, and hunting small game animals. There is new evidence that some of these primitive peoples may have reached Peru about 22 thousand years ago.

> **Main Idea:**
> The first inhabitants of Ancient America were mixtures of several Asiatic physical types.

The second wave of Asian groups of people who migrated into the Americas brought big-game hunters, who also spread out over the continents and later into the islands of the **Caribbean**. By 9000 B.C.E., the descendants of these nomadic hunters reached the **Patagonia**, in present-day southern Argentina. During this time period, many large prehistoric animals roamed and multiplied on the plains and in the forests. The nomadic peoples hunted these game animals as they traveled and moved to different areas of the American continents.

Around 9000 B.C.E., the climate experienced drastic changes. The last great ice blanket, fields of glaciers, began to retreat as a warmer, drier climate settled over large areas. Grasslands decreased and the large game animals that had used them as pastures died out. The decline of game animals was probably also caused by the prehistoric hunters who increasingly became more efficient as their hunting methods and weapons improved. The nomadic hunters had to adapt to the new living conditions to find the food they needed to survive. Smaller animals, such as deer, antelope, and rabbits increasingly became sources of meat. Wild plants, especially their seeds, also took on a new importance. The nomadic peoples gathered, picked, ground up, and ate whatever edible food was available.

Early Developments in Agriculture

This new way of life eventually led to the development of agriculture. At first agriculture supplemented the older hunter-gatherer way of providing food to eat. As elsewhere in the Old World the shift to agriculture was more likely a gradual increase of the use of domesticated plants. This change took place over thousands of years. As this *evolution*, gradual change, developed, some groups of people became less nomadic. Increasingly, some groups of people turned more to farming to have a secure source of food. They settled down in places where they could clear land of trees or grass, plant, garden, weed, and harvest crops.

Among the more important wild plants were pumpkins, beans, and corn.

Among the important wild plants that were domesticated were pumpkins, beans, and corn or **maize**. Maize became the foodstuff that was the mainstay of the great cultures of Ancient America. Between 5000 and 1000 B.C.E. *manioc*, a starchy root, was cultivated in the tropics and became a staple food, particularly on the Caribbean islands. As agriculture developed, the potato first grown in the Peruvian Andes area became an important part of peoples' diets.

Agriculture became the principal economic activity in areas where the soil was fertile and the climate was helpful. The amount of annual rainfall was especially important for successful farming. The Native American peoples living in bands or small tribes were increasingly able to adapt to the climatic and soil conditions. Slowly, they learned methods of farming and how to make tools to help grow crops. In the forests and jungles, the peoples who chose to live there employed a **slash-and-burn** method of cultivation. Trees and brush were cut down and burned. Maize and other food staples were planted in the cleared area with a digging stick. This method exhausted the soil after a year or two. The clearings in the forest were abandoned, and the people moved on in search of new land for planting.

Despite this limitation, farming became a way of life in the forests and jungles although it rarely could support large groups of people. There were two important exceptions to this limitation in agriculture in the tropical forests. In Mexico and Central America, as we will see later in this chapter and in Chapter 9, the Olmec and Maya were able to develop systems of agriculture enabling them to have an advanced civilization in a tropical forest. They were capable of supplementing their slash-and-burn agricultural production by constructing raised patches of land in more swampy areas to grow the food that they needed. By using these methods of agricultural production, the Olmec and Maya grew in number and created more complex societies in the tropical forests of Mesoamerica.

A more productive type of agriculture developed in the highlands of the Americas. In central Mexico, the Andean region, and the desert coast of Peru; the land could be tilled more easily and its fertility preserved even longer by using the **digging stick** technology. In these arid or semiarid lands, the temperate climate and a naturally rich soil favored the development of farming. This led to the growth of larger populations and more complex civilizations. Food production was increased with the aid of irrigation projects and a greater division of labor. Increased agricultural production and the rise of strong central governments helped the Central Valley of Mexico and the Andean region become the leading centers of American civilizations before 1492. (See Chapters 9 and 14.)

The Development of Different Types of Cultures and Societies

As time passed, the numerous groups of peoples spread out on the American continents and onto the islands of the Caribbean. They developed numerous *cultures*, ways of life. These different peoples can be classified by how they were able to feed, clothe, and shelter themselves and the complexity of their social organization. Basically, we can put these human groups into three levels or categories—tribe, chiefdom, and state. These categories correspond to the stages in general cultural evolution of the different groups.

The simplest, most primitive, type of group was the *band* or *tribe*. These human groups generally lived in difficult environments such as dense forests, extremely wet areas, deserts, or frigid areas. The land that they inhabited had a limited productivity level of needed food. These bands or tribes are characterized by small groups of *egalitarian*, or equal, people, who relied on hunting, fishing, and collecting edible plants. Some hunting and gathering groups supplemented their food supply by using slash-and-burn agriculture but moved from place to place in a more nomadic type of existence. These types of groups engaged in limited agriculture and migrated within a given territory according to the seasonal availability of game animals, fish, and edible plants.

This lifestyle limited the growth of the group's population. There were loose associations of different bands or tribes based on ideas of kinship or family relationships. A wide variety of social positions and roles in the group, or **social stratification**, did not exist beyond the level of the chief. All members of the tribe or band had access to its hunting and fishing grounds and its land to gather and sometimes plant. The leaders of these tribes or bands of peoples owed their power to physical strength or other outstanding personal abilities; however, the exercise of their power was limited to times of hunting, fishing, and conflict with other groups. A member of this type of cultural group might serve as a healer or connection to the people's idea of gods. Most often these gods were the forces of nature. Women often were assigned the roles of gathering and preparing foods and raising children.

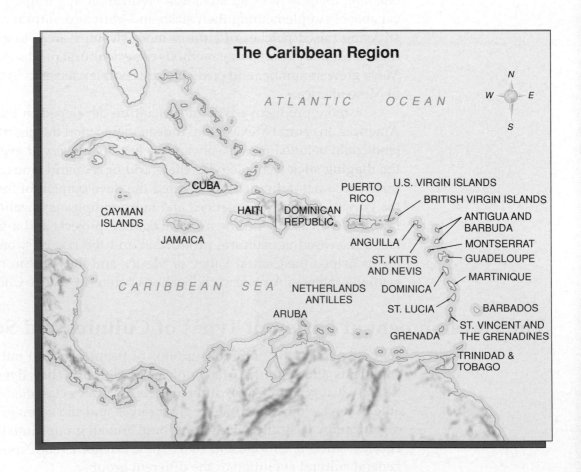

The Caribbean Region

The many tribes of the **Amazon** basin were typical of these egalitarian cultures. This way of life often led to frequent intertribal warfare. The purpose of war was mainly to capture prisoners for sacrifice and food consumption. The use of ritual sacrifice by different Native American peoples in the New World impressed the first Europeans who wrote accounts of this practice. A famous French writer in the sixteenth century, Michel de Montaigne, read accounts of European travels and contacts with these groups in the Americas. He used some of these accounts in his own writings to portray these peoples as "noble savages." Montaigne described the innocent cannibal who had a democratic spirit and moral perfection free from the vices and extreme poverty that existed throughout European societies during this period. Today many people would consider the use of an expression such as "noble savages" as evidence of the feelings of superiority that western Europeans had at this time regarding Native American peoples and their cultures.

> **Main Idea:**
> The ability to produce a secure source of food was an important step toward a more advanced level of social organization.

The *chiefdom*, the second category of Native American social organization, represented the immediate level. Most commonly the subsistence or food base of the chiefdom depended on intensive farming. This ability to produce a secure source of food was an important step toward a more advanced level of social organization. Intensive farming supported a larger and denser population living in villages containing from hundreds to thousands of people. In more organized chiefdoms, villages lost their independence and were ruled by a paramount chief. The leading chief or ruler was aided by a number of subordinate or lesser chiefs who ruled individual villages. The leading chief was often given a sacred character and attended to by a large group of officials and servants.

Social ranking was a very important factor in determining a person's position in the chiefdom. In terms of how the society functioned, the people were basically divided into two groups: commoners and elites. The *elites* were people considered to be more important. The differences among people were based on family ancestry and social connections. The higher-ranking persons were the chiefs, their families, and other officials, particularly those responsible for the rituals or religious practices. *Commoners* had to give tribute, or offerings of goods and labor, for the support of the chiefs and other important people of the chiefdom. Blood relationship to the chief meant a higher rank in the chiefdom. The ruler or paramount chief received the most donations as tribute and also had a right to the surplus production of what was produced by the group. The leading chief used this tribute and surplus production for selective redistribution to those he considered important in his chiefdom.

Warfare between chiefdoms was very common and played a continual role in the origin, expansion, and decline of chiefdoms. Warfare resulted in prisoner taking and ritual sacrifice. Often, the taking of captives, particularly women, resulted in enslavement and the use of this labor by the slave owners. Numerous chiefdoms existed in Ancient America when the Spaniards and Portuguese arrived in the New World at the end of the fifteenth century.

The Chibcha or Muisca chiefdoms in the eastern highlands of present-day Colombia are good examples of this category of social structure. These chiefdoms used intensive agriculture to grow maize, potatoes, quinoa (a hearty type of grain), and a wide variety of other types of plants. Their agricultural techniques included the use of terraced and raised planting beds. They fished and hunted in an organized way, which supplemented the food available for the village. Their crafts—pottery, weaving, and metallurgy—were highly developed. Their magnificent gold work ranks among the finest of such work in Ancient America.

The highest level of social organization was a civilization that can be classified as a *state*. Up to the year 500 C.E. in Ancient America, there was only a limited number of state-type social organizations. It is difficult to draw an exact dividing line between chiefdoms such as the Chibcha and Muisca and state civilizations such as the Olmec, Mochica, Teotihuacán, or Maya. A state-type civilization really was an expansion and deepening of the way that chiefdoms were organized and run. These more advanced civilizations developed in southern Mexico, Central America, and Peru.

In the state type of civilizations, the growth of the division of labor and specialization increased. The state required a high level of organization. The artisan groups who made the products used in the state were no longer very involved in farming. The priestly class in charge of religious activities had a more important position in the state. There was a special warrior class whose high status entitled its members to receive land and share in tribute. The bureaucracy that ran the administration of the state divided into different specialties. There were *scribes*, or writers, architects, treasurers, and other specialists who were involved in intellectual pursuits. A specialized group of traders grew in importance as the state expanded. There was an increased exchange of goods between regions. Often this led to the development of a professional merchant class. The most common specialization remained the farmer-laborer who in times of warfare served as a soldier. The additional jobs in the state type of civilization intensified the levels of social stratification.

Kinship ties still existed and counted particularly for the nobles related to the ruler or king. Nevertheless, a true class structure developed because *kinship*, or blood relationships, was no longer the only way to determine a person's social position in society. The kinship ties that united the priest-king or emperor

A Mayan temple wall showing serpent god (c. 450 C.E.).

and other important people with the commoners were weakened. The ruler assumed divine or godly attributes.

As the population of the state grew, some ceremonial or religious centers became true cities. They also were administrative and market centers where people gathered particularly to celebrate religious events. State temples and other buildings were often monumental architectural constructions. There was a more developed and organized agricultural base to support the city centers. A high level of food production gave the state a sense of prosperity and security.

ADVANCED AREAS OF NATIVE AMERICAN CIVILIZATION: THE VALLEY OF MEXICO, PETEN RAIN FOREST, AND ANDEAN HIGHLANDS

Specialists writing about the developments of agriculture, technology, religion, art, and social and political organization call the time from 7000 to 2500 B.C.E. the *archaic*, or ancient, period. Traces of agriculture, pottery, and weaving have been found in many areas of the Americas. The first agricultural cultures in the Americas date from approximately 7000 B.C.E. Starting around this time, archaeologists have found evidence of early village life, basic farming techniques, and other technological improvements. Some small groups were slowly able to develop what are called the earliest organized sedentary agricultural communities. This is particularly true in areas in central and southern Mexico, Central America, and the Andean zone of South America.

The change to a more agricultural type of lifestyle actually began as early as 9000 years ago. A gradual shift from hunting and food gathering to agriculture started in many parts of Nuclear America as the climatic conditions changed. Nuclear America refers to the key areas of advanced civilizations in the Americas, such as the valley of Mexico, the Peten rain forest, and the Yucatan Peninsula. Slow advances eventually produced an economy in which better living conditions depended on people becoming more sedentary, living in one place, and growing more of their food supply. For thousands of years, most groups of people continued to live as hunter-gatherers. Social groups were small and often seminomadic. The development of pottery, weaving, and the domestication of wild plants to be grown as a secure food source took place over thousands of years. Experimentation with plants led to improved high-yield varieties of maize and other crops. Irrigation was used in some areas. A few animals were domesticated, but in the Americas there weren't many large animals. Domesticated animals did not play a large role as food or transportation sources in the Americas. This meant that humans would be used more than animals for the transportation of goods.

Between 2500 and 1500 B.C.E., cultural and technological advances in various regions of Nuclear America led to the *Formative* or *Pre-Classic Period*. The population began to grow more rapidly in Nuclear America. The advances in agriculture and technology made it possible for more complex societies to develop. The domestication of maize and other plant foods and their careful cultivation provided the food base for larger groups to live together. By the end of

Main Idea:
A gradual shift from hunting and food gathering to agriculture started in many parts of Nuclear America as the climate conditions changed.

An artist's depiction (c. 1550 C.E.) of Aztec daily life.

the period, pottery and weaving were highly developed. It became possible for groups of villages to support chiefs and priests who protected them and acted as intermediaries between people and the gods. More abundant food also released labor to construct mounds of earth topped by temples.

During the Formative Period, the social unit increasingly became the village community made up of one or more kinship groups; however, by the end of the period, small chiefdoms uniting several villages appeared. Because land and food were more plentiful and populations were still small, warfare between competing chiefdoms, which later would increase, did not happen very often. Religion centered on the worship of water and fertility gods.

The early **Classic Period** began around 1500 B.C.E. During the next centuries up to about 500 C.E., there were major cultural developments in parts of the Americas. Improvements in architecture, the arts, and technology made it possible to develop city centers in some regions. Weaving and pottery reached an impressive level of decoration and style. The working of metals, *metallurgy*, flourished in some places especially Peru. The increased food supply made it possible for populations to really expand. There were developments in astronomy, mathematics, and writing in some areas of the Americas. The building of huge stone-faced pyramids began during this time period. These stone pyramids and buildings became the administrative and ceremonial centers of a state ruled by a priest-king. Priestly and warrior classes developed to serve the priest-king and help run the state and religious center. During this time, warfare increased as rival city-states competed for leadership and power.

THE DEVELOPMENT OF EARLY STATE CIVILIZATIONS

By the early Classic Period, a number of more advanced civilizations developed in Nuclear America. During this time period, the Teotihuacán civilization of central Mexico, the Monte Alban culture of southwestern Mexico, and the Olmec and Maya cultures of the southern Yucatan of Mexico and northern Central America flourished. In the Andes, the Nazca and Mochica cultures on the Peruvian coast also reached their high point of development. The available evidence suggests that during the early and middle Classic Periods more advanced civilizations were limited to specific geographical areas of Mesoamerica—the central Andean region and western coast of South America from Peru to Ecuador.

The Olmecs

The **Olmec** civilization of the Mexican gulf lowlands was the earliest known civilization to develop in Mesoamerica. The Olmecs served as the transition culture that led from the Formative to the Classic Period. The Olmecs developed what are considered to be the first ceremonial centers in Mesoamerica. Many archaeologists believe it is the mother culture of this part of the Americas. The Olmec culture is thought to have flourished from about 1500 to 400 B.C.E. Thereafter, the Olmec civilization declined and eventually disappeared.

The Olmec art style was very expressive and made use of carved stone and wood. At the Olmec ceremonial centers of La Venta and Tres Zapotes, huge carved stone heads have been found. The Olmecs are credited with the development of the first writing symbols, picture-like hieroglyphs, and written calendar. One of the earliest known dates in the Americas was found on an Olmec carved stone. The year translates to be 31 B.C.E.

The facial features carved on Olmec stones are like no others found in the Americas. Archaeologists have wondered about the origins of this culture because the facial features seem almost African. This mystery can only be solved if new archeological evidence is found. Presently available archeological evidence indicates that the Olmecs influenced the development of other early Mesoamerican civilizations especially the Maya culture, which replaced it in this tropical forest region.

At the Olmec ceremonial centers of La Venta and Tres Zapotes, huge carved stone heads have been found.

Teotihuacán Civilization

The first true city as opposed to a ceremonial center in the Western Hemisphere was Teotihuacán in central Mexico. It was located about twenty miles north of present-day Mexico City near the ancient **Lake Texcoco**. This lake has since disappeared. The city was built on a grid pattern and occupied a land area of more than nine square miles. Teotihuacán's origins date to the Formative Period, and it reached its peak sometime between 500 and 600 C.E. In **Nahuatl**, the language of the Aztec people, Teotihuacán means "where the gods were

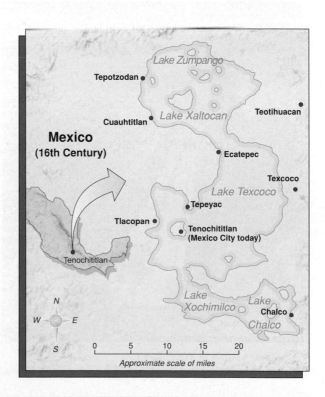

made" (see Chapter 14). The influence of Teotihuacán culture reached into the northern desert region and as far south as the Guatemalan highlands.

At its height, this enormous city may have had between 60,000 and 80,000 inhabitants. There are a number of huge and impressive buildings and pyramid-type structures in the city center. Teotihuacán civilization developed brilliant mural art, magnificent architecture, a system of writing, and a sacred calendar of 260 days. Religion was based on the worship of the sun and moon and agricultural gods. Archaeologists have found evidence of major *deforestation*, the clearing of trees, in the hills that surround the city. This most likely caused serious erosion of top soil and probably contributed to the decline of Teotihuacán.

The Maya

Among ancient American civilizations, the **Maya** are credited with some of the greatest cultural achievements. No other group over a long period of time demonstrated such extraordinary abilities in architecture, sculpture, painting, mathematics, and astronomy. In this chapter, you will learn about the Maya who lived in the early and middle Classic Periods. You will see how the Maya created what many people consider the most developed Native American civilizations in the Americas in a physical environment that was a tropical rain forest.

The ancient Maya of the Classic Period lived in the *Peten*, a lowland tropical rain forest in Mesoamerica. Today, this once larger tropical forest area is in modern-day southeastern Mexico, Guatemala, the western part of Honduras, and Belize. The Maya civilization reached its highest development in this challenging environment, which was not the usual land area for a state-type civilization to develop. This is unusual because the other more advanced Native American civilizations in the Americas developed in higher and drier climatic zones.

A Mayan temple at Tikal, Peten.

The early developments in Maya culture can be traced back to the Olmec civilization. The Maya originally lived in the region where the Olmec culture flourished. It is possible that the Maya even conquered and took over the remains of the Olmec civilization. Much remains to be learned about this formative period of Maya history. The Maya of the Classic Period were descendents of these earlier Mayan groups, which had migrated southeast into the Peten tropical forest. By adapting Olmec knowledge and traditions to meet their own needs, the Maya brought with them the essential elements of an already more advanced culture. As the centuries passed, they expanded upon this knowledge base.

They built their first ceremonial centers in the Peten. The bottom layers of the ceremonial centers can be dated back to the Pre-Classic Period before 300 C.E. Clearing the rain forest with primitive tools must have been extremely difficult. There was no available metal, and the water supply, although plentiful, was seasonal. Yet it was here where the Maya built some of their largest ceremonial centers. There was surplus labor available in the first centuries of Mayan cultural development, although it was a lowland tropical forest. The Peten was rich in wild game and building materials, limestone and fine hardwoods.

From 300 to 700 C.E., the Maya prospered in the tropical forest. The Maya civilization reached its highest levels of development in many areas and the number of ceremonial centers multiplied. The major Mayan centers in the Peten included Tikal, Calakmul, Copan, Piedras Negras, and Palenque. There were many other large and small population centers scattered throughout the Peten. Some Maya sites remain to be discovered in the dense rain forest. The forest Maya made impressive achievements in the sciences, arts, and architecture. However, starting after 500 C.E., the ceremonial centers increasingly became competing, warring city-states. The rivalry among the city-states would eventually lead to a crisis and collapse of the Maya civilization in the tropical rain forest.

The Maya relied on a complex agricultural system to feed the growing tropical forest population. They used the traditional slash-and-burn agricultural system along with the digging stick method.

The Maya believed that the gods gave them life, health, food, and death and represented the forces of nature.

However, advances in Maya farming technology made it possible to grow more food in a highly productive manner. They used kitchen gardens with root crops as staples, terracing, and *raised fields* (artificial platforms of soil built up from low-lying areas to increase their food supply). The Maya also picked fruit from trees that they planted and cultivated, which improved their diet.

Clusters of villages where the common people lived and worked the land surrounded the ceremonial centers. Archaeological evidence has shown that the Classic Period Maya family lived in clusters of three or more houses built on raised platforms within the surrounding areas of the ceremonial centers. These houses were probably inhabited by extended families. A common ancestor determined kinship ties. Their burial remains tell us that males were dominant in Maya culture. Therefore the families were related by descent from the male line. Maya clothing was typically Mesoamerican: cotton loincloths, leather sandals,

Throughout their lives, the Maya sought to please their gods with ritual practices.

The Maya recorded dates on carved limestone rocks such as this one.

and wrap-around cotton garments, which served as upper body covering. Women wore wrap-around skirts and blouses. The upper classes wore the same type of clothing, but it was more richly decorated.

Religious ideas dominated all aspects of Mayan life. The Maya believed that the gods gave them life, health, food, and death, and represented the forces of nature. They also believed in an afterlife. Throughout their lives, the Maya sought to please their gods with ritual practices that included fasting, penance by bloodletting, incense burning and human sacrifice.

They developed a solar calendar for daily life that was more accurate than the European calendar in use at the time. Maya priests were obsessed with time and were capable of making adjustments to account for lost days in the solar year. The Maya actually had two calendars. The other calendar they used was a sacred round of 260 days, which was based on their ceremonial life. They were very interested in science and, above all, with astronomy. The Maya made celestial observations and calculations of great complexity and were capable of predicting eclipses.

Mayan writing was hieroglyphic in nature. This hieroglyphic type of writing is called *glyphs*. There was no alphabet, and their characters represented ideas or objects rather than sounds. Written texts were called **codices**. They were full of different information about myths, legends, poetry, and traditional history that was also orally transmitted.

The Maya recorded dates on parchment-type paper and carved limestone rock called *stelae*. They developed mathematics further than any of their Mesoamerican neighbors. Their math system was based on units of one, five, and twenty and used dots and bars. They were aware of the concept of zero. Mayan mathematical calculations were mostly about astronomy, divination, time, and related topics.

In certain artistic activities, the Maya were very advanced. In architecture, they used the *corbelled* or false arch. The façades of their buildings were decorated with carved stone, and high ornamental roof combs were used on the roofs of palaces and temples.

The Maya were wonderful painters of frescos, which told the famous stories of their kings. In Chapters 9, 14, and 17, you will continue to learn about the history and culture of the Maya.

The Nazca and Mochica

Nazca culture is known mostly from the polychrome-style pottery that it is famous for and gives it its name. This culture dates from about 200 B.C.E. to 600 C.E. and developed along the southwest coast of Peru. The Nazca style of pottery and weaving of textiles is recognized for its rich varieties of red, white, black, orange, and gray. Nazca culture developed from the remains of the earlier **Chavin** culture, which also existed along the Peruvian coast, 900–500 B.C.E.

The Nazca were influenced by Chavin ideas and took over the lands of this earlier and little known people. Nazca culture spread to other areas along the coast and into the highlands of the Andes.

Even more remarkable was the Mochica culture of the northern Peruvian coast. The Mochica built pyramids and temples, roads, and large irrigation canals. They developed a complex, highly stratified society with a strong priesthood and a powerful priest-king. Metallurgy was well developed. They used copper tools and weapons. The manufacture of copper, gold, and silver *alloys*, or mixtures of metals, was well advanced. The Mochica culture is best known for its black and red pottery, which was beautifully decorated. They painted realistic scenes showing that their history was full of wars and struggles over land and water. From about 600 to 700 C.E., invaders probably from the mountainous Andes invaded the Nazca and Mochica cultural areas of influence and destroyed these early classical civilizations. A time of turmoil and cultural decline came to the coast of Peru. The focus of Andean civilization shifted from the coast to the highlands (see Chapter 9).

LINK TO TODAY
The Legacy of the Early American Cultures

Today most of the traces of the earliest American peoples and their cultures have disappeared. There are still some more isolated parts of the Americas in tropical forests and more desert-like regions, particularly the few remaining untouched areas of the Amazon region, where a few of these earliest types of societies and their cultures still exist. Unfortunately, the continuing existence of these small tribes is in danger because of the arrival of immigrants into these lands and the cutting down of forests to make way for farming, cattle-raising, and mining pursuits. What we know today about the first American cultures and civilizations comes mainly from evidence found and interpreted by archeologists, anthropologists, and historians. Despite the disappearance of these first American cultures and civilizations, the people who live in what we today call Latin America and the Caribbean will always have a connection to the peoples of Ancient America and will wonder who they were and how they lived.

CHAPTER SUMMARY

In this chapter, you have seen how the peoples who migrated from the Asian continent slowly developed from small kinship communities to more complex chiefdoms and in some areas to even state-type societies. In some areas of the Americas, a number of more advanced civilizations developed. This did not mean that the smaller bands of people or more complex chiefdoms disappeared. They continued to exist in other areas of the Americas. However, the more advanced civilizations became the centers of growth and expansion and made impressive accomplishments in architecture, mathematics, science, technology, and other artistic endeavors. By the middle of the first millennium C.E., great changes were beginning to take place in Ancient America. These changes would bring an end to some of these early civilizations and alter the course of historical development of other civilizations. You will read more about these important changes that took place after about 500 C.E. in Chapter 9.

IMPORTANT PEOPLE, PLACES, AND TERMS

KEY TERMS	PEOPLE	PLACES
Ice Age	Maya	Caribbean
slash and burn	Olmec	Tierra del Fuego
Ancient Americas	Chavin	Patagonia
New World		Bering Sea
maize		Amazon
Nahuatl		Teotihuacán
Old World		Lake Texcoco
Classic Period		
social stratification		
digging stick		
Codices		

EXERCISES FOR CHAPTER 4

MULTIPLE CHOICE

Select the letter of the correct answer.

1. What kind of agricultural technique did the earliest American cultures first develop?

    a. commercial farming
    b. large plantations
    c. slash and burn
    d. chemical fertilization

2. The earliest advanced civilization in Mesoamerica was the

    a. Maya.
    b. Teotihuacán.
    c. Zapotec.
    d. Olmec.

3. The development of more complex cultures and societies led to

   a. peace among competing peoples.
   b. peoples becoming less sedentary.
   c. more hunting groups forming.
   d. specialization and social stratification.

4. The Olmec and Maya are an exception in terms of where the first state-type societies developed because their homeland was in a

   a. desert area.
   b. mountainous region.
   c. tropical rain forest.
   d. high plateau.

5. The first inhabitants of the Americas most probably came during the last Ice Age from

   a. Africa by sailing boats across the Atlantic Ocean.
   b. Europe by crossing the Atlantic Ocean in ships.
   c. Asia by migrating over the frozen Bering Sea.
   d. Asia by using rafts to cross the Pacific Ocean.

6. Which characteristic did the ancient American civilizations have in common?

   a. All civilizations developed the idea of monotheism.
   b. Urban communities were built by using iron and steel tools.
   c. The religious practices were based on the idea of polytheism.
   d. Agricultural developments did not happen before 500 C.E.

7. Which pair of cultures indicates a chronological order of development?

   a. Chibcha > Montealban
   b. Olmec > Maya
   c. Mochica > Nazca
   d. Teotihuacán > Olmec

8. Traditional religious beliefs in Ancient America were based on

   a. a desire to gain wealth as the key to life.
   b. a written tradition about the fertility god.
   c. an appreciation for the forces of nature.
   d. a willingness to accept the idea of monotheism.

9. The areas of advanced civilization in the Americas were

   a. Tierra del Fuego and the Atacama Desert.
   b. Rocky Mountains and the Brazilian Rainforest.
   c. Central and Southern Mexico and the Andean Region.
   d. The Guiana Highlands and Northern Mexico.

10. In the advanced ancient American civilizations, works of art and architecture served to

    a. satisfy the needs of the rulers.
    b. limit the influence of religion.
    c. reflect ideas of other continents.
    d. express opposition to the government.

11. The invention of a writing system and growth of religious centers took place in which pair of ancient American civilizations?

    a. Nazca and Chibcha
    b. Olmec and Maya
    c. Chavin and Teotihuacán
    d. Maya and Mochica

12. Which statement best describes the status of women in ancient American societies?

    a. Women were encouraged to obtain an education.
    b. Women were expected to run for political office.
    c. Women were expected to dedicate their lives to their families.
    d. Women were encouraged to participate in military affairs.

13. Maya, Teotihuacán, and Olmec civilizations were similar in that they

    a. showed no evidence of urban planning.
    b. lacked strong leaders and a central government.
    c. developed complex mathematic and calendar systems.
    d. used military weapons that made use of iron and gunpowder.

14. A study of the Nazca and Chibcha show that these ancient American civilizations

    a. used a system of writing based on glyphs.
    b. developed a transportation system using the wheel.
    c. produced cultural achievement in the arts.
    d. made use of iron ore to develop steel weapons.

15. A study of the Maya, Olmec, and Teotihuacán civilizations would show that they

    a. developed advanced societies before the arrival of the Europeans.
    b. established extensive trade with the Middle Eastern cultures.
    c. were strongly influenced by cultural diffusion by way of Africa.
    d. had little if any contact or knowledge of other existing civilizations.

16. Which geographic feature had the greatest influence on the development of some ancient American civilizations?

    a. River valleys
    b. Long coastlines
    c. Fertile plateaus
    d. Mountain passes

17. What is one characteristic of the ancient American societies that practiced subsistence agriculture?

    a. Growth of surplus crops for export
    b. Production of crops mainly for their own use
    c. Establishment of state-owned farms
    d. Dependence on slave labor for farming

18. Olmec and Maya glyph systems provided the bases for the development of

    a. subsistence farming.
    b. oral traditions.
    c. written history.
    d. international trade.

19. Ancient American peoples who moved frequently as they searched for food were

    a. village dwellers.
    b. subsistence farmers.
    c. hunter-gatherers.
    d. mound builders.

20. Most migrating peoples who came to the Americas crossed the Bering Sea during the period called

    a. Global Warming.
    b. Thermal Melting.
    c. Ice Age.
    d. Post Glacial.

ESSAYS FOR CHAPTER 4

1. Assume that you are the ruler of a Maya city-state in the Peten. What would you write to the people in your kingdom, priests, military officers, other officials such as scribes who help to administer your realm, and farmer-soldiers to explain to them what their jobs and duties are in your kingdom?

2. Imagine you are a historian very interested in Ancient America. What would you write in an essay about the three different categories or levels of culture and civilization that existed in Ancient America prior to 1492?
3. What were the great achievements of Mayan civilization?
4. What role did the physical geography of the Americas play in the development of the more advanced civilizations?
5. What role did religion play in ancient American societies?

DOCUMENT-
BASED
QUESTIONS

This task is based on the accompanying documents. Some of these documents have been edited for the purposes of this task. This task is designed to test your ability to work with historical documents. As you analyze the documents, take into account both the source of each document and the author's point of view.

Directions: Read the following documents and answer the questions after each document. Use the information in the reading and this chapter in writing your answers.

Document #1

Latin America is made up of five climate regions: high mountains, tropical jungles, deserts, temperate highlands, and temperate coastal plains. The first three are sparsely populated. With the exception of the Maya all the great ancient civilizations arose in the highlands of the Andes and Mexico. The physical geography of ancient America has influenced its economic, political, and social development. Topography, natural resources, climatic conditions, and water bodies have determined how the three different levels of cultures and civilizations of ancient America developed. The physical geography of the lands and bodies of water of what we now call Latin America are varied, which led to some peoples living in areas where it was more possible to develop higher levels of culture and civilization. The varied climate and topography of South America, Mexico, and Central America have helped produce this uneven distribution of population. Three notable examples—the huge Amazonian region of mostly steamy tropical forests and savannah, the vast desert of Patagonia in southern Argentina, and the northern wastelands of Mexico—support few inhabitants. In contrast to these inhospitable regions, a thin strip along Brazil's coast, the plain along the Rio de la Plata estuary in Argentina, and the central plateau of Mexico contain most of the people in these countries. Thus these nations are overpopulated and underpopulated at the same time.

From *A History of Latin America* by Benjamin Keen

Questions

1. How did the different physical geography regions influence where people lived and developed their civilizations in ancient America?
2. Identify four physical geography factors that influenced the development of the levels of civilization in ancient America. Explain how each physical geography factor influenced this development.

Document #2   The mountain ranges and the high plateaus have influenced the economic, social, and political life of much of Latin America from the time of the earliest civilizations of Ancient America. Parallel to the Pacific Ocean, there are a number of large mountain chains in the Americas. In Mexico, the Sierra Madres (Occidental and Oriental) run north and south. Between these two mountain ranges is a vast central plateau. It is here that a number of important pre-Columbian civilizations developed, including the Aztecs. The Sierra Madre del Sur run through Central America. In South America, the Andes Mountains run along much of the continent's western coast. Here, too, Ancient American civilizations rose, prospered, and fell. Mountains and plateaus afforded, water resources, soil for planting crops, and protection.

From *Let's Review Global History and Geography* by Mark Willner et al.

Questions

1. According to this reading, which physical geographical feature played a major role in the development of early life in Latin America?
2. How have mountains and plateaus played an important role in the development of early civilizations in Ancient America?

Document #3   ## MAP OF THE NATURAL SETTING OF SOUTH AMERICA, CENTRAL AMERICA, AND THE CARIBBEAN

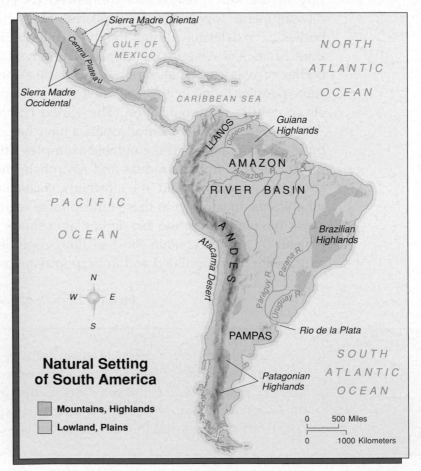

Questions

1. Based on your reading of the chapter, documents 1 and 2, and this map, which geographical areas in Ancient America saw the development of the most advanced civilizations?
2. How can you explain the development of more advanced civilizations in these areas?

Document #4   MAP OF CLIMATE ZONES OF LATIN AMERICA

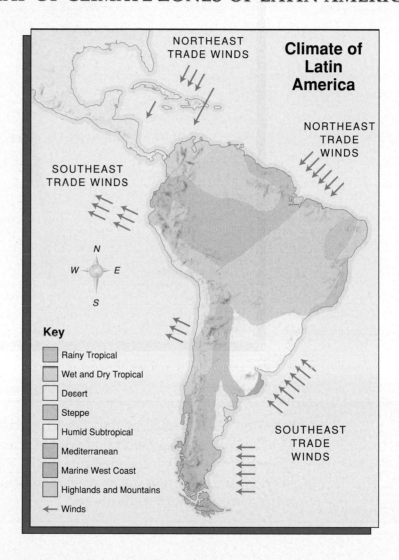

Questions

1. Based on your reading of the chapter, documents 1 and 2, and this map, which were the climatic zones in Ancient America saw the development of more advanced civilizations?
2. How did the climate of the zones that you chose influence the development of the more advanced civilizations?

MAP OF TOPOGRAPHICAL AREAS
IN LATIN AMERICA AND THE CARIBBEAN

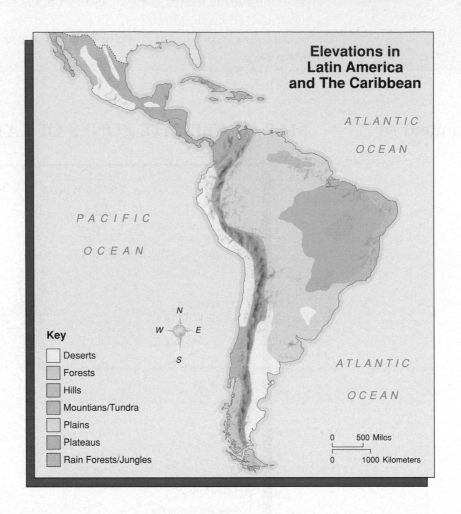

Elevations in Latin America and The Caribbean

ATLANTIC OCEAN

PACIFIC OCEAN

ATLANTIC OCEAN

Key
- Deserts
- Forests
- Hills
- Mountians/Tundra
- Plains
- Plateaus
- Rain Forests/Jungles

N
W   E
S

0   500 Miles

0   1000 Kilometers

Questions

1. Based on your reading of the chapter, documents 1 and 2, and this map, which were the topographical areas in Ancient America that saw the development of more advanced civilizations?

2. How did the topographical areas that you chose influence the development of the more advanced civilizations?

ERA II
EXPANDING ZONES OF EXCHANGE AND ENCOUNTER
(500–1200)

INTRODUCTION

Cultural diffusion or the exchange of ideas, customs, and products between nations, is the chief agent of change and growth within civilizations. As in the ancient world, trade and conquest continued to lead to the transition or decline of old civilizations as well as the creation of new ones.

The period of 500–1200 was known as the Middle Ages in Western Europe. It was a time of transition from Roman domination to a new civilization. It combined Christianity and Greco-Roman learning with the culture of the Germanic peoples who conquered the region. The Eastern Roman Empire, however, continued to flourish in Eastern Europe and Asia Minor, despite the loss of its Middle Eastern Provinces in the sixth and seventh centuries. In the Middle East, the religion of Islam was developed quickly dominating the region and spreading to North Africa, the Indian sub-continent, and Southeast Asia. In Asia, the era brought vast changes with new states developing and challenging the domination of Chinese civilization. Finally in the Americas, many changes within and between existing civilizations transformed that region as well.

The expansion of zones of exchange and encounters between cultures and civilizations began a process that would continue to make the world "smaller." As peoples throughout the world became aware of other societies beyond their immediate neighbors, they began to reexamine themselves. How could our society enjoy the luxuries and advances others had developed? What could be learned from other civilizations? This part of our historical journey will reveal how this process of global interaction began.

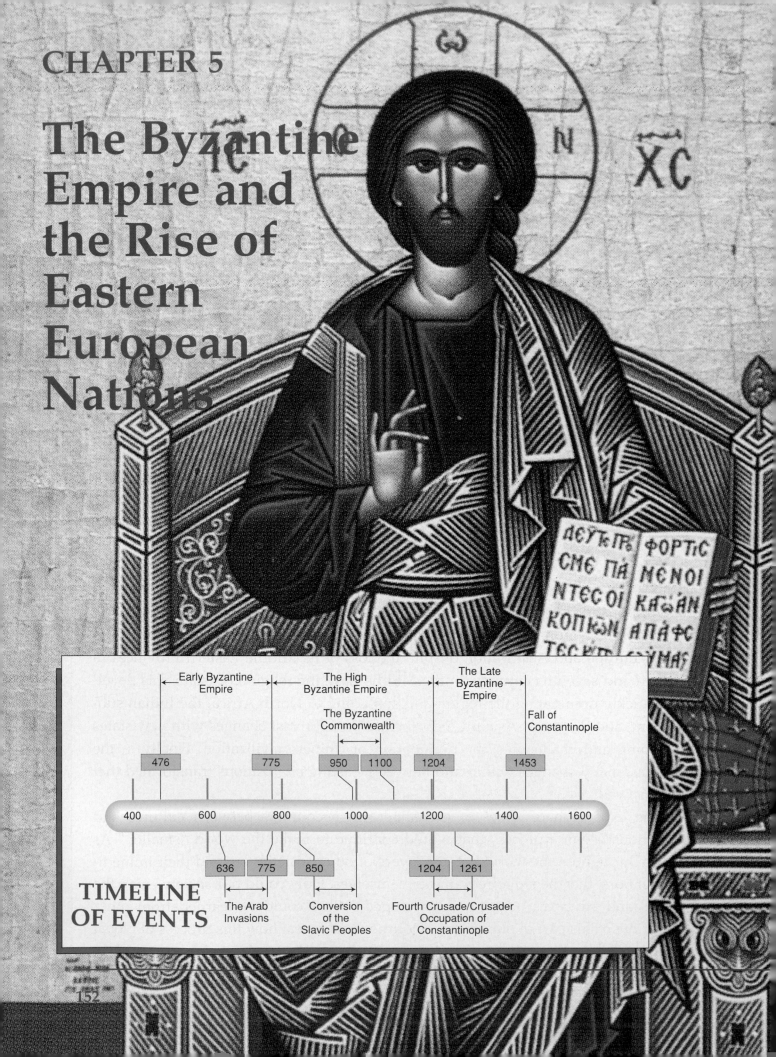

CHAPTER 5

The Byzantine Empire and the Rise of Eastern European Nations

TIMELINE OF EVENTS

Early Byzantine Empire

The High Byzantine Empire

The Late Byzantine Empire

The Byzantine Commonwealth

Fall of Constantinople

| 476 | 775 | 950 | 1100 | 1204 | 1453 |

| 400 | 600 | 800 | 1000 | 1200 | 1400 | 1600 |

| 636 | 775 | 850 | 1204 | 1261 |

The Arab Invasions

Conversion of the Slavic Peoples

Fourth Crusade/Crusader Occupation of Constantinople

Why did the Roman Empire in the West decline? We have seen the answers to that question in Chapter 3. The question for us to answer in this chapter is about the Roman Empire in the East. Why did it survive beyond 476 A.D.? Indeed, the Eastern Empire continued for almost another thousand years. To explain the remarkable continuation of the **Eastern Roman Empire** (476–1453), we must look to such factors as the combination of Greco-Roman and Christian culture, advanced scientific technology, and stable political and religious institutions. An efficient government and the Greek Orthodox Church supported the emperor. The Eastern Roman Empire is commonly referred to as the **Byzantine Empire** because its capital, **Constantinople**, was built on the site of the former city of **Byzantium**. The unique ability of the Byzantine Empire to recover from crises and to adjust to changes that destroyed other civilizations reflects its great balance of the Classical and Christian cultures. In addition to its numerous contributions to art, architecture, literature, music, theology, and science, Byzantium protected and preserved Greco-Roman civilization. The Eastern Roman Empire also physically shielded the West as it repulsed invaders and enemies from all directions. Byzantine civilization brought together the best elements of the Ancient and Christian worlds and created a new society.

Main Idea:
The unique ability of the Byzantine Empire to recover from crises and to adjust to changes that destroyed other civilizations reflects its great balance of the Classical and Christian cultures.

A Russian icon of the Nativity.

The Byzantine Empire and the Rise of Eastern European Nations **153**

THE EARLY BYZANTINE EMPIRE (476–775)

The first period of Byzantine history was in great part devoted to attempts at restoring the Roman Empire to its former size and power. The idea that the West, particularly Italy and North Africa, could be lost was difficult to accept for most people in the eastern part of the Empire. A series of weak and incompetent rulers in the East from 476 to 527 made any real action to restore the Imperial Roman government impossible.

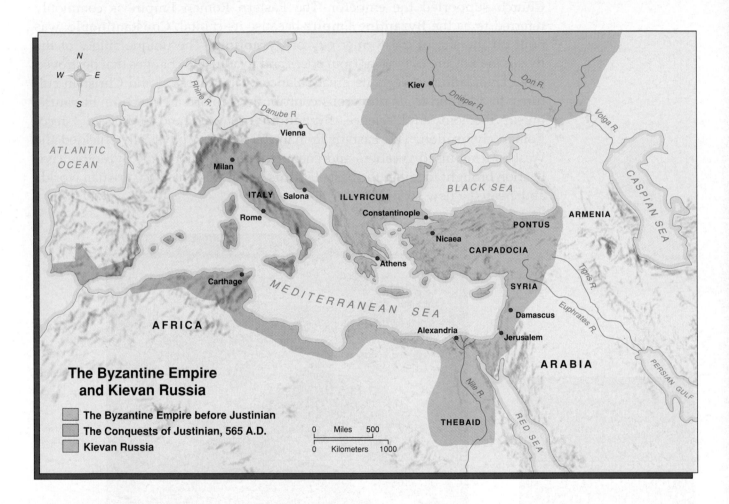

The Byzantine Empire and Kievan Russia

- The Byzantine Empire before Justinian
- The Conquests of Justinian, 565 A.D.
- Kievan Russia

The Reign of Justinian I (527–565)

Justinian I (r. 527–565), known in history as the last Roman Emperor and first Byzantine Emperor, managed to reconquer the western part of the Empire, largely through the efforts of two brilliant generals, **Belisarius** and **Narses**. This effort, however, drained the Empire of both resources and manpower, damaging the economy and ignoring the growing threat of Persian power in the east. The West itself had also changed. The Roman population had become a minority among the Germanic barbarians who had settled there. Despite all his efforts, within a generation of Justinian's death, the Western Empire was lost again to various Germanic tribes.

The Justinian Legal Code

Justinian's domestic efforts had longer lasting results. He perfected the system of strong monarchy and central government that previous emperors had established. Led by the brilliant lawyer **Tribonian**, a legal commission was created by the emperor to revise Roman law. By 533, the commission produced the *Corpus Juris Civilis (Body of Civil Law)*. This consisted of

1. The *Codex Justinianus*, which organized all the main laws of previous Roman Emperors
2. The *Digest*, which contained rulings and precedents of Classical Roman lawyers
3. The *Institutes*, a handbook for law students
4. The *Novels* or *New Laws*, which presented laws recently added to meet the changing needs of a newly Christian state

Interestingly, the first three parts of the *Corpus* were in Latin, the traditional legal tongue of Rome, but the *Novels* were in Greek. Greek, the language of the East, had now become dominant in the Empire. The *Corpus* remained the basis of Byzantine law until the Empire's collapse in 1453 and influenced the development of later legal systems in both western and eastern Europe.

Justinian's Building Program

Justinian also built churches, monasteries, castles, fortifications, palaces, and hospitals, mostly in Constantinople. It was here that he also built the massive **Hippodrome** (stadium for horse racing) and the magnificent **Cathedral of Saint Sophia** (Holy Wisdom).

The magnificent Cathedral of Saint Sophia can be seen in this painting.

The Monophysite Controversy

Following the example of Constantine, Justinian saw himself as the protector and defender of Church and faith. He believed that religious unity was as necessary as loyalty to the Emperor and the state. Viewing theological conflict within the Church as dangerous, he attempted to resolve the **Monophysite Controversy**, which had divided Christians within the Empire. The Monophysites believed that Jesus was only God and just looked like a man, as opposed to the Orthodox teaching of the Church that he was both fully God and fully human. Justinian's wife, the capable and colorful **Empress Theodora**, was a Monophysite. Her position gave her husband

An Orthodox icon of the Annunciation in which an angel tells Mary that she will give birth to Jesus.

the trust of the Monophysite community in holding negotiations to end the controversy. Theodora's unexpected death in 548 destroyed any hopes of resolving the division and forced Justinian to persecute the Monophysites. The Monophysites, who were strongest in Egypt, Syria, and North Africa, became enemies of the Empire and were later in great part responsible for the loss of these provinces.

The Persian War (610–641)

Justinian's reign left the Eastern Roman Empire physically and economically exhausted. His successors were unable to prevent the loss of the West, or the western part of the Roman Empire, in 568 to the Germanic barbarians or the invasion of the Balkans by Slavic tribes led by Asiatic nomads in 587. By 610, the Persians had captured Syria, Palestine, Egypt, and much of Asia Minor. Overthrowing an incompetent and unpopular emperor, the dynamic general, **Heraclius** (r. 610–641), seized the throne and led the Byzantine Army to defeat the Persians completely. Although Heraclius restored the eastern provinces to Byzantine control and ended Persian power permanently, the long and costly war left the Empire paralyzed economically and militarily.

THE ARAB INVASIONS (636–775)

In 636, the *Arab* armies seeking to spread *Islam*, which had started their conquests years earlier in the Arabian Desert, began to invade the territories of the Eastern Roman Empire. The complete exhaustion of the Byzantine military forces and the support of many Monophysites in the eastern provinces allowed the Arab armies to capture Palestine, Syria, Egypt, North Africa, and most of Asia Minor, as well as the Persian Empire, by 711. Jerusalem had been taken by 700. From 717 to 718, Constantinople was even under siege. Due to the leadership of **Emperor Leo III** the Isaurian, which means "of Syria" (r. 717–741), Constantinople was saved, and the Arab forces were repulsed. The Arab navy was destroyed through the use of a new invention, **Greek fire** (a chemical that burned ships and could not be put out with water), which kept the Empire and its ships safe from future Arab attack. By 775, Leo III and his successor, **Constantine V** (r. 741–775), had restored Asia Minor to the Empire. Byzantium, however, became a strictly European power and had to adjust to this new status.

THE HIGH BYZANTINE EMPIRE AND THE RISE OF THE EASTERN EUROPEAN NATIONS (775–1204)

Having lost the eastern provinces of Palestine, Syria, and Egypt, the Byzantine Empire looked north to Europe. The Mediterranean was no longer the "**Roman Lake**," but had become a border dividing the Christian and Islamic worlds. The Slavic nations of eastern Europe became the focus of Byzantine missions as the Empire's forces reestablished military control of the region. Under a strong series of rulers, Byzantine influence extended into central and eastern Europe as well as parts of the East.

The Macedonian Dynasty (867–1055)

Despite great military successes, which included the restoration of Asia Minor and the reconquest of Greece from Slavic tribes, the controversial domestic policies of the *Isaurian dynasty* (717–742), particularly over **iconoclasm,** which was the destruction of **holy icons** or religious pictures, created serious internal quarrels. The Isaurian emperors' stand against the use of icons made them extremely unpopular and was ultimately responsible for their downfall. A new Arab threat to Asia Minor and the rise of powerful and aggressive Bulgars, who were Asiatic-Slavic people, to the north led to the emergence of the *Macedonian dynasty* (867–1055).

The policy of iconoclasm, which was the destruction of holy icons such as this mosaic of Jesus, created serious internal quarrels. (Photo submitted by George Hero.)

The Conversion of the Slavic Peoples (850–1000)

The Macedonian emperors restored the Empire to a position of power and prestige it had not enjoyed since Justinian. This time, however, Byzantium was not economically and physically devastated by the expansion. Beginning with **Basil I** (r. 867–886), the Empire began a campaign to expand both its influence and its borders. The Byzantines launched a series of successful missions to convert the **Slavic peoples** to Eastern Orthodox Christianity. There had already been much missionary work done under the leadership of two brothers, **Cyril** (c. 827–869) and **Methodius** (c. 815–885), who had converted the peoples of Moravia, located in the modern Czech Republic, to Christianity and created the **Slavonic** language and alphabet, used for church services and early historical writing by the Slavic peoples.

The Byzantine Commonwealth (950–1100)

As ruler of Kiev, the most powerful city in the federation of states known as Rus', Prince Vladimir led the mass conversion of his people to Orthodox Christianity.

Since the rise of the **Carolingians** in western Europe (see Chapter 6), a strained relationship had developed between the **Eastern Church**, under the **Patriarch of Constantinople** and the **Western Church**, under the **Pope of Rome**. The disagreement arose over the Pope's claim to be the supreme head of the Christian Church. This led to a **schism** or split between Eastern and Western Christianity in 1054.

The two churches began to compete for the conversion of non-Christian peoples. Eastern Europe soon became divided into two spheres of religious and political influence: the **Eastern Orthodox**, which included **Bulgaria**, **Serbia**, **Romania**, and **Rus'**, which is today's **Ukraine** and **Russia**, and the **Roman Catholic**, which consisted of **Croatia**, **Moravia**, **Hungary**, and **Poland**. The Eastern Orthodox nations formed an alliance with the Empire, the **Byzantine Commonwealth**, which provided mutual military and economic support. The results of this division can still be seen in the political tensions of modern-day eastern European politics.

The Conquest of Bulgaria

The rise of Bulgarian aggression in the late tenth century resulted in its conquest by the Empire under **Basil II** (r. 976–1025) and the annexation of **Armenia**. By the reign of the last ruler of the Macedonian dynasty, Byzantium was the greatest power of that part of the world. Yet, maintaining the vast borders the Macedonian emperors had created put the Eastern Roman Empire under an enormous pressure. We have seen the same kind of pressure faced by the Western Roman Empire as it tried to maintain its many borders.

The Crusades

The invasions of the **Seljuk Turks**, who were Asiatic nomads, into Asia Minor further strained the Empire's resources. The complete defeat of the Byzantine Army by the Seljuks at **Manzikert** in Asia Minor in 1071 was a blow from which the Empire never fully recovered. By 1081, Armenia and most of Asia Minor had been lost.

With the ascent of **Alexius I** (r. 1081–1118), the tide of invasion was reversed. Asking the Pope for western European help to remove the Seljuks from Asia Minor, Alexius received an army of **Crusaders** (see Chapter 6), who assisted him in regaining some of Asia Minor (1098). These Crusader armies then proceeded further east to regain Jerusalem from the Muslims. Although successive dynasties of emperors managed to maintain these shrunken borders, the Byzantine Empire was never able to recover all of Asia Minor or their pre-1071 power.

The relationship with the West and the Pope had grown worse due to the actions of the Crusaders. The final break came in 1204 when the knights of the **Fourth Crusade** attacked and occupied Constantinople. This forced the Byzantine government into exile at **Nicaea** from 1204 to 1261. The slaughter of fellow Christians by the Crusaders and the installation of a **Latin Patriarch** in Constantinople, which had the approval of the Pope, during the occupation resulted in mistrust and resentment between the Eastern Orthodox and Roman Catholic churches that has continued until the present day.

Main Idea:
The slaughter of fellow Christians by the Crusaders and the installation of a Latin Patriarch in Constantinople, which had the approval of the Pope, during the occupation resulted in mistrust and resentment between the Eastern Orthodox and Roman Catholic Churches that has continued until the present day.

Saints Constantine and Helen. Note that these figures are dressed as Byzantine rulers. (Photo submitted by George Hero.)

THE LATE BYZANTINE EMPIRE (1204–1453)

The Paleologian Dynasty (1261–1453)

The restoration of Constantinople under the *Paleologian dynasty* (1261–1453) faced overwhelming odds from the start. The successful efforts to remove the occupying western European Crusaders had exhausted the Byzantines physically and economically. More importantly, new invaders, the Ottoman Turks, had taken most of Asia Minor while the Empire was preoccupied with freeing the capital. To make matters worse, much of the Balkans and Greece had been lost to various western European powers.

The Council of Florence

Beginning with **Michael VIII** (r. 1261–1282), the Paleologian emperors tried to restore as much of the Empire as possible. Although Byzantium regained most of Greece, the Turks made more gains in Asia Minor. Eventually they controlled the entire area except for Constantinople and its immediate surroundings. Desperate for Western assistance against the Ottoman Turks, the Byzantines entered into negotiations with the Papacy, which insisted on ending the schism between the churches as a condition for sending help. There were many attempts at union, the most notable being the **Council of Florence** (1439–1440), where an agreement was reached, but the clergy and people of the Eastern Orthodox Church would not accept it.

The Fall of Constantinople

By the late fourteenth and early fifteenth centuries, Serbia and Bulgaria had fallen to the Turks, leaving Byzantium encircled. The Papacy had lost much of its power and influence in internal battles and was not able to provide the assistance it once could. By 1453, the Turks had captured the area surrounding the capital and lay siege to the city. On Tuesday, May 29, Constantinople fell to the Ottomans. The last Byzantine Emperor, **Constantine XI Paleologus** (r. 1449–1453), died in the fighting. By 1460, Greece had also fallen. The ancient Greco-Roman world had come to an end.

Saint Vladimir of Kiev, the ruler who converted the Rus' to Orthodox Christianity. (Photo submitted by George Hero.)

BYZANTINE SOCIETY

Byzantine society was, in many ways, a continuation of Roman society. We must remember that the region of the Eastern Roman Empire was formerly the Hellenistic Kingdoms. Yet, the Christian faith did make some noticeable differences. The population was unified by a common religion, Orthodox Christianity, as well as a common culture, Greco-Roman. Religious issues also often divided the population. For example, even the simplest farmer might get into an argument about theology when he went to market. The disagreements, however, could have very damaging effects. One example was the Monophysite Controversy, which resulted in that group assisting the Arab takeover of Byzantium's Middle Eastern provinces.

Church and State in Byzantium

For the vast majority who remained within the official Church, religion gave their lives both hope and meaning. Colorful and impressive religious ceremonies reinforced both their faith in God and the image of the Emperor, who became the "**Viceroy**" or representative of God. It was his duty to protect his people and church; in turn, the people were expected to cooperate with the government. With the addition of Christian morals and values, governmental responsibilities expanded. Through the monasteries, the government funded orphanages, hospitals, old age homes, and other institutions of social welfare. In fact, the Byzantine Empire was the first state to sponsor **philanthropic** work, which is the advancement of care for fellow humans.

When the Isaurian emperors decided to forbid the use of religious pictures, or holy icons, the population refused to accept the decision and protested. (Photo submitted by George Hero.)

The relationship between the Emperor and Church leadership became a balance of power. Theoretically the two worked side by side, dealing with different needs. While the emperors tended to dominate, they were limited by theology and tradition. Attempts to violate these, such as the **Iconoclast Controversy** (726–843), ended in failure. This conflict was started when the Isaurian emperors decided to forbid the use of religious pictures, or holy icons. The population, led by the monks and many clergymen, refused to accept the decision and protested. The stubborn refusal by the Isaurians to give up on this unpopular policy resulted in their eventual loss of the throne, despite a record of brilliant military successes and good government.

The Patriarchate System

The emperor worked directly with the **Patriarch of Constantinople**, one of five head bishops who governed the Eastern Church. At the first Christian councils in the late fourth and early fifth centuries it was decided that the major cities of the Empire, which included **Rome**, **Constantinople**, **Alexandria**, **Antioch**, and **Jerusalem**, known as the birthplace of the Christian faith, would have Patriarchs. They were equals, but the Patriarch or Pope, which means "Father," of Rome was the "first among equals" because Rome was the capital of the Roman Empire. After the fall of the West in 476, however, the Papacy took on many special powers, which it later came to regard as its rights.

The Schism of the Eastern and Western Churches

The Pope's claim to be the head of the Church brought it into conflict with the other Patriarchates, especially the Patriarch of Constantinople, which had become the leader of the Eastern Church. From the ninth to eleventh centuries theological disputes began to drive a wedge between the two patriarchates. In 1054, because of differences in practices and the development of Papal supremacy in the Roman or Latin Catholic Church, a schism or split occurred between the Eastern or Greek Orthodox and the Roman Catholic churches. This division was healed soon after, but relations continued to be strained. With the Fourth Crusade of 1204, a final break came as a result of the Latin occupation of Constantinople. Distrust and resentment followed and continue today, especially in parts of Eastern Europe.

The Improved Status of Women

The legal status of women improved greatly in the Byzantine Empire. Women ruled independently as empresses as well. These were **Irene** from 797–802, **Zoe** and **Theodora** in 1042, and Theodora alone from 1055–1056. They were allowed to own property and became legally independent of male relatives or husbands.

Architecture

The Byzantines expanded on Roman architecture continuing to create roads, bridges, aqueducts, palaces, and public buildings; they concentrated on the construction of churches and monasteries. The greatest example of this was the Emperor Justinian's Cathedral of St. Sophia in Constantinople. Justinian was also responsible for the **Monastery of St. Catherine** on Mount Sinai in present day Egypt.

Sculpture and Painting

Like architecture, art was heavily religious in nature. Although sculpture in the Classical style was practiced, the demand was very limited. Patrons as well as churches commissioned icons, **frescoes** or wall paintings, and mosaics depicting Christ, the Virgin Mary, the various saints, and scenes from the Bible. Carvings and statues were also used at first. They were later forbidden for use in religious worship by the Eastern Church, which decided to allow only flat images. A "Byzantine style" of religious painting developed, which emphasized the supernatural nature of the subjects. This dominated Byzantine art, which largely ignored the western European movement to make artistic depictions more

A Byzantine style of religious painting developed that emphasized the supernatural nature of the subjects, as in this icon of the Virgin Mary and Baby Jesus. (Photo submitted by George Hero.)

realistic. Unlike the West, where **secular**, meaning nonreligious, art began to appear in the Late Middle Ages, art in Byzantium remained predominantly religious. Monasteries produced the bulk of icons after the Iconoclast Controversy, so few names of artists are known, as monks did not sign their names to their work.

Literature

Literary forms in Byzantium were dominated, as were all things, by religion. The Byzantines abandoned the simplified **Koine**, Greek used in the Hellenistic period, for the Classical form of the language. The Classics were studied more for grammar than for content. The three forms of literature that were most developed were history, theology, and **haigiography**, which is the study of the lives of saints.

Secular poetry disappeared by the sixth century, replaced by the religious poetry used in hymns. Employing the rules and format of Classical poetry, hymn writing became an art. The greatest Byzantine writer was **Romanus the Melodist** (died c. 555). Responsible for over a thousand hymns, only about eighty-five have survived; Romanus became the model by which future poets would measure their work. Although secular music was composed as well, religious hymns were in the greatest demand. The Byzantines developed a very stylized form of chant that was used in religious services. As time went on, choirs of singers were used to enhance the beauty of the Eastern Orthodox liturgy. Secular poetry reappeared in the Late Byzantine period with the anonymous epic *Digenes Akritos*, about a hero who is half-Arab and half-Byzantine and his romance and struggles. This **humanistic**, which is the study of human beings, work inspired others such as **Theodore Prodromos** (1100–1170), who wrote satires and **panegyrics**, which are poems of praise, in imitation of the Greeks and Romans.

Historical Writing

In the Roman tradition, historical writing continued to flourish. Despite the strong religious fervor of their civilization, most Byzantine historians tried to be objective and were reliable in their facts. Two schools of history developed: the **monastic**, which consisted of **chronicles** (or lists of events in chronological order), that were highly biased toward a religious viewpoint, and the **secular**, written by laymen and reflecting a less narrow perspective. The monastics wrote universal histories, which started with the Creation in the Bible and went until the present. These writers saw history as part of a predetermined plan by God and read religious significance into every event.

Secular historians were quite

> **Main Idea:**
> Two schools of history developed: the monastic, that were highly biased toward a religious viewpoint, and the secular, reflecting a less narrow perspective.

St. Paul the Apostle. Originally known as Saul of Tarsus, Paul was instrumental in organizing the early Church. His letters, known as epistles, served as both guides and inspiration for the first Christians. (Photo submitted by George Hero.)

varied in their subjects and approaches. The last of the historians trained in the old Roman tradition, **Procopius** (c. 500–c. 565) wrote on the Emperor Justinian's military successes in *On the Wars*, and the rebuilding of Constantinople in *On the Buildings*. In his last work, *The Secret History*, Procopius unfairly attacked Justinian as an evil ruler, possibly after being denied a government position he thought he deserved. The Emperor **Constantine VII "Porphyroghenitos,"** meaning "Born in the Purple" (r. 945–959), wrote two accounts (*On the Imperial Administration* and *On the Ceremonies*) of Byzantine government and court life. The historian **Michael Psellus** (1018–1081) gave fascinating portraits of twelve Byzantine rulers in his *Chronographia (Chronography)*. One of the most unusual and well written of Byzantine histories was that of **Anna Comnena** (1083–1154), daughter of Emperor Alexius I. In her *Alexiad*, an account of her father's reign, she analyzed Byzantine society.

LINK TO TODAY
The Bishop's Throne

There are many reminders of the Byzantine Empire in modern Greek Orthodox Churches. One of the most prominent is the bishop's throne. Located on the right side of the altar, it is usually very ornate, decorated with the Eastern Roman Empire's double-headed eagle, which was the symbol of its rulers during the Late Byzantine Period (1261–1453). These thrones, on which only the emperor was allowed to sit, were elevated so that he could be seen throughout the church. The color of the material used for the seat and cushions was porphyron, a deep purple that was reserved exclusively for use by Roman Emperors. On the inside of the high back of the throne above the seat was an icon of Christ dressed as a Byzantine emperor wearing a crown. After the fall of Constantinople and Ottoman conquest of Byzantium in 1453, the bishops replaced the emperor as leaders of the surviving Byzantine community. They began to sit in the imperial throne during religious services wearing the crowns once worn by the Eastern Roman emperors. This practice has continued in Greek Orthodox churches to this day.

These icons of Mary and Jesus show them seated in thrones, similar to the Bishop's thrones that can be seen in modern Greek Orthodox churches.

CHAPTER SUMMARY

The Byzantine Empire preserved the culture, language, institutions, and customs of the Classical World. More importantly, it re-introduced western Europe to its Greco-Roman heritage after the Early Middle Ages. Byzantium laid the religious, cultural, and political foundations for the civilizations of the eastern European nations as well. Through the conquest of the Eastern Roman Empire's cities, Islamic civilization greatly benefited from Byzantine advancements. The combination of flexibility and continuity of the Byzantine Empire maintained the Western cultural practices when they might otherwise have been lost.

IMPORTANT PEOPLE, PLACES, AND TERMS

KEY TERMS	PEOPLE	PLACES
Eastern Roman Empire	Justinian I	Constantinople
Byzantine Empire	Belisarius	Byzantium
Corpus Juris Civilis	Narses	Moravia
Hippodrome	Tribonian	Serbia
Cathedral of Saint Sophia	Empress Theodora	Romania
Monophysite Controversy	Heraclius	Rus'
Greek fire	Emperor Leo III	Ukraine
Roman Lake	Emperor Constantine V	Russia
iconoclasm	Slavic peoples	Byzantine
holy icons	Basil I	Commonwealth
Slavonic	Cyril	Armenia
Crusaders	Methodius	Manzikert
Fourth Crusade	Basil II	Nicaea
Council of Florence	Seljuk Turks	Alexandria
Viceroy	Alexius I	Antioch
philanthropy	Michael VIII Paleologus	Jerusalem
Iconoclast Controversy	Constantine XI Paleologus	Monastery of
Patriarchs	Irene	St. Catherine
Popes of Rome	Zoe	Bulgaria
schism	Romanus the Melodist	Croatia
frescoes	Theodore Prodromos	Hungary
secular	Procopius	Poland
Koine	Anna Comnena	
haigiography	Theodora	
Digenes Akritos	Michael Psellus	
monastic	Emperor Constantine VII	
chronicles	"Porphyroghenitos"	
Eastern Orthodox		
Roman Catholic		
humanistic		

EXERCISES FOR CHAPTER 5

MULTIPLE CHOICE

Select the letter of the correct answer.

1. Which answer would best complete this partial outline?

   BYZANTINE HERITAGE

   I. Blended Christian beliefs with Ancient Greek art and philosophy
   II. Extended Roman engineering achievements
   III. Preserved Greco-Roman texts
   IV. _____

   a. Adapted Roman law
   b. Had Senate as chief governing body
   c. Led the Crusades to liberate Rome from the Huns
   d. Helped maintain Roman rule over Western Europe

2. The Emperor Justinian accomplished all of the following EXCEPT

   a. the revision of Roman law.
   b. a massive building program.
   c. a solution to the Monophysite Controversy.
   d. the temporary restoration of the West.

3. The *Body of Civil Law* consisted of

   a. Digest, Novels, Institutes, Index.
   b. Digest, Novels, Codex, Institutes.
   c. Novels, Codex, Institutes, Index.
   d. Digest, Codex, Institutes, Index.

4. The Emperor responsible for saving the Byzantine Empire from the Persians was

   a. Justinian I.
   b. Leo III.
   c. Heraclius.
   d. Constantine VII.

5. The success of the Arab Invasions in the Roman Empire's eastern provinces was due to all of the following EXCEPT

   a. poor leadership in the Byzantine government.
   b. exhaustion of the Byzantine Army after the Persian War.
   c. monophysite cooperation with the Arab invaders.
   d. lack of economic resources to begin new military operations.

6. The Isaurian emperors grew unpopular as a result of the

   a. loss of the eastern provinces to the Arabs.
   b. Monophysite Controversy.
   c. corruption in the Byzantine government.
   d. policy of iconoclasm.

7. One lasting achievement of the Macedonian dynasty was the

   a. conversion of the Slavic peoples to Eastern Orthodox Christianity.
   b. defeat of the Persians.
   c. conquest of the Bulgarians.
   d. annexation of Armenia.

8. Which group of nations were members of the Byzantine Commonwealth?

   a. Bulgaria, Moravia, Serbia, and Romania
   b. Bulgaria, Serbia, Croatia, and Poland
   c. Bulgaria, Serbia, Romania, and Rus'
   d. Moravia, Serbia, Poland, and Rus'

9. All of the following were responsible for the schism between the Eastern and Western churches EXCEPT

   a. the Schism of 1054.
   b. the concept of Papal Supremacy.
   c. the Monophysite Controversy.
   d. the Fourth Crusade.

10. Which is the correct chronological order of events?

    1. Defeat of the Crusaders by Salhaadin
    2. Sack of Constantinople by the Crusaders
    3. Capture of Jerusalem by the Crusaders
    4. Schism between the Eastern Orthodox and Roman Catholic churches

    a. $1 \rightarrow 2 \rightarrow 3 \rightarrow 4$
    b. $2 \rightarrow 1 \rightarrow 3 \rightarrow 4$
    c. $3 \rightarrow 1 \rightarrow 2 \rightarrow 4$
    d. $4 \rightarrow 2 \rightarrow 3 \rightarrow 1$

11. Anna Comnena was the daughter of which emperor?

    a. Constantine XI
    b. Alexius I
    c. Justinian I (the Great)
    d. Heraclius

12. The Fourth Crusade ultimately resulted in

    a. the Ottoman Turkish conquest of Byzantium.
    b. Crusader domination of the Middle East.
    c. the restoration of Jerusalem to the Christians.
    d. The unification of western and eastern Europe.

13. The last dynasty of Byzantine rulers was described as the

    a. Comnenan.
    b. Angelan.
    c. Paleologan.
    d. Nicaean.

14. In 1453, Constantinople fell to the

    a. Ottoman Turks.
    b. Seljuk Turks.
    c. Arabs.
    d. Crusaders.

15. Which of the following statements about Byzantium is true?

    a. Their society was unified by a common religion and culture.
    b. Their style of painting emphasized the natural world.
    c. The Turks were never able to defeat them.
    d. Church and state always had a smooth working relationship.

16. The Conversion of the Slavic peoples to Orthodox Christianity by the Byzantines is an example of

    a. imperialism.
    b. cultural diffusion.
    c. ethnocentrism.
    d. legalism.

17. Unlike those in Ancient Greece, women in the Byzantine Empire

    a. were legally considered minors.
    b. had limited legal rights.
    c. had full legal rights.
    d. had no legal rights.

18. Byzantine art differed from that of Ancient Greece and Rome in that it

    a. centered on religion.
    b. focused on humans.
    c. emphasized nature.
    d. was primarily concerned with history.

19. The Byzantine (Eastern Orthodox) Church is theologically

    a. pagan.
    b. Arian.
    c. monophysite.
    d. duophysite.

20. One characteristic common to Egyptian, Persian, and Byzantine government was

    a. democracy.
    b. autocracy.
    c. constitutional monarch.
    d. military dictatorship.

1. Explain the statement, "Byzantium was both a continuation of Rome and a new Christian state." Show three ways in which the empire of New Rome (Byzantium) differed from that of Old Rome.
2. The Arab invasions were both destructive and beneficial for the Byzantine Empire.
   a. Give two examples of how the Empire suffered as a result of the Arab invasions.
   b. Show two ways in which the loss of the Eastern provinces ultimately benefited the Empire.
3. Were the western Europeans responsible for the destruction of the Byzantine state? Show two ways in which Byzantium's relationship with the West led to the destruction of the Empire.
4. Byzantium provided the cultural and religious foundations of many Slavic nations.
   a. Select two nations that were influenced by the Byzantine Empire.
   b. Show one way they were influenced religiously and one way culturally each.
5. You are a student in a Byzantine university writing to a friend in Rome. In the letter, you want to brag a little about the accomplishments and advances that have taken place in the Eastern Empire. Be sure to include at least one specific example of each of the following in your writing: the arts, literature, and building.

DOCUMENT-BASED QUESTIONS

This task is based on the accompanying documents. Some of these documents have been edited for the purposes of this task. This task is designed to test your ability to work with historical documents. As you analyze the documents, take into account both the source of each document and the author's point of view.

Directions: Read the following documents and answer the questions after each document. Use the information in the reading and this chapter in writing your answers.

Document #1

MOSAIC OF THE EMPEROR JUSTINIAN AND HIS COURT

Questions

1. In what ways does the illustration of the Emperor Justinian and his court show the mixture of Greco-Roman culture and Christianity in Byzantine civilization? Refer specifically to symbols and objects shown that indicate this cultural diffusion.

2. Why does the Emperor have a halo, which is a Christian symbol of holiness, above his head? What does this show about the relationship between church and state?

Document #2   THE JUSTINIAN CODE

Marriage is the union of a man and a woman, a partnership for life involving divine as well as human law.

Marriage cannot take place unless everyone involved consents, that is, those who are being united and those in whose power they are.

A girl who was less than twelve years old when she married will not be a lawful wife until she reaches that age while living with her husband.

When relationship of brother and sister arises because of adoption, it is an impediment to marriage while the adoptions lasts. . . . We are not allowed to marry our paternal or maternal aunts or paternal or maternal great-aunts although paternal and maternal great-aunts are related in the fourth degree. Again, we are not allowed to marry a paternal aunt or great-aunt, even though they are related to us by adoption.

Where he marries someone because his father forces him to do so and he would not have married her if the choice had been his, the marriage will nevertheless be valid, because marriage cannot take place without the consent of the parties; he is held to have chosen this course of action. Women accused of adultery cannot marry during the lifetime of their husbands, even before conviction.

Women who live in a shameful way and make money out of prostitution, even where it is not done openly, are held in disgrace.

Marriage is dissolved by the divorce, death, captivity, or other kind of slavery of either of the parties.

A true divorce does not take place unless an intention to remain apart permanently is present. So things said or done in anger are not effective until the parties show by their persistence an indication for their considered opinion. So where repudiation takes place in anger and the wife returns shortly afterward, she is not held to have divorced her husband.

[An] insane woman can be repudiated, because she is in the same position as a person who does not know of the repudiation. But she could not repudiate her husband because of her madness, . . . but her father can repudiate for her.

The wives of people who fall into enemy hands can still be considered married women only in that other men cannot marry them hastily. Generally, as long as it is certain that a husband who is in captivity is still alive, his wife does not have the right to contract another marriage, unless she herself has given some ground for repudiation. But if it is not certain whether the husband in captivity is alive or has died, then if five years have passed since his capture, his wife has the right to marry again so that the first marriage will be held to have been dissolved with the consent of the parties and each of the parties will have their rights withdrawn. The same rule applies where a husband stays at home and his wife is captured.

It is not just a person who smothers a child who is held to kill it but also the person who abandons it, denies it good, or puts it on show in public places to excite pity which he himself does not have.

The Digest of Justinian Translated by Alan Watson

Questions	1. In what ways does Justinian's Legal Code show the influence of Christianity on Roman law?
	2. Are these laws similar to those in American society today? Explain

Document #3 **KIEVAN RUS' AND THE BYZANTINE EMPIRE**

1. Based on the map, how did geography allow Byzantium to gain influence over its eastern European neighbors?
2. In what ways did Kievan Rus' trade with the Byzantine Empire lead to religious and cultural exchange?

Document #4

BYZANTINE CORONATION CEREMONY OF MANUEL II (1392)

One of the bishops took the crown [evidently the crown of the Caesar, a lower rank of the hierarchy, worn during the entry] from his head and gave it to the chief of the wardrobe. The patriarch took the incense-burner from the emperor's hands and censed the emperor himself. Then they left the altar and mounted to the pulpit, and there while the emperor bent his head the patriarch alone privately uttered a prayer—the bishops and deacon there heard him—which ran thus:

"King of Kings and Lord of Lords, Who through Your prophet Samuel anointed Your servant David with holy oil as king and ruler of Your people, Yourself, holy Lord King, send down your power from Your holy abode through my sinful hands and anoint Your servant Manuel, emperor and ruler of us, Your faithful people: bring forth in his days justice and the fullness of peace, subdue beneath his feet all foreign peoples who desire war, so that we who lead a quiet and harmless life may glorify Your splendid name by the supplications and prayers of Your all-holy Mother, of the holy and glorious prophet Samuel, and of the holy and glorious ancestor of God the prophet David, of the holy and God-crowned great rulers and equals of the apostles Constantine [the Great] and Helen, and of all Your saints, because Thine is the kingdom and the power and the glory of Father and Son and Holy Spirit now and forever and unto ages of ages. Amen."

Then the patriarch placed the crown atop his head. But if the emperor is a son who has an emperor as father or an emperor is in office [i.e., if an emperor is crowning his son or someone else as co-emperor], the patriarch anoints him, but his father the emperor puts his crown on his head, and the whole people hail him. The patriarch gave him the cross in his right hand, and descending [from the pulpit] they stood at the throne. The empress, having approached, bent her head, and the crowned emperor, her husband, placed the crown customary for the empresses upon her head, and gave into her right hand a golden scepter with precious stones and pearls.

Having worshiped at the altar and ascended the podium, they were seated on their thrones.

Icon and Minaret: Sources of Byzantine and Islamic Civilizations
Translated by P. Schreiner

Questions
1. In what ways does the coronation ceremony of Manuel II reflect the Byzantine view of the Emperor's authority?
2. In what ways does the ceremony reveal the Byzantium's attitude about its empire and its imperial policies?

Document #5

PROCLAMATION OF THE
SECOND COUNCIL OF NICAEA (787)

We, therefore, following . . . the divinely inspired authority of our Holy Fathers and the traditions of the Catholic church for . . . the Holy Spirit dwells in her, define with all certitude and accuracy, that? . . . the vulnerable and holy images, as well as painting and mosaic, as of other fit materials, should be set forth in the holy churches of God . . . the more frequently as they are seen in artistic representation, by so much the more readily are men lifted up to the memory of their prototypes . . . to these should be given . . . honorable relevance . . . for the honor which is paid to the image passes onto that which the image represents.

[T]hose . . . who dare think or teach otherwise, or as wicked heretics as to spurn the traditions of the church . . . we command that they be deposed [and] be cut off from communion.

A Source Book on Ancient Church History
Translated by Joseph G. Ayer, Jr.

Questions
1. How does the proclamation reflect the importance of holy images to Byzantine society?
2. In what ways does this reveal the strong relationship between church and state and Byzantium?

CHAPTER 6
Medieval Europe

The Early Middle Ages

476

Central Middle Ages

Late Middle Ages

Carolingian Empire

Germanic Kingdoms — Feudalism

The Crusades

The Hundred Years' War

850

1046 — 1204

1337 — 1453

| 400 | 500 | 600 | 700 | 800 | 900 | 1000 | 1100 | 1200 | 1300 | 1400 | 1500 |

1347 — 1450

The Black Death

TIMELINE OF EVENTS

The end of Roman government in western Europe began a period of instability and change. The transition period between what is considered as ancient (c. 500) and modern (c. 1500) is known as the **Middle Ages** or **Medieval Period**; it witnessed the transformation of western Europe into a group of nations that soon became the most powerful on earth. As the Ancient World was eclipsing with the gradual shrinking of the **Byzantine Empire**, its knowledge and ideas were passed on to the peoples of the West, who came to regard themselves as the heirs to the Classical World and Greco-Roman civilization. This legacy, combined with their own unique institutions, became the foundation of modern Western society.

THE EARLY MIDDLE AGES (476–1000)

The collapse of the Western Roman Empire threw Europe into a state of violent disorder. The Germanic tribes that had been held back for years flooded into Imperial territory as Roman authority gradually receded. They settled throughout the former Western Empire. These tribes—**Visigothic**, **Ostrogothic**, **Vandal**, **Frankish**, **Burgundian**, and **Anglo-Saxon**—were poorly organized and often at war with each other. Between the years of 500 and 750, they divided western Europe, creating independent kingdoms.

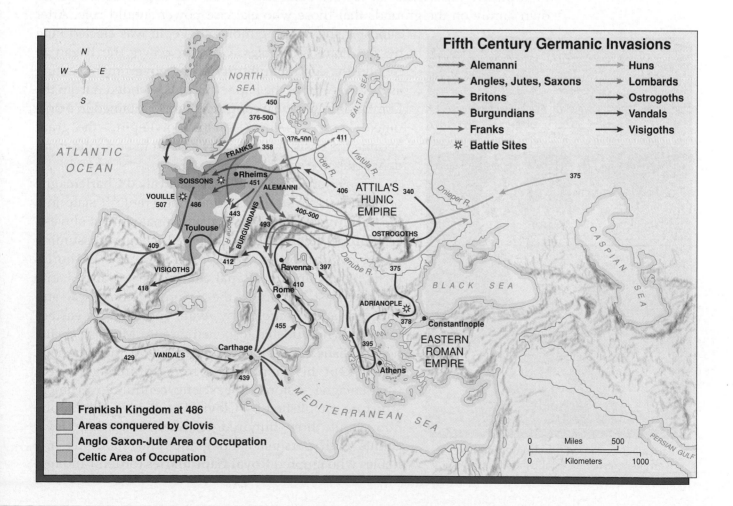

Main Idea:
The Frankish
kingdom became
very powerful
under the
leadership of
King Clovis.

Under the leadership of the **Merovingian** king **Clovis** (r. 481–511), the Frankish kingdom became very powerful. Building up a strong and organized military, he and his successors destroyed the Burgundian kingdom, drove the Visigoths out of Gaul, and expanded their borders into eastern Germany. Clovis was also the first Frankish ruler to convert to Christianity, hoping that his new religion would eventually unite his kingdom further. He ruled by a strong monarchy with an efficient court of officials. Each local district or *county* was administered by a royally appointed governor or *count*, who collected taxes, provided justice, and kept order. Clovis' successors however, were not very capable rulers. Slowly royal power and authority disintegrated. The Merovingian rulers kept dividing the kingdom equally between male children until three weak sub-kingdoms existed. Great landowners were depended upon to rule efficiently in place of the central government, which could no longer do so. The local nobles soon grew used to their power, creating their own private governments on the lands they ruled. The inability of the government to provide protection forced the population to take pledges of loyalty and service to the nobles.

The Carolingians soon filled the lack of leadership on the part of the Merovingian kings. Serving as *mayors* or chief officers of the Frankish Royal Court, they built up great power and influence. In 732, **Charles Martel** (r. 714–768) led Frankish forces to defeat the invading **Moors** or Spanish Muslims while his successor, **Pepin the Short** (r. 741–751) convinced the Pope to authorize the transfer of the Frankish crown from the Merovingians to his own family on the grounds that those who exercise power should rule. After deposing the reigning monarch, Pepin was elected king by the Frankish nobles. Once in power, he began to rebuild the central authority of the government. Acting as the protector of the Papacy, Pepin defended it from the Lombards and gave it captured land. Contained in a document known as the "Donation of Pepin," the grant became the basis of the Papacy's claim to be an independent state.

Carolus or *Charles* (768–814), later called **Charlemagne** or *Charles the Great*, transformed the Frankish state into the **Carolingian Empire**, which dominated most of western Europe. Charles conquered the Lombards, assuming power over all of Italy except the Byzantine territories in the south and the **Papal States**. He expanded into the northeast, subduing the Saxons in that area, and annexed lands occupied by Avars and Slavs in eastern Europe. While unable to penetrate into Moorish Spain, he established a military border beyond the Pyrenees, which kept his empire safe from future aggression. Charlemagne restored the strong central government structure established by Clovis. He divided the Empire into about three hundred counties, rewarding loyal counts with personal land grants and subduing any nobles who ignored **Royal Capitularies** (orders) and reg-

Charlemagne restored the strong central government structure established by Clovis.

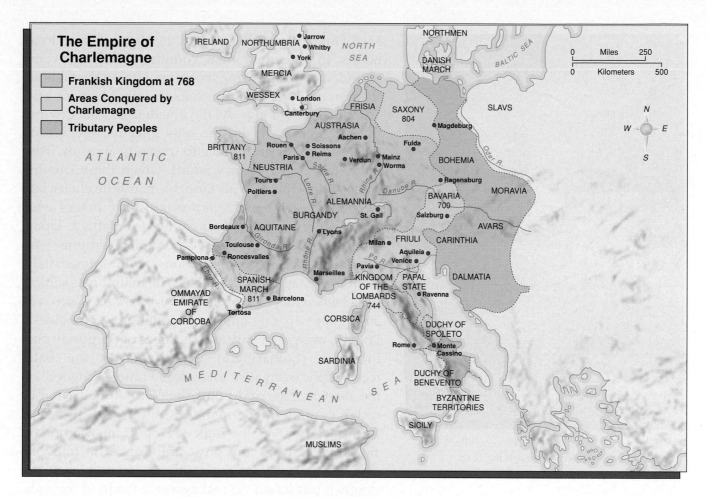

The Empire of Charlemagne

- Frankish Kingdom at 768
- Areas Conquered by Charlemagne
- Tributary Peoples

ulations. Imperial envoys called *missi* were sent out to investigate and report on the actions of local officials. Charles enforced uniformity in religion as well as law, forcing the remaining pagans in the Empire to accept Christian baptism. He encouraged the building of churches and monasteries and imposed a tax of 10 percent of income, the **tithe**, to support the Church. Working closely with the Papacy, Charles enforced uniform ritual in religious services and orthodox theological beliefs, establishing the Roman Catholic Church in Europe. Within his court, Charlemagne supported a revival of Greco-Roman culture and learning, known later as the **Carolingian Renaissance**. This movement established a palace school at **Aachen**, under the direction of the English monastic scholar **Alcuin**. All the young men of the court were required to attend the school, producing a generation of educated and efficient administrators. Charles and his court rediscovered the legacy of the Classical World and attempted to model the Carolingian on the Roman. Seeing his kingdom as the restoration of the Western Roman Empire, Charlemagne had the Pope crown him **Holy Roman Emperor** on Christmas day of 800. This produced a strong negative reaction from both the Byzantine emperor and the Eastern Church, straining relations. Yet, it was significant as, for the first time, a Germanic ruler adopted Greco-Roman learning and identified himself as a Roman Emperor. This brought unity to the region for the first time since Roman domination.

Charlemagne's son, **Louis the Pious** (r. 814–840), was a very weak successor. Extremely religious and indecisive, Louis was unable to enforce central authority over the vast Carolingian Empire as his father did. Instead, as the

A painting of a Viking ship. The only effective method of defense was for each noble to organize an army.

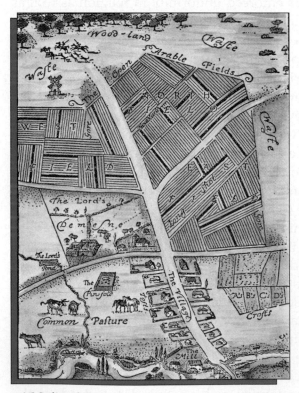

A Medieval English Manor.

Merovingian kings before him, he depended on local nobles to rule their own counties. This was compounded by the growing barbarian attacks throughout the Empire by Islamic Saracens, Asiatic Magyars, and Scandinavian Vikings. As the invaders did not occupy, but attacked and fled, the only effective method of defense was for each noble to organize an army. This made the local ruler a warlord. Given these circumstances, the Holy Roman Emperor had little choice but to cooperate with and even reward local nobles who successfully protected their county from attack. Upon Louis' death in 840, the Carolingian Empire was divided between his three sons, who immediately went to war against each other. The matter was settled in 843 when they signed the *Treaty of Verdun*, which created three separate and equal kingdoms. The eldest, Lothair, was given Italy and the areas of Burgundy and Provence (Lotharingia) while Charles the Bald received the equivalent to modern France (Kingdom of the West Franks) and Louis the German had what is roughly modern Germany (Kingdom of the East Franks). After 843, the rank of Holy Roman Emperor no longer carried any great authority. The Imperial title was transferred from one German dynasty to another, but it had no real power outside of the area the ruler himself controlled. By 900, the Carolingian dynasty was completely discredited and **feudalism** dominated throughout the empire. Feudalism is a lack of central authority with local government based on a system of mutual hereditary obligations.

After 850, the Saracen, Magyar, and Viking attacks intensified. The need for a strong army forced local nobles to offer grants of land, known as **fiefs**, to warriors or **knights** in order to secure their services. In return, the knights took an oath of loyalty to the noble, becoming his **vassals**, or servants. The noble became their seigneur or **lord**, to whom they owed total allegiance. The knights were usually men from the upper levels of society who had been trained to fight and could supply their own armor and horse, but who offered their services to more powerful individuals, especially those who owned castles. To ensure that these arrangements would continue, vassalage or military service owed for the exchange of land grants, and fiefs were made hereditary. Many times a vassal would divide part of his own fief to create vassals of his own. Many lords were more powerful than kings, who had become, in reality, little more than local rulers themselves by the tenth century. Feudalism in western Europe took on the form of **manorialism**, as the peasant population attached itself to self-sufficient agricultural estates run by nobles or the Church, who protected them. The owner of the manor and the peasant also had hereditary obligations. In exchange for the use of the land, the peasant became a **serf**, who was bound to stay on the manor and obligated to provide services for his lord. These included working the lord's lands, providing skilled labor, and repairing roads, fortifications, and buildings for the men, the women were required to perform such duties as spinning, cleaning, and preparing food in the lord's house. Those who were not serfs were **villeins**, who were exempt from the obligatory service. For the peasant, the manorial system was usually harsh and cruel producing, at best, enough to survive.

THE CENTRAL HIGH MIDDLE AGES (1000–1300)

The problems that plagued the Early Middle Ages receded after the year 1000. The population actually began to grow, and there was an excess of food for the first time since the start of the Late Roman Period. Many factors contributed to this. First and foremost, the barbarian attacks ended as the Magyars were prevented from further expansion and the Vikings settled to form independent Christian nations. There was a great improvement in agricultural techniques that resulted in a surplus of produce. They adopted a new system of crop rotation in which different crops were divided into three fields, rather than the

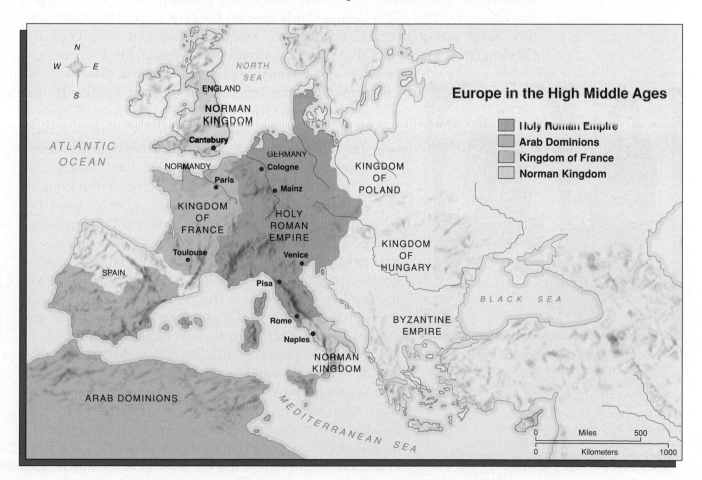

traditional two. This improved soil fertility, increased crop yields, provided more food for livestock, and reduced the amount of time spent plowing. The invention of the heavy moldboard plow was also a major technological advance that allowed the plowing of heavy soil easily. The improved, rigid horse collar and the adoption of the horseshoe allowed that more efficient animal to be used in farm work. An increased use of iron made agricultural tools more effective as well. There was an improvement in western Europe's climate that brought about milder winters, better distribution of rainfall, and less excessive variations in temperature. The barbarian attacks subsided as the Magyars were prevented from further expansion in 955 and the Vikings settled to form independent Christian nations by 1000. The growth in population and peace in the countryside allowed manors to expand by clearing new lands in order to increase their food production. Seeking a more peaceful environment in which to pursue their spiritual development, the monks expanded into the northern European wilderness, cutting down forests and draining swamps. Runaway serfs and peasants who were experiencing difficulties due to the increase in population soon followed them. These groups eventually established towns in previously uninhabited areas. These combined factors created conditions that encouraged the growth of commerce.

The revival of trade and the new wealth it produced, especially in the growing towns and cities destroyed the feudal structure. The Crusades opened up new trade routes and exposed western Europeans to new products. National kings began to rebuild their authority and power. The earliest and most impressive effort was that of the German **Holy Roman Emperors**. Until the tenth century, royal power declined in the three kingdoms that had once been the Carolingian Empire. In Germany, local dukes had formed the independent kingdoms of **Saxony**, **Bavaria**, **Franconia**, **Swabia**, and **Lorraine** out of the kingdom of the East Franks. By the mid-tenth century, **Otto I** (r. 936–973), the Duke of Saxony, ended the Magyars' raids on Germany, gained control over the other independent German kingdoms, restored the northern parts of Italy once held by the Carolingians, and was crowned Holy Roman Emperor by the Pope in 962. **Otto the Great**, as he was later known, used **lay investiture**, which was the appointment of high ecclesiastical positions by the ruler rather than Church officials, to gain control of the German kingdoms. His successors, however, became preoccupied in Italy, allowing feudalism to reappear in Germany. The last of this line, Heinrich (Henry) II (r. 1002–1024), used lay investiture and the influence of the Church to reassert Imperial control.

Medieval illustration of the German Holy Roman Emperor Heinrich or Henry IV asking forgiveness of Pope Gregory VII at Canossa in 1077. While this was a temporary victory for the Papacy in its struggle with the German emporors over the power of clerical investiture, it was under a later pope, Innocent II, that the Church won back this right in the Concordat of Worms (1122).

In 1024, Konrad II (r. 1024–1039) established the *Salian dynasty* of Holy Roman Emperors, also using lay investiture to maintain his power. His son, Heinrich III (r. 1039–1056), was a reformer, who condemned lay investiture. In 1046, he installed his cousin, the dedicated German reformer, Leo IX (r. 1049–1054), as pope. Under Leo's leadership, a reform movement began within the Roman Catholic Church. This movement opposed corruption among the clergy and lay investiture. His successor, **Pope Gregory VII** (r. 1073–1084), pursued these reforms, bringing him into direct conflict with **Emperor Heinrich IV** (r. 1056–1105) in 1076. When Heinrich declared that Gregory VII was no longer pope, the emperor was excommunicated. Faced with the loss of his crown, he was forced to retract his declaration and seek the pope's forgiveness in 1077. In 1084, Heinrich invaded Italy, forced Gregory into exile, and replaced him. In 1122, a compromise was reached between Emperor Heinrich V (r. 1106–1125), the German nobles, and the pope, with the **Concordat of Worms**. This granted that only the Church could appoint ecclesiastical positions, while the land and powers of the office would be given by the emperor. Ultimately, this weakened the position of the monarchy.

By the mid-twelfth century a new dynasty, the *Hohenstaufens* of Swabia attempted to rebuild Imperial power. At first, **Emperor Friedrich (Frederick) I Barbarossa** ("Red Beard") (r. 1152–1190) pacified the German nobility and reestablished control over northern Italy. In 1176, the **Lombard League**, an alliance of northern Italian city-states led by the Papacy, successfully ended German domination. In 1183, a compromise was reached in which Barbarossa's overlordship was recognized in return for actual independence. Friedrich's successors attempted to restore control over Italy, but in the end they were prevented by the most powerful of all the Medieval Popes, **Innocent III** (r. 1196–1216). Initially, **Emperor Friedrich II** (r. 1198–1250) returned control of the German Church to the Papacy and guaranteed Papal independence in return for Innocent's support. Friedrich later began an unsuccessful struggle to reassert Imperial control over Italy, which ended with his death in 1250. The struggle for Italy between the Hohenstaufens and the Papacy created a state of civil war from the late twelfth to the early thirteenth century between two factions; the **Ghibblines** who supported the emperor and the **Guelfs** who supported the Papacy. Even though it established temporary Italian independence, the disunity between the various states led to its domination by foreign powers and a decline in Papal power. Involved with internal struggles, the German nobles did not agree on a successor to Friedrich until 1273, when they elected **Rudolf of Habsburg**, a weak ruler who would not threaten to dominate them. The fatal flaw of the German Holy Roman Emperors, particularly the Ottonians and Hohenstaufens, was their determination to create an empire outside Germany rather than to build a national state as other European rulers. Their obsession with becoming the Roman Empire resulted in the disintegration of their authority and power.

The Kingdom of France was first established by the Treaty of Verdun as the Kingdom of the West Franks. Charles the Bald and his heirs ruled it until 987. Carolingian power however, declined during that period. Feudalism was stronger in France than anywhere else in western Europe. The French kings were officially recognized as overlords of France, but the great landholding lords held the real power. In 987, the French nobles and clergy ended the Carolingian dynasty and elected one of the chief lords, **Hugh Capet** (r. 987–996), **Count of Paris**, as king.

The *Capetian dynasty* ruled France until 1328. Under the first four Capetians, the kings had no power outside their own domain, the area surrounding Paris known as the *Ile de France*. Even though they did manage to

HUGH CAPET

In 987 the French nobles and clergy ended the Carolingian dynasty and elected Hugh Capet as king.

establish a hereditary right to the throne and gain the support of the Church, the rest of the Kingdom remained divided into feudal principalities. Even within the Ile de France, Capetian power was limited. With the reign of Louis VI the Fat (r. 1108–1137), they first gained control over the feudal vassals in the domain. Building a strong government and courts, Louis provided order and justice for his subjects. He also ended the monopoly of nobles holding royal offices by bringing in men of the middle class that were completely loyal to the monarchy. Louis was so effective that the dying Duke of Aquitane entrusted his daughter Eleanor (1122–1204) and his kingdom to him. She was married to Louis' son and successor, **Louis VII** (r. 1137–1180), a religious and dedicated ruler, who was not very capable politically. Unable to control the rebellious Aquitane territory or his wife, who was unfaithful to him, Louis secured an *annulment*, or divorce from the pope and ended the childless union. Eleanor married **Henry II** (r. 1154–1189), King of England, who added the Aquitaine to his other French territories, which included **Normandy**, **Anjou**, **Brittany**, **Maine**, **Touraine**, known as the *Angevin Empire* as Henry was descended from the Dukes of Anjou. Louis' son, Philippe II Augustus (r. 1180–1223), annexed all the northern Angevin possessions after the *Battle of Bouvines* in 1214. Philippe's successors, especially **Louis IX** (r. 1226–1270), later canonized as a saint of the Roman Catholic Church, and **Philippe IV the Fair** (r. 1285–1314) continued to expand the possessions of the French monarchy. They also developed a strong central government with efficient institutions run by experts devoted to the monarchy. The Capetians gave great financial assistance to the Church in return for its support. This relationship ended when Philippe IV became involved in a conflict with **Pope Boniface VIII** (r. 1294-1303) over the king's power to tax Church property and judge the clergy. Philippe turned the French against the Papacy, intimidated the clergy into submission to royal authority, and sent agents to Rome to capture Boniface, preventing him from interfering in French affairs. By 1300, the feudal French monarchy controlled much of the nation under a strong central government.

England had been under the control of Anglo-Saxon kings since the Early Middle Ages. In 1066, the Normans led by the **Duke of Normandy, William I the Conqueror** (r. 1066–1087) conquered the nation at the Battle of Hastings. William established feudalism in England by giving large pieces of land as fiefs to his vassals, or **barons** from Normandy. To avoid the problems that other feudal kings had encountered, he insisted that all **subvassals**, or vassals to other vassals swear allegiance to the king first, establishing both a stable political base and a powerful military for the monarchy. William built a strong government based on the resources and authority of the previous Anglo-Saxon rulers, claiming to be their rightful successor. He created the **Curia Regis (Court of the King)**, which was an assembly of barons and bishops that acted as judges and advisors to the king. William retained the Anglo-Saxon system of local administration, putting the local officials, especially the **sheriffs**, under the monarchy's direct control. By supporting the Papal Reform movement, he won the recognition of

WILLIAM the CONQUEROR.

William the Conqueror established feudalism in England by giving large pieces of land as fiefs to his vassals from Normandy.

the pope and control of the English Church. In 1086, William ordered a comprehensive survey of his subjects and their property, even including the number of their oxen for the purpose of assessing his kingdom's taxable resources. This survey was known as **The Domesday Book** and it represents that William's England had attained a degree of centralized control and financial expertise to be found nowhere else in medieval Europe.

William's successors, known as the *Norman-Angevin dynasty*, were energetic and capable kings who developed royal power. Under Henry I (r. 1100–1135) and **Henry II** (r. 1154–1189) an effective central government was established. Government departments were established; the *Exchequer* to collect taxes, the *Treasury* to guard and dispense royal money, the *Chancery* to issue royal orders and compose correspondence, and the *Royal Law Courts* to dispense justice. Henry I began the *Circuit Court System*, which sent traveling judges around the nation to hear cases. Henry II established central courts at **Westminster** to hear more difficult cases as well as a *jury system*. Just as Philippe IV of France, Henry II came into conflict with the Church over the questions of taxation of Church properties and the royal authority to judge the clergy. In 1164, he issued the *Constitutions of Claredon*, which ordered that clergy accused of civil crimes be tried in royal, instead of ecclesiastical, courts. **Thomas Becket** (1162–1170), the *Archbishop of Canterbury*, the highest-ranking bishop in England, and one-time friend and *Chancellor* (the highest advisor) to King Henry, opposed these laws. Becket was eventually murdered in Canterbury Cathedral. He was later made a saint of the Roman Catholic Church. Henry was forced to make concessions to the English Church. Yet, despite the setback, the English monarchs continued to exercise great control over the Church. Henry II also accumulated vast holdings in France, which became known as the *Angevin Empire*. His son and successor **Richard I the Lion-Hearted** (r. 1189–1199) kept these territories, but was far too involved with foreign affairs to address domestic problems. His successor, **John** (r. 1199–1216), lost most of the Angevin French possessions to Philippe II Augustus in 1214, due to poor judgment and his alienation of the majority of his French vassals. The humiliating loss, despite a heavy burden of service and taxation to his subjects, was compounded by a conflict with Pope Innocent III over the appointment of Stephen Langton as Archbishop of Canterbury, in which the king was also defeated. Responding with tyrannical policies, John also provoked the Church. In 1215, faced with a rebellion led by Archbishop Langton and his most powerful nobles, John signed the **Magna Carta**, meaning "Great Charter," which was an agreement to limit royal power. It affirmed the traditional privileges of the nobles, clergy, and townspeople, and the monarchy's of respect law and custom. It was also an important first step in the development of representative government in Europe, which exists today and had great influence on the United States.

King John's concession did not resolve the conflict between the nobility and monarchy. It continued throughout the reign of John's extravagant, weak, and foolish son **Henry III** (r. 1216–1272). The king's refusal to work with his barons, use foreign advisors, and make concessions to the Papacy and his pursuit of futile military expeditions led the exasperated nobles to rebel. Under Simon de Monfort, the rebels summoned a **parliament**, or representative assembly, made up of nobles, clergy, and townsmen to decide on a new type of lim-

> **Main Idea:**
> The Norman-Angevin dynasty was composed of energetic and capable kings who developed royal power.

ited monarchy. The rebellion was crushed due to their lack of unity, but Henry's successor, **Edward I** (r. 1272–1307), established Parliament as a regular assembly of representatives. While it was initially an advisory body to the king, its powers and rights grew in the following centuries.

The Crusades

The end of the barbarian invasions, disintegration of feudalism, rise of trade and commerce, growth of papal power and development of national monarchies resulted in new problems. The institutions that feudalism had created, particularly knighthood, had become *superfluous* or unnecessary. With the changes that had taken place in western Europe, feudal vassals were nuisances because of excessive warfare and, therefore, were obstacles to progress. There simply was not enough for them to do, and the feudal world that produced the need for them was rapidly disappearing. **Pope Urban II** found a solution, when he received a request for military assistance from the Byzantine Emperor **Alexius I** (see Chapter 5). Since 1071, Seljuk Turks had invaded the Eastern Roman Empire. Byzantine forces

Pope Urban delivered a sermon at Clermont in France where he declared a Crusade to restore the Holy Land to Christianity.

had been unable to drive the Turks out and turned to western Europe for *mercenary troops*, or paid foreign soldiers. In 1095, Urban delivered a sermon at **Clermont** in France where he declared a *Crusade*, or armed pilgrimage to restore the Holy Land, especially Jerusalem, to Christianity. The entire Middle East and North Africa had been under Muslim Arab control since the eighth century (see Chapter 7). The pope promised salvation for taking up the sword against the Muslims. Urban saw the Crusade as an opportunity to rid western Europe of the warring feudal knights, bring greater prestige and power to the papacy, and force the Eastern Church to accept papal supremacy.

The response to Urban's request was overwhelming. By 1096, four large armies of the *First Crusade* arrived at Constantinople to unite with Byzantine forces in a campaign to remove the Muslim Turks from Asia Minor and then liberate Jerusalem. The second part of the plan was a surprise to the Holy Roman Emperor, who was only expecting mercenaries. He was forced to negotiate separately with each group's leader, as there was no unity among the Crusaders. Despite their promise to assist Alexius in regaining Asia Minor, the Crusading army separated from the Byzantine forces in 1097 after defeating the Turks in a

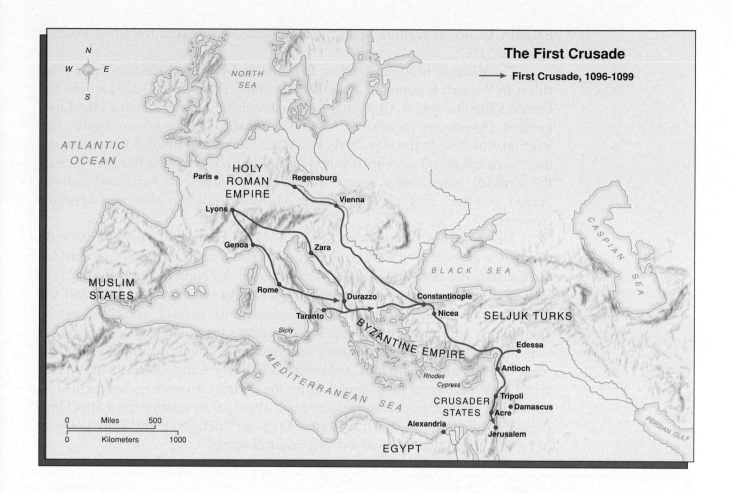

The First Crusade

→ First Crusade, 1096-1099

decisive battle. Once in Syria, the armies split up, each leader anxious to establish his own kingdom. One Crusader state was established at **Edessa** (1097) under Baldwin of Flanders, another at **Antioch** (1098) under the Norman prince Bohemond, and a third at **Jerusalem** (1099) under Baldwin, who made Edessa, Antioch, and **Tripoli** (1100) fiefs of his domain. Disregarding their promises to the Byzantine emperor and the pope, they established an independent feudal hierarchy of Latin Crusader kingdoms under the overlordship of Baldwin, King of Jerusalem.

With the assistance of the Italians, the Crusaders seized the chief Mediterranean seaports in Syria and Palestine, allowing control of the sea routes leading to the Latin kingdoms. They also built a series of castles at strategic locations throughout the area. Three Crusading orders were established; the **Knights Templar**, the **Knights Hospitaler**, and the **Teutonic** (German) **Knights**. Modeled on monastic orders, their members vowed to defend and protect Christians living in and **pilgrims** visiting the Holy Land. Despite all their efforts, maintaining these crusader kingdoms was difficult.

The *Second Crusade* was prompted by the loss of Edessa to the Turks in 1144. Appeals by the pope led to the creation of a crusading army under the Holy Roman Emperor Konrad III and the French King Louis VII. The force was, however, destroyed by the Turks in Asia Minor and unable to assist the Latin kingdoms. In the years following the Second Crusade, an alliance between the Muslim forces of Egypt and Syria, under the leadership of the dynamic general

Saladin, led to the capture of all the Latin kingdoms except for a few isolated castles by 1187.

The disaster brought another Crusade, led by the three most powerful rulers in Western Europe; the Holy Roman Emperor Friedrich I Barbarossa, the French King Philippe II Augustus, and the English monarch Richard I the Lion-hearted. Despite the promise of the *Third Crusade*, it was a failure. Barbarossa left first, but died on the way there. When the French and English kings arrived, their personal disagreements resulted in Philippe's leaving; Richard left to lead the Crusade alone. After several inconclusive battles, Richard and Saladin agreed to a truce that left Jerusalem in Muslim hands but allowed Christians free access.

The **Fourth Crusade** was a wasteful and destructive event that only resulted in further dividing the Christian World. Started by Pope Innocent III, the Crusade did not attract the support expected. Meeting in Constantinople in 1204, the Venetians, who had been hired to transport the Crusaders, and the knights agreed instead to attack the Byzantine capital instead. The city was savagely taken with many lives lost. The Crusaders proclaimed *a Latin Empire of Constantinople* with its own emperor and patriarch. The Byzantine government went into exile in Nicaea and continued to fight the Latin usurpers until 1261, when they recaptured their capital. After the Fourth Crusade, crusading lost its appeal for most Europeans. Despite later attempts to restore the Latin kingdoms, most notably by the Holy Roman Emperor Friedrich II and King Louis IX of France, the movement had lost any real following.

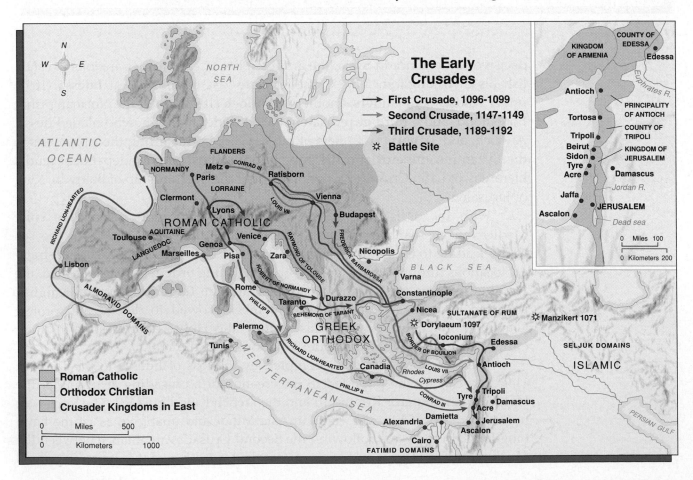

Meeting in Constantinople in 1204, the Venetians, who had been hired to transport the Crusaders, and the knights agreed to attack the Byzantine capital.

The Crusades had many results. On the positive side, they exposed Europeans to the cultures of The Byzantine Empire and the Islamic nations. Many new products and technologies were brought back to the West. The heritage and learning of the Greco-Roman World was re-introduced to the Europeans. A new exchange, both economic and cultural, developed between the East and West. Trade and commerce was encouraged as well as the growth of the merchant class. European exploration was also advanced through the search for alternative trade routes to Asia and the Indian subcontinent. These explorations resulted in the European discoveries of the Americas (see Chapter 17). The feudal system was effectively destroyed with order and stability restored within Europe by the rising national governments. On the negative side, the Crusades created a permanent split between the East and West, the western Europeans earning the hatred of Byzantines and Muslims alike. The Eastern (Greek) Orthodox and Roman (Latin) Catholic churches also divided. The Crusader occupation, which diverted the Byzantines from the advancing Ottoman threat, resulted in the fall of Constantinople to the Turks in 1453.

LATE MIDDLE AGES (1300–1500)

The Late Middle Ages saw great disorder and strife. The changes that took place in the High Middle Ages brought conflict to various groups in society. The internal weaknesses and problems within many of the institutions themselves also created instability. Some of the most serious problems were economic and social in nature, the result of limitations and inadequacies within the traditional systems of agriculture, commerce, and industry. The weak position of the Holy Roman Emperor after the election of Rudolf of Habsburg in 1273 became clearer in succeeding years. In 1356, **Emperor Karl (Charles) IV** (r. 1347–1378) issued a document known as the **Golden Bull**, which provided that the Holy Roman Emperor would be chosen by seven princes who would be designated as *electors*. These rulers were the archbishops of **Cologne**, **Trier**, and **Mainz**, and the princes of **Saxony**, **Brandenburg**, **the Palatinate**, and **Bohemia**. Each elector was also granted complete independence within his own territory. After 1356,

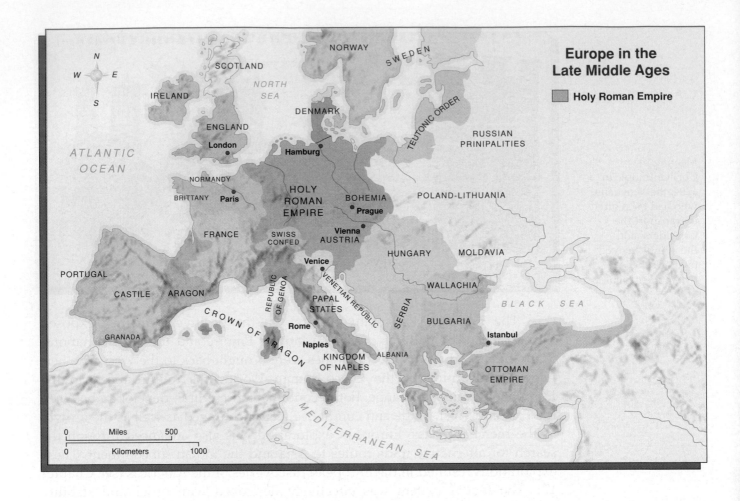

Europe in the
Late Middle Ages

[ ] Holy Roman Empire

the Empire was decentralized further as other princes demanded and gained the same kind of independence as the electors. The Holy Roman Empire became little more than a confederation of hundreds of independent German states. The emperor could call representatives of this confederation together for an *Imperial Diet*, but the decisions this body made could not be enforced. As emperor, he had no army, tax system, or courts other than those within his own kingdom.

France and England

The histories of France and England are linked from 1300 to 1500 by the **Hundred Years' War** (1337–1453), which was a conflict over English possessions in France that began in the twelfth century. The first part of the struggle ended with Philippe II Augustus' annexation of the northern Angevin Empire in 1214. Strong French kings constantly pressured the English, who still held important southern possessions. A rivalry also developed between the two nations over Flanders, which was dominated by France, but depended on English wool. In 1328, the last Capetian king died without an heir. The French nobles chose a cousin of the Capetians, **Philippe of Valois**, who ruled as **Philippe VI** (r. 1328–1350). **King Edward III** of England (r. 1327–1377), a grandson of Philippe IV, also laid claim to the French throne in 1337. This gave the French king an excuse to "confiscate" the remaining English possessions. These actions led to war.

France recovered under Charles V, who rebuilt the military and increased royal income.

The first phase of the Hundred Years' War (1337–1360) almost destroyed France. Establishing control over the Channel, the English invaded France and wiped out the French armies in two major battles; **Crecy** (1346) and **Poitiers** (1356). Most of the French nobility was killed, and **King Jean II** (r. 1350–1364) was captured and taken to England. A peasant rebellion known as the **Jacquerie** followed in 1358, which resulted in groups of unpaid soldiers ravaging the French countryside. King Jean eventually bought his freedom by agreeing to *the Treaty of Bretigny* (1360), in which he paid a huge ransom and gave Edward more French territories for which the English king renounced his claim to the French crown.

The next part of the war (1364–1380) consisted of limited and indecisive battles. This was due to internal problems in both nations. France recovered under Charles V (r. 1364–1380), who rebuilt the military and increased royal income, but lost these gains during the reign of his incompetent successor, **Charles VI** (r. 1380–1422). Corrupt relatives, who used their power for personal profit, controlled the child when he became King Charles VI. As the king began to suffer spells of insanity, two rival groups, the *Burgundians* (followers of his uncle) and the *Armagnacs* (supporters of his brother) struggled for power, throwing the nation into chaos and civil war. Problems also engulfed England. Both Edward III and his successor, **Richard II** (r. 1377–1399), came into conflict with the Parliament, which had gained authority in the spending of money as well as the raising of taxes, over the cost of the war against France. Troubled by social and economic problems that led to the **Peasant's Revolt** in 1381, the autocratic Richard was deposed in 1399 by Parliament and replaced with the cooperative **Henry IV** (r. 1399–1413). His successor, **Henry V** (r. 1413–1422), invaded France, crushing the French forces in the *Battle of Agincourt* (1415). With the support of the Burgundians, he established control over most of northern France. In 1420, he forced Charles VI to accept the humiliating *Treaty of Troyes*, which stated that Henry would marry Charles' daughter and that the child of that union, **Henry VI** (r. 1422–1461) would rule both nations. In the event that Charles died before the child was of age, Henry would rule France as regent.

After both Henry and Charles died in 1422, the French rallied around Charles VII (r. 1422–1461), the son of Charles VI. With the *Battle of Orleans* (1429), the French armies began winning great victories. The force behind this recovery was not the timid Charles, who was unable to organize his nation at first, but a young peasant girl, **Jeanne of Arc**. Dressed like a man, she inspired both the troops and Charles to take the offensive and drive the English out of France. In 1430, Jeanne was captured by the Burgundians and given to the English, who burned her at the stake as a heretic in 1431. By 1453, the English had lost all of their French possessions except the port of Calais. Realizing the need for a powerful central government, the monarchy gained sweeping powers, destroying the feudal basis of French society. When Charles died in 1461, his son, **Louis XI** (r. 1461–1483), inherited a

The French armies began winning great victories as a result of the actions of a young peasant girl, Jeanne of Arc.

strong base from which to rule. The experience of the Hundred Years' War convinced the French that an absolute monarchy was needed to keep the nation unified. The growth of royal absolutism, however, seriously hurt France's ability to progress and compete in later centuries.

The defeat in France resulted in an internal conflict between the two most powerful families in England, the **Houses of Lancaster and York**. The Yorkists, who had a strong claim to the throne through Richard II, blamed the loss of France on the Lancastrians, particularly Henry VI. This struggle, known as the **War of the Roses** (1453–1485), resulted in the extermination of most members of both families. In 1485, Henry Tudor, a Lancastrian commander, defeated and killed the Yorkist king **Richard III** (r. 1483–1485). He assumed the throne as **Henry VII** (r. 1485–1509), marrying Elizabeth of York and establishing a new dynasty of English kings, the *Tudor dynasty*. Although the English defeat in France and the resulting civil war seemed to be catastrophic at the time, it ultimately made England a great power. The loss of their French territories forced the English to concentrate on developing the resources of the island itself. This resulted in the steady growth of a profitable wool trade and the creation of a navy. England's mastery of the seas and development of industry were the source of its later greatness.

Spain and Portugal

The **Reconquista** or "reconquering" of the Iberian Peninsula from the Moors by Christian powers resulted in the creation of the Spanish and Portuguese nations. This was a slow and discontinuous process that began in 900 when Spanish Christians conquered the land north of the Duoro River, establishing the Kingdom of Leon. About 950, part of the kingdom separated into an independent state, **Castile**. Rivalries between the two temporarily stopped the progress of the Reconquista until 1031, when the Muslims became involved in a civil war. In 1037, Leon and Castile united into one kingdom, capturing the greater part of the peninsula as far as **Toledo** by 1085.

The kingdom of **Aragon** rose to prominence in the eleventh century. It consisted of Aragon and the counties of **Navarre**, **Saragossa**, and **Catalonia**. Even though it was less powerful than Castile, Aragon captured **Valencia** and the **Balearic Islands** from the Moors. Its location on the Mediterranean made the kingdom very wealthy and important.

Portugal emerged as an independent nation-state in the twelfth century. Originally part of the Kingdom of Castile, the county was given to **Henri of Burgundy**, a knight who had been instrumental to its capture from the Moors, as a fief by the Castilian king. In 1139, his son, **Alfonso Henriques** (r. 1139–1185), declared himself king of the independent nation of Portugal. With the intercession of the pope, **Alfonso VII of Castile** (r. 1126–1157) agreed to recognize the new title. In 1147, Alfonso Henriques gained more territory from the Muslims, including the port city of **Lisbon**. In 1249, Portuguese troops captured the remaining Muslim territory to the south, the **Algarve**, which fixed the country's borders. The new nation developed a separate cultural identity and language as well as a strong national monarchy. During the second part of the fourteenth

Main Idea:
Portugal emerged as an independent nation-state in the twelfth century.

Queen Isabella I of Castile married King Ferdinand II of Aragon, uniting their kingdoms and creating the nation of Spain.

century, Portugal fought long wars with Castile over its independence. In 1385, the Portuguese defeated the Castilians at the *Battle of Aljubarotta*, assuring Portugal's survival as a nation. Under Joao (John) I (r. 1385–1433), Portugal began a program of overseas exploration that brought great wealth and prestige to the nation. Juan's son, **Prince Henrique (Henry) the Navigator** (r. 1394–1460) inspired the fifteenth-century search to circumnavigate Africa.

Despite the wars with Portugal, the Kingdom of Castile continued to gain territory from the Moors. In 1212, the Castilian king led a Chistian army that destroyed the North African **Berber** Army at the **Battle of Las Navas de Tolosa**. With the Berber's destruction, Moorish resistance collapsed, and the Castile captured **Cordova** and **Seville**. In 1469, **Queen Isabella I** of Castile (r. 1474–1504) married **King Ferdinand II** of Aragon (r. 1458–1516), uniting their kingdoms and creating the nation of Spain. In 1492, Spanish forces conquered the last Muslim stronghold of **Grenada**. With the unification of the nation complete, the Spanish government turned to overseas exploration and competition with Portugal.

The Inquisition, which was originally created to find and eliminate corruption in the Catholic Church eventually became a means of forcing religious conformity throughout western Europe. In Spain, the Inquisition became a means by which the monarch could crush religious and political dissent. Under the control of Head Inquisitor, Tomas de Torquemada, terror and violence was used to kill and drive out dissenting Christians who would not conform to Catholicism as well as Jews and Muslims who would not convert.

The political upheaval experienced in western Europe in the Late Middle Ages was in part the result of social and economic problems. Economic growth from 1000 to 1300 resulted in sustained population growth, which strained the limited capacity for food supply. Famines and economic depressions followed in the fourteenth and fifteenth centuries. In addition, a devastating disease known as the **Black Death**, an epidemic of **bubonic plague**, spread over Europe from 1347 to 1350 and then returned periodically from the fifteenth to the seventeenth centuries. The Black Death was brought to Europe from the East on ships by rats

A devastating disease known as the Black Death spread over Europe from 1347–1350.

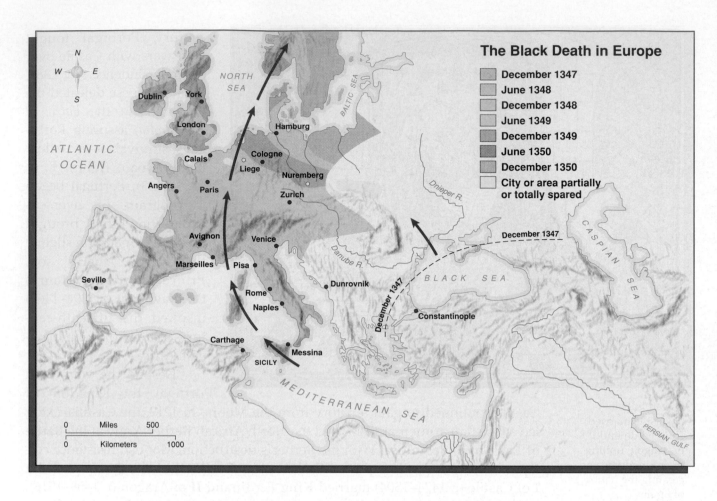

The Black Death in Europe

- December 1347
- June 1348
- December 1348
- June 1349
- December 1349
- June 1350
- December 1350
- City or area partially or totally spared

infested with fleas whose bites transmitted the disease to the human bloodstream. It is estimated that a third of Europe's population was wiped out between 1347 and 1350. By the early fifteenth century, there were half as many people as there had been in 1300. It was not until 1450 that the economic and social stresses began to subside, as royal absolutism restored order and the outbreaks of plague ended.

MEDIEVAL SOCIETY

The greatest influence on Medieval society was the Roman Catholic Church. It shaped the culture and organization of the Middle Ages. After the fall of the Roman Empire, it was the only institution of the old order left. The Church soon converted Germanic rulers and provided them with guidance in creating a new society. Yet, the Germans influenced the Church as well. It had to adjust to meet the needs of its new adherents, which were often very different from those of the Romans. From the start, the patriarch or pope of Rome became the sole representative of the Romans to the new rulers. The papacy took on great responsibilities and powers as well as a role of leadership. As the Germanic tribes converted to Christianity, the pope's flock grew. The concept of **papal supremacy**, which was the belief that the pope was the head of the entire Church, as well as the *Petrine Theory*, which stated that the popes were direct descendants of St. Peter, the leader of Jesus' Apostles, was used to establish their position as the guardians of true doctrine and right worship. Under **Pope Gregory I the Great** (r. 590–604), the papacy gained great prestige. An excellent administrator and skillful politician, he strengthened papal political and economic power. Regarded as a Latin Church Father, he wrote important works of theology and outstanding sermons. He is also credited with developing Church music known as *Gregorian Chant.*

Main Idea:
In addition to religious activities, the Church cared for the poor and weak, maintained hospitals and schools, and injected the concepts of justice, charity, and mercy into the harsh laws of the Germanic tribes.

The Church's activities were not just religious; it cared for the poor and weak. It maintained the only hospitals and schools, injecting the concepts of justice, charity, and mercy into the harsh laws of the Germanic tribes. Clergymen often served on the councils of Germanic kings, influencing their policies and administrations. The most influential Medieval Christian institution was *monasticism.* Monks served as administrators, social workers, and, most importantly, missionaries. Monasteries became centers of learning, preserving the knowledge and culture of the Greco-Roman past. Unlike those of the East, which were centers of asceticism, the monasteries of the West served the community. Needing guidelines for the different style of monasticism that had developed, Benedict of Nursia (480–543) created the **Benedictine Rule**. It established an orderly daily routine of prayer, work, and study, which was particularly suited to the society. The Rule became very popular, and monasteries of the *Benedictine Order* appeared throughout western Europe.

As western Europe became Christian, the Benedictines became very powerful, accumulating land and wealth through donations and endowments. The efficient maintenance of these holdings often diverted the monks from their spiritual development and community service. Seeking to return to the primitive purity of the Benedictine Rule, a new order, the **Cluniac**, was created in 910. It emphasized religious ritual and worship as the main duty of monks. The Cluniacs became famous for their elaborate and beautiful *liturgies* (religious services). Their concepts of piety, conduct, and efficient administration influenced reform within the Church during the eleventh century. As the century progressed, however, the Cluniac Order grew increasingly wealthy and worldly, losing spiritual objectives. In an attempt to return to the original spirit of monasticism as first practiced by the Desert Fathers (see Chapter 3, Section 3), Bruno of Cologne (c. 1033–1101) founded the **Carthusian Order** in 1084. Settling in very isolated and unattractive places, the Carthusians practiced very severe asceticism, making themselves models of humility and self-denial. In fact, the ascetic became a folk hero in the Medieval World, guaranteed salvation through his rejection of pleasure and wealth. Men and women from all classes joined monasteries and *nunneries* (monasteries for women). This new spirit inspired yet another order, the *Cistercian*, founded in 1098 at Citeaux in Burgundy. Founded in wild and isolated places to escape the distractions of the world, the Cistercian monasteries became centers of learning and prayer. The new order owed much of its popularity to the leadership of **Bernard of Clairvaux** (1113–1153), an outstanding preacher who became

Under Pope Gregory I the Great, the papacy gained great prestige.

influential throughout western Europe. He insisted that a monk had to be prepared spiritually through long prayer, contemplation, and physical denial, to go out and fight sin and indifference. With their success, however, the Cistercian monasteries became wealthy and often lax in spiritual discipline. An order called the *Augustinian Canons* was organized in 1100 to improve the moral character of the cathedral clergy, who often found it difficult to be pious while holding administrative responsibilities. By the thirteenth century, *medicant* or begging orders appeared. Fearing that any order, no matter how ascetic, would eventually become worldly if it possessed wealth, they adopted a policy of absolute poverty, living by begging. They lived among the people, setting an example of humility and morality. Their preaching had its greatest impact on urban populations. The *Dominicans* were founded by a Spanish priest, Dominic (1170–1221), to combat heresy in southern France. Their sincerity and lack of wealth made them very popular and effective in preaching orthodox Church doctrine. In Italy, a contemporary of Dominic, **Francis of Assisi** (c. 1182–1226), founded a similar order, the *Franciscans*, based on absolute poverty and theological simplicity. Unlike the educated Dominicans, the early Franciscans were simple preachers, emphasizing basic Christian values. Despite the initial suspicion and dislike of the medicant orders, especially the Franciscans, both were confirmed by the papacy by 1216.

As was the case with most of the aspects of Medieval culture, architecture and art were dominated by religion. Medieval society regarded artists as craftsmen, but some architects attained positions of great authority and respect. Architecture was revived in the eleventh century as Europe came out of feudalism. The term **Romanesque**, which applies to art and architecture between 1000 and 1200, refers to the Roman elements of that style. The term, which was given to the period much later on, is inaccurate as Romanesque architecture and art actually borrowed from many styles including Byzantine and Islamic. Romanesque architecture, which was almost completely churches, used barrel and cross vaults to support the high ceilings, giving a massive appearance. Due to the great pressure and weight on the walls, large windows were impossible, and this gave churches dark interiors. The Cluniac revival and growth of new monastic orders created a demand for churches in the Romanesque style. Examples of this are Notre Dame la Grande (church) in Poitiers (France), Saint-Sernin (cathedral) in Toulouse (France), the Cathedral Church of Worms (Germany), and Sant'Ambrogio (church) in Milan (Italy). Romanesque churches were also built along the great pilgrimage and Crusader routes, such as the Cathedral of Santiago (St. James) at Compostela (Spain). Romanesque art consisted of both sculpture and painting. The walls were decorated with frescoes

The Cathedral of St. James is an example of Romanesque architecture.

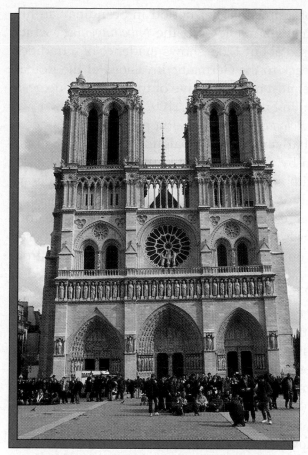

Notre Dame is an outstanding example of Gothic architecture.

while the massive *piers* (supports) were adorned with sculptures. Romanesque sculpture was also noted for its large scale.

In a desire to achieve height and light in churches, the **Gothic** style was created. The Gothic church was an attempt to leave the darkness and mystery of the Romanesque style. Appearing in the mid-twelfth century, Gothic architecture reflected the intellectual and cultural changes western Europe was undergoing. It consisted of slender columns, pointed arches, and huge windows, which gave the impression of light and majesty. This was made possible by the development of the flying buttress which allowed for large windows, since walls no longer supported the roof. Outstanding examples of Gothic architecture are the Abbey of Saint Denis (monastic church), Notre Dame (cathedral) in Paris, and the cathedrals of Chartres, Rheims, Amiens, Strasbourg, and Bourges in France, as well as the cathedrals of Lincoln, Salisbury, and York in England and Cologne Cathedral in Germany. Gothic sculpture was far more proportioned and realistic than the Romanesque. Gothic painting was most noted for its *stained glass windows* (there was little room for frescoes) and *manuscript illumination* (illustrations in books).

Medieval literature was dominated by religion until the Late Middle Ages when vernacular writing revived secular subjects. The majority of written medieval works were in Latin, chiefly dealing with theology, philosophy, law, morality plays, and the lives of the saints. This is not surprising as literacy was limited to clergymen and monastics until the Late Middle Ages. As in Byzantium, poetry was limited to hymn writing, with its monastic composers remaining anonymous. It was the oral poetic traditions of the Germanic and Scandinavian peoples that revived secular poetry. The earliest form of this is the *epic poem* or *chanson de geste* (songs of warrior's deeds). The first existing example is the Anglo-Saxon epic *Beowulf*. It was not written down until much later, but it probably dates back to about 800, reflecting the culture of pre-Christian Germanic society. The *Norse Sagas*, which were not written until the twelfth and thirteenth centuries, also reflect the violence and

The Cathedral of Salisbury is another example of Gothic architecture.

Stories like the legends of King Arthur were extremely creative; the historical events described in them, however, were usually wrong.

paganism of a much earlier period in Scandinavian history. The chief Germanic epic, the *Nibelungenlied*, which was composed about 1200, shows evidence of a tradition that dated back to the Germanic invasions of the Roman Empire. The most representative of the chansons de geste were written in France around 1100. The best known was the *Song of Roland*, which tells of a heroic knight's deeds while on Charlemagne's campaign against the Moors in 778. Written by a Spanish contemporary, the *Song of the Cid* dealt with exactly the same subject. The new literary form of the lyric poem soon rivaled the epic. This became very popular, especially among the nobility. Its creators, traveling bards (singing poets) called **troubadours**, based their works on emotion, longing for love or suffering from a lack of it, rather than the action and adventure used in the epics. The lyric writers developed a new literary form that examined the self, emotions, and values. Unlike the writers of the epics, the troubadours were not anonymous, composing in very distinct styles. By the twelfth century, the epic and lyric traditions were fused together to produce a new kind of poetry, the *romance*. This was a combination of romance and adventure that usually centered on three themes: the deeds of Charlemagne, the legends about King Arthur (legendary English ruler), and the stories of Greek and Roman heroes. The historical events were usually wrong, and the love story was exaggerated; yet they were extremely creative. Among the most outstanding examples were Chretien de Troyes' *Romance of the Rose*, a twelfth-century French work that established a model of the ideal knight; Gottfried von Strasbourg's *Tristan and Isolde*, a thirteenth-century German examination of two lovers; Wolfram von Eschenbach's *Parzival*, another thirteenth-century German romance about a knight's quest for the Holy Grail (legendary cup Christ used at the Last Supper); and Thomas Mallory's *The Death of Arthur*, a fifteenth-century English treatment of the Arthurian legend.

Literature in the vernacular evolved into prose as well. Stories, often with strong social messages, began to appear by the fourteenth and fifteenth centuries. Society's faults and injustices were pointed out. They examined the life of the common person rather than legendary kings or epic heroes. This literature often poked fun at medieval institutions, particularly the Church. Geoffrey Chaucer's *Canterbury Tales* and William Langland's *Piers the Ploughman* are examples of this.

Historical writing was dominated by monks and largely a series of universal histories or monastic chronicles in Latin. Many times they were actually of a record of events in a particular monastery. These accounts often mixed **haigiography** (see Chapter 5) with history. Some universal histories, however, were exceptional such as the *History of the Franks* by Gregory of Tours (c. 539–594), the *History of the English Church and People* of Bede (c. 673–735), and *the History of the Kings of Britain* by Geoffrey of Monmouth (died 1155). There were also works that differed from the standard universal account or chronicle. The *Life of Charlemagne* by the diplomat Einhard (c. 770–840), who knew the subject per-

University of Paris
(14th century).

sonally. Gerald of Wales (c. 1145–1223) combined history with geography and anthropology in his two works, the *History and Topography of Ireland* and the *Journey Through Wales*. By the Late Middle Ages, histories written in the vernacular began to appear, such as Geoffroy de Villehardouin's (c. 1150–1218) account of the Fourth Crusade and the history of the Hundred Years' War by Jean Froissart (c. 1337–1410) in his *Chronicles*. Despite great bias and inaccuracies, these later works rejected the universal historical format and broke free of the monastic tradition.

Theology and philosophy were joined together in the Middle Ages. Until the mid-eleventh century, monastic schools were the only centers of learning. They were replaced by the **cathedral schools**, which were located in urban areas, making education more accessible. During the twelfth century, a new institution appeared, the *university*, which began as a *guild* (Medieval union of artisans) of students and teachers. It grew out of the cathedral schools in northern Europe and, unlike the Italian universities, was run by the teachers, not the students. Founded in 1200, the University of Paris, the first in northern Europe, was soon followed by others (Chartres, Oxford, and Cambridge). Medieval cathedral schools and universities produced the *Scholastic movement*, which taught that philosophy could be used to better understand theology. Called **Scholastics** or Schoolmen, these thinkers argued that faith and reason were compatible. They believed that God had already revealed truth to humanity and it was the task of the individual to apply reason to the Ancient texts, such as the Bible, in order to find it. When their sources conflicted, the Scholastics used the *dialectic*, a method of reasoning adapted from the Ancient Greeks, which tried to show logical connections between opposing statements. The Scholastics also looked to Classical literature for knowledge. The most famous thinkers of the movement were: Anselm of Canterbury (1033–1109), who first developed these ideas and was regarded as the founder of Scholasticism; **Peter Abelard** (1079–1142), whose work *Sic et non (Yes and No)* developed the use of dialectic in theology; and **Thomas Aquinas** (c. 1225–1274), who applied Scholastic principles to practical issues (politics, justice, social relations) as well as theology. In his work, the *Summa Theologica*, Aquinas attempted to show how all knowledge, both Christian and pagan, can be used to find the truth of Christian belief and the existence of God.

Scholasticism was not universally accepted and came under attack by other thinkers. The Franciscan philosopher and scientist Roger Bacon (c. 1214–1294) opposed the use of deductive reasoning and stressed that knowledge of the world must be based on experience. The Franciscan philosopher

Thomas Aquinas applied Scholastic principles to practical issues as well as theology.

John Duns Scotus (c. 1266–1308) developed a different philosophical system, *Scotism*, which taught that faith was more important than reason in order to achieve salvation in the next world. The philosopher William of Ockham (c. 1285–1349) argued that since the existence of God is a *metaphysical* (beyond nature) belief, it is outside the scope of human reason and must be a matter of faith.

LINK TO TODAY
The Christmas Tree

Many modern-day traditions have their origins in the past. When the Germanic tribes that dominated western Europe were converted to Christianity in the Early Middle Ages, they retained many of their customs, giving them new Christian meanings. One example of this is the Christmas tree. It has its origins in the Germanic tribal custom of bringing evergreen trees and shrubs, which they believed contained spirits, into their homes during the winter. This was done during the celebration of the annual winter solstice or the time when the sun is farthest away and the day is shortest. After becoming Christians, the Germanic peoples continued this practice, transforming the custom into a celebration of Christ's birth. The tree came to symbolize both the Tree of Knowledge in Eden, showing humanity's fall, and the cross upon which Christ was crucified, indicating future salvation. Apples, a reminder of Adam and Eve's disobedience to God in Eden, were often hung on the trees. Even though decorations have become more elaborate and less religious, the tradition of the Christmas tree has continued until this day.

Merry Christmas to you.

CHAPTER SUMMARY

The Medieval Period was one of enormous change. Western Europe, which had been a collection of Germanic tribal kingdoms, evolved into a group of powerful nations. The Middle Ages saw the violence and disorder of the early period lead to the creation of a new order. The Medieval Catholic Church had brought order and beauty to a wild and difficult society. Its message of hope and salvation encouraged the population to endure hardship and have faith in medieval institutions. It unified western Europe's many tribes and peoples. The slow rediscovery of the Greco-Roman past, as well as the development of their own institutions, brought western Europe to a new era, one in which experimentation and exploration would take them beyond their greatest expectations. Their medieval childhood ended, the young nations began to grow into powers that would dominate the world.

IMPORTANT PEOPLE, PLACES, AND TERMS

KEY TERMS	PEOPLE	PLACES
Middle Ages	Clovis	Saxony
Medieval Period	Charles Martel	Normandy
Visigoth	Pepin the Short	Anjou
Vandal	Charlemagne	Brittany
Frankish	Otto the Great	Maine
Anglo-Saxon	Pope Gregory VII	Touraine
Merovingian	Emperor Heinrich IV	Clermont
Carolingians	Emperor Friedrich I	Jerusalem
Royal Capitularies	Innocent III	Spain
Tithe	Emperor Friedrich II	Portugal
Carolingian Renaissance	Rudolf of Habsburg	England
feudalism	Hugh Capet	France
fiefs	Louis VII	Castile
knights	Henry II	Leon
lord	Philippe IV the Fair	Compostela
manorialism	Pope Boniface VIII	Notre Dame
serf	William I the Conqueror	Paris
villeins	Thomas Becket	Germany
Holy Roman Emperors	Richard I the Lion-Hearted	York
lay investiture	John	Salisbury
Concordat of Worms	Edward I	Cologne
Lombard League	Alexius I	Orleans
Ghibblines	Pope Urban II	Poitiers
Guelfs	Philippe VI	Angincourt
barons	King Edward III	Papal
subvassals	Charles VI	States
Curia Regis	Richard II	Aachen
sheriffs	Jeanne of Arc	Bavaria
Magna Carta	Richard III	Franconia
		Swabia

KEY TERMS	PEOPLE	PLACES
parliament	Henry VII	Lorraine
Teutonic Knights	Henri of Burgundy	Westminster
Fourth Crusade	Alfonso Henriques	Edessa
Golden Bull	Prince Henrique	Antioch
Hundred Years' War	the Navigator	Tripoli
Jacquerie	Queen Isabella I	Trier
Peasant's Revolt	King Ferdinand II	Mainz
Houses of Lancaster and York	Pope Gregory I the Great	Saxony
War of the Roses	Francis of Assisi	Brandenberg
Reconquista	Jean Froissart	Palatinate
Moors	Peter Abelard	Bohemia
Black Death	Thomas Aquinas	Toledo
Papal Supremacy	Alcuin	Aragon
Benedictine Rule	Louis the Pious	Navarre
Romanesque	Louis IX	Saragossa
Gothic	Saladin	Catalonia
troubadours		Balearic
cathedral schools		Islands
Scholastics		Valencia
Ostrogoth		Lisbon
Burgundian		Algarve
vassals		Cordova
Knights Templar		Seville
Knights Hospitaler		Grenada
pilgrims		

EXERCISES FOR CHAPTER 6

MULTIPLE CHOICE

Select the letter of the correct answer.

1. In western Europe, which development caused the other three?

   a. The decline of trade
   b. The fall of Rome to the Visigoths
   c. The breakdown of Roman government
   d. A rise in the power of the Christian Church

2. The first powerful Germanic kingdoms was the

   a. Gaulish.
   b. Frankish.
   c. Visigothic.
   d. Ostrogothic.

3. Under Charlemagne, all the following were accomplished EXCEPT for

   a. a uniformity of religion.
   b. a strong central government.
   c. the investigation of local officials.
   d. a revival of learning throughout the Empire.

4. The Treaty of Verdun (843)

   a. unified the Carolingian Empire.
   b. divided the Carolingian Empire.
   c. granted the Carolingian Empire greater territory.
   d. forced the Carolingian Empire to surrender territory.

5. Feudalism was based on

    a. a strong central government.
    b. a need for unity against barbarian attacks.
    c. mutual hereditary obligations.
    d. a balance of power.

6. The form that feudalism took in the Middle Ages was

    a. agriculturalism.
    b. seigneurialism.
    c. manorialism.
    d. hereditarianism.

7. The following were all reasons for the decline of feudalism EXCEPT

    a. an improvement in the climate.
    b. the end of barbarian attacks.
    c. a decrease in population.
    d. the invention of better farming equipment.

8. Which statement expresses a direct result of the Crusades?

    a. The volume of trade decreased as the manors became self-sufficient.
    b. Christians gained permanent control of the Holy Land.
    c. The power of European nations declined due to a lack of interest in world affairs.
    d. Contact with the Muslim and the Byzantine worlds brought new ideas to western Europe.

9. The Concordat of Worms (1122)

    a. granted all powers of investiture to the Papacy.
    b. granted all powers of investiture to the emperor.
    c. compromised all powers of investiture between emperor and the Papacy.
    d. granted all powers of investiture to a Church council.

10. The Reform Movement within the Roman Church did all of the following EXCEPT

    a. force celibacy on the clergy.
    b. restore the Church's power of investiture of the clergy.
    c. put an end to corruption among the clergy.
    d. reunite with the Eastern Orthodox Church.

11. The king who successfully ended Papal interference in French affairs was

    a. Philippe II Augustus.
    b. Louis IX.
    c. Philippe IV the Fair.
    d. Louis XI.

12. Jeanne of Arc was the inspiration to lead France to victory in the

    a. War of the Roses.
    b. Third Crusade.
    c. Hundred Years' War.
    d. Thirty Years' War.

13. All of the following were created by the English king Henry I EXCEPT

    a. the Chancery.
    b. the Curia Regis.
    c. the Royal Law Courts.
    d. the Circuit Court System.

14. The Constitutions of Claredon ordered that clergy accused of civil crimes be tried in

    a. a civil court.
    b. an ecclesiastical court.
    c. by a special Papal court.
    d. by a special Royal court.

15. The War of the Roses resulted in the succession of the

    a. Lancastrian dynasty.
    b. Yorkist dynasty.
    c. Tudor dynasty.
    d. Angevin dynasty.

16. The Benedictine monastic order emphasized

    a. prayer and work.
    b. meditation.
    c. liturgical services.
    d. charitable work.

17. The two nations that developed in the Iberian peninsula were

    a. France and Burgundy.
    b. Spain and France.
    c. Portugal and France.
    d. Spain and Portugal.

18. Base your answer on this map below and your knowledge of global history.

What conclusion about the affects of the Black Death can be drawn from this map?

    a. It did not spread beyond Europe.
    b. It was most severe in Europe but was also found in northern Africa and Asia.
    c. It affected only crowded urban areas.
    d. It spread rapidly throughout the Russian states.

19. Which is the correct chronological order of events?

    1. Rise of independent towns
    2. The outbreak of the bubonic plague
    3. Decline of feudalism
    4. Rise of independent nation-states

    a. $1 \rightarrow 2 \rightarrow 3 \rightarrow 4$
    b. $4 \rightarrow 1 \rightarrow 2 \rightarrow 3$
    c. $2 \rightarrow 3 \rightarrow 4 \rightarrow 1$
    d. $3 \rightarrow 4 \rightarrow 1 \rightarrow 2$

20. Unlike the Greco-Roman World, the chief institution responsible for learning in the Middle Ages was

    a. government.
    b. the Church.
    c. the military.
    d. government-sponsored schools.

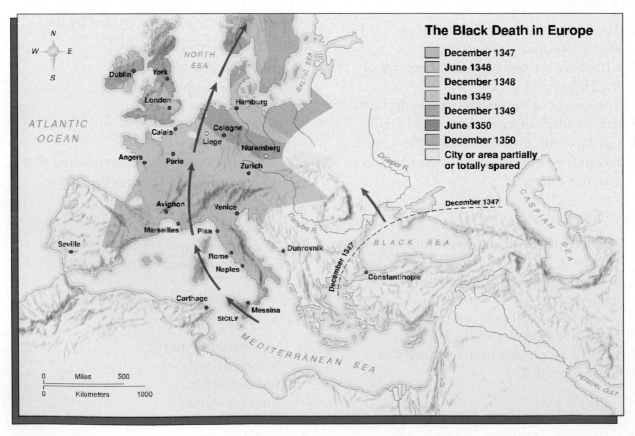

The Black Death in Europe

December 1347
June 1348
December 1348
June 1349
December 1349
June 1350
December 1350
City or area partially or totally spared

1. To what extent were the Middle Ages a combination of Classical, Byzantine, and Germanic civilizations? Show one example of the influence of each on Medieval culture.
2. Was manorialism a practical system for Europe in the ninth and tenth centuries? Show two reasons for its development and two benefits this system offered.
3. What political, economic, social, and technological developments made the prosperity and advanced civilization of the High Middle Ages possible? Show one way each development above led to feudalism's decline after 1000.
4. Why did national monarchies develop in Germany, England, France, and Spain during the High and Late Middle Ages? Show one factor for each nation that made this process different in each nation.
5. Did the Crusades transform Europe? Show three ways that Crusader ideas and institutions led to changes in western Europe.

DOCUMENT-BASED QUESTIONS

This task is based on the accompanying documents. Some of these documents have been edited for the purposes of this task. This task is designed to test your ability to work with historical documents. As you analyze the documents, take into account both the source of each document and the author's point of view.

Directions: Read the following documents and answer the questions after each document. Use the information in the reading and this chapter in writing your answers.

Document #1

DUTIES OF VASSALS AND LORDS

He who swears fealty to his lord aught always to have these six things in memory; what is harmless, safe, honorable, useful, easy, practicable. Harmless, that is to say that he should not be injurious to his lord in his body; safe, that he should not be injurious to him in his secrets or in the defenses through which his is able to be secure; honorable, that he should not be injurious to him in his justice or in other matters that pertain to his honor; useful, that he should not be injurious to him in his possessions; easy or practicable, that that good which his lord is able to do easily, he make not difficult, nor that which is practicable he make impossible for him.

However, that the faithful vassal should avoid these injuries is proper, but not for this does he deserve his holding; for it is not sufficient to abstain from evil, unless what is good is done also. It remains, therefore, that in the same six things mentioned above he should faithfully counsel and aid his lord, if he wishes to be looked upon as worthy of his benefice and to be safe concerning the fealty which he has sworn.

The lord also ought to act toward his faithful vassal reciprocally in all these things. And if he does not do this he will be justly considered guilty of bad faith, just as the former, if he should be detected in the avoidance of or the doing of or the consenting to them.

Letter of Fulbert, Bishop of Chartres (1020) *Feudal Documents,*
from *Translations and Reprints from the Original Sources of
European History,* vol. IV (University of Pennsylvania)

1. How was the Feudal Code designed to keep order and balance power in Medieval Europe?
2. What ideas and values does the Feudal Code emphasize?

Document #2

MEDIEVAL MANOR

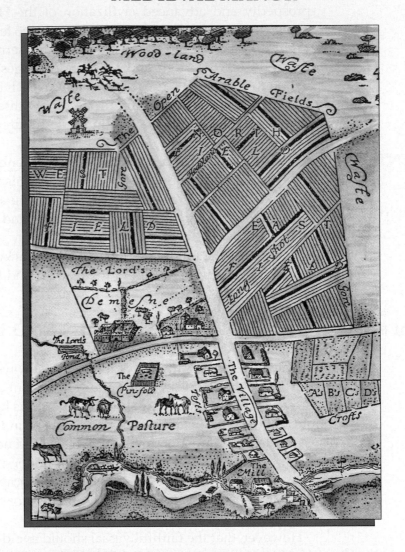

1. In what ways does this illustration of a manor show the organizational style of feudalism in Medieval western Europe?
2. What advantages and disadvantages did this isolated and self-sufficient way of life have for those living on it? Give two examples of each.

Document #3

POPE URBAN II PREACHES
THE FIRST CRUSADE (1095)

In the year 1095 from the Lord's incarnation, with Henry reigning in Germany as so-called emperor, and with Philip as king in France, manifold evils were growing in all parts of Europe because of wavering faith. In Rome ruled Pope Urban II, a man distinguished in life and character, who always strove wisely and actively to raise the status of the Holy Church above all things.

Then on the day set aside for it, he called them together to himself and, in an eloquent address, carefully made the cause of the meeting known to them.

"Most beloved brethren," he said, "by God's permission placed over the whole world with the papal crown, I, Urban, as the messenger of divine admonition have been compelled by an unavoidable occasion to come here to you servants of God. . . ."

"Now that you, O sons of God, have consecrated yourselves to God to maintain peace among yourselves more vigorously and to uphold the laws of the Church faithfully, there is work to do, for you must turn the strengths of your sincerity, now that you are aroused . . . to another affair that concerns you and God. Hastening to the way, you must help your brothers living in the Orient, who need your aid for which they have already cried out many times.

"For as most of you have been told, the Turks, a race of Persians, who have penetrated within the boundaries of Romania even to the Mediterranean . . . occupying more and more of the lands of the Christians, have overcome them, already victims of seven battles, and have killed and captured them, have overthrown churches, and have laid waste God's kingdom. If you permit this supinely for very long, God's faithful ones will be still further subjected.

"I speak to those present, I send word to those not here; moreover, Christ commands it. Remission of sins will be granted for those going.

"O what a shame, if a people so despised, degenerate, and enslaved by would thus overcome a people endowed with the trust of almighty God, and shining in the name of Christ! O how many evils will be imputed to you by the Lord Himself, if you do not help those who, like you profess Christianity!"

"Let those" he said, "who are accustomed to wage private wars wastefully even against Believers, go forth against the Infidels in a battle worthy to be undertaken now and to be finished in victory."

"Let no delay postpone the journey of those about to go, but when they have collected the money owed to them and the expenses for the journey, and when winter has ended and spring has come, let them enter the crossroads courageously with the Lord going on before."

From *The Chronicle of Fulcher of Chartres*
Translated by Martha Evelyn McGinty

Questions

1. What reasons does Pope Urban II present to the knights gathered at Clermont for going on the Crusade?
2. What problems within western Europe would the knights going on the Crusade resolve?

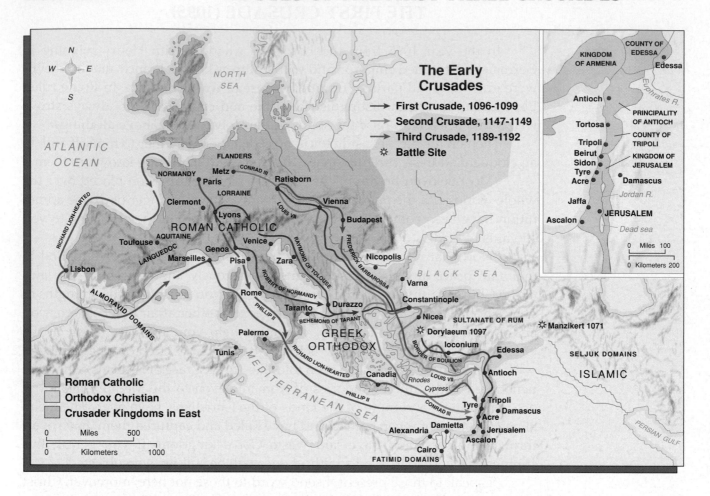

Questions

1. Based on this map, what nations were directly affected by the three Crusades?
2. What benefits and problems did the crusading movement bring to the economic life of the nations shown on this map?

Document #5   **MAGNA CARTA (1215)**

John by the Grace of God, King of England, Lord of Ireland, Duke of Normandy, and Acquitaine, and Earl of Anjou, to . . . his faithful subjects— Greeting. Know ye, that We, in the presence of God, and for the salvation of our own soul, and of the souls of all our ancestors, and of our heirs, to the honor of God, and the exaltation of the Holy Church and amendment of our Kingdom, by this our present Charter, have confirmed, for us and our heirs forever:

That the English Church shall be free, and shall have her whole rights and her liberties inviolable. . . .

We have also granted to all the freemen of our Kingdom, for us and our heirs forever, all the underwritten Liberties, to be enjoyed and held by them and by their heirs, from us and from our heirs.

If any of our Earls or Barons, or others who hold of us in chief by military service, shall die and at his death his heirs shall be of full age, and shall owe a relief, he shall have his inheritance by the ancient relief. . . .

But if the heir of any such be under age, and in wardship, when he comes to age he shall have his inheritance without relief and without fine.

A widow after the death of her husband shall immediately, and without difficulty, have her marriage and her inheritance; nor shall she give anything for her dower, or for her marriage, or for her inheritance, which her husband and she held at the day of his death; and she may remain in her husband's house forty days after his death, within which time her dower shall be assigned.

. . . The City of London shall have all its ancient liberties and its free customs as well by land as by water. Furthermore, we will and grant that all other Cities, Burghs, and Towns, and Ports should have all their liberties and free customs.

. . . To have the common council of the kingdom, to assess and aid . . . we will cause to be summoned the Archbishops, Bishops, Abbots, Earls, and great Barons . . . our Sheriffs and Bailiffs all those who hold of us in chief, at a certain day, that is to say at the distance of forty days (before their meeting), at the least, and to a certain place; and in all the letters of summons, we will express the cause of the summons; and the summons being thus made, the business shall proceed on the day appointed, according to the counsel of those who shall be present, although all who have been summoned have not come.

Magna Carta
Translated by Boyd C. Barrington

Questions

1. In what specific ways does the Magna Carta limit the powers of the monarchy?
2. What groups and individuals benefited from the Magna Carta?

CHAPTER 7

The Rise and Spread of Islam

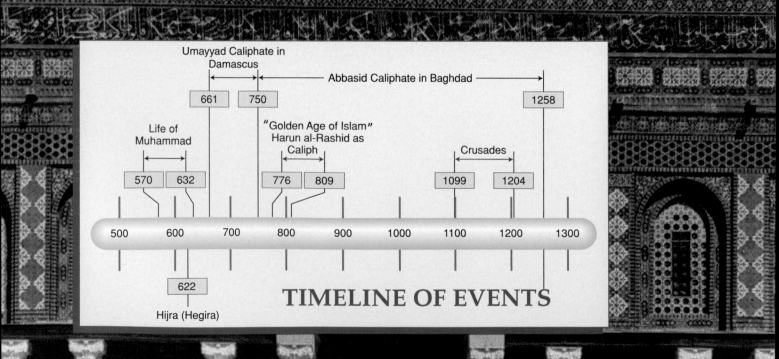

Umayyad Caliphate in
Damascus

Abbasid Caliphate in Baghdad

661   750   1258

Life of
Muhammad   "Golden Age of Islam"
Harun al-Rashid as
Caliph   Crusades

570   632   776   809   1099   1204

500   600   700   800   900   1000   1100   1200   1300

622

Hijra (Hegira)

TIMELINE OF EVENTS

The religion of **Islam** has its beginnings in what is now **Saudi Arabia**, in the seventh century. From there, it spread throughout the Middle East and elsewhere in the next four hundred years and has been a growing religion now in the twenty-first century. To understand its history, we will examine its origins, its basic beliefs, and the reasons for its early growth.

Today, Islam is the religion followed by over one billion people in the world. This figure constitutes approximately 19 percent of the world's population. It is practiced by over 90 percent of the people in the Middle East. It was the third major religion to develop in the area, Judaism being the first and Christianity the second. Many Islamic

Today, Islam is a religion followed by people all over the world. This photo is from an 8th century Grand Mosque in Cordova, Spain.

beliefs come from Judaism and Christianity. The most important element common to all three religions is monotheism, or the belief in the existence of one God, which was first stated by the Jews. The followers of Islam call this one God **Allah**. People who are followers of Islam submit themselves to the will of Allah and are called **Muslims**. *Islam* is defined as "submission." The word *Muslim* is a religious term, while the word *Arab* is a cultural term. There exist both Muslim Arabs and Christian Arabs. Most Arabs are Muslims, but not all Muslims are Arabs. Indeed, the largest Muslim nations are not part of the Arab world. They are Indonesia, Pakistan, and Bangladesh. To appreciate how and why the religion reached these areas from the Arabian Peninsula, it is to that land that we now travel. It was there, in the city of Mecca (*Makkah* in Arabic) that the prophet Muhammad was born.

THE SIGNIFICANCE OF MUHAMMAD

Muhammad lived from 570 to 632. Muslims believe that he was the fourth and most important prophet chosen by God (Allah) to teach and spread holy ideas and thoughts. Muslims accept most of the teachings of Judaism and Christianity and therefore accept the existence of Abraham, Moses, and Jesus as prophets. However, Muslims view these leaders as simply preparing the way for Muhammad. Jews and Christians, accordingly, had not properly preserved and interpreted monotheistic beliefs and practices. It now remained for Muhammad to be the final prophet from the one god and to proclaim the true faith. Knowing about the life of Muhammad is essential for understanding Islam, just as familiarity with the lives of Abraham, Moses, and Jesus is essential for understanding Judaism and Christianity. All four leaders are considered to have had some

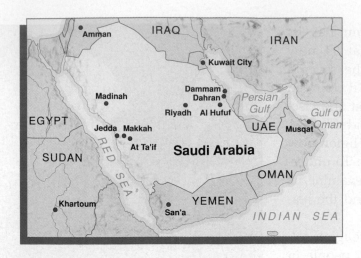

kind of direct contact with God at specific moments. Events in the lives of each have profound religious meaning for the faithful: Abraham with Isaac at Mt. Moriah, Moses at Mt. Sinai, the crucifixion of Jesus near Jerusalem, the revelations to Muhammad in a cave near Mecca.

Muhammad, who was born in *Makkah* (also spelled as "Mecca"), became an orphan at the age of 6 and was raised by an uncle. He married Khadijah, a widow who had a successful career in the caravan trade that passed through Makkah. He helped her in the business. They became parents of several daughters, as well as of a son who died in childhood. In 610, while meditating in a cave outside of Makkah, Muhammad heard a voice in Arabic. This was the first of several revelations that he claimed to hear for approximately three years. He was finally convinced, according to Muslim belief, that he had heard the words of Allah as transmitted by the angel Gabriel. He then began to preach to people in Makkah. The leaders of the city grew to fear Muhammad and his message about what he believed to be the one true God. People in Makkah and throughout the Arabian peninsula had a variety of religious beliefs. There were Jews, Christians, and tribal followers of polytheistic desert gods and spirits. Afraid of the growing hostility toward him and worried about his followers and the attacks upon them, he fled north to the city of **Medina** in 622. This trip, or flight, is the **Hijra** (also *Hegira*). It is one of the most important events in Islamic history. The date 622 is thus the beginning of the Muslim calendar.

The population of Medina proved to be very friendly to Muhammad. They accepted his teachings. The city's original name, Yathrib, was now changed to Medina ("city of the Prophet"). Muhammad's designation as a **prophet** is vital for understanding Islam. A prophet is viewed as a human being who has had some communication with a deity or god and who thus acts as a messenger of the deity to people on earth. Muhammad is thus known as the "messenger of God." Muslims do not worship him; they worship Allah. It therefore would be wrong and improper to label the religion as "Mohammedanism," as some history books do. The inhabitants of Medina saw Muhammad as a religious leader and later as a military leader. As converted Muslims, they now made up a single **umma**. This is a community characterized solely by its acceptance of Islam and Muhammad as God's messenger. The Medina umma and the citizens of Makkah, now considered unbelievers, did not like each other. A series of wars between them ended with the takeover of Makkah by Muhammad and his followers in 630. The great majority of its citizens now declared their loyalty to Muhammad and thus became part of the umma.

The city was now becoming the center of a unified state in the Arabian peninsula. Different groups from all over the peninsula came to Makkah to meet Muhammad and to look at him as a political and religious leader. Arab tribes that had once worshiped idols and spirits now declared their devotion to Islam and the belief in one God, monotheism. Jews acknowledged him as a political

The Dome of the Rock was built by the Muslims in 637 after they conquered Jerusalem.

figure and he in turn welcomed this acknowledgment. However, when he tried to have the Jews convert to Islam and they refused, he turned his back upon them and sought to expel them.

Muhammad remained in Makkah until his death in 632, at the age of 62. He was buried in Medina, which is the second of Islam's three holy cities. Muslims believe that one night toward the end of his life, Muhammad rode to Jerusalem on a winged mare and stepped on a rock before going to heaven and receiving Allah's blessings. He then returned to the rock and rode back to Makkah by dawn. This rock is the one on which Jews believe Abraham was going to sacrifice his son, Isaac. In 637, Muslims conquered Jerusalem and soon thereafter built a structure over this rock. This building is called the **Dome of the Rock**. Consequently, **Jerusalem** is considered Islam's third holiest city.

Makkah is Islam's holiest city. Although it is noteworthy due to Muhammad's being born there, the city had spiritual prominence for centuries prior to his birth. It contained a shrine called the **Ka'ba** (also spelled as Kabbah). The Ka'ba is a black cubical building, approximately 45 feet high. Prior to Muhammad's time, it contained idols brought by many Arab tribes, as well as a black stone. People believed that the Ka'ba and the stone were on the spot where God commanded Abraham and Ishmael, one of his sons, to build a place of worship. Furthermore, in the area immediately surrounding the structure, killing was prohibited. For these reasons, the Ka'ba became a respected holy place for religious pilgrims. Thousands would travel to Makkah for the purpose of making a pilgrimage. Upon Muhammad's return to Makkah in 630, he destroyed the idols in the Ka'ba. Today, the Ka'ba lies within the Great Mosque at Makkah. Muslims now face Makkah when they pray, whereas Jerusalem had previously been the center point of prayer. Today, Muslims thus consider Makkah to be their holiest city with the Ka'ba as their holiest site.

People believed that the Ka'ba is on the spot where God commanded Abraham and Ishmael to build a place of worship.

BASIC BELIEFS OF MUSLIMS

Abu Bakr was an early follower of Muhammad and one of his closest friends. After Muhammad died, Abu Bakr and other followers began to organize Muhammad's revelations into a book. This book was completed around the year 650. It was called the *Quran* (also spelled as "Koran") and means the "recitation." However, it is not viewed as the words of Muhammad, but rather as the words of God. It contains, for example, teachings and regulations covering aspects of daily life. The **five pillars** (obligations) or basic beliefs of Islam are described in the following chart, with corresponding similarities in Judaism and Christianity.

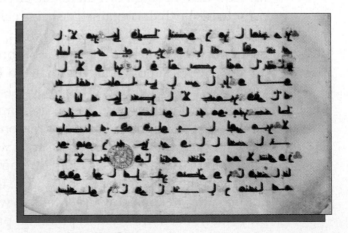

A page from the Quran.

THE FIVE PILLARS	ISLAM	JUDAISM	CHRISTIANITY
Proclamation of faith	"There is no God but Allah, and Muhammad is his prophet."	"Hear oh Israel, the Lord our God, the Lord is one."	"There is but one God, creator of Heaven, earth, and all things."
Prayer	Five times a day, facing Makkah.	Three times a day for some Jews, facing Jerusalem.	Regular prayer encouraged for all Christians.
Fasting	During Ramadan, fasting from sunrise to sunset. Ramadan was the month when the Quran began to be revealed to Muhammad.	Fasting on certain designated days during the year (i.e., Yom Kippur).	Abstinence from certain foods on specifically designated days during the year (i.e., Lent).
Almsgiving (charity)	"Whoever does not know that his need of the reward for giving is greater than the poor man's need of the gift is donating his charity in vain."	"The poor person does more for the giver than the giver does for the poor man."	"It is more blessed to give than to receive."
Pilgrimage (visit to a holy area)	An obligation to make the **haj**, a trip to Makkah once in a lifetime. One who makes the haj is called a *haji*.	Jerusalem is holy because it is the site of the first two Jewish temples and the Western or "Wailing" Wall.	Bethlehem is holy as the birthplace of Jesus. Jerusalem is important as the site of his crucifixion.

OTHER CHARACTERISTICS	ISLAM	JUDAISM	CHRISTIANITY
Holy books	Quran contains 114 *suras* or chapters. The *Shari'a* is a code of law based upon the Quran.	Old Testament (also called the Tanach containing the Torah and other writings). The Talmud has commentaries on the Tanach.	The Bible, containing the Old Testament and the New Testament.
Groupings	Sunni and Shi'ite	Orthodox, Conservative, and Reform	Catholic, Protestant, and Eastern Orthodox
Symbols	Crescent and star	Six pointed star of David	Cross

THE TWO MAJOR GROUPS IN ISLAM

The origin of the two major groups in Islam can be traced to the events that occurred after the death of Muhammad. It was not his intention to have the umma split into different groups. However, he left no instructions about who his successor as leader should be, nor how the successor should be chosen. Within a day after his death from a short illness, several key followers in Medina elected Abu Bakr as *khalifa*. This word means "successor" and in English is **caliph**. Abu Bakr had been very close to Muhammad and was the father of A'isha, Muhammad's favorite wife. (It was not unusual for a man at this time in the Arab world to have more than one wife.) As the first caliph, Abu Bakr sought to maintain unity in the Arabian Peninsula and build up a Muslim empire or **caliphate**. He used military force, for example, against some tribes who had abandoned Islam and refused to pay taxes.

> **Main Idea:**
> Internal conflicts, tensions, and civil wars were features of early Islamic history. Nevertheless, within 150 years of its beginnings, the Muslims built an empire that spanned three continents.

Upon Bakr's death, Umar was elected caliph. When he died, Uthman was elected caliph. His rule as third caliph ended with his murder. The election of **Ali** as the fourth caliph sparked much controversy. His supporters, on the one hand welcomed him. He was Muhammad's first cousin as well as his son-in-law. Ali was the husband of Fatima, Muhammad's daughter. Consequently, as a relative of Muhammad, he would be suitable to succeed as caliph. Such was the view of the Muslims backing him, becoming known as *Shi'a* (the party of Ali; they would also later be known as **Shi'ites**). Opposing him was A'isha as well as relatives of the slain caliph Uthman. They belonged to the *Umayya* clan and challenged Ali on the battlefield. Ali was victorious at the Battle of the Camel (656). This name was given because the fighting took place around the camel on which A'isha sat. Ali was subsequently killed by one of his own supporters for agreeing to have his nomination as caliph reviewed by a set of Muslim arbitrators. Mu'awiya, a member of the Umayya clan became caliph and selected his own son to succeed him. This was the start of the *Umayyad caliphate*. A son of Ali, **Husayn**, mounted a revolt in 680, objecting to these actions, and wanted to reassert the right of Ali's family to rule. Husayn's small army was slaughtered by the Umayyads at Karbala (in Iraq) in 680. The Muslims who supported the first three caliphs and those who supported the Umayyads came to be called "people of tradition and community," or *Sunnis*.

Internal conflicts, tensions, and civil wars were features of early Islamic history. Nevertheless, within 150 years of its beginnings, the Muslims built an empire that spanned three continents. Today, about 85 percent of all Muslims are Sunnis, the remainder are Shi'ites.

THE SPREAD OF ISLAM

It once was said that at its height, "the sun never set on the British empire." This was an accurate statement at a time when Britain had many colonies in various parts of the globe. It no longer is true, as the empire no longer exists. Yet, one can say today that "the sun never sets on the world of Islam." The reason is not that there is an Islamic Empire all over the globe. Rather, the reason is that by

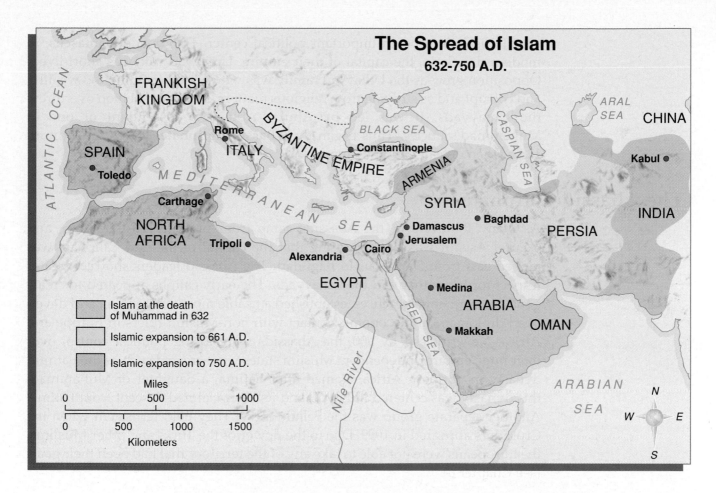

The Spread of Islam
632-750 A.D.

Islam at the death of Muhammad in 632

Islamic expansion to 661 A.D.

Islamic expansion to 750 A.D.

the twenty-first century, Islam has expanded over the many years to every corner of the world. The factors accounting for this growth are many. We will try to examine them.

The Umayyad Caliphate

From 661 to 750, the **Umayyads** created an empire that ranged from the Atlantic Ocean eastward to India. Prior to 661, Arab armies had taken Syria and Egypt from the Byzantine Empire. Military advances continued across northern Africa and made a historic breakthrough in Europe with the conquest of Spain in 711. The skilled Arab armies were frequently able to enlist the aid of armed forces from previously conquered territories. Their further movement into Europe was stopped by Christian armies at the *Battle of Tours* in Southern France in 732, approximately 100 miles southwest of Paris. Spain nevertheless remained under Muslim or Moorish control until 1492. It was known as al-Andalus.

In areas to the north of Arabia, controlled mainly by the Byzantines and Persians, disunity and internal problems made conquest by Arab armies relatively easy. Upon taking Jerusalem, the Umayyads built a monument over the rock on which Muhammad was alleged to have stepped on prior to ascending to heaven. This structure is called, appropriately, the Dome of the Rock. Completed in 691, it is on a site holy to Jews. It was here that the Second Temple stood until it was destroyed by the Romans in 70. The Umayyads never considered Jerusalem to be an important political center. They made **Damascus**, in modern-day Syria, the capital of their empire. Umayyad rule was short-lived. Opposition grew as the Umayyad family was viewed as becoming too wealthy and corrupt and as straying from religious matters. In 750, a rebellion overthrew the Umayyads. It was led by Abu al-Abbas, a descendent of one of Muhammad's uncles. Thus began the **Abassid Caliphate**. It was to last until 1258, when defeated by the Mongols.

The Abassid Caliphate

As many followers of the Abassids came from present-day Iraq, Iran, and Central Asia, it was not surprising that the capital of the new caliphate was moved east from Damascus to **Baghdad**. The Abassid leaders showed greater respect for Islam than did the Umayyads. The early caliphs appeared to create good governmental practices, established a usable monetary system, and developed diplomatic and economic contact with non-Muslim rulers in Europe and Africa. Nevertheless, by 900, the Abassids were losing political control over their huge empire. Independent Muslim states were created such as the Fatimid dynasty in northern Africa. Named after Fatima, a daughter of Muhammad, this dynasty was centered in Egypt, and its ruler claimed descent from Fatima. Another separate group was the Seljuk Turks. They held Jerusalem when the Crusaders appeared in 1099. Due to the power of the Turks and other Muslims, the Europeans were not able to take any of the territory that had been their goals (see Chapter 6).

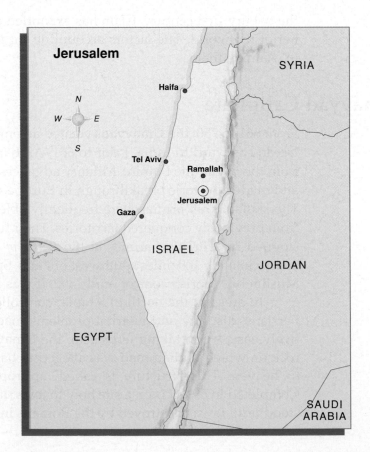

Parts of the present-day Middle East that were once under the rule of the Umayyads (including Israel and the Palestinian territories).

Reasons for Islamic Expansion

The spread of Islam in the time period covered above came about for many reasons. Superior military force was the chief factor. Islamic armies were well equipped and highly disciplined. They were also filled with religious purpose and zeal as they felt compelled to extend the scope of Islam.

This compulsion can be understood in the concept of **jihad** or holy war. This stems from the belief that the world is split into two parts. One is *dar al-Islam*, the land of Islam, containing all areas that are Muslim. The other part is the war territory, *dar al-harb*, containing non-Muslim lands. Such a belief can support the supposed responsibility of Muslims to increase the frontiers of the faith. Therefore, a war to accomplish this is holy. Anyone who dies in this effort will go to heaven. These ideas have, regrettably, been the basis of a series of horrific deadly acts in the late twentieth and early twenty-first centuries. Iraqi leader Saddam Hussein urged the Iraqi people to fight a jihad against the United States and its allies during the Gulf War (1990–1991) and thereafter until his overthrow in 2003. Arab terrorists were responsible for the murder of Israeli athletes at the 1972 Olympic Games in Berlin, the attempt to blow up the World Trade Center in New York City in 1993, as well as several hijackings of airplanes in the 1980s and 1990s. Radical Islamists, Muslims of both Arab and non-Arab background planned and carried out the atrocious and murderous attack on the World Trade Center on September 11, 2001. Such "jihadists," comprising a very

> **Main Idea:**
> Islamic armies were well equipped and highly disciplined. They were also filled with religious purpose and zeal as they felt compelled to extend the scope of Islam.

The Islamic Badshahi Mosque, located in Lahore, Pakistan.

small minority of the world's Muslims, view Americans and Jews as "enemies of God." Such thinking represents, to most Muslims, an extreme distorted interpretation of jihad. Moderate Muslims would explain jihad as the obligation to struggle to better oneself and follow God's will. In fact, some Muslims have suggested that this struggle could be seen as the sixth pillar of Islam.

The expansion of Islam after Muhammad's death did not simply occur because of jihad. The armies of the Byzantine and Persian Empires were weak and offered little resistance. In both of these empires, there were minority populations who were willing to accept Islam and become converts. They had been persecuted because they did not support the official religions of Christianity and Zoroastrianism. In many other conquered areas, the people found the message of Islam appealing and willingly converted. Furthermore, if they converted, they would not have to pay certain taxes. As Islam reached new areas, the inhabitants would usually be offered three choices:

Main Idea:
Modern Muslims would explain jihad as the obligation to struggle to better oneself and follow God's will.

1. Conversion, with full membership including rights and duties in the umma

2. Acceptance of Muslim rule as "protected" people and payment of taxes

3. Fighting or the sword if neither of the first two options was accepted

The second option showed partial respect and toleration by Muslims of Jews and Christians. They were accepted as "people of the book" and could usually continue their religious ways. Yet, they had to pay certain taxes and had to observe some restrictions.

A final reason for the spread of Islam lies outside of military activity. This was trading activities by Muslim merchants. Such merchants, traveling along both land and sea routes, were not primarily interested in spreading the religion. Yet, some of the people with whom they developed commercial ties wanted to learn more about the faith. Trade routes by land went along the Silk Road into the Orient. Water routes passed along the Mediterranean Sea and the Indian Ocean.

MUSLIM ACCOMPLISHMENTS AND CONTRIBUTIONS

For approximately 500 years, (700–1200), the Muslim world ushered in one of history's great civilizations. This can be seen in areas of scholarship, science, and art. Many of the early Abassid caliphs, most notably **Harun al-Rashid**, promoted research and learning. His reign, from 776 to 809, has been described as a "golden age."

A great deal of writing about philosophy and other areas of knowledge from Ancient Greece and Rome was preserved by Muslim scholars and translated into Arabic. Such preservation was vital, particularly with the fall of the Roman Empire in 476. Valuable scholarship might have been lost had it not been for the Muslims. In later years, they would transmit much of this to western Europe (see Chapters 6 and 10).

Accomplishments by Islamic scientists were very advanced. A concern with astronomy was spurred by the need to perform three of the five pillars of

Advances in medicine could be seen in the work of al-Razi, a Persian physician.

Islam: praying five times a day toward Makkah, fasting during the month of **Ramadan**, and making the haj. A lunar calendar was developed as was geographical direction and locations of cities. This also led to a series of carefully drawn maps, by the cartographer al-Idrisi. The astrolabe was developed as an instrument for measuring the angles of the sun, as well as observatories. Advances in medicine could be seen in the work of al-Razi, a Persian physician. He wrote a textbook on smallpox and measles as well as an encyclopedia on medical knowledge from other lands. Buildings that we know today as pharmacies, drug stores, and hospitals were to be found throughout the Muslim world. A Jewish physician, Moses ben Maimon (Maimonides), living mostly in Egypt, also made medical contributions and served as an advisor to several governmental officials.

In the field of mathematics, Muslim scholars significantly were very renowned. Al-Khwarizmi, born in Baghdad, wrote a book about unknown and known quantities. He employed a procedure he labeled as *al-jabr*. This word has come down to us today as *algebra*. He admired the mathematical achievements of Indian scholars, particularly in the use of numbers. He studied the concept of zero and other Indian numerical symbols. Eventually, these notations were passed on to Europe and then to America and became known as Arabic numerals. Another Muslim mathematician, Ibn al-Haytham, wrote a book about optical measurements and described how the passage of rays helps us to see things. Geometric designs were blended into Muslim architecture, mainly in mosques.

Literature, philosophy, and history were additional prominent fields. The best known literary work was *The Arabian Nights*, compiled anonymously. It consisted primarily of tales about the wealth and splendor of Baghdad. The philosopher Ibn Rushd (Averroes), living in Spain, compared Islamic ideas and reasoning with those of Plato and Aristotle. The historian Ibn Khaldun compiled an enormous history of North Africa. He also produced a six-volume history describing those world civilizations that he knew about.

DISUNITY AND DECLINE

The cultural and political greatness of the Muslim world began to diminish after 1200. There were reasons for this change.

1. Disunity was apparent as many local leaders did not wish to obey the caliph in Baghdad.

2. The Crusades had caused much destruction in Middle Eastern lands.

3. Christian Europe grew stronger and was able to defeat Muslim armies in France and to reclaim Spain and Portugal.

4. The destruction of Baghdad by the Mongols in 1258 brought the Abassid Empire to an end.

The best known Muslim literary work was *The Arabian Nights*. This image from the story shows a sultan in his harem. Drawing by J.J. Ford.

LINK TO TODAY

The past is so very often a guide to the present. The U.S. Marine Corps, as well as the United States Army became aware of this truism in 2004 during the Iraq War, and faced a dilemma. The Iraqi city of Najaf is holy to Shi'ite Muslims. It contains the tomb of Ali, located in the Iman Ali Mosque, a holy site. As the fourth Caliph of Islam, and as Muhammad's son-in-law, Ali is a greatly revered figure. Thousands would come to the mosque on pilgrimages. However, during the spring and summer of 2004, several hundred Muslims opposed to U.S. involvement in Iraq, fought pitched battles in Najaf against American forces. In the face of overwhelming firepower from these forces, these Islamic insurgents retreated to the inside of the Iman Ali Mosque. Despite repeated requests by the Iraqi government and U.S. commanders to surrender, they refused and continued to fire their weapons. The problem now facing the U.S. soldiers was not a military one, it was cultural and political. Clearly, from a military standpoint, the Americans could have mounted a successful attack against the fighters, even if it meant causing damage to the mosque. Yet, such a decision would have caused serious resentment among the millions of Shi'ites in Iraq. This would be true, even among the vast majority of Shi'ites who welcomed the American overthrow of Saddam Hussein and did not like what the insurgents were doing. Shi'ites make up more than 50 percent of that nation's population. Their support was definitely needed if the U.S.-led plan for peace and democracy in Iraq was to be fruitful. The United States could not risk alienating such an important segment of Iraq's population.

What should the U.S. commanders do? What would you advise them to do? To learn what happened in Najaf, do some newspaper research in the library or search for Najaf on the Internet.

CHAPTER SUMMARY

As a cultural, political, and economic force, Islam has had a crucial impact in and on world history. As a religion born in the Arabian Peninsula, in a desert community, it spread beyond that territory very quickly. As a result, it gave birth to a distinct culture that nevertheless had some ties to previous faiths and cultures. It found acceptance by diverse peoples for different reasons. In its first 500 years of existence, as covered in this chapter, it made noteworthy achievements in politics, art, and science. These were mainly in the lands of the Middle East and ended with the fall of the Abassids. Yet, it would remain, as we will see, for future Islamic empires to make their own specific additions to the history of our planet. In time, we will meet the Ottomans, the Safavids, and the Mughals.

IMPORTANT PEOPLE, PLACES, AND TERMS

IMPORTANT TERMS	PEOPLE	PLACES
Hijra	Muhammad	Damascus
caliph	Abassids	Baghdad
Crusades	Harun al-Rashid	Saudi Arabia
Allah	Abu Bakr	Makkah
Muslim	Ali	Medina
Islam	Husayn	Jerusalem
five pillars (obligations)	Umayyads	Dome of the Rock
Ramadan		Ka'ba
prophet		
umma		
haj		
Sunni		
Shi'ite		
caliphate		
jihad		

EXERCISES FOR CHAPTER 7

MULTIPLE CHOICE

Select the letter of the correct answer.

1. The caliph associated with the "golden age of Islam" is

   a. Moses ben Maimon.
   b. Ibn al-Haytham.
   c. Harun al-Rashid.
   d. Ibn Rushd.

2. Which is the correct chronological order concerning Muhammad's life?

   a. Hijra, revelations from Allah, conquest of Makkah
   b. Revelations from Allah, Hijra, conquest of Makkah
   c. Conquest of Makkah, Hijra, revelations from Allah
   d. Hijra, conquest of Makkah, revelations from Allah

3. The Dome of the Rock is found in

   a. Israel.
   b. Egypt.
   c. Saudi Arabia.
   d. Indonesia.

4. Which word is connected with pilgrimage?

   a. Ramadan
   b. Haj
   c. Hijra
   d. Quran

5. The split between Sunnis and Shi'ites was over

   a. reasons for jihad.
   b. selection of a leader.
   c. construction of the Ka'ba.
   d. Muhammad's burial site.

6. The issue in the split described in Question 5 concerned

   a. interdependence.
   b. succession.
   c. scarcity.
   d. urbanization.

7. What is the correct ranking order of holy cities to Muslims?

   a. Makkah, Jerusalem, Medina
   b. Jerusalem, Makkah, Medina
   c. Medina, Jerusalem, Makkah
   d. Makkah, Medina, Jerusalem

8. Muslims go to the Ka'ba, Jews go to the Western Wall, Christians go to Bethlehem. These travels are examples of

   a. revelations.
   b. pilgrimages.
   c. holy wars.
   d. sacrifices.

9. Under which heading would a textbook have detailed information on Judaism, Buddhism, Christianity, Hinduism, and Islam?

   a. Imperialism
   b. Movement of people and goods
   c. Environment
   d. Belief systems

10. A person who practices Islam would be most likely to

    a. visit a shrine on the shore of a lake.
    b. pray five times a day.
    c. bathe in the Ganges River.
    d. make a pilgrimage to Jerusalem.

11. The actions of most radical Islamist fundamentalists show that they support

    a. equal rights for women.
    b. American policies in the Middle East.
    c. traditional Muslim teachings.
    d. renewed attempts at modernization.

12. Judaism, Christianity, and Islam share a belief in

    a. the central authority of the Pope.
    b. a prohibition on the consumption of pork.
    c. reincarnation and the Four Noble Truths.
    d. monotheism and ethical conduct.

13. Which heading would be most appropriate?

    1. _____

       A. Jihad
       B. Dissatisfaction with local rulers
       C. Appeal of new ideas

    a. Teachings of Muhammad
    b. Spread of Islam
    c. Disunity between Sunnis and Shi'ites
    d. Defeat of Abu Bakr

14. The "golden age of Islam" was known for

    a. exploration for oil.
    b. military conquests.
    c. literary and artistic achievements.
    d. construction of underground mosques.

15. Which of the following was characteristic of the Abassid Caliphate, the Han dynasty in China, and the Gupta Period in India?

    a. Free elections
    b. Religious intolerance
    c. Overseas expansion
    d. Cultural achievements

16. The Umayyads and the Romans were similar in that they controlled land in

    a. northwestern Europe.
    b. southern Africa.
    c. southwestern Asia.
    d. eastern Asia.

17. During the "golden age of Islam," scholars were encouraged to

    a. reject all knowledge that was Western in origin.
    b. ignore the achievements of Chinese culture.
    c. preserve and expand ancient Greek and Roman learning.
    d. accept medieval western European religious ideas.

18. Which chapter title in a history textbook would describe events such as those that occurred in Rome in 476 and Baghdad in 1258?

    a. Destruction by outsiders
    b. Urban expansion
    c. Scientific achievements
    d. Reasons for civil war

19. A sociologist interested in Arabic culture would most likely focus on the study of

    a. parliamentary government in Lebanon.
    b. oil prices in Iran.
    c. Islam's influence in Saudi Arabia.
    d. economic development in Syria.

20. Study the following picture and then answer the question.

Which religious group would be most concerned and worried about the people in the picture?

    a. Muslims
    b. Christians
    c. Jews
    d. Hindus

1. Describe one way in which Islam, Judaism, and Christianity are similar and one way in which Islam differs from either of the other two religions.
2. Make a ranking list of the three most significant reasons for the spread of Islam. Explain why you picked these reasons in the order you chose.
3. Make believe that you are in Saudi Arabia sometime this year. Write a letter to your social studies teacher about Islam. In your letter, tell him/her about any three of the five pillars of Islam that you have learned from your trip. In the letter, describe three realistic things or actions (one for each pillar) that you saw, or witnessed, being done by Arab people there.
4. The life of Muhammad is important for an understanding of Islam. Describe three events in his life and show they affect Muslim traditions.
5. Describe three achievements of Muslim society during the "golden age of Islam."

DOCUMENT-BASED QUESTIONS

This task is based on the accompanying documents. Some of these documents have been edited for the purposes of this task. This task is designed to test your ability to work with historical documents. As you analyze the documents, take into account both the source of each document and the author's point of view.

Directions: Read the following documents and answer the questions after each document. Use the information in the reading and this chapter in writing your answers.

Document #1

Mecca's leaders feared that accepting Muhammad as the sole agent of the one true God would threaten their power and prosperity. They pressured his kin to disavow him and persecuted the weakest of his followers. Stymied by this hostility, Muhammad and his followers fled Mecca in 622 to take up residence in . . . Medina.

From *The Earth and Its Peoples*, by R. Bulliet et al.

Questions

1. Why were Mecca's leaders afraid of Muhammad?
2. What action did they take against him?

Document #2

Ye shall do battle with them, or they shall profess Islam . . . whosoever shall obey God and His Apostle, He shall bring him into the gardens of {Paradise}; but whosoever shall turn back, He will punish him.

From the *Quran*

Questions

1. Who is doing battle with whom?
2. What does Muhammad promise to those who choose to follow him?

Document #3

The Moslems struck their enemies and laid waste to the country and took captives without number . . . everything gave way to their scimitars [swords] . . . . All . . . the Franks trembled as that terrible army . . . attacked Tours . . . and the fury and cruelty of the Moslems towards the inhabitants of the city were like the fury and cruelty of raging tigers.

From Fifteen Decisive Battles of the World, by E. Crecy

Questions

1. What is the place and country where this battle occurred?
2. How does the writer describe the actions of the Moslems?

Document #4

Questions

1. What were the three continents where Islam had spread by 750 C.E.?
2. Describe the contrast in the size of areas containing Moslems before and after the death of Muhammad.

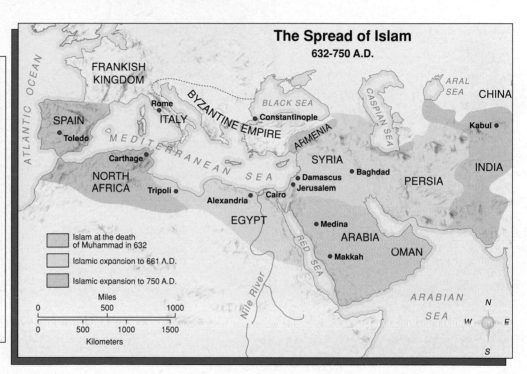

The Spread of Islam
632-750 A.D.

Islam at the death of Muhammad in 632
Islamic expansion to 661 A.D.
Islamic expansion to 750 A.D.

Document #5

Koranic revelation commanded them to "Fight in the cause of God against those who fight you, but do not be the aggressors." The early Muslims thus fought their heathen enemies . . . war against unbelievers was sanctioned by divine revelation and the example of the Prophet. But many Arabs were Christians or Jews. What was to be done with them? Mohammed respected the older monotheistic faiths . . . he called them "People of the book" . . . they were not forced into Islam but were allowed to retain their ancestral religion on payment of tribute.

From The Caliph Omar: Arab Imperialist, by J. J. Saunders

Questions

1. Why were actions against unbelievers required?
2. What would happen to Jews and Christians?

CHAPTER 8
Asia

Section 1—Southern Asia 227

Section 2— China 228

TIMELINE OF EVENTS

Tang Dynasty		Song Dynasty

618   907 960   1279

Muslims in South Asia   Gunpowder in China   Mahmud of Ghazni

711   850   997 1030

600   700   800   900   1000   1100   1200   1300

Southern Asia

The spread of Islam, which we have just learned about in Chapter 7, was to have an impact on southern Asia. This impact first began in the early eighth century, due to invasions. The initial Muslim invasion was successful, chiefly because the southern Asian region at that time was disunited and fragmented. The unity and control under the Gupta Empire (see Chapter 3, Section 1), starting in 320, began to fade away. Its control in southern Asia steadily weakened after 500. The result was the growth of many separate kingdoms. Political unity in the subcontinent no longer existed, as Gupta rule was over by the end of the seventh century. Frequent attacks by outsiders, such as the Huns, Turks, and Mongols severely weakened the empire.

Shortly thereafter, in 711, angered by an attack on an Arab ship near the Indus River, the Umayyad leader of Iraq mounted an attack on Sind (an area in Pakistan). The inhabitants were forced to convert to Islam or face death. A more devastating series of raids into the **Punjab** plains of northern India was carried out by the Afghan **Mahmud of Ghazni** (997–1030). Known as the "sword of Islam," he

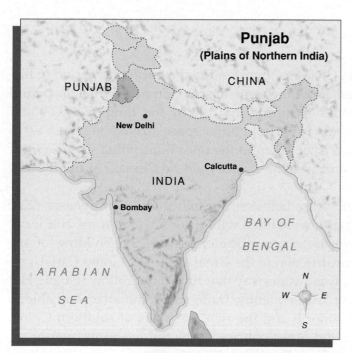

Punjab
(Plains of Northern India)

PUNJAB

CHINA

New Delhi

Calcutta

INDIA

Bombay

BAY OF BENGAL

ARABIAN SEA

N W E S

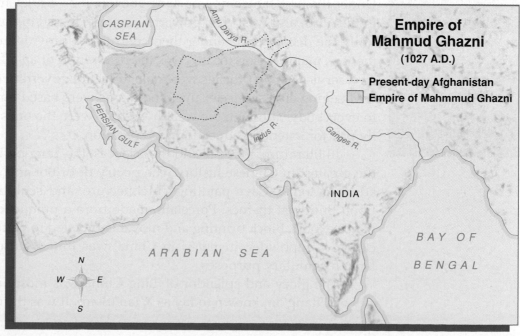

Empire of Mahmud Ghazni
(1027 A.D.)

- - - - **Present-day Afghanistan**
☐ **Empire of Mahmmud Ghazni**

CASPIAN SEA

Amu Darya R.

PERSIAN GULF

Indus R.

Ganges R.

INDIA

ARABIAN SEA

BAY OF BENGAL

N W E S

was said to make these jihads for both riches and the reward of reaching paradise. Hindu temples were burned to the ground, as Mahmud added the Punjab to his own empire. His empire in turn was taken over by other Muslims, who were of a mixed Turko-Afghan background. They were to be the first of several Islamic dynasties in southern Asia. The first of these was the Delhi Sultanate. It was to last for 320 years. Its conquerors were the Mughals, whom we will learn more about in Chapter 19.

SECTION 2

China

In our discussion of Islam in Chapter 7, we described a particular period of history as a golden age. We can apply the same description to a particular period of Chinese history. This would be during the rule by the **Tang** (618–907) and **Song** (960–1279) dynasties. If a visitor from outer space arrived on planet earth in this time period and asked to be taken to the one country that was the most advanced, most powerful, and wealthiest, it would be China. Let us find out why this would be true.

The approximately 400 years between the fall of the Han dynasty (220) and the rise of the Tang Dynasty were filled with disorder, civil wars, and weak emperors. The only noteworthy accomplishments were the building of the **Grand Canal** and further construction of the Great Wall. The Grand Canal, created during the Sui dynasty, was a waterway that linked the Yellow (Huang He) River with the Yangtze River. Consequently, trade and commerce were able to expand between cities of the north and the rich rice areas of southern China. Nevertheless, the harsh tax and other policies of the Sui led to its overthrow. Under the first Tang emperor, Tang Taizong (627–649), China regained territory in the north and west with powerful armies. He and his successors were able to unify the distant parts under their control and provide more efficient management. A major reason for this was the restoration of an efficient and productive civil service. Good officials were able to secure government jobs by passing the challenging civil service exams. The exams were based on merit and were open to everybody, although the wealthy people were the ones who could more easily pay for extended educational preparation.

In literature, the arts, and the sciences, the Tang period is seen as perhaps the greatest in Chinese history. The poetry of Li Boi and Dufu is still read and admired today. Cave paintings, architecture, and sculpture were often based upon Buddhist themes. Porcelain, made from a unique kind of clay, became a major export. Block printing and movable type led to better forms of communication. Gunpowder, invented in China, was initially used for fireworks and, later, for military purposes.

The glory and splendor of Tang China was most apparent in the capital city of **Chang'an**, known today as **X'ian** (Sian). It was the eastern end of trading

Main Idea: Tang Taizong and his successors were able to unify the distant parts of China under their control and provide a more efficient management.

Statue of Buddha in Japan.

Main Idea:
The Song dynasty maintained a dynasty remembered for its cultural achievements and economic prosperity.

routes such as the Silk Road. As a result, it became a huge urban metropolis with people from all over Asia. Among these were Indians, Persians, Syrians, Jews, Vietnamese, Koreans, Japanese, and Turks. As a planned city with a checkerboard grid of broad avenues going north-south and east-west, it contained over one million people. Admired by the Japanese, it was to be the model for such Japanese cities as Nara. Up to this point in world history, the Tang was the planet's largest empire and exceeded those of Rome and the Han.

In spite of its cultural, political, and military achievements, the Tang dynasty began to decline in the eighth century. Heavy taxes were imposed, especially for military purposes. This caused much unrest in a population that now grew more restless. Rebellions grew throughout the empire. Its total land area became too big to control. The Chinese army was weak and suffered a humiliating defeat at the hand of the Arabs at the 751 **Battle of Talas** in central Asia. The Chinese lost control over much of central Asia. In 907, a rebel force stormed and captured Xian and killed the last Tang ruler.

With the fall of the Tang, rival armies now competed for control of China. One of these, to be known as Song Taizu, won out. He reunited most of what had been Tang territory and began the Song dynasty. It was to last from 960–1279. Although the Song rulers never took back any western land and presided over a smaller empire than that of the Tang or the Han, they nevertheless maintained a dynasty remembered for its cultural achievements and economic prosperity.

In this period, landscape paintings became a high art form. Daoist ideas of nature exerted a strong influence on such paintings. Trees, branches, and flowers were often painted. Scholar officials wrote poetry. There were rapid improvements in agriculture and manufacturing. Pumps were increasingly used for crop cultivation and for producing textiles. Paper money made an appearance, aiding widespread commercial activities. The magnetic compass, although developed prior to the Song, was now used more extensively and made China a major Asian sea power. The compass and other Chinese nautical inventions slowly made their way to Europe. Ironically, Europeans would use these one day, as they traveled to China and other parts of Asia. A gigantic astronomical clock was built at the capital city of **Kaifeng**. As an engineering feat, it reflected then-current knowledge of mathematics and calendar making. Running water helped to regulate movements.

The Song era was less known for its military strength. It was unable, for example, to stop attacks from across its northern border. The Jurchen, a Manchurian people, invaded part of Song territory in the twelfth century and created the Jin Empire. Song rulers fled south and built a new capital at **Hangzhou**. Eventually, the Mongols, a more powerful force than the Jurchens, would conquer China in 1279.

CHAPTER SUMMARY

The advance of human progress during the seven centuries comprising this chapter was more evident in China than in India. The eras of the Tang and Song dynasties were two of the greatest in Chinese history, as measured by many criteria. Political unification provided some stability, even though both dynasties eventually suffered internal problems and failed to resist superior military forces. Their culture, scientific, and technological achievements did much to bring pride to Chinese people, then and now. These were times of immense population growth and the rise of several urban areas. Scholars believe that there were ten cities containing at least one million people in each one. For sure, any appreciation of Chinese civilizations must include a study of these two remarkable dynasties.

IMPORTANT PEOPLE, PLACES, AND TERMS	KEY TERMS	PEOPLE	PLACES
	Tang	Mahmud of Ghazni	Punjab
	Song		Grand Canal
			Chang'an (Xian)
			Silk Road
			Kaifeng
			Hangzhou

EXERCISES FOR CHAPTER 8

MULTIPLE CHOICE

Select the letter of the correct answer.

1. The Tang and Gupta Empires both declined as a result of

   a. European penetration.
   b. natural disasters.
   c. foreign attacks.
   d. religious wars.

2. "The recently built Grand Canal will increase trade and provide better irrigation." The person who wrote this lived during which Chinese dynasty?

   a. Han
   b. Sui
   c. Tang
   d. Song

3. Which sequence is placed in correct chronological order?

   a. Tang dynasty, Muslim advance in southern Asia, Song dynasty
   b. Song dynasty, Tang dynasty, increased use of gunpowder
   c. Muslim advance in southern Asia, Tang dynasty, Song dynasty
   d. Song dynasty, Chang'an as a major urban center, Tang dynasty

4. The Tang dynasty in China, the Gupta Empire in India, and the city-state of Athens in Greece during their golden ages were known as eras of

   a. major industrial development.
   b. intense nationalism.
   c. economic poverty and upheaval.
   d. artistic and intellectual achievement.

5. Which religious group suffered most due to the actions of Mahmud of Ghazni?

   a. Jews
   b. Buddhists
   c. Hindus
   d. Catholics

6. The location of Xi'an at the eastern end of the Silk Road would be of interest to a scholar studying the city's

   a. economy.
   b. school system.
   c. defenses.
   d. political system.

7. Although primarily a Chinese city, Xi'an once contained Indians, Persians, Jews, and Japanese. This was an example of

   a. interdependence.
   b. diversity.
   c. imperialism.
   d. nationalism.

8. The Japanese built their city of Nara, using as a model the city of

   a. Beijing.
   b. Kaifeng.
   c. Chang'an.
   d. Hangzhou.

9. The modeling described in Question 8 is an example of

   a. cultural diffusion.
   b. interdependence.
   c. empathy.
   d. economic growth and development.

10. The Silk Road was important because it allowed for the

a. exploration of China by the Persian army.
b. development of agriculture by the nomadic people of central Asia.
c. movement of Chinese armies through Southeast Asia.
d. exchange of goods between Asia and the Middle East.

11. Which heading best completes the following partial outline?

1. _____

   A. Han
   B. Tang
   C. Song

a. Empires of India
b. Latin American civilizations
c. Japanese emperors
d. Dynasties of China

12. A military historian studying China would most likely want to visit the

a. Grand Canal
b. Himalaya Mountains.
c. Great Wall.
d. Silk Road.

Use this map and your knowledge of social studies to answer Questions 13, 14, and 15.

13. Xi'an, the Tang capital, lies in what direction from The Great Wall?

a. North
b. East
c. West
d. South

14. Which statement is true concerning The Grand Canal? It

a. ran east and west.
b. ran north and south.
c. flowed north of Loyang.
d. was used by sailors along the Silk Road.

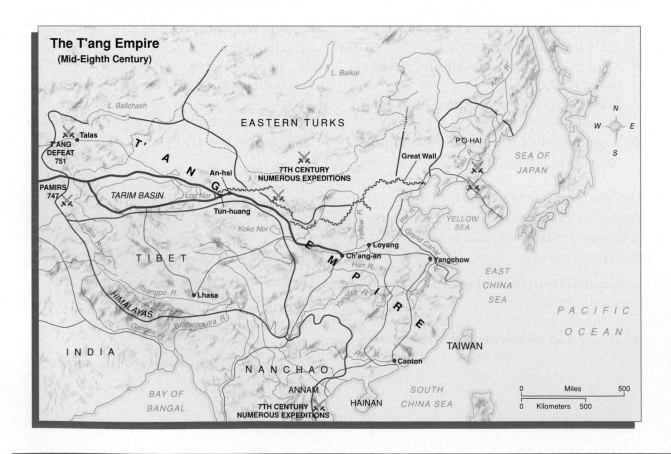

15. The Tang dynasty

    a. was victorious in all its military expeditions.

    b. was larger than present-day China.

    c. took over Japan.

    d. extended into the Middle East.

16. The civil service exam used by the Tang emperors to select government officers was based on

    a. The Twelve Tables.

    b. The Quran.

    c. The Hippocratic Oath.

    d. The Confucian set of values.

17. What term would best describe the cultural achievements of the Tang and Song dynasties as well as those of Ancient Greece in the fifth century B.C.E.?

    a. An era of economic prosperity

    b. A Renaissance

    c. A Golden Age

    d. An era of civil war

Base your answer to Questions 18 and 19 on the map below and your knowledge of social studies.

18. Which statement is accurate?

    a. The eastern end of the Silk Road was in China.

    b. The Silk Road passed through India.

    c. Rome sold silk to China.

    d. The Silk Road was south of the Himalaya Mountains.

19. Which was a result of increased contact and trade along the Silk Road?

    a. Nationalism

    b. Religious devotion

    c. Diversity

    d. Hunger and poverty

20. In which order were the following dynasties in control of China?

    (a) Yuan   (b) Han   (c) Song

    a. abc

    b. bca

    c. bac

    d. cab

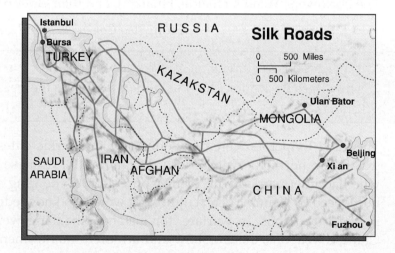

ESSAYS FOR CHAPTER 8

1. The Tang dynasty has been described as China's "golden age." Describe two reasons for this description.

2. Between 500 and 1200, China and India had different historical experiences. Which of these two places would you like to visit if you could go back in a time machine? Give two detailed reasons for your answer.

3. Describe one effect on Xi'an, due to its location at the eastern end of the Silk Road.
4. Describe one similarity and one difference between the Tang and Song dynasties.
5. What was true of both Mahmud of Ghazni and Tang Taizong in regard to military activities? How were these activities different?

DOCUMENT-BASED QUESTIONS

This task is based on the accompanying documents. Some of these documents have been edited for the purposes of this task. This task is designed to test your ability to work with historical documents. As you analyze the documents, take into account both the source of each document and the author's point of view.

Directions: Read the following documents and answer the questions after each document. Use the information in the reading and this chapter in writing your answers.

Document #1

FAN HUAIDONG BORROWS A PIECE OF SILK

On the first day of the third moon of the year, Fan Huaidong and his brothers, whose family is in need of a little cloth, have borrowed from the monk Li a piece of white silk thirty-eight feet long and two and one-half inches wide. In the autumn, they will pay as interest forty bushels of corn and millet. As regards the capital, they will repay it (in the form of a piece of silk of the same quality and size) and before the end of the second moon of the following year. If they do not repay it, interest equivalent to that paid at the time of the loan (that is, forty bushels of cereals) shall be paid monthly. The two parties having agreed to this loan in presence of each other shall not act in any way contrary to their agreement. The borrowers: Wenda, Huaida, Huaizhu, and their elder brother Huaidong.

From *Two Contracts from Dunhuang* (900)

Questions

1. Why can this document be called a contract?
2. How does this contact help us understand how the peasants lived in China?

Document #2

The Tang Emperors were descendents of the Turkic elites of small kingdoms existing in northern China after the Han, and of Chinese officials and settlers who had intermarried with them. Consequently, the Tang nobility were heavily influenced by Central Asian culture but were also knowledgeable about Chinese political traditions. In warfare, for instance, the Tang were ready to combine Chinese weapons, the crossbow and armored infantrymen, with Central Asian expertise in horsemanship and the use of iron stirrups. As a result, from 650–750, the Tang armies were the most formidable on earth.

From *The Earth and Its Peoples* by R. Bulliett et al.

Questions

1. What was the background of the Tang emperors?
2. Why were the Tang armies so strong?

Document #3 At its height, for its first half century, the Tang Empire was the greatest yet seen anywhere on earth, in area, population, and its achievements. This was to be typical of most Chinese dynasties: a first half of new vigor and a second half in which the system began to run down and collapse.

From *East Asia, A New History* by R. Murphey

Questions
1. Why was the Tang Empire so great?
2. How was the Tang similar to some other Chinese dynasties?

Document #4 Perhaps an even more important change was the development under the Song, for the first time, of a civil service recruited for its higher posts almost entirely from the educated group who had passed the three levels of the imperial examinations. Under the Tang, when recruitment through examination was developed well beyond its Han origins, such people filled at most a third of the civil service jobs.

From *East Asia, A New History* by R. Murphey

Questions
1. Why were examinations used by the Tang and Song dynasties?
2. What change in the examination system was developed by the Song?

Document #5 Wu Zhao was one of several wives of the Tang emperor Taizong. She came to the royal court when she was only 13. After his death she became the most well-liked wife of a son of the emperor. As he was very sick, she began to take over some of his ruling responsibilities. Sometime after his death, she took over the throne. She was 65 years old and ruled as empress until she reached the age of 80.

Questions
1. Although she was not part of the Tang bloodline, why did Wu Zhao have a position at the royal court?
2. What was unusual, in Chinese history, about her life from the age of 65 to 80?

CHAPTER 9

Changing Times in the Americas

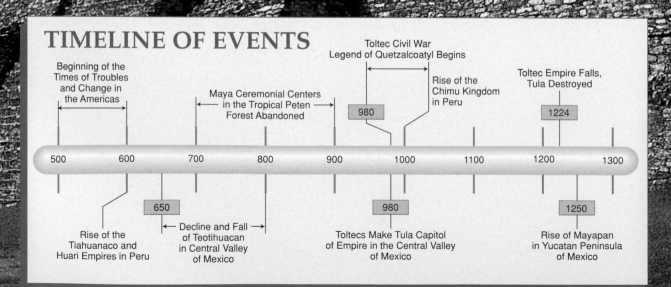

TIMELINE OF EVENTS

Toltec Civil War
Legend of Quetzalcoatyl Begins

Beginning of the
Times of Troubles
and Change in
the Americas

Maya Ceremonial Centers
in the Tropical Peten
Forest Abandoned

Rise of the
Chimu Kingdom
in Peru

Toltec Empire Falls,
Tula Destroyed

| 980 |

| 1224 |

| 500 | 600 | 700 | 800 | 900 | 1000 | 1100 | 1200 | 1300 |

| 650 |

| 980 |

| 1250 |

Rise of the
Tiahuanaco and
Huari Empires in Peru

Decline and Fall
of Teotihuacan
in Central Valley
of Mexico

Toltecs Make Tula Capitol
of Empire in the Central Valley
of Mexico

Rise of Mayapan
in Yucatan Peninsula
of Mexico

The period after 500 C.E. was a time of change and troubles in the more advanced areas of civilization in the Americas. The Mesoamerican world was shaken to its foundations by a number of crises that seemed to spread from one classic center to another. Some civilizations disappeared forever and are only remembered by the remains of buildings, monuments, and other artifacts that were found in more recent times. Other peoples survived, although they lived differently or migrated to new areas where they once again developed a high level of civilization. In Mesoamerica, many of the events and the reasons that caused them are still not very well known. Nevertheless, historians, archaeologists, and anthropologists are learning more about this period.

What is true for Mesoamerica is also true for the Andean region where new cultures and peoples not well known from the period before 500 C.E. took control of older centers of civilization or established new ones. By about 600 C.E., the focus of Andean civilization shifted from the coast to the highlands. Although historians, archaeologists, and anthropologists will never completely know the full story as to why all these changes happened in the Andean region, they have come up with some good explanations in some cases.

Before 1492 C.E., there were many more Native American peoples and cultures than there exist today in the Americas. These peoples, as in Asia, Africa, Europe, and elsewhere, gave themselves their own distinctive names and spoke a wide variety of languages. Today the names of some of the civilizations and peoples who you will read about in this chapter may seem long and difficult to pronounce. Wherever possible, specialists who study the life, history, and culture of these peoples have tried to be as accurate as possible with the names of different groups of people and individuals.

MESOAMERICA

Mesoamerica is generally defined as the physical area that includes the northern regions of present day Mexico into Central America to the border of the nation of Costa Rica. In Mesoamerica, more is known about what happened during the centuries after 500 C.E. than elsewhere in the Americas. Historians think that this period was a time of important changes and troubles. In the Americas, the historical events from about 500 to 900 C.E. can be compared to other long periods of change and troubles on other continents. Throughout human history, civilizations have disappeared or evolved. As happened elsewhere in the world, this period of political instability and problems came to an end in Mesoamerica as peoples began once again to unite large areas, develop their civilization, and prosper.

There are a number of possible explanations concerning what happened during these troubling times. One explanation is that some Native American peoples who lived in what today is the northern desert region of Mexico were able to penetrate into the civilized Central Valley of Mexico. This migration of nomadic tribes contributed to the collapse of the more advanced civilizations. These Native American tribes or peoples were nomadic and lived in wandering tribes, which had little interest in a more sedentary lifestyle. They were peoples

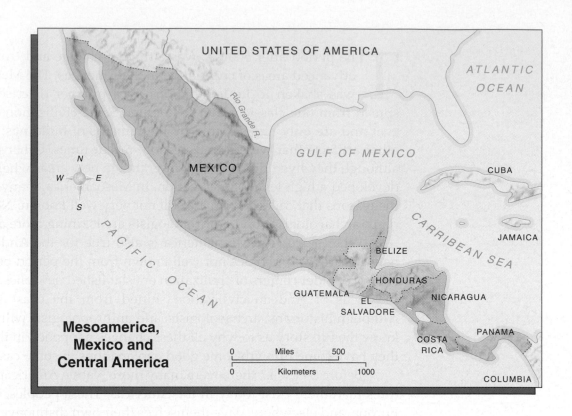

UNITED STATES OF AMERICA

ATLANTIC OCEAN

Rio Grande R.

GULF OF MEXICO

MEXICO

CUBA

N
W   E
S

PACIFIC OCEAN

CARRIBEAN SEA

JAMAICA

BELIZE

HONDURAS

GUATEMALA

EL SALVADORE

NICARAGUA

COSTA RICA

PANAMA

COLUMBIA

Mesoamerica, Mexico and Central America

Miles
0   500

Kilometers
0   1000

Main Idea:
Teotihuacan, which is sometimes called the greatest classic Mesoamerican civilization, ended sometime between 650 and 800 C.E. at the hands of invaders who burned down the city.

who found shelter in caves or built temporary bush huts. Often they wore little clothing and spent their lives in a nearly naked state. These warlike nomads were hunters and superior marksmen with the bow and arrow. Both the Toltecs and Aztecs claimed with pride their nomadic ancestry. You will learn more about the Toltecs, who are important to this time period, and the Aztecs, who developed later (see Chapters 14 and 17).

A second possibility is that the populations of the classic civilizations grew to the point that the land they lived on could no longer support that many people. A large growth in population combined with a decline in available food resources would have led to hunger and even starvation. Environmental problems caused by deforestation and resulting soil erosion or a prolonged drought and soil exhaustion could have worsened this critical food shortage problem. This need for more food resources may have led to increased warfare among the classic civilizations. A need to expand to gain more land and food could have possibly involved the nomadic tribes who often were used as *mercenaries*, people who are hired to fight for other people.

Based on available evidence, it is thought that the Teotihuacan and the Maya centers of civilization were either attacked and destroyed by invading groups or abandoned. Most likely, these events happened because of changes in climatic and soil conditions. The lack of rainfall led to drought conditions and decreased food production. This resulted in increased warfare. Teotihuacan, which is sometimes called the greatest classic Mesoamerican civilization, ended sometime between 650 and 800 C.E. at the hands of invaders who burned down the city. In the case of the Maya, recent archaeological evidence has revealed that the Maya city-states lived in a situation of continual ritual war, which pitted one city-state and its allies against another. The constant warfare was very

Statues of Toltec gods.

disruptive for the people who lived in the Maya heartland. By 800 C.E., the Maya heartland of southern Yucatan and northern Guatemala was being abandoned as people moved northward into a drier part of the Yucatan Peninsula. Slowly over the next centuries, the ceremonial centers of Maya civilization once again became a tropical forest.

The Toltecs

After 600 C.E., more militaristic societies developed in Mesoamerica. This time is also called the Post-Classic Militarist Period. Civilizations arose in which the role of the warrior grew to be very important. Warriors dominated the new military type of states. The new warrior civilizations celebrated the idea of and participated in warfare. No longer would only priest-kings control societies. The key gods to be worshiped in these warlike societies were the terrifying war gods. The new military-led societies were still *polytheistic*; the belief in many gods continued. Nevertheless, above all other gods, the war gods had to be pleased. This meant more blood and human sacrifice.

Toltec Rain God.

By the late 900s, the **Toltecs** developed a powerful military empire in the Central Valley highlands, which rose to great heights. The Toltecs ruled from their ceremonial center capitol, **Tula**, which today is located about fifty miles northeast of present-day Mexico City. The Toltecs were a non-sedentary tribal grouping. This means their lifestyle was at first nomadic. They worked as mercenaries for the rulers of Teotihuacan and helped guard against other roaming nomadic tribes on Teotihuacan's northern frontier. Following the collapse of Teotihuacan, the Toltec people entered the Central Valley of Mexico and gradually took it over. In the following centuries, they became the dominating civilization in this part of Mesoamerica.

Toltec power and prosperity reached its peak under a ruler named **Topiltzin**, who moved his capitol to Tula in about 980 C.E. The priest-king Topiltzin, also known by the name of **Quetzalcoatyl** ruled the Toltec Empire for about nineteen years. Tolpitzin-Quetzalcoatyl presided over a society that brought back the memories of the once powerful Teotihuacan civilization. His reign was a time of splendor and prosperity, and he and his city became legendary. Legend has it that the Toltec land and its capitol, Tula, was a true paradise. It was a place where the people grew colored cotton and the soil yielded fruit and vegetables in such large quantities that ears of corn were used as fuel.

At the end of Quetzalcoatyl's reign, Tula became the scene of a great religious controversy. The religious struggle pitted the followers of two different gods against each other. Each side wanted its god to be worshiped as the supreme god. One side worshiped the Toltec tribal warrior god, Tezcatlipoca, who demanded increased human and blood sacrifice. The other side supported a god also called Quetzalcoatyl, who brought men and women the culture of *maize* (or corn), all learning, and the arts. This second god only demanded peaceful offerings of jade, snakes, and butterflies. A civil war broke out between these Toltec groups, and the warrior followers of Tezcatlipoca won the struggle.

The priest-king Quetzalcoatyl and his followers were driven out and went into exile.

The legend of Quetzalcoatyl played an important role in the history of Mesoamerica. The exiled priest-king promised to return someday to reclaim his kingdom. This story lived on in the minds of the peoples of Mesoamerica. The belief in the idea of a king who would come back someday to regain his throne was crucial in the destruction of the Aztec Empire when Hernando Cortes arrived more than five centuries later. By a coincidence, the year that Quetzalcoatyl promised to return was the very year that Cortes landed in Mexico and the conquest of the Aztecs began. The Aztec ruler and people believed in this legend and hesitated to attack the Spaniards when they first arrived in Mexico (see Chapters 14 and 17).

The new rulers of Tula could not overcome the long-term disastrous effects of the civil war. The Toltec military empire became weaker as time passed. A prolonged and severe drought and crop failures added to the Toltec problems. The need to feed a large population forced the Toltec rulers to fight wars to gain control of better agricultural land. In about 1224 C.E., these increased economic and military problems resulted in the collapse and disappearance of the Toltec state. Nomadic tribes once again entered the Valley of Mexico and destroyed Tula.

> **Main Idea:**
> The nomadic tribes respected and tried to absorb the superior culture of the defeated Toltecs. They were eager to intermarry with the surviving Toltec royalty and nobility and carry on their traditions of kingship.

The fall of Tula opened the way for a general invasion of the valley by Nahuatl-speaking northern desert peoples who had a less developed culture. The newcomer nomadic tribes may be compared to the barbarian Germanic tribes who broke into the dying Roman Empire (see Chapter 3, Section 3). The nomadic tribes respected and tried to absorb the superior culture of the defeated Toltecs. They were eager to intermarry with the surviving Toltec royalty and nobility and carry on their traditions of kingship. These invaders founded a number of city-states in the highland lake country in the central valley of Mexico. Their kings claimed Toltec descent to legitimize their rule. In about 1250 C.E., a powerful kingdom centered around **Lake Texcoco** gained power in the Central Valley by creating a military alliance of city-states. This kingdom ruled the Central Valley for the next century. Among the mercenary nomadic tribes who worked for them was a group who called themselves the Mexica. Today these people are better known as the Aztecs (see Chapters 14 and 17).

The Maya Decline and Transformation

The Maya civilization of the tropical forest region—the **Peten** in southern Mexico, Guatemala, and northern Honduras—declined over the centuries starting around 600 C.E. Specialists in Maya studies have given a number of reasons for the mysterious decline and abandonment of the tropical forest ceremonial centers and the people's migration into the more northern areas of the Yucatan Peninsula in Mexico. Anthropologists, historians, and archaeologists offer explanations, which include soil exhaustion as a result of slash-and-burn farming, invasion of cornfields by grasslands, failure of the water supply, peasant revolts against the ruling priest-kings, and disruptive effects caused by events taking place in the Valley of Mexico.

Peten Rain Forest

MEXICO

Tikal

PETEN
RAIN
FOREST

BELIZE

GUATEMALA

Guatemala

HONDURAS

EL SALVADORE

PACIFIC OCEAN

N
W E
S

Today most specialists believe that the principal cause for the Maya decline was the warfare among the competing city-states of the tropical forest region. During the later centuries of the Classic Period, the constant wars led to the slow but steady abandonment of the Peten forest. A growing population strained food resources and forced the adoption of more intensive agricultural methods. This, in turn, increased the competition for land and led to the growth of warfare and militarism. The rival city-states and their satellite-city allies engaged in increasingly destructive warfare. The object of war was to capture and sacrifice the rival city's rulers. Some ceremonial center construction and development in architecture and the arts continued, but the increased warfare caused a steady decline in farming. This resulted in growing hunger—malnutrition and starvation. The political and economic instabil-

A typical Mayan temple.

The Mayan temple of Quetzalcoatyl at Chichen Itza.

ity in Maya society led to the depopulation of the tropical forest and abandonment of the city-state religious centers.

The Maya migrated northward into the drier area of the Yucatan Peninsula or southward into the highlands of Guatemala. It was in the northern Yucatan that the Maya civilization reestablished itself and entered into what specialists call its Post-Classic Period. The northern Yucatan is a low-lying limestone plain covered in most places by dense areas of thorny scrub forest. The Maya settled around places where they found natural depressions in the limestone and large pools of fresh water. In was here that they cleared the land, began to farm, and rebuilt their ceremonial centers. Maize continued to be the principal crop and food source. Beans, squash, fruits, and game animals supplemented the Maya diet. The Maya were skillful hunters and called their homeland the "Land of the Turkey and the Deer." Although these centers never reached the artistic beauty and glory of their fallen forest kingdoms, some centers did flourish, particularly **Chichen Itza** and Uzmal.

During this time of change in the Maya world, there is an interesting connection to the legend of Quetzalcoatyl. Sometime after 1000 C.E., an invading army arrived from the central northern highlands. These people were migrants from the defeated group that supported Topiltzin-Quetzalcoatyl in the Toltec civil war. These Toltec warriors overran the northern Yucatan and established their rule over the Maya. They governed from the ceremonial temple center of Chichen Itza. The invaders introduced the Toltec styles in art and architecture, including reclining stone figures, which held a stone bowl in the center to receive human hearts. Toltec influence can be seen in an increased obsession with human sacrifice and the offering of the human heart to the gods. In both

Tula and Chichen Itza, the same figures and other architectural and artistic artifacts have been found. This connection makes the legend of Quetzalcoatyl more believable.

By 1200 C.E., Maya political power and cultural influence revived. Chichen Itza was abandoned, and political power in the Yucatan passed to the rising military city-state of **Mayapan**. In the next centuries, the Maya rulers governed the Yucatan Peninsula and highlands of Guatemala. Specialists in Maya studies think of the Post-Classic Period as a time when the level of Maya culture, architecture, and the arts declined. After the fall of Chichen Itza, the new centers of Maya political and religious power never achieved the glory and splendor of the Classic Period.

Until the arrival of the Spaniards in the sixteenth century, the Maya controlled their own destiny. The Mayan people continued to live in extended family units and practice their polytheistic religious beliefs. The class system that developed in the Classic Period continued on in the Post-Classic Period. At the top of a city-state stood a hereditary ruler who combined political, religious, and military leadership. Below the ruler was the nobility who supported his leadership. The bureaucrats who helped administer the state and the military leaders were chosen from among the nobility. There were other specialists such as scribes who wrote and recorded events and dates and artisans who produced textiles and pottery.

The farmers who performed all the agricultural and other heavy labor, for example the construction of temples, were at the bottom level of society. The difficult burdens of Maya society fell on the farmer family groups who were the vast majority of the people. Unhappiness among this lower class of Maya society about their living conditions often led to uprisings. Nevertheless, Post-Classic Maya society remained intact. This durability of the Maya people and their culture will be discussed in later chapters.

THE ANDEAN REGION OF SOUTH AMERICA AND THE CARIBBEAN BASIN

The Andean region of South America also experienced changes starting around the year 500 C.E., In South America, there is less written and other evidence for historians, anthropologists, and archaeologists to rely on. Despite the lack of a more complete record, we know that in the Andes the older societies either disappeared or were absorbed after being conquered by more warlike cultures. The Nazca and Mochica civilizations, which developed along the Peruvian coastline, gave way to new militaristic cultures, which shifted the focus of Andean civilization from the coast to the highlands.

The Carib

The word *Carib* refers to a large grouping of peoples and languages. These peoples lived in an area centered mainly in the Guianas in northeastern South America. It is thought that the Carib-speaking peoples migrated into this area to escape the pressure on their tribes by more aggressive South American tribes.

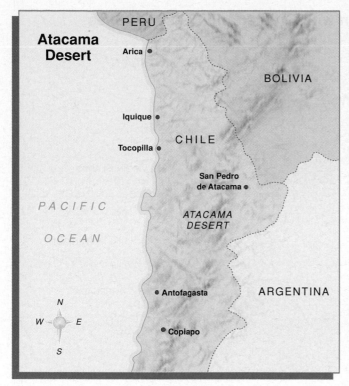

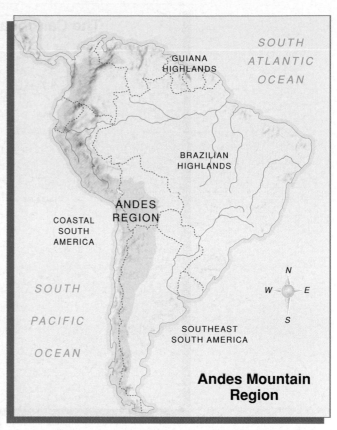

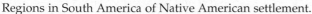

Regions in South America of Native American settlement.

Andes Mountain Region

About a century before the arrival of Columbus, some **Carib** peoples left the mainland and pushed north into the **Lesser Antilles**. They began to replace the **Arawak** on some islands. In turn, the Arawak moved to other islands, particularly the **Greater Antilles**.

The island Carib were a skillful maritime people who made long voyages, even as far away as the Yucatan coast. The Carib used sailing canoes, which they decorated with the symbols of their culture. The Carib raided other islands and the coast to take captives. Male valor had the highest value in Carib culture, and participating in war and raids was how warriors proved themselves. Male captives were tortured and then cooked and eaten. Women were kept as servants. The Carib men lived apart from women in lodges. The women labored to grow and harvest manioc, which was ground into flour, and tended fruit plantations. Women lived together with the children. The men spoke Carib, and their wives spoke Arawak. When Columbus first arrived in the Caribbean basin, the Arawak people who first greeted him had a deep fear of the warlike Carib.

The Arawak

The Arawak were a group of peoples who spoke a related group of languages. They originally lived in the northeastern part of South America. Around 1000 C.E., under pressure from the migrating Carib tribes, a number of Arawak peoples moved into the Caribbean Islands. When Columbus arrived in 1492, the Arawak peoples inhabited the islands of the Greater Antilles—Cuba, Hispaniola, the present-day Dominican Republic, and Haiti, Puerto Rico, and

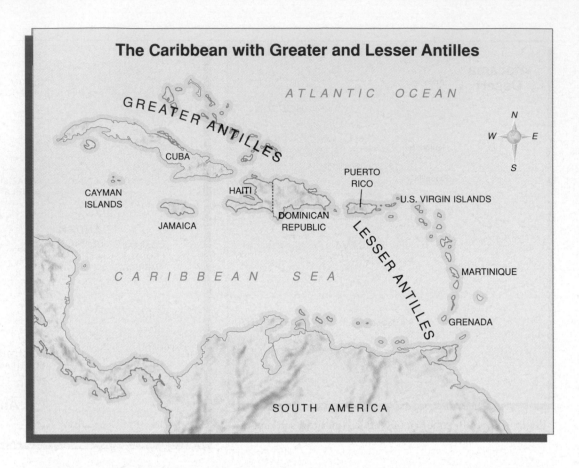

The Caribbean with Greater and Lesser Antilles

Jamaica. They also lived on some of the islands of the Lesser Antilles. Arawak peoples were organized in chiefdoms, and their villages were set back from the coast because they feared the raids of the Caribs. The Arawak did not practice monogamy and lived in groups in which relationships among men and women weren't permanent. All people shared the responsibility of raising children.

The Arawak used large canoes and engaged in interisland trade. They knew how to grow maize and manioc. The Arawak were believers in guardian spirits. Every person possessed one or more spirits, which inhabited pieces of small wood, stone, or bone objects. The spirits played the role of state deities. The higher the rank of a person, the more important was his or her spirits. There may have been a connection also between the Arawak and the people of Mesoamerica because they also used the ball court, a game played by men whose object was to put a ball through a hole suspended on a wall by using one's hips.

LINK TO TODAY
Living in a Time of Change and Troubles

In human history, there have been many periods when political, social, and economic problems have resulted in great changes. Peoples who developed civilizations throughout history have had to confront problems and respond to the troubling challenges of the time period in which they lived. Sometimes they succeeded, and the civilization and culture changed or evolved. At other times on different continents, some peoples could not find the solutions to the problems they faced, and their civilizations disappeared. What you have read about in this chapter is only one example of a time period when important changes took place in the existing civilizations and cultures. Today some of these same troubling political, economic, and social problems that cause instability and migration exist in different parts of the world and will have to be resolved. People will always have to respond to troubling challenges that will bring about great changes.

CHAPTER SUMMARY

The period between about 500 and 1200 C.E. was a time of change and trouble in many parts of the Americas. More aggressive warlike cultures replaced older civilizations and cultures in the more developed areas of Mesoamerica and the Andean region. These new civilizations eventually fell and were ultimately replaced by even more developed civilizations (see Chapter 14). In the Americas, there is evidence that during this time period there was also a lot of movement of peoples, or migration. There were different reasons for all of this movement: war, fear, drought, soil exhaustion, and a gradual decline of some cultures.

Despite the changes and troubled times, there is evidence that the population of the Americas grew steadily. Although it will probably never be known with absolute certainty, anthropologists and historians support the idea that the population in the more developed cultural areas and elsewhere in the Americas expanded. Despite the uncertainties of life, the inhabitants of the Americas increased in the areas already inhabited and also migrated to new places. Eventually, the areas that all these peoples inhabited would be known as Latin America and the Caribbean, but this only happened after the Spanish and Portuguese conquered these lands.

IMPORTANT PEOPLE, PLACES, AND TERMS	KEY TERMS	PEOPLE	PLACES
	Polytheistic	Toltec	Tula
	Mercenary	Quetzalcoatyl	Atacama Desert
	Manioc	Chimu	Peten
		Arawak	Chichen Itza
		Topiltzin	Lesser Antilles
		Carib	Mayapan
			Greater Antilles

EXERCISES FOR CHAPTER 9

MULTIPLE CHOICE

Select the letter of the correct answer.

1. The legend of Quetzalcoatyl linked which two civilizations?

   a. Toltec and nomadic tribes
   b. Maya and Toltec
   c. Tiahuanaco and Maya
   d. Tihuanaco and Toltec

2. During the period called the time of troubles and change in the Americas

   a. more people migrated to the tropical rainforests.
   b. military societies led by warriors became more common.
   c. advanced civilizations rebuilt their city centers in the Andes.
   d. the nature gods became more important in Mesoamerica.

3. The Arawak and Carib cultures were similar in that both people

   a. lived in peace with their neighbors in the Caribbean.
   b. developed a writing system based on hieroglyphics.
   c. gave all members of the group child-raising duties.
   d. never permitted males to engage in cannibalism.

4. In South America, the centers of advanced civilization were located in the

   a. tropical Amazon rain forest.
   b. fertile Brazilian highlands.
   c. grasslands of the Pampas.
   d. highlands of the Andes.

5. The primary reason for the decline of the Maya ceremonial centers was

   a. the development of trade routes to more prosperous regions.
   b. the constant warfare among rival city-states.
   c. invasion of the tropical rainforest by nomadic tribes.
   d. religious battles that resulted after the change to monotheism.

6. One effect that mountain ranges, rainforests, and river systems had on Latin America has been to

   a. encourage cultural diffusion.
   b. limit the development of transportation and communication.
   c. permit nations of the area to use a single form of government.
   d. allow the development of large amounts of arable land.

7. The nomadic tribes of Mexico and the Hittites of Asia were similar in that they

   a. used horses to travel and hunt.
   b. developed calendars to travel and hunt.
   c wrote in a hieroglyphic language.
   d. invaded lands of more civilized peoples.

8. One long-term result of the Toltec civil war was that

   a. the Toltecs established a new kingdom north of the Valley of Mexico.
   b. the Valley of Mexico became an inhabited area for several centuries.
   c. the Yucatan Peninsula was invaded and conquered by Toltec tribes.
   d. the Quetzalcoatyl became the undisputed ruler of the Toltec Empire.

9. Which geographical area is correctly linked with the people who inhabited that land?

    a. Andes Mountains—Toltecs
    b. Yucatan Peninsula—Maya
    c. Central Valley of Mexico—Arawak
    d. Northern Mexico—Olmecs

10. The Maya civilization was similar to the Egyptian and Mesopotamian civilizations in that they

    a. made use of a glyph or pictograph writing system.
    b. did not have the mathematical knowledge to develop a calendar.
    c. used iron to develop their military technology.
    d. learned from each other how to advance their agricultural techniques.

11. The Maya culture was noted for all of the following accomplishments EXCEPT

    a. developing a writing system using glyph pictographs.
    b. making observations in astronomy including eclipses.
    c. perfecting the development of agricultural techniques including chinampas.
    d. building an advanced road system to cross the Valley of Mexico.

12. The following lines are from a Mayan poem, "The Popul Vuh":

"When it was still night and dark the gods wanted light."

"Let dawn rise on heaven and earth so the gods can assemble."

"There shall be no glory for the gods until the human creature exists."

"There was nothing in the beginning until the gods created light."

The headline that best describes the above lines from the Mayan poem would be

    a. Mayas support monotheism.
    b. Mayas have an organized religion.
    c. Mayan gods control the forces of nature.
    d. Mayas see conflict between gods and humans.

13. Base your answer on the following reading passage:

"It was Quetzalcoatyl, the Plumed Serpent, the creator of humankind who discovered and gave the first grain of corn, with the help of an ant, succeeding where all the other gods had failed. Before this there was nothing to eat and humankind went hungry always looking for food. If it was not for Quetzalcoatyl humankind would still roam the earth in search of what to eat."

Quetzalcoatyl was considered the god that

    a. helped humankind survive.
    b. demanded food as a sacrifice.
    c. created corn and ants.
    d. angered other gods.

14. The rise of more advanced cultures in the Andean region

    a. was added by the migration of peoples from other regions of South America.
    b. led to the conquest of the Amazon rainforest by Andean peoples.
    c. was helped by the development of agricultural techniques and staples.
    d. led to the decline of trade among the peoples who inhabited the coast.

15. The Maya belief that Quetzalcoatyl was a god that helped humans is similar to the idea that

    a. Prometheus helped the Greeks.
    b. Zeus helped the Romans.
    c. Mars helped the Trojans.
    d. Vishnu helped the Persians.

16. The ancient peoples of Mesoamerica believed in sacrifice because

   a. it would uphold the world, the sun, and life itself.

   b. they wanted to eliminate any possibility of revenge.

   c. this was the only way males could gain the respect of females.

   d. life had little meaning to these uncivilized peoples.

17. The Maya differed from many other more advanced peoples in that

   a. their homeland was in a tropical rain forest.

   b. their religious sytem was based on monotheism.

   c. they did not have any system of writing.

   d. they were very peaceful and did not engage in warfare.

18. The Classical Period of civilization in Ancient Mesoamerica was

   a. a time during which the Maya civilization reached its greatest heights.

   b. a period during which the Toltecs developed their capitol in Tula.

   c. a period during which the Toltecs successfully invaded the Yucatan Peninsula.

   d. a time when the potato became the principal crop in the highlands.

19. The social structure of the Maya was organized

   a. democratically.

   b. in an egalitarian system.

   c. hierarchically.

   d. based on socialistic ideals.

20. The Toltec, Egyptian, and Mesopotamia civilizations all were

   a. iron age cultures.

   b. bronze age cultures.

   c. egalitarian cultures.

   d. hunter-gatherer cultures.

ESSAYS FOR CHAPTER 9

1. Assume that you are Quetzalcoatyl, the exiled leader of the Toltec people. Write an essay explaining to the people of Tula the reasons for your exile and why you will return someday to rule again.

2. Assume that you are a government official, a scribe, in a Maya ceremonial center in the tropical rainforest. Write an essay about why you have decided to leave your home and job and migrate further north into the Yucatan.

3. Why were the Maya considered to be an advanced Mesoamerican culture?

4. How does the story of the god Quetzalcoatyl link the Maya and Toltecs?

5. Why was ritual sacrifice so important for Native American cultures?

DOCUMENT-BASED QUESTIONS

This task is based on the accompanying documents. Some of these documents have been edited for the purposes of this task. This task is designed to test your ability to work with historical documents. As you analyze the documents, take into account both the source of each document and the author's point of view.

Directions: Read the following documents and answer the questions after each document. Use the information in the reading and this chapter in writing your answers.

Document #1   The collapse of Classic Mayan civilization in the tropical rain forest and the abandonment of the great ceremonial centers has puzzled scholars. There are many reasons that have been offered to explain why this happened. An epidemic is one cause given. Other factors suspected are soil erosion, civil war, climatic change, food shortages and rebellion by the lower class of Maya society. Probably there were many causes, but the total collapse and abandonment of the Maya city-states at the end of the Classic period had to have one primary cause. Scholars continue to search more evidence to explain the mystery of the abandonment of the Mayan ceremonial centers in the rain forest. Today more Maya scholars are supporting the idea that the Maya city-states engaged in constant warfare against other city-states as the key reason for the collapse. The rulers of the larger more powerful city-states built alliances and tried to destroy their rivals and thereby increase their own political power. The warfare led to increased political instability and to a growing insecurity. The vast majority of Mayan people were farmers but were now forced to be soldiers and defend their city and its rulers. The continual warfare reduced the overall food production and caused widespread suffering. Ultimately the farming communities began to drift away and the city-states were slowly abandoned.

From the *Encyclopedia of Latin America*

Questions
1. Why do scholars think the collapse of the Maya city-states of the tropical rainforest is a puzzle?
2. What are some of the reasons given to explain the collapse of the Maya city-states in the tropical rainforest?

Document #2   Of these peoples the most known were the Toltecs. Advancing from a northerly direction, but from what exact region is uncertain, they entered the territory of the Central Valley of Mexico probably by the end of the seventh century. Of course, little can be said with certainty respecting a people who are known to us only through the traditional legends of the nations that succeeded them. However by general agreement the Toltecs were well instructed in agriculture and many of the useful mechanic arts. They were fine workers of metals and invented the complex arrangement of time adopted by the Aztecs.

From *The Conquest of Mexico* by William Prescott

Questions
1. Why is so little known about the Toltecs?
2. In what ways were the Toltecs advanced?

Document #3   The Toltecs established their capitol at Tula, to the north in the Valley of Mexico. The remains of their extensive buildings were discovered during the Conquest. The noble ruins of religious and other edifices [buildings] give these people the credit of being architects who like the ancient Egyptians, also used stone blocks to construct impressive monuments that have resisted the ravages of time and the elements.

From *The Conquest of Mexico* by William Prescott

Questions
1. How can we compare the Toltec and Egyptian architecture?
2. Where were the Toltec ruins first discovered?

Document #4   After a period of four centuries, the Toltecs, who had extended their sway over the remotest borders of the Central Valley of Mexico, were greatly reduced it is said by famine, pestilence and unsuccessful wars. They disappeared from the land as silently and mysteriously as they had entered it. A few of them remained but others spread over the region of the Yucatan and influenced the buildings and cultural developments of the Mayan people.

From *The Conquest of Mexico* by William Prescott

Questions
1. What were some of the possible reasons for the decline and fall of the Toltecs?
2. How did the Toltecs influence the development of Mayan culture?

Document #5   After a lapse of another hundred years, a numerous and rude group of nomadic peoples, entered the deserted country from the regions of the far northwest. They were followed by other non sedentary peoples of the same language family. Their language is known as Nahuatl. The nomadic tribes adopted the civilization that had been developed by the Toltecs from those remaining people in the Valley of Mexico. In this manner they slowly abandoned their rudimentary culture and became a civilized people.

From *The Conquest of Mexico* by William Prescott

Questions
1. Why were the peoples of the northern region of Mexico considered to be nomadic?
2. How did the nomadic tribes benefit from their entry into the Valley of Mexico?

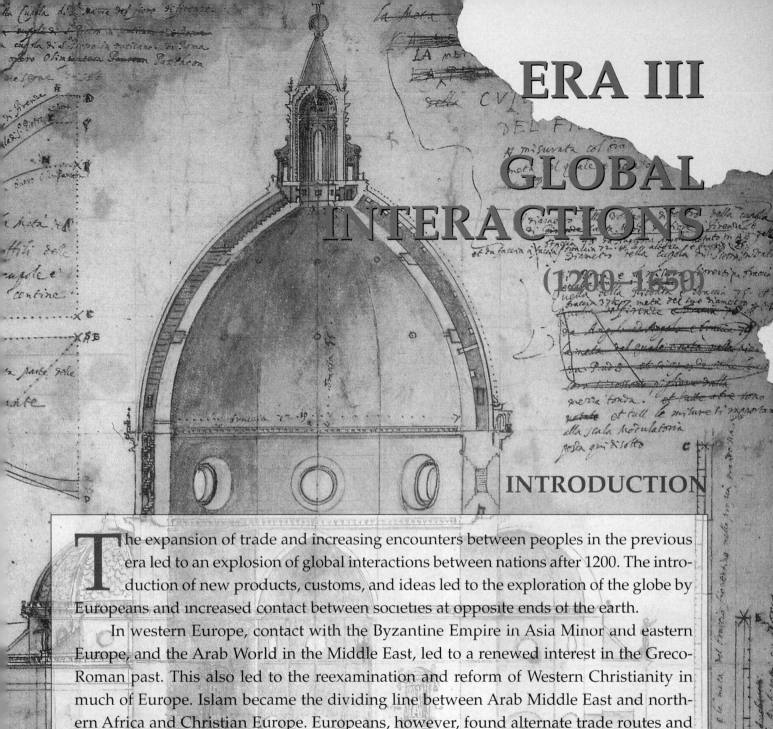

ERA III
GLOBAL INTERACTIONS
(1200–1650)

INTRODUCTION

The expansion of trade and increasing encounters between peoples in the previous era led to an explosion of global interactions between nations after 1200. The introduction of new products, customs, and ideas led to the exploration of the globe by Europeans and increased contact between societies at opposite ends of the earth.

In western Europe, contact with the Byzantine Empire in Asia Minor and eastern Europe, and the Arab World in the Middle East, led to a renewed interest in the Greco-Roman past. This also led to the reexamination and reform of Western Christianity in much of Europe. Islam became the dividing line between Arab Middle East and northern Africa and Christian Europe. Europeans, however, found alternate trade routes and established contact with the peoples of the Indian subcontinent and Asia. Throughout Asia, Eurasia, and the Indian subcontinent, the Mongols created their own empire. Exploration led to the European discovery and conquest of the Americas, resulting in the decline of the independent civilizations in those continents.

The expansion of global interaction between nations from 1200 to 1650 raised new questions about culture, traditions, and ideas. Were accepted ways of doing things necessarily true or correct? Could one society learn from another? Should individuals be able to improve their economic, political, and social status through ambition and hard work despite traditional social restrictions? These were some of the new ideas the period brought.

253

CHAPTER 10

The Renaissance

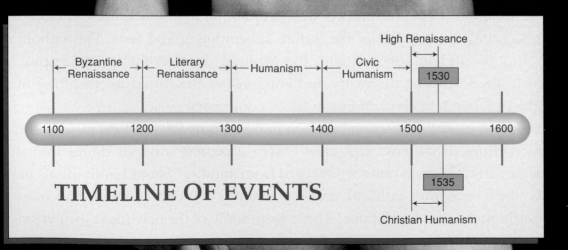

Byzantine Renaissance	Literary Renaissance	Humanism	Civic Humanism	High Renaissance

1530

TIMELINE OF EVENTS

1535

Christian Humanism

1100   1200   1300   1400   1500   1600

The great changes that western Europe experienced during the Middle Ages, as well as its contact with Byzantium and the Islamic World, resulted in a new period of experiment and exploration that became known as the **Renaissance**. The term *renaissance* means "re-birth," and in the development of Western civilization it refers to Europe's revived interest in its Greco-Roman heritage. Although knowledge of and interest in the Classical World had never completely died out in the Middle Ages, the Church and theology dominated Medieval society. The Renaissance brought a new appreciation of the Ancient Greeks and Romans to balance the overwhelming preoccupation with religion. The period was not antireligious, but rather combined the secular pursuits of the Greco-Roman World with the religious devotion of the Medieval Period.

Main Idea:
The term *renaissance* means "re-birth," and in the development of Western civilization it referes to Europe's revived interest in its Greco-Roman heritage.

The Renaissance began in Italy about 1100. The Italians became interested in the culture and learning of the Eastern Roman Empire due to the increased contact during the Crusades. This led to a rediscovery of the Classical past by 1200. Literature and the arts were the first area to reflect this movement, which dominated Italian culture from 1300 until the sixteenth century. While the rest of Europe was in the Late Medieval period, Italy was experiencing the Renaissance. When it reached the northern nations, the Renaissance took a somewhat different form.

By the fourteenth century, Italy saw the rise of **humanism**, which was the Classical World's glorification of the human form as beautiful and the human mind as capable of discovering truth. The thinkers of the Medieval World distrusted physical beauty and thought of the needs of the body as obstacles to the development of the spirit. They also believed that human wisdom was unable to find truth without guidance from God. Humanism emphasized individual and personal achievement. The Medieval belief was that pride was a deadly sin and the individual ego had to be suppressed into the common Christian body. This was illustrated by the practice of Medieval artists, usually monks, who did not sign their names to their works, but gave them to the "greater glory of God." In the Renaissance, not only did the artist sign his name to his work, but he also became famous and expected to be praised. No longer monastic for the most part, artists in the Renaissance became wealthy and celebrated. In fact, the artist became more important than the *patron*, or financial supporter, in that when he became famous, there was a demand for any work by him.

The Renaissance encouraged the individual to pursue a variety of interests. The term **Renaissance man**, meaning a multitalented person, had its origins in this period. An excellent example of the type of all-around individual that the Renaissance produced was **Benvenuto Cellini** (1500–1571). He was an artist, both a sculptor and a goldsmith, as well as a writer. Cellini is known chiefly for his *Autobiography*, which described his experiences as a soldier and a *courtier*, someone who served in the court of a ruler. This type of well-rounded background and *versatility*—ability to do many different things—is still encouraged in contemporary society. The educated person of the Middle Ages

An excellent example of the type of all-around individual that the Renaissance produced was Benvenuto Cellini.

was usually a specialist, such as a theologian or artist, but the learned individual in the Renaissance was expected to be knowledgeable in many areas, like poetry, history, dancing, athletics, vernacular languages, theology, art, and Classical languages. Many Renaissance universities expanded their offerings from the traditional theology-dominated seven **liberal arts**—grammar, rhetoric, logic, arithmetic, geometry, music, and astronomy—to include Classical literature, history, and philosophy. One of the most popular books of the period in Europe was the *Book of the Courtier* by **Baldassarre Castiglione** (1478–1529), which described the ideal gentleman. The courtier was supposed to be a scholar, athlete, soldier, and statesman, knowledgeable in all areas without appearing to have too great an interest in any one topic. The best example of this ideal was the versatile genius **Leonardo da Vinci** (1452–1519), who is best known now as a painter, but who also excelled as a sculptor, architect, engineer, inventor, philosopher, botanist, geologist, and anatomist. Leonardo's drawings of the human anatomy are still used by both medical and art students.

Leonardo da Vinci is best known as a painter. However, he also excelled as a sculptor, architect, engineer, inventor, philosopher, botanist, geologist, and anatomist.

In the fifteenth century, **civic humanism** appeared. This was an interest in improving and developing civic pride in Italian cities. The Ancient Greek *polis* and Roman *civitas* served as models. This attitude led to civic improvement projects, such as better sewerage systems, and works of art to beautify the cities. More importantly, civic humanism resulted in a new awareness of and participation in political life. This was reflected in the attempts to develop a **republican** form of government, which is a representative democratic government, in many of the Italian cities. Classic literature was given a new interpretation, and the Roman Republic, rather than autocracy, was seen as the model to be followed. The **active life**, which is the concern with the present world, became the ideal, replacing the **contemplative life**, the concern with salvation in the next world that had been dominant in the Middle Ages. The civic humanists argued that the individual could be an active citizen with a family and career and still be a good Christian. They believed that asceticism was not necessary for the salvation of the soul. Civic humanism therefore made the Renaissance relevant to contemporary problems and issues of the time.

In the sixteenth century, the Italian Renaissance reached its last stage. Known as the **High Renaissance** (1500–1536), it was a period of high artistic and cultural achievement. Yet, during this century, Italy declined politically, and the center of activity shifted north. The Renaissance in northern Europe took a different form. The Italians had been interested in the secular aspects of Greco-Roman civilization; the northern humanists tried to "humanize" Christianity. Known as **Christian humanism**, this movement was an attempt to combine the best values of the Classical World with Christianity. Classical scholarship was combined with Christian concerns. Literature and philosophy were far more important to Christian humanism than art and architecture. Civic humanism, with its emphasis on republicanism and civil participation, had no place in the strong national monarchies of Europe. Ultimately, northern European humanism led to an intellectual examination of Christianity, which in turn produced a demand for Church reform. Without realizing it, the Christian humanists planted the seeds for the **Reformation** movement.

A PERIOD OF DECENTRALIZATION

Politically, the Renaissance was a period of decentralization, or a breakdown of central government in northern Italy. Despite the fact that the German Holy Roman Emperor was still technically the ruler of most of Italy, after the death of **Friedrich (Frederick) II** in 1250, the emperors rarely tried to interfere in Italian affairs. Ironically, as the various Italian city-states later struggled against one another and against foreign powers, some of them actually tried to get the emperor to exert his influence. After 1250, Italy became divided into many independent states. Among them, some became very powerful and important.

Southern Italy was divided in 1282 into the **Kingdom of Naples**, ruled by a French prince, and the **Kingdom of Sicily**, under a member of the Aragonese royal family. The rivalry and misrule of these two kingdoms resulted in a decline of this once rich area. In 1435, the two kingdoms were united under the Aragonese. The area, however, had been so devastated by the two centuries of fighting that it remained poor and unimportant.

The **Papal States** dominated central Italy. The local nobles, however, actively opposed the pope's control. During the fourteenth century, Papal power declined. A conflict arose between Philippe (Philip) IV of France (r. 1285–1314) and Pope Boniface VIII (r. 1294–1303) about the king's jurisdiction over the French clergy, which resulted in a humiliating defeat for the Papacy. After Boniface's death, Philippe used his influence to elect a French bishop, Clement V (r. 1305–1314), who moved the Papacy to **Avignon** in France. This move gave the French kings enormous influence over the papal decisions. Seven French popes resided at Avignon (1305–1377), a period that was called the **Babylonian**

Main Idea:
After 1250, Italy became divided into many independent states.

The coronation of Pope Clement V.

A brilliant military commander as well as a patron of the arts, Pope Julius II was one of the most powerful rulers in Europe.

Main Idea:
The city of Milan grew wealthy because of its location on a crossroad of trade.

Captivity, because the popes, like the Ancient Hebrews held captive in Babylon, were controlled by a foreign monarchy. In 1377, Pope Gregory XI (r. 1377-1378), returned to Rome. This angered the French Church, which elected a rival pope in Avignon. For forty years, a rivalry known as **The Great Schism** existed between the two popes, and after 1409 a third developed until the **Council of Constance** (1414–1418) solved the issue by electing Martin V (r. 1417–1431), an Italian, to the papal throne and designating Rome as the Papacy's permanent residence. The absence of the Papacy during the Babylonian Captivity had hurt Rome's authority and prestige. During the fifteenth and early sixteenth centuries, a succession of ruthless popes restored their authority over the Papal States. Under **Pope Julius II** (r. 1503–1513), papal power was at its height. A brilliant military commander as well as a patron of the arts, Julius was one of the most powerful rulers in Europe. Beginning in 1516, however, the Papal States, along with the rest of Italy, fell to invasion and domination by the Spanish, French, and Germans.

Northern Italy was divided into many small city-states, most of which were constantly in conflict with one another. The earliest notable city was **Siena**, which established a **commune**—a system where the citizens share the responsibilities of government—from 1287 to 1355. Siena became wealthy through trade and was the first center of Renaissance art and culture. After suffering enormous losses of population during the **Black Death** in 1348, Siena declined and was absorbed by more powerful neighbors.

The city of **Milan** grew wealthy because of its location on a crossroad of trade. It began as a republic but this was destroyed as a result of the conflict between supporters of the Papacy and the German emperors in Italy in the middle of the thirteenth century. In 1277, the pro-Ghibelline Visconti family seized power and ruled Milan until 1447 as **despots,** rulers who are absolute and often tyrannical. Despite attempts to restore the republican system, a new family of despots, the Sforzas, took power later that year. Even though the Sforzas were ruthless, they provided Milan with competent rule, promoting public works and patronizing the arts. In 1499, the last of the Sforzas, **Ludovico Sforza the Moor** (r. 1494–1499), was expelled after unsuccessful campaigns against the invading French. In 1535, the Spanish took Milan.

The city of **Florence** was the "cradle of Renaissance culture" producing the greatest artists of the period. It was a wealthy city that grew rich through banking, trade, and the wool industry. Florence began as a self-governing commune in the twelfth century. As a result of the **Guelf-Ghibelline** struggles in the thirteenth century, a Guelf-dominated republic replaced the commune. By the fourteenth century, the Guelf party divided into two groups: the *Blacks*, who favored an oligarchy of wealthy merchants, and the *Whites*, who supported a more democratic rule of artisans. They fought for power between 1302 and 1434. The struggle resulted in financial and military losses that made both groups very unpopular. In 1434, the Medici family rose to power. Without altering the republican structure of government, the Medicis ruled the city. This was

The "Golden Age" of culture in Florence was achieved under the rule of Lorenzo de Medici il Magnifico or "the Magnificent," who was himself a scholar, poet, and musician.

similar to what Augustus did when he took control of the Roman Empire in 31 B.C.E. A family of wealthy bankers, they provided able government, supported building programs, and patronized the arts. The "Golden Age" of culture in Florence was achieved under the rule of **Lorenzo de Medici il Magnifico** or **the Magnificent** (r. 1469–1492), who was himself a scholar, poet, and musician. In 1494, the Medicis were expelled from power for surrendering Florentine possessions to the French. The reestablished republic lasted until 1498, when the Medicis were restored to power. They ruled Florence until the eighteenth century. Despite the competent rule of this family, Florence, like the rest of Italy, declined in the sixteenth century. The influence of the Medici family, however, extended beyond the city they ruled. They produced three popes, Leo X, Clement VII, and Leo XI, and two queens of France, Catherine de Medici and Marie de Medici.

The **Republic of Venice** was an exception to the Renaissance trend toward despotism. Unlike its neighbors, Venice had been ruled for centuries by a powerful merchant oligarchy or small group of elites. They exercised power through a representative body known as the **Great Council**, which was limited to the descendants of about 200 families. This system provided Venice with a strong and efficient government that protected and encouraged trade. By the fourteenth century, Venice controlled Mediterranean commerce and had become extremely wealthy. In order to protect the flow of trade, the Venetians conquered territories throughout Italy. This involved them in the power struggles among Italian cities, diverting them from the greater threat of the Ottoman Turks. After the fall of Constantinople in 1453, trade in the Mediterranean became very limited and Venice entered a period of decline. Along with the rest of Italy, this grew worse after foreign domination began in the sixteenth century.

RENAISSANCE SOCIETY

The Renaissance began with the recovery of Classical texts and their study in the original Greek and Latin. The civilization of Ancient Greece and Rome inspired the efforts of humanists and gave them models to follow. They tried to find the best and most accurate copies of Ancient manuscripts and developed new fields of study to assist them in correcting errors and inconsistencies in the texts. Among the new disciplines were **philology**, (the study of written texts), grammar, textual and historical criticism, dictionaries, and handbooks on Classical mythology, geography, history, architecture, and art. Classical Latin became the standard by which literary works were judged. The study of Classical Greek also became important, and Greek works were used as models for imitation. The civic humanist **Lorenzo Valla** (1407–1457) reflected this critical spirit when he examined the official Latin translation of the Bible known as the *Saint Jerome Vulgate* and found that it contained errors in translation. He also proved that the *Donation of Constantine*, a document that gave the Papacy supreme secular power in the West, was actually a later forgery. It was this spirit of reevaluation and scholarship that characterized the Renaissance.

Before the fifteenth century, Italian architecture had been a blend of the Byzantine, Romanesque, and Gothic styles. The innovations of the architect **Filippo Brunelleschi** (1377–1446) brought architecture into a new era. After studying Ancient buildings and determining their mathematical proportions, he designed structures that combined these techniques and forms. Brunelleschi is noted for his construction of the dome on the **Cathedral of Florence**, which was the first attempt on such a large scale since Antiquity. Two other Renaissance architects, **Donato Bramante** (1444–1514) and **Michelangelo Buonarroti** (1472–1564), were responsible for the design of **Saint Peter's Basilica** in the **Vatican**. The Renaissance also made great contributions to domestic architecture, such as ornate palaces and **villas** or country houses, and urban planning, notably **piazzas** (or town squares) and public buildings. Classic Renaissance architecture is best exemplified by the work of **Andrea Palladio** (1508–1580), whose decorative windows, villas, and churches became models for later generations.

The genius of the Italian Renaissance is most obvious in its painting and sculpture. In the thirteenth century, Italian art greatly resembled the Byzantine. This *Italo-Byzantine* tradition was limited to frescoes, panel paintings, and mosaics. Adopting the principles of Byzantine theology, the art was supernatural and made no attempt to be realistic. In the fourteenth century, however, Italian painting entered a new phase. The revived interest in the Classical World encouraged some artists to paint secular themes such as history, mythology, and natural scenes in their work. Even though most continued to depict religious subjects, the work showed both realism and emotion. This style became known as **naturalism**. Beginning with **Giotto** (c. 1267–1337), Italian art became more concerned with accurate depictions of the natural world. Religious figures were often placed in natural scenes wearing contemporary dress. Giotto also introduced the concept of **chiaroscuro**, the use of contrasting light and shade to give the illusion of depth. This made art far more realistic. Considered the true founder of Renaissance painting, **Masaccio** (1401–1428) gave Giotto's methods a scientific basis. Using Brunelleschi's mathematical laws of architecture, he developed the concept of **linear perspective** in painting. This gave the work an appearance of distance and space.

By the fifteenth century, Italian art had developed a wide variety of individual styles that reflected both the personalities of the artists and the tastes of their patrons. In addi-

Brunelleschi's architectural plans for the Cathedral of Florence.

Donato Bramante and Michelangelo Buonarroti were responsible for the design of St. Peter's Basilica in Rome.

tion to religious, mythological, historical, and natural subjects, artists painted portraits of their patrons with the same convincing realism. This change is reflected in the work of **Sandro Botticelli** (c. 1445–1510), who painted scenes from Classical mythology on a scale that was only used previously for religious themes. His two most famous works are *The Birth of Venus* and *Primavera* or *Spring*. Other outstanding Florentine painters of this period were **Fra Angelico**

The Birth of Venus by Sandro Botticelli.

The Last Supper
by da Vinci.

(1387–1455), and **Piero della Francesca** (c. 1420–1492). In Venice, artists adopted the innovations of the Florentines but used more color to give the paintings an illusion of radiance. They also began to paint smaller works that could be hung in the homes of wealthy citizens. The Venetian artists included **Giovanni Bellini** (c. 1427–1516), **Giorgione** (1477–1510), **Tintoretto** (1518–1594), and the best known of Venetian painters, **Titian** (c. 1490–1576), whose works went on to influence later generations.

The High Renaissance of the sixteenth century produced the greatest artists of the period. Leonardo da Vinci had his greatest impact as a painter even though he only finished a small number of paintings. His most famous is the large fresco *The Last Supper*, painted on the wall of a monastery's *refectory* or dining room in Milan. His other well-known works are the *Virgin and Child with Saint Anne* and *La Giaconda*, which is more commonly known as the *Mona Lisa*. No less a giant in painting than his Florentine rival da Vinci, Michelangelo Buonarroti distinguished himself with the frescoes on the ceiling of the **Sistine Chapel** in the Vatican. Working on a scaffold for four years, he covered the ceiling with nine scenes from the Book of Genesis, the most famous of which was the *Creation of Adam*. A contemporary of both artists, **Raphael** (1483–1520) painted two famous frescoes on the walls of the Vatican Library, *The School of Athens* and *Disputa*.

Northern Europe produced its own tradition of art in this period. While Italian Renaissance painters studied perspective and anatomy, the northern European artists experimented with real space in their workshops in order to paint realistic images. They are especially famous for their fine detail. In the fifteenth century, a *Flemish School* developed. The most famous of these

The Mona Lisa (or *La Giaconda*)
by da Vinci.

The Creation of Adam, by Michelangelo, appears on the ceiling of the Sistine Chapel in the Vatican.

painters were **Jan van Eyck** (c. 1390–1441) and **Rogier van der Weyden** (1400–1464). Both artists were known for their precision, detail, and emotion in their paintings. One of the first northern artists to incorporate Renaissance ideals in his work was the German painter **Albrecht Dürer** (1471–1528). Dürer was also known for his woodcuts and copper engravings. Another German painter, **Hans Holbein** (1497–1543), was famous for his realistic portraits. Two of the most original artists of the northern European Renaissance were from the Netherlands, **Hieronymus Bosch** (c. 1450–1516) and **Pieter Bruegel the Elder** (1525–1569). Bosch's work is full of fantastic creatures and horrifying scenes of violence, reflecting the northern European obsession with sin, hell, and damnation. Bruegel's best work was painting landscapes and scenes from daily life.

Of all the arts in the Renaissance, sculpture was most directly influenced by Classical art. The first Italian sculptor who incorporated Classical sculpture into his work was **Nicola Pisano** (c. 1220–1278). A southern Italian, Pisano saw numerous examples of Ancient sculpture, which he used in his own work. By the late fourteenth century, Italian sculpture adopted the ideas of naturalism. The relief carvings of **Lorenzo Ghiberti** (1378–1455) achieved both clarity and realism. His most famous work was *The Gates of Paradise,* which were bronze doors of the Baptistry of Florence. In the fifteenth century, the work of **Donatello** (c. 1386–1466) had fused the sculpture of the Classical World with that of the Renaissance. Donatello's bronze statue *David* was the first freestanding nude sculpture since Antiquity. His work reflected the revival of the Classical glorification of the human body. His *Saint George* applied Classical

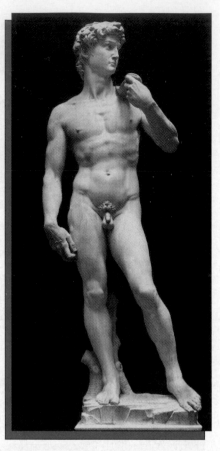

Raphael painted two famous frescoes on the walls of the Vatican Library, *The School of Athens* (seen here) and *Disputa*.

Donatello's bronze statue *David* was the first freestanding nude sculpture since Antiquity.

detail and realism to a Christian subject. The height of Renaissance sculpture was achieved by Michelangelo Buonarroti. Like Donatello, his best-known work is his sculpture *David*, which came closest to the Classical ideal of masculine beauty. His statue *Moses* is also a masterpiece of sculpture, showing great power and emotion, as does his *Pieta*, which is a sculpture depicting the Virgin Mary weeping over the dead body of Jesus.

Ironically, most of greatest works of Renaissance literature were written in the vernacular, or spoken languages, rather than the newly rediscovered Classical languages. The first literary pieces of the Renaissance were in Italian, produced by three writers known as the "Tuscan Triumvirate" because they all lived in Florence in the old **Etruscan** province of **Tuscany**. It is for this reason that modern spoken and written Italian is the Tuscan dialect. The first was **Dante Alighieri** (1265–1321). His masterpiece, the *Divine Comedy*, was an epic poem that combined Classical mythology, Christian theology, and Medieval folklore in a imaginary trip from Hell through purgatory to heaven. The combination of references in this work reflect the various influences that created Renaissance society. Dante's other works are entirely secular. The second member of the Triumvirate, **Francesco Petrarca** or **Petrarch** (1304–1374), is known as the **father of humanism**. He was the first writer to abandon the methods and objectives of Medieval thought in favor of the Latin Classics. To Petrarch,

Classical literature was a source of morality and virtue, despite being the product of a pagan civilization. He searched for Ancient manuscripts, studied Classical literature and grammatical style. He wrote poetry in Latin, most notably *Africa*, an epic celebrating the life of the Roman general Scipio Africanus, as well as beautiful love lyrics in his native Tuscan, known as the *Canzoni* or *Songs*. In 1341, Petrarch was awarded the title of **Poet Laureate** in Rome. The last member of the Triumvirate was **Giovanni Boccaccio** (1313–1375), who developed Italian prose. In the *Decameron*, a collection of one hundred tales, Boccaccio examines every side of human nature in a very entertaining narrative style.

The northern European Renaissance further developed both poetry and prose. England produced some of the most important literature of the period. **Sir Thomas More** (1478–1535), the Christian humanist who served as Chancellor of England, developed a "blueprint" for a perfect society on earth in his novel *Utopia*. In creating this ideal commonwealth, More criticized his own society. Interestingly, *Utopia*, which means either "some place" or "no place" in Ancient Greek, depending on how it is used, is modeled on monastic life,

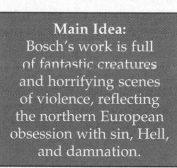

Main Idea:
Bosch's work is full of fantastic creatures and horrifying scenes of violence, reflecting the northern European obsession with sin, Hell, and damnation.

Garden of Delights by Hieronymus Bosch.

Sir Thomas More developed a "blueprint" for a perfect society on earth in his novel *Utopia*.

revealing the author's religious spirit. In contrast, the poetry of **Sir Thomas Wyatt** (c. 1503–1542) reflected the influence of Classical literature. The reign of **Queen Elizabeth I** (1558–1603) was a period of great literary creativity. Known as the **Elizabethan Era**, it saw the highest development of English drama in the masterpieces of **William Shakespeare** (1564–1616), whose plays contain some of the greatest poetry in the English language. These include *Hamlet, Macbeth, Romeo and Juliet, Henry V, Othello, King Lear, The Merchant of Venice, Julius Caesar, As You Like It,* and *A Midsummer Night's Dream*. Equally outstanding are the dramas of **Christopher Marlowe** (1564–1593), including *Doctor Faustus, The Jew of Malta, Tamburlaine the Great,* and *Edward II*. The poetry of **Edmund Spenser** (c. 1552–1599) glorified the ideas of the versatile individual of the Renaissance, particularly in his masterpiece, *The Faerie Queen*. In France, **Michel de Montaigne** (1533–1592) created the literary form of the essay. His near contemporary, **Francois Rabelais** (c. 1490–1553) wrote satirical novels that combined the defense of humanist ideas with comedy. His most notable work was the satire *Gargantua and Pantagruel*. In Spain, literature reached a "golden age," as illustrated by the work of **Miguel de Cervantes** (1547–1616). His masterpiece, *Don Quixote de la Mancha*, a satire about an eccentric gentleman who believes he is a knight, brilliantly criticized Cervantes' own society.

The Renaissance also saw the development of modern historical writing. One of the first to write history in secular terms, **Leonardo Bruni** (1374–1444) was a civic humanist who served as Chancellor of Florence. His *History of the Florentine People* is considered the first modern historical account, due to its scholarly approach. Bruni, who studied the Roman historians, believed that the past had much to teach the present and that human history was basically a struggle for liberty. This was followed a century later by another Florentine, **Francesco Guicciardini** (1483–1540), who regarded history as a unique series of events based on human actions that should be studied on its own terms, not for the lessons it could teach. His work, the *History of Italy*, revealed much of the greed, hatred, ambition, and egotism in Renaissance Italy. As an historian of his own time, he made great use of official archives. Guicciardini's concern for factual accuracy and his worldview of historical causes set new standards in historical writing. *The Lives of the Artists* by **Giorgio Vasari** (1511–1574), a series of short biographies about artists by an artist who knew many of them, is indicative of the changes the Renaissance had brought.

Philosophy flowered in the Renaissance as well. The founding of Greek studies at Florence in 1396 by the Byzantine scholar and diplomat **Manuel Chrysoloras**

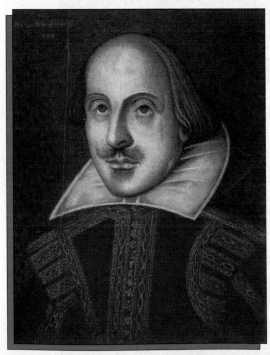

The Elizabethan era saw the highest development of English drama in the masterpieces of William Shakespeare.

(c. 1350–1450) sparked a new interest in the study of the language. As Byzantium fell to the Turks, streams of Greek émigrés came to Italy, bringing Classical works with them. With a new knowledge of the Greek language and literature, interest in philosophy grew as well. Under the leadership of **Marsilio Ficino** (1433–1499), a brilliant scholar who had translated the complete works of Plato, the Platonic Academy of Florence was founded. Ficino and his circle found that Platonic and Neoplatonic philosophy indirectly supported Christian belief. Ficino's most accomplished student was **Giovanni Pico,** Count of Mirandola (1463–1494). Well-educated (he knew Hebrew and Arabic as well as Greek and Latin), Pico argued that the unity of truth exists at the core of all religion and philosophy. He developed these ideas in his massive work *900 Theses*. These views placed him in constant danger from religious authorities. His preface to the *900 Theses* "Oration on the Dignity of Man" is an excellent example of the Renaissance belief in human potential for good. With the revival of Platonism in Florence, a similar interest in the philosophy of Aristotle began. Developing a system called **Aristotelian humanism**, these Renaissance philosophers used the works of Aristotle instead of Plato as models.

Political philosophy was transformed in the Renaissance, most notably by **Niccolo Machiavelli** (1469–1527). A Florentine bureaucrat who had become disillusioned by his experiences, Machiavelli was a realist who believed that decisiveness and force were needed in order for a city or nation to achieve greatness. His most famous work, *The Prince*, was a guidebook for rulers to be successful. He argued that the ideal prince had to use whatever means were necessary to gain and hold on to power *("The end justifies the means")*. The best known of

the northern European humanist philosophers was the scholar **Desiderius Erasmus** (1466–1536). Called the Prince of humanists, he studied the Classics and applied their wisdom to Christian belief. Erasmus sought to "humanize" Christianity, instructing the individual to pay less attention to ritual and theology and to seek the "historical" or human side of Christ, following that example. He also criticized corruption in the Church, calling for religious and social reform. His most famous works are the *Praise of Folly*, which ridiculed the superstition and ignorance of his own time, and *The Education of a Christian Prince*, a book of instruction for rulers that applied Christian humanistic principles, unlike Machiavelli.

Political philosophy was transformed in the Renaissance, most notably by Niccolo Machiavelli.

LINK TO TODAY
The Development of Banks

Few today would question the importance of banks. It was not until the Renaissance, however, that this institution was created. With the revival of trade in the High Middle Ages (1000–1300), coin currency reappeared in western Europe. Increased trade within Europe and with the Byzantine Empire created a greater demand for hard cash as well as a system for exchanging different currencies. By 1200, the northern Italian cities had developed into economically powerful independent states. In Florence, its wool industry and geographic location as a major trade route had made it population wealthy. The need for currency resulted in the creation of Florentine banks owned by the powerful Medici family. In the German city of Augsburg, the wealthy Fuggers opened banks, becoming extremely powerful. Banks became increasingly important to the economic life of European cities. The availability of currency and fixed rates of exchange encouraged further growth of trade and production. Despite the later development of paper currency and electronic money, banks remain an important modern institution.

CHAPTER SUMMARY

The Renaissance was the fusion of centuries of cultural and ethnic diffusion. The civilizations of the Classical World, which include Greek, Roman, and Byzantine, and those of the Medieval World, which include Celtic, Germanic, Scandinavian and Slavic, came together to form the modern European nations. The Renaissance removed the cultural limitations that religion had created in the Middle Ages. A new spirit of curiosity and belief in human potential was created. These attitudes would take Europeans far, both in exploration and scientific progress. They would, however, also remove the controls on society, which would result in religious division, war, and the brutal exploitation of other peoples in the New World. Yet, like a child that must get bruised learning how to walk, Europe stood up and took its first steps. It had entered the modern world.

IMPORTANT
PEOPLE,
PLACES,
AND TERMS

KEY TERMS

Renaissance	Council of Constance	linear perspective
humanism	commune	Poet Laureate
Renaissance man	Black Death	Elizabethan Era
liberal arts	Guelf-Ghibelline	Aristotelian humanism
civic humanism	philology	"The end justifies the
active life	*Saint Jerome Vulgate*	means"
contemplative life	*Donation of Constantine*	republican
High Renaissance	villa	Reformation
Christian humanism	piazza	despots
Babylonian Captivity	naturalism	Great Council
The Great Schism	chiaroscuro	

PLACES

Kingdom of Naples	Milan	Vatican
Kingdom of Sicily	Florence	Sistine Chapel
Papal States	Republic of Venice	Etruscan
Avigon	Cathedral of Florence	Tuscany
Siena	Saint Peter's Basilica	

PEOPLE

Benvenuto Cellini	Piero della Francesca	Giovanni Boccaccio
Baldassarre Castiglione	Giovanni Bellini	Sir Thomas More
Leonardo da Vinci	Giorgione	Sir Thomas Wyatt
Friedrich (Frederick) II	Tintoretto	Queen Elizabeth I
Pope Julius II	Titian	William Shakespeare
Ludovico Sforza the Moor	Raphael	Christopher Marlowe
	Jan van Eyck	Edmund Spenser
Lorenzo de Medici il Magnifico	Rogier van der Weyden	Michel de Montaigne
	Albrecht Dürer	Francois Rabelais
Lorenzo Valla	Hans Holbein	Miguel de Cervantes
Filippo Brunelleschi	Hieronymus Bosch	Leonardo Bruni
Donato Bramante	Peter Bruegel the Elder	Francesco Guicciardini
Michelangelo Bounarroti	Nicola Pisano	Giorgio Vasari
Andrea Palladio	Lorenzo Ghiberti	Manuel Chrysoloras
Giotto	Donatello	Marsilio Ficino
Masaccio	Dante Alighieri	Giovanni Pico
Sandro Botticelli	Francesco Petrarca (Petrarch)	Niccolo Machiavelli
Fra Angelico		Desiderius Erasmus

EXERCISES FOR CHAPTER 10

MULTIPLE CHOICE

Select the letter of the correct answer.

1. A major reason that the Renaissance began in Italy was that

    a. Italian city-states had grown wealthy from trade between Europe and Asia.
    b. farmers produced great agricultural surpluses on vast plains.
    c. merchants developed prosperous trade in southern Italy.
    d. many European scholars migrated there.

2. The term *renaissance* means

    a. revival.
    b. restoration.
    c. rebirth.
    d. return.

3. The Renaissance was chiefly inspired by

    a. Hellenistic civilization.
    b. Medieval scholasticism.
    c. Christianity.
    d. Greco-Roman learning.

4. The Italian Renaissance introduced

   a. no effective political institutions.
   b. democratic ideals.
   c. a strong sense of Italian nationalism.
   d. no fundamental change in society.

5. Which of the following was true of humanism in Italy?

   a. It was religious based on the equality of all humans.
   b. It was an examination of human values.
   c. It was the glorification of humanity and a belief in its potential.
   d. It was an interest in studying the variety of human beings.

6. The inability of the Italians to unite into a single nation resulted in

   a. the domination of the Papacy.
   b. the economic domination of the north.
   c. the deterioration of political organization.
   d. the development of independent city-states.

7. The Italian Renaissance was chiefly centered in

   a. central Italy.
   b. southern Italy.
   c. northern Italy.
   d. Sicily.

8. The term *Renaissance man* refers to

   a. someone who is well-rounded and versatile.
   b. an expert in one area.
   c. an individual who believes in Renaissance Period values.
   d. a teacher of Classical literature.

9. The city known as the cradle of Renaissance culture was

   a. Rome.
   b. Milan.
   c. Venice.
   d. Florence.

10. Which is the correct chronological order of the following events?

    1. civic humanism
    2. literary Renaissance
    3. Byzantine Renaissance
    4. High Renaissance

    a. $3 \rightarrow 2 \rightarrow 1 \rightarrow 4$
    b. $2 \rightarrow 1 \rightarrow 3 \rightarrow 4$
    c. $4 \rightarrow 2 \rightarrow 1 \rightarrow 3$
    d. $1 \rightarrow 2 \rightarrow 3 \rightarrow 4$

11. The city-state of Siena established a

    a. republic.
    b. commune.
    c. oligarchy.
    d. monarchy.

12. The internal political struggle in fourteenth century Florence was between the

    a. Guelfs and Ghibellines.
    b. Medicis and Republicans.
    c. Reds and Greens.
    d. Blacks and Whites.

13. The Republic of Venice was dominated by an oligarchy of

    a. aristocrats.
    b. merchants.
    c. clergy.
    d. military leaders.

14. The Papacy's claim to supreme secular power in western Europe was based on the forged document known as the

    a. Donation of Constantine.
    b. Donation of Clovis.
    c. Donation of Pepin.
    d. Donation of Charlemagne.

15. The architect best known for his construction of the dome on the Cathedral of Florence was

    a. Michelangelo Buonarroti.
    b. Andrea Palladio.
    c. Donato Bramante.
    d. Filippo Brunelleschi.

16. The first Renaissance artist to develop the naturalistic style was

   a. Giotto.
   b. Masaccio.
   c. Fra Angelico.
   d. Piero della Francesca.

17. In his book *The Prince*, Niccolo Machiavelli advises that a wise ruler is one who

   a. keeps taxes and food prices low.
   b. encourages education and the arts.
   c. allows advisors to speak their minds.
   d. does what is necessary to stay in power.

18. The sculpture that came closest to the Classical Ideal of masculine beauty was

   a. Donatello's *David*
   b. Donatello's *Saint George*
   c. Michelangelo's *David*
   d. Michelangelo's *Moses*

19. The Tuscan Triumvirate consisted of

   a. Dante, Petrarch, and Cellini.
   b. Dante, Boccaccio, and Cellini.
   c. Dante, Petrarch, and Boccaccio.
   d. Petrarch, Boccaccio, and Cellini.

20. The art of the Renaissance was similar to that of Ancient Greece and Rome in that both

   a. celebrated human beauty.
   b. focused on religion.
   c. emphasized nature.
   d. were primarily concerned with history.

ESSAYS FOR CHAPTER 10

1. Was the Renaissance truly a "re-birth" of Classical civilization? List two ideas and two institutions of the Greco-Roman World adapted to Christian European society?

2. In what ways did humanism alter European society in the Renaissance? Show two attitudes of Europeans changed by humanistic ideas?

3. Why was the Italian peninsula ideally suited to the development of the Renaissance? Give three reasons that prove this is true.

4. Compare and contrast the Italian Renaissance with that of northern Europe. In what ways were they different? How did the northern European movement completely change the direction and focus of the Renaissance?

5. How was the culture of the Renaissance different from the Middle Ages? Show three ways in which the pursuits of writers, poets, historians, artists, and architects differed from their counterparts in the Middle Ages?

DOCUMENT-BASED QUESTIONS

This task is based on the accompanying documents. Some of these documents have been edited for the purposes of this task. This task is designed to test your ability to work with historical documents. As you analyze the documents, take into account both the source of each document and the author's point of view.

Directions: Read the following documents and answer the questions after each document. Use the information in the reading and this chapter in writing your answers.

Document #1

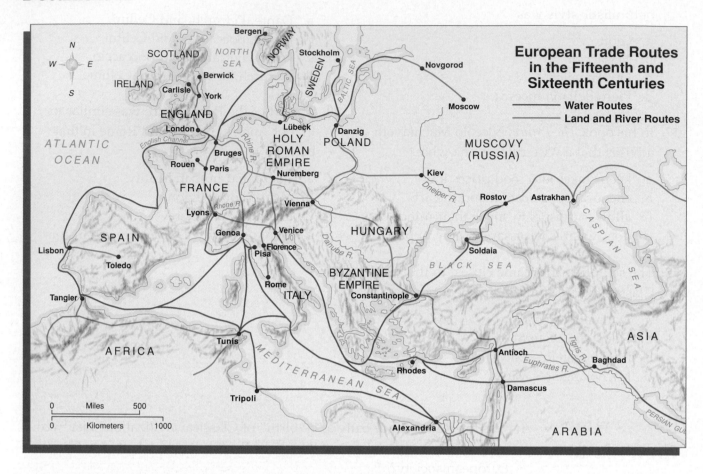

European Trade Routes in the Fifteenth and Sixteenth Centuries

Water Routes
Land and River Routes

Questions

1. Based on this map, list the two causes of economic growth in Western Europe during the thirteenth and fourteenth centuries?
2. Which Italian city-states prospered from this growth of trade?

Document #2   LEONARDO BRUNI, "A HUMANIST EDUCATION"

Devote yourself to two kinds of study. In the first place, acquire a knowledge of letters. . . . Secondly, acquaint yourself with what pertains to life and manners—those things that are called humane studies because they are perfect and adorn man. In this kind of study your knowledge should be wide, varied and taken from every sort of experience, leaving out nothing that might seem to contribute to the conduct of your life, to honor, and to fame. I shall advise you to read authors who can help you not only by their matter but also by the splendor of their style and their skill in writing; that is to say, the works of Cicero . . . thoroughly explore the fundamental and systematic treatment of those matters in Aristotle; as for beauty of expression, a rounded style, and all the wealth of words and speech. . . . For I would wish an outstanding man to be both abundantly learned and capable of giving elegant expression to his learning. However, no one can hope to achieve this without reading a lot, learning a lot, and taking a lot away from everywhere. Thus one must not only learn from the scholars (which is the foundation of all study) but must also get instruction from poets, orators and historians, so that one's style may become eloquent, elegant, and never crude in substance.

Translated by E. Garin

Questions

1. What types of study does Bruni recommend for a student?
2. Why is this type of education referred to as "humanist"?

Document #3   ST. PETER'S BASILICA

Questions

1. Based on this photograph of St. Peter's Basilica, identify the characteristics of both Greco-Roman and Christian culture that are reflected in the architecture.
2. How does this building reflect the ideals of the Italian Renaissance?

Document #4   NICCOLO MACHIAVELLI, *THE PRINCE*

A great many men have imagined states and princedoms such as nobody ever saw or knew in the real world, for there's such a difference between the way we really live and the way we ought to live that the man who neglects the real to study the ideal will learn how to accomplish his ruin, not his salvation.

. . . [A] prince must be shrewd enough to avoid the public disgrace of those vices that would lose him his state. If he possibly can, he should also guard against vices that will not lose him his state; but if he cannot prevent them, he should not be too worried about indulging them. And furthermore, he should not be too worried about incurring blame for any vice without which he would find it hard to save his state.

The question arises: is it better to be loved than feared, or vice versa? I don't doubt that every prince would like to be both; but since it is hard to accommodate these qualities, if you have to make a choice, to be feared is much safer than to be loved. For it is a good general rule about men, that they are ungrateful, fickle, liars and deceivers, fearful of danger and greedy for gain. While you serve their welfare, they are all yours, but when the danger is close at hand, they turn against you.

How praiseworthy it is for a prince to keep his word and live with integrity rather than by craftiness, everyone understands; yet we see from recent experience that those princes have accomplished most who paid little heed to keeping their promises, but who knew how craftily to manipulate the minds of men. In the end, they won out over those who tried to act honestly.

Nothing gives a prince more prestige than undertaking great enterprises and setting splendid example for his people.

A prince ought to show himself an admirer of talent, giving recognition to men of ability and honoring those who excel in particular art. Moreover, he should encourage his citizens to ply their callings in peace, whether in commerce, agriculture, or in any other business.

. . . [T]he prince should bestow prizes on the men who do these things, and on anyone else who takes the pains to enrich the city or state in some special way. He should also, at fitting times of the year, entertain his people with festivals and spectacles.

Translated by Robert M. Adams

| Questions | 1. According to Machiavelli, what qualities should a ruler possess? |
| | 2. How does Machiavelli's view of human nature influence his ideas? |

Document #5   **BALDASSARRE CASTIGLIONE'S**
                          BOOK OF THE COURTIER

I wish, then, that this Courtier of ours should be nobly born and of gentle race; because it is far less unseemly for one of ignoble birth to fail in worthy deeds, that for one of noble birth, who, if he strays from the path of his predecessors, stains his family name, and not only fails to achieve but loses what has been achieved already; for noble birth is like a bright lamp that manifests and makes visible good and evil deeds, and kindles and stimulates to virtue both by fear of shame and by hope of praise.

. . . [T]he principle and true profession of the Courtier ought to be that of arms; which I would have him follow actively above all else, and be known among others as bold and strong, and loyal to whomsoever he serves, and he will win a reputation for these good qualities by exercising them at all times and in all places the reputation of a gentleman who bears arms, if once it be in the least tarnished with cowardice or other disgrace, remains forever infamous before the world and full of ignominy. . . . [Y]et I do not deem essential in him that perfect knowledge of things and those other qualities that befit a commander; since this would be too wide a sea, let us be content, as we have said, with perfect loyalty and unconquered courage. . . .

Then coming to the bodily frame, I say it is enough if this be neither extremely short nor tall, for both of these conditions excite a certain contemptuous surprise, and men of either sort are gazed upon in much the same way that we gaze on monsters. Yet if we must offend in one of the two extremes, it is preferable to fall a little short of the just measure of height than to exceed it, for besides often being dull of intellect, men thus huge of body are also unfit for every exercise of agility, which this I should much wish in the Courtier. And so I would have him well built and shapely of limb, and would have him show strength and lightness and suppleness, and know all bodily exercises that befit a man of war: I think the first should be to handle every sort of weapon well on foot and on horse, to understand the advantages of each and especially to be familiar with those weapons that are ordinarily used among gentlemen; for besides the use of them in war . . . there frequently arise differences between one gentleman and another, which afterwards results in duels often fought with such weapons as happen at the moment to be within reach. . . .

It is fitting also to know how to swim, to leap, to run, to throw stones, for besides the use that may be made of this in war, a man often has occasion to show what he can do in such matters, whence good esteem is to be won . . . another admirable exercise, and one very befitting a man at court, is the game of tennis, in which are well shown the disposition of the body, and the quickness and suppleness of every member, and all those qualities that are seen in nearly every other exercise. Nor less highly do I esteem vaulting on horse, which although it be fatiguing and difficult, makes a man very light and dexterous more than any other thing; besides its utility, if this lightness is accompanied by grace, it is to my thinking a finer show than any of the others.

From *Book of the Courtier*, translated by George Bull

| Questions | 1. Based on Castiglione's book, what characteristics should an individual serving in the court of a ruler develop? |
| | 2. How do these ideas reflect the ideals of the Italian Renaissance? |

CHAPTER 11

The Reformation

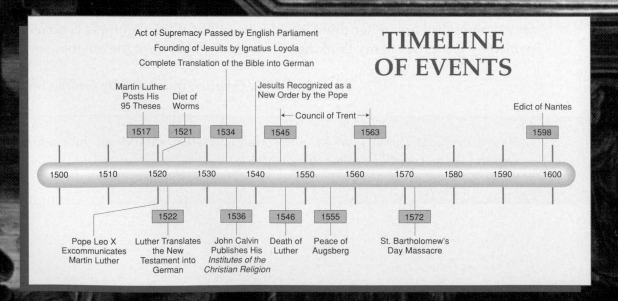

TIMELINE
OF EVENTS

Act of Supremacy Passed by English Parliament

Founding of Jesuits by Ignatius Loyola

Complete Translation of the Bible into German

Martin Luther
Posts His
95 Theses

Diet of
Worms

Jesuits Recognized as a
New Order by the Pope

←— Council of Trent —→

Edict of Nantes

| 1517 | 1521 | 1534 | 1545 | 1563 | 1598 |

1500   1510   1520   1530   1540   1550   1560   1570   1580   1590   1600

| 1522 | 1536 | 1546 | 1555 | 1572 |

Pope Leo X
Excommunicates
Martin Luther

Luther Translates
the New
Testament into
German

John Calvin
Publishes His
*Institutes of the
Christian Religion*

Death of
Luther

Peace of
Augsberg

St. Bartholomew's
Day Massacre

As we saw in the last chapter, The Renaissance helped to form what we now call Modern Europe. The Reformation also helped to do this. The **Reformation**, also called the Protestant Reformation, is a period of time in history. The reasons for this will be explained in the following chapter. Simply defined, the Reformation was a movement to reform, or change, certain ideas and practices of the Roman Catholic Church. The movement was successful in some parts of Europe. In addition to affecting religion, the Reformation had an impact on economics and politics in Europe. Ultimately, it was going to have an effect on life in the "New World" of the Americas. Of all the people who played major historical roles during the Reformation, the most important was Martin Luther. His actions in October 1517 marked the start of the Reformation. Let us now turn to him to understand more about his place in European history.

THE LIFE OF MARTIN LUTHER

> **Main Idea:**
> Although Luther did not initially wish to start a new religion, his ideas and other beliefs eventually became known as Lutheranism.

Born in 1483 to a wealthy German peasant family, **Martin Luther** originally planned to study law. However in 1505, during a terrible rainstorm, he was knocked to the ground. He cried out for help and declared, "I will become a monk." Soon thereafter, he gave up the study of law and entered a monastery. He led a holy life and became very interested in the religious doctrine or idea about salvation of the soul. Eventually, he became a monk as well as a professor of religion at the University of Wittenberg.

His interest in the doctrine of salvation grew to the point where he became disturbed with the then-current teachings of the Roman Catholic Church about this idea. These teachings stated that in order to overcome a person's sins, and thereby achieve salvation, the person had to have faith, perform good works, pray, and fast. It was also permissible to buy an **indulgence** (a Church pardon to escape punishment for a sin). From Luther's point of view, however, all that should be necessary to gain salvation was to have faith in God. He rejected the need to perform good works, attend fancy ceremonies, and buy indulgences as signs of good faith. In fact, his idea came to be called simply "justification by faith."

These ideas and other beliefs of Luther eventually became known as Lutheranism. Initially, Luther did not wish to start a new religion. Rather, he only wanted to make some changes in Church practices. Nevertheless, his teachings angered papal authorities in Rome. An additional reason for papal anger was Luther's criticism of the vast amount of wealth accumulated by Church officials. Besides protesting the sale of indulgences, for example, Luther was also against such practices as **simony** (selling Church offices), and **nepotism** (appointing relatives to high positions). He felt that these practices were wrongful because they were not in keeping with what he thought was the spiritual mission of the Church.

Luther's ideas, particularly those on indulgences, attracted much public attention. This was due mainly to his posting his **Ninety-Five Theses** on a Wittenberg church door on Sunday, October 31, 1517. The posting of these *theses*, or statements, was a specific reaction to the activities of a monk named **Johann Tetzel**. Tetzel had been sent by **Pope Leo X** to raise money for rebuilding the cathedral of St. Peter's in Rome. Tetzel's travels took him to German villages near Wittenberg, where he attempted to obtain money by offering indulgences for sale. He claimed that buyers of indulgences would be making charitable contributions and at the same time would be gaining forgiveness for their sins. Luther criticized such claims. He stated that indulgences could neither help people escape purgatory nor cancel out their sins; that it was improper to seek money from people in return for false promises. Consequently, as was common in those days, Luther wrote down his thoughts and nailed them to the church doors. These were the Ninety-Five Theses.

In posting these theses, Luther did not seek to start a revolution or a division in the Catholic Church. Basically, he was objecting to the impropriety of Tetzel's actions. He also wanted people to consider the propriety of the claims connected with these practices. Little did he realize or intend the widespread impact of his actions. News about what he had done spread quickly throughout Europe, due in large measure to the printing press. The Ninety-Five Theses were reprinted and aroused much controversy. The sale of indulgences began to diminish, while the irritation of papal authorities began to increase. Although he was under great pressure from these authorities, Luther refused to recant or take back his views. In a famous debate in 1519 with John Eck, who was sent by the pope to confront Luther in Leipzig, Luther held to his opinions. He also admitted that they were similar to those of John Huss. Huss had preached against the Church in the fifteenth century, was accused of heresy, and was burned at the stake.

Luther now increased his attacks upon the Church. For example, he declared that the authority of the Bible and the authority of a person's conscience were more important than the authority of the pope. In June 1520, Pope Leo X **excommunicated** Luther by issuing a *Papal Bull* (an official document from the Pope). When Luther received this document, he took the dramatic step of burning it in front of a large crowd in a public square in Wittenberg. He felt confident and fearless in doing this because of the strong support he had been getting in this part of Europe from people who agreed with his views.

The next year, 1521, proved to be very momentous. Luther was summoned to appear before the Imperial Diet at Worms by Emperor **Charles V**. He was emperor of the Holy Roman Empire, the large region in central Europe that includes modern-day Germany. Charles V wanted to carry out the excommunication because he feared that Luther's teachings and actions would create trouble throughout the empire. At Worms, Luther was put under severe questioning as attempts were made to get him to recant his views. However, he stood his ground. A loose translation of his emotional response to one question was as follows: "Here I stand; I cannot do otherwise. God help me. Amen."

Frederick the Wise of Saxony hid Luther in his castle for almost a year.

Stunned by Luther's firm resistance, Charles V now issued the **Edict of Worms**. This document condemned Luther as a heretic, forbade the distribution and reading of his works, and ordered his arrest and banishment from the empire. Fortunately for Luther, several German princes were willing to protect him from danger. One of these, Frederick the Wise of Saxony, hid Luther in his castle for almost a year. Luther eventually returned to Wittenberg without being bothered by any authorities. He married a former nun and raised a large family. All of these actions intensified his break with the Roman Catholic Church. In 1529, some of his followers published a protest against the Edict of Worms. Thereafter, his followers became known as Protestants. And what was described generally as the new Protestant religion, based on Luther's teachings, spread rapidly in the northern parts of the Holy Roman Empire. Indeed, by the time of his death in 1546, this new religion had been accepted by many princes in this area.

There are now some important questions for us to ask about this Protestant Reformation: What were Luther's basic teachings? What factors were responsible for bringing about the Reformation? What was its impact?

LUTHER'S TEACHINGS—BASIC PRINCIPLES OF PROTESTANTISM

Most of Luther's basic ideas can be found in his writings. The most important of these, published in 1520, were *Address to the Nobility of the German Nation, On the Babylonian Captivity of the Church,* and *The Freedom of a Christian Man.* Their chief ideas, which are listed here, were accepted by most of the Protestant sects that emerged in Europe. These sects viewed Protestantism as a revision and reformulation of Christian beliefs and traditions. The contrasting views of the Roman Catholic Church at the time are in parentheses:

1. Salvation comes about through faith alone. (Salvation results from faith and good works.)

2. Religious authority rests with the Bible, not with the pope. (The pope and Church officials under his leadership are the sources of authority.)

3. Only two **sacraments** are permitted—baptism and communion. (Seven sacraments are practiced—baptism, communion, confirmation, penance, marriage, ordination, and extreme unction.)

4. The **clergy**, known as ministers, are only guides for the faithful. People should be free to understand and interpret the Bible for themselves. Accordingly, Luther held services in German rather than in Latin. In 1522, he translated the New Testament into German. His complete translation of the Bible, from Hebrew and Greek texts, appeared in 1534. (Priests were needed to explain writings.)

5. Priests could marry. (Because of their vow of celibacy, priests could not marry.)

FACTORS LEADING TO THE REFORMATION

We generally date the beginning of the Reformation to 1517. Its origins and fundamental causes, however, can be found prior to the day when Luther posted his Ninety-Five Theses. Such tracing of causes is important whenever studying great historical movements. For example, we realize that the origins of the fall of the Roman Empire can be seen prior to 476, and that the origins of the American Revolution occurred before 1776. Martin Luther's protests against Church practices and beliefs were shared by many people in northern Europe. You may recall that he was concerned about such practices as simony, nepotism, sale of indulgences, and the worldliness of the clergy, as well as teachings about salvation and the role of the pope. These religious reasons by themselves, however, cannot explain why the movement known as the Reformation had such a major historical impact. In many areas, Luther's actions against the Church were supported by people for reasons that had little to do with religion. Nonreligious factors that helped to bring about the Reformation are as follows:

1. *Economic conflicts*: Many rulers were upset about the economic power and wealth of the Roman Catholic Church. This power and wealth came from taxes imposed by the Church on its worshipers as well as from the vast amounts of land it owned throughout Europe. Local rulers were angry about the huge amount of money that flowed out of their regions into the papal treasury in Rome. To many rulers, who lived at great distances from Rome, the papacy seemed to be a foreign power interested chiefly in draining wealth from others. And in truth, these rulers hoped to obtain this wealth for themselves and for their people.

2. *Political conflicts*: Many people believed that the pope had too much power over political and other *secular*, or nonreligious, matters. In the late Middle Ages, political leaders often challenged the pope's claim to be supreme in secular as well as religious affairs. They resisted the Church's claim to power over them and other civil officials and to its interference in political matters concerning their territories. They also strongly objected to the Church's authority to remove rulers, to excuse their subjects from allegiance on issues of loyalty and obedience, and to transfer their land to others.

3. *Humanism and Renaissance thought:* The Renaissance emphasized the ability of humans to think and reason for themselves. Along with this came the questioning of traditional authority. In this atmosphere, many people began to disagree with certain Church practices and ideas.

4. *Previous Church problems and reform attempts:* Even before Luther, there had been problems within the Church. One example was the Babylonian Captivity of 1309 to 1377, when popes lived in France and were under control of the king of France. Another instance was the Great Schism of 1378 to 1417, when two popes competed for control of the Church. Other reformers had attacked some of the same practices that Luther protested against. These included John Wycliffe in England, John Huss in Bohemia, and Desiderius Erasmus in Holland. Wycliffe claimed that Jesus Christ, not the pope, was the real head of the Church. Huss preached that the Bible's authority was higher than that of the pope. Erasmus was critical of the Church's wealth and worldliness.

Main Idea:
In many areas, Luther's actions against the Church were supported by people for reasons that had little to do with religion.

THE GROWTH AND IMPACT OF PROTESTANTISM

The protests by Luther are the basis for the word *Protestant*. His movement was to have serious political and religious consequences in the German states. These consequences are discussed in the following paragraphs.

Many German Princes Supported Luther

> **Main Idea:**
> Both the pope and the Holy Roman Emperor were seen as foreigners who had exerted too much control over the German princely states.

The German princes wanted to break away from the religious and economic powers of the pope. They also wanted to break from the control and power of Charles V, the Holy Roman Emperor. Both the pope and the Holy Roman Emperor were seen as foreigners who had exerted too much control over the German princely states. Feelings of patriotism and nationalism grew, mostly in the northern German areas. Fighting soon broke out between German princes and Charles V because the emperor wanted to stop the spread of Protestantism. However, neither side was able to win decisively. The fighting eventually stopped as a result of the Peace of Augsburg, recognized in a treaty signed in 1555. Two terms of this document were vital in the history of religion in Europe.

1. Lutheranism was recognized as a legal religion.

2. The ruler of an area was the one who would determine the religion for the people of that area. Therefore, if the head of the German state of Saxony chose to follow Protestantism, then his subjects would be Protestant. If the ruler of Bavaria chose to remain a Catholic, then his subjects would be Catholic. Subjects who refused to accept the faith chosen by the ruler could not stay in the area. Practically all the northern German princes selected the new Lutheran faith.

Protestant Sects Began to Appear

As Protestantism gained popularity, various groups or sects appeared. Some of these often fought with each other as well as with Catholics. Most of these sects did not become large, organized established churches, but they often united behind a leader and tried to live by their own interpretations of the Bible. One such group was the Anabaptists, eventually to be called the Baptists. Among their beliefs were the separation of church and state, religious tolerance, and baptism and Church membership for adults only. They reasoned that children should not be baptized because of their inability to understand the faith. For these and other beliefs, along with the fact that they were seen as threats to established customs, the Anabaptists suffered persecution; as an extreme example, in the German city of Munster in 1535, many Anabaptists were executed. Nevertheless, several Anabaptist groups survived. They existed in ways they thought were typical of early Christian communities—by sharing, working, and praying together and by emphasizing *ascetism* (denial of worldly ways and pleasures, avoidance of materialism). The spirit of their beliefs can be seen today in the United States in such various groups as the Baptists, Quakers, Mennonites, and Amish.

The Peasants' Rebellion of 1524

Angered with the heavy taxes put upon them by nobles and the Church, southern German peasants began to react with violence. Although Luther initially supported the peasants' stand, he soon reversed his support. He was upset with their many instances of burning and killing. Critical of such actions, Luther backed the successful efforts of nobles in putting down the revolt. Consequently, many peasants grew disappointed with Luther and returned to Catholicism.

Luther and the Jews

Among Luther's many harsh criticisms of the Catholic Church was its poor treatment of the Jews. Laws and actions taken against Jews were wrong, he claimed, as were the Church's beliefs about the Jews and its attempts to convert them. The small community of German Jews initially responded favorably to Luther, welcoming him as a defender and feeling that he respected them. However, when Luther also attempted to convert them, they resisted. Luther then became bitter toward Jews for not accepting entry into his version of Christianity. He made vicious anti-Semitic statements and even suggested extermination. Luther's anti-Semitism emerged late in his life and had little effect upon his followers. Indeed, those Scandinavian countries in which the majority of citizens became Lutherans, were helpful to Jews during the twentieth-century Holocaust initiated by the Germans.

THE GROWTH OF PROTESTANTISM BEYOND GERMANY

The Protestant Reformation began as a movement in Germany and spread to other parts of Europe. The spread was most evident in northern Europe and to some of the European colonies in North America.

Our survey of the influence of Luther's movement in non-German areas will begin with Switzerland. It was here, in the city of Zurich, that the priest Ulrich Zwingli was active. Like Luther, Zwingli believed that the Catholic Church had strayed from its original purposes. Both men wished to provide reforms. Until the time of his death in 1531, Zwingli had spoken out against indulgences and was in favor of simplifying church building decorations and allowing priests to marry.

Calvinism

The ideas of Zwingli and Luther spread throughout Switzerland and influenced a Frenchman, **John Calvin**, who lived in Geneva. Calvin's thoughts about religion are contained in his book, *The Institutes of the Christian Religion*, published in 1536. As Luther did, Calvin opposed the belief that good works would lead to **salvation**. However, Calvin's emphasis on some issues was different from Luther's. Luther, for example, claimed that people could achieve salvation through faith in God. Calvin maintained that God alone would decide who would be saved; God had already selected these people. This was the theory of **predestination**. According to this theory, God chose certain people, called the elect, to be saved. Those who had not been chosen could never achieve salvation, no matter what they did on earth. Although people obviously did not know whether they were among the elect, they should nevertheless behave as though they were among the chosen. This behavior would consist of leading a life according to extremely strict and high moral standards. These standards included careful devotion to the Bible, self-discipline, avoidance of material occupations, living simply, and working hard and honestly in one's occupation.

John Calvin (1509–1564).

It was in Geneva in 1541 that Calvinism became a way of life for citizens there. The city was governed as a **theocracy**. This meant that the government and all laws and rules came under the influence of religious ideas. There was no separation of church and state. For example, Calvinist regulations against dancing, obscene language, bad manners, and so on were strictly enforced by the government. Geneva became a center for many Europeans who wished to learn about Calvinist ideas. Geneva was practically a Calvinist Rome.

Calvinism could be considered simply one form or pattern within the Protestant Movement against the Catholic Church. Its influence was very great, however. It spread to the Netherlands (Holland), appealing primarily to those living in urban, commercial areas. Calvinism also gained followers in France, particularly among those concerned with the worldliness of the Catholic Church. These followers organized churches, mostly in southern France, and were called **Huguenots**. Their attempts to exist were challenged, most critically during the wars of religion that raged in France between 1562 and 1598. A terrible incident of religious violence was the St. Bartholomew's Day Massacre of August 1572. Thousands of Huguenots were killed in Paris and other parts of France. Religious tension continued until issuance of the **Edict of Nantes** in 1598. This stated that Protestants in France (as well as those practicing other religions) were permitted to practice their faith. This was a victory for religious toleration.

Main Idea:
Calvin's thoughts about religion are contained in his book, *The Institutes of the Christian Religion.*

Protestantism in England

Besides France and the German states, the other major region experiencing religious change in the sixteenth century was England. What has even become known as the English Reformation was begun by King **Henry VIII** (r. 1509–1547). However, his reasons for a change were very different from those of Martin Luther. Henry's protest against the Catholic Church was more for political than for religious reasons. In fact, Henry had been a devout Catholic and had written a criticism of Martin Luther in 1521. This criticism had impressed the pope, who gave Henry the title "defender of the faith." This is a title that is still carried by the British monarch.

Henry's problems with the Church stemmed from his wish to have a male heir to his throne. He was unable to have a son with his first wife, Catherine of Aragon. He therefore wanted to divorce Catherine and marry Anne Boleyn. To his dismay, his request to Pope Clement VII for an *annulment* (voiding) of his marriage to Catherine was denied. Angered by this denial, Henry spoke out against the pope and authorized the Archbishop of Canterbury, Thomas Cranmer, to annul the marriage. Henry then married Anne Boleyn. The pope responded by declaring the divorce from Catherine invalid and excommunicating Henry. With resentment growing against the pope, Parliament passed the Act of Supremacy in 1534. This legislation established the king as the head of the Church of England, or Anglican Church. **Anglicans**, as its followers were called, were no longer under the authority of the pope. Anglicanism became a religion that kept some Catholic ideas and ceremonies but also mixed them with Protestant ways, as in the use of the English language instead of Latin.

Henry's actions were supported by a large majority of English people. They also welcomed his closing down many monasteries and selling the monastery lands. Those who opposed Henry resented the break with Rome. This group included Sir Thomas More. He had hoped to have reforms come from within the Catholic Church itself. Henry feared More and had him executed, along with others who opposed the Act of Supremacy. After Henry died, having married six times, the crown passed to his son, Edward VI. During his reign (1547–1553), Protestant officials published *The Book of Common Prayer*. This

King Henry VIII of England.

> **Main Idea:**
> Henry's problems with the Church stemmed from his wish to have a male heir to his throne.

> **Main Idea:**
> With resentment growing against the pope, the Parliament passed the Act of Supemacy in 1534. This legislation established the king as the head of the Church of England.

Catherine of Aragon, the first queen of Henry VIII.

described practices to be observed in Anglican services and was a combination of both Protestant and Catholic ideas. The transformation of England into a Protestant nation was stalled by Edward's successor, Mary Tudor (r. 1553–1558). She tried to make England Catholic again and to restore the authority of the pope. Upon her death, another daughter of Henry VIII became queen. This was **Elizabeth I** (r. 1558–1603). She was interested, as was the case with her father, in devoting her energy to political issues rather than to religious ones. Nevertheless, she did much to make England a Protestant nation. She enforced her belief that the monarch was the head of the Anglican Church. In addition, she continued her father's policy of seizing Church lands and had Parliament pass an act that forced people to pay a fine if they did not attend the Anglican Church. By strengthening both her role and that of the Anglican Church, Elizabeth hoped to bring about greater political unity in England. It can thus be said that by the time of her death in 1603, England had indeed become a predominantly Protestant nation. This did not mean, however, that religious controversy and its effect on politics had died down. For almost one hundred years after Elizabeth's death, the English people were to experience much tension and even a civil war (see Chapter 16).

Sir Thomas More was executed at the orders of King Henry VIII.

Queen Elizabeth I was one of Henry VIII's daughters. She hoped to bring political unity to England.

PROTESTANTISM ELSEWHERE

Elsewhere in Europe, Protestantism was making inroads. **John Knox** brought Calvinism to Scotland, having lived for some time in Geneva. A form of Calvinism, Presbyterianism, became the national religion of Scotland. In Ireland, Protestants who came over from England became the ruling class. Anglicans in the American colonies became Episcopalians. The great majority of Irish people, however, remained as Catholics. The Scandinavian countries of Denmark, Norway, and Sweden witnessed a spread of Protestant beliefs. Led by royal leaders, Lutheran national state churches were created in these lands.

In lands overseas, particularly in some New World colonies of North America, the Protestant Reformation had an impact. The Puritans who settled in Massachusetts, for example, had left Europe fearing persecution. Their attempt to "purify" the Anglican Church of all features of Catholicism had caused them problems with English officials. In Virginia, the Church of England became the established Church. Roger Williams, a strong believer in religious freedom and a founder of Rhode Island, is memorialized in a statute of him on "Reformation Wall" in Geneva. In the Dutch colony of New Amsterdam, the settlers were of a Protestant faith. Even today, one can find Dutch Reformed Churches and cemeteries in New York City. They are in the borough of Brooklyn, named after the Dutch town of Breukelen. And finally, we should not be surprised to find that the greatest number of Lutherans living in the United States can be found in the Midwest. The explanation lies in the great emigration of Scandinavian people from, for example, Norway to Minnesota and Iowa.

Main Idea:
Protestantism spread not only to other European countries, but to New World colonies of North America as well.

John Knox brought Calvinism to Scotland.

Lutheranism and Anglicanism were religious offsprings of the Protestant Reformation. So were many other religious groups we have mentioned —the Anabaptists, the Calvinists, and the Presbyterians. Each of these is considered as a form of Protestantism. Although these various groups or denominations had differences, they shared several things in common. One of these was their refusal to come under the authority of the pope. Obviously, the pope and Catholic Church saw Protestantism as a threat to their view of Christian unity in western Europe. Their attempts to fight this threat are the topic to which we will now turn.

THE CATHOLIC AND COUNTER REFORMATIONS

The reaction of the Catholic Church to the Protestant Movement took two basic patterns.

1. The attempt to make some reforms and changes within the Church, maintaining obedience to the pope while recognizing some of the abuses that Luther had attacked. This attempt can be called the Catholic Reformation.

2. The attempt to stop the spread of Protestantism by creating new religious orders. This attempt can be called the **Counter Reformation**.

Main Idea:
Although the Council of Trent upheld the traditional beliefs and practices of the Roman Catholic Church, it also corrected some abuses.

These reactions by the Catholic Church had the support of political leaders, mainly in southern Europe, just as Luther's efforts had support from political leaders in northern Europe. The move to press for changes within the Church came from Pope Paul III (r. 1534–1549). He appointed scholarly figures to high Church positions, such as cardinals and bishops. These leaders sought to maintain a strong devotion to Catholicism. They were willing, though, to provide for a spiritual renewal. An opportunity to do this occurred with Pope Paul's call for a Church council at the city of Trent in 1545. The **Council of Trent** (1545–1563) upheld the traditional beliefs and practices of the Roman Catholic Church, including the supreme power of the pope over the Church and the necessity of both faith and good works for salvation. It also corrected some abuses, banning the sale of indulgences and forbidding simony. It called for improvement in the training of priests as well as in the keeping of Church finances. New ground was broken by the Council of Trent with the creation of the **Index**. This was a list of books that Catholics were not permitted to read. Books would be placed on the Index if they contained ideas deemed by the Church to be heretical. The Index was seen as an effective weapon to use against the widespread publication of books that had been made possible by the fifteenth-century invention of the printing press. (The Church kept the Index until 1966. In that year, the Second Vatican Council abolished it.) The work of the Council of Trent was designed, in part, to reach some reconciliation with Protestants. Protestant leaders who were invited, however, did not attend.

The establishment of new religious orders or groups, begun in the 1520s, proved to be important. The Capuchins, a branch of the Franciscans, was organized to carry out the ideals of St. Francis and preach to the poor. The Ursuline order of nuns gained an admirable reputation for educating women. But the most scholarly and educated of these new groups was the **Jesuits**. Known formally as the Society of Jesus, this order was founded in 1534 by the Spaniard **Ignatius Loyola** (1491–1556). After receiving a serious wound as a soldier, Loyola became deeply involved in studying about religious issues during his period of recovery. Ultimately, he wrote a book, *Spiritual Exercises.* In it, he emphasized self-discipline and complete obedience to papal leadership of the Roman Catholic Church. These became major characteristics of the Jesuit order, whose followers became known as the "soldiers of the Catholic Church."

The Jesuits were officially recognized as an order by the pope in 1540. They went about their tasks as if they were a finely tuned military organization. Their tasks were to prevent the spread of Protestantism, to help Catholics keep their faith, and to win converts. Their weapons were not guns but devotion, education, and a strong sense of purpose. They were respected for their learning and willingness to engage in debates on religious topics. In southern Germany and eastern Europe, they were successful in winning some Protestants back to Catholicism. Their efforts, along with the measure of the Council of Trent, were highly welcomed in Spain, France, and Italy. The Jesuits also traveled overseas to East Asia and the Americas, where they proved to be successful **missionaries**.

Another method used by the Roman Catholic Church to combat Protestantism was the Inquisition. This was a series of Church courts, originally established during the Middle Ages to put heretics on trial. The courts of the Inquisition tried to impose religious uniformity. They proved to be successful mainly in areas of southern Europe, where Protestantism was not much of a threat. The Inqusition had little impact in areas where Protestantism had a firm hold.

Saint Ignatius Loyola founded the Jesuits.

RESULTS OF THE PROTESTANT REFORMATION

The chief result of the Protestant Reformation was the breakdown of the religious unity of western Europe. By 1600, the territorial divisions between Protestants and Catholics were clear to see (see the accompanying map). The various Protestant faiths were primarily in northern Europe, whereas Catholicism remained dominant in southern Europe. Religious hostility was to continue, one example being the Thirty Years' War (1618–1648). Additional results were as follows:

Political. The monarchs and local officials , especially in central and northern Europe, gained power as the strength of the Catholic Church declined.

Economic. The selling of Church property and the end of Church taxes in Protestant areas resulted in an increase in wealth in these areas.

Cultural. Progress was made in education and literacy, especially because of the greater interest in reading the Bible. The growth of universities was supported by reformers, and was a continuation of learning brought on by the Renaissance. For Jesuits, scholastic institutions were instrumental for promoting self-discipline and enriching religious faith.

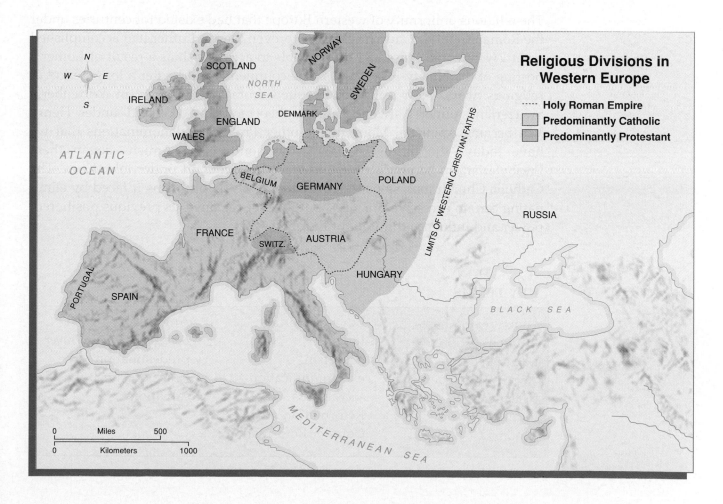

LINK TO TODAY
The Legacy of the Jesuits in the United States

The great devotion to learning and scholarship of the Jesuits is seen in many of the colleges they founded in Europe and elsewhere. Today in the United States, there are several Jesuit institutions of higher learning—Boston College, Fordham University, Georgetown University, Marquette University, Notre Dame University, Loyola University in Chicago, and Loyola University in New Orleans. It should also be noted that those parts of the Americas that were colonized by France, Portugal, and Spain are primarily Catholic in today's world.

CHAPTER SUMMARY

The religious uniformity of western Europe that had existed for centuries under the Roman Catholic Church was gone forever. Martin Luther had accomplished what Wycliffe and Huss had been unable to accomplish as a result of Luther's posting of the Ninety-Five Theses. The continent would enter a long period of religious wars. New religions resulted from what began in Wittenberg. Switzerland under Calvin became a theocracy, and England under Henry VIII became Anglican. Many of the other Protestant denominations that we have today—the Baptist, Quaker, Mennonite, and Amish—began then. Presbyterianism became strong and spread in Scotland under John Knox. The Catholic Church took steps to remedy some of the problems it faced by eliminating certain excessive practices, but it never regained its previous position of power and influence throughout Europe.

IMPORTANT PEOPLE, PLACES, AND TERMS

KEY TERMS

Ninety-Five Theses	Edict of Worms	Anglican
Council of Trent	Index	*Book of Common Prayer*
Edict of Nantes	nepotism	predestination
Act of Supremacy	excommunication	Peace of Augsburg
theocracy	sacraments	salvation
indulgences	Reformation	
simony	Counter Reformation	

PEOPLE

John Calvin	Leo X	Henry VIII
Johann Tetzel	Jesuits	Elizabeth I
Charles V	John Knox	Huguenots
Ignatius Loyola	clergy	
Martin Luther	missionaries	

PLACES

Wittenberg	Rome	Holy Roman Empire

EXERCISES FOR CHAPTER 11

MULTIPLE CHOICE

Select the letter of the correct answer.

1. Which pair shared the most in common?

   a. Tetzel and Luther
   b. Luther and Calvin
   c. Calvin and the pope
   d. Luther and the pope

2. Which factor most helped in leading to the Protestant Reformation?

   a. The Catholic clergy had lost faith in its religion.
   b. Islam was attracting many converts in western Europe.
   c. The nobility in northern Europe resented the power of the Catholic Church.
   d. Exploration of the Americas led to the introduction of new religious ideas.

3. The development of the printing press helped the success of the Protestant Reformation mainly by

   a. providing in writing that the Catholic clergy was not completely correct in matters of faith.
   b. making the spread of new ideas possible.
   c. describing the evils of simony.
   d. providing translations of the Bible.

4. In general, the religious Reformation that occurred under Henry VIII in his country was mainly for reasons that could be described as

   a. economic.
   b. social.
   c. political.
   d. military.

5. As a result of the Protestant Reformation, western Europe today can be described as a region that

   a. is all Protestant.
   b. is obedient to the pope.
   c. has religious diversity.
   d. has many gods or deities.

6. In which pair of people did the actions of the first person lead to actions by the second person?

   a. John Knox—John Huss
   b. Martin Luther—Ignatius Loyola
   c. John Calvin—Johann Tetzel
   d. Henry VIII—Martin Luther

7. The greatest significance of the Reformation for later European history was that

    a. most Europeans abandoned Catholicism for Protestantism.
    b. conflict between religious and secular authorities was reduced.
    c. the Church's control over idea was diminished.
    d. Christianity was no longer a powerful force.

8. Calvinism was brought to North America by

    a. Jews in New Amsterdam.
    b. Spaniards in Mexico.
    c. French in Canada.
    d. Puritans in Massachusetts.

9. According to Luther, salvation comes about through

    a. good works.
    b. faith.
    c. indulgences.
    d. a saintly life.

10. Which heading best describes these individuals?

    I. _____

        A. Moses
        B. Jesus
        C. Muhammad
        D. Luther

    a. Writers of religious scriptures
    b. Religious leaders who initially faced opposition to ideas they presented
    c. Conquerors who spread their religious thoughts
    d. Religious figures who preached polytheism

11. Which of the following could be considered an effect of the Protestant Reformation?

    a. Posting of the Ninety-Five Theses
    b. Decline in the power of the Roman Catholic Church
    c. Sale of indulgences
    d. End of religious warfare

12. Prior to the Protestant Reformation, the Medieval church in western Europe was criticized for:

    a. sponsoring explorations in the Middle East.
    b. allowing the Bible to be printed and distributed to the people.
    c. being too concerned with worldly power and riches.
    d. refusing to sell indulgences to peasants.

13. Which of the following is common to both Catholics and Protestants?

    a. The pope as a spiritual leader
    b. Religious authority rests with the Bible
    c. Acceptance of only two sacraments
    d. Belief in monotheism

14. Which action would best complete this partial outline?

    I. Luther and his ideas

        A. Posting of the Ninety-Five Theses
        B. Excommunication by the pope
        C. Translation of the Bible into German
        D. _____

    a. New interpretation of the Old Testament
    b. Spread of Protestantism in America
    c. Acceptance of Luther's teachings by the Spanish monarchy
    d. Expansion of Protestantism under Charles V

15. King Henry VIII of England and Prince Shotoku of Japan were similar in that, during their rule, they permitted

    a. Protestant beliefs to be taught in schools.
    b. a new faith to be practiced that began in a foreign area.
    c. Hindu ideas to be spread in major cities.
    d. Ignatious Loyola to preach in churches.

16. The Jesuit order originated under the leadership of

    a. John Calvin.   c. Desiderius Erasmus.
    b. Ignatious Loyola. d. Martin Luther.

17. Besides the two-part division of Christianity in western Europe into Catholicism and Protestantism, which belief system underwent a similar division?

    a. Confucianism
    b. Taoism
    c. Hinduism
    d. Islam

18. "Luther did not wish to start a new religion. He only wanted to make some changes in Christian teachings and practices. The resulting faith thus retained some *traditional* Catholic ideas as well as *new* Protestant ideas." Which if the following figures had a similar impact in regard to the history of his religion?

    a. Muhammad
    b. Guatama
    c. Moses
    d. Lao-tzu

Base your answers to Questions 19 and 20 on the map below and your knowledge of social studies.

19. In which nation was the Counter Reformation successful?

    a. Sweden
    b. Italy
    c. Holland
    d. Denmark

20. If this map were updated for all of Europe, and also showed areas inhabited by Orthodox Christians, Jews, and Muslims, which social science concept would be apparent and relevant?

    a. Interdependence
    b. Imperialism
    c. Diversity
    d. Conflict

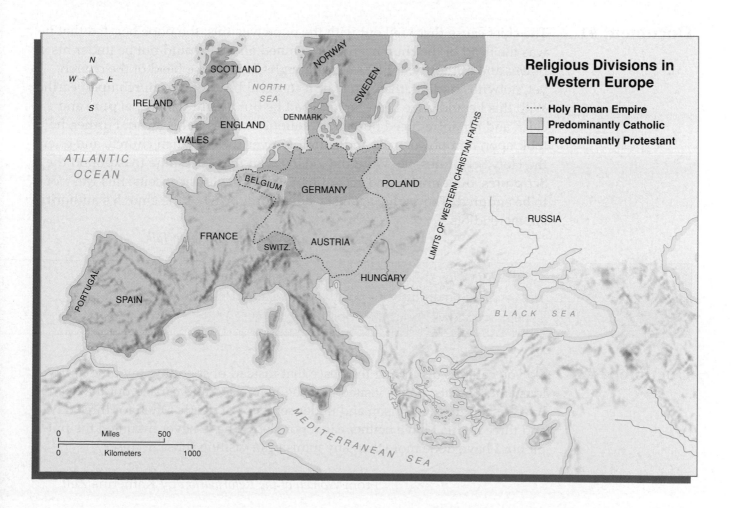

1. Assume you are Martin Luther. Write a letter to Pope Leo X explaining two reasons for your actions in posting the Ninety-Five Theses in Wittenberg.
2. Assume you are the editor of a northern German newspaper. You have learned that several northern German princes have begun to support Martin Luther's movement. However, many other princes are not sure whether to join in this support. Write an editorial, indicating whether or not they should support Luther.
3. Describe two long-range results of the Reformation.
4. State one goal of the Catholic Church during the Counter Reformation and describe two methods used to achieve this goal.
5. Explain this statement: "The Renaissance contributed to the Reformation."

DOCUMENT-BASED QUESTIONS

This task is based on the accompanying documents. Some of these documents have been edited for the purpose of this task. This task is designed to test your ability to work with historical documents. As you analyze the documents, take into account both the source of each document and the author's point of view.

Directions: Read the following documents and answer the questions after each document. Use the information in the reading and this chapter in writing your answers.

Document #1

The chief cause that I fell out with the pope was this: the pope boasted that he was the head of the church, and condemned all that would not be under his power and authority; for he said, although Christ is the head of the church, yet, notwithstanding, there must be a corporal head of the church upon earth. With this I could have been content, had he but taught the gospel pure and clear, and not introduced human inventions and lies in his stead. Further, he took upon him power, rule and authority over the Christian church, and over the Holy Scriptures, the Word of God; no man must presume to expound the Scriptures, but only he, and according to his ridiculous conceits; this was not to be endured. They, who, against God's word, boast of the church's authority, are mere idiots.

Observations by Luther in Table Talk

Questions

1. What can you tell about Luther's personality from this excerpt?
2. Describe one of Luther's positive views about the pope and one of his negative views about the pope.

Document #2

Do you call this disturbing the peace that instead of spending my time in frivolous amusements. I have visited the plague infested and carried out the dead? I have visited those in prison and under sentence of death. Often for three days and three nights I have neither eaten nor slept. I have never mounted the pulpit but I have done more than any minister in visiting those in misery.

From Women of the Reformation by Katherina Zell

1. Explain whether or not Katharina Zell was a member of the clergy?
2. Did she act in a religious manner?

Document #3

Beginning as a protest against arbitrary . . . [and increasing self-powerful] authority in the person of the pope, the Reformation came to be closely identified in the minds of contemporaries with what today we might call states' rights or local control. To many townspeople and villagers, Luther seemed a godsend for their struggle to remain politically free and independent; they embraced his Reformation as a conserving political force, even though they knew it threatened to undo traditional religious beliefs and practices.

From *Protestants: The Birth of a Revolution* by Steven Ozment

Questions

1. State the action Luther took toward the pope and one reason for this action.
2. Why did townspeople and villagers accept Luther's ideas?

Document #4

Could the Reformation spread so far and so fast had it not started anywhere but in Germany? At any rate, the fact that it had its beginnings in the middle of Europe made a very rapid [movement] in all directions; (a) . . . whole circle of [surrounding] countries came one after the other under its influence. Germany's position at the center of European trade also helped greatly. German merchants carried not only goods but Lutheran ideas and books to Venice and France.

From *Reformation Europe* by G. R. Elton

Questions

1. How did geography affect the Reformation?
2. How did commerce and trade contribute to the spread of Lutheranism?

Document #5

You may obtain letters of safe conduct from the vicar (representative) of our lord Jesus Christ, . . . and convey . . . from all pains of purgatory, into the happy kingdom . . . with these confessional letters you will be able at any time in life to obtain full indulgence for all penalties imposed upon you.

From a sermon (edited) of Johann Tetzel

Questions

1. What is Tetzel promising?
2. What was Luther's reaction to Tetzel's promises?

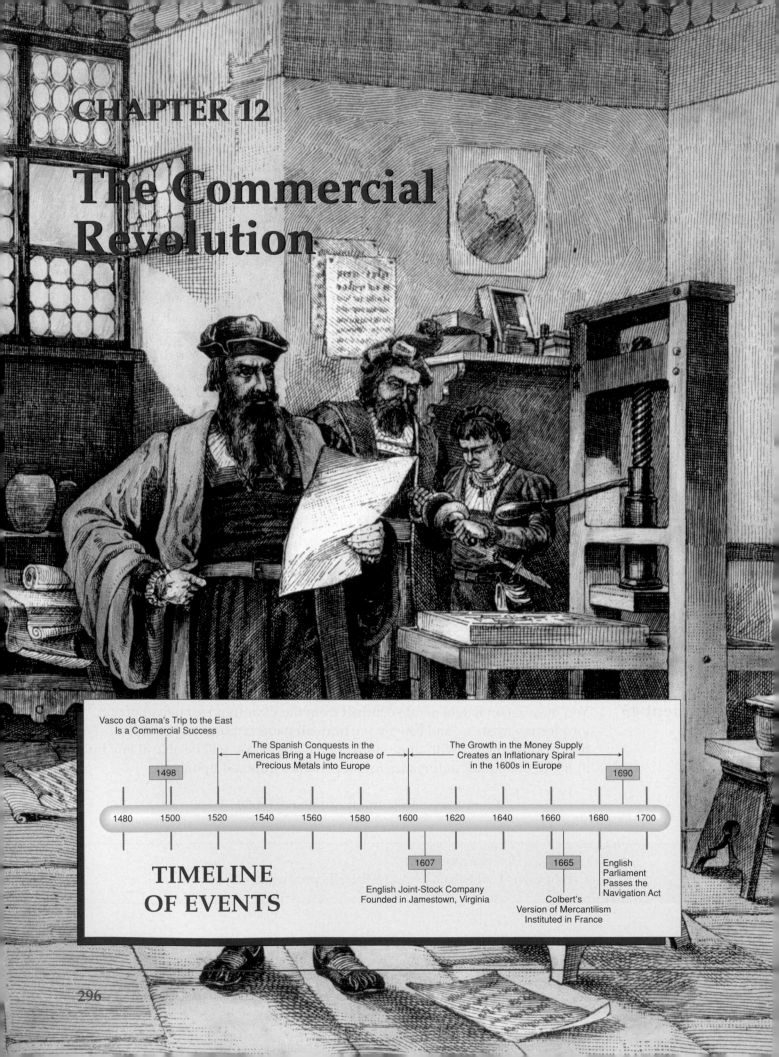

CHAPTER 12

The Commercial Revolution

TIMELINE OF EVENTS

Vasco da Gama's Trip to the East
Is a Commercial Success

The Spanish Conquests in the
Americas Bring a Huge Increase of
Precious Metals into Europe

The Growth in the Money Supply
Creates an Inflationary Spiral
in the 1600s in Europe

1498

1690

1480 1500 1520 1540 1560 1580 1600 1620 1640 1660 1680 1700

1607

1665

English Joint-Stock Company
Founded in Jamestown, Virginia

Colbert's
Version of Mercantilism
Instituted in France

English
Parliament
Passes the
Navigation Act

296

Whenever we watch television, we often see commercials. A commercial's purpose is to persuade us to buy products or services that individuals or companies make and sell. Buying and selling things, along with producing them, is what business, commerce, and trade are all about. These types of economic activities have undergone changes throughout world history. One of the periods of great economic changes is called the Commercial Revolution and took place over centuries from the early 1400s to the end of the 1600s. This term refers to the new business ideas that revolutionized commerce and trade. During the Commercial Revolution the ways of conducting commerce and trade were transformed. The origins of the Commercial Revolution can be traced back to the end of the Middle Ages and the beginning of the Renaissance in Europe.

The economic changes caused by the Commercial Revolution did not happen as rapidly as those brought about by a political revolution. They took place over a longer period of time. In some respects, the Commercial Revolution can be considered an evolution in the way business, trade, and commerce came to be conducted in western Europe and later elsewhere in the world. In this chapter, you will read about why and how all of these important economic changes took place. You will learn how some of the nations of western Europe developed their economies during the Commercial Revolution, a time period that can be called the first global age of business, commerce, and trade.

ECONOMIC REVIVAL IN EUROPE

After the long period of the Crusades and the Middle Ages ended, an era of economic change began in western Europe. The Renaissance, the period of rebirth and renewal that followed, led to the development of new ideas about many things including business, commerce, and trade. By the 1400s, the population of Europe began to rise steadily. Economic recovery and growth once again became possible. The rise of towns, the beginnings of private banking, the growth of a money economy, and trading organizations all signaled the end of feudalism and the start of a new economic era. Trade and commerce were stimulated by the ending of local trade barriers that characterized the Middle Ages.

Starting in the Renaissance, some merchants became very wealthy. A number of the richest merchant families went into banking. Their growing financial power led to their increased political influence in determining economic policies. As time passed, the merchant banking class replaced the land-owning aristocracy as the wealthiest group in society. As more people left rural areas and no longer engaged in agricultural pursuits, the cities and towns of western Europe grew in size and importance. People in the growing urban areas sought work in commercial occupations such as business, trade, and textile production.

The monarchs in western Europe supported the growth of towns and trade in the lands that they ruled. They were seeking to increase their power and wealth. Political stability made it possible for merchants to conduct business and trade and to travel more freely. The rising merchant class supported the growing power of the monarchy because it suited the interests of the merchant class. In the following centuries, the rise of the nation-state in Europe had

Main Idea:
The Renaissance led to the development of new ideas about many things including business, commerce, and trade.

a positive effect on the development of new centers of business, commerce, and trade. By the late 1500s, the political and military power of Spain and Portugal declined, while that of the Netherlands, France, and England increased. The Netherlands, France, and England were the first European nations to really benefit from the developing Commercial Revolution. In these nations, business and commerce benefited from the economic changes taking place in the sixteenth and seventeenth centuries. Trade and markets grew in Europe and elsewhere as the Europeans expanded their commercial relations in other parts of the world.

Commercial expansion was aided by technological improvements in *seafaring*, the ability to navigate and sail in the oceans of the world. By the sixteenth century, European explorations resulted in increased trade with other global regions (see Chapter 17). The Portuguese voyages down the Atlantic coastline of Africa in the 1400s brought trading opportunities that enriched that nation's monarchy and merchant class. In 1498, the Portuguese explorer **Vasco da Gama** commanded the ship that completed the first European voyage to Asia. Da Gama's success in returning with a cargo of peppercorns valued about ten times the original investment was the beginning of a new economic era. Thereafter, an increasing number of European merchants and banking families took part in economic developments, which expanded global business, commerce, and trade.

In the 1500s, the Arab and **Venetian** merchants lost control of the profitable European Asian trade. The Portuguese discovery of the sea route around Africa made it possible for this small maritime nation to open up direct trade between Europe and Asia. There was no longer a need for Asian products to pass through areas under control of the Ottoman Empire in order to reach Europe. The stranglehold that the **Ottoman Empire** had over trade with the East was broken. Reliance on the eastern Mediterranean route was no longer necessary. Goods from the East became more readily available in western Europe. The focus of commerce shifted from the Mediterranean to Atlantic ports as more companies were granted charters to conduct business and trade.

The voyages of exploration and conquest of the Americas gave European nations new sources of wealth. The Portuguese and Spanish discoveries and conquests led to the exploitation of the mineral wealth, mainly gold and silver, of their American colonies. Starting in the 1500s, the growth of business and trade was aided by the huge quantities of gold and silver coming out of Spanish and later Portuguese America. Agricultural products, principally sugar and tobacco, also contributed to the rise in business and trade ventures as more commercial plantations were started. As the sixteenth century progressed, other European nations took advantage of opportunities to further their economic

Main Idea:
Da Gama's success in returning with a cargo of peppercorns valued about ten times the original investment was the beginning of a new economic era.

Vasco da Gama commanded the ship that completed the first European voyage to Asia.

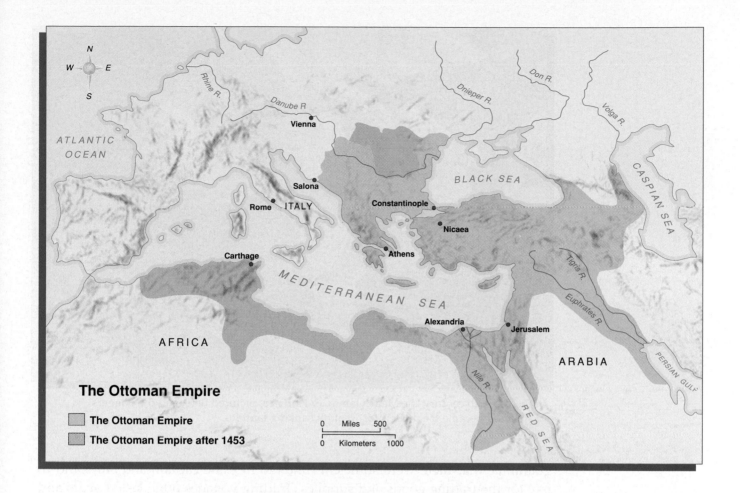

The Ottoman Empire

■ The Ottoman Empire
■ The Ottoman Empire after 1453

0 Miles 500
0 Kilometers 1000

development. The English defeat of the Spanish Armada in 1588 made it possible for England and other European nations to become even more involved in the trans-Atlantic trade.

In some western European countries, there was an increasing growth in the number of commercial trading companies that received charters. A **charter**, issued by a government, was a written agreement given to investors who shared ownership in a business and conducted joint trading enterprises. As the western European nations gained control of colonial possessions, they developed economic policies to safeguard their business and commerce. Credit facilities, state banks, stock markets, and other business innovations became commonplace in the economic life of those nations that took part in the growing Commercial Revolution.

BUSINESS METHODS CHANGE

In western Europe, economic life no longer only depended solely on agricultural production or the owning of land to raise sheep and other livestock. A new class of wealthy merchants and bankers arose; it had the economic means to start commercial exchanges and finance overseas trading expeditions. This led to the development of economies based increasingly on commerce and industry. Merchants who invested in the financing of a trading vessel's voyage needed to

In the fifteenth century, the Medici family of Florence, pictured here, and the Fuggers of Ausburg became the models for wealthy banking families.

guarantee that there were sufficient funds to hire the captain and crew and to pay for the trading goods and supplies. Trading voyages often lasted years and involved buying and selling at many ports of call long distances from home. Only upon a ship's return could the merchants and the bankers who backed them regain their investment and make a profit. It was not practical for wealthy merchants or even monarchs to provide for all of the investment for these trading expeditions alone. Bankers increasingly provided the loans and credit for groups of merchants to conduct their business and trading enterprises.

In the fifteenth century, the **Medici** family of Florence, Italy, and the Fuggers of Ausburg, Germany, became the models for wealthy banking families who financed the increasing number of merchant capitalist ventures. The Medici and Fuggers offered loans to the merchants who turned to them for **capital**, the money used in business. The powerful European banking families grew very wealthy and were able to perform such banking services as accepting deposits, making loans, and transferring funds to other cities. Moreover, the banking families were able to loan European monarchs large sums of money, thereby increasing their political and economic influence.

By the 1600s, government-chartered banks began to replace banks controlled by private banking families. New banking services were designed to make trading transactions easier. Bank notes and checks replaced large payments in gold and silver coinage. The government-chartered banks also performed the service of exchanging foreign currencies, often at the official rate of exchange. In general, economic activity greatly increased as banking, business, trade, commerce, and industry flourished.

THE JOINT-STOCK COMPANY

Another important economic change was the rise of the **joint-stock company**. These companies made it possible for individual merchants to invest in organizations that sold shares of stock to investors in a trading expedition. In this way, the risks of a venture were shared by a number of investors. The joint-stock company, with its shared investment, allowed merchants to put funds into more than one trading opportunity and limit their losses in the event that any one venture failed. Increased capital became available because the joint-stock company was a more stable way of financing trading ventures. Joint-stock companies often sought charters for overseas trading investments that led to the development of colonial enterprises.

Some nations even provided certain joint-stock companies with government support. In the 1600s, the **Dutch East India Company** and **British East India Company** became rich and powerful and acted in the names of their governments in the colonies where they operated. These companies could make war, establish forts, seize foreign ships, and monopolize trade. The British and Dutch governments profited from customs revenues collected as a result of the companies' trade. Joint-stock companies made it possible to organize colonial investment ventures in areas that were considered to be somewhat risky. One such venture took place in 1607, when the Virginia Company of London, a joint-stock company, financed an expedition that led to the founding of the **Jamestown** colony on the Atlantic coastline of the future United States of America.

> **Main Idea:**
> The joint-stock company allowed merchants to put funds into more than one trading opportunity and limit their losses in the event that any one venture failed.

A sample of a charter. Joint-stock companies often sought charters for overseas trading investments that led to the development of colonial enterprises.

THE MONEY SUPPLY INCREASE

Main Idea:
Although the American mineral riches were important for Spain and Portugal's trade and commerce, most of this wealth did not remain in the Iberian peninsula.

Trade and other commercial activities increased to such an extent that there was a need for a greater **money supply**. Individuals needed money to conduct their daily business. The shops that sold goods depended on a reliable and steady flow of funds. Coins continued to be a medium of exchange for the average business and individual who bought and sold goods, but the use of paper money grew.

Starting in the early 1500s, the wealth of Spain increased as large gold and silver shipments flowed into the Iberian peninsula. At first, Spain benefited enormously from the wealth of the Americas. The Aztec and Inca treasures and the mining deposits that were later discovered and exploited made the 1500s Spain's "golden century." Portugal also found large gold and diamond deposits in Brazil in the 1600s. Although the American mineral riches were important for Spain and Portugal's trade and commerce, most of this wealth did not remain in the Iberian peninsula. Spain and Portugal did not have the type of population that had the knowledge and skills to develop a pre-industrial economy based on a factory system. The expulsion of the Jews and Moslems who refused to convert to Christianity had a long-term negative effect on the development of industry and business in both countries. The expulsion of the Jews and Moslems left Spain without an experienced business class who engaged in commerce and trade. Much of the available Iberian manpower was engaged in the exploration, conquest, and settlement of other areas of the world. Many of the Spanish and Portuguese nobles did not consider business and commerce to be worthy pursuits. At home, agriculture and ranching were the primary economic occupations.

Spain and Portugal, the nations that brought most of the bullion to Europe from their mines in the Americas became poorer as the centuries passed. Their inability to develop industry in the Iberian peninsula had a long-term negative effect on overall economic growth. This meant that they imported more goods than they exported. Another factor for Spain's economic decline was its militant Catholicism, which continued from the time of the Catholic monarchs, Ferdinand and Isabella, to Philip II. Spain assumed the military role of defender of the Roman Catholic religion during war with the Ottoman Empire. During the period of the Protestant Reformation and later Catholic Reformation, Spain also sought to defend the interests of Catholicism and suppress a rebellion in the future Dutch Republic, Holland.

The mineral riches of Spain and Portugal found their way into Holland, England, and France. They helped in the development of commercial and industrial activities and served as a means of exchange along with copper coinage. In western Europe, the mineral riches of the Americas stimulated early developments in factory-like production. Flanders, Amsterdam, Rotterdam, Paris, and London particularly benefited from the gold, silver, and later diamonds that flowed their way to pay for industrial products. In the 1600s, the overall increase in personal wealth in western European nations led to a price revolution. The rise of prices meant still more profits and increased wealth for those engaged in the growing Commercial Revolution. More people had the ability to spend increasing sums of money, which led to **inflation**, a rise in the price of goods because of the increased money supply. Nevertheless, despite the price increases and inflation, the economies of the Netherlands, France, and England continued to grow.

THE RISE OF THE ENTREPRENEUR

The changes in banking, the growth of joint-stock companies, and the rise in the money supply created many new business opportunities. The Roman Catholic Church had, throughout the Middle Ages, prohibited the lending of money for interest. The rise of lending institutions was aided by the Church's declining influence concerning the lending of money and charging of interest. This was particularly true in the Protestant areas where this type of commercial activity was encouraged. The lending of money for profit by charging interest, *usury*, became more acceptable and widespread in Holland, England, and elsewhere. The methods of business changed. It became more acceptable for enterprising individuals to pursue profits. **Entrepreneurs**, individuals who organized, managed, and assumed responsibility for businesses, were able to pursue new ideas. They could make use of money to buy raw materials and pay labor to produce goods in order to earn a profit.

The entrepreneurs engaged in the Commercial Revolution no longer worried that the making of profit in a business enterprise would be a cause for religious criticism or damage their standing in society. The textile industries offered some of the best opportunities for entrepreneurs. Entrepreneurs in the areas of rising textile production were able to combine all the necessary business and commercial ingredients and thereby to take advantage of market conditions. For example, a businessman in England or Holland could buy wool or cotton, hire weavers and dyers to make cloth, and sell the goods on the open market at a profit.

THE BEGINNING OF CAPITALISM

The Commercial Revolution led slowly to the growth of **capitalism** as the principal economic system in western Europe. Capitalistic types of economies began to develop. Capitalism is the economic system in which the means of production are privately owned and operated for profit. As the capitalist system developed, entrepreneurs, merchants, bankers, and joint-stock companies were free to use capital, or money, to generate profits. Property increasingly was privately owned, and the remains of feudalism, such as the fief, faded away. Capitalism also came to be known as the **free enterprise** system. In this system, individual initiative, investment, and risk generated ideas and energy, which resulted in economic activity. Investors with money were free to risk their capital. The banking system developed, in part, to meet the needs of entrepreneurs engaged in capitalistic ventures in commerce and industry.

Another significant change was the decline of the Medieval guilds. **Guilds** were associations of merchants or artisans that governed a town or craft in the Middle Ages. The guild system, which was the principal economic system that supported commerce, the production of goods, and the training of workers, was gradually replaced by the domestic system. The *domestic system* allowed the entrepreneur to exercise greater control over the laborers who produced the goods. Individuals with money to invest in business could, for example, buy raw wool and hire peasants in the countryside to dye and spin it into cloth. The regulations that governed the manner in which the guilds produced and sold goods were no longer adequate for a growing urban population. In an economy controlled in large measure by entrepreneurs who had enough money to invest in a business to make a profit, laborers were increasingly paid according to market conditions.

Certain new industries demanded sizable capital investment. In 1445, the German Johannes Gutenberg developed a printing press that used a metal alloy to make movable type. Gutenberg's hand-set type led to the rise of the printing industry. The rapid expansion of the printing industry in the sixteenth and seventeenth centuries required an investment in expensive equipment and supplies. With the backing of banks and joint-stock companies, entrepreneurs often provided the necessary investment capital in the printing industry. This was similar to the way in which banks' and joint-stock companies' investment capital financed major mining and shipbuilding projects.

In 1445, Johannes Gutenberg developed a printing press that used a metal alloy to make movable type.

MERCANTILISM DEVELOPS IN EUROPE

Spain, Portugal, Holland, France, and England followed an economic policy called **mercantilism**. Mercantilist regulations were designed to benefit the nation that issued these rules governing colonial trade and business. Mercantilism was based on the belief that national wealth and power were best served by increasing exports and collecting **precious metals** in exchange for them. Raw materials were very sought after. *Duties*, or taxes, on imported goods provided revenue for the government. Colonies existed to enrich the mother country. The nation that owned and controlled colonies only did so to benefit from the economic arrangement. Another major mercantilist aim was to make the mother country economically independent. As trading empires developed, mercantilist ideas influenced the development of economic policy in western Europe.

> **Main Idea:** Mercantilist regulations were designed to benefit the nation that issued the rules governing trade and business.

Increasingly, the monarchs of the western European countries recognized that their nations' political power depended on controlling its economic wealth. European rulers believed that the most important measure of their nations' wealth was the total amount of **bullion**—gold or silver—that it owned. Bullion was best acquired by foreign trade and manufacturing or processing. The major trading nations, from the sixteenth through eighteenth centuries, sought to increase this national wealth, and thereby their power, by promoting exports and collecting precious metals.

The period from 1500 to 1800 was a time of costly religious wars as well as bitter commercial rivalries. During these years, increasingly large revenues were needed by the developing nations of western Europe to pay for these wars and the related growing expenses of civil government. The expanding government offices and the growing number of state officials, the *bureaucracy*, enabled the monarchs to govern their nations more effectively. However, the growing bureaucracy also added to the need for greater revenues. More government workers meant that the monarchy had to pay more salaries.

Mercantilist theory also supported the idea that it was more profitable to make and sell a finished manufactured product than to market a raw material. For example, English cloth that was exported as woolen blankets was more profitable than English wool as a raw material or even the unfinished cloth. Therefore, it was necessary for mercantilist nations to regulate their trade and control the economies of their colonies. A favorable balance of trade, in which exports were worth more than imports, was a major goal of the mercantilist nations.

THE IMPORTANCE OF COLONIES

Colonies played an increasingly important role in the mercantilist economies. Colonies and colonists not only could supply raw materials for the developing industries but also were markets for the manufactured goods produced in the mother country. In western Europe, all of the competing commercial powers had mercantilist regulations that were designed to control their trade. Their goal was to maximize their profits at the expense of their economic rivals.

Spain

Spain tried to prevent other European nations from trading with its American colonies through a complicated set of trading laws and a system of fleets to control trade. This restrictive commercial policy only worked while Spain was capable of enforcing its regulations. Smuggling and piracy were constant problems. By the end of the reign of Philip II and with the defeat of the Spanish Armada in 1588, Spain was no longer western Europe's leading military and naval power. Spain's decline thereafter was, in large measure, related to its inability to effectively enforce its mercantilist policies.

France

In 1665, France's monarch, Louis XIV, chose **Jean Baptiste Colbert** as his finance minister. Colbert was one of the most successful practitioners of mercantilism and sought to make France economically self-sufficient. He encouraged the growth of industry through subsidies and tariffs. Colbert regulated the prices and quality of manufactured goods and agricultural products. His economic policies sought to break down trade barriers within France. To accomplish this goal, he started a serious road-building program and restricted the use of natural resources. In 1669, as secretary of state for naval affairs, he initiated policies to construct shipyards, arsenals, harbors, and a large navy. His naval policies enabled France to take major steps in the development of commerce and colonization. Colbert's mercantilist-type policies did lead to significant economic growth, but his efforts to regulate the French economy were ultimately undone by Louis XIV's extravagances and the expensive wars that the king pursued during his long reign. Heavier taxation, increased borrowing, and the sale of government offices were the result of a constant need for more revenue. Colbert's popularity declined, and he was eventually dismissed from office by the king.

Main Idea:
Colbert's naval policies enabled France to take major steps in the development of commerce and colonization.

Jean Baptiste Colbert was one of the most successful practitioners of mercantilism.

England

England's commercial expansion began during the rule of Elizabeth I in the late 1500s. The English economy grew slowly but steadily despite the troubled reigns of the Stuart kings and the Cromwell period in the 1600s. The joint-stock company was the principal method that the capital-deficient English used to finance their overseas trading enterprises and early textile industry development. The English colonial ventures to the Atlantic coastline of North America were initially financed by joint-stock company investments. English mercantilist policy had a great influence on the economies of the thirteen American colonies. The **Navigation Acts** passed by the English Parliament during the 1680s were designed to benefit the mother country. The American colonies were prohibited from manufacturing certain finished goods such as iron products. They were restricted in their trade, even with areas under English rule, and were required to use British vessels for the shipment of their goods. The Americans also did not like the restrictions that the British placed on the trade of the Atlantic Circuit from Europe to Africa to the Americas and back to Europe.

Colonial merchants often ignored many of the restrictive regulations. However, they had to be careful not to arouse the suspicions of the British customs officials. British mercantilist trade regulations, enforced by the powerful royal navy, were a constant problem for the American colonists. This was particularly true concerning the profitable **triangular trade**. This trade route linked Great Britain, the Atlantic coast of North America, and Africa. Rum was shipped to Africa for gold and slaves. The slaves and gold were transported to the Caribbean for molasses. After, the molasses was then was taken back to the thirteen colonies to be manufactured into rum. Ultimately, the colonial resistance to British trading regulations became a major factor in encouraging the independence movement in the thirteen colonies.

> **Main Idea:**
> British mercantilist regulations were a constant problem for American colonists.

LINK TO TODAY

We live today in a time when new changes are taking place in the way our global economies operate. Today we often see, read about, and listen to economic news that concerns the ways in which the world economies are becoming more global. The term *globalization* has become very important today for anyone who wants to understand the economic changes taking place throughout the world today.

It is interesting to compare some of the changes taking place today with the changes that you are reading about in this chapter. If we really look at what is happening today in terms of the globalization of the world economies, we can see links with what happened during the Commercial Revolution.

During the Commercial Revolution, the nature of work changed as the guild system came to an end and more people began to work in commerce and industry and left agricultural jobs. Today, new economic changes are taking place worldwide. In our present technological age, in the United States more people are working in service industries in which they are paid to provide services rather than to produce goods. This is also true in the nations that led the growth in the world economy during the Commercial Revolution, which really was the first global economic age.

In addition, because of the differences from country to country concerning the price of labor, many manufacturing and service industry jobs are moving to the East, particularly China and India. This outsourcing of jobs from western Europe and the United States to Asian countries is forcing many people in the United States and western Europe to reconsider what careers and jobs they should prepare for. How young people should plan for a successful future in the world of work is an increasingly complex problem in countries where salaries are considered to be high. Employers are looking to produce goods and services in countries with lower labor costs.

Have you thought about how these economic changes might affect your own future job choice and career?

CHAPTER SUMMARY

The Commercial Revolution in European history led to fundamental economic changes. These changes not only greatly affected the way that the economy worked but also affected the political and social policies and practices in some West European nations. The increased commercial activity led to significant political and social changes in the European societies and other world areas that experienced these changes. By 1700, the developing Commercial Revolution prepared the stage for the Industrial Revolution, which first took place in Europe.

Economic Effects

The revolution in commerce led to the growth of more business- and trading-oriented economies in a number of western European nations. The principles of mercantilism were adopted. Increased trade and the control of overseas empires stimulated economic development, first in Portugal and Spain, and then in the Netherlands, France, and England. These nations became competing economic powers as the commercial expansion continued to develop in the following centuries. The rise of private banking, a money economy, and chartered trading organizations increased economic growth. Trade expanded as markets grew wider and became more secure. Commercial expansion was supported by technological improvements in navigation and sailing vessels.

In western Europe, quickened commercial activity resulted in more economic specialization. This led to the transformation of how goods were produced. A new method of making goods, the domestic system, developed, and production increased. The domestic system brought workers together in a cooperative type of manufacturing arrangement. These economic developments contributed to the rise of modern capitalism.

Political Effects

The economic rivalries over commercial matters that developed among the western European nations led to major conflicts within Europe and throughout the globe. Wherever the European nations traded and established colonies, economic and political disagreements and problems increased. European nations became involved in wars to protect their colonial empires and take colonies and trade away from their rivals. The European nations capable of overseas expansion waged war over trade routes, the control of the lucrative slave trade, and colonies in global areas. Ultimately, the two remaining European rivals, England and France, fought the first world war, the Seven Years' War, from 1756 to 1763 for control of most of the existing global trading network. This first global war was fought in Europe, Asia, and the Americas. European influence in world affairs continued to increase in the following centuries.

Social Effects

The growth in commercial activity led to significant social changes. The development of new economic activities allowed the upper classes, nobles, and rich merchants to acquire great wealth, which they often spent on a lavish lifestyle. Large palaces and homes were built. New foods were introduced for consumption at European tables. Expensive and exotic clothing such as silks and American furs became more readily available. The upper classes of these nations became patrons of the arts and decorated their homes to display their wealth.

The vast majority of people did not benefit very much from the increased economic activities and expansion. Although the conditions of life that feudalism brought to Europe in the Middle Ages disappeared in the nations where the Commercial Revolution took place, the living conditions of the towns were often harsh. Workers earned low wages, housing was often of poor quality, and health care was inadequate. There was no significant increase in the life span of the majority of urban residents.

Major movements of population occurred because of the European colonization of the Americas. The exportation of millions of enslaved Africans to the Americas to work in agricultural, mining, and other enterprises increased as the centuries progressed. The forced movement of people to locations where the European nations had colonies and needed labor led to the development of new peoples of mixed ancestry. In the process, the Native American population of the Americas drastically declined.

During this era of economic development, we see where the statement "necessity is the mother of invention" might apply. Once European nations spread their political control to other lands, new business practices were needed to take full economic advantage of the situation. Two challenges were present. The first challenge was the need to raise capital and develop a global commercial economy. The second challenge was to make the mother country economically independent of other nations. To accomplish the first, new business techniques such as joint-stock companies and bank notes and checks were established. To accomplish the second, mercantilism became the dominant economic practice. Colonies were established in the Americas by England, Spain, France, and Holland to enhance the power of the mother country. While Europe became richer as a result of this, it had a negative effect on the inhabitants of other parts of the globe.

IMPORTANT PEOPLE, PLACES, AND TERMS

KEY TERMS

credit facility	entrepreneur	precious metals
colony	inflation	price revolution
money supply	charter	trade route
joint-stock company	stock market	capital
customs duties	guild	British East India
capitalism	mercantilism	Company
triangular trade	free enterprise	Dutch East India
navigation acts	bullion	Company

PEOPLE

Vasco da Gama	Medici	Jean Baptiste Colbert
Venetians		

PLACES

Venice	Ottoman Empire	Jamestown
Mediterranean Sea		

EXERCISES FOR CHAPTER 12

MULTIPLE CHOICE

Select the letter of the correct answer.

1. European nations adopted mercantilist policies to
   a. safeguard their commerce and new colonial possessions.
   b. break down existing trade barriers.
   c. provide their colonies with financial support to develop industry.
   d. stimulate the guilds that produced most European goods.

2. By the 1400s, the monarchs of Europe
   a. sought to limit the growth of towns in their realms.
   b. began to support urbanization to increase their power.
   c. created state credit facilities and national banks.
   d. tried to prevent the disintegration of the feudal system.

3. One reason for the change in business methods was the

   a. transition from an industrial to an agricultural economy.
   b. need to finance overseas trading expeditions.
   c. demand by the landed aristocracy for financial support.
   d. general decline in trade and industry after 1450.

4. All of the following are associated with the Commercial Revolution except

   a. joint-stock companies.
   b. an increased money supply.
   c. the rise of the entrepreneur.
   d. the growth of the manorial system.

5. The Triangular Trade involved which three global regions

   a. Asia, Europe, and Africa.
   b. Africa, the Americas, and Asia.
   c. Europe, Africa, and the Americas.
   d. the Americas, Asia, and Europe.

6. Which economic theory, developed in the seventeenth century, supported European colonialism?

   a. Socialism
   b. Mercantilism
   c. Bartering
   d. Feudalism

7. Base your answer to this question on the following map.

   Which is the most appropriate title for this map?

   a. The Industrial Revolution
   b. Imperialism in Africa
   c. Voyages of Exploration
   d. Atlantic Trade Routes

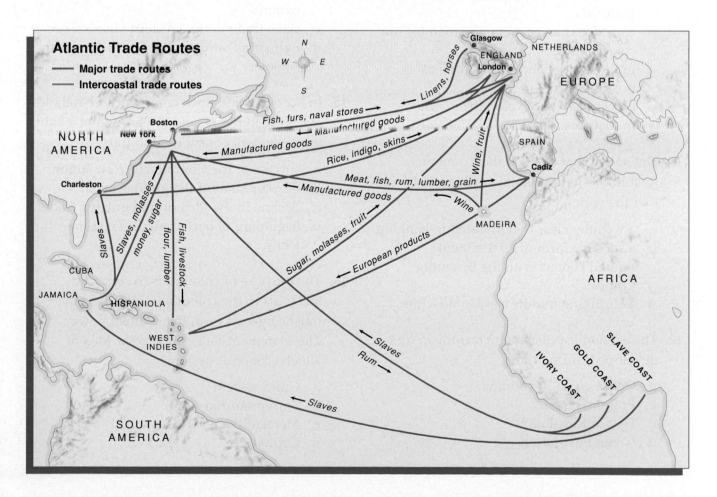

8. Which was the result of the Commercial Revolution?

   a. Decline in population growth in Europe
   b. Shift in power from western Europe to eastern Europe
   c. Spread of feudalism throughout western Europe.
   d. Expansion of European influence overseas.

9. The Commercial Revolution in Europe led directly to

   a. development of a socialist economy.
   b. establishment of the guild system.
   c. weakening of the power of the middle class.
   d. increased trade within European markets.

10. According to the theory of mercantilism, colonies should be

   a. acquired as markets and sources of raw materials.
   b. considered an economic burden for the colonial power.
   c. granted independence as soon as possible.
   d. encouraged to develop their own industries.

11. One factor that enabled the Commercial Revolution to flourish in northern Italy was that the region had

   a. a wealthy class that invested in banking.
   b. a socialist form of government.
   c. limited contact with the Byzantine Empire.
   d. a shrinking middle class in the cities.

12. The economic policy of mercantilism first developed during the

   a. Commercial Revolution.
   b. Enlightenment.
   c. French Revolution.
   d. Green Revolution.

13. Which economic system is described by the following statements?

   Statement A: The might of a country consists of gaining surpluses of gold and silver.

   Statement B: A nation's strength is found in economic independence and the maintenance of a favorable balance of trade.

   Statement C: We need to gain colonies both as sources for raw materials and as markets for our manufactured goods.

   a. Traditional
   b. Feudal
   c. Command
   d. Mercantile

14. The success of the triangular trade system depended on increasing the

   a. political independence of the Caribbean nations.
   b. emphasis on free trade in European nations.
   c. slave trade in the Western Hemisphere.
   d. industrialization of the South American colonies.

15. In Europe, joint-stock companies, shareholders, entrepreneurs, and the growth of a banking system all contributed to the

   a. success of the Commercial Revolution.
   b. development of the guild system.
   c. decline in the idea of unregulated trade.
   d. beginning of barter and interest-free loans.

16. The purpose of colonies is to ship raw materials to the colonial power and buy finished goods from the colonial power. This statement reflects the basic idea of which economic system?

   a. Guild system
   b. Entreprenurial
   c. Mercantilism
   d. Capitalism

17. Under the policy of mercantilism, colonial powers considered their colonies to be

 a. independent nations that traded throughout the world.
 b. independent nations that had special relations with European powers.
 c. possessions to benefit the colonial power and make it more wealthy.
 d. possessions to benefit the colony at the expense of the colonial power.

18. Which pair is correctly matched?

 a. France > Colbert
 b. Italy > Fuggers
 c. Austria > Medici
 d. Spain > Vasco da Gama

19. Which factor was a development of the Commercial Revolution?

 a. There was a decreasing importance of towns and cities.
 b. There was a decline of trade between Europe and Asia.
 c. There was an increase in the influence of serfs.
 d. The entrepreneurial class began to control business and trade.

20. The term *mercantilism* is defined as an economic system in which

 a. all prices are determined by the law of supply and demand.
 b. the amount of gold and silver held determines a nation's wealth.
 c. the means of production are owned by the government
 d. working class benefits at the expense of the middle class.

ESSAYS FOR CHAPTER 12

1. Assume that you are an entrepreneur. Write to a merchant banking family as if you are asking to borrow money for a trading expedition or new business. State two reasons for wanting to borrow the money and explain how you will repay the loan.
2. Assume that you are a merchant and want to form a joint-stock company to finance a trading expedition. Write an essay to attract potential merchant partners and other investors to join your company.
3. Why would nations such as England, France, and Holland support a policy of mercantilism?
4. Why did the possession of colonies become more important as the Commercial Revolution developed?
5. How did the Commercial Revolution lead to the growth of capitalism?

DOCUMENT-BASED QUESTIONS

This task is based on the accompanying documents. Some of these documents have been edited for the purpose of this task. This task is designed to test your ability to work with historical documents. As you analyze the documents, take into account both the source of each document and the author's point of view.

Directions: Read the following documents and answer the questions after each document. Use the information in the readings and this chapter in writing your answers.

Document #1

From his castle on the Sagres, the Atlantic coast of Portugal, Prince Henry the Navigator gathered together all of the nautical wisdom of his times, perfected cartography and navigational instruments, developed swift, easily maneuverable seafaring vessels such as the caravel and trained crews to man them. Henry's grand design was to outflank the Turks by sailing south to Africa and then east to the Orient (Asia). With the help of Flemish bankers, Portugal worked its way down the Western African coast until Batholomeu Dias rounded the Cape of Good Hope in 1488. From there the Portuguese proceeded quickly to India where Vasco da Gama established trade in 1498. Along the way sugar was planted and slaves were bought and sold.

From *The Buried Mirror* by Carlos Fuentes

Questions
1. Why was Prince Henry able to realize his navigational plans?
2. How did the da Gama voyage help expand global trade?

Document #2

In the Venetian tradition, Spain claimed a monopoly over commerce with its American empire, and control of all trade and navigation. The control of trade was exercised through the ports of Seville and Cadiz. The monopoly was enforced during the colonial period although it became much less effective after the sinking of the Spanish Armada in 1588. The Spaniards sought to transport the riches of the Americas particularly the precious metals, gold and silver, in their own ships, which they assigned to fleets for safety. The Spanish monarchy created a Casa de Contraction, an agency to authorize and regulate all trade with the American colonies and to collect customs duties. The intent of the crown's commercial policies was to establish rules and regulations in order that the Spanish nation would have exclusive control over and benefit from its American Empire.

From *The Spanish Sea-borne Empire* by John Parry

Questions
1. Why did the Spanish crown establish the Casa de Contraction?
2. Why can the Spanish commercial policy be considered a trading monopoly?

Document #3

English manufacturers also went to Spanish America via England's trade with Portugal. Payment for goods was largely made in silver, swelling the unrecorded bullion sent from Portugal to England during this period. Altogether, the Spanish American empire contributed to England's commercial growth by providing capital in the form of bullion and providing an additional market for finished goods. Demands for English manufactured goods continued to grow during the 1700s. English merchants profited enormously from the Spanish American trade. They also made handsome profits from the growing slave trade and trade in foodstuffs.

From *The Portuguese Trade* by H. E. S. Fisher

Document #4   The enormous injection of Spanish metals revolutionized the European economy, bringing inflation, high prices, growing demand and flourishing banks throughout the western part of Europe. Many of the banks were creditors to the Spanish monarchy willing to extend generous loans to Philip II on the promise of an unending stream of bullion from Mexico and Peru. Gold and silver quickly spread all over Europe provoking the sixteenth century "price revolution." Throughout Europe prices rose more and more rapidly.

From *The Buried Mirror* by Carlos Fuentes

| Questions | 1. How did the wealth of the Americas effect the European economy? |
| | 2. Why was the accumulation of gold and silver so important during this period? |

Document #5   The Fugger's and other bankers financed and milked the Spanish Empire. The nations of Europe were dazzled by the accumulation of gold and silver as the essential goal of economics. This mercantilist idea grew as the European and thus the world economy became more and more a network of commercial, financial, industrial, and technological relationships.

From *Spanish Imperialism and Political Imagination* by Anthony Pagden

| Questions | 1. Why did the theory of mercantilism appeal to European nations? |
| | 2. How did the rise of a banking class stimulate the development of global trade? |

CHAPTER 13

Global Interactions in Asia

Section 1—The Mongols 317

Section 2—The Yuan Dynasty 319

Section 3—Japan and Korea 321

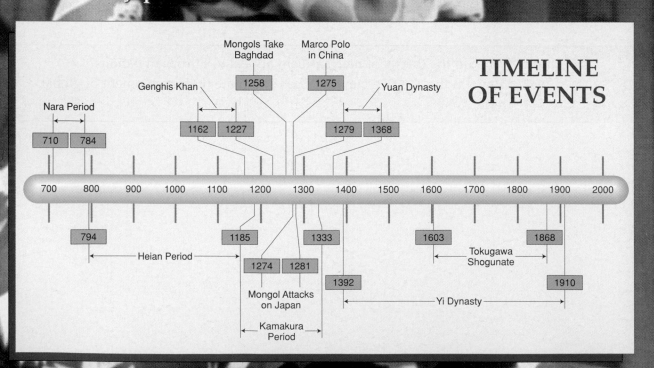

TIMELINE OF EVENTS

Nara Period
710 — 784

Genghis Khan
1162 — 1227

Mongols Take Baghdad
1258

Marco Polo in China
1275

Yuan Dynasty
1279 — 1368

700 800 900 1000 1100 1200 1300 1400 1500 1600 1700 1800 1900 2000

794

Heian Period

1185

1274 1281

Mongol Attacks on Japan

Kamakura Period

1333

1392

Yi Dynasty

1603

Tokugawa Shogunate

1868

1910

The Mongols

While Europe, as you have read in the last three chapters, underwent a cultural renaissance, a religious reformation, and a commercial revolution, the same could not be said of Asia throughout the entire time span of 1200–1650. The most distinctive feature of Asian history in the first two hundred years of this span was the emergence of the **Mongols**. They were to forge an empire that was to stretch from Poland to northern China. Its founder, **Genghis Khan**, became the most famous conqueror in world history. The Mongol Empire was the largest continuous land empire ever known. Our task then is to explain the rise and fall of the Mongols, their legacy, and their place in the history of our planet.

Environmental conditions, most notably geography, contributed to the rise and eventual expansion of the Mongols. They hailed from the **steppes** of the Eurasian land mass. The steppes are a long expanse of grassland that extends from eastern Europe to eastern China. They are divided into the western steppes (from Europe to Central Asia) and the eastern steppes (comprising the present-day boundaries of Mongolia).

These areas receive very little rainfall. Inhabitants of the steppes were **nomads** and **pastoralists**. This meant that they often would move their herds of animals, looking for good pasture for feeding purposes. They became excellent riders, herdsmen, and good hunters. Some historians claim that the Mongols would put their little children, as infants, on goats in order to accustom them to riding. As their patterns of movement often took them from farming areas, they needed to be self-sufficient and provide things such as meat and milk for themselves. They often faced scarcity and harsh conditions. Yet, they were proud of their toughness and ability to survive. Often, they would leave the steppe to raid border areas containing villages and settled communities. The Chinese, very wary of nomadic intruders, built the Great Wall as a protective measure.

The Mongols consisted of several ethnic groups or clans. In one of these clans, powerful families formed a council that made important decisions in accord with their leader or *khan*. In 1206, they agreed that a man born with the name *Temujin* would be the Great Khan. He took the name Genghis (meaning "universal"). He unified many clans, often by force. He then began to seek tribute from and later, control over several Central Asian peoples. By 1221, for example, his armies had conquered almost all of present day Iran. Mongol soldiers were feared for their fierceness and fighting ability. They would go into battle as armies of ten thousand men apiece. Their skill on horseback, combined with use of superior bows, flaming projectiles from catapults, and armored infantrymen were key factors in their conquests. Genghis Khan was a brilliant military planner and strategist, as well as a cruel and ruthless conqueror. He frequently had whole villages massacred and cities burned to the ground. Fear of the Mongols proved to be a very valuable tactical and psychological weapon.

Upon the death of Genghis Khan in 1227, his empire was divided up among his sons and grandsons. These descendants then led their respective armies in several different directions; some went to Europe and others went to the various parts of Asia. Major victories were achieved, for example in Moscow, Kiev, and other Russian cities between 1255 and 1260. In 1258, Baghdad was destroyed, thus bringing to an end the Abbasid Caliphate. By 1260, the empire was split into four big territories or *khanates*. Each was ruled by a descendant of Genghis Khan. The four were the Khanate of Chagatai (Central Asia), the Khanate of the Great Khan (Mongolia and China), the Ilkhanate (Persia), and the Khanate of the Golden Horde (Russia). Mongol rule in the first three of these ended in the 1300s; it ended in Russia in 1480. Although we will explain the reasons for this decline, we first need to stop and examine the impact of Mongol rule throughout the empire.

A significant political and economic achievement of the Mongols was the establishment of a period of peace and stability across most of the Eurasian land mass. Historians have labeled this the **Pax Mongolia** or Mongol Peace. Peaceful movement of travelers, merchants, and missionaries was guaranteed by the Mongols. The **Silk Road** was once again a highway of economic and cultural diffusion. Much cultural enrichment occurred, for example, in exchanges between Iran and China. This involved artistic patterns, political ideas, and governmental practices. Frequently, over a period of time, some Mongols were to adopt features of the culture of those societies they had conquered. The Ilkhans and the Golden Horde became Muslims. In China, as we will soon see, under the Yuan dynasty, the Great Khans involved themselves with certain native traditions.

On the negative side, it is clear that the Mongols wrought great destruction in many areas. Populations were often decimated. Cities were destroyed, with only a few ever recovering.

Main Idea:
Although Genghis Khan was a brilliant military planner and strategist, he was was also a cruel and ruthless conqueror.

Genghis Khan became the most famous conqueror in world history.

The Yuan Dynasty

The Yuan dynasty was the ruling authority in China, as established by the Mongols, from 1279–1368. This was the first time in Chinese history that foreigners controlled China. Yuan was the name chosen by **Kublai Khan**, a grandson of Genghis Khan. Mongol attempts to subdue China began as early as 1234. They were finally realized in 1279, when Kublai Khan's army was successful and he declared himself to be emperor. Ironically, although he was not Chinese, he is considered to be one of China's great emperors. Why was this so? As for

Kublai Khan was a grandson of Genghis Khan.

politics, he was able to bring unity to China for the first time in 300 years. Prior to the Mongol conquest, China did not exist as it does today. There were three divided political areas, two in the north and the Song in the South. They had diverse languages, writing systems, and patterns of government. Kublai Khan destroyed all these and promoted a sense of unity. He adopted many Chinese traditions, something that would be characteristic of other foreign conquerors of China such as the Manchus. Kublai gave one of his sons a Chinese name. He even had his son educated by Confucian scholars. Furthermore, he was also tolerant of Buddhist and Daoist practices.

Economic prosperity was enhanced with the Pax Mongolia. Safe routes for exchanges of goods and inventions between areas to its west were established. Transmission of ideas, information, skills, and advisors was possible. Porcelain from China reached the western end of the Silk Road while engineering patterns, astronomy theories, and weaponry came to China from the Il-Khan-ruled Middle East. Kublai Khan enabled Iranians to travel to Beijing his capital, to build an observatory. Iranians, in turn, learned about Chinese ways of viewing clouds, trees, and rocks. Persian medical books, particularly in anatomy and ophthalmology, were used in China.

Of all the foreigners who found their way to the Chinas during the Yuan dynasty, the most famous was **Marco Polo**. A native Italian from Venice, he traveled as a trader along the Silk Road and came to China in 1275. Kublai Khan met him and sent him to several cities in China to report back to him. In 1292, Marco Polo returned to Venice and told of his stay in China and later wrote a book. His descriptions of that society were full of praise. The accounts of great wealth, large cities, and Chinese traditions were widely read in Europe. Some people, however, did not believe these accounts. To this day, there is still some debate concerning the truthfulness of his trip and his descriptions.

The Decline of Mongol Rule

In the years after Kublai Khan's death in 1294, Mongol rule and control in China began to decline. Mongol princes started to fight among themselves. In addition, many Chinese who opposed Mongol rule ignited rebellions. Attempts by the Yuan dynasty to take over Southeast Asia and Japan were unsuccessful and very costly in terms of money, lives, and equipment. A Chinese rebel leader, Zhu Yuanzhang, led forces that overwhelmed the Mongols and brought their empire in China to an end in 1368. Taking the name of Hongwu, he founded a new dynasty, the Ming dynasty. As we will see in Chapter 19, it was to last until 1644. Some Mongols remained in China, while others fled to parts of inner Asia still ruled by Genghis Khan's heirs. Yet, with the exception of the Golden Horde in Russia, by the end of the fourteenth century, the huge global Mongol Empire had ceased to exist. Internal problems and discord led to the end of the Ilkhanate in Persia (1330) and the Chagatai in Central Asia (1370s).

Hongwu, whose real name was Zhu Yuanzhang, was the founder of the Ming dynasty.

Japan and Korea

The Mongols failed in their two attempts to invade Japan, during the thirteenth century. Had they been successful, however, they would have found Japan to be a nation with patterns of life that were both similar to and different from those in China. It is to those patterns and history that we now turn.

Buddhism in Japan and the Nara Period (710–784)

In the fourth and fifth centuries, when the Japanese had some territory in Korea, they came into contact with Chinese culture. Up to this time, Korean culture had been greatly influenced by China. Japan admired many features of Chinese culture and began to send scholars and government officials to China and Korea to learn more about these features. Consequently, a host of Chinese cultural items were adopted by Japan. These included silk and metalwork production, tea drinking, painting, weaving, and China's writing system. The Japanese would adopt these foreign ways to meet their own needs, while preserving many of their traditional customs. The Japanese, for instance, adopted Chinese written characters yet pronounced them differently. Such an example of cultural diffusion has proved to be a legacy that exists until the present day.

The Yumedono Pavilion (Hall of Visions) at Horyuji Temple, near the city of Nara, Japan.

Shoktoku Taishi, the crown prince and Regent of Japan, between one of his brothers and his son.

Another long-lasting example of cultural diffusion that is also found today in Japan was the adoption of **Buddhism**. Originating in South Asia, Buddhism was to make its way to China and Korea and then on to Japan. Its basic ideas (see Chapter 2, Section 1), with some modifications, would be accepted by the Japanese. They would come to practice this faith along with their own native religion, Shintoism (see Chapter 2, Section 4). Buddhism came to Japan by 552 from Korea. Travelers from Korea introduced this new faith. From 607–614, Prince Shotoku, the Japanese ruler, sent officials to China to learn more about Buddhism and other aspects of Chinese culture. Initially, it became popular with the nobles and upper classes. Eventually, as has happened with other religions when they spread afar from their origin, Buddhism underwent changes in Japan. It was adapted to meet needs and feelings of Japanese with the result that more people came to accept it. By the eighth century, the imperial Japanese government officially accepted Buddhism. Beyond the eighth century and for centuries afterward, the changes that Buddhism underwent were many. Different sects developed that appealed to various groups in the population. Among the sects were Pure Land, Nichiren, and Zen.

Although **Zen** is a sect that only a minority of Japanese belongs to today, it nevertheless is the one that is best known to the Western world. It arose in Japan during the Kamakura period (1192–1333), having begun in China. Zen focuses on having a person achieve an enlightened state of mind by meditation and discarding logical reasoning and common-sense thinking. This state of mind is very difficult to achieve. It may come as a sudden flash or what is termed **satori**. In reaching this state of mind, a follower is challenged to consider **koans** or riddles. Here is an example: "What is the sound of one hand clapping?" Zen requires strict physical and mental discipline as well as hours of meditation. It has influenced Japanese art, architecture, literature, education, and other features of Japanese life.

A major influence on the adoption of Buddhism and other features of Chinese culture rested with Japan's great admiration of the Tang dynasty in China (618–907). The Tang capital city, **Chang'an (Xian)** became the model for the first real city in Japan. This was **Nara**. It was the capital of Japan from 710 to 784. Its streets and many Buddhist temples were based on Chinese patterns from Chang'an. The temple complex at Horyuji, near Nara, has some of the oldest wooden buildings in the world. Its architecture has clear, unmistakable Chinese features. In 784, a new emperor moved the capital to **Heian**. It was also built from a Chinese model. Heian is known as *Kyoto*, which means "western Capital." It was to remain as Japan's capital until 1868. In that year, Tokyo (eastern capital) became the capital of Japan.

The Heian Period

The period from 784 to 1185 is called the Heian Period. Among the upper classes, a very aristocratic, sophisticated, and elegant court culture developed. This meant that at the emperor's court, quiet restraint and careful manners were expected by people who wore clothing that matched the seasons. Nobles were supposed to be able to write poetry and paint. Two literary masterpieces were produced at this time. One was *The Tale of Genji,* written by **Lady Murasaki Shikibu** in the eleventh century. It is about the life and adventures of a prince at the imperial court. Considered to be the world's first novel, it was the basis for extensive artistic portrayals in later centuries. Another book about court life in the Heian Period was *The Pillow Book* by **Sei Shonagon**. It is a diary account that shows much psychological insight about the Japanese upper classes.

While the cultural and social history of the Heian Period warrants attention, we need to turn now to crucial political developments. The descendants of the Yamato clan (see Chapter 2, Section 4) continued to rule as emperors. However, they were generally weak and came under the influence of the wealthy **Fujiwara** family. The Fujiwaras were able to manipulate several people at the emperor's court and to affect policies and decisions. Frequently, they arranged for princes of the imperial family to marry daughters of their widespread clan. Affairs at court became increasingly corrupt, especially as the Fujiwaras were freed from paying taxes and took over large amounts of imperial land. Other large land owners and nobles became disrespectful of the central government, raised their own armies, and sought to further their own private interests. Much of Japan now became unsafe and lawless. Farmers and small land owners grew fearful and needed protection. They were thus willing to gain protection under powerful lords or **daimyos**, by giving up their land and pledging their labor and loyalty. These relationships led to a system known as **feudalism**.

A Japanese scroll painting on paper showing a scene from *The Tale of Genji.*

Feudalism in Japan

As with European feudalism that you studied in Chapter 6, the Japanese version was based on a set of relationships, promises, and obligations between different groups of people. Some had more power, rights, and privileges than others. Nevertheless, there were some differences. One of these involved the status of those who were the member of each lord's army. In Europe, these were the knights. In Japan, these were the **samurai**. This word meant "one who serves." The samurai lived a very strict and disciplined life, under a code called **bushido** ("the way of the warrior"). If a samurai violated any part of this code, or brought shame on his lord, he would seek to commit ritual suicide (*hari-kari*) and die in what he would consider an honorable death. These ideas were not part of a knight's behavior under European feudalism. Another difference could be seen in the value that samurai placed on painting, writing poetry, carrying out the tea ceremony, and doing calligraphy. In general, such skills and attitudes toward the arts were not expected of knights. Other contrasts between the two forms of feudalism are as follows:

1. In Europe the lord-vassal-knight relationship was a legal arrangement. For the Japanese, the ties between a lord and his samurai warriors were based on morality and complete loyalty. The lord was thought to possess superior wisdom and ethical behavior.

2. Samurai would fight in exchange for an allowance from a large land owner. A knight would fight in exchange for land from a noble.

3. In Japan, women could be samurai and would thus be expected to be as tough and disciplined as men. In Europe, women were to be protected and were considered to be inferior beings.

A Japanese samurai in armor.

Much about Japanese life today can be explained if we understand the customs followed in feudal times. The ideals of loyalty, duty, responsibility, and self-discipline are remainders from feudalism. They are evident in the character and personality of modern-day Japanese people.

The Kamakura Period

The feudal patterns of Japanese culture emerged, as we have seen, in the Heian Period. They were to grow at a fast pace during the Kamakura Period (1185–1333). In the twelfth century, as Heian-centralized control was weakening, two powerful clans or families struggled for domination in Japan. The *Minamoto* family, whose leader was *Yoritomo*, was victorious. The emperor bestowed on him the title of

Shogun. This could be translated as "supreme general of the emperor's army." He could place his own lords and warriors in high government positions. Japan was now ruled under a *shogunate*, also called a *bakufu*. Yoritomo was to become the equivalent of a military dictator. This pattern of government was to remain in effect until 1868. During the period which we can also call the Kamakura Shogunate, the emperor retained his title while living at Kyoto (formerly Heian). However, the actual control of the country was at the military headquarters of Yoritomo, in the city of Kamakura. Decisions on topics such as taxes, transportation, the armed forces, and land policy were his to make. The emperor, powerless, was said to reign but not rule.

It was during the Kamakura Period that, for the first time in its history, Japan was faced with military invasion. The attackers were the Mongols. They sought to attack from bases in China and Korea that they had taken over. In 1274, a 30,000 man invasion force landed on the coast of the southern island of Kyushu. They easily defeated the Japanese army. However, a devastating storm arose in the area that prevented supplies from reaching them and forced the Mongols to sail back to the Asian mainland. Kublai Khan, the Mongol leader, then sent representatives to Japan demanding surrender. The Japanese refused and killed all the representatives. Sensing another attack, the Kamakura Shogun gathered forces from many parts of Japan and built fortified walls along the Kyushu coast. The attack came in 1281 and was unsuccessful. The walls prevented the Mongols from landing, while a ruinous typhoon struck the area. Almost half the Mongol fleet was sunk. The remainder sailed away, never to confront Japan again. The Japanese would claim that the typhoon contained *kamikaze* ("winds of the gods") and that spiritual heavenly forces had intervened to save them.

Painting of Minamoto Yoritomo on silk.

The preparations for battle with the Mongols had been costly for the Kamakura treasury. Funds were scarce. Several samurai were angered by the Shogunate's inability to pay them. Local rulers withdrew their allegiance to the Shoguns and began to fight among themselves. Power eventually passed onto another strong family. The result was the formation of the *Ashikaga* Shogunate. Yet, the Ashikaga Shoguns were weak and could not stop various military lords from constant warfare among themselves. The fighting became so intense that the timeframe from 1467 to 1590 is called the *Sengoku* or "Warring States Period." Ultimately, the bloodshed ceased when a set of powerful daimyo used their superior forces to subdue their opponents in the late sixteenth century. The creation of the **Tokugawa Shogunate** shortly thereafter, in 1603, would bring about over 200 years of unity, peace, and stability to Japan.

The Tokugawa Shogunate

Although the Tokugawa Shogunate did indeed provide for an orderly and peaceful Japan for over two centuries, it was born out of bloodshed. The story begins with Oda Nobunaga, a powerful daimyo who was able to take over most of the main island of Honshu by defeating other daimyos. He was the first Japanese to use guns and firearms in battle, obtained mainly from the Portuguese. He was helped in his victories by two generals, **Toyotomi Hideyoshi** and **Tokugawa Ieyasu**. Upon Nobunaga's death, Hideyoshi continued with his former leader's attempt to unify Japan. To do this, he had to fight other daimyos who stood in his path. He proved to be successful in spreading his control over most of Japan, while combining ruthless tactics and political maneuvering with friendly daimyos. He had also hoped to conquer China, and thus mounted an invasion of Korea in order to get to China. Yet, as fierce Korean resistance severely affected his armies, Hideyoshi was forced to give up his expansionist goals. He died peacefully in 1598.

At this time, command of his armies went to Tokugawa Ieyasu. It was he who was able to complete the unification of Japan by 1600. In that year he won a historic battle over opposing armies at Sekigahara, near Kyoto. In 1603, he was appointed shogun. He now enjoyed the support and loyalty of all daimyo. With his moving the capital from *Kyoto* ("southern capital") to Edo, now called *Tokyo* ("northern capital"), he was to establish the Tokugawa Shogunate.

When evaluating a long period of history in a nation, historians will often examine the country's foreign policies as well as its domestic policies. As historians, we will now do this as we look first at Tokugawa relations with the outside world and then with conditions inside Japan itself. The Tokugawa policy toward other nations may be described as isolationism as well as a "closed-country policy." There is evidence for this attitude as well as a reason. In 1639, the Shogunate closed Japan to all outsiders except for Dutch and Chinese merchants. These foreigners were allowed to bring in a limited number of trading ships each year to a small island near the port of Nagasaki but were not permitted to leave the island. Rules were also written that forbade any Japanese from traveling to a foreign country. Japanese who were not in Japan were prohibited from returning there.

Christian missionaries, who had initially come to Japan in 1549, were now banned. Christianity was viewed by the Tokugawa shoguns as a threat to their rule, particularly as several Japanese Christians had been part of the revolt in 1637. These Christians faced persecution by the rulers. Because Christianity and other foreign ideas, primarily from Europe, were seen as harmful, the shoguns wanted to restrict their adoption in Japan. The main reason for this policy toward foreigners, as well as the main reason for the foreign policy of any nation, rested upon what the Japanese

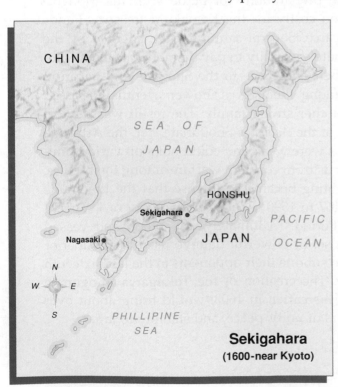

Sekigahara
(1600-near Kyoto)

felt to be in their own self-interest. In other words, the Tokugawa rulers saw foreign ideas as harming both their interest in keeping Japan under their rule and their interest in preserving order, stability, and traditional ways of life. They were successful in these goals. They were able to promote trade and industry in the country, as well as to ensure peace and maintain unity. Nevertheless, there were downsides and disadvantages to the Tokugawa foreign policy.

The refusal to have contact with Europeans occurred at a time when the Europeans were making great strides in science, technology, and commerce. The Japanese thus missed out on learning things of value and achieving things in those areas that might have contributed to helping their own development as a nation. Another consequence of this closed-door policy was the loss of trade with countries in East and Southeast Asia.

In domestic affairs, Tokugawa Japan was characterized by a rigid class structure. Society was grouped into four classes in a ranked order. These were the samurai, peasants, artisans (craftspeople, artists, blacksmiths, etc.), and merchants. The merchants were on the bottom of this social scale because they earned their money from things made by other people. Such was the Confucian view of merchants, adopted by the Japanese from China. The daimyos were required to stay for part of each year in Edo, the center of Tokugawa power. They had to pay for their travel, food, and lodging. The Tokugawa rulers could keep an eye on the daimyos, while the expense borne by the daimyos took away from their ability to raise armies and challenge the shoguns. The system of alternate attendance in Edo was called **sankin kotai**. It helped the Tokugawa to maintain their hold on the country.

Throughout the Tokugawa era, the Japanese were able to refine many cultural achievements. Noh dramas, emphasizing tragic stories, were popular with the samurai. **Kabuki** theater featured music, dance, and attractive costumes. Wood-block prints, known as **Ukiyo-e**, were colorful and highly prized. They reflected aspects of urban life. Haiku poetry focused on images, described within a framework of seventeen syllables divided into three lines. One of the great Haiku poets was **Matsuo Basho**.

Japanese Kabuki actor.

Korea

Although Japan escaped Mongol penetration, Korea did not. Mongol rule lasted there from 1231 to 1356, primarily under control by the Yuan dynasty in China. The Mongols had destroyed a Korean kingdom that had emerged in 935. This was the **Koryo dynasty**. This name was a shortened version of the name, Koguryo, a former kingdom (see Chapter 2, Section 5). The name *Korea* comes from "Koryo." Under the Koryo dynasty, Chinese political and cultural ideas were influential. A civil service system modeled on Confucian patterns was established, and Chinese characters came to be used.

The Mongol conquest proved to be very severe and harsh. Koryo leaders were forced to pay vast sums of tribute money. The Mongols forced thousands of Koreans into service in their army and navy. The Mongol ships that sailed to attack Japan included Koreans on board. With the collapse of Mongol rule throughout many parts of Asia, the Koryo dynasty maintained power but did govern wisely. Unfair taxation spurred dissatisfaction and revolts. In 1392, the government was overthrown by Yi Song-gye. He established the *Yi* or *Choson dynasty*, which was to continue for 518 years, until 1910.

Several significant things were accomplished under the Yi dynasty; these accomplishments would bring pride to Koreans, then and now. Seoul became the capital. An alphabet, **Hangul**, created by *King Sejong* in 1446, is the basis for the native Korean language used today. In a series of great and bloody naval battles in 1593 and 1598, the Korean admiral **Yi Sun-shin** was able to defeat a Japanese invasion force. He has been given a hero's status in Korea for his victories. He was the first to use iron-clad ships in combat. The ships were known as the "turtle boats" because of their shape and image.

LINK TO TODAY
Japan—The samurai legacy

The loyalty and obedience of the samurai warriors were very fixed parts of Japanese culture in the feudal era. Although there are no samurai today in Japan nor any current practice of feudalism, there are still examples of Japanese modern-day culture that can be traced back to the samurai. In the years after World War II, as the Japanese achieved great economic growth, workers for Japanese firms worked diligently and were loyal and obedient. They could expect to have life-long employment and would never consider working for another company. Because they would never leave their own families, they would never leave the firms they worked for. Indeed, their links to their companies were very similar to their links to their families.

However for a period of years in the 1990s, there was a bit of a breakdown in the pattern of life-long employment. Japan's economy declined somewhat, as it experienced a burst in its "bubble economy." The result was that some employers were forced to lay off and fire workers. Some dismissed workers felt so ashamed and disgraced by this action that they committed suicide. The number who did this was very negligible, not even one percent of the fired labor force. Yet, such events received much publicity and made people think of the samurai code of honor from feudal times.

CHAPTER SUMMARY

The Mongol empire can be viewed in both positive and negative ways. Covering a vast amount of territory, it promoted trade and commerce, provided a sense of unity and stability, as well as an exchange by people of ideas and culture. The opposition to the Mongols, especially after the fall of the empire, formed bases for ethnic identity and a sense of nationalistic feeling. Yet, scholars also view the Mongols as cruel and devastating conquerors. Their frequent massacres and thorough destruction of many cities made them feared and hated.

IMPORTANT PEOPLE, PLACES, AND TERMS

KEY TERMS

Heian	satori	Tokugawa Shogunate
Yuan dynasty	feudalism	sankin kotai
Yi dynasty	bushido	kabuki
Pax Mongolia	shogun	Ukiyo-e
Buddhism	*The Tale of Genji*	*The Pillow Book*
Zen	Hangul	
koans	Koryo dynasty	

PEOPLE

pastoralists	Yi Sun-shin	Toyotomi Hideyoshi
nomads	Fujiwaras	Tokugawa Ieyasu
daimyo	Lady Muraski Shikubu	Matsuo Basho
Genghis Khan	samurai	Sei Shonagon
Kublai Khan	Mongols	
Marco Polo	Oda Nobunaga	

PLACES

Nara	Silk Road	Sekigahara
steppes	Chang'an (Xi'an)	

EXERCISES FOR CHAPTER 13

MULTIPLE CHOICE

Select the letter of the correct answer.

1. Kublai Khan and Yi Sun-shin were similar in that they achieved success in

   a. literature.   c. government.
   b. warfare.   d. agriculture.

2. Baghdad and Bejing were capital cities that

   a. had Muslim holy sites.
   b. were centers of commerce and trade with Japanese merchants.
   c. were captured by the Mongols.
   d. were built on the Nara model.

3. "I was able to defeat the Japanese and thus instill pride in my people." This statement would most likely be found in the diary of

   a. Genghis Khan.   c. King Sejong.
   b. Kublai Khan.   d. Yi Sun-shin.

4. Trade and commerce during the Pax Mongolia was an example of

   a. interdependence.
   b. ethnocentrism.
   c. scarcity.
   d. imperialism.

5. Which statement related to the Mongols is an opinion?

   a. They brought an end to the Abassid Caliphate.
   b. China was once ruled by them.
   c. Japan's economy would have improved under their rule.
   d. Their empire was broken up into khanates.

6. Koguryo, Koryo, and Choson were the names of dynasties in

   a. China.
   b. Japan.
   c. Korea.
   d. Russia.

7. The Tokugawa Shogunate and the Roman Empire were different with regard to

   a. expanding beyond their own borders.
   b. permitting all males to vote.
   c. having one city as a capital.
   d. maintaining a class structure.

8. The Mongol conquest in China and the Roman conquest in Gaul both resulted in the

   a. spread of democracy.
   b. suppression of Islam.
   c. rule of foreigners.
   d. growth of monarchies.

9. Which term best describes the foreign policy of the Tokugawa Shogunate?

   a. Imperialism
   b. Internationalism
   c. Isolationism
   d. Expansionism

10. The Japanese built Nara using Xi'an as a model, while adopting the Confucian view of merchants. These actions were examples of

   a. cultural diffusion.
   b. nationalism.
   c. empathy.
   d. movement of people and goods.

11. Julius Caesar and Kublai Khan were similar in that they

   a. controlled territory outside of their original homeland.
   b. improved the status of women.
   c. spread the teachings of Christianity.
   d. introduced new ideas in education.

12. Which was most characteristic about society in Tokugawa Japan?

   a. Militarism was discouraged.
   b. Social mobility was discouraged.
   c. Cultural diffusion was encouraged.
   d. Democratic institutions flourished.

13. Which chapter title would be appropriate for these Japanese items?

   I. _____

   A. Haiku
   B. Ukiyo-e
   C. Kabuki
   D. Noh

   a. Military weapons
   b. Cultural achievements
   c. Geographic regions
   d. Scientific advances

14. The decline of the Mongol and Song dynasties was similar in that

   a. floods and earthquakes devastated their economic systems.
   b. new belief systems affected the morale of their armies.
   c. disputes over who was to rule or weak leaders led to loss of power.
   d. nomads from the north destroyed the empires.

15. Under Tokugawa rule, a rigid class structure existed from highest to lowest in this order:

   a. samurai, peasants, artisans, merchants.
   b. samurai, artisans, farmers, merchants.
   c. merchants, artisans, farmers, samurai.
   d. samurai, merchants, artisans, peasants.

16. Which social scientist would be most interested in studying the structure in Question 15?

   a. Historian
   b. Economist
   c. Political scientist
   d. Sociologist

17. The adoption of Buddhism in Japan and the coming of Christianity to the Roman Empire occurred in ways that were due to

a. peaceful means.
b. military conquest.
c. imposition by foreigners.
d. mass conversions by missionaries.

18. What would be the appropriate religious heading for these items?

I. _____

    A. Zen
    B. Mahayana
    C. Pure Land
    D. Nichiren

a. Hinduism
b. Buddhism
c. Catholicism
d. Islam

19. In which sequence did the eras of Japanese rule occur?

    (1) Heian   (2) Nara   (3) Kamakura

a. 1, 2, 3
b. 2, 3, 1
c. 2, 1, 3
d. 3, 1, 2

20. Lady Murasaki Shikubu and Sei Shonagon were famous women writers who wrote of life in the

a. Mongol Empire.
b. Yuan dynasty.
c. Nara Period.
d. Heian Period.

ESSAYS FOR CHAPTER 13

1. Name two dynasties covered in the chapter. For each one, (a) give the place where it existed; (b) give the time period; (c) describe one impact it had on the people it ruled; (d) discuss whether it had a positive or negative impact.
2. Define the term *feudalism.* Explain (a) two reasons why it developed in Japan; (b) whether it had a positive or negative affect on Japanese history.
3. The Tokugawa Shogunate promoted a policy of isolationism rather than internationalism in foreign affairs, and thus had very little contact with other parts of the world. Discuss one advantage for a country of following an isolationist policy and one disadvantage.
4. Explain the following statement: "Nobunaga 'harvested' the rice; Hideyoshi 'cooked' the rice; Ieyasu 'ate' the rice."
5. Marco Polo and Kublai Khan were foreigners who came to China. For each of them answer the following questions. (a) From where did he come? (b)When did he come? (c) Why did he come? (d) What was one result of his coming to China?

DOCUMENT-BASED QUESTIONS

This task is based on the accompanying documents. Some of these documents have been edited for the purposes of this task. This task is designed to test your ability to work with historical documents. As you analyze the documents, take into account both the source of each document and the author's point of view.

Directions: Read the following documents and answer the questions after each document. Use the information in the reading and this chapter in writing your answers.

Document #1 More precious and costly items are imported in Beijing than into any other city in the world. . . . All the treasures that come from India . . . are brought here. So too are the choicest and costliest products of China itself and every other province. Every day, more than one thousand cartloads of silk enter the city, for much cloth of gold and silk is woven here.

From *The Travels of Marco Polo*

Questions 1. Why was Marco Polo impressed with Beijing?
2. What items were brought to Beijing? Where were they from?

Document #2 The men under your command . . . must be carefully chosen for your service. Do not take "difficult" fellows. If men under your orders, however loyal, are wanting in intelligence, you must not trust them with important duties, but rely upon experienced older men. If you are in doubt, refer to me, Shigetoki.

When accusations are brought to you, always remember that there must be another side to the question. Do not merely indulge in anger. To give fair decisions is the most important thing not only in commanding soldiers but also in governing a country.

From *Hojo Shigetoki: A Samurai Instructs His Son*

Questions 1. What advice does the samurai father give to his son? Describe one example.
2. Describe one samurai value or virtue that the speaker possesses.

Document #3 And the troops (of Genghis Khan) were more numerous than ants or locusts being in their multitude beyond estimation or computation. Detachment after detachment arrived each like a billowing sea and encamped round about the town. At sunrise, twenty thousand men from the Sultan's army issued forth from the citadel together with most of the inhabitants; being commanded by Kok-Khan. Kok-Khan was said to be a Mongol and to have fled from Genghis Khan and joined the Sultan. As a consequence of which his affairs had greatly prospered. When these forces reached the banks of the Oxus, the patrols and advanced parties of the Mongol army fell upon them and left no trace of them. On the following day when from the reflection of the sun the plain seemed to be a tray filled with blood, the people of Bukhara opened their gates and closed the door of strife and battle.

From *The Destruction of Bukhara, 1220* by Juvaini

Questions 1. How does the writer describe the Mongol army?
2. What happened to the Sultan's army?

Document #4

1. Japanese ships will not be sent abroad.
2. No Japanese shall be sent abroad. Anyone violating this prohibition shall suffer the penalty of death.
3. The samurai shall not purchase goods on board foreign ships directly from foreigners.

From *Japan's Act of Seclusion*, 1636

Questions

1. How did the Japanese isolate themselves from foreign contact?
2. Why did they do this?

Document #5

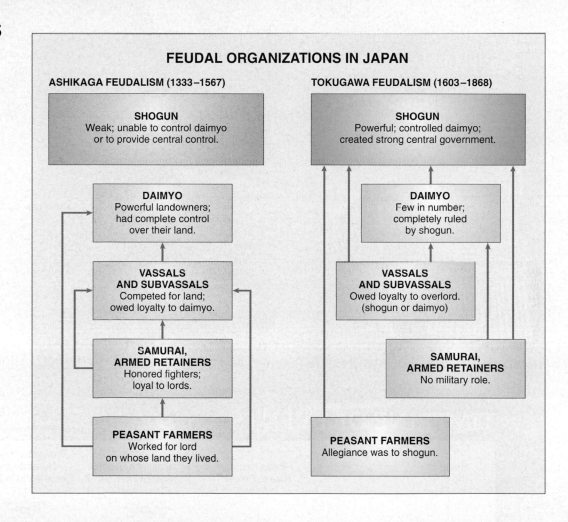

FEUDAL ORGANIZATIONS IN JAPAN

ASHIKAGA FEUDALISM (1333–1567)

SHOGUN
Weak; unable to control daimyo or to provide central control.

DAIMYO
Powerful landowners; had complete control over their land.

VASSALS AND SUBVASSALS
Competed for land; owed loyalty to daimyo.

SAMURAI, ARMED RETAINERS
Honored fighters; loyal to lords.

PEASANT FARMERS
Worked for lord on whose land they lived.

TOKUGAWA FEUDALISM (1603–1868)

SHOGUN
Powerful; controlled daimyo; created strong central government.

DAIMYO
Few in number; completely ruled by shogun.

VASSALS AND SUBVASSALS
Owed loyalty to overlord. (shogun or daimyo)

SAMURAI, ARMED RETAINERS
No military role.

PEASANT FARMERS
Allegiance was to shogun.

Questions

1. Compare the difference in the position of the Shogun between the Ashikaga and Tokugawa eras.
2. Describe the changing status of the daimyo and give one reason for this change.

CHAPTER 14
Empires in the Americas

TIMELINE OF EVENTS

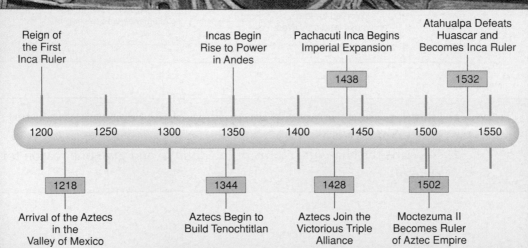

Reign of
the First
Inca Ruler

Incas Begin
Rise to Power
in Andes

Pachacuti Inca Begins
Imperial Expansion

1438

Atahualpa Defeats
Huascar and
Becomes Inca Ruler

1532

| 1200 | 1250 | 1300 | 1350 | 1400 | 1450 | 1500 | 1550 |

1218

Arrival of the Aztecs
in the
Valley of Mexico

1344

Aztecs Begin to
Build Tenochtitlan

1428

Aztecs Join the
Victorious Triple
Alliance

1502

Moctezuma II
Becomes Ruler
of Aztec Empire

Two major civilizations developed in Mesoamerica and South America in the centuries before the arrival of the Europeans. The rise of the Aztec and Inca Empires, two rich and powerful ancient American empires, was the result of important political changes that took place in two important areas of the Americas. One empire developed in the lake country of the Valley of Mexico. The other grew strong in the highland plateau region of the Andes Mountain chain stretching from Ecuador to Peru. From the thirteenth to the sixteenth centuries (the 1200s to 1500s), both the Aztec and Inca Empires became the most important and highly developed civilizations in the Americas prior to the European arrival and conquest of the Americas.

We know much about these civilizations because they still existed when the European explorers and conquerors arrived in the New World. In Mesoamerica, the Aztecs developed a military trading empire, which they ruled from the city of Tenochtitlan in Lake Texcoco. The lake was in the central valley plateau region of Mexico. They ruled over a wide area when **Hernando Cortes** and the Spaniards whom he led first encountered them. Cortes and his men conquered and destroyed the Aztec Empire. In South America, the Incas also developed an empire whose main city was Cuzco in the highlands of the Andes in modern Peru. The Incas suffered the same fate as the Aztecs when Francisco Pizarro and his group of Spanish soldiers and adventurers conquered and destroyed the Inca state (see Chapter 17).

In this chapter, you will learn more about these once great American empires and how they came to dominate the more developed cultural regions of the Americas. In this chapter, as you learned in Chapter 9, there will be some names and words that are long and hard to pronounce. Once again, remember that the peoples of the Americas had their own languages, and names for themselves and the places and things in their world.

THE AZTECS OF MEXICO

Early Beginnings

The **Aztecs** were a tribe that was among the last of the nomadic peoples to arrive in the Valley of Mexico in the thirteenth century. The Aztecs called themselves the Mexica. The name of the nation of Mexico has its origins in this name. An Aztec legend, probably in part based on truth, tells the story of their departure from the northern desert region of present-day Mexico at the beginning of the twelfth century. Led by four priests and a woman who carried a medicine bundle and was guided by the spirit of their fierce tribal war god, they finally arrived in the Valley of Mexico in 1218.

The arrival of another nomadic tribe whose culture was basically centered on hunting and gathering did not bring any immediate political change to the lake country of the central valley. At this time, the Aztec people consisted of a small number of kinship land-holding groups. They found most of the desirable land already taken by other more settled tribes. Therefore, the Aztecs took refuge and made their home on the marshy areas around Lake Texcoco. It was here that they slowly changed their way of life. They started to develop a more advanced economic and social organization and culture. Starting in about 1344 in the marshlands of the lake, the Aztecs began to build the town of **Tenochtitlan**, which ultimately would become the capitol of their military and trading empire.

The Aztecs were for a long time a subservient people. They had to obey the orders of a more powerful Valley of Mexico neighbor. The Aztecs provided warriors to this dominant city-state in the lake country in the late fourteenth and early fifteenth centuries. During these centuries, the Aztecs worked on the development of patches of solid ground in their marshland home area. They had to create dry land to build their cane and reed huts and also for agricultural purposes. It was during this time that the Aztecs made use of the technique of making artificial garden beds formed of masses of earth rich in sediment dredged from the lakebed and held in place by reeds. Eventually the roots striking downward took hold on the lake bottom and created solid ground. On these patches of solid ground called *chinampas*, the Aztecs grew the maize, beans, and other products to feed their growing population.

The Rise of the Aztecs

A turning point in Aztec history came in 1428. The Aztecs joined two other rebellious city-states to end the domination of the lords who had long ruled the Central Valley lake country. The victory of these city-states in 1430 led to the rise

Detail from Diego Rivera's mural of market day in Tenochtitlan. The Great Temple is seen in the background.

A colored Spanish engraving of Montezuma II.

of a powerful triple alliance, which soon gained almost total control of the Central Valley of Mexico. The Aztecs gradually gained complete control of the **Valley of Mexico** as their military power grew. They then began to dominate their two allies, and their kings ruled the valley.

In part, the strength of the Aztecs was based on the strategic position of Tenochtitlan. They made this city, their capitol, into a fortified island. The Aztecs also pursued a shrewd policy of forming beneficial alliances and sharing the riches gained from conquests with towns centered near Lake Texcoco. This policy added military support when needed and gave them the political support of potential rival towns in the lakeside country.

Their control of the Valley of Mexico and the ability to command the surrounding towns gave the Aztecs more of an open path to conquer other areas of Middle America. The Aztecs had the advantages of an island fortress capitol, short internal lines of communication surrounded by easily defensible mountain barriers and the ability to raise large armies. The Aztecs often used warriors from other tribes as mercenaries. These warriors who fought on their side did so because of the possibility of gaining rewards. In the mid 1400s, the Aztecs began to expand their rule in all directions as their warrior armies won victories in the adjacent valleys.

The Aztecs, often in alliance with other towns, extended their rule over and beyond the Valley of Mexico. By the time that **Moctezuma II** became ruler in 1502, the Aztecs and their allies were levying tribute on scores of towns, large and small. Aztec tribute was demanded from the distant areas of the arid northern Mexican plateau to the southern lowlands of Tehuantepec, and from the Atlantic to the Pacific. Within this extensive area only a few states or kingdoms, like the independent city-state of Tlaxcala, retained complete independence. Tributary peoples were left in peace in return for their benevolent neutrality and cooperation.

The Aztecs waged war with or without cause. Refusal to pay tribute to the Aztec ruler was a sufficient reason for invasion by the Aztecs. The Aztecs required tributary peoples to set aside certain lands for the benefit of the Aztec ruler and nobility. Injuries to the demanding and far-ranging Aztec merchants by the people of a region sometimes served as the motive for an invasion. Victory in war led to long lines of captives who made the journey to Tenochtitlan to be offered on the altars of the gods in sacrifice. In addition, periodic tribute was imposed on the defeated people. The type of tribute depended on the region and people. Tribute could be anything considered valuable or needed and included items such as maize, cacao beans, or cotton mantles.

The Aztec Political System

The Aztec political system on the eve of the conquest was a mixture of royal despotism and theocracy. The ruler presided over his empire with absolute power and resembled a bronze-age–type king in many ways. The ruler was selected from among the sons, brothers, and nephews of the previous ruler by a council of close relatives, priests, and noble-warriors. The kings of other important towns also had a voice in the choice of the new ruler. Political power was concentrated in the hands of the ruler who also was the highest religious authority. Political power was shared to some extent with a ruling class of noble-warriors and priests; however, the king was the supreme authority in all respects in the Aztec world. The Aztec monarch was considered a godlike figure.

The Aztec Empire was not a government that directly ruled all the peoples they dominated. Nor did the Aztecs seek total territorial control. The Aztec government operated more as a federal type of government. In all matters crucial to the Aztecs, conquered tribes had to obey the Aztec commands. Examples of important matters were contributing warriors to fight for the Aztecs in times of war and supplying people for sacrifice. The Aztec imperial system represented an alternative to centralized imperial administrative control. It was above all a tributary and trading empire. **Tribute** was something of value that was given to please the Aztec ruler. Examples of tribute were beautiful women and precious stones such as jade. If a ruler and his subjects were obedient, the people were allowed to enjoy autonomy in local government, culture, and customs. The Aztecs allowed them to select their own leaders.

The Aztec army only mobilized and attacked already conquered regions if a rebellion occurred or there was resistance to the idea of being a tributary people. According to some estimates, the Aztecs and their allies ruled over a population of perhaps twenty-five million people. Many of the peoples suffered from Aztec domination. Most peoples only cooperated with them because they feared an Aztec military response if they failed to obey. This deep-rooted hatred of the Aztecs helped Cortes in his conquest of the Aztec Empire.

Aztec Religion

Polytheistic religious beliefs played an essential role in the lives of the Aztecs. The Aztecs honored and worshiped many gods and had a rich mythology about them. The Aztec people thought that their gods had to be pleased by offering human sacrifices. The favor of their gods was needed if they were to be successful in all aspects of their daily lives. Their gods were believed to influence all events including birth, marriage, the planting of crops, war, and death.

Tlaloc, the Aztec god of water and rain.

The priesthood had a crucial role in linking religion to Aztec society. The priests were responsible for conducting the religious rites such as human sacrifice and for interpreting the will of the gods whom they served. Their decisions were very important for guiding the life of the Aztecs. They were the guardians of the religious temples housing the statues of the gods. Warfare was a sacred activity. The war god was at the top of the pantheon of Aztec gods. The Aztecs believed that their war god wanted more and more human blood and hearts torn out of sacrificial victims. As the Aztec Empire expanded, it became increasingly necessary to capture more prisoners or purchase slaves. They were later sacrificed on the altars of the Aztec gods. **Sacrifice** was done in order to ensure the continuance of the universe and to please the war god and guarantee further success on the battlefield.

The Aztecs also worshiped the forces of nature. There were many nature gods such as the rain, maize, sun, and moon. The priests determined the sacred time that the gods of rain, maize, and other fertility gods should be worshiped. The rain and maize gods were particularly important in Aztec society.

Aztec Social Organization

As the class system became more structured, the social and economic status of the Aztec people became ever more dependent on the role each individual played within the developing military and trading empire. At the top of the Aztec society was the ruler and the royal family. Noble-warriors and priests were also part of the upper classes. Royal officials who served in the state government, the *administrative bureaucracy*, also held a superior status in Aztec society. These government officials were responsible for the administration of the empire.

Most of the newly conquered land and the peasant farmers living on it were assigned to nobles who distinguished themselves in battle. These rich agricultural lands became hereditary. As a result, the noble-warrior class grew in power. Therefore, warfare to gain control of land and people became increasingly important in Aztec society. The elevated social status of the noble-warrior meant that military skills and accomplishments were highly regarded. The noble-warrior was a pillar of support for an increasingly powerful monarchy. Their increased control of lands on the lakeshore and elsewhere expanded their control of agricultural production and food resources.

The myth that the noble-warrior class descended from a separate divine origin, from the god Quetzalcoatl, also gave this group a higher social status. The belief in Quetzalcoatl and all of the legends about him played an enormous role in Aztec history. The Aztecs' unwillingness to attack Cortes and his small group of conquerors when they first arrived in Mexico was a result of their beliefs concerning this influential god (see Chapter 17).

The older tradition of the land-holding kinship groups continued to exist, but these lower-status kinship groups were increasingly subject to the rule of more elite noble families. The vast majority of Aztec commoners were farmer-soldiers who owed tribute, labor, and military service to the Aztec ruler and state. There was a growing difference in the social status of the Aztec upper classes as compared to the lower-class farmer-soldiers.

The status of the merchant class increased over time. Their role in trading for and purchasing products not found or grown in the Valley of Mexico expanded with the growth of the empire. The merchants controlled the Aztec open air markets. Merchants wandered far and wide to bring the desired products to the great Aztec open air market in Tenochtitlan. The ruler and upper nobility often depended on the merchant class to make available items that were considered the luxuries of life. Cacao beans used to make chocolate, exotic feathers of birds particularly from the sacred Quetzalcoatl, and rare animals were among these products. The merchants also served as the eyes and ears for the monarchy. They were quick to report resistance to paying tribute, resistance to providing people for sacrifice, and other signs of rebellion. In other ancient empires in Africa and Asia, the merchant class also provided useful information to the ruler to help prevent rebellion.

Some commoners were also artisans. An artisan's primary responsibility was to produce simple goods such as clothing or foodstuffs to be sold in the Aztec markets. Some artisans had a higher social status if their particular skill had value to the ruler and upper classes. These artisans were artists, sculptors, and jewelers. Entertainers also had a higher social status.

On the margins of Aztec society was a large class of slaves. Slavery was a punishment for a variety of offenses, including failure to pay debts. In return for food poor commoners were sometimes willing to become slaves. Slaves were treated as chattels to be bought and sold. They were used for personnel service or as sacrificial offerings to the gods.

Aztec Culture and City Life

By the beginning of the sixteenth century, it is estimated that the Aztec capitol, Tenochtitlan, had a population of between 150,000 to 200,000 people. Like Venice in Italy, the city was an oval island with an extensive canal system. It was connected to the mainland by three *causeways*, or roadways, that converged at the city center and served as the main arteries of traffic. Although there were very few streets or wide avenues, the city's system of interconnecting canals were bordered by footpaths. The numerous canoes that used the canals served as the main means of transportation and also were used for trading purposes.

Lower-status social groups, mostly artisans, lived as family units in the simple homes built alongside the city's many canals and on the outskirts of the city. Their houses were often made of reeds covered with dried mud, but if they had more means, they built homes of adobe. The middle-status social groups of Aztec society were the special artisans, entertainers, civil servants, and higher-grade soldiers. They lived in the city in better homes built of adobe, which were always lime-washed and painted. The upper social groups, noble-warriors, and wealthy merchants lived in far more spacious homes closer to the center of the city. An aqueduct in solid stone masonry brought fresh water from the mountain springs to the city.

As in housing, individual dress depended on a person's social and economic status. The average commoner wore essential garments. A man wore a loincloth with a front and back flap, a plain blanket of coarse cotton fiber, and sandals. Women wore wrap-around skirts of white cotton with a narrow belt and loose-fitting tunics. Women went barefoot. The upper- and middle-status Aztecs dressed in a richer style. Wealthier men wore elaborate cotton mantles, shirtlike garments, decorated with symbols and had ear and nose plugs of precious stone, often green jade traded for in the south. Richer women wore more colorful and beautifully decorated tunics, better-quality cotton wrap-around skirts, and more jewelry.

The Aztec diet was varied and included mostly vegetables, fowl, fruit, fish, and some meat. Turkey, venison, and quail were eaten with sauces often made with chilies. As in other cultures in Europe and Asia, the higher-status socio-economic groups had a greater ability to purchase a wider variety of food items that were considered to be expensive and hard to obtain. For example, chocolate was made into a delicious beverage but was forbidden to commoners. The commoners ate a diet consisting mostly of maize meal, beans, and vegetables cooked with chilies.

Education was very formal and intended to prepare a child for his or her place in the Aztec world. One goal of educating the young was to teach them Aztec ideals. The type of school attended depended on the social status of the student. The language of instruction was Nahuatl, which was the native tongue of the Aztec people. Boys and girls attended different schools. Students went to school from about the age of 10 or 12 to 20 or 22, at which time they were expected to enter into a marriage contract.

At the time of the arrival of the Spaniards in the second decade of the sixteenth century, the Aztec people lived in a very complex society in which the ruler and upper classes were lords and masters of a far-reaching trading empire based on military power. All this would change after the Spanish conquest. Nevertheless, up to this time, it is clear that the Aztecs had reached the highest pinnacle of civilization in Mesoamerica.

> **Main Idea:**
> The Aztec people lived in a very complex society in which the ruler and upper classes were lords and masters of a far-reaching trading empire.

TIIE INCAS OF PERU

In the 1200s, the **Incas** were still a small tribe living in the highlands of modern Peru. Yet by the mid 1400s, the Incas managed to create the mightiest empire in South America. Prior to the arrival of the Europeans, the Incas developed an advanced bronze-age culture that was similar in many ways to cultures that developed in the Ancient World in the Middle East, Africa, India, and Southeast Asia (see Chapter 2). The history of the Inca's rise to power in the Andean region is a story of strong leadership and skillful organization. From the time of the discovery and conquest of Peru in the 1530s by **Francisco Pizarro** to the present, the Inca achievements in the arts, building, and political and social organization have been recognized by historians, anthropologists, and archaeologists.

For many years, historians and social scientists that study ancient civilizations saw the Inca society as a *socialist empire*, a type of government that sought to help all people according to their needs. The Inca government was thought of as an early version of the modern-day welfare state, in which people were shielded from severe economic problems in time of need such as drought. Today most historians and others that study the Inca state believe that this view is incorrect. They support the idea that the Inca state was similar to that of a despotic ancient empire. The Inca state was theocratic in the sense that the ruler was thought to be divine and the worship of the Inca was encouraged. The Inca is considered to be an all-powerful ruler. Within the theocratic state that the Incas controlled, all people had to obey the godlike Inca. After reading this section, you can decide for yourself what type of civilization and society the Inca ruled.

The Origins of the Inca Civilization and Empire

The Incas were heirs to a cultural tradition that started before their rise to power in the Andean region. This cultural tradition originated on the coast of present-day Peru and spread into the highlands. The earlier Andean kingdoms provided instructive precedents, cultural and political ideas that the Incas built upon to create their theocratic state (see Chapter 9). The Incas had their own myths and legends. One such story gave their rulers a *divine*, or godly, origin and their warriors a supernatural favor and protection.

The reign of the first important Inca ruler dates back to the 1200s. He was a capable and strong leader and is considered to be the first Inca monarch. Thereafter, Inca rule was followed in succession by the same kinship and blood lineage group. By the time of the eighth Inca ruler in about 1400, the Inca Empire began to emerge as one of the important powers of the Andean highlands. True imperial expansion dates from 1438 when the hero and monarch of the Inca nation ruled. His name was Pachucati Inca, and he was a great conqueror who expanded the Inca Empire. He is credited with making important

Main Idea:
The Incas managed to create the mightiest empire in South America.

An image of an Inca god.

A wood engraving for Pachacuti Inca Yupanqui, an Inca emperor.

reforms and innovations, which established the territorial divisions and administrative bureaucracy to run the expanded empire.

Inca Imperial Rule

The Incas created the greatest and most extensive empire in the Americas prior to the arrival of the Spaniards. Their empire stretched for over 2000 miles in the **Andes** mountainous region from north to south. By 1527, the boundary of the Incas, who thought of themselves as the children of the sun, stretched from Ecuador and Colombia in the north to the present day Santiago in Chile in the south. The Incas ruled an empire that had more than 9 million subjects. Inca rule over the masses of peasant-farmers was often indirect and exercised through local chieftains.

The Incas did not have a writing system. Special officials kept records with a memory device called a *quipu*, which was a stick or cord with a number of knotted strings of different colors. The knots were a complicated number system representing ones, tens, hundreds, thousands, and so on. Quipus contained all of the important records of the Inca Empire. These records included population counts, tribute collected, and granary storage figures.

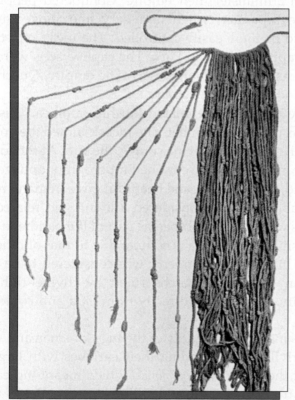

This device is called a quipu, which was used for counting and recording facts and events.

In this drawing by Felipe Guaman Poma de Ayala (c. 1600), an Incan nobleman receives a report from an official, who holds a quipu.

The Incan capitol
of Cuzco, in Peru.

The great success of the Incas in controlling such a large land area with so many different tribes and peoples was due to their ability to act quickly to put down rebellions. The Inca road network and messenger system played important roles in helping them administer their empire. Conquered peoples who rose up in rebellion were separated when necessary and moved to other provinces where they could be more easily controlled. The Incas kept the sons of chiefs hostage in their capitol, **Cuzco**, in Peru. The captive sons were forced to learn Quechua, which was the official language of the empire. Quechua was the language used by the Incas and local nobility.

The Incas were made up of twelve related kinship families. This blood-related group of people was limited in number. The Incas claimed they obtained their right to rule and privileges from a divine source, the sun. At the top of the imperial social structure was the **Inca** himself. The Emperor monopolized trade in luxury items such as gold, cocoa leaves, and beautiful girls. In many respects, the Inca was unapproachable and was considered a living god related to the sun. The former Inca rulers were also worshiped as part of the pantheon of gods related to the sun. The position of the Inca is comparable to that of other monarchs in Europe and Asia. In Japan, the emperor was considered to be a direct descendent of the sun. In Europe, monarchs ruled by divine right. They believed that their authority to rule came directly from God and could not be questioned.

The Inca nobility was made up primarily of the Inca kinsmen and women. Only the Incas had the privilege of extending their earlobes with large ornaments. The Spanish called the Inca nobles *orejones*, which meant big ears. The Inca nobility were exempt from any tribute and military service. Below the Inca nobility in the social hierarchy were the conquered local chieftains. These conquered chiefs were given a high status as long as they made sure that their peoples remained peaceful and paid tribute. Labor on the roads and in the mines was the most common form of tribute.

Next in the line of status were a numerous class of specialists who were professional military officers, royal servants and retainers, quipu keepers, other administrative officials, and entertainers. Their loyalty and services to the Inca were rewarded with rich gifts of land, llamas, and a class of farm laborers whose status resembled that of permanent servants.

The vast majority of people in the Inca Empire were farmers who produced the agricultural products, labored on public works projects, and fought in the Inca's armies when called upon. Peoples ruled by the Incas were grouped in kinship relationships, which were traced through a common ancestor. Marriage took place within the kinship group. This created additional links among the families of each extended kinship group.

Inca Religion, Arts, and Learning

The Inca religion supported the power of the Inca and state. The Inca Empire is often considered to be a theocracy because government and religion were so tied together. *Inti*, the sun god, was believed to be the father of all Incas. Inti guided the Incas in all areas of their life and was the symbol of their greatness. The worship of Inti was required in every conquered province. Nevertheless, the Inca state religion existed side by side with the much older ancestor cults and the worship of a large number of local objects and places.

The priestly class tended to the religious ceremonies, prayers, and temples. A class of holy women who took vows of permanent chastity assisted them in their religious duties. The Inca idols were housed in numerous temples. One special group of religious buildings or dead households held the mummified remains of the

An Incan ceremonial knife.

former Inca rulers. The royal mummies became part of the pantheon of gods to be worshiped and maintained by their servants. The priests also performed human sacrifice rites and were responsible for the religious cure of diseases.

Inca art and architecture were at a high level of artistic and technical excellence. Inca architecture was solidly built and meant to last. Buildings were functional and were constructed for multiple purposes. Massive stone characterized Inca buildings. Experts have marveled at the precise fitting of the stone blocks that make up the monuments and walls of Inca-built structures. Stone-type sculptures had broad features and were heavy looking in their appearance. The weaving of tapestries was done in a very fine and detailed way. Inca weavers made beautiful textile masterpieces. Inca metallurgy was also of a high technical and artistic level. The Inca capitol, Cuzco, had numerous structures with gold objects

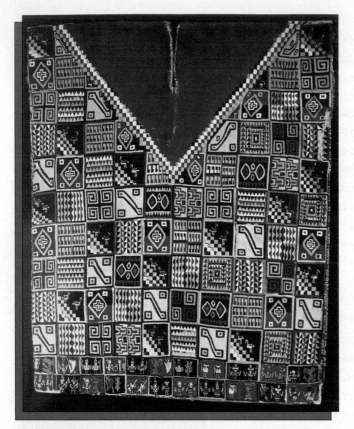

Inca clothing.

and panels. For example, both the imperial palace and the Temple of the Sun contained golden life-like plants and animals and wall designs.

The Incas had no system of writing and lacked written literature. Instead the Incas had a strong oral tradition of prayers and tales that were handed down from generation to generation. They also lacked the type of calendar that other Mesoamerican peoples used. Nevertheless, they kept time through a series of annual festivals and rites. This system of festivals and ceremonies instructed them when to plant based on the positions of the sun and moon. Traditional Inca music had a melancholy and nostalgic spirit and tone and to our modern ear may sound sad.

The Inca Economic System

The economic basis of the Inca Empire was its intensively irrigated agriculture production. This food-producing system supported the population and also resulted in a surplus production that was stored in granaries in strategic places throughout the empire. The agricultural production was more than sufficient to feed the large Inca armies, administrative bureaucracy, and many other persons engaged in nonproductive agricultural activities. The key to this large agricultural production was the irrigation systems that existed in the coastal and highland areas. Many of the irrigation ditches and canals existed prior to the Incas rise to power, but the Incas did introduce advanced practices of irrigation.

In addition the Incas made use of a terracing system, which they used on the slopes of the numerous hills and mountains. This enabled more farmers in the food-producing population to be productive because terracing extended agricultural land and limited the erosion of the rich soil vulnerable to rains and floods. The Inca Empire also made use of fertilization, which also increased crop production.

The agricultural implements used by farmers were few and simple. The foot-plow to break up soil was the most common farm tool. A hoe with a bronze plate was also used for general cultivation. The potato and *quinoa*, a grain, were the principal staple crops in the higher valleys. Maize was the main crop in lower altitudes. Cotton, beans, and cocoa leaves were grown in lower and hotter valleys.

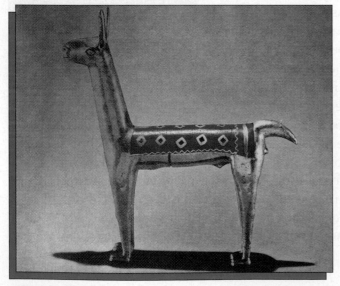

Alpaca artifact.

Aztec sun calendar.

The Inca state regulated the exchange of the agricultural products of these different farming environments. The administrative bureaucracy controlled a system of open-air markets and the transportation network. A significant part of the agricultural production was taken as tribute and used by the Inca, nobility, soldiers, and others entitled to a share of the food production. Despite the regulations, the Inca food production system allowed for community autonomy and self-sufficiency. All subject peoples determined how they would use the food production that remained after tribute was taken. It was once thought that the Inca economy was an early example of a socialist- or welfare-type economy. Today the idea that the Incas controlled an economic system for the benefit of all members of society is no longer believed to be true by a growing number of historians and others who study Inca society. The Incas set up an economic system principally for their own benefit and exploited the labor of other peoples. The granaries were not available to people in need of food unless the Inca state thought it was in its interest.

At the time of the arrival of the Spaniards, the Incas were rulers of an empire, which like that of the Aztecs in Mesoamerica can be called a bronze-age type of despotism. The peoples who lived within their empire feared the Incas and for good reason. Resistance and rebellion were met with an attack by an Inca army, which was professionally led and trained. Harsh measures of repres-

An Incan farmer irrigating a cornfield.

Incan farmers digging and transporting potatoes in Peru.

sion and forced removal to other pacified lands often followed. It is not surprising that many of the conquered peoples did little to help the Incas when Pizarro and his men arrived in Peru.

LINK TO TODAY

The Aztecs and Incas created empires in the Americas before the arrival of the Europeans in the 1500s. After contact was made, the Aztec and Inca Empires were destroyed by conquerors from Spain. One reason for the success of the Spaniards was their superior military capabilities. The military weapons and tactics used by the Spaniards were more advanced than that of the Aztec and Inca armies.

In our world today we can see similar situations. There are nations that, because of their technological capabilities to create weapons, have a great advantage in a time of military conflict. If we look at two of the military conflicts that took place in the Middle East during the early 1990s and later in 2003 and 2004, the Gulf War and the war in Iraq to remove Saddam Hussein from power, we can see how superior military technology and equipment played a significant role in determining the outcome of the actual fighting in these conflicts.

History has repeatedly shown us that superior weaponry is a definite advantage in a military conflict that is hard if not impossible to overcome. Nevertheless, despite initial military victories, there is no guarantee that weapons of military superiority will lead to a successful peace. After the Spaniards conquered the Aztecs and Incas, their societies could not adjust to the loss of their leaders and destruction of their cultures and religious practices. There was a huge drop in the populations in both regions, which was only reversed after over a century.

In Iraq today, we see some of the same things happening although in a different way. Saddam Hussein, like the Inca and Aztec rulers, was a supreme dictator. His removal from power was necessary if the Iraqi nation and people are to progress. However, this progress may take many years to happen. The link here is that superior military advantages can help win a war, but there is no guarantee that the change in power will lead to more happiness or better lives for the people affected by these changes—at least not during and in the years immediately following a military conflict.

CHAPTER SUMMARY

In this chapter, you have seen how two great civilizations created empires in the Americas prior to the arrival of the Spaniards in the early decades of the sixteenth century. The Aztecs developed more of a trading empire based on military power and the paying of tribute. They did not seek to rule over peoples but rather forced them to trade, pay tribute, and provide people for their sacrificial ceremonies.

The Incas created more of a state-like administrative system to control the peoples they conquered. Although they allowed for local autonomy by permitting the chiefs of tribes to rule, they administered their empire as an organized state system. Inca rule was based on a highly efficient agricultural system, which depended on human labor and irrigation and terracing techniques. The Aztec and Inca monarchs had a divine nature, but the Inca Empire was more of a theocratic state because the ruler and his entire kinship family claimed descent from the sun. Both the Aztecs and the Incas were the most advanced civilizations in Mesoamerica and the Andean region of South America. They developed cultures and civilizations that are comparable to those of this bronze-age type on other continents (see Chapters 1 and 2).

Neither the Aztecs nor Incas benefited from ideas that came from other parts of the world. The isolation of the Americas meant that the Native American peoples never had the opportunity that Europeans, Africans, and Asian civilizations had to learn from each other's ideas and inventions. This learning through cultural diffusion that the Europeans profited from enabled the Spaniards to develop more rapidly and to conquer these two great American civilizations easily. Nevertheless, we should look at the Aztecs and Incas for what they were prior to the conquest. Before the Europeans came to the New World, both civilizations made numerous cultural advances and should be respected for their artistic, administrative, and other accomplishments.

IMPORTANT PEOPLE, PLACES, AND TERMS

KEY TERMS	PEOPLE	PLACES
Inca	Aztecs	Valley of Mexico
tribute	Incas	Andes Mountains
sacrifice	Moctezuma	Tenochitlan
	Hernando Cortes	Cuzco
	Francisco Pizarro	Peru

EXERCISES FOR CHAPTER 14

MULTIPLE CHOICE

Select the letter of the correct answer.

1. The Aztecs and Incas were similar in that both built an empire based on
   a. democratic ideals and principles.
   b. military power, trade, and tribute.
   c. the idea of sharing political power.
   d. the use of iron to make weapons and tools.

2. The Aztecs believed that their gods
   a. did not interfere at all in human matters.
   b. should only be worshiped in a time of war.
   c. required human sacrifice to win their favor.
   d. were really the spirits of dead human beings.

3. Based on items 1–4 which title would best complete this partial outline?

Title:_____

    1. Built public granaries that provide for all people.
    2. Built roads to better control their empire.
    3. Imposed their gods but respected local gods.
    4. Forced rebellious people to move to other areas of empire.

    a. The Aztecs create a powerful empire in Mesoamerica.
    b. The Incas develop a powerful theocratic empire in the Andes.
    c. Rival city-states unite to form important alliance.
    d. Ancient American empires develop social welfare states.

4. The Aztec and Inca Empires were similar to other Ancient World empires in that

    a. the Aztecs and Incas used farming implements made of iron.
    b. like other ancient civilizations they developed after the Crusades.
    c. like other ancient civilizations they believed in monotheism.
    d. the monarch was all powerful and ruled based on divine right.

5. Base your answer to Question 5 on the following reading passage.

> Religion played a crucial role in Inca life. The term "Inca" refers to the ruler of the empire and his extended family, which numbered in the thousands. The Inca was believed to be a descendent of the sun god, Inti. He was worshiped like a living god. The Incas sought through their worship to influence their gods to help them.

The reading passage supports which of the following statements?

    a. The Incas believed in the idea of separation of church and state.
    b. All of the members of the extended Inca family were worshiped as gods.
    c. Religion played a determining role in all areas of life in the Inca Empire.
    d. The Inca descended from the god Inti.

6. The expeditions of Hernando Cortes and Francisco Pizarro resulted in the

    a. destruction of the Aztec and Inca Empires.
    b. capture of Brazil by Portugal.
    c. colonization of North America by Portugal.
    d. exploration of the Philippines and East Indies.

7. One similarity of the Aztec, Maya, and Inca Empires is that they

    a. developed in fertile river valleys.
    b. maintained democratic political systems.
    c. coexisted peacefully with neighboring empires.
    d. created complex civilizations.

8. Base your answer to this question on the facing map.

Which conclusion about Inca society could be drawn from this map?

    a. An extensive road system connected all parts of the empire for trade.
    b. Their trade depended on many seaports.
    c. Tropical climatic conditions existed throughout the empire.
    d. A similar language unified the Inca civilization.

9. Which idea was shared by the ancient Maya, Aztec, and Inca civilizations?

    a. Practicing rituals to please the gods
    b. Equality among the social classes
    c. Direct democracy
    d. Monotheism

10. The archeological evidence found at the Mesoamerican sites of Tenochitlan and Cuzco suggests that these societies

  a. consisted of hunters and gatherers.
  b. were highly developed and organized cultures.
  c. practiced a monotheistic religion.
  d. followed a democratic system.

11. How did the Inca adapt to their physical environment?

  a. They built large fishing fleets to feed their populations.
  b. They built footbridges that connected their roads across the Andes.
  c. They established extensive trade agreements with Europe.
  d. They raised cattle and horses on the pampas.

12. Inca terrace farming and Aztec floating gardens are examples of

  a. the ability of civilizations to adapt to their region's physical geography.
  b. slash-and-burn farming techniques.
  c. Mesoamerican art forms symbolizing the importance of agriculture.
  d. colonial economic policies that harmed Latin American civilizations.

13. Which statement about the Incas and Aztecs is accurate?

  a. The Aztecs and Incas were lead by rulers who supported monotheism.
  b. The Inca and Aztec rulers had no blood heritage to the gods.
  c. The Inca and Aztec capitols were set in the coastal plain.
  d. The Inca and Aztec social systems were based on a classless society.

14. The Aztec, Inca, and Maya civilizations all achieved great progress in developing

  a. a written language and great literature.
  b. strong naval forces.
  c. the arts and architecture.
  d. a monotheistic religion.

15. A major reason for the end of the Aztec Empire was

  a. the refusal of people to obey their leaders.
  b. the conflict with the Inca Empire.
  c. the arrival of the Spanish conquistadores.
  d. political corruption and an unstable government.

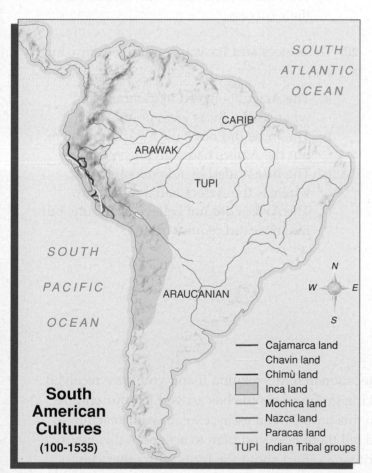

SOUTH ATLANTIC OCEAN

CARIB

ARAWAK

TUPI

SOUTH PACIFIC OCEAN

ARAUCANIAN

N
W —◆— E
S

South American Cultures
(100–1535)

—— Cajamarca land
  Chavin land
—— Chimù land
▨ Inca land
—— Mochica land
—— Nazca land
—— Paracas land
TUPI Indian Tribal groups

Base your answers to Questions 16 and 17 on the following passage.

The Inca government was held together by a tight social system based on communal land holding and a far reaching system of forced labor. Discipline was enforced by a strict code that was backed by the Inca military organization. The Incas required their conquered subjects to worship the cult of the Inca ruler, which included the sun god Inti and previous Inca rulers. The Inca government was more highly organized than the Aztec Empire. The well-maintained Inca road system made it easier for the Inca to send his armies at the first sign of rebellion to put down any sign of unrest.

16. Which answer best compares the Incas to the Aztecs?

   a. The Aztecs had better control over their empire.
   b. The Inca road system was a handicap for the army.
   c. The Aztec tight communal system helped them maintain order.
   d. The Inca military enforced order in their empire.

17. Which sentence best describes the Inca society?

   a. The Incas created a very egalitarian society.
   b. All subject peoples were allowed freedom of religion.
   c. Land ownership played a major role in the social structure.
   d. The military had a limited role in Inca society.

18. The Incas were particularly noted for which of the following accomplishments?

   a. They were skilled shipbuilders who explored the Pacific.
   b. They used their knowledge of metals to create objects of stainless steel.
   c. They developed a road system that helped them to rule a large empire.
   d. They glyph writing system led to beautifully designed golden paper in books.

19. Which statement is true of the Aztec Empire?

   a. The Aztecs lacked a merchant class to conduct trade.
   b. The Aztecs were noted for their lenient treatment of prisoners.
   c. The Aztec rule was not determined by blood lineage.
   d. The Aztecs believed in sacrifice to ensure their success.

20. The Aztecs and Incas were different in which way?

   a. The Aztecs believed in monotheism, whereas the Incas were polytheistic.
   b. The Incas did not have a writing system, but the Aztecs had a glyph system.
   c. The Incas ruled in a democratic way, whereas the Aztecs had a monarchy.
   d. The Aztecs did not believe in tribute, but the Incas did require tribute.

ESSAYS FOR CHAPTER 14

1. Assume you are the Aztec monarch Moctezuma II and you have received news that a strange-looking group of people has arrived in your empire. How would you react to this news? In an essay, explain your reaction to your noble-warriors and tell them how you plan to act about this news.
2. Assume that you are writing a report about the Incas with other classmates as part of a cooperative learning group assignment. Write an essay to your classmates about the accomplishments of the Incas.

3. How were the Aztecs able to maintain control of their empire?
4. How big of a role did religion play in the Inca Empire?
5. Why are the Inca and Aztec Empires considered to be bronze-age–type empires?

DOCUMENT-BASED QUESTIONS

This task is based on the accompanying documents. Some of these documents have been edited for the purposes of this task. This task is designed to test your ability with historical documents. As you analyze the documents, take into account both the source of each document and the author's point of view.

Directions: Read the following documents and answer the questions after each document. Use the information in the reading and this chapter in writing your answers.

Document #1

The Aztec occupation particularly respected was that of merchant. It formed so important a feature of their overall economy and the merchant was honored for the luxuries and other goods he traded in. The Aztec merchant was sort of an itinerant trader, who made his journey to the remotest areas of the Aztec Empire and to the countries beyond. He carried with him merchandise of rich stuffs, jewelry, slaves and cacao beans. Dealing in slaves was an honorable calling among the Aztecs. The merchants often received gifts of tribute for the Aztec sovereign from local chiefs and carried them to the capitol, Tenochtitlan. The merchants' goal was always to pursue trade and should this be denied to him or should he be met with violence the Aztec ruler would soon send his army to punish these people who resisted the offer of exchanges of goods.

From *The History of the Conquest of Mexico* by William H. Prescott

Questions

1. Why were merchants important in the Aztec Empire?
2. How did the Aztec ruler react if he received complaints from merchants about trading problems with subject peoples?

Document #2

Victory in war always had the same results: long lines of captives made the long journey to Tenochitlan to be offered up to the gods. In addition periodic tribute payments of maize, cotton mantles, cacao beans or other products, depending on the geography and resources of the region, were imposed on the vanquished. Certain lands were also set aside to be cultivated by them for the support of the Aztec crown, priesthood and state officials. A resident garrison was stationed in the town. As a rule the conquered people continued to enjoy autonomy in government, culture and customs.

From *A History of Latin America* by Benjamin Keen and Keith Haynes

Document #3   Because the gods had sacrificed themselves so that the world and humanity might exist, humans were obligated to plunge, if needed, into the bonfire of life and death. The need for sacrifice was an undoubted thing in Indian societies, not subject to the discussion or skepticism of any sort. For the ancient Americans, the forces of the universe were a constant source of danger as well as a constant source of the very survival they menaced. This ambiguity and uncertainty was resolved in sacrifice. The continuity of life and order of the universe depended on it.

From *Buried Mirror* by Carlos Fuentes

Questions   1. Why did the Aztecs believe the gods were owed sacrifice?
2. Why was sacrifice so important for the civilizations of the Aztecs and Incas?

Document #4   The ruler of the Incas descended from an unbroken succession from father to son, throughout their whole dynasty. It appears probable that the right of inheritance was claimed by the eldest son of the Coya, who was the lawful queen. The queen was further distinguished by the circumstance of being selected from among the sisters of the Inca. This arrangement secured an heir to the crown of pure heaven born race, uncontaminated by any mixture of earthly blood.

From *The Conquest of Peru* by William Prescott

Questions   1. How was the Inca ruler selected?
2. What role did the Coya play in the succession of the Inca?

Document #5   The Inca government was in reality despotism. The sovereign was placed at an immeasurable distance above his subjects. Even the proudest of the Inca nobility claiming a descent from the same divine original as the Inca could not venture into the royal presence unless barefoot and bearing a light burden on his shoulders as a token of homage. The Inca as a representative of the Sun stood at the head of the priesthood. He was the source from which everything flowed. He was in short himself the state and the embodiment of its dignity.

From *The Conquest of Peru* by William Prescott

Questions   1. What happened when even a noble of the Inca class had an audience with the Inca?
2. Why was the Inca placed so above all other members of the Inca state?

ERA IV

THE FIRST GLOBAL AGE

(1450–1770)

INTRODUCTION

Historians generally define the time period from about 1450 to 1770 as the First Global Age. The Age of Exploration started in the mid 1400s with the Portuguese voyages down the Atlantic coast of Africa. This was the beginning of the search for an all-water route to Asia. Throughout the last decades of the 1400s and in the 1500s, explorers and sailors such as Bartholomeu Dias, Christopher Columbus, Ferdinand Magellan, Vasco da Gama, John Cabot, and others opened up areas of the globe by finding new routes and lands that Europeans did not know even existed. By the 1540s, Hernando Cortez and Francisco Pizarro conquered empires in the newly discovered lands called the Americas. These and other conquests brought great mineral wealth to Europe. The increased wealth from trade in agricultural products such as tobacco and sugar and colonial mineral resources, particularly gold and silver, led to the spread of European influence and power over the globe. During this time great progress was made in technology. New types of sailing vessels and navigational instruments began to be used, which greatly aided the exploration of the globe. These advances allowed European explorers and conquerors to sail the world.

During this unit, you will read about many interesting events and people from this era. The First Global Age was an exciting time of political and economic change when the world began to come closer together. Globalization today owes much to the heritage of these first centuries when the nations and peoples learned about the importance of sharing the world and its resources.

The Rise of Nation-States

Section 1—England 357

Section 2—France 363

Section 3—Spain 370

Section 4—Austria 374

Section 5—Prussia 376

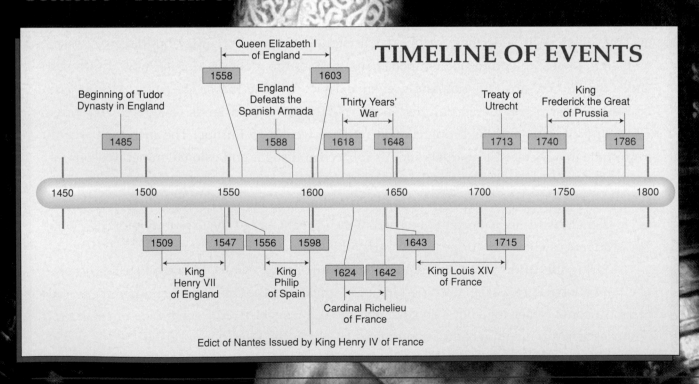

TIMELINE OF EVENTS

Queen Elizabeth I of England
1558 — 1603

Beginning of Tudor Dynasty in England
1485

England Defeats the Spanish Armada
1588

Thirty Years' War
1618 — 1648

Treaty of Utrecht
1713

King Frederick the Great of Prussia
1740 — 1786

1450 1500 1550 1600 1650 1700 1750 1800

1509 1547 1556 1598 1643 1715

King Henry VII of England

King Philip of Spain

Cardinal Richelieu of France
1624 — 1642

King Louis XIV of France

Edict of Nantes Issued by King Henry IV of France

Today, in the early years of the twenty-first century, Europe is a continent of many countries. The word *country* describes a fixed geographical area and its population, controlled by a government. An example would be modern France or Spain. Countries such as these can also be referred to as nation-states. Their development took place over the course of many centuries, usually under strong rulers, as they grew from small areas to much larger ones. For some of them, the greatest period of development occurred between the late 1400s and the early 1700s.

This was a period of much change in Europe. The changes we have already studied have been cultural (the Renaissance), religious (the Reformation), and economic (the Commercial Revolution and Age of Exploration). It is the major political changes during this period that will be of concern to us in this chapter.

As we will see, those changes that led to the political development of nation-states were most evident in England, France, and Spain. The term *nation-state* now needs to be defined. It refers to a specific area of land with fixed boundaries, inhabited by people united under an independent central government. The people of a **nation-state** usually share many common factors, such as language, religion, race, and culture. When all these factors are actually present, we may say that the people have a common **nationality**. This was the situation in England, France, and Spain and was, therefore, a key reason for the shaping of unified nation-states under powerful monarchs. In Austria, Prussia, and Russia, however, the population consisted of different nationalities—people who spoke different languages and were of different cultures. As a result, the nation-states that monarchs built in these areas were not characterized by strong feelings of national unity.

We will now examine events in England, France, Spain, Austria, and Prussia.

SECTION 1

England

One of the earliest significant instances of royal power and nation building in England was seen in the reign of **William the Conqueror** (r. 1066–1087). As Duke of Normandy in France, he laid claim to the English throne. Although opposed by the British King Harold and other Anglo-Saxon nobles, William and his army landed in England and won the decisive Battle of Hastings in 1066. Soon thereafter, he was crowned King William I. The people he ruled over had many customs in common, although they originally belonged to different groups that had invaded the British Isles: Celts, Romans, Germanic Angles, Saxons, Jutes, and Danes. William's actions in 1086, compiling the **Doomsday Book** and making feudal lords and knights take the Salisbury Oath, showed his ability as an effective and commanding ruler. (See Chapter 6.)

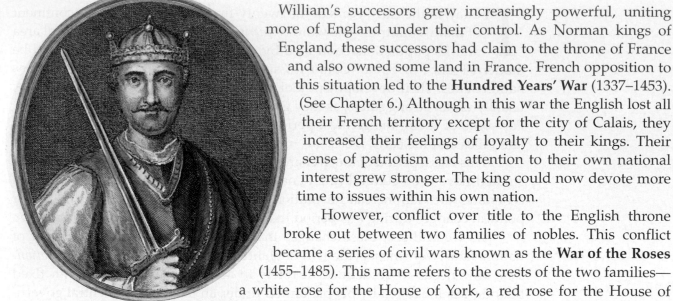

William's successors grew increasingly powerful, uniting more of England under their control. As Norman kings of England, these successors had claim to the throne of France and also owned some land in France. French opposition to this situation led to the **Hundred Years' War** (1337–1453). (See Chapter 6.) Although in this war the English lost all their French territory except for the city of Calais, they increased their feelings of loyalty to their kings. Their sense of patriotism and attention to their own national interest grew stronger. The king could now devote more time to issues within his own nation.

However, conflict over title to the English throne broke out between two families of nobles. This conflict became a series of civil wars known as the **War of the Roses** (1455–1485). This name refers to the crests of the two families— a white rose for the House of York, a red rose for the House of Lancaster. The wars concluded with the victory of Henry Tudor, a member of the House of Lancaster. A major result of the War of the Roses was a strengthening of the position of the monarch at the expense of the nobles because

William the Conqueror showed his ability as an effective and commanding ruler.

- Middle-class merchants, upset with the war's harmful effect upon commerce, were glad to support the new king.

- The deaths of many nobles reduced the numbers of contenders for the crown.

- The king added to his wealth by taking over the properties of nobles who died and who had opposed him.

- Most people were weary of the long and costly wars and were willing to support the strong central government that the new king created.

The new king, crowned as **Henry VII**, ruled from 1485 to 1509. His reign began the **Tudor dynasty**, which was to consist of five monarchs and lasted from 1485 to 1603. Tudor England, as this period is called, was another step forward in the evolution of both royal power and the nation-state as political forces. This period was the era of strong monarchy. Let us consider the reasons for this.

Henry VII was able to restore order and stability, desperately welcomed after many years of international and civil wars involving these compatriots. Some of this stability was the result of his marriage to Elizabeth of the House of York and his appointment of members of the rising, prosperous merchant class to important positions at his court. He won favor with lawmakers in the Parliament as he rarely asked for a raise in taxes. He had little need to ask, since he was able to add to the royal treasury from properties he seized after the Wars of the Roses. Indeed, when he died, he left to his son a full treasury and a well-managed kingdom.

The Rule of King Henry VIII

That son became **Henry VIII** (r. 1509–1547). His defiance of the pope, having Parliament pass the Act of Supremacy and creating the Anglican Church, showed him to be an authoritative and powerful figure. (See Chapter 11.) These actions won him the support of the vast majority of his subjects. His taking over land once owned by the Roman Catholic Church helped him to continue the good royal financial record established by his father. Henry VIII got along well with **Parliament**, being careful to remember the parliamentary limitations on royal power that had been carried over from the Middle Ages—for example, the king could not impose new taxes without Parliament's consent. (See Chapters 6 and 16 for a full discussion of these limitations.) Many members of Parliament admired Henry VIII, so he was usually able to get what he wanted from that body. The English economy was prosperous, and Henry encouraged commercial activity. This situation, along with the fact that he kept his nation out of costly overseas wars, helped to make him a popular ruler.

Henry strove to make England great. Historians generally agree, however, that he did this more for his own self-advancement than for love of his people. Personally, he was egotistical, self-centered, and selfish. Although he had many faithful advisors, he did not hesitate to turn against them and have them executed when they displeased him. He has six wives, two of whom he had beheaded for controversial reasons. Some of those who opposed his royal actions concerning religious matters lost their lives and property. Whatever one may think of his moral character, he did leave the nation more united and the monarchy more powerful at his death than when he ascended to the throne.

Many members of Parliament admired Henry VIII, so he was usually able to get what he wanted from them.

The Rule of Queen Mary I

The next two Tudor rulers had neither Henry's leadership qualities nor his popularity. Upon Henry's death in 1547, his only son, born of his third wife, became king as Edward VI. He was a 10-year-old, sickly child at the time. Under the influence of strong-willed advisors, his government made England a more Protestant nation. At his death, only six years later, in 1553, his older half-sister became the first woman to sit on the throne of England. **Queen Mary I** (r. 1553–1558) was Henry's daughter by his first wife, Catherine of Aragon. Although she had some of her father's forceful manner, she used her energies to pursue a policy that angered many people and brought her disfavor. She inherited her mother's devotion to the Roman Catholic faith and proceeded to pursue a policy designed to restore that religion:

Queen Mary I became the first woman to sit on the throne of England.

- She married Philip II of Catholic Spain.

- She had Parliament *repeal* (take back) anti-Catholic laws passed during her father's reign, such as the Act of Supremacy.

- She persecuted Anglican clergymen, burning almost three hundred of them at the stake. Archbishop Cranmer, who had obeyed King Henry VII and annulled the king's first marriage, suffered this fate.

For these actions, the Queen was called "Bloody Mary." It is a curious twist of history that Mary's religious policy backfired. Her persecutions, for example, designed to spread the Catholic faith and extinguish Anglicanism, dismayed her subjects—both Protestants and non-Protestants. The population was opposed to seeing people burned for their religious opinions. Indeed, Mary's determination to impose her religious beliefs hardened the English public's attitude toward the Roman Catholic Church and probably guaranteed the future of Protestantism in her nation. In the year of her death, 1558, she was a very sad figure. Disliked by her subjects for her religious policies and for engaging England in a brief war that saw the nation lose land in France, she was deserted by her husband after an unhappy marriage. She had no children as heirs and feared that her probable successor, her Protestant half-sister Elizabeth, would expand upon the religious policies of their common father. Her fears were to be realized.

The Rule of Queen Elizabeth I

Elizabeth I was the daughter of Henry VIII and his second wife, Anne Boleyn. Like her father, Elizabeth had a forceful, compelling personality. She proved to be an authoritative figure who enjoyed flattery and liked to stage big pageants and social events—probably to satisfy her love of display as well as to impress her subjects. It was believed that at the time of her death she owned more than one thousand dresses. Nevertheless, despite these characteristics, she was not perceived in those times to be very "womanly." Possessed of a sharp tongue and what was then considered a masculine toughness, she was said by an advisor, Robert Cecil, to be "more than a man, and sometimes less than a woman." During her reign, 1558 to 1603, she used her skills to promote the power of the throne and to increase pride in the nation. Examples can be seen in her handling of key issues both within her realm and with foreign powers.

In religious matters, she did things that would have pleased her father. She had Parliament repeal laws passed during Queen Mary's reign. England became a more Protestant nation under Elizabeth. English, for instance, became the language of worship, and clergymen were allowed to marry. (See also Chapter 11.) When the pope excommunicated her in 1570, she and Parliament retaliated by making more harsh laws against Catholics. As Elizabeth did not

During her reign, Queen Elizabeth I used her skills to promote the power of the throne and to increase pride in the nation.

Mary, Queen of Scots, was imprisoned and beheaded at the orders of her cousin, Queen Elizabeth I.

marry and had no children to leave as heirs, concern grew that her successor would be a devout Catholic—her cousin, Mary, Queen of Scots. Elizabeth imprisoned Mary, and, after learning of Mary's alleged plot to capture her throne, had Mary beheaded in 1587.

The interaction of religion and politics was also seen in Elizabeth's actions toward Ireland. English control over the Irish began as early as 1167. In 1495, the Statute of Drogheda (Poynings's Law) made laws passed by England applicable to Ireland. All Tudor rulers considered themselves to be monarchs of both England and Ireland. Henry VIII tried to introduce into Ireland the religious changes he made in England. Native Irish, who were strongly Catholic, resented English policies. This resentment caused a revolt to break out in 1597, led by Hugh O'Neill. Elizabeth's forces put down the revolt with much bloodshed. This strong-armed action added to the tension between the Irish and English—a tension that continues into the twentieth century.

Elizabeth did not have any deep personal religious feelings. In her private life, she considered herself Protestant while admiring certain Catholic rituals. In her public role as queen, politics determined her religious policies. She did not want religious issues to harm the stability and unity of her nation. Her ideal was a national church, the (Anglican) Church of England, which would be at once Catholic and Protestant and would claim the loyalty of the majority of her subjects. She wanted to keep to a middle ground between what she felt were two extremes—Catholics, whose first loyalty was to the pope, and strict Protestant groups, such as the Calvinists and Puritans, who felt the Reformation in England had not gone far enough. In keeping to this middle ground, she did not hesitate to act against anyone from these extremes who might threaten national harmony.

In the field of foreign affairs, Elizabeth acted with similar attitudes regarding politics, religion, and her nation's well-being. Examples can be seen in her policies toward France and Spain, two predominantly Catholic nations who were England's main opponents at the time. When religious wars occurred in France in 1562, she provided encouragement and some help to the **Huguenots** (French Protestants). When the Dutch, who were mostly Protestant, revolted against Spanish rule in 1581, Elizabeth sent them money and a small army. In siding with the Huguenots and the Dutch, Elizabeth did not act as a champion of Protestantism. She supported these groups not because they were Protestant but because they could weaken those powers who were threats to England.

Defeat of the Spanish Armada

Tension with Spain reached a peak toward the end of the sixteenth century. Rivalry between the two nations existed on the high seas, where English seamen often attacked Spanish merchant ships, and in the New World colonies of the Americas. More significantly, King **Phillip II** of Spain (r. 1556–1598) wanted to make England Catholic again and to enlarge his territorial domains in Europe. He therefore prepared a fleet of 130 ships to attack England. Called the "Invincible Armada" by Spaniards, the fleet sailed for England in May 1588. Elizabeth and the English were ready, and inflicted a crushing defeat on the **Spanish Armada** in August. The English ships were able to move faster and had superior guns. Faced with several ships sunk in the English Channel and others seriously damaged, limited ammunition, and declining morale among their men, the remaining Armada vessels tried to escape toward the North Sea. Here they faced a violent storm (later called "the Protestant Wind") that destroyed additional ships. Those that survived tried to sail back to Spain around Scotland and Ireland, but not without difficulties. Bad weather and continued attacks by the Irish and English caused more losses for the fleet. Only when the remnant of the Armada reached Spain was the full impact of the disaster understood. Sixty-three ships had been captured or destroyed, with the loss of over ten thousand lives. The crushing defeat of the Armada had three crucial consequences for the English:

1. As queen, Elizabeth gained greater prestige and popularity.

2. Protestantism in England was no longer endangered.

3. England was free to continue exploration and settlement overseas, particularly in North America and the West Indies.

The Spanish Armada.

In her last years as monarch, Elizabeth continued to get along fairly well with Parliament. Yet that legislative body became more active by frequently questioning things that the queen wanted and by becoming increasingly more concerned about the increasing power she had acquired. Parliament also wished to have a greater role in setting government policies. Eventually, after Elizabeth's death in 1603, an outright clash did develop between the throne and Parliament. We will examine this crisis in the next chapter.

It is clear that the Tudor rulers, particularly King Henry VIII and Queen Elizabeth I, increased their authority as monarchs. Nevertheless, strong-willed and domineering as they were, they did not govern as absolute monarchs. **Absolutism**, as we will soon see, was more characteristic of monarchs in France, Prussia, and Austria. An absolute monarch is one who makes all decisions by himself or herself and claims to have complete authority to control the lives of his or her subjects. The absolute monarch does not observe any restriction on his or her power nor consult with any representatives of the people. Answerable only to heaven, he or she would claim to have a "divine right" to rule. This type of ruler can also be described as an **autocrat**.

SECTION 2

France

This first major name in the history of absolute monarchy in France is King **Louis XI** (r. 1461–1483). He was able to increase his power and make his government more wealthy, efficient, and centralized. A chief reason for this was the ending of the Hundred Years' War (1337–1453). The war had seen the deaths of almost all English territories in France. This made the French proud of their nation and also enriched the royal treasury.

King Louis XI.

The Rule of King Henry IV

The Protestant Reformation that began in 1517 was to affect France and the position of the monarchs. A series of religious wars broke out in 1562 between Huguenots and Catholics. For the next thirty-six years, France suffered much bloodshed and religious bigotry. The kings during these times were weak and ineffective. The fighting ended in 1598, when Henry of Navarre, a member of the **Bourbon** family, took the throne as **Henry IV**. Although a Huguenot, he quickly realized that he could not restore peace and unity to his nation nor respect for the monarchy if he maintained his Protestant faith in a predominantly Catholic country. He decided to put the national interests of France above his personal religious beliefs and converted to Catholicism. In doing this, he is reputed to have remarked, "Paris is well worth a mass."

His decision to convert was one of several politically wise actions taken by Henry IV. Another was his issuing the **Edict of Nantes** in 1598, a document that was, for that time, a landmark in the history of religious toleration. Its chief provisions were as follows:

1. Huguenots were permitted freedom of worship.

2. They could establish churches in certain places, but not in Paris.

3. They were granted the same civil rights that Catholics had.

4. They could fortify their major cities with their own soldiers.

Curiously, at first the Edict of Nantes was criticized by both Catholics and Huguenots. Catholics felt that the edict gave too much freedom to Huguenots and that its issuance was proof that Henry's conversion was not sincere. For Huguenots, on the other hand, the edict did not go far enough and should have permitted even more religious freedom. Nevertheless, in time, the edict did achieve its purpose. By 1610, the year of Henry's death, a good measure of religious peace and civil order was evident in France.

Two other actions by Henry IV strengthened this government. He was able to reduce the power of the nobles, many of whom had been troublesome for previous kings and had ignored royal directives. Henry placed some of them in his government and gave bribes to some others. Henry's appointment of the Duke of Sully as his chief minister improved France's financial condition. Sully made the tax collection system much better and cut down spending by the royal household. The result was a surplus of money in the crown's treasury. Large sums were then used to build roads, bridges, and public buildings. Both agricultural and industrial production improved. France was a prosperous nation in the early years of the seventeenth century.

Henry's reign in that century was cut short by an assassin in 1610. The killer was a religious fanatic, who thought Henry was an enemy of the Catholic Church, and stabbed him on a Paris street. As we have seen, Henry's kingship made France a more stable and powerful nation. And yet, we must note his place in the growth of absolutism in his country. He had the temper of an autocrat. To a meeting of citizens in the town of Toulouse, he once said, "I must insist on being obeyed." He never gave the **Estates-general** (the national legislative

Main Idea:
The Edict of Nantes was a landmark in the history of religious tolerance.

body) a chance to challenge his will. Indeed, never once did he summon it to meet. Such royal attitudes were to have serious repercussions in France in the seventeenth and eighteenth centuries.

The Rule of King Louis XIII

Henry's son became king as **Louis XIII** (1610–1643). As the new king was only 8 years old, it was decided that his mother, Marie de Medici, would rule as regent. This meant that she would rule in his behalf until he came of age. She proved to be ineffective, getting into trouble with the nobles and using up the reserves of money that Sully had created. It was in this setting, in 1614, that a meeting of the Estates-general took place. Almost 500 members met. They were unable to accomplish anything, as they argued among themselves. The clergy and nobility wanted to retain their special

King Louis XIII.

privileges and refused to give in to demands from the *Third Estate* (i.e., commoners, shopkeepers, and peasants). The Estates-general did not meet again until 1789, 175 years later, on the eve of the French Revolution.

The Impact of Cardinal Richelieu

When Louis XIII did come of age, he did not appear to be a strong ruler in the mold of his father. However, he appointed as chief minister a man who possessed political skills and substantial leadership abilities. This was **Cardinal Richelieu**. For almost the entire remainder of Louis XIII's reign, Richelieu was the real power in France (1624–1643). He had two goals:

1. To make the king's power supreme in France

2. To make France the supreme power in Europe

Let us now look at these goals carefully, with particular regard to the method used in attempting to achieve them.

To achieve the first goal, Richelieu aimed to end the rights of the Huguenots and to reduce the power of the nobles. Under the Edict of Nantes, Huguenots were given the right to fortify their towns with their own armies. To

Richelieu, this stood in the way of his desire to build a strong centralized royal government. The Protestant towns were almost states within a state. Accordingly, Richelieu mounted a military campaign against the towns with the backing of the king. With the royal forces successful, the Huguenots were stripped of their special political rights in the towns but were allowed to keep their religious freedoms. As for the nobles, Richelieu had many of their castles destroyed and removed several nobles from positions as governors of provinces. Provinces were subsequently headed by intendants. These were officials selected by the king, forming a kind of civil service, who owed allegiance only to him and who would therefore favor a strong monarchy.

To achieve his second goal, whereby France would become the dominant power in Europe, Richelieu planned to strike at the power of the Catholic **Habsburg** rulers of Austria and the Holy Roman Empire. A chance to do this came during the **Thirty Years' War** (1618–1648). This was actually a series of on-again-off-again conflicts that occurred mostly on German soil and that began as a struggle between Protestant and Catholic powers. You may recall that previous religious fighting in the German states had been temporarily settled by the 1555 Peace of Augsburg (see Chapter 11). However, religious issues remained and sparked a Protestant rebellion in Bohemia, which lasted from 1618 to 1620. Its suppression by Habsburg ruler Ferdinand II provoked Danish King Christian IV and soon thereafter Swedish King Gustavus Adolphus to join the struggle on the Protestant side. Protestant Denmark and Sweden fought against Ferdinand for both religious and territorial reasons. Along with Richelieu, they feared the growth of Habsburg power in Europe, especially if that power were to extend to all of Germany. Accordingly, Richelieu gave economic aid to the Swedes. Richelieu did not have France actively enter the fighting until 1635. He made this decision as a result of the failure of Christian IV to invade Germany and the death of Gustavus Adolphus. Here we see how Richelieu gave priority to his political goals over his religious ideals. Although a Catholic clergyman, he now had Catholic France fighting for Protestant forces in Europe against the Catholic Holy Roman Emperor! Cardinal Richelieu had now become statesman Richelieu, trying to make the best of a given situation when it would benefit him. Such a person could be call an **opportunist**, as well as a pragmatist or realist.

Although Richelieu did not live to see the end of the Thirty Years' War in 1648, he would have been pleased with its results. The concluding Treaty of Westphalia recognized victory by the French and Swedes and reduced the power of the Habsburgs. Its main provisions were as follows:

Cardinal Richelieu was the real power in France from 1624–1643.

- France obtained Alsace.

- Switzerland and the Netherlands were recognized as independent Protestant nations.

- German rulers could determine the religion of their people, free from Habsburg influence.

The Rule of King Louis XIV

Like Richelieu, King Louis XIII was not alive when the Thirty Years' War ended. Upon his death in 1643, his son became king as **Louis XIV** (r. 1643–1715). As the new king was only 4 years old at the time, rule in France was actually exercised by his mother, Anne, with Cardinal Mazarin as chief minister. Trained by Richelieu to be his successor, Mazarin continued the former's centralizing policies. He was successful in stopping a short series of rebellions called the *Fronde* (1648–1652). Its leaders had hoped to displace Mazarin and weaken the monarchy by securing more power for the nobles. Mazarin's victory added to the absolutism of the crown. The Fronde was to be the last attempt to challenge royal power prior to the revolution of 1789.

At Mazarin's death in 1661, Louis declared that he would rule on his own. His entire reign, covering seventy-two years, was the longest in French history. This reign reached the heights of absolutism, as the result of both the absolutist tendencies that had been growing since the Hundred Years' War and the personality of Louis XIV himself. No monarchy ever had a more glorified view of himself and his position. He was convinced, for example, that he was "the visible image of God on earth." All his ideas and policies were the result of heavenly guidance and were therefore not open to question or dissent. These beliefs made up the theory of **divine right** of kings. Consequently, it is not surprising that Louis recognized no limits to his authority.

Considering himself to be the greatest of all men, Louis took the sun as his emblem. He became known as the Sun King as well as the Grand Monarch. He is supposed to have said, *"L'etat, c'est moi"* (I am the state). Whether or not he made this assertion, it accurately described the conditions of his rule. There was hardly any opposition to his will. Possible threats were held in check. The Estates-general was never summoned. If he wanted to impose new taxes, there was no need to consult with anyone or any group. Fittingly, the right of many cities to choose their own mayor was ended. These posts were sold by the king to those who bid the most and who could prove their loyalty to him.

King Louis XIV was only 4 years old when he became king.

The Palace of Versailles

Clearly, Louis XIV was the state—and the state was Louis XIV. Much of our description about this towering figure would be verified if you could take a trip back in time and visit him at **Versailles**. This was the site, eleven miles from Paris, where he built a magnificent palace. This became the seat of the French government, taking over twenty-five years to build and requiring more than 30,000 workers. The expense severely drained the French treasury. The actual figures are not known, as Louis destroyed all construction bills and accounts. You would enter through the palace grounds, amazed at the lovely gardens. You would find the large halls filled with colorful paintings, named after figures from Greek mythology. You might be dazzled by the 240-foot-long Grand Hall of Mirrors, containing seventeen large windows and as many framed mirrors. Should you wander outside, you would find it easy to get lost among the many fountains, ponds, waterfalls, and marble statues.

You would see many visitors from other countries, astonished at this grand display of wealth and royal power, and hoping to build similar palaces in their own countries. They also hoped to learn to speak French, as well as wear French clothing and adopt French customs. No doubt you would be introduced to many of France's great nobles. Louis wanted them to live at Versailles, especially if they desired favors from him. Also, he could keep an eye on them and their families this way. You shouldn't be surprised to find them happy to have the honor of praying with the king or watching him eat or get dressed. Finally, if you were not tired at night, you could witness one of the many balls, dances, masquerades, or parties that frequently were held.

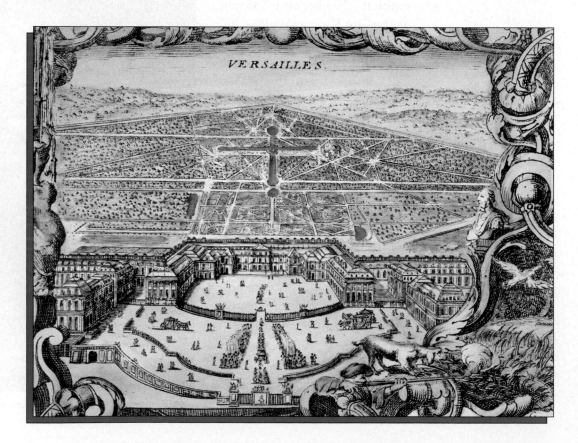

A painting of the city of Versailles.

Even though he spent huge sums on the Versailles palace and other items that he deemed necessary for a grand monarch, Louis XIV was lucky to have a finance minister generally able to keep the royal treasury full. This minister was Jean Colbert (see Chapter 12). Colbert wanted to maintain the financial policies of Sully, by making reforms in the tax system and by ending corruption among tax collectors. His decision to raise taxes fell mainly on the middle and lower classes. This was because the clergy and nobles were exempt from paying taxes. He expected large royal revenues to be obtained from trade with other nations and from colonies overseas. He was a firm believer in mercantilism, promoting government regulation of and aid to industry so as to make France self-sufficient. He pressed for high tariffs in order to protect French industries. French agriculture suffered, however, when other nations retaliated against Colbert's high industrial tariffs by placing heavy taxes on French farm exports.

Main Idea: Louis XIV was lucky to have a finance minister who was able to keep the royal treasury full.

For most of his term of office, Colbert was able to increase the national income. Yet, there were three things that hurt his economic program and that were to seriously affect the French economy. The first of these was the 1685 revocation of the Edict of Nantes. Louis XIV was worried about the Huguenots for political rather than religious reasons. He felt that their existence was a threat to national unity. They began to face mild persecution—their schools were closed, their churches were attacked, and they were offered bribes and requests to convert to Catholicism. When these measures failed to persuade the Huguenots to give up their Protestant beliefs, the king ordered the Edict of Nantes to be revoked. Louis XIV did not realize it, but the harshness of this decision was to damage France's prosperity. With their religious freedom now ended, almost 200,000 Huguenots secretly fled France. They were among the nation's most energetic, productive, and industrious citizens. Although emigration was forbidden to them, they managed to flee to England, Holland, and the Americas.

The second and third major blows to the French economy were also the result of actions taken by the king. His personal expenditures for his palace, clothing, and other luxuries drained the treasury. But the most catastrophic shock to France's finances was the series of wars fought with other European nations between 1667 and 1713. The wars of Louis XIV imposed a huge burden on the treasury and saw the nation's productive energies used for fighting rather than for the welfare of the people. The wars lasted off and on from 1667 to 1713, with the longest being the War of the Spanish Succession (1701–1717).

Why did so many wars take place? The basic answer is that France wanted more land, even if this meant taking it from other rulers. Louis XIV felt that to be safe and secure, France needed to extend to "natural frontiers." This meant taking all the land eastward up to the Rhine River. France already felt protected on the north, west, and south by the **English Channel**, the Atlantic Ocean, and the Pyrenees, and the Mediterranean Sea. The expansionist desires of

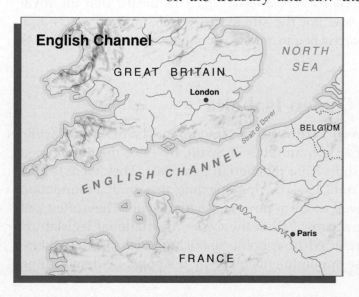

English Channel

France worried other countries. Therefore, at one time or another, the French found themselves fighting against England, Spain, Denmark, Sweden, Austria, and several German states. This resistance to French aggression by various combinations is an early example of what we now call balance of power diplomacy.

The most violent conflict was the War of the Spanish Successions. With his grandson inheriting the throne of Spain and all its colonies, Louis hoped to unite France and Spain. This wish was thwarted by an alliance of European nations that wanted to maintain a balance of power and prevent France from gaining a dominant position. Fighting took place in Europe, on the seas, and even in the Americas. The Treaty of Utrecht, 1713, ended the war. The grandson of Louis XIV was recognized as King Philip V of Spain, but Louis agreed that France and Spain would never unite. England received some French territory in North America. France was permitted to retain some of the land acquired prior to the war.

Two years after the Treaty of Utrecht, Louis XIV died. At his death, France was viewed as a political power. Its cultural prestige was the greatest of any European nation. Inside France, however, there was misery, unstable financial conditions, and a population weary of warfare. These conditions were not improved during the reign of Louis XV (r. 1715–1774) and were to be some of the factors that caused the historic revolutionary explosion in 1789 under Louis XVI. The absolutism of Louis XIV extended beyond his life, but eventually it would tragically affect the life of his nation.

SECTION 3

Spain

As you may remember, Spain was where a terrorist attack by Islamist radicals at a train station occurred in 2004. It was ruled under a monarchy then, and still is today. However, you would not call this style of rule an absolute monarchy. Better today to call Spain a *constitutional monarchy*. This means that the royal power is limited. But this was not the situation several hundred years ago, when the institution of monarchy began and accompanied Spain's emergence as a unified nation.

The Rule of King Ferdinand and Queen Isabella

The marriage in 1469 between **Ferdinand** of Aragon and **Isabella** of Castille brought together the Christian communities of Spain. By 1492, their combined armies had driving the Muslims from the Iberian peninsula. They were to rule as king and queen together until 1504. During this time, they built a foundation for absolute monarchy as well as for a powerful nation-state. They often put forth laws without seeking approval from the *Cortes*, the national legislature. Although Catholic, they preferred to appoint Spanish Church officials themselves rather than have these appointments made by the pope. By demolishing

King Ferdinand and Queen Isabella.

several castles belonging to nobles, they weakened the power of that class.

They felt that religious unity would help achieve political unity. Accordingly, they pursued a policy to make Spain a Catholic country by persecuting minorities such as Jews and Muslims. This persecution took forms that, from a modern democratic point of view, were clear violations of human rights. With authorization from the pope, the Spanish **Inquisition** was created as a court for detecting and punishing heresy and thus prohibiting religious freedom. It was aimed mostly at Jews, and primarily at those who did not accept offers to convert to Christianity. Accused people brought before the Inquisition and its dreaded head, Tomás de Torquemada, had no procedural safeguards such as the right to have a lawyer. They underwent terrible tortures and were frequently burned at the stake in a ceremony known as the **auto-da-fé** (act of faith).

Another form of persecution was the signing by both monarchs of the Edict of Expulsion on March 31, 1492. Jews were ordered to convert or to leave the kingdom by the following August. Among the thousands who departed were skilled workers, government officials, and merchants. Spain thus lost a valuable group of citizens. (It is of historical value to note that exactly 500 years later, on March 31, 1992, King Juan Carlos of Spain officially revoked the Edict of Expulsion at a Jewish temple in Madrid.)

In foreign affairs, 1492 turned out to have additional significance for Spain. In that year, Christopher Columbus sailed on behalf of the monarchy and landed in the Americas. This voyage, to what from the European perspective was the New World, soon led to extensive exploration and colonization by other Spaniards. Spain thus gained a large empire and obtained much wealth. Spain also secured an important alliance with the powerful Habsburg family when Joanna, a daughter of Ferdinand and Isabella, married Philip of Habsburg. Their son became King Charles I of Spain in 1516.

Christopher Columbus sailed on behalf of Ferdinand and Isabella and landed in the Americas.

The Rule of King Charles V

In 1519, Charles was also elected as Holy Roman Emperor. As he was the fifth Charles to hold that title, he became **Charles V**. He thus became one of the most powerful rulers in European history, having the following lands under his authority: Spain and all its colonies in the New World, the Netherlands, the German states, Austria, and part of Italy. During his reign as both king and Holy Roman Emperor, he was successful in defending Christian Europe from invasion by the Ottoman Turks. The key event in this defense was his victory at the Battle of Vienna in 1529. He was less successful in stopping the spread of Protestantism in the German states, agreeing to the Treaty of Augsberg in 1555. These military involvements, along with a shore war against France, forced him to spend tremendous amounts of money. As an absolute ruler, he spent freely, never consulting with any group representing his subjects.

In 1556, Charles gave up his throne and retired to a monastery. He determined that his domains were much too vast for control by any one person. Fatigued and suffering from attacks of gout due to his excessive eating habits, Charles divided his empire between his brother and his son. His brother became Holy Roman Emperor as Ferdinand I, and began the Austrian Habsburg dynasty. His son received Spain and all its possessions in Europe and overseas, as Philip II. He began the Spanish Habsburg dynasty.

The Rule of King Philip II

During his reign, 1556–1598, Philip II acted as an absolute monarch in his attempts to increase Spain's role as a world power and to protect Catholicism. By the middle of the sixteenth century, Spain was looked on with great awe. It was said, "When Spain moves, the whole world trembles." Yet by the end of the century, with Philip's passing, a general decline in his nation's fortunes was evident. His style of leadership was such that he trusted no one. Distrustful of even his advisors, he tried to do too many things by himself. His desire for absolute control of all decision making was seen in his endless reading of long reports and his writing replies to various petitions addressed to his government. Decision making thus became a very slow process. He was unable to distinguish important matters from trivial ones that could be given over to his ministers. These characteristics were not appropriate for the efficient administration of a huge empire. Once, for a period of eight months, he left important messages from his ambassadors unanswered.

He was known to spend lavishly and unwisely, thereby weakening the royal treasury. This could be seen in the huge palace, the Escorial, that he built near Madrid, as well as in the many wars in which he was engaged. Royal expenditures exceeded the income that came in from taxes and his overseas colonies. As a result of creating enormous debts, Philip found himself bankrupt on more than one occasion. Frequently, he had to borrow money from German and Italian bankers. To pay back these loans with their high interest rates, Philip would use the gold and silver taken from Mexico, Peru, and other Spanish colonies in the Americas. This led to an increase in the amount of money in circulation and, ultimately, to a rise in the prices of goods and services. This situation is called *inflation*. It contributed to a severe decline in the Spanish economy, with suffering for businesses and the middle-class merchants.

A large portion of the merchants and skilled craftsmen were people who faced persecution on the basis of religion. These were **Marranos** (converted Jews who secretly maintained Jewish beliefs and practices) and **Moriscos** (converted Muslims or Moors). If suspected of being insincere in their new beliefs, they risked being subjected to the Inquisition and the auto-da-fé. These institutions had begun in the reign of Philip's great-grandparents, Ferdinand and Isabella, and he did not hesitate to use them against those he deemed heretics. He further issued an expulsion edict against Moriscos in 1570, similar to the one issued in 1492 against the Jews. As a declared upholder of the Catholic faith, Philip said that he "would rather reign in a desert than in a country peopled with heretics." Royal policies stemming from such a pronouncement caused the flight of many Marranos and Moriscos from Spain, adding further to the country's economic problems.

In the field of foreign affairs, the sad record of Philip was part of Spain's decline as a great power. His goal of protecting Catholicism brought him into conflict with the Muslim Ottoman Turks. Although he was proud of his naval victory against them in 1571 at the Battle of **Lepanto**, fought near the coast of Greece, he was unable to keep the Turks completely out of the Mediterranean region. He had brief encounters against France on issues concerning religion and land. These struggles, along with other ones, were to place severe drains on his treasury. Serious losses, political and human as well as financial, came about in his relations with England. The frequent raids on Spanish merchant ships and New World colonies by the English were very damaging. And the defeat of the Spanish Armada was a disaster of enormous proportions, as indicated earlier in this chapter.

The most troublesome foreign problem for Philip was the revolt in the seventeen provinces that made up the Netherlands. He inherited this region from

King Philip II had the Escorial Palace built near Madrid.

Spain **373**

Under the leadership of William the Silent, the seven northern provinces joined in the rebellion.

his father and was aware of its prominence as a rich commercial center. The taxes he imposed on its people were deeply resented, especially as the people were not consulted and as the monies were used for Philip's expenses, not for the people's benefit. Another cause of resentment was Philip's effort to stop the spread of Protestantism.

In 1566, almost fifty years after Martin Luther's actions had sparked the Reformation, the growth of the Calvinist form of Protestantism so alarmed Philip that he ordered action against the new faith and its followers. The consequence flowing from Philip's policies was an open rebellion. For the remainder of his lifetime, terrible fighting went on, leading to thousands of deaths, destruction of churches, and loss of property. In 1581, under the leadership of William the Silent, the seven northern provinces joined in the rebellion. Even after Philip's death in 1598, armed struggle continued. Finally, in 1609, a truce was signed. The seven northern provinces, granted limited self-rule by Spain, became known as the Spanish Netherlands and in 1830 became the independent nation of Belgium.

Absolutism in Spain did not end with Philip's passing. But Spain's glorious days as a world power were over. Spanish culture, however, did reach a high level during Philip's reign. During his time and into the seventeenth century, many great works were created by Spanish artists and writers: El Greco (painter of saints), Diego Velázquez (a famous royal court painter), Miguel Cervantes (the author of *Don Quixote*), Lope de Vega (a dramatist), and Francisco Suarez (a philosopher).

SECTION 4

Austria

The Habsburg family began its control of Austria in the late 1200s. From the sixteenth to eighteenth centuries, its members ruled their lands as heads of the Holy Roman Empire. Absolutism was a key feature of their reign. However, they suffered some loss of power and prestige with their inability to halt the growth of Protestantism in northern Germany and their defeat in the Thirty Years' War. To their credit, they were instrumental as part of a Christian alliance in stopping a Turkish advance into Europe at the 1683 Battle of Vienna. In the eighteenth century, their Empire contained several different subject nationalities: Austrian, Belgians, Croats, Czechs, Germans, Hungarians, Italians, Poles, Romanians, Serbs, and Slovenes. With so many diverse groups—all with different languages and customs—and local nobles who wanted more power, it was not easy for the Habsburg monarchs to build a strong sense of unity. They were worried about revolts by some of the nationalities, as well as threats from other European powers seeking to take parts of their Empire.

The Rule of Maria Theresa

Such worries were on the mind of Austrian ruler and Holy Roman Emperor Charles VI (r. 1711–1740). Accordingly, in order to safeguard the inheritance of his empire to his daughter **Maria Theresa**, he persuaded many European rulers to sign the Pragmatic Sanction. The signing powers to this agreement promised to let Maria Theresa inherit her lands intact. The year 1740 marked the start of her forty-year reign, 1740 to 1780, as well as an invasion of Silesia by Frederick the Great of Prussia. This was one of Maria Theresa's richest provinces, noted for its iron ore and farmland, and had long been desired by Frederick. Although his father had signed the Pragmatic Sanction, Frederick claimed that he was not bound to honor it. The taking of Silesia by Prussia was contested by Austria and led to a long war known as the War of the Austrian Succession (1740–1748). For a number of reasons, mainly hopes of seizing Austrian land for themselves, several powers allied themselves with Prussia: France, Spain, Sweden, and the German states of Bavaria and Saxony. Weary of France, England supported Austria. The war ended with the Treaty of Aix-la-Chapelle in 1748. It allowed Frederick to keep Silesia and recognized Maria Theresa as ruler of the other Habsburg lands.

Angered by her loss of Silesia, Maria Theresa sought to regain it and to form an alliance against Prussia. She decided it was in her best interest to ally herself with Bourbon France. England, maintaining its desire for a balance of power in Europe and jealous of France, allied itself with Prussia. This odd changing of alliances between former friends and foes came to be called the Diplomatic Revolution. Shortly thereafter, another war broke out, the Seven Year's War (1756–1763). The causes included disputes over Silesia, other land in Europe, and overseas colonies. This war was the greatest conflict the modern world had seen up to that time. Fighting took place in Europe, India, and the Americas. (In North America, the struggle was known as the French and Indian War.) The Treaty of Hubertusburg, ending the war in 1763, restored matters in Europe much the way they had been prior to the fighting. Prussia, for example, kept Silesia. The Treaty of Paris, signed in the same year, saw England emerge as the dominant power in North America and India.

Angered by her loss of Silesia, Maria Theresa sought to regain it and to form an alliance against Prussia.

The Rule of an Enlightened Despot—Joseph II

Maria Theresa's land passed on to her son, who became King Joseph II of Austria and Holy Roman Emperor. As yet another example of an absolute monarch, he single-handedly increased royal authority. He ended local self-government, took control of the Catholic Church and its lands, and taxed nobles heavily and altered their relations with their serfs. Yet Joseph II did try to provide *reforms* (changes) that he thought would improved the lives of his people. Claiming to rule in the people's best interests as he alone saw them, and declaring that only he knew how best to protect these interests, Joseph was one of several monarchs at the time who became known as **enlightened despots**. He saw himself as paternalistic and fatherly, but not democratic. Although an autocrat, he improved the lot of serfs and made advances in religious toleration, education, and the judicial system. After his death, most of these reforms were not continued.

SECTION 5

Prussia

One of the best-known enlightened or benevolent despots was Frederick II of Prussia. Better known as **Frederick the Great** (r. 1740–1786), he was a member of the **Hohenzollern** family. This family of nobles initially ruled the northern German state of Brandenburg. Through marriages, alliances, and wars, their holdings came to include Prussia and other German territories. They ruled as absolute monarchs, establishing a powerful centralized government. Although Frederick was the best known of the Hohenzollern monarchs, his predecessors had begun a number of measures that transformed Prussia from a minor kingdom into a strong European power:

Frederick II was one of the best-known enlightened or benevolent despots.

1. A civil service was created to make the carrying out of policies more efficient.

2. The army grew to become one of the best trained and most feared in Europe. Officers were selected from the upper-class Junkers. The values of obedience, loyalty, and discipline were emphasized in the military as well as elsewhere in society.

3. Primary education was required for most children.

4. The economy prospered, with careful financial planning and development of agriculture and new industries.

As he grew up, Frederick did not appear to have those talents and interests that would enable him to continue the autocratic patterns of his father and grandfather. He played the flute, loved poetry, and enjoyed philosophy. His father, unimpressed by these interests, disciplined his son severely. Curiously, when Frederick came to the throne in 1740, he maintained his involvement with these activities while governing in a manner that was stricter and more authoritarian than that of his father. Hints of this manner, as well as his practice of enlightened despotism, can be seen in his own words. He once said, "The people are not here for the sake of the ruler, but the rulers for the sake of the people." In a letter to the French philosopher Voltaire, he wrote the following: "My chief occupation is to fight the ignorance and the prejudice in this country. . . . I must enlighten my people, cultivate their manners and morals, and make them as happy as human beings can be; as happy as the means at my disposal permit me to make them."

Some of Frederick's achievements within Prussia did show him to be true to his words. He made improvements in the civil service system and expanded public education. He placed high taxes on imports in order to encourage and protect Prussian industries, while improving agriculture by giving seeds and money to needy farmers. He encouraged settlers to emigrate from other countries and promoted a high degree of religious toleration relative to his time. His reforms in the court system saw the creation of uniform legal fees, speedy disposition of lawsuits, and reduction in the use of torture. Known as a supporter of literature and the arts, Frederick's rule inspired writers; he was often glorified as a national hero in songs and stories.

In foreign affairs, he sought to increase the power and prestige of his kingdom at the expense of his neighbors. As we have seen, pursuit of his goals involved him in two major European wars—the War of the Austria Succession and the Seven Years' War. The acquisition of Silesia in these wars, as well as his taking of Polish territory in 1772 in the first Partition of Poland, made Prussia a much enlarged nation by the time of his death in 1786. By this time, it was clear that Prussia had become an equal of Austria, France, and Spain as a power on the European continent.

LINK TO TODAY

The nation-state is the most prevalent category of political unification that exists today. With established boundaries, a postal system, armed forces, a flag, and other features of a national entity, this category began to be created in the time period you have just read about. While "enlightened despots" once reigned during the time period in areas to which you "traveled," that is not the case today. One reason for this rests with what you will learn in the next chapter on the growth of democracy in England.

CHAPTER SUMMARY

You have now finished reading one of the longest chapters in this book. Its length was necessary, as we learned a great deal about the growth of nation-states and the rise of royal absolutism. Knowledge of these changes will help us to understand the history of Europe right up to our own times. Some of the general reasons for these changes can now be summarized:

1. The powers of nobles had been reduced.

2. An increased feeling of national unity made people view the king or queen as an important symbol of the nation.

3. In some areas, because of Reformation, the monarch took over powers traditionally held by the Catholic Church.

4. Rising merchants often supported the king or queen to protect their own business *interests*.

5. The establishment of a professional, well-trained army, with a national rather than a purely local loyalty, became a powerful tool in the hands of a monarch. This was a process that had slowly been going on since the Middle Ages.

It is interesting to note that during this period of time women played a more important role. Isabella of Spain sent out Columbus, and unfortunately began the Inquisition. Maria Theresa was deeply involved in central European political intrigues, which resulted in major conflicts. Mary I of England became known in history as Bloody Mary because of her persecution of the Protestants. Elizabeth I of England took over a throne in difficulty, and when she died she left her successor a major player in the game of power politics. More than ever, power became centered in the hands of what came to be called absolute monarchs. This was exemplified by Louis XIV of France and his "I am the state" statement. Wars were on a world scale because overseas colonies of the major European powers were brought into the fighting.

Europe entered into a period of change and transition in the 1600s and 1700s. Some of the great changes that took place were evolutionary, which means they took place over a long period of time. Other changes and transitions were more rapid and often the result of war and conquest. One significant change was the rise of the nation-state in western Europe. The rise of powerful nation-states in western Europe had a significant effect on the political and economic developments that took place throughout the world.

By the end of the First Global Age, the leading nation-states that developed in western Europe became colonial powers. Spain and Portugal, both nation-states by the end of the fifteenth century, dominated the early part of the First Global Age into the late 1500s. These nations were the first colonial powers of this era. Starting in the 1600s, France, Holland, and England all became powerful nation-states and global colonial powers. In England, the idea of democracy also developed and took root. The development of democratic traditions in England and the spread of these ideas to that nation's colonies on the

Atlantic coast of North America eventually led to a political revolution in these colonies as the First Global Age came to a close.

In other parts of the world, important changes also took place. In 1453, the Ottoman Turks captured Constantinople, thereby bringing about the fall of the Byzantine Empire. The Ottoman victory gave them control over the area referred to as the Middle East. During the First Global Age, about 1450 to the mid-1700s, the Ottoman Empire was at the peak of its power. The "Turk" took over large areas of eastern Europe, particularly the Balkan region and the coastal regions of northern Africa. Ottoman rule in the Middle East and eastern Europe lasted for centuries. A major reason for the European explorations was the Ottoman dominance of the trade routes that passed through the Middle East.

In Africa, wealthy kingdoms existed in the northwest area below the Sahara Desert. The kingdoms of Ghana, Mali, and Songhai all flourished in this region of Africa before the coming of the Europeans. The arrival of the Portuguese and the beginning of the slave trade led to catastrophic changes in Africa as the centuries passed. Slavery destroyed the heart of Africa and robbed it of much of its wealth and potential from the early 1500s throughout the next centuries. During this era in Africa, a major cause of its decline was the slave trade

In Asia, the Mughal Islamic Empire of India dominated the regions of the northern Indian subcontinent at the start of this era. By the 1600s, the British and French established colonies and fought to gain control on the Indian subcontinent. The Mughal Empire was eventually taken over by the British after the Seven Years' War. In China, the Ming dynasty, which was established in the mid-fourteenth century, ruled until 1644. It was then replaced by the Manchu, or Qing, dynasty. Unlike India, China was able to retain control of its lands during this era. In Asia, the influence of Westerners who came to the East was important during these centuries, particularly in Southeast Asia.

IMPORTANT PEOPLE, PLACES, AND TERMS

KEY TERMS

nationality	Parliament	opportunist
Anglo-Saxon	absolutism	Thirty Years' War
Doomsday Book	autocrat	L'etat, c'est moi
nation-state	Bourbon	auto-da-fé
Hundred Years' War	Hohenzollern	Marranos
War of the Roses	Edict of Nantes	Moriscos
Tudor dynasty	Estates-general	Inquisition
Huguenots	Habsburg	divine right
Spanish Armada	Holy Roman Empire	enlightened despots

PEOPLE

William the Conqueror	Phillip II	Ferdinand
Henry VII (England)	Louis XI	Isabella
Henry VIII (England)	Henry IV	Maria Theresa
Mary I	Cardinal Richelieu	Frederick the Great
Elizabeth I	Louis XIV	Charles V

EXERCISES FOR CHAPTER 15

MULTIPLE CHOICE

Select the letter of the correct answer.

1. Bourbons, Hohenzollern, and Tudor were names of famous

   a. castles.   c. capitals.
   b. dynasties.   d. battles.

2. Sully, Mazarin, and Colbert were consulted by their kings for advice on

   a. taxes.   c. ships.
   b. weapons.   d. palaces.

3. "L'état, c'est moi," an example of absolutism, was reported to have been said by

   a. Frederick the Great.
   b. Henry VIII.
   c. Cardinal Richelieu.
   d. Louis XIV.

4. Which was the most important consequence of both the War of the Roses and the Hundred Years' War?

   a. Royal rule weakened.
   b. A new trade route to the Americas was discovered.
   c. Royal rule became more powerful.
   d. Queens replaced kings as rulers.

5. Autocratic monarchs claimed their power to rule was based upon

   a. the consent of the middle class.
   b. the support of the Church.
   c. the theory of mercantilism.
   d. the theory of divine right.

6. Which family and nation are correctly paired?

   a. Tudors—England
   b. Bourbons—Prussia
   c. Hohenzellerns—Austria
   d. Habsburg—France

7. Which was a belief common to seventeenth- and eighteenth-century absolutism?

   a. Separation of Church and state was encouraged.
   b. Dissenters are dangerous and should be punished.
   c. A two-party political system is essential for a stable society.
   d. The government should establish a strong public school system.

8. A goal of Cardinal Richelieu's foreign policy was to make France stronger by

   a. reducing the power of the Habsburgs.
   b. helping Protestants against Catholics.
   c. making a Frenchman the king of Spain.
   d. having King Louis XIII become Holy Roman Emperor.

9. In 1772, Russia, Prussia, and Austria signed the first partition of

   a. Italy.
   b. Germany.
   c. Palestine.
   d. Poland.

10. Revocation of the Edict of Nantes hurt France because

    a. Huguenots held violent protests.
    b. Catholics lost their religious freedom.
    c. thousands of productive citizens left France.
    d. other nations formed an alliance against France.

11. Which of the following social sciences would be most concerned with a study of absolutism?

    a. Anthropology
    b. Sociology
    c. Political science
    d. Geography

12. Which heading best completes the partial outline below?

    I._____

       1. John Wycliffe
       2. Martin Luther
       3. Henry VIII

    a. Leaders of the Crusades
    b. Opponents of Roman Catholic Church Policies
    c. Translators of the Bible
    d. Allies in the Hundred Years' War

13. "In 1469, Isabella of Castile married Ferdinand of Aragon. This marriage between the rulers of two powerful kingdoms opened the way for a unified state. Using their combined forces, the two monarchs made a final push against the Muslim stronghold of Granada. In 1492, Granada fell."

    What is being described in this passage?

    a. A crusade to the Holy Land
    b. The reasons for the voyages of Columbus
    c. The start of the Italian Renaissance
    d. The unification of Spain

14. King Louis XIV of France and Emperor Shi Huangdi of China can be considered absolute rulers because they

    a. broke from the Roman Catholic Church.
    b. helped feudal lords build secure castles.
    c. began programs that gave more power to peasants.
    d. created policies without the consent of their people.

15. As a result of the Spanish Inquisition, which group was denied rights of citizenship?

    a. Hindus   c. Jews
    b. Christians   d. Buddhists

16. The seventeenth-century kings claimed that their maintaining absolute power was justified because

    a. they had a divine right to rule.
    b. of the threat of Mongol attacks.
    c. the peasants were gaining too much power.
    d. of the pope's consent.

17. Most empires are characterized by many different cultures, peoples, and languages. Most nation-states have

    a. people with different cultures but all speaking one language.
    b. people who have a common culture and common language.
    c. people who have very different languages, religions, and customs.
    d. groups of people, with each group seeking its own national identity.

18. Henry Tudor of the House of Lancaster tried to hold off another War of the Roses and ensure that his son would be the second Tudor King of England by

    a. murdering all members of the House of York.
    b. killing off all members of the Lancaster family.
    c. marrying a Lancaster woman.
    d. marrying a woman from the York family.

19. Elizabeth I can be considered a leader who

    a. fought wars to protect her nation.

    b. was a weak monarch who was resented by her people.

    c. promoted religious conflict.

    d. encouraged trade, exploration, and the arts and sciences.

20. The Battle of Lepanto and the defeat of the Spanish Armada were both fought

    a. on land.

    b. on water.

    c. in Spain.

    d. in France.

ESSAYS FOR CHAPTER 15

1. Describe two factors that led to the rise of nation-states in Europe.

2. Absolutism was characteristic of many European monarchs.
   a. Define absolutism.
   b. Describe one example of absolutism as practiced by each of the following monarchs: (1) Henry VIII, (2) Louis XIV, and (3) Philip II.

3. Did absolutism help or hinder the growth of nation-states? Explain by presenting two reasons for your opinion.

4. A nation's foreign policy often depends on what it sees as its own self-interest. Support this statement by describing one action taken by each of the following:
   a. Elizabeth I
   b. Cardinal Richelieu
   d. Philip II

5. Define enlightened despotism.
   a. Name one enlightened despot and his/her country.
   b. Would you like this person as your ruler? Explain.

DOCUMENT-BASED QUESTIONS

This task is based on the accompanying documents. Some of these documents have been edited for the purposes of this task. This task is designed to test your ability to work with historical documents. As you analyze the documents, take into account both the source of each document and the author's point of view.

Directions: Read the following documents and answer the questions after each document. Use the information in the reading and this chapter in writing your answers.

Document #1

These thoughts were expressed by King Louis XIV of France:

> The head alone has the right to deliberate and decide, and the functions of all the other members consist only in carrying out the commands to them. . . . The more you grant . . . [to the assembled people], the more acclaims . . . the interest of the state must come first.

Questions

1. What type of government does the king describe?
2. Why does he recommend this type of government?

Document #2 I repeat, then, the sovereign represents the state; he and his people form one single body which can only be happy insofar as it is harmoniously united. The prince stands in relation to the society over which he rules as the head stands to the body.

Frederick the Great

Questions
1. What is Frederick's view of the relationship between the people and the ruler?
2. Is Frederick practicing absolutism? Explain.

Document #3 The first characteristic of the sovereign prince is then power to make general and special laws but . . . without the consent of the superiors, equals, or inferiors. If the prince requires the consent of superiors, then he is a subject himself; if that of equals, he shares his authority with others; if that of his subjects, senate or people, he is not sovereign.

From *Six Books of States* by J. Bodin

Questions
1. What is Bodin's view of power?
2. Does the writer believe in democracy? Explain.

Document #4 When God called us to the head of state, we cherished the purpose not only of putting an end to the disorders caused by the civil wars which had so long distracted the country, but we also aimed to adorn the state with all the ornaments appropriate to the oldest and most illustrious of existing monarchies.

Announcement by King Louis XIII of France

Questions
1. Does Louis XIII claim to rule by divine right? Explain.
2. What does he hope to accomplish as king?

Document #5 My loving people . . . Let tyrants fear; I have always so behaved myself, that under God I have saved my [chief] strength and safeguard in the loyal hearts and good will of my subjects, and therefore I am come amongst you, as you see, at this time, not for my own recreation . . . but being resolved in the midst and heat of battle, to live or die amongst you all, to lay down for my God and for my kingdom, and for my people, my honor and my blood, even in the dust.

Elizabeth I, The Armada Speech (1588)

Questions
1. Does Elizabeth believe in "divine right" rule? Explain.
2. Why did she make this speech?

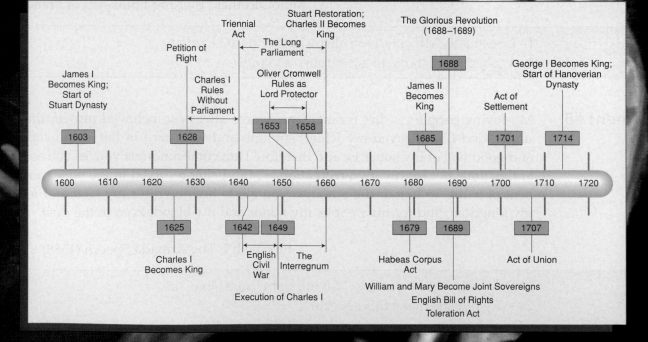

James I
Becomes King;
Start of
Stuart Dynasty

1603

Petition of
Right

1628

Charles I
Rules
Without
Parliament

Triennial
Act

The Long
Parliament

Oliver Cromwell
Rules as
Lord Protector

1653   1658

Stuart Restoration;
Charles II Becomes
King

The Glorious Revolution
(1688–1689)

1688

James II
Becomes
King

1685

George I Becomes King;
Start of Hanoverian
Dynasty

Act of
Settlement

1701

1714

1600   1610   1620   1630   1640   1650   1660   1670   1680   1690   1700   1710   1720

1625

Charles I
Becomes King

1642   1649

English
Civil
War

The
Interregnum

Execution of Charles I

1679

Habeas Corpus
Act

1689

William and Mary Become Joint Sovereigns

English Bill of Rights

Toleration Act

1707

Act of Union

384

In the United States, the right to vote and the right to enjoy freedom of religion and other basic freedoms are things we seem to take for granted. Such rights are part of the system of government we know as **democracy**. The evolution and growth of this kind of system took place over the course of many centuries, mainly in England. As the twentieth century began, there were very few democracies in the world. Most of the world's people lived under other forms of government. As the twentieth century came to a close, the number of democracies had increased. However, the total number of people living under democratic governments is still less than half of the world's population.

If we go back to the seventeenth century, the comparison between democratic governments and other kinds of governments was even more tilted. Indeed, there were no nations at the start of that century that could be called democracies! Most countries or nation-states were ruled by kings or queens. And as we have seen, several of them practiced absolutism in one form or another. By the end of the seventeenth century, however, there was one nation where the change from government by monarchs to government by the people had taken a bold step forward. This was England. Such a political change was so revolutionary for the 1600s that we can label this development in England the English Revolution. It was followed by similar revolutions in North America and in France in the 1700s.

Because the progress toward democracy in seventeenth-century England was so significant, we will devote this entire chapter to examining it. A good way to begin is to define the word *democracy*. It may be thought of as a system of government that has two basic features:

1. *Popular sovereignty:* The people have the freedom to choose those who govern. Generally, they elect representatives to carry out their wishes.

2. *Equality and respect for the individual:* Each person has specific freedoms and rights that are protected by the government.

PRE-SEVENTEENTH-CENTURY HISTORICAL BACKGROUND

Like a garden, democracy takes a long time to grow and must be cultivated. It requires care, nourishment, and much attention by both those who govern and those who are governed. Its earliest seeds were planted in Ancient Greece and Rome. Regrettably, its growth was hurt by the rise of tyrannical and autocratic governments later in the Roman Empire and by the feudalism of the Middle Ages. It was unable to blossom under conditions connected with the expansion of royal power and absolutism, as we have just studied. Why, then, did it ever so slowly ripen in England during the seventeenth century, prior to its gaining life elsewhere? Part of the answer lies with the roots planted in English soil prior to that period. Let us review this background.

Jury Systems

The idea of a trial by jury began under King **Henry II** (r. 1154–1189). The early juries were not strict trial juries in the modern sense, but were rather a group of twelve sworn witnesses who were summoned into a royal court. The royal courts were established originally as a means of strengthening the king's authority.

Limit on Royal Power

The **Magna Carta** (Great Charter) was signed by King John I in 1215 (see Chapter 6). It placed limits on the king's power to imprison people and to levy taxes. It stated, "No freeman shall be imprisoned . . . unless by the lawful judgment of his peers and by the laws of the land." The king needed the consent of the *Great Council*, an advisory body composed of England's leading nobles and bishops, in order to raise taxes. This body was to evolve eventually into **Parliament**. The Magna Carta established the principle that the king was not above the law; like his subjects, he had to obey the law.

King John signing the Magna Carta.

Legislative Power

The Great Council gained more power under the rule of King Edward I. In 1295, he decided to include members of the middle class, the *burgesses* (representatives of the towns), and knights of the *shire* (small landowners). When this enlarged Great Council met, it became known as the Model Parliament. For many years afterwards, all parliamentary meetings included representatives of all these groups. Parliament was eventually divided into two parts, the House of Lords (nobles and clergymen) and the House of Commons (burgesses and knights). Even though members of the Lords did not have to face elections and members of the Commons were elected by only a small portion of the population, the very existence of Parliament was nevertheless an important step toward representative government and therefore popular sovereignty in England.

Judicial Power

During the later Middle Ages (1000–1500), the decisions of judges were written down, collected, and became the basis for future legal decisions. These common practices and legal decisions, which were based on judges' conclusions rather than on a code of laws passed by a legislature, formed a body of law known as *common law*. The English common law, or judge-made law, involving both civil and criminal cases, was held to apply equally to all people.

THE BEGINNING OF STUART ABSOLUTISM: CONFLICT BETWEEN THE CROWN AND PARLIAMENT

The democratic advances described in the previous section did not make England a true democracy. However, they did enable Parliament to have some say in the affairs of the nation. It was generally accepted that passage of laws required the consent of Parliament and agreements by the monarch. And as long as monarchs respected this situation, even though they may not have always liked it, bitter clashes between the crown and parliament were avoided. Even the most popular and powerful of the Tudor rulers, **Henry VIII** and **Elizabeth I**, sought to consult Parliament on important matters. This relationship between the chief parts of the English government worsened after the death of Queen Elizabeth in 1603.

Because Queen Elizabeth died without any heirs, the crown passed to her cousin, King James VI of Scotland. He was the son of Mary, Queen of Scots, and a member of the Stuart family. Mary's grandmother, Margaret Tudor, had married into the Stuart family. And as Margaret was the sister of Henry VIII, father of Elizabeth, Elizabeth and James were therefore related. James now became King **James I** of England as well as King of Scotland (r. 1603–1625). The English became distrustful of James soon after he ascended to the throne because he was a foreigner, from Scotland, with a strange accent and undignified manner. Although well educated, particularly in theology, James was not thought to have much common sense. King Henry IV of France had called him "the wisest fool in Christendom."

The Rule of James I

James I ruled as an absolute monarch. He did not respect the democratic traditions that had evolved in England, distrusted Parliament, and claimed to rule by **divine right**. He believed that God has ordained kings to rule. He summarized his concept of government with the Latin phrase, "a deo rex, a rege lex" (the king is from God, and law from the king). With such attitudes, James was to face troubles during his reign. They occurred mainly in three areas: religion, money, and foreign policy.

As head of the **Anglican** (English) Church, James could appoint all bishops. The bishops wanted a certain amount of uniformity in religious services. The Puritans objected to the standards wanted by the bishops, and felt that the Anglican service was too similar to Catholic ways. The Puritans wanted to "purify" the Church of what they considered "popish" practices. James's support of the bishops made the Puritans fear that James was determined to bring the English Church back to Roman Catholicism with control by the pope. James saw the Puritans as a threat to England's political unity and imprisoned Puritan writers who criticized the bishops. Tension increased when James proclaimed that clergymen who refused to conduct services according to the Anglican Prayer Book would be dismissed. With bitterness, thousands of Puritans left England. Some went to Holland and then to North America, where, as the Pilgrims, they founded a settlement at Plymouth in 1620.

There was one request of the Puritans that James did grant early in his reign. This was for a new translation of the Bible. Upon his orders, the work was completed by a committee in 1611. It was based on original Greek and Hebrew texts, the Latin Vulgate, and various English translations. Known as the King James version, it is considered one of the greatest prose works in the English language and is still used today.

In monetary matters, James was far from being a thrifty monarch. He spent lavishly and frequently found himself asking Parliament for money. Parliament often refused to give him everything he wanted, based on its dislike of him and his ways of ruling. He then angered Parliament by raising money without its approval, increasing taxes on imports and selling titles of nobility.

King James I of England.

Some of the tension with Parliament might have been diminished if James had been more agreeable in the field of foreign affairs. Unfortunately, his attempts to create greater friendship with Catholic Spain proved to be very unpopular. His 1604 peace treaty with that country was criticized by Englishmen who bore a general dislike of Spain from the past, particularly by those merchants in the House of Commons who were profiting from raids on Spanish commerce. In addition, James provoked controversy when he sought to have his son Charles marry a Spanish princess. The House of Commons spoke out against this, preferring that Charles marry a Protestant, and issued in 1621 the Great Protestation. Incensed by this action, James tore up the document, dissolved Parliament, and imprisoned four of its leaders. The marriage never occurred, and Parliament was ultimately called back into session. A basis had now been laid for Parliament's grown power in the making of foreign policy.

The Rule of Charles I

When James died in 1625, there was hardly any sorrow. He was succeeded by his son, **Charles I** (r. 1625–1649). Little did this twenty-five-year-old new monarch realize it, but his reign was to be the most disastrous in English history. He inherited a harsh set of problems from his father, amid an atmosphere of friction, and he made no attempt to resolve these problems peacefully or to cool down political tempers. Like his father, Charles I was a believer in the divine right of kings and ruled in an arrogant, absolutist manner. His marriage to a French princess, who was Catholic, alarmed Puritans. Under his influence, he relaxed some of the penal laws against Catholics. Parliament began to question whether, even though he was an Anglican, Charles would maintain England as a Protestant nation.

In the first two years of his rule, Charles dissolved Parliament twice. He was upset with its refusal to grant him all the monies he wanted and was worried that his chief advisor would be removed from office. He began to raise money by forcing loans from wealthy subjects and by quartering troops in private homes at the homeowners' expense. Desperate for even more money for his expenditures both at home and abroad, Charles summoned Parliament in 1628. In exchange for granting him more *revenues* (money), Parliament made Charles agree to the **Petition of Right**. This historic document laid down some of the basic rules of modern constitutional government. With its limitations on royal power, it has even been referred to as the "Stuart Magna Carta." Its main provisions stated that the crown could not:

1. Tax without the consent of Parliament

2. Place soldiers in private homes without permission

3. Imprison people without a specific charge and a trial

Hardly had the ink dried on this document than Charles began to ignore it. He began to collect some monies not authorized by Parliament. John Eliot, a parliamentary leader who wrote resolutions of protest against the monarch, was arrested and imprisoned in the **Tower of London**, where he died. In 1629,

Charles dissolved Parliament and did not summon it for the next eleven years. During these years, 1629–1640, he continued to violate the provisions of the Petition of Right. One of his more notorious measures was the creation of a royal court called the **Star Chamber**. Here, he would have his own judges secretly try individuals who disagreed with him. Common law guidelines were not followed, nor were juries used. Many of those who suffered under Star Chamber proceedings were Puritans. Puritans and others who did not conform to Anglican Church practices, as directed by Charles in his role as head of the Church, experienced persecution.

THE LONG PARLIAMENT AND THE ENGLISH CIVIL WAR

The eventual downfall of Charles I was hastened by events involving both Scotland and Ireland. When Charles attempted to impose Anglican Church organization and rituals in Scotland, he met armed opposition from the Scots. The Scots, who were Presbyterians, stopped Charles's forces from invading their territory. The Scots were willing to fight to preserve their religious freedom. Charles saw their actions as a rebellion and thus summoned a new parliament in 1640 to request funds for an army to fight the Scots. This parliament would meet periodically until 1660 and was therefore called the **Long Parliament**. It did give Charles, in 1640, the money he wanted, but only after it did the following:

1. Abolished the Star Chamber court

2. Had two of Charles's chief advisors jailed

3. Passed the **Triennial Act** (This act stated that Parliament was to meet at least once every three years.)

These were further checks on the power of royal absolutism and could be seen as additions to the power of Parliament. Such additions came about mainly because Charles recognized Parliament's power of the purse, the ability to raise and provide money.

Although he was able to put down the Scots, Charles then faced a rebellion in 1641 by the Irish. Most of Ireland was Catholic, but under the English crown. Over the years, the northern region of Ulster had been settled by many English, and Scottish people. This Anglo-Irish minority grew wealthy, increased its control in the island, and was resented by the majority of native Irish. When this resentment broke out in a rebellion, Charles anticipated leading an army into Ireland to fight the Irish. Uncertain whether to finance an army under Charles for this purpose, Parliament drew up a document, the **Grand Remonstrance**, containing its many complaints against the king. Charles responded by personally leading an armed force into Parliament in order to arrest five opposition leaders. As the five had been forewarned, they were not present on that day. Having to leave the building without arresting them, Charles reportedly said, "The birds have flown." In the summer of 1642, he

The English Civil War

- ☐ Controlled by the king
- ▨ Controlled by Parliament

SCOTLAND

Edinburgh

Carlisle

Durham

NORTH SEA

IRISH SEA

Lancaster

Marston Moor

Leeds

Liverpool

Manchester

Sheffield

Lincoln

Newark

Shrewsbury

Leicester

WALES

Coventry

Naseby
Northampton

Gloucester

Oxford

Cambridge

Cirencester

London

Bristol

Thames R.

Canterbury

Exeter

FRANCE

Plymouth

Severn R.

0   Miles   100

0   Kilometers   160

moved north of London and raised an army. Parliament took over the government and announced it would raise its own army in preparation for the coming military conflict.

This conflict escalated into the **English Civil War** (1642–1649). The central issue was whether sovereignty, the power to govern the nation, should be in the hands of the king or Parliament. Although people of every class were on each side, supporters of the king included mostly nobles, wealthy landowners, Anglican and Catholic clergy, and citizens who were against the Puritans for political and religious reasons. Collectively, these supporters were referred to as **cavaliers**. They were given this name because many leaders of the royal cause were from the king's cavalry, wore fine clothing, and let their hair fall over their shoulders. Parliament's support came primarily from merchants, farmers, small landowners, and the Puritans. They were known as the **roundheads** because they cut their hair short and wore it underneath helmets. They received additional support from the Scots. Although the political fate of the nation was at stake, most Englishmen remained neutral. It has been estimated that less than 3 percent of the population was under arms during the fighting.

The fighting at first was a stalemate, but eventually the parliamentary forces won decisively at the battles of **Marston Moor** (1644) and Naseby (1645). Charles surrendered to the Scots in 1646 and was given over to Parliament in 1647. Why did the Cavaliers lose the war? The chief reason was that Charles's forces really had to fight two armies—that of Scotland and that of Parliament. In addition, there was no one on the royalist side who could match the leadership of the Puritan **Oliver Cromwell** (1599–1658). He reorganized most of the parliamentary forces into the new model army. A tall, powerful, heavyset person with a square jaw, Cromwell developed a force of well-trained, disciplined, religion-inspired fighters. He once remarked: "I think that he that prays and preaches best will fight best." His men were known to go into battle chanting psalms.

Even though Charles had surrendered, a serious political problem arose in the victorious Parliament. A split existed between a moderate group and a more radical group. The moderates were willing to place the king back on the throne with strict limitations. They were Anglicans and Presbyterians who wished to have some kind of uniformity and formality. They were opposed by a radical group that severely distrusted Charles. The radicals included Cromwell and many members of the new model army. They were of many different religious beliefs. Known as the independents, they were opposed to the goals of the moderates. They felt that they had fought to establish complete religious freedom. In December 1648, the independents moved in a forceful way. They had Colonel

The execution of King Charles I.

Pride lead soldiers into the House of Commons to exclude all members who did not agree with them. When Pride's Purge was finished, only sixty members remained—all independents. These remaining members, once part of the Long Parliament, were now known as the **Rump Parliament**. They declared that they represented all the people of England, when in reality their authority rested upon the support of the army.

Moving quickly, they accused Charles I of treason and placed him on trial. Without offering any defense other than to protest his being tried under any authority, Charles was found guilty and was beheaded on January 30, 1649. This act of regicide, the killing of a king, stirred deep emotions throughout the nation. This was particularly so because Charles had shown dignity and courage while quietly praying as he faced his executioner on that fateful January day. Also, it is doubtful whether the Rump Parliament's actions had the support of the nation. Indeed, Charles the Martyr soon became more popular than Charles the King. Curiously, for many people, the sympathetic reaction to his death cancelled out the resentment of his harsh qualities. Already, a wish slowly arose for restoration of the Stuart line. The Rump Parliament, however, would have none of this and proceeded to create a new political order. Clearly, Cromwell had won the day. Royalists had lost their power.

THE INTERREGNUM: ENGLAND AS A COMMONWEALTH AND THEN A PROTECTORATE, 1649–1660

The first signs of a new political order came with the decision by the Rump Parliament to abolish the monarchy and the House of Lords. England was not to experience an interruption in the pattern of centuries-old rule by a monarch. This period of interruption was to last for eleven years (1649–1660) and became known as the **interregnum**. In place of a monarchy, England was declared to be a **commonwealth**. In this situation, a commonwealth may be defined as a government that is a republic; the power to govern rests with Parliament and a council of state. In reality, the governing power here rested with Cromwell. And his basis of support was the army. England had become a military dictatorship.

Cromwell and the army began to face problems with the Rump Parliament. It was replaced by another parliament that was dissolved in 1653. Thus ended the commonwealth. A constitution was now drawn up by the army, known as the instrument of government. It provided for executive power to be exercised by someone in the new position of lord protector. England now was a **protectorate**. Did the nation benefit from Cromwell's rule during both the commonwealth and protectorate periods?

For answers, we need to look at his deeds, both *domestic* (within England) and foreign. A strict moral tone was established in England in accordance with Puritan ideals. Outlawed were such things as gambling, dancing, and horse races. Theaters were closed. In matters of religious freedom, his record was mixed, although generally tolerant. He extended his protection to the new sect of Quakers and permitted Jews to return to England by reversing the exclusion policy that had been in effect since 1290. Yet he did give some property of the Anglican Church to Puritans and prohibited use of the Anglican Prayer Book. Roman Catholics were placed under certain restrictions, but penalties against them were rarely enforced in England.

Catholics in Ireland saw a very ugly side of Cromwell as a result of political and religious factors. A rebellion against English rule broke out there in 1650. Cromwell ruthlessly suppressed it, leading an army himself throughout the island. Thousands of Irish people were killed, and some were sent into forced labor to British colonies in the West Indies. Hundreds of Catholic priests were, as Cromwell put it, "knocked on the head." Much land was taken and given to followers of Cromwell. Cromwell's acts were bitterly embedded in the Irish people's memory. "The curse of Cromwell on you!" remains one of the worst things you can say to someone you do not like.

In foreign affairs, Cromwell sought to build up English commerce while taking actions against Holland and Spain. He had Parliament pass the Navigation Act of 1651, requiring that imports into England be carried in English ships or in ships from the nation producing the goods. This hurt the Dutch, as their ships had made much profit from carrying goods across the seas. In a short, inconclusive war against the Dutch, the English navy performed ably.

As lord protector, Cromwell never enjoyed support by the majority of his subjects. Insurrections against him occurred in some parts of the country. His ruling under *martial* (military) law for a while violated the Petition of Right. To finance this and some other actions, he authorized a tax without Parliament's consent. In doing these things, he was committing the kind of injustices that he had criticized when they were committed by the king. Upon his death in 1658, his son Richard became lord protector. Unable to provide effective leadership, Richard resigned his post. The mood in England seemed willing to welcome the return of monarchy. The Long Parliament met and issued an invitation to become king to the son of Charles I who was living in exile abroad. He accepted and, in May 1660, entered London as King Charles II. The monarchy had been restored.

THE STUART RESTORATION (1660–1688)

The reign of **Charles II** (r. 1660–1685) was characterized by a decline in absolutism and a willingness to get along with Parliament. Fully mindful of his father's fate and Cromwell's problems during the interregnum, Charles promised to abide by the Magna Carta and the Petition of Right. He moved quickly to end the restrictions on activities that had been imposed during Cromwell's rule. Although he had pro-Catholic sympathies, he wisely refrained from letting these influence his public actions. His desire to permit complete religious toleration was not, curiously enough, shared by Parliament. In 1673, with passage of the **Test Act**, only persons who joined the Anglican Church could vote, hold public office, attend universities, and assemble. Although this legislation narrowed a person's freedom of religion, another law did much to expand a person's rights as an accused in a court of law. The **Habeas Corpus Act** of 1679 stated that an arrested person could get a writ or court order and be brought before a judge within a certain period of time to hear the charges against him or her. The order was called a writ of habeas corpus. The court would then determine whether the accused should go free or stand trial. The Habeas Corpus Act, which was carried over into American law, provided protections from an individual against unlawful, arbitrary arrest and imprisonment. The purpose of the act was to create a check on the power of the monarch.

In foreign affairs, as in domestic affairs, Charles was careful not to anger Parliament or do anything that would place his crown in danger. He maintained Cromwell's commercial and trade policies and was able to reduce the sea power of the rival Dutch. This was one result of the Anglo-Dutch War of 1664 to 1667; another result was the taking of Dutch New Amsterdam in North America and changing its name to New York, in honor of Charles's brother James, the Duke of York.

Two peaceful political developments that occurred during the reign of Charles II were unwritten but have since become part of both English and American government practices:

Fully mindful of his father's fate, King Charles II promised to abide by the Magna Carta and the Petition of Right.

1. Charles appointed five men from Parliament to serve as his major advisors. This small group turned out to be the forerunner of the cabinet system.

2. In Parliament, two groups emerged with different ideas and interests. These were the Tories and the Whigs. This emergence marked the beginning of political parties.

The **Tories** were mainly Anglicans, tolerant of Catholics, and preferred a strong but not absolute hereditary monarchy. The **Whigs** were very anti-Catholic and wanted a weak monarch with a powerful parliament. The formation of these two groups was sparked mainly by the realization that Charles would die without a legitimate child as heir, and that the likely successor would be a Catholic, his brother James.

When Charles died in 1685, his brother did come to the throne as King **James II** (r. 1685–1688). Although he was taller and more handsome than Charles, he nevertheless lacked his brother's charm as well as his cleverness and respect for history. James had two distinct goals:

1. To rule as an absolute monarch

2. To reestablish the Roman Catholic Church in England

In 1687, he issued a Declaration of Indulgences without consulting Parliament. Although this document guaranteed religious toleration for all groups, both Tories and Whigs in Parliament viewed it as a cover for promoting Catholicism and thought that the King should have obtained their consent. Further tension was in the air when James ignored the **Test Act** of 1673 and appointed Catholics to high positions in the army and at Oxford University. Displeasure and fear greeted his creations of a standing army of 30,000 men, placing it near London in what appeared to be an attempt to intimidate his critics. Fear also gripped Parliament when James's second wife, a Catholic, gave birth to a son. It was assumed that this son's ascent to the throne would lead to a line of Catholic monarchs in a predominantly Protestant nation. To prevent a Stuart Catholic dynasty, a group of Tory and Whig leaders wrote to the Dutch ruler, the Protestant William of Orange, inviting him to become King of England.

THE GLORIOUS REVOLUTION (1688–1689)

William was married to Mary Stuart, a Protestant daughter of James II by his first wife. William himself was the son of the sister of Charles II and James II. William accepted Parliament's offer and landed in England with a large army in November 1688. As William advanced toward London, he was greeted by throngs of people and scores of government officials. Deserted by many of his closest followers, James tried to escape on a ship for France but was captured by some fishermen. He was brought to London, and he was afraid that he would be executed. William, having arrived in London without any opposition, now made a smart political decision. He did not have James beheaded but rather let him flee to France in exile. William did not want to make a martyr and hero of James as had happened when Cromwell had Charles I executed. In France, James received a palace and a pension from King Louis XIV. James was thus permitted to keep his head, but not his throne. Without bloodshed, the English had now made a change in the monarchy—a bloodless revolution had been accomplished.

William's acceptance of the English crown had less to do with his wanting power and more to do with his desire to obtain England as an ally of his native Holland against the France of Louis XIV. On February 13, 1689, he and his wife were officially proclaimed King **William III** and Queen **Mary II** (r. 1689–1694). (After his wife's death, William continued to rule until his death in 1702.) Their becoming joint sovereigns, or rulers, was the climax to several active steps taken by Parliament after the Glorious Revolution. It had declared the throne officially vacant as James had "abdicated the government," broken "the original contract between king and people," and had "withdrawn himself out of the kingdom."

The crown was then offered to William and Mary on condition that they agree to be bound by a "declaration of right." Having secured agreement, Parliament soon drew up a formal law including this declaration. This law became famous as the **English Bill of Rights** (1689).

In *deposing* (removing) James II and placing William and Mary on the throne, Parliament clearly established its right to dethrone and enthrone a monarch. This was the crushing deathblow to the theory of the divine right of kings and queens. From this point on, all authority would be centered in Parliament. This key political concept was authenticated and spelled out in the Bill of Rights, along with rights important for the protection of individual liberties. The chief provisions of this document can be read as restrictions on the power of the king or queen as an absolute monarch. The king or queen may not:

1. Make or suspend laws without the consent of Parliament

2. Keep a standing army nor levy taxes without the consent of Parliament

3. Interfere with parliamentary debates and elections

4. Deny a jury trial to anyone accused of a crime

5. Inflict cruel or unusual punishment

6. Deny people the right to petition

Main Idea:
In deposing James II and placing William and Mary on the throne, Parliament clearly established its right to dethrone and enthrone a monarch.

King William III and Queen Mary II.

Other provisions require that Parliament meet frequently, and that for a person to become the monarch, he or she must neither be a Catholic nor have married a Catholic.

The Bill of Rights now resolved the issue of the relationship between monarch and Parliament. From 1689 onward, no English king or queen ever tried to govern without the consent of Parliament. Therefore, we can call England a limited or **constitutional monarchy**. This means that a king or queen sits on the throne, but that person's powers are limited by a written constitution as well as by unwritten traditional practices. The monarch reigns but does not rule.

Although the **Glorious Revolution** of 1688 to 1689 made some enormous strides, it left certain issues unresolved. Some undemocratic features remained. There were limits, for example, on religious freedom. The Toleration Act of 1689 permitted freedom of worship to all Christians, except for Catholics. This meant that all Protestants, Anglicans, and non-Anglicans could worship freely. And as long as Catholics and other religious groups such as Jews and Unitarians remained loyal to the government, they did not, in reality, suffer any interference. Another undemocratic feature was the makeup of Parliament. Its members were nobles and wealthy land owners and merchants. There were not women or commoners. Very few people had the right to vote. The members of Parliament in the seventeenth century wanted to reduce the monarch's power but were not interested in letting the great mass of people have a voice in choosing and running the government. Also, the House of Lords' membership was based on heredity and the Lords had equal power with the elected House of Commons. For all these reasons, the English Revolution of the seventeenth century may properly be labeled an aristocratic revolution.

In the years following the dramatic events of 1688 to 1689, there were additional political developments of note concerning England. James II went to Ireland, where he led a rebellion against English rule, hoping to retake the throne. After his defeat at the *Battle of the Boyne*, Parliament enacted severe restrictions on the majority Catholic population of Ireland. Catholics could not buy or inherit property from Protestants and could not run for election to the Irish parliament. That body, under control of London, would consist only of people from the Anglo-Irish Protestant minority. These policies added to the resentment felt in Ireland toward England.

To avoid future problems regarding succession to the throne, the English passed the **Act of Settlement** of 1701. Passage was prompted by the fact that there were no children born to William and Mary. The chief provisions were the following:

1. Mary's sister Anne would become queen.

2. If Anne should die without heirs, the crown would go the Protestant Sophia of Hanover and her heirs. Sophia was the granddaughter of James I and had married into the German House of Hanover.

3. All future English monarchs had to be members of the Anglican Church and could not belong to any other Protestant groups.

Although Queen Anne (r. 1702–1714) had seventeen children, none of them survived her. At her death, and with Sophia of Hanover dead, the crown was given to Sophia's son, who became King George I (r. 1714–1727). (See the chart that shows sovereigns of England and Scotland.) Both he and his successor, George II (r. 1727–1760), spoke very little English, were unfamiliar with the workings of English society, and were willing to depend heavily on their advisors—the cabinet. The result was an even further decline in royal power and an increase in the power of the cabinet and Parliament. This pattern, as it progressed in the reign of George III (r. 1760–1820) and thereafter, will be taken up in a future chapter concerned with advances in British democracy.

The descendants of George I have ruled to the present and have taken the dynastic name the **House of Windsor**. George's official title at his coronation was King of Great Britain and Ireland. The reason for this was passage of the **Act of Union** in 1707 by the parliaments of the kingdoms of Scotland and England. Scotland was now merged with England, which also had control over Wales and Ireland; the new kingdom could now be called Great Britain or the United Kingdom (U.K.). The English Parliament could now be called the British Parliament. In the world today, for reasons about which we will learn, the United Kingdom consists of England, Wales, Scotland, and Ulster (Northern Ireland).

POLITICAL IDEAS IN SEVENTEENTH-CENTURY ENGLAND

To understand a writer's ideas about politics and government, we first have to know something about the times in which he or she lived. Since we now have learned about the historic political events in seventeenth-century England, we can examine carefully the thoughts of two major writers from that time. They are **Thomas Hobbes** (1588–1679) and **John Locke** (1632–1704). They stand at opposite ends of political philosophy from each other.

Hobbes published *Leviathan* in 1651, two years after Charles I was beheaded and amid much political tension. Hobbes was very pessimistic about the behavior of human beings. He felt that by themselves, in a pure state of nature, without any controlling authority, in a condition of anarchy,

John Locke published the *Two Treatises of Government*.

they were selfish and would do bad things to each other. People would thus be in a continuous state of war. The only way to resolve this bad situation was for people to agree with each other to give up "all their power and strength upon one man, or upon one assembly of men, that may reduce all their wills . . . into one will." What would be formed would be a very strong government, a leviathan, with absolute and undivided powers. Hobbes was a defender of **absolutism**. He was a supporter of Charles I and has even been seen as establishing a set of justifications for twentieth-century totalitarian dictators.

John Locke published the *Two Treatises of Government* in 1690, having lived through the Glorious Revolution. Locke's view of humans differed from that of Hobbes. In a state of nature, Locke thought humans would be basically good and not engaged in constant warfare. They would agree with each other, in a social contract, to set up a government "for their comfortable, safe, and peaceful living . . . in a secure enjoyment of their properties." In creating this government, people would give up some rights but keep many others. These others were natural rights, such as the rights to life, liberty, and property. Government existed to protect these rights, as part of its contractual promises. If government failed in its responsibilities, then the people had the right to resist it and overthrow it. For Locke, the power of government was not absolute. That power was based upon the consent of the governed. These theories would explain why it was proper for Parliament to depose James II and to make itself more powerful in dealings with the monarchy. Although Locke died before 1776, he is considered to be a founding father of the American Revolution. His ideas were known to Thomas Jefferson and found their way into the American Declaration of Independence.

LINK TO TODAY

Many democratic ideas and political practices developed in England were included in American documents—the English Bill of Rights is similar to the U.S. Constitution and Bill of Rights and Locke's ideas can be found in the Declaration of Independence. We should also mention two famous American sites that are reminders of the Glorious Revolution. They are both in the state of Virginia—Williamsburg and the College of William and Mary. Whether or not you have visited these places, you now know something about the origins of their names.

William and Mary College in WIlliamsburg, Virginia.

CHAPTER SUMMARY

The growth of democracy in England, particularly as seen in the seventeenth century, has had a worldwide influence. The advances we have described influenced political revolutions in the British colonies in North America (1776) and in France (1789). (See Chapter 21.) Democratic ideals also affected the emergence of several nations from imperialism in the twentieth century, India being a good example. A trend toward democracy was also evident in the closing years of the twentieth century, mainly in Eastern Europe. In our own nation, we should remember that a major factor in the American Revolution was the emphasis by colonists on their "rights as Englishmen."

IMPORTANT PEOPLE, PLACES, AND TERMS

KEY TERMS

democracy	Rump Parliament	*Two Treatises of Government*
popular sovereignty	English Civil War	
absolutism	interregnum	anarchy
Parliament	protectorate	martial law
divine right	commonwealth	Stuart Restoration
Anglican	Star Chamber	Habeas Corpus Act
Petition of Right	Test Act	Glorious Revolution
Triennial Act	Magna Carta	Bill of Rights
Long Parliament	Act of Union	constitutional monarchy
Grand Remonstrance	*Leviathan*	Act of Settlement

PEOPLE

Henry II	James I	John Locke
Charles I	Oliver Cromwell	William and Mary
Henry VII	Charles II	House of Windsor
Elizabeth I	Tories	Thomas Hobbes
cavaliers	Whigs	
roundheads	James II	

PLACES

Tower of London	Marston Moor	Battle of the Boyne

EXERCISES FOR CHAPTER 16

MULTIPLE CHOICE

Select the letter of the correct answer.

1. The "divine right" theory of government had its greatest follower in
   a. John Locke.
   b. James I.
   c. Charles II.
   d. George I.

2. In a constitutional monarchy
   a. the king writes the constitution.
   b. the constitution limits the king's power.
   c. the constitution gives the king unlimited power.
   d. the king is free to rule without the constitution if he so wishes.

3. The Glorious Revolution saw Parliament

   a. proclaim William and Mary as joint rulers.
   b. declare war against James I.
   c. offer Charles II the title of Lord Protector.
   d. pass the Instrument of Government Act.

4. Of the following choices, the greatest influence on the American Declaration of Independence came from

   a. Thomas Hobbes.   c. James II.
   b. Oliver Cromwell.   d. John Locke.

5. Star Chamber proceedings were instituted against

   a. sailors who deserted their ships.
   b. soldiers of a defeated nation.
   c. political opponents of the king.
   d. clergymen who supported Parliament during the Glorious Revolution.

6. George Santayana said that those who do not learn from the past are doomed to repeat it. Who showed that he "understood" Santayana's comment?

   a. James I
   b. Oliver Cromwell
   c. Charles II
   d. James II

7. English common law grew out of

   a. decisions by judges.
   b. acts of Parliament.
   c. announcements by the monarch.
   d. jury verdicts made by commoners.

8. The chief reason for the success of Parliament in its seventeenth-century struggles against the crown was its

   a. calling for demonstrations by farmers, angry with the king.
   b. power over money appropriations.
   c. freedom to debate proposed bills.
   d. control over newspapers.

9. The Stuart Restoration came about mainly because the Commonwealth under Cromwell had

   a. imposed Puritan ideas.
   b. weakened English Naval strength.
   c. lost the thirteen colonies in America.
   d. caused an economic crisis.

10. Base your answer on this map and on your knowledge of social studies.

Which statement is true, as determined by this map of England in 1642 during the English Civil War?

   a. France gave help to the Parliamentary forces.
   b. The British capital city was controlled by Parliament.
   c. Oliver Cromwell was welcomed by the people in Wales.
   d. The King fled to Edinburgh.

11. The Civil War was fought between which two groups?

    a. Puritans and Protestants
    b. The kings of England and France
    c. Roundheads and cavaliers
    d. The Irish and the British

12. Which form of government would be most appealing to John Locke?

    a. Autocracy
    b. Democracy
    c. Monarchy
    d. Theocracy

13. Which statement best describes a result of the Glorious Revolution of 1688?

    a. England formed an alliance with France.
    b. The power of monarchy was increased.
    c. Principles of limited government were strengthened.
    d. England lost its colonial possessions.

14. Which belief would best characterize these monarchs?

    I. _____

       1. Louis XIV (France)
       2. James I (England)
       3. Charles I (England)

    a. Popular sovereignty
    b. Divine right
    c. Trial by jury
    d. Freedom of religion

15. The death of Charles I was unusual because it was an example of

    a. suicide.   c. infanticide.
    b. genocide.   d. regicide.

16. On which topic did John Locke and Thomas Hobbes express different views?

    a. Cultural diffusion
    b. Political systems
    c. Global interdependence
    d. Belief systems

17. Base your answers on this picture and on your knowledge of social studies.

    Which social scientist would be most interested in these people?

    a. A geographer
    b. An anthropologist
    c. An economist
    d. A political scientist

King William III and Queen Mary II.

18. The chief significance of the Magna Carta and the English Bill of Rights was that they limited the power of the English

    a. nobles.
    b. kings.
    c. middle class.
    d. clergymen.

19. Which title of a history book chapter would contain these actions?

I. _____

    1. Attempted arrest of members of Parliament
    2. Use of the Star Chamber
    3. Violation of the Petition of Right

a. Causes of the interregnum
b. Causes of the English Civil War
c. Results of the Glorious Revolution
d. Results of the restoration

20. What was true of both William of Orange and the Chinese ruler Kublai Khan? They were rulers who

a. practiced absolutism.
b. controlled land far from their birthplace.
c. instituted democratic reforms.
d. supported the growth of Parliamentary power.

ESSAYS FOR CHAPTER 16

1. Write a newspaper story for these headlines:
    a. "Civil War Starts in England"
    b. "Charles I Executed"
    c. "William and Mary Become Joint Sovereigns"
2. Write a conversation between Thomas Hobbes and John Locke on the best kind of government for a nation. Each speaker should explain his point of view and give two reasons for it.
3. Define the word *democracy*.
    a. Describe two advances in English democracy in 1700.
    b. Describe two undemocratic features in England that still existed in 1700.
    c. Did the coming of George I to the throne help or hinder democracy in England? Explain.
4. Oliver Cromwell was a controversial person, depending upon the perspective from which he was viewed. Give your opinion of him as if you were on of the following individuals.
    a. Thomas Hobbes
    b. John Locke
    c. a Catholic living in Ireland
    d. a Puritan
    e. a member of the new model army
5. Make a ranking list of three decisions made by Charles I that worsened his conflict with Parliament, from most serious to least serious. Give reasons for your ranking.

DOCUMENT-BASED QUESTIONS

This task is based on the accompanying documents. Some of these documents have been edited for the purposes of this task. This task is designed to test your ability to work with historical documents. As you analyze the documents, take into account both the source of each document and the author's point of view.

Directions: Read the following documents and answer the questions after each document. Use the information in the reading and this chapter in writing your answers.

Document #1   These thoughts were expressed by King James I of England.

The state of monarchy is the supremest thing upon earth; for kings are not only God's lieutenants upon earth, and sit upon God's throne, but even by God himself they are called gods. . . . Kings are justly called gods, for that they exercise a . . . divine power upon earth. . . . God hath power to create or destroy, make or unmake at His pleasure, to give life or sent death, to judge all and to be judged nor accountable to none, to raise low things and to make high things low at His pleasure. . . . And the like power have kings.

Questions

1. What type of government does King James describe?
2. Why does he believe it should be organized this way?

Document #2   Men being . . . by nature all free, equal, and independent, no one can be . . . subjected to the political power of another without his own consent. . . .
To protect natural rights governments are established. . . . Since men hope to preserve their property by establishing a government, they will not want that government to destroy their objectives. When legislators try to destroy or take away the property of the people, or try to reduce them to slavery, they put themselves into a state of war with the people who can then refuse to obey the laws.

From *Two Treatises on Government* (1690) by John Locke

Questions

1. According to Locke, why is government established?
2. Under what circumstances can the people revolt?

Document #3

Cromwell led an army of well-trained, religious fighters in the new model army. Here, he is seen dissolving the Long Parliament.

Document #4

That the . . . power of suspending of laws or the [carrying out] of laws by regal authority without consent of Parliament is illegal . . .

That it is the right of the subjects to petition [make requests of] the king, and all commitments (imprisonments) and prosecutions for such petitioning are illegal.

That the raising or keeping a standing army within the kingdom in time of peace unless it be with consent of Parliament, is against the law.

That election of members of Parliament ought to be free.

From The English Bill of Rights

| Questions | 1. How did Parliament limit the power of the king? |
| | 2. How did Parliament attempt to protect itself? |

Document #5

I did hint to you my thoughts about the reformation of manners; and those abuses that are in this nation through disorder . . . should be much in your hearts. . . . I am confident our liberty and prosperity depends upon— reformation. To make it a shame to see men to be bold in sin and profaneness—and God will bless you. You will be a blessing to the nation.

From Oliver Cromwell (1656)

| Questions | 1. What does Oliver Cromwell want to change? |
| | 2. What does he predict will happen for those people who accept his changes? |

CHAPTER 17

The Age of Exploration

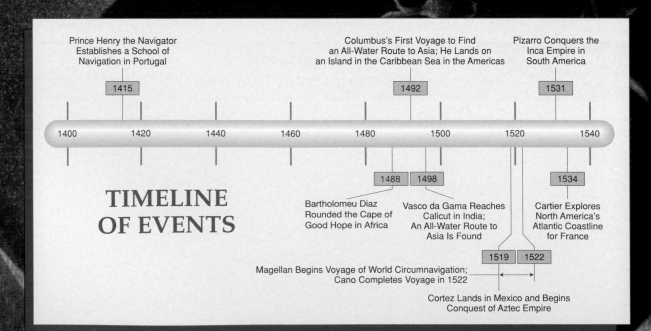

Prince Henry the Navigator Establishes a School of Navigation in Portugal

`1415`

Columbus's First Voyage to Find an All-Water Route to Asia; He Lands on an Island in the Caribbean Sea in the Americas

`1492`

Pizarro Conquers the Inca Empire in South America

`1531`

| 1400 | 1420 | 1440 | 1460 | 1480 | 1500 | 1520 | 1540 |

`1488` `1498`

`1534`

TIMELINE OF EVENTS

Bartholomeu Diaz Rounded the Cape of Good Hope in Africa

Vasco da Gama Reaches Calicut in India; An All-Water Route to Asia Is Found

Cartier Explores North America's Atlantic Coastline for France

`1519` `1522`

Magellan Begins Voyage of World Circumnavigation; Cano Completes Voyage in 1522

Cortez Lands in Mexico and Begins Conquest of Aztec Empire

D. FRAN^co PIZARRO.

From the mid-1400s for a period of 300 years, Europeans changed the world as they explored the globe. The **Age of Exploration** began with a search for an **all-water trading route** to Asia. Europeans hoped to find a direct sea route to riches of the East. The East, which is Asia today, was one of the centers of world trade. From China, India, and the East Indies came the precious goods that the Europeans wanted to buy. The expression **"God, gold, and glory"** represented the mixed intentions of the Europeans during the Age of Exploration. The European monarchs and merchants wanted to trade directly for and profit from the valuable commercial products—spices, gold, ivory, silk, silver, and slaves. They wanted to eliminate the middlemen in this trade with the East. The middlemen were the Turkish, Arab, and Italian merchants who profited by first buying and then selling these goods at a higher price to other merchants.

The Europeans were also interested in spreading their faith, the Christian religion. Religious leaders wanted to spread Christianity to peoples previously unknown. The Catholic Church and the European monarchs even hoped to find allies in their struggle against the Ottoman Empire. They wanted to find a way to surround and defeat the **Ottoman Empire**, a powerful Islamic state established in 1453 whose capitol Istanbul is in present-day Turkey. Some Europeans were also driven by a sense of adventure. These men had an attitude that they had everything to gain and nothing to lose. Many of these adventurers were noblemen who had titles but little wealth. The participants in the explorations hoped for heroic adventures that would bring them fame and riches.

The Europeans explored many parts of the world as they searched for the all-water route to the fabled East Indies. By 1498, they did eventually discover an all-water route to the East when **Vasco da Gama**, a Portuguese captain, reached India. European explorers also discovered new lands and wealth to the west of Europe across the Atlantic Ocean. In 1492, Columbus's first voyage led to the discovery of what the Europeans called the New World. Columbus's voyage led to further explorations, conquests, and settlements. Some years later these newly discovered lands were named the Americas after the Italian

Camel caravans were typical along the Silk Road routes.

explorer **Amerigo Vespucci**. Vespucci made a voyage to the Americas and profited from the claim that he had discovered a New World.

European rulers, merchants, adventurers, and Christian religious leaders were stimulated by the possibilities that the discoveries opened up. They were most of all interested in developing commercial trading ventures. As a result, the Columbian Exchange began as economic links tied the world more closely together. The expression "Columbian Exchange" is used to refer to the international trading network that developed for finished goods and raw materials. Some examples of the traded items were corn, potatoes, textiles, and rum. The Columbian Exchange led to important cultural changes. European nations also became increasingly involved in colonizing the new lands of the Americas. Western European nations were very influenced by the ideas of mercantilism once colonization began (see Chapter 12).

European interest in finding a new trading route to Asia grew after the Middle Ages ended. From the 1200s, a time when Marco Polo visited the Chinese Empire of Kublai Khan, Europeans made use of the old established trade routes to Asia. This usually meant traveling to the eastern end of the Mediterranean Sea and joining caravans that followed the silk road routes to the wealthy lands of the fabled East. Merchants from Venice and Genoa dominated the European portion of the Asian trade. In addition, the European merchants were also dependent on the Turkish and Arab merchants operating out of trading centers in cities such as Antioch and Alexandria. By the time the precious Asian goods reached western Europe, their prices had increased many times.

The domination of the older trade routes in the eastern Mediterranean Sea by the Islamic Ottoman Empire troubled the Europeans. The Ottoman merchants benefited greatly from their involvement as middlemen in this trade. Western European nations wanted to end their dependence on the Ottoman Empire and the seafaring Italian city-states such as Venice and Genoa. Many Europeans were increasingly interested in the possibilities of direct trade with other wealthy areas of the world. These factors contributed to encourage European explorations westward in the Atlantic Ocean in search of new trade routes to the East. Portugal and later Spain took the lead in searching for a new all-water route.

NEW TECHNOLOGY PERMITS EXPLORATION

A number of key factors enabled western European nations, primarily Portugal, Spain, Holland, France, and England, to undertake these voyages of discovery. The Age of Exploration led to a growing knowledge about geography and natural science. Improved sailing vessels and technological advances in navigational instruments made longer voyages of exploration possible. Venturing out into the Atlantic was made easier by use of these new technological advances in determining position and direction at sea. The use of ships with sails were more suitable for sea voyages and made it more possible to remain at sea for longer periods of time.

During the 1400s, Portugal became increasingly interested in finding a new sea route to trade directly with the East. In western Europe, Portugal was the first nation where political and economic conditions encouraged the beginning of sea exploration. These favorable conditions aided a diverse group of individuals who possessed the necessary wealth, knowledge, skills, and willingness to venture overseas to find riches and fame. The desire for God, gold, and glory motivated these merchants, sailors, and adventurers to participate in the often dangerous voyages of exploration. Fortunately, they were supported by a monarchy that encouraged sea exploration.

In the 1400s, a number of technological advances in shipbuilding and navigation made longer sea voyages possible and marked the end of European regional isolation. These voyages led to the beginning of European global domination. Starting in the mid-1400s, Portugal and then Spain began to create trading bases and colonies in the south Atlantic off the coast of Africa, on the African continent and then in the Americas.

Several of the technological innovations that aided the process of exploration made use of advances that had been perfected by Arabs and Asians. The **compass,** of Chinese origin, helped sailors to better determine geographical direction. The **astrolabe,** perfected by the Arabs, enabled sailors to determine the altitude of the sun and other celestial bodies. Europeans, particularly the Portuguese, made progress in shipbuilding. The caravel type of ship took advantage of advances made in outfitting Islamic sailing vessels. Multiple triangular-shaped sails and masts adapted by European shipwrights enabled ships to travel much faster. The crews of the caravels also made use of European innovations in weaponry, such as cannons and rifles.

European *cartography*, map-making skills, also gradually improved. The older maps and charts were often inaccurate and based on rumor and legend. The Mercator projection resulted in more accurate map making. During the Age of Exploration, a new and better view of the globe became possible. Europeans later added to this knowledge as they explored more of the unknown world. It should be noted that the idea that the earth was round was accepted by many educated people, particularly map makers such as Christopher Columbus.

Prince Henry the Navigator.

PORTUGAL'S EARLY EXPLORATIONS

Portugal was the first nation in western Europe that was capable of venturing out into the Atlantic Ocean in search of new sea routes and trading opportunities. Portugal, which bordered the Atlantic Ocean, began its explorations in the 1420s. **Prince Henry** the Navigator, a younger brother of the king of Portugal, established a school for navigators in

Sagres, Portugal. It was from this point in the southwest of Portugal overlooking the Atlantic that Prince Henry promoted numerous voyages of exploration. During the 1400s, sea captains flying the Portuguese flag made a number of important discoveries of islands in the Atlantic and pushed farther and farther along the coastline of West Africa in search of a sea route to Asia.

By the mid-1400s, the Portuguese discovered and made settlements in the Azores, the Madeira, and the Cape Verde islands. They laid the foundation of what would become the Portuguese seaborne empire in the 1500s. The Portuguese established trading posts called *factorias* along the African coast and bought gold and ivory from African tribes. In the 1400s, the Portuguese also became increasingly involved in the African slave trade. The slave trade was not something new in Africa. Slavery had existed in sub-Saharan Africa for many centuries and was an integral part of the Trans Saharan trade controlled by Arab and Berber merchants. However, the Europeans made the slave trade more of a commercial international trade. The slave trade grew enormously over the next 400 years. By the early 1800s, the continually expanding slave trade devastated the African continent and destroyed many tribes.

After Prince Henry's death in 1460, sea exploration temporarily slowed. However, in the 1480s, under the rule of King John II, new exploratory ventures were launched in search of an all-water route to Asia. By 1488, **Bartholomeu Dias** rounded the southern tip of Africa, which was renamed the **Cape of Good Hope**. In 1497, Vasco da Gama set sail and visited cities along the east coast of Africa. With the aid of an Arab pilot, he crossed the Indian Ocean and reached the Indian port of Calicut in 1498. At last an all-water route to Asia had been found. The profits gained from Vasco da Gama's return cargo of spices showed Europeans that great riches could be obtained from direct sea trade with the East.

COLUMBUS'S VOYAGES LEAD TO THE DISCOVERY OF THE AMERICAS

In Spain, three significant and symbolic events happened in 1492. In that year, under the rule of the Catholic monarchs, **Ferdinand** and **Isabella**, Spain became a united nation when the Moorish Islamic Kingdom of Granada was finally conquered. Shortly afterward, Queen Isabella, a devout Catholic who was influenced by Roman Catholic Church officials, decided to expel from Spain the Jews and Moslems who refused to convert to Christianity. Also in that year, Queen Isabella also agreed to finance the first voyage of **Christopher Columbus**, which led to the discovery of the Americas. Columbus's discovery of the Americas, which the Europeans called the New World, led to increased exploration and conquests and the Columbian Exchange.

In the 1490s, under the leadership of King Ferdinand and Queen Isabella, Spain embarked on a series of explorations that led to the establishment of a vast colonial empire. Queen Isabella's support for Columbus's voyage was tied to Spain's recent conquest of Grenada. The re-conquest of the Iberian peninsula from the Muslims did not mean that Catholic Spain gave up its role as a defender of Christianity. After the Catholic monarchs eliminated the last Islamic state in the Iberian peninsula, they continued to make plans to solidify their rule and strengthen Christianity.

Columbus was a sailor and maker of maps, a cartographer, by profession. He assumed the world was round and hoped to reach the East by sailing west. For a number of years, Columbus had unsuccessfully tried to convince other European monarchs to finance his voyage to find a westerly all-water route to the East. At last in 1492, Columbus finally succeeded in gaining the support of the Spanish monarchs now that their attention could turn elsewhere. In August 1492, Columbus set sail from Spain with three small ships. Later that year, he made his famous discovery when his ship reached an island in the Caribbean Sea. Upon his return to Spain, Columbus was treated as a hero. He was given the title of Admiral of the Ocean Sea, and made Viceroy and Governor of the lands that he discovered.

Columbus was an excellent navigator, but he miscalculated the distance he had to travel to circle the globe. Columbus never did achieve his goal of finding a westerly all-water route to Asia. During his remaining three voyages to the Americas, Columbus further explored the Caribbean Islands and sailed along the coast of northern South America. Based on the knowledge that was available then, Columbus thought the trip to the East would be only about 2200 nautical miles. Although Columbus may have suspected that the real distance to Asia was actually much greater, he refused right up to his death in 1506 to recognize what he had really discovered. The lands that he discovered were in the Caribbean Sea and part of the South American continent. They were not off the coast of Asia. He died a broken man, suffering from his failures as a colonizer and a disease supposedly contracted in the Americas.

Ferdinand and Isabella.

A statue of Christopher Columbus.

Columbus's voyages led to explorations in search of more new lands by Europeans. The voyages of discovery changed the course of world history by linking the Americas to the rest of the world. Today we know that Columbus was not even the first European to set foot in the Americas. The Vikings from Scandinavia and possibly other people from Africa and Asia reached the Americas earlier. The question of who should be given credit for the discovery of America has caused controversy in recent years. What is really important is that after Columbus's voyages European interest in the New World grew. The Americas became thereafter linked to other areas across the globe. Columbus should be remembered as a person who was a product and symbol of exploration and global change. During the Age of Exploration, the Europeans brought the world closer together. They established trading relations and colonies in other global areas. As a result, important economic changes took place first in Portugal and Spain and later in other western European nations.

Today we know that there were millions of people already living in the so-called New World. These peoples were spread out throughout the Americas. The inhabitants whom Columbus first found on the Caribbean Islands were called Indians by Columbus. This incorrect name, has endured to our present day. Some of these Native American peoples lived in advanced agricultural and trading civilizations, while others hunted and gathered in more primitive tribes. These peoples had developed independently and were isolated from the changes that took place in other world areas (see Chapters 4, 9, and 14). After Columbus's voyages, most of these Native American peoples and their cultures underwent enormous changes. Many of these peoples and their cultures disappeared after contact was made with the Europeans. Other peoples survived and adapted as best as they could to the European presence in the Americas.

PORTUGAL AND SPAIN: EARLY COLONIAL RIVALRY

Portugal and Spain played the major roles in the first century of European global exploration. During the 1400s, Portugal made most of the explorations and discoveries. The Portuguese had no rivals to challenge them as they worked their way down and around the coast of Africa. Until Columbus's first voyage, Spain had little interest in financing voyages of exploration. Spain was preoccupied with the wars of re-conquest and unification until 1492. An exception to this was the conquest and settlement of the **Canary Islands** in the Atlantic Ocean. Columbus's early voyages led to increased rivalry over sea routes, exploration, and land claims between Portugal and Spain. In the early 1490s, King John II of Portugal rejected Spanish claims to the newly discovered Caribbean Islands. Spain and Portugal refused to accept each other's claims and disputed the rights to explore and settle new lands.

The solution to this early colonial rivalry was arranged by Pope Alexander VI. The pope wanted to keep the peace between these two Christian nations. The **Treaty of Tordesillas** of 1494 was signed after difficult negotiations and an initial rejection by Portugal. This treaty set the boundary limits or demarcation line separating Portuguese and Spanish interests. Essentially, Spain received the right to explore and colonize all newly discovered lands to the west of the treaty line. Portugal gained the same privileges for lands that were to the east of the demarcation line. Spain ultimately gained the lion's share of North and South America and the Caribbean. Portugal obtained Brazil and claimed the trading rights in the rich Asian lands of India, China, and the East Indies. Despite the papal-sanctioned accord, the Dutch, French, and English refused to recognize the treaty. These nations all soon began to explore and seek to exploit wealth from areas in Asia, Africa, and the Americas.

THE PORTUGUESE SEABORNE EMPIRE AND BRAZIL

In the 1500s, Portugal concentrated for the most part on its trading empire in Africa and Asia. The Portuguese gained control of the trade in the Indian Ocean from Arab merchants after demonstrating they had superior ships and weapons. They were led by adventurous sea captains such as Pedro Cabral and Vasco da Gama. The Portuguese built naval bases in the Indian Ocean along the east coast of Africa, expanded eastward to the Spice Islands or Moluccas, and eventually established trading ports in China and Japan.

Portugal also explored and began its colonization of Brazil's coast. Pedro Cabral had claimed Brazil for Portugal in 1500. At first, trade with Brazil was primarily for wood. However, in the late 1500s, Brazil's importance grew as Portugal lost control of most of its Asian trading bases to the Dutch. The Portuguese began to take advantage of Brazil's vast potential for agricultural products such as sugar cane and tobacco. Rich deposits of gold and diamonds were later found in the interior of Brazil. The highland plateau of Brazil, particularly the area of the present-day state of Minas Gerais, became another valuable region to explore because of its mineral wealth.

The Native American inhabitants of Brazil—the Tupi and Carib tribal groups—could not be used as a reliable labor force. The majority of this original population either died because of warfare and disease or fled to the interior. Because of this, African slaves increasingly were imported to Brazil to replenish the labor supply. The Portuguese were few in number, and men predominated in the early colonial population. The even smaller number of Portuguese women led to increased racial mixture in Brazil. This resulted in the creation of new racial types, the mestizo and mulatto. A *mestizo* is a person of mixed European and Native American heritage. A *mulatto* is a person of mixed European and African heritage

SPAIN CONQUERS THE AMERICAS

The 1500s was Spain's golden century. Spain's dominance was in large measure due to the powerful monarchs who ruled its growing empire. During this time, Spain explored and conquered huge regions in the Americas. The Spanish explorers and conquerors came to the Americas "to serve God and his majesty" and to enrich themselves. These explorers and adventurers were responsible for gaining control of vast land areas and the peoples who inhabited these lands.

After Columbus's first voyages, Spanish explorers conquered and settled the islands in the Caribbean Sea. By the first decades of the 1500s, Spanish conquistadors began to explore the mainland. Vasco Nunez de Balboa crossed the jungles of Central America and sighted the Pacific. **Ponce de Leon**, who helped conquer Puerto Rico, discovered Florida. The period of Spanish explorations continued for most of the 1500s and resulted in the conquest of the more advanced civilizations in the Americas by the mid-sixteenth century.

FERDINAND MAGELLAN AND THE CIRCUMNAVIGATION OF THE GLOBE

Ferdinand Magellan was a Portuguese soldier of fortune.

Ferdinand Magellan, a Portuguese soldier of fortune serving the Spanish crown, led a historic three-year sailing expedition around the globe. Beginning in 1519, Magellan began a voyage that proved the world was indeed round. Magellan's expedition of five ships and a crew of 265 men crossed the Atlantic and explored the east coast of South America, sailing into bays and inlets in search of a route to the South Sea. Magellan overcame a mutiny along the way and sailed past the tip of South America into the Pacific through the dangerous **Cape of Storms** (Strait of Magellan). The strong currents and severe gales in the strait resulted in the destruction of one ship and the return of another to Spain.

Magellan's ship and two others continued into the South Sea, which Magellan named the Pacific Ocean because he found it to be so calm. The ships sailed on for four months before finally reaching land in the Mariana Islands. Shortly after, in the Philippines, Magellan was killed in a battle between two rival native groups. After Magellan's death, **Juan Sebastian del Cano** took charge and completed the voyage. Cano eventually arrived in Spain in September 1522, after a number of adventures, with one ship, the *Victoria*, and a crew of eighteen men.

The Magellan-Cano voyage from 1519 to 1522 resulted in the first **circumnavigation**, or complete circling, of the world by ship. This voyage revolutionized ideas about the relative proportions of land and water. It also revealed that the Americas were separated from Asia. The Magellan-Cano voyage is considered one of the greatest achievements of navigation. Although he did not live to complete the journey, Magellan provided the skill and determination that took his expedition into an unknown area of the world. He justly deserves recognition as a great explorer. Cano also deserves recognition for successfully completing the voyage.

CORTEZ CONQUERS THE AZTECS OF MEXICO

The exploits of the *conquistador*, or conqueror, **Hernando Cortez** excited the imagination of all Europeans who heard the story. Conquistador is the Spanish term used to describe the men who took part in the Spanish conquest of Mexico, Peru, and other global regions in the sixteenth century. In 1519, the Cortez expedition to Mexico led to the downfall of the Aztec Empire. This resulted in an enormous amount of wealth falling into Spanish hands. Cortez, like many Spanish conquistadors, was a minor member of the Spanish nobility. He was a *hidalgo*, which means a person of noble birth. In Spain, the rule of *primogeniture*, giving all the land to the first-born male, had led to the growth of landless nobil-

Cortez's expedition of 11 ships and about 500 men conquered the Aztec Empire ruled by Montezuma.

ity. The hidalgos had this title but little else. Therefore, it is not surprising that they were interested in heroic adventures that could lead to glory and riches. Cortez's expedition of eleven ships and about 500 men conquered the Aztec Empire ruled by the all-powerful Montezuma II. The history of the conquest of the Aztec Empire is a story of adventure that tells about acts of enormous courage and terrible cruelty.

Although Cortez's men were greatly outnumbered, they were able to defeat Montezuma's large armies by means of superior weaponry and tactics that made use of horses, then unknown to the Aztecs. Cortez used a divide-and-conquer strategy and made use of the Aztec's many enemies in his campaign. The Tlaxcalans, who were the Aztec's principal opponents in Mexico in the highlands of central Mexico, supplied the manpower for the conquest of such a large empire.

The religious beliefs of the Aztecs also helped the Spaniards conquer the most powerful civilization in Mesoamerica. The Aztecs thought that Cortez and his men were the returning former rulers of this central plateau and valley region in Mexico. The legend of the god Quetzalcoatyl and the prophecy of his return influenced Montezuma (see Chapter 14). He allowed Cortez to march up from the coast unopposed to the Aztec capitol Tenochtitlan. After his capture, Montezuma, the Aztec ruler, gave Cortez a large quantity of gold objects in the hope of gaining his freedom. Montezuma was eventually killed, and the golden treasure was melted down into bullion bars. Within three years, warfare and disease destroyed the Aztec trading and tributary empire. Cortez in the name of the Spanish monarch became the new ruler of Mexico.

Cortez's lieutenants penetrated into other areas of Mesoamerica and repeated the pattern of conquest. The Maya of the Yucatan and present-day Central America and other Native American peoples could not resist the Spanish conquerors. Spanish explorers also led expeditions into the northern regions of the Americas that resulted in great hardship for the participants and the finding of little wealth. Vast areas of northern Mexico and part of the future United States were explored by Hernando de Soto and Francisco Coronado in search of fabled cities of gold.

PIZARRO CONQUERS THE INCAS IN SOUTH AMERICA

The Incas ruled a great empire stretching from Colombia along the spine of the Andes Mountains into Chile. **Francisco Pizarro** eventually defeated the Inca armies by using the same weaponry and tactics employed by Cortez. The tragic death of Atahualpa, the Inca ruler, soon led to the end of Inca resistance. The Inca Empire soon disintegrated as a result of the Spanish conquest. From their new capital, Lima, in present-day Peru, the Spanish began to rule a vast area of land with many peoples that stretched along the Andes Mountains from Colombia to Chile (see Chapter 14).

As in Mexico, the Native American population was drastically reduced because of warfare and newly introduced diseases that spread rapidly, such as small-pox. Mistreatment of the Native

Francisco Pizarro eventually defeated the Inca armies by using the same weaponry and tactics employed by Cortez.

American peoples caused by the abuses in the encomienda and mita labor systems was also a primary cause for the population decline. The *encomienda* was tribute granted to some Spanish colonists in the New World. The tribute was often provided as a labor payment or in goods by the Native Americans. The *mita* was a labor obligation for Native Americans for a fixed time period. The mita often involved working in the silver mines, which was particularly deadly.

THE DUTCH COLONIES IN ASIA, THE AMERICAS, AND AFRICA

By the late 1500s, Spain's power in Europe began to decline. In the Netherlands, the Dutch, who were deeply affected by the Protestant Reformation, gained their independence from Catholic Spain. During these years, the Dutch, an industrious people, increasingly built up their commerce with other nations and peoples. By the 1600s, the Dutch Republic established a global trading empire, and Amsterdam became the major commercial city in Europe. During this period, the Dutch had Europe's most powerful navy. By the 1640s, the Dutch had driven the Portuguese out of most of their bases in Asia and gained control of the Spice Islands. The Dutch East India Company, chartered in 1602, monopolized the Netherlands' Asian trade.

In the Americas, the Dutch attacked Spanish and Portuguese settlements. For a time, they gained control of Brazil's northern coastal region and its valuable sugar production and trade. Further north, Henry Hudson, an English navigator working for the Dutch, claimed territory along the Atlantic coast of North America and searched for a northern water route to Asia. Dutch farming and trading settlements were established in **New Amsterdam**, present-day New York City, and elsewhere in the area. The Dutch West India Company was chartered by the government of the Netherlands to rule the American colonies and regu-

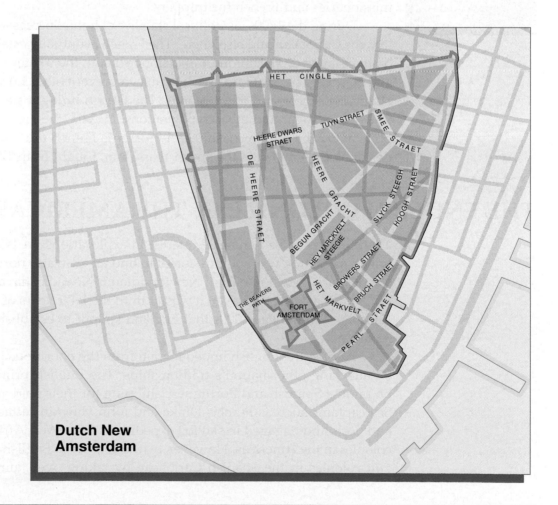

Dutch New Amsterdam

late the growing trade of farm products and valuable furs. By the middle decades of the 1600s, the Dutch colonies increasingly came under pressure from the British and French, who were busily establishing their own colonial empires.

THE FRENCH AND THE AMERICAS

At first the French did not play a major role in the early voyages of exploration and settlement. During the Protestant Reformation and its aftermath, the Catholic Counter Reformation, the French were too involved with religious conflicts and civil wars at home to focus on exploration. However, some French-financed sea voyages took place. The French explored and made discoveries along the North Atlantic American coast and into the continent's interior waters. French fisheries were set up in Nova Scotia, Newfoundland, and elsewhere.

In 1524, Giovanni Verrazano tried to find a northwest passage through America to Asia. The northwest passage represented another hope of reaching the East by sailing westward. Jacques Cartier later explored the St. Lawrence River area and claimed eastern Canada for France. By the early 1600s, Samuel de Champlain founded Quebec in Canada. Later in the 1670s, the explorations of the Jesuit missionary Jacques Marquette and the explorer Louis Joliet resulted in French claims in the Mississippi Valley and its valuable fur trade. The French contacts with Native American tribes came mostly through the work of Jesuit missionaries and French fur trappers.

> **Main Idea:**
> As political stability at home increased, France expanded into the Caribbean and elsewhere.

During the 1600s, as political stability at home increased, France expanded into the Caribbean and elsewhere. The French eventually established themselves on the islands of Martinique, Guadaloupe, Haiti, the western part of Hispaniola, and St. Kitts. The Spaniards were unable to prevent other European nations from taking over these and other islands. The French brought slaves to these islands to work on sugar and tobacco plantations. In Asia, the French gained control of ports along the Indian coastline. In India, the French presence lasted until their defeat by the English in the Seven Years' War, fought from 1756 to 1763.

THE ENGLISH COLONIZE IN THE AMERICAS

The English showed an early interest in explorations. In 1497, John Cabot, the Italian navigator, was commissioned to find an all-water northern route to Asia. Cabot's voyages took him to Newfoundland, Nova Scotia, and along the New England coastline. However, it wasn't until the later years of the reign of Queen Elizabeth I in the late 1500s that England sought to establish colonies in North America.

At first, the English hoped to gain from the enormous profits to be earned by attacking other nation's trading ships. The English primarily concentrated on raiding Spanish and Portuguese shipping for their gold and silver treasures. Sea captains such as Francis Drake and John Hawkins attacked Spanish ships and ports and engaged in slaving expeditions from West Africa to the European colonies in the Americas. However, by the 1660s, the English established important colonies in the Spanish Caribbean by taking over Jamaica, the Bahamas, and Barbados. English sugar plantations were soon established. These commercial farming enterprises were worked by slave labor brought from Africa. The establishment of English colonies in the Caribbean, or West Indies, and on the Atlantic coast of North America led to the growth of the **triangular trade**. This three-continent trading system involved the exchange of shipments of English-manufactured goods, African slaves, West Indian sugar and molasses made into rum, and North American lumber, tobacco and other crops. The triangular trade is an example of the Columbian Exchange that developed as a result of the Age of Exploration.

The North American continent was initially settled by the English in 1607. The **Virginia Company** of London financed an expedition that settled in Virginia at a place they called **Jamestown**. Other English colonies were later established in New England by religious dissenters. These people were called **Pilgrims** and were the first of the **Puritan** settlers in this colder and less hospitable region. In the 1660s, as a result of a conflict with the Dutch, the English gained control of New Amsterdam, which they renamed New York. By the end of the century, England had colonies along the Atlantic coast of North America from Massachusetts to the Carolinas. England's rise to the position of Europe's most important colonial power came in the mid-eighteenth century after the defeat of their major rival, the French.

RESULTS OF THE AGE OF EXPLORATION

The Age of Exploration brought far-reaching changes to the peoples of Europe, the Americas, Africa, and Asia. A vast global trading network, which would expand to our present day, was created. Colonies and trading posts were established throughout the world and maintained for the benefit of the European colonial powers. Europe, which began the period as one of the poorer and more backward regions of the world, gradually became the center of the world's military and economic power. The wealth of other continents and peoples fueled the economic growth of western European nations.

The linking of Africa, Asia, and the Americas to Europe had some serious negative consequences for these regions. Africa was devastated by the slave trade. The enormous loss of African population led to increased political instability. The negative effects of the slave trade, which lasted over four centuries, have continued to today. The slave expeditions wreaked havoc on the African tribes, who suffered because of the breaking up of families and exportation of tribal members. The social and economic consequences for Africa were particularly tragic. Africa's loss of population robbed the continent of the talent and industry of millions of people.

In the Americas, the native populations and cultures drastically declined. The Spanish Empire was controlled through the Council of the Indies in Seville and administered by crown-appointed viceroys. The viceroys served as the king's governing agents, and they directed the Spanish Empire's interests in terms of military, economic, and social matters. The Spanish officials ignored, for the most part, the injustices inflicted upon the Native American populations. The introduction of African slaves completely changed the population in the

West Indies and, to a large measure, on the mainland where the Spanish made use of slave labor. A new people, the Latin Americans, were born out of the resulting racial mixture of Europeans, Africans, and Native Americans.

In Asia, the Europeans had less impact. China and Japan restricted European merchants to a couple of trading ports and severely limited the spread of the Christian religion after the missionaries' early successes. Nevertheless, a European trading presence was established, and the European nations would expand their power and influence in the nineteenth century.

LINK TO TODAY

During the Age of Exploration global trade began to expand. Starting in the fifteenth century, the Portuguese explored the western coastline of Africa. They set up trading places and began to trade for such products as gold, ivory, and slaves. After the voyages of Christopher Columbus, Vasco da Gama, Ferdinand Magellan, and others, trade became more global in nature. The expansion of global trade continued over the next centuries. Mercantilist principles governed the first centuries of the expanding international trade (see Chapter 12 for a complete explanation of mercantilism). The balance of trade in the first centuries of global trade was primarily measured by amounts of gold that a country possessed in their treasury.

As the Industrial Revolution developed, European nations and later the United States increasingly traded with other nations. The developed industrial countries generally sold finished goods that they manufactured. In turn, these industrial nations bought raw materials, which cost less than the finished products. By the 1800s, the nations that profited most from the growing global trade were the countries that explored the world, made discoveries, and created colonial and later imperialistic economic relationships. Western European countries and the United States became wealthier at the expense of the rest of the world because the trade balance favored them.

As the twentieth century came to an end, new patterns of global trade developed. Asian nations, first Japan and more recently China and India, have increasingly become industrialized nations. These countries are capable of producing goods and selling them to other nations at prices that are difficult to compete with. The countries that first industrialized and expanded global trade no longer have the same advantages they had in their earlier global trading relationships. Today, for example, the United States no longer has a favorable balance of trade or produces most of the goods that American people purchase. The United States has a very unfavorable trading balance, which is steadily getting worse. The nations of Asia, particularly China, India, and Japan, have profited enormously from the increase globalization of the world economies.

It is difficult to predict how the globalization of the world economy will develop in the future. Nevertheless, it seems clear that the nations that spurred the Age of Exploration will no longer be able to control global trade as they did in the past. This means that the wealth and trading advantages once enjoyed primarily by western European nations and the United States will be shared by nations from other continents, particularly Asia.

CHAPTER SUMMARY

A number of factors had combined to make the Age of Exploration necessary and possible. Europeans had a need for goods that came from other parts of the world. They were not satisfied with the way that they could obtain these products for political and economic reasons. The Islamic Ottoman Empire had a stranglehold over the then-existing trade routes. Europeans were ready to leave their shores and were curious about what existed across the globe. The Europeans developed financial institutions and businesses that added in their explorations and resulted in the expansion of trade. Each European nation's desire to control its own trade routes fueled exploration. Technological advances made ocean travel and exploration more possible. Europeans were also motivated by religious reasons.

In addition, the political, economic, and religious rivalry between the Christian and Islamic nations led to renewed wars between the Ottoman Empire and Spain in the 1500s. The European monarchs hoped to find Christian allies in Africa and ultimately end Ottoman control of the eastern Mediterranean. A group of extraordinarily brave and determined Europeans were willing to risk life and limb to obtain what they wanted—wealth. It took a brave person to sail off into the unknown. A combination of political, economic, religious, and social reasons contributed to stimulate Europeans into taking the necessary risks. Sometimes this beginning stage or the first centuries of the Age of Exploration is referred to as the old imperialism because the European voyages and discoveries led to Europeans taking over areas of land and peoples to promote the political and economic interests of their nations.

Once new lands were uncovered, the nations of Europe competed with each other for colonies and trading privileges to promote both the wealth and grandeur of the mother country. Often, the Native Americans, Africans, and Asians that were already living in these lands were badly treated and suffered at the hands of their new masters. In the centuries to come, the European nations that participated in the Age of Exploration became the dominant economic and sometimes political powers of the world. This period was the beginning of what we call today the global economy.

IMPORTANT	KEY TERMS	PEOPLE	PLACES
PEOPLE, PLACES, AND TERMS	Age of Exploration all-water trading route God, gold, and glory Ottoman Empire silk route roads compass triangular trade Treaty of Tordesillas circumnavigation Virginia Company Puritan Pilgrim astrolabe	Prince Henry Bartholomeu Dias Christopher Columbus Vasco da Gama Ferdinand Magellan Juan Sebastian del Cano Hernando Cortez Francisco Pizarro Ponce de Leon King Ferdinand Queen Isabella Amerigo Vespucci	Cape of Good Hope East Indies West Indies New Amsterdam Jamestown, Virginia Tenochtitlan Canary Islands Cape of Storms

EXERCISES FOR CHAPTER 17

MULTIPLE CHOICE

Select the letter of the correct answer.

1. Christopher Columbus's voyages of discovery are important because he

   a. was the first European to reach Japan.
   b. found the lost Native American peoples.
   c. linked the Americas thereafter with other global regions.
   d. found the all-water route to Asia.

2. The Age of Exploration was spurred on by the European Commercial Revolution because

   a. countries wishing to increase their trade and wealth supported exploration.
   b. the Italian cities of Venice and Genoa invested in finding new trade routes.
   c. private investment in commercial enterprises decreased in western Europe.
   d. Asian nations were interested in developing trade with the Americas.

3. The expeditions of Hernando Cortez and Francisco Pizarro

   a. proved that the Native American peoples did not possess any real wealth.
   b. demonstrated that a very large military force is always the key to victory.
   c. showed Europeans that the New World had an abundance of precious metals.
   d. resulted in the conquest and colonization of the Philippines and East Indies.

4. Spain and Portugal were the first European nations to participate in the Age of Exploration. Both nations had all of the following characteristics except that

   a. both were disunited nations ruled by a monarch.
   b. they were motivated by the idea of gold, God, and glory.
   c. both wanted to find new trade routes.
   d. they established colonial empires in the New World.

5. Which title would best complete the partial outline?

   I. _____

      A. Magellan-Cano circumnavigate the globe
      B. Cortez conquers the Aztec Empire
      C. Pedro Cabral discovers Brazil
      D. The Spanish monarchs finance Christopher Columbus

   a. European nations follow a policy of isolation
   b. Causes of the Commercial Revolution
   c. Major events in the Age of Exploration
   d. European Colonization of the New World

6. Which was a result of the Age of Exploration?

   a. Decline in population in Europe
   b. Shift of power from western Europe to eastern Europe
   c. Spread of feudalism throughout western Europe
   d. Expansion of European influence overseas

7. Which was an immediate result of European arrival in the western Hemisphere?

   a. Islamic culture spread from Europe to the Americas.
   b. Europeans sought to spread the Christian religion.
   c. African peoples began to immigrate to the New World.
   d. Europe shifted away from the mercantilist system.

8. A major result of the Age of Exploration was

   a. a long period of peace and prosperity for the nations of western Europe.
   b. extensive migration of people from the western Hemisphere to Europe.
   c. the fall of European national monarchies and the rise of the Catholic Church.
   d. the end of regional isolation and the beginning of European global domination.

9. The Age of Revolution in western Europe lead directly to the

   a. development of a socialist economy.
   b. establishment of the Guild System.
   c. weakening of the power of the middle class.
   d. expansion of a global trading network.

10. Which of these events during the Age of Exploration was the cause of the other three?

   a. Europeans brought food, animals, and ideas from one continent to another.
   b. European diseases had an adverse effect on the native populations.
   c. Warfare increased as European nations competed for land and power.
   d. Advances in learning and technology made long ocean voyages possible.

11. The Native American population in the Americas declined in the 1500s because of

   a. crop failures brought on by poor weather conditions.
   b. emigration of Native Americans to Europe and Africa.
   c. wars among the different Native American tribes.
   d. diseases introduced by the Spaniards and Portuguese.

12. Which is a characteristic of the policy of European mercantilism?

   a. The colonies were forced to develop local industries by themselves.
   b. Spain sought trade agreements between its colonies and English colonies.
   c. The colonies were required to provide raw materials and buy finished goods.
   d. Spain encouraged the colonies to experiment in developing economic policy.

13. Which statement best describes a result of not using Native American labor?

   a. Unskilled laborers were brought in from Asia and Africa.
   b. Many people from Spain and Portugal migrated to find work.
   c. Native American populations from the interior migrated to the coasts.
   d. Large numbers of African slaves were increasingly brought in to work.

14. Portugal's mercantilist policies affected the development of its Brazilian colonies by promoting

   a. the production of raw materials and cash crops.
   b. free trade with African and Asian nations.
   c. respect for the economic rights of Spanish emigrants.
   d. the developing of a colonial factory system.

15. In colonial Latin America, the main purpose of the encomienda system was to

   a. ensure that Native Americans were paid wages.
   b. provide a steady supply of labor for the early colonists.
   c. prevent slavery in Spain's New World colonies.
   d. build and maintain forts to expel foreign invaders.

16. Which statement is true about the Treaty of Tordesillas of 1494?

   a. It provided for self-government by Native American peoples.
   b. It declared in the New World that monarchs ruled by divine right.
   c. It divided areas of the world into European-controlled segments.
   d. It encouraged economic development in the Americas and Africa.

17. During the 1500s, the interest of Europeans in Africa grew primarily because of

   a. a need to sell surplus agricultural products.
   b. a desire to obtain workers for colonies in the Americas.
   c. an African willingness to develop global trading relations.
   d. attempts by European nations to absorb surplus populations.

18. The printing press, the astrolabe, and the Mercator projection were technological advances that contributed to the

   a. exploration and overseas expansion of the colonial empires.
   b. growth of industry in most regions of the world.
   c. decline in demand for goods that came from the east.
   d. rise of a trading system based on ideas of free trade.

19. The death of large numbers of Native Americans in the first century of the Age of Exploration resulted in

   a. a decline in Spanish and Portuguese immigration to the Americas.
   b. the increased use of Asian labor in the mines and on plantations.
   c. greater efforts to improve health care for Native American peoples.
   d. the rise in the importation of Africans to do the necessary labor.

20. The influence of African culture on the development of the Americas was largely a result of

   a. the willingness of Africans to share their music and arts with Native Americans.
   b. the rise of global artistic networks that sought to encourage cultural infusion.
   c. the lack of any artistic and musical traditions among the Native Americans tribes.
   d. the desire of enslaved Africans to artistically and musically express themselves.

1. Why were the western European nations so interested in finding new sea routes?
2. It is 1499 and you are living in Spain. Imagine that you were born a person who has a title and little wealth. You have a good education and are adventurous. Write a letter to your monarchs asking them to lend you support for leading a voyage of exploration. State the reasons as to why the monarchs should finance and supply your voyage.
3. It is 1550 and you are the King of Spain. Write a letter of instructions to your representatives in the New World informing them about how you want them to deal with issues such as treatment of the Native American population, loyalty to the monarchy, and honesty in their financial dealings.
4. Why were the Europeans able to expand into other world regions during the Age of Exploration?
5. How did the Age of Exploration lead to major changes for Native American and African peoples?

DOCUMENT-BASED QUESTIONS

This task is based on the accompanying documents. Some of these documents have been edited for the purposes of this task. This task is designed to test your ability to work with historical documents. As you analyze the documents, take into account the sources of each document and the author's point of view.

Directions: Read the following documents and answer the questions after each document. Use information in the reading and this chapter in writing your answers.

Document #1

The relationship between the Spanish crown and the explorers and conquerors was one of great conflict. This conflict had to do with the use of land and labor, and thus of political power. It was the question of the rightful ownership and use of wealth and use of power in Spanish America. How and to whom should this wealth and power be distributed? Is the distribution of wealth and power just? Will the distribution of power and wealth benefit the monarchy and nation? In the sixteenth century the Spanish monarchy faced a difficult dilemma seeking the answers to solve these questions in their New World empire.

From The Buried Mirror by Carlos Fuentes

Questions

1. What conflicts existed between the Spanish monarchy and the explorers?
2. Why were there conflicts between the monarchy and those people engaged in exploration and conquest?

Document #2   During the reigns of Charles V and Philip II, northern Europe began to see a spectacular rise in capital accumulation. Spain did not benefit exclusively from this capital accumulation despite its mercantilist policies. In essence Spain saw the capital of its New World empire leave the peninsula. Spain did not have the necessary capitalist class of bankers and entrepreneurs to truly benefit from this new found wealth. Seventy-five percent of the gold and silver from the American mines ended up in four European capitols: London, Rouen, Antwerp, and Amsterdam.

From *Buried Mirror* by Carlos Fuentes

Questions   1. Why was there a spectacular rise in the capital available in Europe?
2. Why didn't Spain benefit greatly in the long term from its newly acquired wealth obtained in its American colonies?

Document #3   What sort of men were the conquistadors? The conquest of the Americas attracted a wide variety of types. There was a sprinkling of professional soldiers, desperate men, commoners, hidalgos, artisans, notaries and even criminals. At the head of the expedition stood a military leader who usually possessed a royal sanction which gave him the right to pursue conquest in the name of the crown. Bravery and the incredible ability for enduring hardships were among the characteristics of the conquistadors. Often the expeditionary group were hard and ruthless in dealing with the Native Americans as well as among themselves. The harshness of the conqueror reflected the conditions that formed his character and what he faced during the conquest. The climate of violence and inequality of Spanish society played a large determining role in the way the conquerors acted when they came to the New World.

From *A History of Latin America* by Benjamin Keen and Keith Haynes

Questions   1. What types of people became the explorers and conquerors of the New World?
2. Why were the explorers and conquerors usually harsh people?

Document #4   The Black Legend is the idea that the Spanish conquistadors treated the Native Americans with great cruelty and violence. This treatment caused the death of millions of Native Americans and the destruction of their societies. This view was spread throughout Europe in the early 1500s. It was supported by the famous defender of the Native Americans, Bartolome de Las Casas in his "Brief Account of the Destruction of the Indies." Is the Black Legend true or false? Supporting it are eyewitnesses such as Las Casas. Skeptics rebut the testimony and offer the idea that disease played the greatest role in the death of most of the Native American population in the 1500s.

From *The Encyclopedia of Latin America* edited by Helen Delphar

Questions

1. Why has the idea of Black Legend caused a historical controversy?
2. What evidence is there that the Black Legend is true?

Document #5

The five-hundredth anniversary of Columbus's 1492 voyage to America produced a large number of writings seeking to throw a new light on that momentous event. There has been agreement that the event had enormous consequences for future developments in Europe, the Americas and elsewhere in the world. There has also been dispute as to whether Columbus's voyage should be a cause for celebration or regret. Despite the writings of people such as Bartolome de Las Casas, which were critical of the conquest of the Indies, until recently few Europeans and Americans questioned the splendor and value of Columbus's achievement. The "Discovery" of the New World was viewed with pride and satisfaction and rarely challenged. After World War II, anti-colonial revolutions unleashed by the conflict led to a new way at looking at the "Discovery" and its repercussions. This new frame of reference is commonly known as the "Vision of the Vanquished" because it takes into account the point of view the impact of Columbus's voyages on the peoples and cultures of the Americas and Africa. "The Vision of the Vanquished" seeks to balance the assessment of the discovery of America and its consequences. It offers the view the "Discovery" and its sequel the "Conquest" were an unmitigated disaster for the native peoples and culture. To assess the significance of Columbus's achievements properly, it must be understood that he was the instrument of historical forces of which he wasn't aware and that the whole success of the "Discovery" and "Conquest" is tied to the rising world of capitalism and the creation of a global market.

From *A History of Latin America* by Benjamin Keen and Keith Haynes

Questions

1. Why has the celebration of Christopher Columbus's first voyage of discovery become so controversial in recent years?
2. Explain what is meant by the "Vision of the Vanquished."

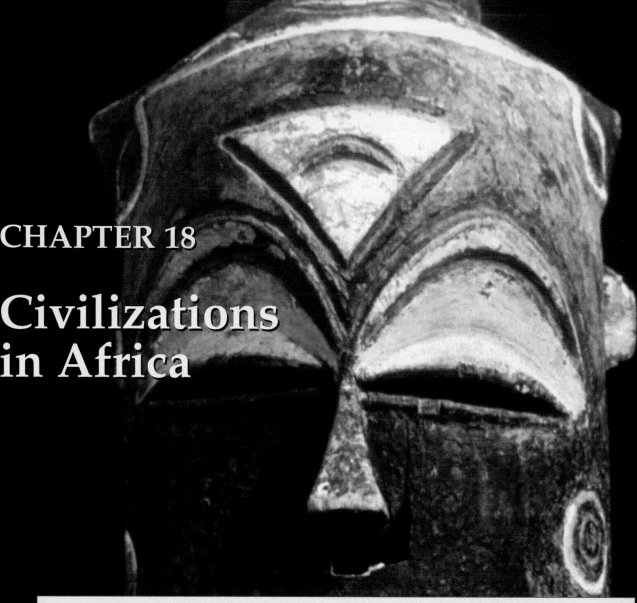

CHAPTER 18

Civilizations in Africa

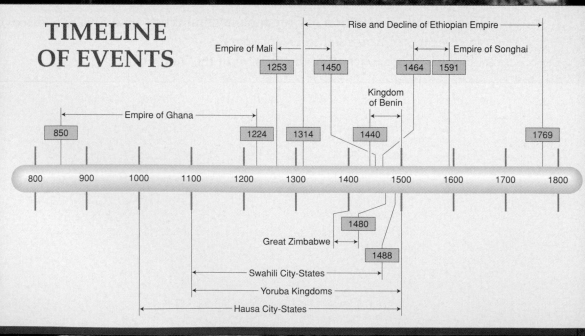

TIMELINE OF EVENTS

Rise and Decline of Ethiopian Empire

Empire of Mali

| 1253 | | 1450 |

Empire of Songhai

| 1464 | 1591 |

Kingdom of Benin

Empire of Ghana

| 850 | | 1224 | 1314 | 1440 | | | 1769 |

| 800 | 900 | 1000 | 1100 | 1200 | 1300 | 1400 | 1500 | 1600 | 1700 | 1800 |

| 1480 |

Great Zimbabwe

| 1488 |

Swahili City-States

Yoruba Kingdoms

Hausa City-States

The period from 1000 to 1500 was a time when many kingdoms were formed in Africa. Throughout the continent, many tribes ruled by chiefs became unified kingdoms. Numerous kingdoms developed into empires. Various cultures, languages, and religions mixed as Africa underwent a period of great cultural diffusion. From 1500 to 1700, many of these kingdoms and empires declined and were replaced by new ones. The coming of European explorers after 1500 would sow the seeds of imperialism that would later end almost all these civilizations by the nineteenth century.

WEST AFRICAN CIVILIZATIONS

The process of kingdom building and their growth into empires was extensive in West Africa. Beginning in the eighth century, **trans-Saharan** trade grew rapidly due to new markets created by the Arab takeover of North Africa. West Africa's wealth of gold and the demand for it from both Arab and European merchants encouraged its peoples to merge into larger, more efficient political units. These kingdoms soon became empires.

Empire of Ghana

The trans-Saharan trade routes crossed through a region formed by the **Soninke** people. They called their ruler **Ghana** or "war chief." Merchants referred to the Soninke region as Ghana, which became the name it was known by as it developed into an independent kingdom by the mid-eighth century. Ghana grew wealthy by taking the goods traders brought through the region. Royal guards protected the roads and trading cities in which merchants met to exchange goods.

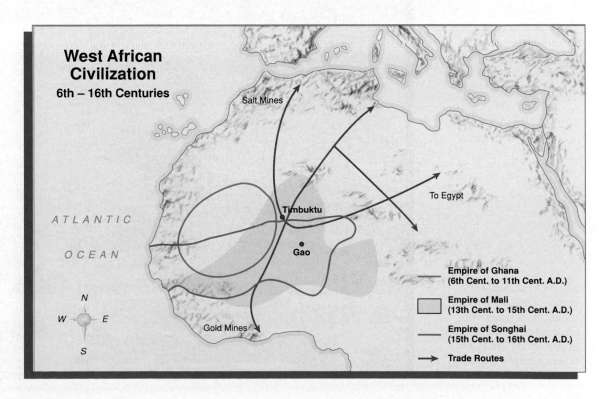

West African Civilization
6th – 16th Centuries

Salt Mines

To Egypt

Timbuktu

ATLANTIC

OCEAN

Gao

N
W E
S

Gold Mines

Empire of Ghana
(6th Cent. to 11th Cent. A.D.)

Empire of Mali
(13th Cent. to 15th Cent. A.D.)

Empire of Songhai
(15th Cent. to 16th Cent. A.D.)

→ Trade Routes

By 800, Ghana had become an empire, controlling trade in the region and collecting taxes from the tribes of surrounding lands. The king limited the supply of gold to maintain its great value. With a large bureaucracy and a huge army, the empire was run efficiently. Ghana's Muslim trading partners, merchants, and advisors to the king gradually converted the monarchs to Islam by the end of the eleventh century. Much of the population practiced **animism**, the belief in the existence of spirits that inhabit natural objects. Even those who had converted continued many animistic practices and beliefs. Islam did however bring a rise in literacy. In order to study the **Koran**, people had to be able to read Arabic.

From 1054 to 1076, the **Almoravids,** who were fanatic Muslim **Berbers** (North African nomads), occupied Ghana. While the Almoravids were eventually driven out, Ghana's economy and trade permanently declined.

Empire of Mali

By 1235, the **Mande** people developed into a new kingdom. No longer under Ghana's control, it became independent and wealthy. Ghana's decline led to a shift in the trade route. A magician, **Sundiata**, became ruler or **mansa**. He soon conquered Ghana and its neighbors, establishing an empire. Sundiata established an efficient bureaucracy to run the government. He encouraged agricultural development through the cultivation and weaving of cotton, and the reestablishment of the gold-salt trade. As Sundiata's empire became a center of trade, it was called **Mali** or "Where the king lives."

Mansa Musa used the empire's great wealth to build up its cities into centers of Islamic learning, in particular, Timbuktu, where a university was established.

After Sundiata's death in 1255, Mali's rulers converted to Islam. They built **mosques**, adapted the Sha'aria (Islamic law), and supported Muslim holy men. Under **Mansa Musa** (1312–1337), Mali's empire expanded. He used the empire's great wealth to build up its cities into centers of Islamic learning, in particular **Timbuktu**, where a university was established. Mansa Musa's efficient administrative bureaucracy resulted in high standards of public morality, law and order, and scholarship. Disputes between his successors after his death, however, led to the decline of central authority.

Songhai Empire

As Mali declined in the fifteenth century, one of the peoples who had been part of its empire, the **Songhai**, broke away to form a new kingdom. They built up an army and began conquering neighboring peoples, forming their own empire. The city of **Gao** became their capital. Under **Sunni Ali** (1464–1492), Songhai became a vast empire. Building a professional army with a riverboat fleet, he captured many important cities, including Timbuktu and **Djenné**, both trade cities with universities.

After Sunni Ali's death in 1492, his son and successor was overthrown by a Muslim revolt protesting the new ruler's mild practice of Islam. The leader of the revolt, **Askia Muhammed**, became the new emperor. He set up an efficient bureaucracy to administrate the empire and created a tax system. Because the Songhai state selected highly competent officials, it was well governed and wealthy. Despite Askia Muhammed's strong establishment of Islam in Songhai's cities, the majority in the countryside remained animists, practicing traditional African religions. Despite serious internal problems between Muslims and animists, Songhai prospered reaching its height under **Askia Daud** (1549–1582).

Songhai, however, overextended itself. It could not control its vast areas. In 1591, Moroccan Arabs, using gunpowder (rifles and cannons) invaded Songhai. Its defeat ended the West African civilizations. The great cities and trade declined in the region. Muslim scholars and merchants moved eastward to the city-states of the **Hausa**.

Hausa City-States

The Hausa kingdoms, located in modern-day northern Nigeria and the Niger Republic, were established by a group of peoples named after the language they spoke. The Hausa city-states developed between 1000 and 1200. After regaining independence from the Songhai Empire, these cities built walls around them and began governing the surrounding villages. City-states such as **Kano**, **Katsina**, and **Zazzau** (later **Zaria**) became major trading states. They grew wealthy, supplying caravans and trading crops grown by local farmers. They also traded in slaves. All the Hausa city-states had similar governments in which local kings ruled but were limited in power by officials and nobles. The constant warfare between Hausa cities prevented them from becoming a powerful empire.

Yoruba Kingdoms

The **Yoruba** people also spoke a similar language. They developed small city-states in modern-day Benin and southwestern Nigeria. Consisting of farming communities, they joined together under local kings. These rulers were religious as well as political leaders. Yoruba chiefs were believed to be descended from the first ruler of the city of **Ife**, who, according to legend, was the first ruler the Creator sent to earth. All the chiefs saw the king of Ife as their religious leader.

Ife and **Oyo** were the most important Yoruba cities. These were surrounded by high walls and protected local farmers, who supplied the cities with surplus food. Yoruba culture produced terra-cotta sculpture and carving in wood and ivory.

Kingdom of Benin

The kingdom of **Benin** was located in the forests southwest of Ife. Like the Yoruba kings, the rulers of Benin also claimed their descent from the first king of Ife. In the fifteenth century, **Ewuare the Great** (1440–1473), **Oba**, or ruler of Benin, made it an important West African state. Building a powerful army, he expanded his control over a huge area extending from the Niger River delta to modern-day Nigeria. Ewuare turned Benin into a wealthy capital city with magnificent buildings and public artwork. It became a center of trade, arts, and learning. Carving in ivory and wood was especially developed at this time. By the 1480s, trade began with **Portugal** for pepper, ivory, animal skins, and slaves. This opened West Africa to later Portuguese imperialism.

EAST AFRICAN CIVILIZATIONS

After the ninth century, the East African coast from **Somalia** southward experienced mass immigration. These groups include **Bantus** from southern Africa and Arabs from the Somalia coast, **Persian Gulf**, and **northwestern India**.

Swahili Civilization

By 1100, the Bantu-speaking people had settled along the east coast of Africa, establishing fishing and farming villages. Trade with East African, Arab, and Persian merchants built them up into seaport cities, which became centers of trade. Bantu and Arabic were blended to create the **Swahili** language.

Arab and Persian merchants traded luxury items for African raw materials such as ivory, gold, animal skins, and rhinoceros horns. By 1300, over thirty-five trading cities covered the eastern coast of the continent.

Between the thirteenth and fifteenth centuries, a distinctive Swahili civilization developed. These cities were Muslim in religion, but they created their own unique artistic and architectural styles. Written in Arabic letters, the Swahili language and culture were distinctive.

The Swahili city-states, like those of Hausa, were Muslim, cosmopolitan, and culturally homogenous, but politically independent. The cities of **Sofala**, in modern-day **Mozambique**, and **Kilwa**, in modern-day **Tanzania**, became the leaders as all the city-states competed with one another economically. Other prominent Swahili cities were **Mogadishu** and **Barana** in modern-day Somalia; **Gedi**, **Pate**, **Malindi**, and **Mombasa** in modern-day **Kenya**; and **Zanzibar** in modern-day Tanzania.

In 1488, the Portuguese began to explore the East African **Congo** in search of trade routes to India. Upon discovering the riches of the Swahili cities, they conquered Kilwa, Sofala, and Mombasa, making them colonies.

Ethiopian Empire

The Kingdom of **Axum** had converted to Orthodox Christianity in the fourth century, later changing its name to **Ethiopia**. Shortly after, it conquered the neighboring empire of **Kush**, which was replaced by a group of smaller kingdoms known as **Nubia**. Soon after, the Nubians were also converted to Orthodox Christianity. The seventh-century expansion of Islam led to the Arab conquest of Persia and Orthodox Christian Egypt, Syria, Palestine, and Nubia. Muslim hostility cut off Ethiopia from trade in the Mediterranean and Middle East, shifting its political center southward. As it became isolated from the Greco-Roman world, it came to see the spread of Islam as a threat.

Ethiopia began to expand into the interior of the African continent in 1314, conquering non-Christian, non-Islamic states to the west. The Ethiopian Orthodox Church sent missionaries to convert the people in the conquered areas while the monarchy imposed a new political order on the region.

Islamic pressure continued with the Muslim conquest of much of western Ethiopia in 1529. Christian Ethiopia was saved from complete destruction in 1541, when its forces under Emperor **Lebna Dengel** (1508–1541) defeated the Muslims with Portuguese assistance. For the next centuries, Ethiopia became isolated, experiencing **xenophobia** or fear of foreigners, civil war between local warlords, and economic stagnation. The authority of the monarchy war also weakened during this period. By 1769, the emperors had become powerless.

SOUTHERN AFRICA

Kingdom of Katanga

The Indian Ocean trade, like that of the trans-Sahara, encouraged Africans to centralize their tribes into kingdoms to better trade and

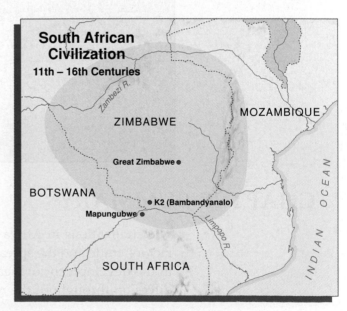

South African Civilization
11th – 16th Centuries

ZIMBABWE
Zambezi R.
MOZAMBIQUE
Great Zimbabwe
BOTSWANA
K2 (Bambandyanalo)
Mapungubwe
Limpopo R.
INDIAN OCEAN
SOUTH AFRICA

compete economically. In the thirteenth century, **Katanga** was the first state in southern Africa to be formed, spreading their ideas of divine monarchy to neighboring peoples. Katanga was developed on the **Rhodesian plateau** in modern-day **Rhodesia.**

Great Zimbabwe

Around 1000, the **Sha'ana** people settled in a fertile, well-watered plateau between the **Zanbezi** and **Limpopo** in modern-day **Zimbabwe**. They established a city, Great Zimbabwe, which grew into an empire due to the gold trade. From 1100 to 1300, it became the capital of a wealthy state.

According to tradition in 1425, **Mutota**, King of **Karanga**, extended his kingdom in southeastern Africa, including Great Zimbabwe. Mutota and his successors were called **Mwanamutapa**, or "lord of the plundered lands," by the conquered **Shona**. From 1425 to 1480 under Mutota and his son **Matope**, Great Zimbabwe became the capital city of a rich and powerful state known as the **Mutapa Empire**. It included most of modern-day Zimbabwe as well as the Zambezi River to the Indian Ocean coast. The Mutapa rulers became unpopular, forcing the conquered people to mine gold for them. After Matope's death in 1480, the empire experienced civil war between powerful **barons**. This resulted in the breakup of the empire into smaller kingdoms.

LINK TO TODAY

Folk singers are nothing new. All civilizations have had them. They preserve history, cultural identity, and customs in their songs. In western Africa, the **griots** are traditional singing entertainers who have preserved these cultural memories. In the days of the empire of Mali, the griots were advisors to kings and the tutors of royalty. Their knowledge of history and custom often made them the best qualified to give rulers advice. All wealthy families had one. Today the griots, both male and female, are respected folk musicians. They sing at weddings, parties, and other social functions. Much like American folk singers, they keep the memories of the national collective past alive.

CHAPTER SUMMARY

The civilizations in Africa during the first Global Age were influenced by two factors: trade and the spread of Islam. In western Africa, the two factors resulted in the development of wealthy trading cities that were responsible for cultural diffusion throughout the region. This was seen in the development of the civilizations of Ghana, Mali, and Songhai. The coast of eastern Africa saw a similar development in the Swahili city-states.

The spread of Islam became an obstacle for Ethiopia, leading to its isolation and decline. In southern Africa, trade led to the development of the powerful Katangan state that conquered Great Zimbabwe, turning it into an empire that oppressed the population. The interference of the Europeans, beginning with the Portuguese, could change all this, opening the continent up to imperialism.

IMPORTANT PEOPLE, PLACES, AND TERMS

KEY TERMS

animism	Soninke	Shona
Koran	Ghana	Mutapa
mansa	Almoravids	Berbers
mosques	Mande	Mali
Oba	Yoruba	Songhai
Swahili	Bantus	xenophobia
Mwanamutapa	Sha'ana	griots
barons	Katanga	

PEOPLE

Sundiata	Askia Daud	Mutota
Mansa Musa	Ewuare the Great	Matope
Askia Muhammed	Emperor Lebna Dengel	Sunni Ali

PLACES

trans-Saharan	Portugal	northwestern India
Ghana	Somalia	Mozambique
Timbuktu	Sofala	Gedi
Gao	Kilwa	Pate
Djenné	Tanzania	Malindi
Hausa	Mogadishu	Mombasa
Kano	Barana	Kenya
Katsina	Congo	Zanzibar
Zazzau	Ethiopia	Kush
Zaria	Nubia	Rhodesia
Bombia	Rhodesian plateau	Zimbabwe
Ife	Zanbezi	Karanga
Oyo	Limpopo	
Benin	Persian Gulf	

EXERCISES FOR CHAPTER 18

MULTIPLE CHOICE

Select the letter of the correct answer.

Base your answers to Questions 1 and 2 on this map and on your knowledge of this chapter.

1. Which civilization was located at the mouth of the Niger River?

   a. Ghana
   b. Congo
   c. Benin
   d. Ashanti

2. Which statement about the civilizations of Africa before 1901 can best be inferred by the information on the map?

   a. Christianity and Islam played a minor role in the development of African civilization.
   b. Most African civilizations existed for only a few years.
   c. Very little interaction occurred between these civilizations.
   d. African civilizations were located in a variety of physical environments.

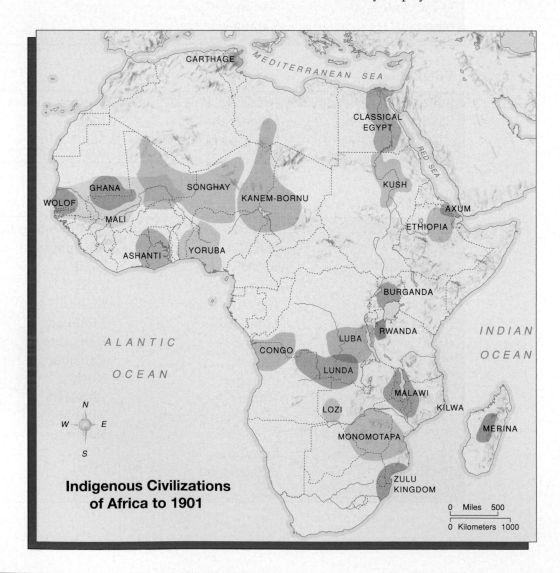

Indigenous Civilizations of Africa to 1901

3. West African kingdoms, such as Mali and Songhai, based their economic systems on

   a. exporting slaves.
   b. agriculture and trade.
   c. commercial fishing.
   d. hunting and gathering.

4. Which West African ruler is incorrectly paired with his state?

   a. Mansa Musa—Mali
   b. Sunni Ali—Songhai
   c. Sundiata—Ghana
   d. Ewuare—Benin

5. One similarity between the Hausa city-state and those of Ancient Greece was

   a. absolute monarchy.
   b. democracy.
   c. warfare between cities.
   d. large overseas empire.

6. All of the following were true of the western African civilizations EXCEPT

   a. Islam was the main religion.
   b. they were centers of trade.
   c. they were cosmopolitan.
   d. they were isolationists.

7. Which is the correct chronological order of the following events?

   1. Decline of Ethiopian Kingdom
   2. Empire of Great Zimbabwe
   3. Conversion of kings of Ghana to Islam
   4. Rise of Hausa city-states

   a. 1 → 2 → 3 → 4
   b. 2 → 4 → 3 → 1
   c. 4 → 2 → 1 → 3
   d. 3 → 4 → 2 → 1

8. The traditional religion of the African peoples was

   a. Christianity.
   b. Judaism.
   c. Islam.
   d. animism.

9. The term *mansa* means

   a. magician.
   b. father.
   c. ruler.
   d. doctor.

10. Alexander the Great, Charlemagne, and Mansa Musa were all responsible for which of the following?

    a. Making religious reforms
    b. Expanding their kingdoms
    c. Creating cultural diffusion
    d. Allowing greater freedoms

11. Which western African civilization was Timbuktu originally capital city of?

    a. Songhai
    b. Ghana
    c. Mali
    d. Benin

12. Which of the following civilizations did not benefit from the spread of Islam in Africa?

    a. Mali
    b. Ghana
    c. Great Zimbabwe
    d. Ethiopia

13. Which of the following pairs were the "forest civilizations"?

    a. Swahili and Mali
    b. Yoruba and Benin
    c. Yoruba and Katanga
    d. Ethiopia and Great Zimbabwe

14. Swahili is a combination of which two languages?

    a. Bantu and Arabic
    b. Hausa and Portuguese
    c. Yoruba and Arabic
    d. Bantu and Persian

15. Which of the following best completes the outline?

    1. Establishment of trade routes
    2. Expansion of military to protect trade
    3. Creation of efficient bureaucracy
    4. _____

    a. Creation of tax collection system
    b. Building of universities and schools
    c. Military expansion of empire
    d. Support of arts and culture

16. Which European nation was the first to become involved in Africa?

    a. Spain
    b. Portugal
    c. England
    d. France

17. Which was responsible for starting the growth of trade in West Africa?

    a. Trans-Saharan trade
    b. Mediterranean trade
    c. Indian Ocean trade
    d. Atlantic Ocean trade

18. Which was responsible for starting the growth of trade in East Africa?

    a. Trans-Saharan trade
    b. Mediterranean trade
    c. Indian Ocean trade
    d. Atlantic Ocean trade

19. The dynasty that made Great Zimbabwe an empire was the

    a. Almoravid.
    b. Songhai.
    c. Mutapa.
    d. Hausa.

20. All of the following reasons explain the decline of African civilization EXCEPT

    a. European imperialism.
    b. decline of trade.
    c. civil war.
    d. natural disasters.

ESSAYS FOR CHAPTER 18

1. How did the spread of Islam influence the development of African civilizations? Show one way it was influenced throughout two different African cultures.

2. What role did geography play in the development of African civilization? Describe two ways in which the land and its location shaped the development of an African culture.

3. Individual leaders have had an enormous impact on the development of their people. Choose two African leaders from the First Global Age.

4. What influence did African civilizations have on each other? Select two examples showing one African culture's influence on another.

5. Imagine you are a company representative for a European trading firm visiting an African city in the First Global Age. You are keeping a record of all you see in order to report back to your superiors. List four observations about African society in that place. Be specific about the city and people in it.

This task is based on the accompanying documents. Some of these documents have been edited for the purposes of this task. This task is designed to test your ability to work with historical documents. As you analyze the documents, take into account both the source of each document and the author's point of view.

Directions: Read the following documents and answer the questions after each document. Use the information in the reading and this chapter in writing your answers.

Document #1

MUHAMMAD IBN ABDULLAH, *OBSERVATIONS OF KILWA* (1355)

Then I set off by sea . . . for the land of the Swahili and the town of Kilwa, which is in the land of Zanj. We arrived at Mombasa, a large island . . . quite separate from the mainland. It grows bananas, lemons, and oranges. The people also gather a fruit . . . which looks like an olive. It has a nut like an olive, but its taste is very sweet. The people do not engage in agriculture, but import grain from the Swahili [in the interior]. The greater part of their diet is bananas and fish. They follow the Shafiite rite [one of the four schools of law], and are devout, chaste, and virtuous.

Their mosques are very strongly constructed of wood. Beside the door of each mosque are one or two wells, one or two cubits deep. They draw water from them with a wooden vessel which is fixed on to the end of a thin stick, a cubit long. The earth round the mosque and the well is stamped flat. Anyone who wishes to enter the mosque first washes his feet; beside the door is a piece of heavy material for drying them. . . . Everyone here goes barefoot.

We spent a night on the island and then set sail for Kiilwa, the principal town on the coast, the greater part of whose inhabitants are Zanj of very black complexion. Their faces scarred. . . . A merchant told me that Solfala is half a month's march from Kilwa, and that between Sofala and Yufi in the country of the Limin is a month's march. Powdered gold is brought from Yufi to Solfala.

Kilwa is one of the most beautiful and well-constructed towns in the world. The whole of it is elegantly built.

From *Muslim Societies in African History*, Translated by David Robinson

Questions

1. Select two observations made by the Arab traveler about fourteenth-century eastern Africa. Show whether each is positive or negative.
2. Based on the observations you selected, was the author's overall impression favorable? Give two reasons why.

Document #2

AHMAD BABA, *VIEWS ON SLAVERY* (1597)

[Y]ou should be aware that the reason for enslavement is unbelief, and the unbelievers of the Land of the Blacks [Sudan] are like any other unbelievers in this regards—Jews, Christians, Persians, Berbers, or those whose continued adherence to unbelief may rightly be owned, whoever he is, as opposed to those of all groups who converted to Islam first, such as the people of Bornu, Kano, Songhay, Katsina, Gobir, and Mali. . . . They are free Muslims who may not be enslaved under any circumstances.

From *Muslim Societies in African History*, Translated by David Robinson

Questions

1. Why does the author justify the slavery of non-Muslims? Give two reasons for his argument.
2. What does this reading reveal about the attitudes of Muslims towards non-Muslims in Africa in the sixteenth century? Identify two beliefs that are implied.

Document #3   **ABD L-QASIM BIN AHMAD AL-ZIANI, CORRESPONDENCE (c. 1700)**

The Sultan had clothes and weapons distributed to the Blacks, appointed their leaders, and gave them building materials. He ordered them to build their camp, cultivate their fields and raise their children. The Sultan took personal charge of the boys and girls at the age of 10. Some of the children were placed for a year in apprenticeship to masons, carpenters or other builders, while others were employed as workers. The second year, they were trained as mule caravan leaders. The third year they learned construction. The fourth year they learned horsemanship, while the fifth year was devoted to perfecting horsemanship and firing muskets from the mounted position. At the age of 16 young men were put in regiments under their commanders, and married to young Black girls who had learned cooking, housekeeping and washing in the sovereign's palace. The prettiest girls also learned music. When their musical education was finished, they received clothes and a dowry, and were led to their husbands while their marriages were inscribed in a register.

The newly wed had to give their children over: the boys to military service, the girls to service the palace. This system of recruitment lasted until the end of the reign of Ismail. Each year the Sultan went to the camp and led the appropriate children away. The military register of the Black army numbered 150,000 men, of whom 70,000 were at the camp, 25,000 at another camp, and the remainder in various fortresses which the Sultan had built from Oudjda to the Oued Noun [the northeastern to the most southwestern point of the Moroccan shore] . . . [the fortresses] numbered 76.

From *Muslim Societies in African History*, Translated by David Robinson

Questions

1. What was the purpose behind Sultan Ismail's military recruitment system? Give two benefits of the system.
2. What does this reading tell the historian about the way the Arabs ruled North Africa? Give two reasons why this was or was not an effective way to rule over others.

Document #4   TRADE ROUTES OF AFRICA (1000–1500)

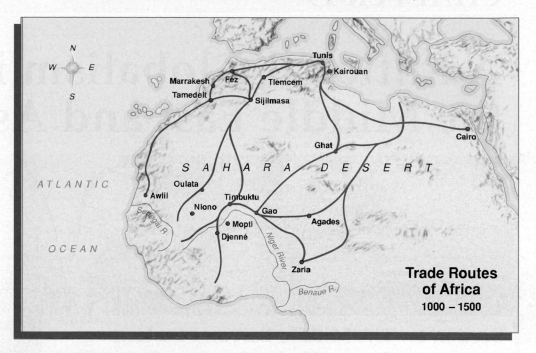

Questions

1. According to this map, which areas on the African continent were the most active for commerce? Identify two areas of trade.
2. Show two ways that geography influenced which areas were most active commercially.

Document #5   THE OLD MOSQUE AT TIMBUKTU

Questions

1. What does the illustration above show us about western African civilization? Use two features of the mosque or the surrounding city in your answer.
2. What connection can you make between the city and its geographical environment?

CHAPTER 19

Additional Globalism in the Middle East and Asia

Section 1—The Middle East and Eastern
        Europe Under Ottoman Rule 443

Section 2—The Muslims in India 447

Section 3—The Ming Dynasty in China 451

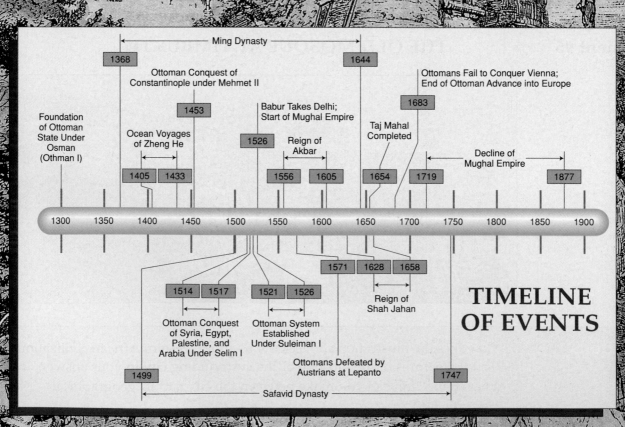

Ming Dynasty

1368

Ottoman Conquest of
Constantinople under Mehmet II

1644

Ottomans Fail to Conquer Vienna;
End of Ottoman Advance into Europe

1453

1683

Babur Takes Delhi;
Start of Mughal Empire

Foundation
of Ottoman
State Under
Osman
(Othman I)

Ocean Voyages
of Zheng He

1526

Reign of
Akbar

Taj Mahal
Completed

Decline of
Mughal Empire

1405   1433

1556   1605

1654   1719

1877

1300   1350   1400   1450   1500   1550   1600   1650   1700   1750   1800   1850   1900

1571   1628   1658

1514   1517

1521   1526

Reign of
Shah Jahan

**TIMELINE
OF EVENTS**

Ottoman Conquest
of Syria, Egypt,
Palestine, and
Arabia Under Selim I

Ottoman System
Established
Under Suleiman I

Ottomans Defeated by
Austrians at Lepanto

1499

1747

Safavid Dynasty

442

SECTION 1

The Middle East and Eastern Europe Under Ottoman Rule

For 600 years, the **Ottoman Empire** was a force in world history. It began with a tribe of **Turks**, who were a nomadic people of **Mongolian** origin in **Central Asia**, and developed into an empire that, at its height, dominated the Middle East, eastern Europe, and northern Africa. Even though the Ottoman Empire was a Turkish empire, most of its diplomats and specialists were Greek, its military officers and elite troops, known as the **Janissaries,** were Balkan Slavs, and its merchants were Armenians and Jews. Islamic in religion, its court ceremonies and architecture were Byzantine, its wealth was Egyptian, its letters were Arabic, and its art and fashions were Persian. A multicultural society, its

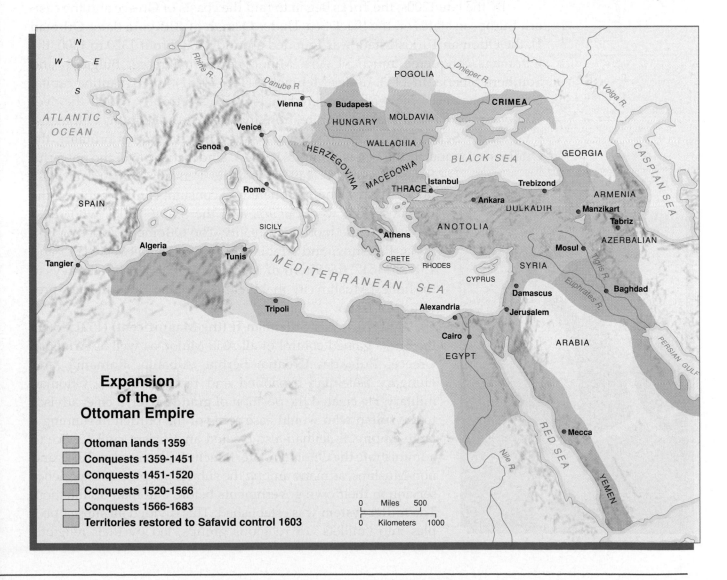

Expansion of the Ottoman Empire

- Ottoman lands 1359
- Conquests 1359-1451
- Conquests 1451-1520
- Conquests 1520-1566
- Conquests 1566-1683
- Territories restored to Safavid control 1603

0   Miles   500

0   Kilometers   1000

The Middle East and Eastern Europe Under Ottoman Rule **443**

local lords or **pashas** could be repressive, but were generally tolerant. The emperor or **sultan** ruled the Ottoman state from the old Byzantine capital city of **Constantinople** in Asia Minor. The height of Ottoman power and conquest was from the 1300s, when it began its successful domination of eastern Europe, until the late eighteenth century, when the western European powers began using their superior weaponry to push the Turks out of that region.

Rise of the Ottoman Empire

The Ottomans were one of many nomadic Turkish tribes who wandered the Steppe of Central Asia in the ninth century. The Turks became warriors for the Abbasid Caliphs of Baghdad (see Chapter 7), who converted them to Islam. The Turks proved excellent fighters and were soon recruited throughout Asia. Under the Persians, they learned political organization. The Turks soon started developing into small states throughout Asia Minor. The most successful of these were the **Seljuks**, who gained part of the Byzantine Empire in **Asia Minor** in 1071 after surprising Byzantine forces. Their occupation forced Byzantium to ask western Europe for assistance. This led to the first **Crusade** (see Chapter 6).

By the late 1200s, the Turks began to raid the coasts of Greece and the eastern European states on the Black Sea. Under **Osman of Bithynia** (later **Othman I**), the Ottoman Turkish state was founded around 1300. From 1320 to 1400, the Ottomans conquered much of Asia Minor, northern Greece, Bulgaria, and Southern Siberia. In 1453, under **Mehmet II** (1451–1481), the Byzantine capital city of Constantinople was conquered in 1453. This officially ended the over 1000-year-old Eastern Roman Empire, bringing great prestige to the Ottomans.

Under **Selim I** (1511–1521), known as **the Grim** due to his brutality, the Ottomans conquered the Persian Empire in 1514. Under the rule of the powerful

Sultan Mehmet II.

Safavid dynasty (1499–1747), the Persians were never fully under Turkish control. There was constant conflict between the Persians, who were *Shi'ites*, and the *Sunni* Turks, who ruled Persia in name more than reality. The Ottomans added Egypt, Syria, Palestine, and Arabia to the Empire between 1515 and 1517. In 1517, the **Sherif of Mecca** gave Sultan Selim the keys to the holiest Muslim city, making the Ottoman Turks the new protectors of Islam.

By 1520, under **Suleiman II (the Magnificent)** (1521–1566), the Turks gained control of all Asia Minor, as well as Armenia, Greece, Bulgaria, Croatia, Serbia, Albania, Romania, and Hungary. Suleiman expanded and reorganized the Ottoman military. He created the position of **grand vizier**, a chief advisor to the sultan who would ease some of the burden in running a large empire. Suleiman also created an efficient civil service to administrate the Ottoman state. It included many non-Turks and non-Muslims, as many among the subject people had experience serving in their own governments before Ottoman domination. The **millet system** was established. This divided all subject peoples into "millets" or religious groups, led by their religious

Suleiman II created an efficient civil service to administrate the Ottoman state.

leaders. All Muslims, Turkish and non-Turkish, were directly under the sultan, who was responsible for seeing that Islamic law or the **Sha'aria** was followed. In cases of conflict between Muslim and non-Muslim, Islamic law also prevailed.

Around 1670, the Ottoman Empire reached the height of its power and size. With the acquisition of northwestern Africa, it had grown vast. The first Ottoman defeat by the Austrians in 1571 at **Lepanto** was followed by the failure to capture Vienna in 1683. These two defeats led to the end of the empire's expansion. Having fallen behind western Europe technologically, the Ottoman armies could no longer advance further into Europe. This began the period of the Empire's greatest decline.

Decline of Ottoman Power (1683–1744)

By the late seventeenth century, it was clear that the Ottoman Empire had grown as large as it could. Defeats by Austria ended the Ottoman advance into Europe. By the eighteenth century, the Austrians slowly began to drive the Ottomans out of Hungary and central Europe. They were joined by the Russians in the nineteenth Century, who also took advantage of the Turkish military weakness. By the middle of the nineteenth century, the Ottomans would be known as the "**sick man of Europe**."

Many historians believe that the reasons for the decline are more complex than the lack of modern weapon technology. Some argue that the sultans were no longer warriors but had become absolute monarchs who were out of touch with current events and real problems. The Ottoman Imperial Court had become too isolated and interested in luxurious living. The grand viziers had become the real rulers of the Empire, freeing up the sultans to pursue a life of pleasure. These advisors often followed policies that benefited themselves rather than the Empire. Other historians believe that the constant struggle to control the Safavids in Persia, who continued to resist Ottoman rule, while continuing to expand into central Europe, resulted in a constant war on two fronts. Still others maintain that the continued warfare greatly hurt trade, making these conflicts extremely costly and creating discontent among the Empire's wealthier residents. Another argument is that the western European exploration and discoveries in the New World (the Americas) provided new and plentiful sources of raw materials, especially gold and silver. This made these resources cheaper, greatly hurting the Turkish economy by making the Ottoman Empire far less important in international trade. Finally, the heavily traditional military, which had been so successful for centuries, would not accept that new technology and organization were needed for their armies to defeat those of western Europe. It is likely that all these factors played a role in the Empire's decline.

The eighteenth century saw a rise in rebellions by subject peoples, particularly in eastern Europe, to which the local Ottoman authorities reacted harshly. This only resulted in more resistance and rebellion. The European Powers, in particular Austria and Russia, took advantage of the discontent by secretly funding rebellions and then openly interfering on behalf of the Christian Europeans. This pattern continued into the 1800s, resulting in the creation of new independent eastern European nations by the end of the nineteenth century.

Ottoman Society

The Ottoman Empire was a mix of many different conquered peoples under Turkish rule. These groups were allowed to practice their religions freely provided they remained peaceful and paid their taxes. The Ottoman government provided order and protection throughout its vast Empire. They also regulated trade both within and outside the Empire.

While generally tolerant, life under the Ottomans could be difficult, especially for non-Muslims. For example, in addition to taxes collected annually, the Ottomans demanded a **"boy tribute"** from each home every three years. This was the practice of taking the strongest and best-looking non-Muslim boys from throughout the Empire to serve in the sultan's elite

The Janissaries, shown in this picture, were the Sultan's elite troops and were made up of "boy tributes" from non-Muslim homes.

troops, the Janissaries, or in his personal **harem** as boy sex slaves (Islamic law forbade Muslims from being enslaved). The boys were taken from their families, taught Turkish, and adopted new identities as personal slaves to the sultan. Local Ottoman officials often had similar practices for enslaving non-Muslim girls. This was sometimes beneficial for the children of very poor families, but it was generally hated by most non-Muslim subjects.

The central government in Constantinople ruled through local officials and nobles throughout the empire. Often the government had little or no control over what the local rulers or pashas actually did. This resulted in varying qualities of local government. The sultan's court, known as the **Sublime Porte** or **High Gate**, became a center of trade, learning, and the arts. It also served as a model for Ottoman cities to follow.

Most Ottoman towns were multicultural centers of trade. Strict curfews in the evening made crime rare. Zoning laws kept the communities apart, especially at night. The Ottoman military saw to it that violence did not erupt between the groups. This became known as the **Pax Ottomanica**. Cities in the Empire lacked public art and architecture, reflecting private rather than public life.

In the Ottoman Empire, most of the merchants were either Christian or Jewish. Along with other non-Muslim minorities, they were known as *dhimmis*. The majority of Turks were farmers or in the military. Due to their previous experiences running governments or businesses before Ottoman domination, many Christian non-Turks, in particular the Greeks, served as diplomats and in important government positions. Ironically, it was the non-Turkish subject peoples that ran a good part of the Empire's economy and government. Even though Turkish nobles held the greatest power, most were at least partly dependent on their non-Turkish subjects.

SECTION 2

The Muslims in India

As we continue with this chapter, there are two questions to ask about a very famous building:

1. If you had one day to visit a building in India, which would it be?

2. What is the best known Islamic building in the world?

The answer to both questions is the **Taj Mahal**. It was constructed in the 1600s by a ruler of the **Mughal Empire**. This was one of several Muslim empires in world history. Indeed, we have seen the growth of Muslim empires in previous chapters. You have just finished reading about the Ottomans. You also learned about the Umayyad, Abbasid, and Safavid empires. All of these empires covered territory from Spain in western Europe, through North Africa, and as far as the Middle East. We now move to explore an empire that dominated India and all of South Asia, that of the Mughals.

The Mughal Dynasty

For approximately 300 years, from 1206 to 1526, most of South Asia was under the rule of a kingdom known as the Delhi Sultanate. Controlled by a succession of thirty-three different sultans, this kingdom was divided into many religious and political factions. This disunity was a major reason for the Sultanate's end, coming as the result of a crushing defeat at the battle of Panipat, April 21, 1526. The victor was Babur, who was now to establish the Mughal Empire. Hailing as a Muslim from central Asia, Babur himself was a Mughal or Mongol, a descendant of Genghis Khan. Although he now controlled Delhi, the seat of the former imperial power, he was uncomfortable with the city's hot weather patterns. He left to live in the cooler climate of Kashmir, in the northwest. While his son Humayun proved to be weak and inept, the same could not be said of his grandson Akbar.

Akbar, meaning "the great one," ruled from 1556 to 1605. This time period could be labeled a "golden age" due to Akbar's popularity, his ruling style, and the achievements during his reign. Although a Muslim, he was a believer in religious freedom and tolerance. He tried to undo some of the harshness that previously had existed at times between Muslims and Hindus. Among his many wives, for instance, were Hindu, Muslim, and Christian women. Another example of his tolerance could be seen in his abolition of a pilgrim tax on visitors to holy places as well as the *jizya*, a tax on non-Muslims. Many Hindus were appointed to high government positions and helped in the running of an efficient civil service.

Akbar's cultural achievements included the creation of a great library. It contained Muslim and Hindu texts. **Persian** was the official court language, but most common people spoke **Hindi**, a combination of Persian and local dialects. Hindi is widely spoken today in India. **Urdu** was another blended language, with elements of Arabic, Persian, and Hindi. It is at present the official language of Pakistan. Magnificent artwork was evidenced in book illustrations, particularly in paintings described as Persian miniatures.

Babur was a descendant of Genghis Khan.

Historians can note the preceding descriptions as peaceful accomplishments under Akbar, but they also recognize that he was a warlike figure. He transformed the Mughal Empire into a military power. His armies were equipped with cannons and other weaponry that enabled him to expand his territorial holdings. By the time of his death, the empire included most of present-day Pakistan, India, and Bangladesh.

Akbar the Great.

Successors to Akbar

Three of the successors to Akbar were to have a significant impact on the empire. His son Jahangir was a weak ruler, who was willing to let his wife be the real power behind the throne. His wife, **Nur Jahan**, was a talented poet, a dress designer, and a skillful politician. She hoped to rule through a son. Yet when he turned against his father, Jahangir, she lost faith in him and supported another son. Khusrau, the first son, won support from the Sikhs. At the time, this religious group grew embittered toward Jahangir and Nur Jahan. These two rejected the tolerant policies of Akbar and wanted to have Islam become the dominant religion in the realm. Tension was thus to develop between the Mughals and the Sikhs.

Shah Jahan, the second son, was in power from 1628 to 1658; he was more willing to continue the policies of his grandfather Akbar. He increased the borders of the empire and was known to have a fondness for large buildings. He made **Delhi** into a major urban center. His most famous structure, however, was near the city of **Agra**, south of Delhi. This was the site of the Taj Mahal. It was built as a memorial to his wife, **Mumtaz Mahal**.

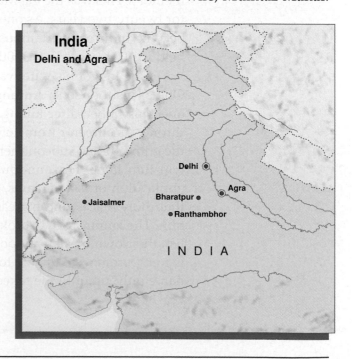

India
Delhi and Agra

Delhi ◉

Agra

● Jaisalmer   Bharatpur ●

● Ranthambhor

I N D I A

Shah Jahan.

Shah Jahan had the Taj Mahal built in memory of his wife.

A Persian princess who bore Shah Jahan fourteen children, she died at the age of thirty-eight. Heartbroken at her death, he ordered a tomb to be built in her memory. This was the Taj Mahal, opened in 1654 after undergoing construction for twenty-two years. As one of the most beautiful buildings in the world, it has become India's most famous tourist attraction. Festivals and celebrations were held in 2004 to mark its 350th "birthday."

The loss of his wife was not the only family event to sadden Shah Jahan. One of his four sons, **Aurangzeb**, proved to be harsh and ruthless. He imprisoned his father, after killing another brother in a bloody civil war to gain the throne. As emperor from 1658 to 1707, he expanded the empire to cover almost the entire Indian subcontinent. Aurangzeb's military exploits, however, did not win him fame. His unpopularity was the result of such policies as his strict application of Islamic laws, oppressive actions against Hindus and Sikhs and their holy places, and increasing taxes. In due time, few subjects felt loyalty to him. The empire slowly broke apart, with Hindus and Sikhs beginning to establish their own breakaway political units. After Aurangzeb's death, the succeeding emperors were unable to restore unity in the empire. The empire existed in name only, up until the takeover by the British in the 1800s.

The Ming Dynasty in China

As we saw in Chapter 13, China was ruled by foreigners, the Mongols, during the Yuan dynasty (1279–1368). Their presence ended with a rebellion by a native Chinese peasant. That man, **Hongwu**, became the first emperor of a new dynasty, the **Ming**. This restoration of native rule instilled pride in the Chinese people. Although he continued to rule from the Yuan capital city of Nanjing, Hongwu embarked on policies that improved life for the Chinese in ways that were not possible under Yuan control. He introduced agricultural changes that made for added rice production. Tax reforms led to resettlement of land previously abandoned. Urban centers grew as did the nation's total population. His admiration of Confucianism was seen in his promotion of Confucian moral ideas and the reintroduction of the civil service examination system. In spite of these welcome changes from the Yuan era, Hongwu turned into a feared emperor in later years. He suspected conspiracies against him and ordered the deaths of hundreds of government officers. With his death in 1398, his son, **Yonglo**, succeeded to the throne.

The reign of Yonglo was noteworthy for both *domestic* (things happening inside China) and foreign activities. Inside China, the production of fine porcelain reached new heights. Blue and white porcelain vases, for example, achieved renown worldwide and became major exports. Yonglo moved the capital to its present location, **Beijing**. It was here that he built the magnificent complex to be known as the **Forbidden City**. Constructed between 1404 and 1420, it was a walled palace consisting of several ornate buildings and thousands of rooms. Foreigners and common people were not allowed to enter its grounds because it was lived in solely by the emperor, his family, and his royal court.

Although Yonglo did not want foreigners in Beijing or anywhere else in China, he was willing to trade with them. He was curious about the world outside China, wanting to make it aware of Ming wealth and power. In addition, in his vision of China as the major empire in East Asia, and as the "Middle kingdom" at the center of the earth, he also sought tribute payment from other nearby societies. Consequently, between 1405 and 1433, China sent seven expeditions overseas. These were the most impressive sea voyages of any country for these times. They reached such areas as the Middle East, Africa, India, and Southeast Asia. They were led by a Chinese Muslim, Zheng He (pronounced "jung huh"). As a result of his trips, Chinese products such as porcelain, silk, and gold reached faraway shores. Some European traders themselves were eventually permitted to come to China and work only in three designated coastal ports. A few missionaries were also allowed in, including the Italian Jesuit Matteo Ricci. He learned Chinese and was able to write detailed accounts about the Ming.

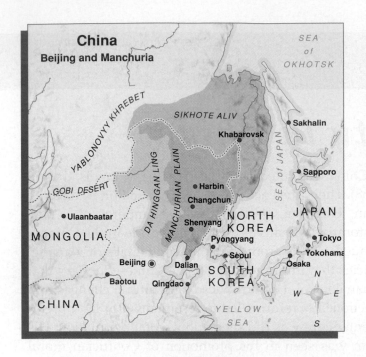

China
Beijing and Manchuria

SEA of OKHOTSK

YABLONOVYY KHREBET

SIKHOTE ALIV

Sakhalin

Khabarovsk

GOBI DESERT

DA HINGGAN LING

MANCHURIAN PLAIN

SEA of JAPAN

Sapporo

• Harbin
Changchun

• Ulaanbaatar

Shenyang

NORTH
KOREA

JAPAN

MONGOLIA

Pyongyang

• Tokyo
Yokohama

Beijing ◉
Dalian

• Seoul

Osaka

Baotou
Qingdao •

SOUTH
KOREA

N

W   E

CHINA

YELLOW
SEA

S

Strangely enough, by the middle of the 1400s, China's overseas expeditions came to a halt. In addition, her manufacturing processes did not attain a high degree of industrialization. How can all this be explained? Historians have suggested the following reasons: (1) The voyages had become very expensive to maintain. (2) Merchants were held in low esteem on the Confucian scale of occupations. Commercial activities violated Confucian ideals. (3) China was basically a farming or agrarian society. (4) The Chinese felt they were self-sufficient and did not need anything from other countries. This attitude also reflected the traditional Chinese view of itself as a superior society.

By the opening years of the 1600s, the Ming dynasty grew weak. Internal wars, ineffective emperors, high taxes, and struggles against the Mongols in the north were the chief causes. Eventually, the Ming fell to the **Manchus**, foreign invaders from **Manchuria**. The Ming were to go down in history as the last native Chinese-controlled dynasty. The Manchus were to be the second and last group of foreigners to maintain a dynasty. They would rule from 1644 until the revolution of 1911.

LINKS TO TODAY
Have You Ever Been to a Bazaar?

Long before shopping malls, people bought and exchanged goods at market places. In the Ancient and Medieval Middle East, these were known as **bazaars**. The bazaars of the Ottoman Empire were the most famous during the First Global Age due to the enormous variety of products available from all over the world. The multicultural nature of the Turkish Empire was reflected in the goods available in its markets. Foods, spices, carpets, furniture, jewelry, art, books, animals, and human slaves of every kind were available. Merchants were able to make both business contacts and profits at the bazaar. Residents and tourists could find any item. A system of currency exchange was established making it possible for all travelers to trade freely. In the evening, the bazaars closed, and watchmen protected the stalls from robbers. It was a system that would be imitated in western Europe after the Crusades and the revival of trade in the Late Middle Ages. The present-day shopping malls are the modern successors to these ancient marketplaces that were developed so efficiently in the Ottoman world.

War and the Taj Mahal

It is one of the ironies of history that the most well-known Muslim building in the world, the Taj Mahal, is in a country, India, whose major religion is Hinduism. Because India is a democracy, there is no attempt by its government to interfere with or suppress the practice of Islam. Indeed, India recognizes the Taj as its greatest tourist attraction as well as an integral part of its history. Such recognition was shown in an interesting way during a war in 1971. India was helping East Pakistan in its rebellion against the nation of Pakistan. Indian troops were fighting Pakistani troops in this region, which would soon become the new nation Bangladesh. India was afraid that Pakistan might fly planes over the Taj, and bomb it, so India installed a huge camouflage covering over the Taj and placed anti-aircraft guns near it. Although Pakistan never tried to attack the Taj, the situation was a most unusual one. Here was a majority Hindu nation protecting a famous Muslim building against possible attack by a Muslim nation!

Is the Forbidden City Still Forbidden?

Entry to the Forbidden City is no longer forbidden. Foreigners and ordinary Chinese can enter freely today. When the communists took over China in 1949, the Forbidden City was declared open. Its former exclusionary status was criticized as representing an oppressive feature of the past. Mao Zedong, the first communist head of state, actually proclaimed China's new political status in 1949 from the entrance to this famous walled palace complex. In front of the entrance is a huge open area, about as large as a football field, called Tiananmen Square. Major parades are held here, surrounded by government buildings and Mao's tomb. With Beijing as China's capital today, the site of the Forbidden City and Tiananmen Square may be considered to be the very "center of the center." Every modern-day American president who has ever traveled to China, starting with former President Richard M. Nixon, has always visited this site.

CHAPTER SUMMARY

The empires described in this chapter covered territories in three continents. They ruled diverse populations whose lives need to be examined in order to understand the nations that make up these territories in our own world.

The Ottoman Turks began as nomadic warriors, developing an empire that extended from Persia to central Europe in one direction and from northern Africa to southern Ukraine in another. At its height, it was a multicultural society that, while dominated by the Turks, was fairly tolerant and acted as an agent of cultural diffusion. Its inability to make internal political, economic, and social changes, as well as military overextension due to the warlike imperial nature of

Turkish culture, led to its stagnation in the seventeenth century and its decline through the eighteenth and nineteenth centuries. Its weakness and vulnerability made it an attractive target for European imperial powers. The declining Ottoman Empire would become a source of contention between them, especially Austria and Russia in the nineteenth century.

As the two most populous nations in the world today, China and India have long histories that need to be understood. Both the Ming and Mughal periods of rule left legacies that remain with their respective heirs. These can be categorized in many ways—cultural, economic, and political to name a few. The Ming were native Chinese who overthrew outsiders and promoted unity while being remembered for the admired production of porcelain. The overseas expeditions of Zheng He can be recalled as China today trades all over the world, with many of her products finding their way into the United States. The Mughals originated from outside of India; nevertheless, they brought a sense of unity to an area that was larger than western Europe. Their being Muslim accounts in part for Pakistan being a majority Muslim nation today, while the Taj Mahal remains as one of the most recognized structures in our contemporary world.

IMPORTANT PEOPLE, PLACES, AND TERMS

KEY TERMS	PEOPLE	PLACES
Janissaries	Osman (Othman I)	Central Asia
Ottoman Empire	Mehmet II (the Conqueror)	Asia Minor
millet system	Sellim I (the Grim)	Constantinople
Turks	Suleiman I (the Magnificent)	Greece
Seljuks	Sherif of Mecca	Bulgaria
Mongolian	Humayun	Serbia
sultan	Akbar	Romania
harem	Shah Jahan	Hungary
bazaar	Aurangzeb	Croatia
Abassids	Nur Jahan	Syria
boy tribute	Mumtaz Mahal	Egypt
grand vizier	Hongwu	Palestine
"Pax Ottomanica"	Yonglo	Persia
"sick man of Europe"	Zheng He	Armenia
"Sublime Porte"	Matteo Ricci	Austria
pashas		Makkah
Crusade		Lepanto
Sha'aria		Panipat
Mughal Empire		Delhi
Hindi		Taj Mahal
Urdu		Agra
Persian		Beijing
Safavid dynasty		Forbidden City
Ming dynasty		Manchuria
Manchus		

EXERCISES FOR CHAPTER 19

MULTIPLE CHOICE

Select the letter of the correct answer.

1. The Ottoman Empire was

    a. ethnocentric.
    b. isolationist.
    c. multicultural.
    d. democratic.

2. Which is the correct chronological order of the following sultans?

    1. Mehmet II (the Conqueror)
    2. Suleiman I (the Magnificent)
    3. Osman (Othman I)
    4. Selim I (the Grim)

    a. 3 → 1 → 4 → 2
    b. 1 → 2 → 3 → 4
    c. 4 → 1 → 2 → 3
    d. 2 → 1 → 4 → 3

3. King Louis XIV of France, Peter the Great of Russia, and Suleiman the Magnificent of the Ottoman Empire were all considered absolute rulers because they

    a. broke from the Roman Catholic Church.
    b. helped feudal lords build secure castles.
    c. instituted programs that provided more power to their parliament.
    d. determined government policies without the consent of their people.

4. All of the following were reasons for decline of the Ottoman Empire from the seventeenth to eighteenth centuries EXCEPT

    a. use of superior weapons by Europeans.
    b. military overextension on two fronts.
    c. heavy tax burden of population from cultural welfare.
    d. constant war with the Europeans over Asia Minor.

5. Which is the correct chronological order of the following events?

    1. Ottoman Conquest of Constantinople
    2. Ottoman Sultan given keys to Mecca
    3. Battle of Lepanto
    4. Ottomans became warriors for Abassid Caliphs

    a. 2 → 3 → 4 → 1
    b. 1 → 2 → 3 → 4
    c. 3 → 4 → 1 → 2
    d. 4 → 1 → 2 → 3

6. At one point in time, the Ottomans and the Mughals both controlled land in

    a. Africa.
    b. Asia.
    c. Europe.
    d. North America.

7. What effect did the Mughals have on the territory they ruled?

    a. Parliamentary republics were established.
    b. Unity was accomplished under one language.
    c. Muslim culture was dominant in some parts.
    d. Hinduism was dominant in the north.

8. Which heading best completes this partial outline?

    I. _____

    A. Maurya
    B. Gupta
    C. Delhi Sultanate

    a. Empires of India
    b. Latin American Civilizations
    c. Empires of the Fertile Crescent
    d. Dynasties of China

9. "I am tolerant of beliefs, attitudes and opinions that differ from my own." Which of the following would most likely accept this assertion?

   a. Pope Leo X
   b. Akbar
   c. Shi Huangdi
   d. Oliver Cromwell

10. The cities of Agra, Jerusalem, and Makkah have sites of religious importance built during periods of rule by

   a. Jews.   c. Muslims.
   b. Christians.   d. Sikhs.

11. The greatest contributor to creating a sense of nationalism in the Mughal Empire was

   a. Aurangzeb.   c. Shah Jahan.
   b. Babur.   d. Akbar.

12. Which statement would most likely be spoken by a Hindu and not by a Muslim?

   a. "I will go to Makkah to participate in the Haj."
   b. "I appreciate the acceptance of diversity shown by Akbar."
   c. "I cannot eat any pork dish."
   d. "I always enjoy the feast that follows the end of Ramadan."

13. Which concept best describes the difference between the rule of Akbar and that of a successor, Aurangzeb, concerning non-Muslims?

   a. Justice
   b. Empathy
   c. Change
   d. Urbanization

14. Base your answer on this map and on your knowledge of social studies.

   Which conclusion is best supported by the map?

   a. Eastern Chinese cities had extensive contact with the Persian Empire in 1405.
   b. Rivers and mountains prevented the expansion of overland Chinese trade.
   c. The Chinese came into contact with people of other cultures between 1405 and 1422.
   d. China was isolated from outside contact under the rulers of the Ming dynasty.

15. The Chinese export of porcelain in return for goods from other countries was evidence of

   a. ethnocentrism.
   b. imperialism.
   c. empathy.
   d. interdependence.

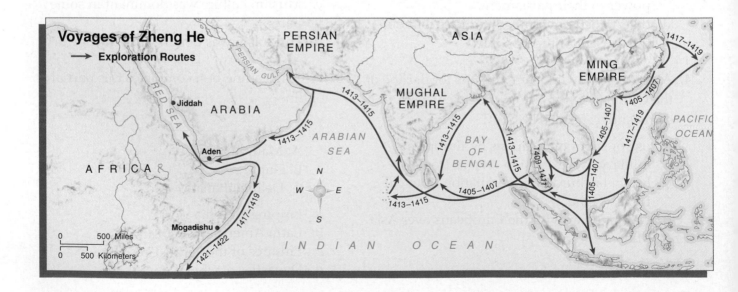

16. The growth of Chinese influence and trade during the Ming dynasty was a consequence of the

a. defeat of the Manchus.
b. removal of foreigners.
c. voyages of Zheng He.
d. return to Confucian values.

17. What was a policy followed by Muslim rulers in Makkah and Ming rulers in Beijing's Forbidden City?

a. Free entry for foreigners who followed Confucian practices
b. Exclusion of certain people
c. Admission based on knowledge of the Qu'ran
d. Posting paintings of Muhammad

18. As of the year 1400, one difference between China and Japan was that China had

a. rejected Buddhism.
b. accepted Shinto ideas.
c. overthrown Mongol rule.
d. developed into a shogunate.

19. "Unless handled properly, this famous product of the Ming Dynasty would break apart while being transported." The speaker is referring to

a. silk.   c. rice.
b. tea.   d. porcelain.

20. If the products described were to reach Rome, they would most likely be sent by a Chinese merchant

a. east, across the Pacific Ocean.
b. west, along the Silk Road.
c. northeast, to Japan.
d. southwest, to Bangladesh.

ESSAYS FOR CHAPTER 19

1. To what extent was the Ottoman Empire an agent of cultural diffusion for the Middle East, northern Africa, and eastern Europe? Show two examples of how it created a multicultural society.

2. Why did the Ottoman Empire begin to decline in the seventeenth century? Give two reasons for the end of the Turkish state's imperial expansion and its slow loss of power after 1650.

3. Justice and tolerance amidst diversity was evident at certain times in South Asia during Mughal rule. Name one Mughal emperor for whom this statement is true, and one emperor for whom it was not true. Explain the reasons for your choices.

4. In what ways was the golden age of Akbar's India similar to and yet different from the Ottoman Empire under Suleiman I? Give one similarity and one difference.

5. Did rule by the Ming dynasty bring benefits to China? (Did China benefit under Ming rule?) Give two reasons for your answer. You may consider categories such as political, economic, and social, as well as domestic and international.

This task is based on the accompanying documents. Some of these documents have been edited for the purposes of this task. This task is designed to test your ability to work with historical documents. As you analyze the documents, take into account both the source of each document and the author's point of view.

Directions: Read the following documents and answer the questions after each document. Use the information in the reading and this chapter in writing your answers

Document #1   HACI HALIFE, *DÜRSTUR ÜL-AMEL*, 1653

The social condition of man corresponds to his individual condition, and in most matters the one is parallel to the other. . . . First of all, the natural life of man is reckoned in three stages, a year of growth, the years of stasis, and the years of decline. Though the times of these three stages are ordained in individual constitutions . . . and these stages also vary in different societies . . . when the reckoning from the migration of the Prophet (upon him the best of greetings) had reached the year 1063, and the lofty Empire of Osman had attained its 364th year, in accordance with God's custom and the natural laws of civilization and human societies, signs of indisposition appeared in the complexion of this lofty Empire, and traces of discord in its nature and its power.

From *The Emergence of Modern Turkey (3rd edition)*, Translated by Bernard Lewis

Questions
1. How does the author compare the Ottoman Empire to a human being?
2. What is the author observing about the Empire when he makes the comparison?

Document #2   VIEWS OF TURKS AND FOREIGNERS

It is certainly a good maxim [saying] for an Ambassador in this Country, not to be over-studious in procuring a familiar friendship with Turks; a far comportment towards all in a moderate way, is cheap and secure; for a Turk is not capable of real friendship toward a Christian.
Paul Rycaut, *The History of the Present State of the Ottoman Empire* (1668)

Familiar association with heathens and infidels is forbidden to the people of Islam, and friendly and intimate intercourse between two parties that are to one another as darkness and light is far from desirable.
Asim Efendi, *History* (1809)

From *The Emergence of Modern Turkey (3rd edition)*, Translated by Bernard Lewis

Questions

1. In what ways is each of the quotes similar in its view of foreigners?
2. How does this influence the historian's analysis of the Ottoman Empire as a multicultural state?

Document #3

Akbar ruled that in legal disputes between two Hindus, decisions would be made according to village customs or Hindu law as interpreted by local Hindu scholars. Muslims followed [their own] law. Akbar made himself the legal court of last resort in a 1579 declaration that he was God's . . . earthly representative. Thus, appeals could be made to Akbar personally, a possibility not usually present in Islamic [empires].

From *The Earth and Its Peoples* by R. Bulliett

Questions

1. Although he was a Muslim, how did Akbar try to settle problems between Hindus?
2. Why can it be said that justice, fairness, and tolerance were part of Akbar's manner of treating the people he ruled?

Document #4

AKBAR (THE GREAT), MUGHAL EMPEROR OF INDIA (1556–1605)

The majority of Islamic scholars . . . concluded that the monarch was divinely appointed by God to serve humanity. . . . In particular, they subscribed to the notion that God had created a Divine Light that is passed down in an individual form from generation to generation; this individual is known as the Imam. The [main historian] of Akbar's reign was Abu'l Faz'l. . . . He believed that [Imams] existed in the world in the form of just rulers. The Imam, in the form of a just ruler, had secret knowledge of God, was free from sin, and was primarily responsible for the spiritual guidance of humanity.

From *World Civilizations: An Internet Classroom and Anthology* by R. Hooker

Document #5

MING GARDENS

Quiet and calm were characteristics of Chinese gardens during the Ming dynasty. They were viewed as places of retreat from everyday activities. The ruler could indulge his "longing for mountains and waters" without turning his back on his obligations to state and family. Originally designed by Taoist poets, Chinese gardens were meant to create an atmosphere of tranquility for contemplation and inspiration.

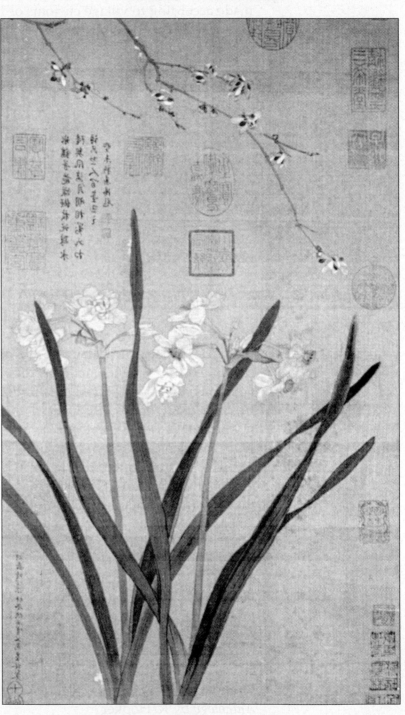

Questions

1. What conclusion can you draw about the role of nature in the culture of Ming China?
2. How can you determine whether this painting is from China?

AN AGE OF REVOLUTIONS

(1750–1826)

INTRODUCTION

In this unit, you will learn about all the new ideas, processes, and revolutionary events that helped shape and change Europe during this era. You will also see how the map of Europe and the Americas changed during these years. Many new countries came into being in the Americas as a result of revolution. Political and social changes were taking place in so many places.

The change in thinking led people to question whether they should accept a political system they had previously thought to be their only alternative.

Revolution was also a vital part of the era. The French Revolution and the Napoleonic years were revolutionary periods in Europe and the Americas. In a sense, the American Revolution (1776–1781) that led to the creation of a republic was a forerunner of the revolutionary events that took place in France, Europe, and the future Latin America after 1789. The changes that occurred in France were truly revolutionary because they resulted in the end of the monarchy, the upheaval of the social order, and the creation of a republic and later an empire. The French Revolution was truly a very influential event in the course of world history.

CHAPTER 20

The Enlightenment and the Scientific Revolution

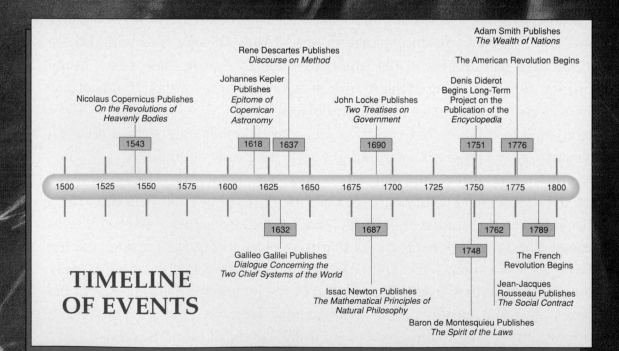

TIMELINE OF EVENTS

Nicolaus Copernicus Publishes *On the Revolutions of Heavenly Bodies*
1543

Johannes Kepler Publishes *Epitome of Copernican Astronomy*
1618

Rene Descartes Publishes *Discourse on Method*
1637

John Locke Publishes *Two Treatises on Government*
1690

Denis Diderot Begins Long-Term Project on the Publication of the *Encyclopedia*
1751

Adam Smith Publishes *The Wealth of Nations*

The American Revolution Begins
1776

1500 1525 1550 1575 1600 1625 1650 1675 1700 1725 1750 1775 1800

Galileo Galilei Publishes *Dialogue Concerning the Two Chief Systems of the World*
1632

Issac Newton Publishes *The Mathematical Principles of Natural Philosophy*
1687

Baron de Montesquieu Publishes *The Spirit of the Laws*
1748

Jean-Jacques Rousseau Publishes *The Social Contract*
1762

The French Revolution Begins
1789

Europe entered into a period of transition beginning in the 1750s. The Seven Years' War fought from 1756 to 1763 led to many significant political changes. During this era, major developments also took place in the economic, medical, scientific, and the social spheres in Europe and elsewhere in the world. To a large measure, this was due to an evolution in thinking, which had begun earlier during the Renaissance and continued throughout the Enlightenment and the Scientific Revolution. The new ways of thinking and doing things resulted in changes in how people thought about things, made decisions, and developed their ideas. Reasoning, experimentation, and the scientific method were substituted for thinking previously based on faith.

THE ENLIGHTENMENT AS THE AGE OF REASON

The **Enlightenment** was a period in human history when new ideas spread and resulted in great change. You have already studied about the Renaissance, a period when Europeans became more interested in worldly matters and less concerned with religion. The Enlightenment was another such period when European intellectuals awakened themselves to the political, economic, cultural, and social problems of their times and the need for change. The writings of philosophers, scientists, and other thinkers were directed toward finding

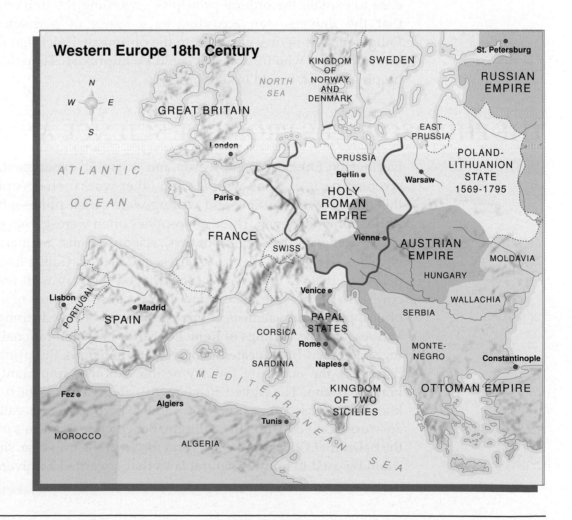

solutions to the serious political, economic, and social issues that they saw around them. The Enlightenment, also called the **Age of Reason**, began in Europe in the last decades of the seventeenth century and continued to the closing years of the 1700s.

In western European nations, many of the ideas and thoughts that developed during the Enlightenment were a result of revived learning. During the Renaissance, educated people began to change their ways of thinking about things. The ideas that developed during the Enlightenment represented an attack on the beliefs, which had previously existed. This pre-Enlightenment thinking was to a large measure based on ideas and beliefs supported by the Roman Catholic Church. For over a thousand years, Church teaching had greatly influenced educational, political, scientific, economic, cultural, and social ideas and thinking in Europe. People were required to accept Church beliefs, ideas, and thoughts.

Now many of these ideas, thoughts, and beliefs were open to question. Reason and nature began to be used to study and explain the workings of human behavior. These new ideas led to calls for basic changes in the ways that governments operated and the rights that the individual had in society. Philosophers during the Enlightenment studied the world as if they were looking at it for the first time. They were no longer held back by traditional religious beliefs. The Enlightenment thinkers fundamentally believed in the use of science to explain the orderly principles governing the universe. They reasoned that the universe ran according to a series of permanent natural laws. Enlightenment figures also held to the optimistic belief that the world and the human beings who inhabited it could be improved. They thought that the triumph of reason would lead to progress.

THE PHILOSOPHERS PROMOTE SCIENCE AND REASON

During the Enlightenment, reason and scientific experimentation became the accepted basis of many writings and other works. The people responsible for this new way of thinking and writing were called philosophes, which means **philosopher** in French. These philosophes often were scientists and mathematicians. Some of these philosophers, scientists, and mathematicians such as Nicolaus Copernicus, Rene Descartes, and Galileo Galilei lived before the time period of this era and chapter. They paved the way with their ideas and discoveries and deserve recognition also because they are representative of the philosophers and scientists of this period who believed strongly in natural law and reason. The writings of **Rene Descartes** based on rationalism were increasingly accepted by educated people. **Rationalism** is the principle of accepting reason as the authority for any action. Another important philosophe was **Francis Bacon**. He argued in favor of **empiricism**, which is the search for knowledge based on observation and experiment, and called into question answers based on faith. In addition, Benedict de Spinoza's *pantheism*, which is the belief that God is all the laws and forces of the universe, showed that reason could be used to find the natural laws that governed a universal order.

The philosophes attacked the basis of traditional thinking about spiritual and political authority. They no longer believed that unproven ideas or opinions were facts. Nothing could be considered as truth just because the Church or monarch said it was. They refused to accept ideas and beliefs based on intolerance. Philosophes argued against ideas supporting censorship, economic restraints, and social injustice. This confidence in human reason gradually became more accepted in Europe during the eighteenth century and found its way into other areas of the world, especially the Americas, by the later decades of the 1700s.

FRANCE: THE CENTER OF THE ENLIGHTENMENT

During the eighteenth century, France was the intellectual center of Europe. The French capital, Paris, was Europe's cultural gathering place. In Paris, at social gatherings called *salons*, performances of music, readings of poetry, and other cultural events took place. The most important artists, writers, and scientists often met to discuss ideas and dine together at these salons. Influential women played key roles in the spread of Enlightenment ideas. Marie Therese Geoffin, Suzanne Necker, Louise de Warens, and Madame de Pompadour, a mistress to Louis XV, are the most famous examples of the patronesses and hostesses at these salon events. These women offered financial support, and their homes and drawing rooms served as the gathering places during the period of the Enlightenment.

Marie Therese Geoffin was one of the sponsors of the philosophe **Denis Diderot**. His contribution to the Enlightenment was the ambitious project called the *Encyclopedia*. Diderot symbolized the spirit of the age of the Enlightenment. For more than twenty years, he worked to edit and complete his grand

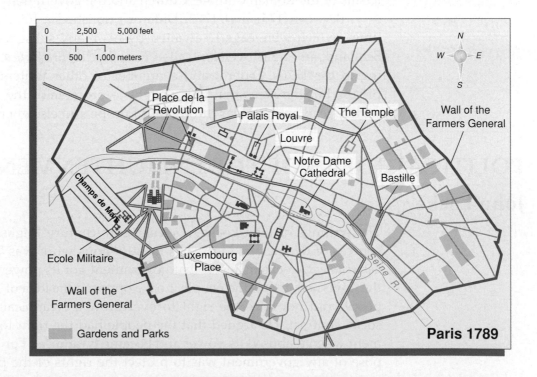

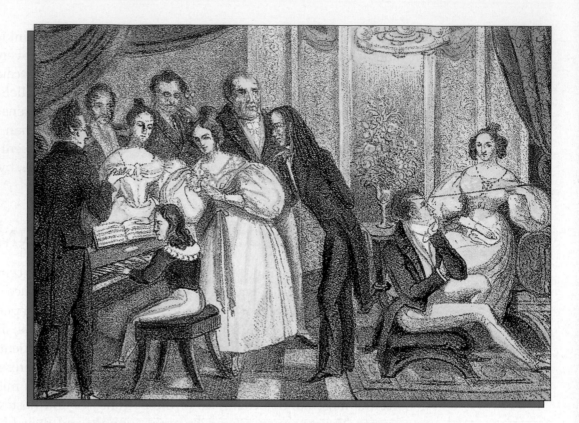

Influential women offered financial support, and their homes and drawing rooms served as the gathering places during the period of Enlightenment.

project. He sought to bring together all of the most important knowledge concerning science, technology, art, music, mathematics, law, government, and geography. Diderot continued to publish his volumes despite government censorship. The contents of a number of the more controversial volumes had angered the Church and the French King Louis XV because they contained criticisms of the Roman Catholic Church and the government.

Between 1751 and 1772, Diderot published a total of twenty-eight volumes, which were eagerly awaited by his many subscribers. In England and Scotland, an English version called *Encyclopedia Britannica* was produced starting in the 1770s. Diderot and a number of other writers eventually went to prison, but the ideas that they sought to promote in the *Encyclopedia* became widely read and popular throughout Europe and elsewhere.

POLITICAL IDEAS OF THE ENLIGHTENMENT

John Locke

The writings of John Locke, a seventeenth-century English philosopher, were sources of democratic ideas. His most famous work was *Two Treatises on Civil Government*. Locke believed that government got its power from the consent of the governed, that is the people. Locke opposed the idea of Thomas Hobbes that people did not have the right to overthrow a tyrannical ruler and change a social contract. He argued that the people had the right to change the government when it abused its power and became tyrannical. For Locke, the chief purpose of any government was to protect the rights of the people. His idea of a social contract concerned the exchange of rights and responsibilities between a government and its citizens. Locke believed people possessed the natural rights of life, liberty, and property. In France, a number of writers expanded upon John Locke's controversial ideas regarding natural rights. His ideas also found their way into the United States Constitution (see Chapter 16).

Voltaire

Francois Marie Arouet, known more familiarly as **Voltaire**, was a brilliant French writer. Voltaire became very famous in France and elsewhere in Europe as a writer of satirical and witty novels. In *Candide* and *Letters Concerning the English*, Voltaire promoted the concept of a limited monarchy and the importance of freedom of speech and religion. Voltaire was forced to seek exile in Great Britain to escape the angry retaliation of the monarchy. Despite his exile, his writings continued to influence those people who saw him as a voice of truth.

Baron de Montesquieu

Montesquieu was the author of the *Spirit of the Laws*. In this influential book, he stated that there should be a separation of powers in government. Montesquieu argued that a system of checks and balances was also needed to prevent abuses of power. He believed that by adopting these ideas it would prevent tyranny and absolutism in government. Montesquieu's ideas were written into the United States Constitution.

Jean Jacques Rousseau

Rousseau was the author of *Social Contract*. His political writings criticized how governments obtained the power to rule the people. He wrote that inequality among people could be ended by citizens coming together and agreeing to promote what he called a general will. The general will is what the majority desires and should be carried out by government. Rousseau's ideas about equality and the will of the majority inspired the revolutionaries who sought to change the manner in which their nations were governed.

Baron de Montesquieu believed that there should be a separation of powers in government.

ECONOMIC IDEAS OF THE ENLIGHTENMENT

The Physiocrats

Not all of the philosophers concerned themselves primarily with political ideas. One group, the **physiocrats**, looked for natural laws to explain how an economy could best function. During this period, mercantilism was the most influential economic theory. The majority of European governments subscribed to mercantilist ideas in making their economic policies. The physiocrats argued against mercantilism because they reasoned that land, and not gold or silver, was the true measure of a nation's wealth. The physiocrats supported farming and argued for the removal of restrictions on trade in order that farmers could sell their products more freely. They believed that a free market would result in increased trade and more wealth for everybody. The physiocrats wanted an economy in which the government would give merchants and entrepreneurs a free hand to produce and sell their goods in an open market.

Adam Smith

Adam Smith was the most brilliant defender of the idea of a free economy.

Adam Smith, a Scottish economist, was the most brilliant defender of the idea of a free economy. In his book *The Wealth of Nations*, first published in 1776, Smith wrote that a free economy without governmental regulations would produce greater wealth for a nation. This was the idea of **laissez-faire**, or "leave the economy alone." Smith's ideas were based on what he called three natural laws of economics. They were as follows:

1. *The law of **supply and demand**:* This law determined the price of any good that was sold in an open market. Producers had to adjust their production to meet the demands of the customers. For example, overproduction lowered the price of a good if people did not want it all.

2. *The law of competition:* This law forced producers to make better products at a lower price. It drove inefficient and selfish individuals, who could not work efficiently and meet the demands of their customers, out of business.

3. *The law of self-interest:* This meant that businesses were primarily created to make profits for their owners. Therefore, the reason for the production of goods was to make money. Left alone, this self-interest guaranteed that there were sufficient goods for customers in an open market.

Essentially, Adam Smith believed that if these natural laws were left free to operate without government interference in the economy, a nation would prosper. A large quantity of well-made goods produced at the lowest possible price was essential for economic progress. England was the European nation that ultimately paid most attention to Smith's ideas in formulating its economic policies in the late eighteenth and nineteenth centuries. The United States also adopted Adam Smith's economic ideas in the nineteenth century.

CULTURAL AND SOCIAL IDEAS OF THE ENLIGHTENMENT

Social Ideas

The ideas of the Enlightenment spread across Europe starting in the mid-eighteenth century and had a significant social and cultural impact. Some of the philosophies of the Enlightenment concerned themselves with ideas that related more directly to the lives of the people.

Jean Jacques Rousseau

Rousseau's writings also addressed social ideas. Rousseau's social ideas rejected society's formal structures and rules. In his writings, for example the novel *La Nouvelle Heloise*, Rousseau encouraged people from all walks of life to live humbler lives, closer to nature. His belief that all people were equal under the law made him an opponent of the class system, which controlled social relations throughout Europe.

Rousseau's aim was to give the individual more freedom in a society where the rational general will of the people would enable people to choose for the common good. He believed that people were born good and that the injustices or difficult experiences of life were reasons that people did not work toward his idea of the common good. He looked to education not as a means of imparting things to be known but rather to draw out what was already there. In *Emile*, Rousseau outlined his educational philosophy. He stressed the need to allow the free development of the human potential.

Baruch Spinoza wanted people to think for themselves and not to accept ideas that resulted in loss of social and religious freedom.

Baruch Spinoza

Baruch Spinoza was a Dutch philosopher who was educated as an Orthodox Jew. Despite his religious education, he grew up to be an independent thinker. His refusal to observe certain religious ideas and ceremonies led to his excommunication from the Jewish community. Spinoza believed that people share a common drive for self-preservation. He believed in the freedom to be guided by the law of one's own nature. In Spinoza's ethical system, the individual and community could obtain freedom through understanding and the use of an active intellect. He wanted people to think for themselves and not to accept ideas that resulted in loss of social and religious freedom.

CULTURAL IDEAS

More people became educated and capable of reading and writing. These individuals began to read the growing numbers of books, journals, and newspapers that contained the ideas of the Enlightenment. The increase in travel to other countries and the spread of books also had far-reaching effects. Public lectures, theater presentations, cafe gatherings, and neighborhood meetings were additional sources of information. More people became informed about new ideas and were interested in discussing them.

The Enlightenment influenced the development of music, literature, and the arts. The writers, composers, musicians, and artists turned to order and reason when thinking about and creating their works. Musical composers like Johann Sebastian Bach, Joseph Haydn, and Wolfgang Amadeus Mozart stressed balance and contrast in their symphonies and operas. Literary figures like Jean Baptiste Moliere, Pierre Corneille, and Alexander Pope wrote in an orderly and reasonable style and helped people to understand their work.

During the Enlightenment, painters and sculptors often drew their inspiration from the classical ideas of the Greeks and Romans. The paintings of Jacques-Louis David symbolized the ideas and inspiration that artists took from classical subjects and forms. In architecture, the use of simple classical forms such as the circle and square contrasted with the more ornate and complicated baroque style. Palaces, opera houses, and other public buildings were designed by architects who attempted to capture the refined and simplified ideas of an earlier Classical Period.

IMPACT OF THE ENLIGHTENMENT ON THE AMERICAS

The ideas of the Enlightenment traveled across the Atlantic Ocean to the Americas. In the English colonies in North America, many of the future leaders of the American Revolution were familiar with Enlightenment authors and their writings. The educated colonial elite often had their own libraries. Discussions of these new ideas took place in homes, taverns, and political meetings. The political thought of the Enlightenment greatly influenced Americans who became the nation's first political leaders.

Benjamin Franklin, the symbol of the enlightened American, was thoroughly familiar with Enlightenment thought. Franklin was a writer, scientist, publisher, and political leader who promoted the ideas that developed in Europe and spread to the Americas. Thomas Paine, the author of *Common Sense,* claimed that Americans possessed natural political rights and had a right to revolt against English tyranny. Thomas Jefferson, James Madison, and other Americans supported the political ideas of the Enlightenment. Jefferson, the principal author of the Declaration of Independence, and Madison, the "Father" of the United States Constitution, were very familiar with the ideas of Locke, Montesquieu, and Rousseau.

In Spanish America, the ideas of the Enlightenment bore fruit in the early nineteenth century during the Napoleonic Era. The ideas of the Enlightenment spread more slowly in the Spanish and Portuguese colonies because the wealthy and educated colonial elite feared the consequences of enlightened thought in Latin America. Francisco Miranda, Simon Bolivar, Jose de San Martin, and other leaders in the various movements for independence in Spanish America were all influenced by the Enlightenment's political ideas (see Chapters 21 and 22).

Benjamin Franklin is the symbol of the enlightened American.

THE SCIENTIFIC REVOLUTION AND THE SCIENTIFIC METHOD

The Enlightenment produced much change in the ways many people thought about themselves and their natural environment. Thereafter, the world in which they lived underwent enormous change. The Enlightenment emphasized reason and a willingness to question previously held ideas. This new way of thinking had a major effect on future historical developments. Although the political, economic, and social ideas of the Enlightenment first developed in Europe, they eventually spread to other parts of the world. The same can be said of the ways in which the people of Europe viewed the natural world and the universe itself. Their knowledge of science and mathematics, and the methods used to obtain that knowledge, was transformed dramatically during the sixteenth, seventeenth, and eighteenth centuries.

This change in scientific knowledge and methodology is called the **Scientific Revolution**. A new system of ideas and theories was created. This *methodology,* or way of doing things, was based on the direct observation of nature and a belief in the power of reason. A **scientific method** was adopted, which consisted of three stages:

Nicolaus Copernicus stirred up a controversy with his claim that the sun was the center of the universe.

1. Statement of a hypothesis or idea

2. Experimentation and observation

3. Interpretation of results, using reason and mathematics to determine the truth of the hypothesis

By using the scientific method, a succession of astronomers, physicists, mathematicians, and physicians changed many ideas that had been accepted for centuries. In fact, a twentieth-century philosopher, Alfred Whitehead, labeled the 1600s the "century of genius." His reference was to the scientific advances made during that time. Let us now learn what these advances were and who the people who made these advances possible were.

Astronomy and Physics

Nicolaus Copernicus

Copernicus was a Polish astronomer and mathematician. He stirred up controversy with his claim that the sun was the center of the universe. This was known as the *heliocentric theory*. It was a challenge to an older theory that had been stated by the ancient Greek scientist Ptolemy. Ptolemy held that the earth was the center of the universe. This was the *geocentric theory*. Ptolemy's theory had lasted well over one thousand years. It received strong backing from the Roman Catholic Church. Church officials claimed that the Bible supported this view.

Copernicus used mathematical calculations to prove that this view was incorrect. He asserted that the earth rotated on its axis and therefore was not stationary. The ideas of Copernicus appeared in his 1543 book *On the Revolutions of the Heavenly Bodies* but were not widely accepted at the time. Both Luther and Calvin condemned Copernican theories. The Roman Catholic Church went so far as to place Copernicus's book on the *Index of Prohibited Books*. The book remained on the *Index* until its removal in the eighteenth century.

The ultimate acceptance of the heliocentric theory was the result of contributions made by other scientists. They were able to prove the truth of Copernicus' theory by further observations and calculations. This progression of scientific knowledge often follows such a pattern. The theoretical ideas put forth by researchers at one point in time are often proven by scientists at a later date. The scientific work accomplished by Tycho Brahe, Johannes Kepler, and Galileo Galilei provided the proof needed for Copernicus' theory.

Tycho Brahe

Tycho Brahe was a Danish astronomer who built an observatory for studying the skies. His scientific ideas developed from his observations of the planets and stars. Brahe's observations helped confirm Copernicus' theory. Unfortunately for Brahe, his ideas about the universe led to problems with the Roman Catholic Church.

Brahe's refusal to admit that his ideas were wrong cost him his life. Brahe was condemned by the Church and burned at the stake. Brahe's execution is an example the power that the Roman Catholic Church had concerning the scientific ideas that were allowed to circulate freely during this time.

Johannes Kepler

Brahe's assistant, the German **Johannes Kepler**, continued his work and did further investigations to confirm his conclusions. Kepler's book *Epitome of Copernican Astronomy*, published in 1618, contained his findings. Although in general agreement with Copernicus,

Johannes Kepler, although in general agreement with Copernicus, described one error in Copernican claims.

Kepler described one error in Copernican claims. Copernicus had stated that the planets revolve around the sun in circles. Kepler's calculations convinced him that the planets actually moved in another kind of pattern, an ellipse.

Galileo Galilei

Galileo Galilei was the greatest astronomer and scientist of his time. He built a telescope using optical lenses to make distant objects seem close. Based upon what he was able to see of the planets and stars, Galileo verified that the planets do indeed move around the sun. His observations made believable the mathematical conclusions arrived at by Kepler. Galileo made these additional discoveries with his telescope:

1. The moon owes its light to reflection.

2. Its surface is not smooth but has valleys and mountains.

3. The sun has movable spots.

4. The planet Jupiter is surrounded by four moons.

The Roman Catholic Church ordered Galileo to renounce his views, which were in contrast with the accepted beliefs of the Church.

All of Galileo's astronomical findings were published in 1632 in his book *Dialogue Concerning the Two Chief Systems of the World.*

Publication of his findings caused trouble for Galileo. His work disproved earlier theories proposed by Ptolemy and the famous Greek thinker, Aristotle. These theories and beliefs associated with them had long been accepted and supported by the Roman Catholic Church. The Church ordered Galileo to renounce his views. Upon his refusal, he was summoned to stand trial by the Inquisition in Rome in 1634. Charged as a heretic and facing the death penalty, Galileo humbly submitted to the Inquisition's demand. On his knees, he took back what the Church said were heresies and errors. He was made to swear that he would never say anything either orally or in writing that would make him suspected of being a heretic. For a time, the Church's insistence that the sun moved around the earth continued to be the only acceptable theory. There is a story that soon after he made these statements, Galileo muttered under his breath that the earth does move. Today of course we know that Galileo's ideas were correct. In the twentieth century, the Church retracted its position on Galileo's teaching.

In the last few years of his life, Galileo's interest turned to mechanics. *Mechanics* is the physical science concerned with matter in motion. His 1636 publication, *Dialogues on Motion,* summarized his work on this topic. He noted that without any air friction, objects of different weight will fall at the same speed. This law of falling bodies negated an older theory of Aristotle's. Galileo's work helped set the stage for Isaac Newton's development of his famous laws of motion. Galileo's investigations of the natural world have led many historians to regard him as the founder of experimental science. He showed that reliance upon traditional concepts about nature cannot be accepted unless there is clear, definitive, scientific proof of these concepts.

Isaac Newton

Isaac Newton carried on the scientific work of his predecessors. During his life he made great scientific accomplishments, which won him enormous respect and prestige. He was undoubtedly the greatest scientist of his time. His reputation was based mainly on three significant discoveries:

1. *Calculus*: This mathematical theory is the basis of modern mathematics. Calculus is concerned with examining changing mathematical quantities.

Isaac Newton's reputation was based mainly on three significant discoveries: calculus, the law of composition of light, and the law of gravitation.

2. *The law of the composition of light*: Newton's demonstrations with light and with color led to the science of optics.

3. *The law of gravitation*: This law provided humankind with a new insight into the universe. Newton's law of gravity was his most monumental achievement. The idea of gravity, as a force that causes the return of an object to the ground, was recognized prior to Newton's time. However, it remained for Newton to discover the law regulating this force and the attraction it exerts. Briefly stated, the law declares that a force of attraction exists between bodies, and that this force increases as the bodies move closer together. This force can be measured in a mathematical formula. This is the force that pulls objects to the earth and is also the force that keeps planets revolving around the sun. Newton was thus able to explain the workings of the solar system—something that Kepler and Galileo had only been able to describe. The heliocentric theory could no longer be denied.

Newton's findings were published in 1687 in his *book The Mathematical Principles of Natural Philosophy*, sometimes referred to as *The Principia*. This work also contained his laws of motion. One important law stated that a body in motion will be attracted to a body that has greater mass (weight), if it is within the larger body's gravity field. Newton came to this conclusion supposedly by watching an apple fall to the ground from a tree. Whether or not this is a true story, Newton's law thereafter had an enormous impact on scientific thinking. Newton believed that the universe was a well-regulated machine that worked in connection with specific laws of nature. His accomplishments helped pave the way for our current ability to travel through and explore outer space.

Other Important Scientific Discoveries

There were scientists in other fields who sought to find explanations for naturally occurring events. These scientists made discoveries that changed older ways of thinking. Their important discoveries based on scientific research brought benefits to people.

Medicine

Important discoveries were made in the field of medicine and health care. Prior to the Scientific Revolution, the ideas of Galen, a Greek physician set the standard for medical science. During the time of the Scientific Revolution much of Galen's work, which had for so long dominated ideas about medicine, the human body, and health care were disproved by exper-

Paracelsus proved that by using heat and mixing chemicals their properties could be changed.

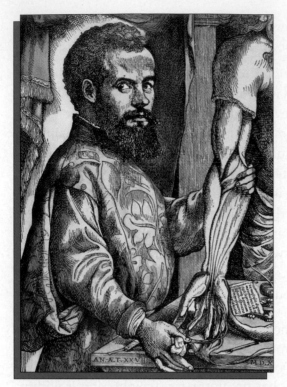

The anatomy work of Andreas Vesalius gave accurate descriptions of the human brain and the digestive and reproductive systems.

imentation. Two of Galen's ideas that were found to be erroneous concerned chemistry and anatomy. Galen believed that chemical changes in a substance were impossible to produce. He also thought that the human body was put together and functioned in a way that scientists and medical researchers proved to be wrong.

Research by a Swiss physician, Paracelsus, disproved Galen's chemical theory. Paracelsus' experiments with chemicals proved that by using heat and mixing chemicals their properties could be changed. In addition, the pioneering anatomy work of Andreas Vesalius, a Flemish professor, gave accurate descriptions of the human brain and the digestive and reproductive systems. Vesalius made his discoveries about the human body and organs by means of dissection. His book *On the Structure of the Human Body,* advanced the knowledge of the human body. The medical studies carried out by the English physician William Harvey were also very significant in discovering how fluids move around the body. By observing humans and by experimenting with the hearts of birds and frogs, Harvey learned much about the circulation of blood. In his *An Anatomical Exercise on the Motion of the Heart and Blood in Animals,* Harvey described the pumplike features of the heart. He proved that blood is driven by the heart in a circulatory pattern. The Italian Marcello Malpighi added to Harvey's discoveries about the circulation of blood. Malpighi described the capillaries and their role in circulation of blood.

These and other medical discoveries were made possible by the use of the microscope. Around 1600, the first microscopes were assembled and used in the Netherlands. The microscope enabled scientists to observe things that could not ordinarily be seen by the human eye. Anton van Leeuwenhoek from Holland was able to investigate protozoa and bacteria as well as to describe blood corpuscles. In England, Robert Hooke discovered that living matter was made up of cells.

There were other notable advancements in the field of chemistry. Robert Boyle known as the founder of modern chemistry, did pioneering research into the composition of chemical compounds. He was accurate in predicting the discovery of many more elements than were known at the time. This prediction was validated by the discoveries of hydrogen, oxygen and other elements by Henry Cavendish, Joseph Priestly, and other chemical researchers. This soon led to the understanding of how hydrogen and oxygen combined to form compounds such as water and carbon dioxide. In France, Antoine Lavoisier helped advance these chemical discoveries.

Robert Boyle is known as the father of modern chemistry.

GROWING SUPPORT FOR THE SCIENTIFIC REVOLUTION

The writings of Rene Descartes were important in promoting the idea of scientific experimentation.

European scientists, physicians, and other researchers increasingly realized the importance of using observation, reason, and careful experimentation when investigating nature. The writings of Rene Descartes, in France, were important in promoting the idea of scientific experimentation. Descartes was not willing to accept anything as knowledge unless it could be proven. He considered mathematics to be the queen of the sciences. Descartes was convinced that the use of mathematical methods was crucial for all other sciences. He emphasized the application of logic and reason in human affairs and considered himself to be a rationalist. According to Descartes, the mere fact that he could think was proof that he existed. This belief was stated in a famous sentence from his *Discourse On Method*. He wrote "I think, therefore I am," which has become the key to understanding the idea of rational belief about human existence.

Lord Francis Bacon, in England, also wrote in support of using the scientific method to gain accurate knowledge. However, for Bacon this knowledge would be especially worthwhile only if it could be practical and utilitarian. This meant that it had to benefit mankind in specific ways—fighting disease and conquering suffering. In his *Novum Organum*, Bacon predicted that science would more widely extend the limits of the power and greatness of man.

The advances in science led to greater interest in all areas of scientific knowledge. This growing interest resulted in the creation of organizations to help exchange ideas, encourage experimentation, and spread information. Some of the earliest organizations or societies were started in Italy. Galileo, for instance, was a member of the Academia dei Lincei. In England, King Charles II favored scientific research. In 1662, he granted a charter to a group that became known as the Royal Society of London for Promoting Natural Knowledge. King Louis XIV of France approved the founding of the French Academy of Sciences in 1666. Within the next one hundred years, similar societies were established in other countries. Scientific journals began to be published by these groups, a practice very much in evidence in our own times.

Lord Francis Bacon predicted that science would more widely extend the limits of the power and greatness of man.

LINK TO TODAY

If we look at the important advances that have been made in the past century, we are often amazed about how far science has come since the time of the Scientific Revolution. Today many of the ideas and discoveries that seemed so incredible then are taken for granted. We live in a time in which space travel, digital cameras, microscopes and audio visual systems, advanced medical treatments, and other scientific accomplishments are commonplace. We expect that tomorrow we will always be able to find the answers to the scientific questions that we are researching today. In our world, we think practically all problems can be resolved if we think logically about them and apply the scientific method.

We owe a great historical debt to the first scientific pioneers whose research and discoveries during the time period of the Scientific Revolution made so much possible for us today. For example, if Issac Newton had not shown the way with his experiments and stated the law of gravity, we would not have been able to have made the scientific and technological advances of the past century that have led us to travel outside the earth's atmosphere. The same can be said for scientists and physicians such as Galileo, Harvey, Boyle, and many others who devoted their lives to developing the scientific knowledge that we benefit from today.

In the twentieth century, Albert Einstein developed a theory about how the universe works. His ideas were based on the scientific thinking and experimentation of so many people who paved the way. In the same way, scientists today are working to see if Einstein's theory is correct. This is the way of science. We think about things in a logical and rational manner. We apply the scientific method to see if the idea is sound. If it is a good idea that can be proved, we can make a scientific advancement. It is in this way that the Scientific Revolution that you read about in this chapter is linked to the present and future.

CHAPTER SUMMARY

The Enlightenment and Scientific Revolution were a time of great change and discovery. People began to rely on a more logical and organized way of thinking to understand ideas and apply knowledge to solve problems. The scientific method was increasingly used to find the answers to important questions and problems. Important discoveries were made in the areas of mathematics, science, and medicine. The medical, scientific, and other changes that took place were long lasting. We are living in a time in which the impact of these discoveries and changes are still being felt. The philosophers and scientists such as Descartes, Bacon, Galileo, Newton, Harvey, and others wrote about ideas and made discoveries that have proven to be a valuable legacy in our day. It was because of these ideas and discoveries that we are able to move ahead and continue to look forward to making progress in the future.

Enlightenment authors such as Locke, Voltaire, Montesquieu, and Rousseau influenced political developments in Europe and the Americas. Their political ideas had a major impact in France particularly after 1789. Some of the political ideas that developed during the Enlightenment also found their way into the United States Constitution. The philosophes attacked the old world of political tradition and privilege. They believed in the idea of a more logical and rational approach to governing people.

IMPORTANT PEOPLE, PLACES, AND TERMS

KEY TERMS	PEOPLE	PLACES
Enlightenment	Nicolaus Copernicus	Paris
Scientific Revolution	Johannes Kepler	England
Age of Reason	Tycho Brahe	The Americas
philosopher	Galileo Galilei	Rome
laissez-faire	Isaac Newton	The Netherlands
rationalism	Rene Descartes	
scientific method	Denis Diderot	
empiricism	Jean Jacques Rousseau	
Encyclopedia	Francis Bacon	
physiocrats	Baron de Montesquieu	
supply and demand	Benjamin Franklin	
natural laws	Adam Smith	
	Baruch Spinoza	
	John Locke	
	Voltaire	

EXERCISES FOR CHAPTER 20

MULTIPLE CHOICE

Select the letter of the correct answer.

1. The Enlightenment was a period when

   a. individuals turned to ideas based on faith.
   b. philosophers sought to justify the power of the monarch.
   c. traditional ideas expressed by the Church were most accepted.
   d. reason and nature began to be used to explain human nature.

2. The philosophers attacked spiritual authority and intolerance because they supported

   a. freedom of thought.
   b. the divine right of kings.
   c. the Protestant Reformation.
   d. a more democratic church.

3. Thomas Hobbes and John Locke differed on the idea

   a. of a government based on a social contract.
   b. that the state held back human progress.
   c. that a government once established could always be changed.
   d. when a people had the right to overthrow a tyrannical government.

4. John Locke believed that people possessed natural rights that included

   a. liberty, equality, and fraternity.
   b. life, democracy, and enfranchisement.
   c. equality, liberty, and creativity.
   d. life, liberty, and property.

5. Enlightenment thinkers supported which of the following ideas?

   a. Separation of powers in government
   b. Papal supremacy in church matters
   c. The idea of divine right for monarchs
   d. The principle of absolutism in government.

6. Jean Jacques Rousseau was a philosopher who believed in

   a. a broader democracy based on equality and the general will of the people.
   b. the idea that a social contract between the monarch and people could not be changed.
   c. a system of government based on the principle of divine right.
   d. giving the Roman Catholic Church a voice in determining people's rights in society.

7. One reason that the Roman Catholic Church opposed Copernicus' ideas was that

   a. the Church had scientific evidence that Copernicus' ideas were wrong.
   b. Copernicus was a strong supporter of the Protestant Reformation.
   c. it feared an acceptance of Copernicus' ideas would diminish its authority.
   d. Copernicus' ideas of the universe violated natural law.

8. The law of supply and demand means

   a. competition has to be regulated.
   b. overproduction cannot be controlled in an open market.
   c. the price of any good would be determined in an open market.
   d. producers would control the supply and demand of their products.

9. The economic idea that is in opposition to mercantilist theory is

   a. storing bullion.   c. restricted trade.
   b. laissez-faire.   d. government subsidies.

10. Artists, musicians, and writers drew inspiration from

    a. Classical traditions.
    b. the Middle Ages.
    c. Gothic styles.
    d. Eastern influences.

11. Base your answer on the following quotation:

    We hold these truths to be self-evident, that all men are created equal, that they are endowed by their creator with certain inalienable rights, that among these are life, liberty, and the pursuit of happiness.

    This statement best expresses the philosophy of

    a. Adam Smith.
    b. Thomas Hobbes.
    c. John Locke.
    d. William Harvey.

12. Which statement best describes the effects of the works of Nicolaus Copernicus, Galileo Galilei, Sir Isaac Newton, and Rene Descartes?

    a. The acceptance of traditional authority was strengthened.
    b. The scientific method was used to solve problems.
    c. Funding in public education was increased by government.
    d. Interest in Greek and Roman ideas was renewed.

13. Base your answer on the following quotation:

    If man in the state of nature is free, if he is absolute lord of his own person and possessions, why will he give up his freedom? Why will he put himself under the control of any person or institution? The obvious answer is that rights in the state of nature are constantly exposed to the attack of others. Since every man is equal and since most men do not concern themselves with equity and justice, the enjoyment of rights in the state of nature is unsafe and insecure. Hence each man joins with others to preserve his life, liberty, and property.

This statement provides support for

a. elimination of laissez-faire capitalism.
b. formation of government based on a social contract.
c. continuation of absolute monarchy.
d. rejection of the natural rights philosophy.

14. One similarity of the Scientific Revolution and Enlightenment is that both

a. had the support of the Roman Catholic Church.
b. placed great value on traditional beliefs.
c. emphasized the value of human reasoning.
d. contributed to the end of feudalism.

15. John Locke and Jean Jacques Rousseau would be most likely to support

a. a return to feudalism in Europe.
b. a government ruled by a divine monarchy.
c. a society ruled by the Catholic Church.
d. the rights of people to decide their government.

16. One similarity between the Renaissance and the Enlightenment is that both periods

a. produced major cultural changes.
b. encouraged traditional values.
c. limited technological advancements.
d. ignored individual achievements.

17. What was a direct result of the Scientific Revolution in Europe?

a. A gradual decline in the growth of cities in western Europe
b. An increase of the absolute power of the monarchy in Europe
c. The rise of the manorial system and the reemergence of feudalism
d. The application of reason and experimentation to political thinking

18. The Enlightenment philosophers believed that the power of government is derived from

a. the natural rights of monarchs.
b. the middle class of society.
c. a strong military establishment.
d. those who are governed.

19. During the Enlightenment, philosophers opposed the theory of divine right because they

a. believed that the Church should have more authority than the monarch.
b. argued that absolutism was better than a limited constitutional monarchy.
c. reasoned that humans possessed inalienable natural rights including liberty.
d. stated it was harmful to the development of a mercantilist-based economy.

20. Base your answer on the following statement:

The person of the King is sacred, and to attack him in any way is an attack on religion itself. Kings represent the divine majesty and have been appointed by God to carry out his purposes. Serving God and respecting kings are bound together.
                                    —Bishop Jacques Bosseut

This statement goes against ideas that developed during which period?

a. The Middle Ages
b. The Enlightenment
c. The Age of Absolutism
d. The Age of Exploration

1. How did the Enlightenment philosophers break with traditional values?
2. How did the basic ideas of John Locke influence the development of democracy?
3. Why were the ideas of Jean Jacques Rousseau considered to be so radical during his lifetime?
4. Explain how Adam Smith's law of supply and demand, law of competition, and law of self-interest were expected to work?
5. How did the Enlightenment change people's ideas about the relationship of people to government and from where a government gets its power?

DOCUMENT-BASED QUESTIONS

This task is based on the accompanying documents. Some of these documents have been edited for the purposes of this task. This task is designed to test your ability to work with historical documents. As you analyze the documents, take into account both the source of each document and the author's point of view.

Directions: Read the following documents and answer the questions after each document. Use the information in the reading and this chapter in writing your answer.

Document #1

The Enlightenment heralded a new age for humankind. The past was left behind as mostly irrational and barbarian. The future was acclaimed. People were perfectible, if only they applied reason to the tasks of progress. Happiness on Earth was possible, thanks to science, education and economic development. The Enlightenment put Europe on the threshold of the Industrial Revolution. The issue for countries like Spain and Portugal was whether to join these momentous events or remain once more on the outside, tied to its medieval past.

From *Buried Mirror* by Carlos Fuentes

Questions

1. Why was the period of the Enlightenment considered to be a new age for humankind?
2. How was it possible for people to become perfectible?

Document #2

Instead of Saint Augustine and Thomas Aquinas, the civil philosophers Montesquieu, Voltaire and Rousseau—especially Jean Jacques Rousseau, the citizen of Geneva, and his ringing cry "man is born free, but everywhere he is in chains." Rousseau perhaps had the greatest influence that any single writer had on the history and literature of Spanish America. He represented the writers of the Enlightenment, declaring new principles of social and religious organization, against the monarchy and against the Church, against divine right of kings and in favor of popular sovereignty."

From *Buried Mirror* by Carlos Fuentes

1. Why did Rousseau have such an important influence on the Enlightenment in Spanish America?
2. How did he represent the writers of the Enlightenment?

Document #3

Such an approach opened the way to purposeful experiment. Instead of waiting to see something happen, make it happen. This required an intellectual leap. How else could the scientific theories of men such as Isaac Newton be proven if not by means of experimentation. How to experiment was a different matter. One first had to invent research strategies and instruments of observation and measurement. The new approach found early application in astronomy and navigation, mechanics, warfare optics and surveying—all of them practical matters.

From *A History of Civilizations* by Fernand Braudel

Questions

1. Why was the idea of experimentation so important during the Enlightenment?
2. How did Isaac Newton advance the idea of experimentation?

Document #4

It has to be repeated that production was always held to be beneficial. All goods produced, in fact, stimulated trade, according to the law of outlets. This has been the doctrine of liberal economists from the time of Adam Smith. In this competitive model of the economy, everything was self-regulating, including the ability to save and invest. And if by some mischance that ability required regulation, it was enough to adjust the interest rate, by raising or lowering it, in order to make it the right amount.

From *A History of Civilizations* by Fernand Braudel

Questions

1. What is meant by the idea of a self-regulating economy?
2. How did the liberal economists like Adam Smith think the economy would correct its mistakes?

Document #5

When Adam Smith came to write about economic matters in the eighteenth century, he pointed out that the division of labor and widening of markets encouraged technological innovation. This is exactly what happened. This often led to a sharp reduction in the cost of doing business. A widening of the market promoted specialization and division of labor.

From *A History of Civilizations* by Fernand Braudel

Questions

1. What is meant by the division of labor?
2. What economic benefits did Adam Smith think the widening of markets would bring about?

CHAPTER 21

The French Revolution

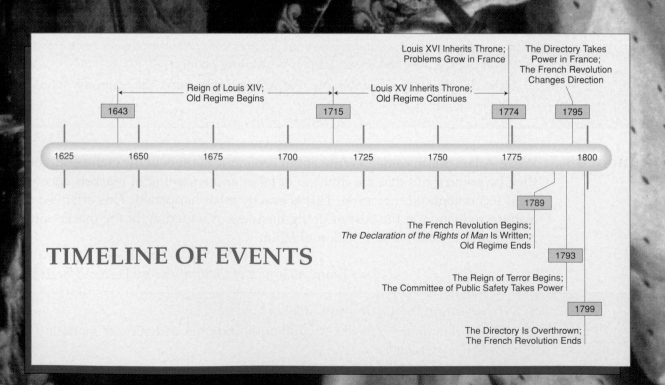

Reign of Louis XIV;
Old Regime Begins

Louis XV Inherits Throne;
Old Regime Continues

Louis XVI Inherits Throne;
Problems Grow in France

The Directory Takes
Power in France;
The French Revolution
Changes Direction

1643   1715   1774   1795

1625   1650   1675   1700   1725   1750   1775   1800

1789

The French Revolution Begins;
The Declaration of the Rights of Man Is Written;
Old Regime Ends

1793

The Reign of Terror Begins;
The Committee of Public Safety Takes Power

1799

The Directory Is Overthrown;
The French Revolution Ends

TIMELINE OF EVENTS

In France and elsewhere, many people were unhappy with their lives and decided to do something about it. They refused to continue to live in a society ruled by a king in which only the nobility and high Church officials enjoyed political freedoms, a high social status, and the better things of life. By 1789, the French people rose up and began a revolution that not only changed their nation's political, economic, and social foundations but also led to revolutions elsewhere particularly in the Spanish and Portuguese American colonies.

THE OLD REGIME: A HIGHLY STRUCTURED AND DIVIDED SOCIETY

In France, the government and society that existed before the French Revolution in 1789 is referred to as the **Old Regime**. During the Old Regime, the French king ruled over the nation and its people by **divine right**. This means that the king believed the right to rule came to him directly from God. The Old Regime began in 1643 when **Louis XIV** became King of France. Louis, the Sun King, made the monarchy's power unlimited or absolute. The time period when monarchs ruled with unchecked power is called the Age of Absolutism (see Chapter 15).

Before the French Revolution, a person's position in society depended on his or her family heritage. In France, all members of society were divided into three classes of people called Estates. This meant that from birth a person's place in life was already determined. Each Estate was a very defined group of people. The **First Estate** included the important members of the clergy. They were high officials of the Roman Catholic Church, small in number and very wealthy. The important Church officials enjoyed all the privileges of the upper class in France. The **Second Estate** was made up of the nobility who were the aristocracy of the Old Regime. The nobles also were small in number. The Second Estate was part of the upper level of French society. The aristocracy, like the important Roman Catholic Church officials, shared in the nation's wealth and privileges. During the Old Regime, less than 10 percent of the population, the First and Second Estates, had access to all of the good things that life had to offer.

The **Third Estate** was made up of the rest of society and counted for more than 90 percent of the French population. The social groups of the Third Estate were the middle class or **bourgeoisie**, the peasants or farm workers, artisans, and city workers. Most of the people who were members of the Third Estate had a much more difficult life than the first two Estates. This was particularly true for the peasants, city workers, and even artisans who lived in very poor conditions. They had few political rights or economic opportunities to improve their lives and a low social status. They also were subject to special work laws and taxes.

The middle class included people better off economically with a decent quality of life. They were the doctors, lawyers, merchants, businesspeople, teachers, and other professional people. Nevertheless, the middle class also had little political power and an inferior social status. They were denied the social positions and prestige that their money and property could give them because they were considered members of the Third Estate. People in the middle class resented that they had to pay taxes that the First and Second Estates did not have to pay. Certain well-educated middle class members of the Third Estate played very important roles throughout the French Revolution.

GROWING UNHAPPINESS IN FRANCE DURING THE 1700s

During his long reign, King Louis XIV was able to reduce the power and prestige of the nobility. Nevertheless, the aristocracy continued to benefit from its social status in French society. Louis allowed the aristocracy to keep many of its traditional privileges. Many nobles continued to own large land holdings and had other sources of wealth that were not taxed. One of the aristocracy's most important privileges was the right to avoid paying almost all taxes. This tax privilege or exemption from most taxes was also given to the clergy of the Roman Catholic Church.

The nobility supported the monarchy because the king was responsible for defending the privileges and wealth of their class. The Catholic clergy also supported the king because they did not have to pay taxes; they also received income from their large land holdings. The Church was also allowed to collect a special 10 percent tax on the income of the Third Estate called a **tithe**. The King relied on the First and Second Estates to support his right to rule by divine right, tax the Third Estate, and spend money as he pleased. When Louis XIV died in 1715, he left France in a terrible financial situation with a large amount of debt. He had waged costly wars and also built a most luxurious home at Versailles.

Louis XV became King of France in 1715. The Old Regime continued to operate as it had before. The political, economic, and social life of the nation hardly changed. The First and Second Estates retained the privileges and powers granted to them by Louis XIV. Louis XV also increasingly needed to raise money to pay for all of his enormous government expenses and extravagant lifestyle. The nobility and clergy resisted all efforts by the monarchy to make them pay a fairer share of

When Louis XIV died, he left France in a terrible financial situation with a large amount of debt.

For most of the 18th century, Louis XV was able to use his absolute powers to put fear into the peasants, city workers, and artisans.

taxes and refused to share the economic burden of supporting an increasingly indebted government.

Therefore, the king had to resort to raising the taxes of an already overly burdened Third Estate. This meant that any new plan for taxation or fees mostly fell on those people least capable of paying—the peasants, city workers, and artisans. These three groups were increasingly unhappy about the increased taxes that they had to pay, the required labor and services they had to perform, and their poor living conditions. In addition, the peasants were required to pay a land tax called the *taille*. They were obligated to perform a labor service for the crown called the *corvée* and also paid rents to their landlords. Some peasants even paid feudal dues to certain lords.

For most of the eighteenth century, the king was able to use his absolute powers to put fear into the Third Estate. The king prevented the development of any rebellious movement. The king wrote royal secret letters to search for and arrest people suspected of being against the monarchy. People were often imprisoned without charges. The aristocracy and Church officials helped the king and nobles keep control of the Third Estate. The Church even promised the people a better life in the hereafter. In this way, the king eliminated all threats to the power and privileges of the monarchy and first two Estates.

In spite of the king's efforts to suppress dissent and rebellion, resentment and anger continued to grow during the 1700s. Educated members of the middle class could not be prevented from learning the truth. The educated middle class had access to books and newspapers. They were influenced by the political ideas of the Enlightenment. The peasants and city workers were subject to rumors that only fueled their anger and feelings of frustration as their living conditions deteriorated and hunger increased.

The Enlightenment was a period of time when philosophers and other writers explored new ideas that challenged old ways of thinking. Many Enlightenment writers were critical of the king's claim of divine right as his reason for absolute rule. The writings of John Locke, the Baron de Montesquieu, Voltaire, and Jean Jacques Rousseau circulated despite attempts to censor them. Enlightenment writers questioned the royal and Church claims to their authority. The monarch and Church based their claim to divine rule on their belief that they were God's messengers on earth. Enlightenment thinkers believed these ideas were in conflict with natural law and had to undergo change (see Chapter 20).

LOUIS XVI INHERITS A TROUBLED THRONE IN 1774

Louis XVI was 13 years old when he inherited the throne and became the king of France in 1774. During the reign of Louis XVI, the financial situation in France grew worse. There were some attempts to undertake economic reforms. However, the attempt by **Robert Turgot,** the king's capable finance minister, to bring about a series of economic reforms to reduce the nation's debt failed. The king was too interested in his own personal pleasures to support reforms to curb the royal family's lavish spending, particularly that of Queen **Marie Antoinette**. The government's poor financial situation was aggravated by the decision of Louis XVI and his advisors to support the Americans in their revolution against the British.

Louis XVI was too interested in his own personal pleasures to support reforms to curb the royal family's lavish spending.

During the 1780s, life for most French people became more difficult. In 1787 and 1788, two successive poor harvests only worsened life for the vast majority of people who were members of the Third Estate. This agricultural disaster, primarily caused by a long period of drought, led to severe food shortages particularly in the cities. When food became scarcer, city people suffered greatly from hunger. Even if they could find where to buy available food, they could not pay the higher prices that were demanded. The Third Estate's resentment against the king and First and Second Estates only grew worse as the food shortages worsened. By 1789, the people of France in the Third Estate would no longer tolerate the situation.

THE FIRST STAGE OF THE FRENCH REVOLUTION

By May 1789, Louis XVI was left with no choice but to call for a meeting of the **Estates-General**, a national representative legislature. His goal was to have this national legislature help solve the economic crisis, which threatened bankruptcy. Louis hoped that the legislature would cooperate and give its approval for the additional taxes that he needed to improve France's financial situation. The meeting of the Estates-General did not turn out the way the king planned. The attempt to reform the tax system proved to be the beginning of the end for the Old Regime.

During this early stage of the French Revolution, the Abbé de Sieyés played a crucial role in defining the key issue for the Third Estate. Sieyés stated that the delegates to the Estates-General first had to address the problem that each Estate only had one vote. The first two Estates had a two to one advantage in the block voting system. The delegates of the Third Estate were more numerous but were frustrated by their inability to bring about changes in the Estates-

The Abbé de Sieyés played a crucial role in defining the key issue for the Third Estate.

General. The Third Estate delegates wanted a different voting procedure in which every delegate would have one vote.

Some of the members of the Third Estate were radicals of the left wing who wanted to enact major changes. Other members of the Third Estate were more moderate or conservative and wanted limited reform. These delegates were part of the right wing of the Third Estate in the Estates-General. The terms *left wing* and *right wing* are often used to distinguish between more radical or left-wing ideas and political positions from more moderate or conservative or right-wing ideas and political positions.

The first two Estates supported by the king refused to change the voting procedures. Increasingly frustrated by the existing political system, the Third Estate delegates decided to take matters into their own hands. In June 1789, they took an oath, the Tennis Court Oath, not to disband until they had written a French Constitution. Count Honoré de Mirabeau, a nobleman and elected delegate to the Third Estate, was a leader of this breakaway movement, whose purpose was to create a limited constitutional monarchy. Louis XVI recognized the danger of a **National Assembly** in which there were only representatives of the Third Estate. He ordered the other Estates' delegates to participate in the National Assembly's work.

As the summer of 1789 approached, political events began to spin out of control. The anger and frustration of peasants grew in the countryside. In Paris, city workers and artisans increasingly protested their difficult living conditions.

The Third Estate took an oath, the Tennis Court Oath, not to disband until they had written a French Constitution.

This anger soon led these groups into violent actions. Rumors spread rapidly. One rumor was about the king's bringing more troops into Paris in order to close the National Assembly.

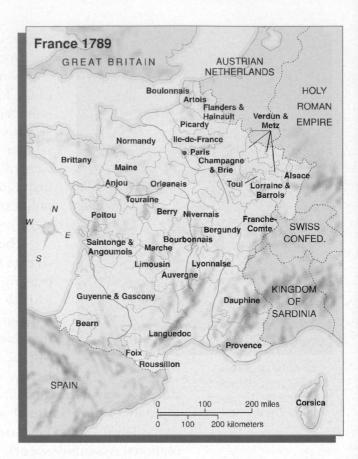

France 1789

In Paris, mobs began to riot over the high price of bread. On July 14, 1789, a Paris mob attacked the hated and infamous **Bastille** prison fortress, freed prisoners, and seized weapons and gunpowder. The Bastille was seen as a symbol of injustice and inequality in the Old Regime. This attack led quickly to peasant upheaval in the countryside. In many places, the castles and large manor houses of the aristocracy were burned, and public documents were destroyed. France would never be the same after these first violent events of the French Revolution.

Main Idea:
As the summer of 1789 approached, political events began to spin out of control.

On July 14, 1789, a Paris mob attacked the hated and infamous Bastille prison fortress.

THE NATIONAL ASSEMBLY ADOPTS REFORMS

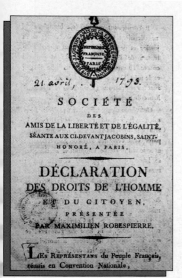

The Declaration of the Rights of Man was passed in 1789.

After the storming of the Bastille, the frightened king recognized the National Assembly. The increasing violence spurred the National Assembly to take action. During one particularly long session on August 4, 1789, the nobles and clergy were forced to give up their privileges. Several weeks later, on August 26, 1789, the National Assembly passed the **Declaration of the Rights of Man and Citizen**. In this declaration, all French citizens were guaranteed the rights of liberty, property, security, and freedom from oppression. Other articles of this famous document gave the French people freedom of religion and speech and the right of equal justice. The class structure and privileges connected with the three Estates were ended, and the remains of feudalism were abolished.

This historic declaration did not end the violence of the Parisian mobs and many peasants in the countryside. Louis XVI and his court were increasingly fearful. The King came to Paris and accepted the *tricolor*, a red, white, and blue ribbon symbol of the revolution. Despite this symbolic gesture, Louis XVI and his family soon had to give up their protected way of life in their luxurious Versailles palace. The royal family was forced to come to Paris and live under guard in a smaller palace in the **Tuileries**.

The National Assembly continued its work for over two years to draft a constitution. Finally, after long sessions and heated debates, a constitution was completed. This first French Constitution of 1791 created a limited monarchy

The symbols of the French Revolution.

Fearful, King Louis XVI accepted the tricolor symbol of the revolution.

During one particularly long session on August 4, 1789, the nobles and clergy were forced to give up their privileges. This is an artist's rendition of the "Destruction of Privilege."

and a *unicameral*, one house, legislature. The Roman Catholic Church lost its lands and political independence. In mid-1791, the first stage of the French Revolution came to a close. Louis XVI reluctantly gave his approval to the Constitution.

During these years, repeated poor harvests led to hunger and mob riots in Paris and other cities and towns. Armed peasants roamed the countryside and continued to frighten the nobles and Church officials. Many of the nobles and clergy felt their lives were in danger and fled the country. They became **émigrés**, people who lived outside the nation's borders. The growing acts of violence were one direct result of the worsening economic conditions.

In June 1791, the king and queen decided to flee Paris with their family. While on the road, the royal family was recognized, arrested, and brought back under guard to Paris. The French Revolution was ready to enter into a more radical and violent stage as different political groups began to fight for control of the National Assembly. During the months that followed, mass arrests of *royalist sympathizers*, people known to support the monarchy, took place. In September, angry mobs massacred many of these prisoners.

THE SECOND STAGE OF THE REVOLUTION

During the second stage of the French Revolution, a republic was eventually established. A *republic* is a government in which people choose their leaders. In 1791, the idea of creating a republic led to fierce political battles for control of the National Assembly. Three groups of deputies competed for power. One group was called the *Girondists*. They were political moderates seeking gradual

George Danton was one of the leaders of the Jacobins, who wanted to eliminate the monarchy.

reform. Another group of deputies was thought of as the *Conservatives*. The goal of people who took a conservative political position was to prevent change and hold to past traditions. The third group was called the **Jacobins**. Jacobins were deputies who wanted extreme changes such as the elimination of the monarchy and establishment of a republic. The Jacobin leaders were Georges Danton, Jean-Paul Marat, and **Maximilian Robespierre**.

In the spring of 1792, the Jacobin deputies, encouraged by the **Paris Commune**, a radical political grouping, demanded more extreme political changes. The outbreak of war with Austria in April 1792 helped their cause. Soon other European monarchies supported the Austrians in the fight against the French army. By July 1792, the foreign armies had advanced on Paris and threatened to put an end to the French Revolution. The worsening war situation led to increased violence within Paris. Jacobin-led mobs attacked the Tuileries, where the king and his family were staying. The royal couple was accused of plotting with foreign powers and imprisoned in a stone tower.

In this stage of the revolution, the radical Jacobin deputies in the assembly became very influential. They played on the fears of the moderate deputies who felt increasingly threatened by the approaching foreign armies. The Jacobin deputies managed to gain control of the National Assembly and used their political power to enact extreme measures. The Jacobin leaders were helped by a favorable turn in the war. Fortunately for the radicals, the French army rallied and defeated the advancing Austrians and Prussians. The Jacobins took the credit for the victory of the French army.

THE FRENCH REVOLUTION TAKES A RADICAL TURN

In September 1792, a newly elected legislature, the **National Convention**, was chosen by means of *universal manhood suffrage*. All adult males were given the right to vote for the first time in France. The National Convention ended the monarchy and established a republic. The king was put on trial and charged with treason. The Jacobins called for the king's death. In a trial, Louis XVI was convicted and sentenced to death. As evidence, the Jacobins used a box of letters that they said proved the king was working with other European monarchs to crush the French Revolution.

The execution of the king in January 1793 was a very momentous event. The king was executed in public by *guillotine*, a devise that uses a sharp falling blade to cut off the head of the victim, thereby severing it from the body. The execution led to a royalist uprising. The Jacobins put down the uprising after a very bloody struggle. The guillotining of Louis XVI also led to renewed attacks on France. The monarchs of other European nations increasingly feared the spread of revolutionary ideas to their nations. They were more than ever determined of put down the French Revolution.

The National Convention was able to remain in power from September 1792 until 1795. The Jacobin leaders controlled the legislative sessions of the National Convention. They allowed no interference in their direction of the Revolution. However, on the battlefield, France's military opponents—Great Britain, the Netherlands, Spain, Austria, and Prussia—were increasingly successful. At this critical moment, Georges Danton issued a famous call for Frenchmen to defend the revolution. An army of volunteers answered his call. In the summer of 1793, the National Convention established a dictatorship to defend the nation and revolution. The deputies voted for the establishment of a **Committee of Public Safety**. This committee was given dictatorial powers.

THE REIGN OF TERROR

During the summer of 1793, the French armies faced an increasingly worsening military situation. The military crisis caused the Committee of Public Safety to take extraordinary measures to defeat their foreign enemies and maintain their political control in France. A conscription program was started to strengthen the army by adding more soldiers. War was waged against the opponents of the

The guillotining of Louis XVI led to renewed attacks on France by monarchs of other European nations who feared the spread of revolutionary ideas.

Revolution in different parts of France. Peasants angered by the draft, economic hardship, and measures taken against the Roman Catholic Church took up arms against the Jacobin military forces. Even in the cities, troubles increased because of food shortages and rising food prices. The rising discontent led to the murder of one of the Jacobin leaders, Jean-Paul Marat.

The Jacobins were now determined to eliminate their opponents in France totally. The Committee of Public Safety unleashed a violent campaign, a **Reign of Terror**, to completely crush all opposition to the Revolution. During the following months, all enemies of the Revolution in France were hunted down. Estimations are that about 40,000 people were

During the Reign of Terror, Queen Marie Antoinette was publicly guillotined.

executed in public, often by guillotine. No one was really safe during the Reign of Terror because people often accused their neighbors for personal reasons. During the Reign of Terror, Queen Marie Antoinette was publicly guillotined.

THE RISE AND FALL OF DANTON AND ROBESPIERRE

Georges Danton and Maximilian Robespierre were the two key Jabobin leaders responsible for directing the Committee of Public Safety. Robespierre gradually gained more dictatorial powers than the other committee members. The Committee of Public Safety was able to overcome the threat of foreign invasion. The inspired French armies were now victorious in the continuing war with the European monarchies.

In the spring of 1794, the Jacobin leaders argued about the direction the Revolution was taking. A serious split occurred between Robespierre and Danton. Robespierre and his followers accused Danton of being disloyal to the Revolution. Danton was arrested and put on trial. His conviction and execution left the Committee of Public Safety completely in the hands of Robespierre and the most fanatical Jacobins.

During the next months, the Reign of Terror increasingly brought fear to even those who considered themselves republicans and supporters of the Revolution. By July 1794, Robespierre's continuing use of terror and executions led the National Convention to order his arrest. After a trial, Robespierre was guillotined. The Reign of Terror came to an end to the relief of the French people.

THE THIRD STAGE OF THE REVOLUTION: GOVERNMENT BY DIRECTORY

The National Convention once again took control of the French government. The middle-class groups that now controlled the National Convention wanted more political stability and security. A new constitution was drafted in 1795. The people who supported this more conservative constitution wanted a return to some of the ideas of the past and an elimination of policies they believed to be too radical or extreme. The Constitution of 1795 created a **Directory**, a council of five men, to rule the nation with the help of a legislature. The Constitution also ended universal male suffrage by requiring men to own property in order to vote. This change put the government back in the control of the propertied classes.

The Directory governed France from 1795 to 1799. In its last years, the Directory had to deal with growing political and economic problems. The nation was threatened by bankruptcy. The Directory increasingly depended on the army to maintain its control over the nation. By late 1799, a popular young army general, Napoleon Bonaparte, joined in a **coup d'état**, or quick seizure of power, and ended the Directory's rule in France. The French Revolution was now over as the final stage of the Revolution came to a close.

THE LASTING IMPACT OF THE REVOLUTION

The French Revolution had a deep and lasting impact. Its results influenced future historical developments. In France and later elsewhere, the Revolution brought about a basic change in the relationship between the government and the governed. The French Revolution advanced the development of democratic traditions by recognizing the value and worth of all individuals. During the nineteenth century, in France and elsewhere, ideas in support of political democracy took root and developed.

The French Revolution brought a temporary end to the monarchy. Even after the monarchy was restored in the early 1800s, it did not last to the end of the century. Political power passed from an absolutist monarch who ruled by divine right to the people. For the French people, the nation and not the monarch became the symbol of unity. A greater sense of patriotism and nationalism developed. This spirit of nationalism became a major factor in Europe and elsewhere. The political slogan **"liberty, equality, and fraternity"** continued to influence and express the hopes of peoples throughout the world in the next centuries.

The French Revolution permanently changed the political, economic, and social structure of French society. The Old Regime ended, and the aristocracy never regained the positions they once held. The last traces of feudalism were wiped out. Thereafter, the middle class, or bourgeoisie, and the wealthy capitalists became the most important and influential political, economic, and social groups in France. Workers and farmers waited longer to gain greater political rights, but they would never again be ignored as they had been in the past. The French nation would never be the same as it was before 1789.

LINK TO TODAY

We live today in a world where revolutions seem to be occurring all the time. Throughout the nineteenth and twentieth centuries, revolutions took place in Europe, Asia, Africa, and North and South America. All of these revolutions had a philosophical connection to the French Revolution. We can trace the reasons why people continued to make revolutions in the nineteenth and twentieth centuries to many of the conditions that were true for the majority of French people who rose up in revolt in 1789. Feelings of injustice and inferiority, government indifference and repression, heavy tax burdens, and overwhelming poverty, hopelessness, and hunger continued to lead people to raise the banner of revolution.

At the start of the current century, on the continents of Africa and Asia, revolutionary movements began because some people believed that they were not being treated fairly by the established governments that ruled these nations. In the nations of the Sudan, the Ivory Coast, and Nigeria, people who believed that there was no other alternative but to fight rose up in order to change their government's policies. Many of these people believed that their living conditions were no longer tolerable. These living conditions in many ways were similar to the conditions that the majority of French people faced during the period prior to the French Revolution. In Asia in the nations of Indonesia, the Philippines, and Sri Lanka, revolutionary movements also started because people believed that they suffered from political, economic, and social discrimination and injustices. Here also the political, economic, and social conditions discussed in this chapter that caused the French people to arise and make a revolution were often the causes of uprisings of these discontented people.

In Europe in Chechnya, a revolution devastated the country. In this region of the Caucasus, the violent events that took place shocked the world because of their brutality. Elsewhere in Europe, particularly in the nations of the area historically referred to as the Balkans, the potential for revolution always strongly exists.

In all likelihood, revolutions will continue to take place throughout the world. The people taking part in these revolutions will probably not be familiar with the causes of the French Revolution of 1789. Nevertheless, these people will know about the conditions and reasons why they rise up and decide to take part in a revolution in their own country. Their link to the French Revolution is that they too will want to bring about meaningful changes to improve their lives. If this cannot be accomplished peacefully, then almost certainly these people will believe that a violent revolution is their only alternative. This is one of the lasting links to the spirit of revolution awakened in France in 1789.

CHAPTER SUMMARY

There have been a number of important events in world history that have marked a turning point in world history. These events led to important changes during the time period that they took place and after they ended. In this chapter, you have read about the time period of the French Revolution. From 1789 to 1799, a period of ten years, a revolution broke out, led to many changes, and finally came to an end. The French Revolution will always be remembered for its political, economic, and social ideas that led to enormous changes in the relationships between people and their government and among people themselves. The key people who participated in the revolution continue to be studied and written about. The lives of Danton, Robespierre, Louis XVI, Marie Antoinette, Marat, and others who played major roles during the revolutionary years continue to fascinate us.

The French Revolution led to the rise of feelings of nationalism, increased calls for the right of self-determination, violent revolution, and harsh repression. In France, Europe, and elsewhere in the world important revolutionary events led to major political changes. As the nineteenth century progressed, these revolutions continued to take place with increasing frequency throughout the world. Some of these nationalist struggles for independence and unification were successful, whereas others failed. You will read more about these revolutions in the following chapter and Volume II.

IMPORTANT PEOPLE, PLACES, AND TERMS

KEY TERMS

Declaration of the Rights of Man and Citizen	Old Regime	bourgeoisie
	divine right	Directory
liberty, equality, and fraternity	Age of Absolutism	Estates-General
	First, Second, and Third Estates	National Assembly
Reign of Terror	tithe	émigré
Committee of Public Safety	Paris Commune	National Convention
	coup d'état	Jacobin

PEOPLE

Louis XIV	Marie Antoinette	Jean-Paul Marat
Louis XV	Robert Turgot	Maximilian
Louis XVI	Georges Danton	Robespierre

PLACES

Bastille	Tuileries	Versailles
Paris		

EXERCISES FOR CHAPTER 21

MULTIPLE CHOICE

Select the letter of the correct answer.

1. The ideas of Montesquieu, Voltaire, and Rousseau most influenced the

   a. growth of power of the Roman Catholic Church.
   b. willingness of Louis XVI to make democratic reforms.
   c. rise of industrial capitalism during the Old Regime.
   d. ideas that led to a desire for political reform.

2. Which of the headlines best reflects the following statements:

   1. Peasants have to pay corvée.
   2. City workers suffer from hunger.
   3. The Nobles and Clergy avoid taxes.
   4. Marie Antoinette buys luxurious gowns.

   a. "France Develops a Market Economy
   b. "Income Gap Narrows in France"
   c. "Old Regime Benefits the Privileged"
   d. "Economic Equality Grows in France"

3. Which statement best reflects the sentiments of the author of the poem?

   If the High-ups still make trouble
   Then the devil confound them
   And since they love gold so much
   May it melt in their traps
   That's the sincere wish
   Of the women who sell fish.

   a. Women who work in fish markets are cruel.
   b. The First Estate in France is treated unjustly.
   c. The wealthy in France deserve to be hated.
   d. Gold is not good to use as bait in fish traps.

4. Which is the correct chronological order of the events listed below?

   1. The Directory takes over in France.
   2. Louis XVI calls for an Estates-General.
   3. The Reign of Terror begins.
   4. The Tennis Court Oath is taken.

   a. 4, 3, 1, 2
   b. 3, 1, 2, 4
   c. 2, 4, 3, 1
   d. 1, 2, 3, 4

5. Which statement best describes France during the Reign of Terror?

   a. The Committee of Public Safety supported the monarchy.
   b. Everyone felt more protected from the threat of invasion.
   c. Robespierre was successful in reducing the violence against émigrés.
   d. Many people were unjustly accused and guillotined.

6. The Old Regime in France refers to

   a. the period of the French Revolution.
   b. pre-1789 French society and social structure.
   c. the time prior to the regime of Louis XIV.
   d. when the Directory took power in 1795.

7. The French monarchy prior to 1789 believed in

   a. constitutional democracy.
   b. absolute rule.
   c. constitutional monarchy.
   d. legislative power.

8. Which statement is true of the class system in France prior to 1789?

    a. The First and Second Estates paid the most taxes.
    b. The Third Estate was subject to very little taxation.
    c. The Third Estate was made up only of nobles and artisans.
    d. The bourgeoisie was considered as part of the Third Estate.

9. Louis XVI was unable to resolve France's financial crisis during his reign because

    a. the second Estate was only willing to pay limited taxes.
    b. the First Estate wanted to increase the labor tax.
    c. the peasantry and workers refused to lend money to the monarchy.
    d. the First and Second Estates blocked all taxation reform affecting them.

10. The Third Estate refused to meet and vote separately in the Estates-General because they

    a. were less numerous than the first two Estates.
    b. hoped to join with the First Estate and form a majority.
    c. were following the previous procedures of the French legislature.
    d. wanted each delegate to have one vote.

11. The National Assembly was responsible for which of the following:

    a. The Declaration of the Rights of Man and the Citizen
    b. The petition to call up the Estates-General in 1789
    c. The establishment of the Directory system of government
    d. The writing of the Constitution of 1795

Base your answers to Questions 12 and 13 on the following passage:

During the greater part of the day the guillotine had been kept busy at its ghastly work. . . . Every aristocrat was a traitor. . . . For two hundred years now the people had sweated, and toiled, and starved to keep a lustful court in lavish extravagance; now the descendants of those who had helped to make these courts brilliant had to hide for their lives.

12. Which event is referred to in this passage?

    a. Reign of Terror
    b. Tennis Court Oath
    c. Directory takes power
    d. Coronation of Louis XVI

13. Which generalization best summarizes the views of the author of this passage?

    a. The common people of the nation deserved to be punished for violating the country's laws.
    b. The goals of fraternity, liberty, and equality were achieved during this period.
    c. The nobility was being punished for bringing benefits to the nation.
    d. Because of past abuses by the nobility, the common people staged a bloody revolt.

14. A primary cause of the French Revolution in 1789 was the

    a. increasing dissatisfaction of the Third Estate.
    b. rise to power of Napoleon Bonaparte.
    c. execution of Louis XVI.
    d. unhappiness of the First and Second Estates.

15. One important result of the French Revolution was that

    a. France enjoyed a lengthy period of peace and prosperity.
    b. the Church was restored to its former role and power in the French government.
    c. political power shifted to the bourgeoisie.
    d. France lost its spirit of nationalism.

16. Which idea is described in the following passage:

God hath power to create and destroy, make or unmake, at his pleasure: to give life or send death; to judge . . . and to be judged by none . . . and like the power of Kings.

    a. Theory of divine right
    b. Enlightened despotism
    c. Constitutional monarchy
    d. Democratic plurality

17. The radical Jacobins wanted a

    a. limited monarchy.
    b. republican form of government.
    c. return to absolute rule.
    d. coalition with the Girondists.

18. During the first stage of the French Revolution

    a. the Estates-General became the National Assembly.
    b. the Jacobins gained control of the Legislative Assembly.
    c. the Reign of Terror began in the French countryside.
    d. the Directory took charge of the French government.

19. The Reign of Terror refers to the time when

    a. Jacobin radicals persecuted all suspected opposition.
    b. King Louis XVI sought to crush the National Assembly.
    c. the Directory hunted down the radical Jacobins.
    d. peasants revolted against the Directory.

20. The Constitution of 1795 established

    a. a Directory of five men to rule the nation.
    b. a constitutional and limited monarchy.
    c. universal manhood suffrage in France.
    d. a military dictatorship to run France.

ESSAYS FOR CHAPTER 21

1. The year is 1793. You are a lawyer who has been assigned to defend the king in the upcoming trial in which he will be accused of treason and disloyalty to France. The prosecution is calling for the death penalty. Write a document in defense of the king, which you will read as your opening statement at the trial.
2. The year is 1789. You are a lawyer representing the peasants in a farming community outside of Paris, near Versailles. The peasants have asked you to write a document listing all of the injustices and sufferings that they have to face. They want to present the document to King Louis XVI.
3. Why did the radical Jacobins think that the Reign of Terror was necessary?
4. Why did the other nations of Europe try to put an end to the French Revolution?
5. Why did the French Revolution finally come to an end?

This task is based on the accompanying documents. Some of these documents have been edited for this purpose. This task is designed to test your ability to work with historical documents. As you analyze the documents, take into account both the source and the author's point of view.

Directions: Read the following documents and answer the questions after each document. Use the information in the reading and this chapter in writing your answers.

Document #1

The backwardness of France is beyond credibility. From Strasburg where I started my travels, I have not been able to see a newspaper. Well-dressed people are talking of news already three weeks old. The whole town of Besancon has not been able to furnish me a single newspaper. It is obvious to any traveling stranger that the people are either too uneducated or being denied news. It is no wonder when one sees the terrible living conditions of most of the peasants and city dwellers.

From *Diary of an English Tourist in 1789* by Arthur Young

Questions

1. Why do you think there was so little news available in the countryside of France?
2. How do you account for the terrible living conditions?

Document #2

Choose! For surely it is necessary that a small number perish so that the mass of people may be saved. Strike, destroy without pity these sorry victims, hurl them into the abyss. . . . Why do you recoil in horror from my words? Are not these horrible men who have been impassive [uncaring] egoists about the despair and misery of the people. These people without bread will no longer leave you in peace to enjoy the dishes of delicacies. Soon you will perish in the fires that come and your honor will not even save even one of your pleasures.

Part of a speech given in the National Assembly by Count Honore de Mirabeau

Questions

1. Why is Count Honore de Mirabeau so angry?
2. What is Count Mirabeau predicting will happen?

Document #3

The Great Fear can be explained by the economic, social and political circumstances existing in France in 1789. Fear that the royalist forces were plotting against them, made the peasants come together, allowed them to achieve full realization of their strength and reinforced the attack already launched against the remaining traces of feudalism. This continuing fear played its part in preparations for the continuing revolution and on these grounds alone must count as one of the most important episodes in the history of the French nation.

From *The Great Fear of 1789* by Georges Lefebvre

1. Why was the Great Fear so important in the continuing French Revolution?
2. Why did the Great Fear particularly effect the peasants in the countryside?

Document #4

The high price of corn has occasioned many insurrections in some provincial towns, particularly at Rheims and Vendome: at St. Quentin a barge laden with 2,000 sacks of the above-mentioned commodity belonging to a very rich individual of the place, who was accused in the neighboring villages of having made his fortune by profiting excessively from the corn purchasing was seized and the whole cargo disappeared.

From "A Letter from Lord Dorset to Lord Carmarthen" in *British Nobility Correspondence"*

Questions

1. Why did the French seize the cargo of corn?
2. What do you think happened to the crop of seized corn?

Document #5

In the early spring of the Duc d'Orleans was very popular in Paris. The previous year he had sold many paintings, and it was generally believed that the eight millions raised by the sale had been devoted to relieving the suffering of the people during the hard winter which had just ended. In contrast, whether rightly or wrongly, there was no mention of any charitable gifts from the royal princes or from the King and Queen. Nor did the King ever show himself. Hidden away at Versailles or hunting in the nearby forests, he suspected nothing, for saw nothing, and believed everything he was told.

From *Escape from Terror: The Journal of Madame de la Tour du Pin*

Questions

1. Why was King Louis XVI so disliked by the French people?
2. Why did Louis XVI know so little about what was happening in France to his subjects?

CHAPTER 22

Revolution and War in the Age of Napoleon

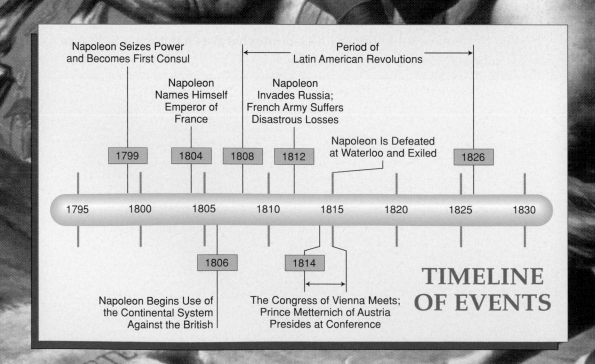

Napoleon Seizes Power and Becomes First Consul

Period of Latin American Revolutions

Napoleon Names Himself Emperor of France

Napoleon Invades Russia; French Army Suffers Disastrous Losses

Napoleon Is Defeated at Waterloo and Exiled

| 1799 | 1804 | 1808 | 1812 | | 1826 |

| 1795 | 1800 | 1805 | 1810 | 1815 | 1820 | 1825 | 1830 |

| | 1806 | | 1814 | |

TIMELINE OF EVENTS

Napoleon Begins Use of the Continental System Against the British

The Congress of Vienna Meets; Prince Metternich of Austria Presides at Conference

Ultimately the French Revolution came to an end. However, it led to the taking of power and the establishing of an empire by one of history's most fascinating personalities, Napoleon Bonaparte. Napoleon's rise and fall from power was also a revolutionary time period. Napoleon fought wars in many European countries and unleashed the revolutionary spirit on the European continent and in the Americas. After his defeat, the Congress of Vienna (1814–1815) sought to restore a balance of political power, political order and stability, and legitimacy in Europe and areas colonized by European nations. In Europe, the leaders of the Congress were successful in preventing **nationalism** in most countries until the outbreak of the revolutions of 1830. However, they could not prevent the Spanish and Portuguese colonies from proclaiming their independence. The era ended as it had begun with more political, economic, and social changes on the way and more revolutions soon to break out in Europe and elsewhere in the world.

NAPOLEON'S EARLY LIFE AND MILITARY CAREER

Napoleon Bonaparte was born in 1769. He grew up on the French Mediterranean island of **Corsica** in a traditional family in which his father made all the important decisions. At the age of 10, Napoleon's father decided to send him to a French military academy. His early military education was an important influence in his life. This training and preparation led Napoleon to pursue a military career. In 1785, Napoleon was commissioned as a French artillery officer. During the Old Regime, Napoleon had little chance for career advancement. Higher military rank was not open to someone of his background. He was from Corsica, and he did not come from an aristocratic family.

After the French Revolution broke out in 1789, France became involved in a series of wars against different coalitions of European nations. The European monarchs joined together to defeat the French army and put an end to what they considered a dangerous revolutionary example. The wars against the European nations gave Napoleon greater opportunities to move up in military rank. Napoleon was able to advance his career because of his talent and abilities as a military leader and strategist. In 1793, Napoleon's military success against the British brought his name to the attention of the Jacobins, who were then in control of the French government. During these years,

Napoleon was willing to serve the cause of the French Revolution and demonstrated that he was a military officer who had the loyalty of the men he commanded.

the French revolutionary governments often changed as political instability increased. Despite the political instability, Napoleon continued to show the radical politicians of the French governments that he was an excellent military officer. Napoleon was willing to serve the cause of the French Revolution and demonstrated that he was a military officer who had the loyalty of the men he commanded (see Chapter 21).

NAPOLEON AND THE DIRECTORY

After the fall of Robespierre in 1794, the **Directory** took over the control of the French government. Napoleon survived the change of government and served the Directory as an artillery officer. Once again, he knew how to demonstrate his military skills and usefulness. When the Directory called on Napoleon to put down a riot by a Parisian mob, the artillery unit that he commanded crushed the rioters. In 1795, Napoleon married Josephine de Beauharnais, who came from a well-known family. This marriage into an influential family soon led to his appointment by the Directory as a general in the army.

Over the next three years, Napoleon was given a number of commanding positions. His military victories against the Austrians, a key member of the anti-French coalition, added to his growing reputation. The Directory next assigned him to the Egyptian campaign. At first, Napoleon was successful against the British army because of his skills as a military strategist. However, Lord Nelson's destruction of the French fleet made Napoleon's land victories in Egypt meaningless. The control of the seas gave the British a major advantage because Napoleon could not resupply his army.

By early 1799, the political status of the Directory greatly deteriorated. Members of the Directory faced serious charges of corruption. There was a growing threat of national bankruptcy. The government increasingly could not pay its bills. To make matters worse, lacking Napoleon's leadership, the French army was defeated in Italy by the combined armies of Great Britain, Austria, and Russia. It was at this time that Napoleon was asked to return to France. After Napoleon's arrival in Paris, he joined in a *conspiracy*, a plot, against the Directory. Even some Directory members were involved in this plot to overthrow the Directory.

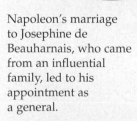

Napoleon's marriage to Josephine de Beauharnais, who came from an influential family, led to his appointment as a general.

A NEW GOVERNMENT TAKES POWER

In 1799, Napoleon and others who were discontent with what was happening replaced the Directory. The corrupt and hated Directory quickly fell after a *coup d'état*, a quick seizure of power. The French legislature then created an executive consul to govern France. Napoleon was appointed to one of the three consul positions. However, Napoleon was not happy about the idea of sharing power with the other consul members. With the support of powerful friends and the army, he soon became the First Consul and used his political power to further his real plan. Napoleon wanted to become the ruler of France. To accomplish his goal, Napoleon's first step was to change France into a constitutional republican government. Under his guidance, a constitution was soon written and adopted. France became a republic.

Napoleon increasingly worked to consolidate his political power. He reorganized the government and put its administration under his personal control. Although Napoleon considered himself a republican and reformer, he was willing to use dictatorial power. His determination to control the nation politically and economically violated the spirit of the new French Constitution. Napoleon was moving away from democratic rule. He was intent in realizing his true ambition. He wanted to create a French empire with himself as emperor.

During his rule as First Consul, Napoleon's domestic policies led to a number of reforms that helped to modernize the French nation. He established a Bank of France and used the funds issued by the bank to make government loans. In this way, he brought the nation's financial system under his personal control. Napoleon stabilized prices to gain popular support for his economic reforms. He also brought about reforms in France's educational system by creating a national system of schools controlled by the government. Technical and secondary schools called *lycées* were opened to all those who qualified for admission. These changes toward a public system of education improved the overall quality of education in France. Education was now more open to all social classes in France.

During this time, one of Napoleon's greatest achievements was his reform of the French legal system and laws. The **Napoleonic Code**, which unified all French law into one legal system, was enacted. The legal concepts of Napoleon's law code were based on ideas that developed in France since the time of the Enlightenment. The Napoleonic law code took into account the principles of natural law. All men were considered equal under the law, but the state was placed above the individual. The accused had to prove innocence if charged by the state.

The Napoleonic Code eliminated the rights that woman and children had gained in the early years of the French Revolution. Napoleon was a strong believer in authority and saw the father as the leader of the family. His belief in the father as the supreme figure in the family most likely was based on how he himself was brought up in Corsica.

In 1801, Napoleon also signed the important **Concordat** agreement with the Roman Catholic Church. Napoleon negotiated this agreement with Pope Pius VII. Roman Catholicism was recognized as the religion of most French people. However the Concordat provided for the continuation of religious toleration. In addition, the agreement confirmed that the French nation would retain the lands seized from the Church

Pope Pius VII negotiated with Napoleon on the Concordat agreement.

by the state during the French Revolution. The bishops also continued to be appointed by the government and had to swear loyalty to the nation. By finding a solution for the church versus state conflict in France, Napoleon increased his popularity among the religious French *peasants*, or farmers.

THE RISE OF THE NAPOLEONIC EMPIRE

In 1800, Napoleon began a military campaign to avenge defeats suffered earlier by French armies in battles against the Second Coalition, an anti-French European military alliance. His ultimate goal still was to create a French empire, but he first had to defeat the armies of the European coalition to realize this ambition. Napoleon's use of masterful military tactics led to the crushing defeat of Austria and that nation's withdrawal from the coalition. Under Napoleon's brilliant command, the French army continued to win military victories. The French military success soon led to Czarist Russia's withdrawal from the weakened coalition.

Under the leadership of Lord Nelson, the British continued to maintain their naval supremacy.

Only Great Britain now presented Napoleon with any real military challenge. Under the leadership of **Lord Nelson**, the British continued to maintain their naval supremacy. Control of the seas enabled the English to protect their war weary island kingdom from Napoleon's powerful army. In 1802, the two rival nations signed a peace treaty that was favorable to Napoleon's long-term interests. The Treaty of Amiens confirmed and restored all of France's territorial conquests in Europe and the Middle East. France was now the recognized leading power on the European continent. Napoleon finally could accomplish his real ambition.

NAPOLEON AS EMPEROR

Napoleon consolidated his power at home and abroad as he moved toward becoming emperor. In 1802 in France, Napoleon became First Counsel-for-Life after a direct vote of approval by the people, a *plebiscite*. In international matters in Europe, Napoleon did not allow the other continental countries to make decisions or take any action that he considered to be against France's national interests. Napoleon insisted on the recognition of France's claims in all commercial agreements, land disputes, and other matters.

By 1804, Napoleon finally realized his dream of becoming the Emperor of Europe's strongest military power.

By 1804, Napoleon finally realized his dream of becoming the emperor of Europe's strongest military power. During his coronation ceremony, Napoleon took the crown from the hands of Pope Pius VII and placed it on his own head. By placing the crown on his head, Napoleon indicated that he owed the title of Emperor of France to no one but himself, not even the Catholic Church. One again by a largely favorable popular vote, another plebiscite, the French approved of Napoleon's decision to name himself Emperor of France.

The French Republic ended with Napoleon's coronation as emperor. Napoleon had no intention of returning France to the time when the aristocracy of the Old Regime had all the privileges. Nevertheless, he generously allowed nobles who were émigrés to return to France. In addition, he granted many new titles to people who were his favorites, thereby increasing the number of French nobles. In spite of his moves to strengthen the aristocracy, Napoleon won middle-class support by establishing a national bank and creating economic stability. His popularity among the lower classes remained strong. Napoleon continued to win impressive military victories, which added to his popular support among the Parisian working class.

Emperor Napoleon soon had the French armies on the move. Napoleon's political ambitions in Italy, Germany, the Netherlands, and Switzerland were the main reasons for the new military campaign. Another reason was that he wanted to take preventive action after the British once again declared war on France. The British took up arms against Napoleon because they claimed that France violated the Treaty of Amiens. Napoleon's armies won easy military victories against the newly formed Third Coalition: Austria, Russia, Great Britain, and Sweden. When Prussia joined the coalition against Napoleon in 1806, it also was quickly defeated. On land, Napoleon's armies were too strong to be defeated, but at sea he still could not overcome the powerful British Royal Navy. The British continued to command the seas. Lord Nelson's destruction of the French fleet at Trafalgar in 1805 limited Napoleon's ambitions to the European continent.

NAPOLEON DOMINATES EUROPE

By 1807, Napoleon was the master of the European continent. His well-organized and capable army enabled Napoleon to influence and dominate the monarchies of Czarist Russia, the Austrian Empire, and Prussia. He forced these European monarchs to sign a treaty of alliance or face renewed military

Classic image of Napoleon.

Napoleon put his brother, Joseph Bonaparte (pictured here), on the Spanish throne.

campaigns. Napoleon soon annexed the Dutch Republic and a number of Italian city-states. Napoleon also gained control of Spain when he forced the Spanish king and his son to reside in France and put his brother **Joseph Bonaparte** on the Spanish throne. Only Great Britain, a dangerous military rival because of its sea power, continued to reject Napoleon's demands and remain out of reach.

THE CONTINENTAL SYSTEM

In 1806, Napoleon decided to change his tactics against the British. He came up with a plan to defeat the English by launching an economic boycott called the **Continental System**. Napoleon's idea was to cut off England's trade. He wanted to severely damage England's commercial system. His ultimate goal was to destroy Great Britain's industrial economy. All nations under French control and influence were required to follow Napoleon's lead or face military consequences. By hurting the British economy, he intended to force the British to accept his demands. Napoleon also wanted to strengthen commercial ties with the European nations already under his control. He wanted to make the French empire Europe's leading economic power.

The importation to and the exportation of goods from Great Britain were banned throughout Europe. Unfortunately for Napoleon, the Continental System did not work out in the way that he intended. European nations were able to evade the French decrees banning trade. They did this by working out a trading system to import products from Britain and export their own goods to the British by falsifying commercial documents and smuggling. Although the volume of trade with England was reduced, it was not ended.

In addition, the British responded with a blockade of their own. They used their naval power to stop suspicious ships on the high seas. British sea power effectively searched ships for goods leaving or coming to France. Britain's policy of stopping and searching all merchant ships caused growing resentment and anger among neutral nations, particularly the United States. Nevertheless, the British aggressively continued to maintain their blockade, which became increasingly effective. In effect, the Continental System backfired. The French economy was hurt far more than that of Britain. There was a sharp decline in France's sea trade.

The Spirit of Nationalism Rises in Prussia

In Prussia, there was a growing spirit of patriotism and nationalism. There was increasing resentment caused by Napoleon's demands. This rising spirit of nationalism and self-interest gave **King Frederick William III** the support he needed to rebuild Prussia's army. The Prussian government was reorganized, and the people were given more political freedom. When Napoleon invaded Russia in 1812, the Prussian king and military decided it was in the nation's best interests to side with Russia in the conflict.

Napoleon's Downfall

In the spring of 1812, Napoleon's decision to invade Russia with his **Grand Army** marked the beginning of his downfall. **Czar Alexander I** of Russia was not an enthusiastic supporter of Napoleon's Continental System. At first, the

czar cooperated because he was afraid to antagonize Napoleon. He did not want to face the military consequences of a French military attack. By 1812, the czar changed his position. The reason for this reversal was that the British blockade had severely hurt the Russian economy. In defiance of Napoleon's wishes, the czar decided to resume trading with the British.

Napoleon's response was to invade Russia. His military strategy was based on a plan for a quick and decisive defeat of the czar's military forces. Czar Alexander I realized that his military forces could not effectively combat Napoleon's powerful army. He ordered the Russian army to retreat and follow

Czar Alexander I was not an enthusiastic supporter of Napoleon's Continental System.

a strategy of "scorched earth." This meant that while falling back and avoiding battle with Napoleon's Grand Army, the Russians burned everything that might be taken and used by French troops.

In September 1812, the czar ordered the burning of the Russian capital, **Moscow**. Alexander I did not want the city to fall into the hands of the French army and serve as a shelter during the coming winter. Napoleon wrote a letter to Alexander in an effort to convince the czar to change his mind. Napoleon stated that the decision to burn the beautiful Russian capital was regrettable. He asked the czar to send him a peace offer, but Alexander I did not respond, and the war continued.

By October 1812, a long and particularly harsh winter began. "General Winter," with its subzero temperatures and fierce wind-driven snow and ice storms, proved to be too much for Napoleon's freezing soldiers and a full retreat was ordered. The long march back toward France led to the loss of tens of thousands of troops who literally starved or froze to death as they tried to retreat.

Napoleon was never able to recover from the loss of France's most seasoned officers and soldiers. A coalition of France's European enemies soon formed to take advantage of Napoleon's weakened position. Britain, Russia, Prussia, Austria, and Sweden united against Napoleon and created a powerful alliance. Napoleon had to rush home and raise a new French army. However, at the decisive Battle of Leipzig in October 1813, the combined European armies dealt the French army a stunning defeat. By March 1814, the allied armies were within Paris. Napoleon was forced to surrender and relinquish his role as emperor.

The winter, with its subzero temperatures and fierce wind-driven snow and ice storms, proved to be too much for Napoleon's freezing soldiers and a full retreat was ordered.

NAPOLEON'S EXILE, RETURN, AND FINAL DEFEAT AT WATERLOO

The fallen Napoleon was sent into exile on the island of Elba off the Italian coast. The victorious allies brought back **Louis XVIII** of the Bourbon monarchy as ruler of France. Shortly thereafter, the victors reduced the French borders to those that existed before 1792, thereby erasing all of the territorial gains made during Napoleon's rule.

Napoleon made one more desperate attempt to regain the power and glory of his fallen empire. The French people had not yet given up hope that Napoleon would return and bring the nation back to its former position as Europe's leading power. In March 1815, Napoleon escaped from Elba and returned to France where he received widespread popular support. The army of Louis XVIII quickly went over to Napoleon. Within days Napoleon was once again emperor of France.

The Duke of Wellington.

In a period known as the **Hundred Days**, Napoleon once again ruled France. In response, the European powers once again joined together to form a powerful coalition against Napoleon. Under the command of the **Duke of Wellington**, the allied army of the **Quadruple Alliance** met the French forces led by Napoleon at **Waterloo** in present-day Belgium. The result was that the French army was completely crushed. Napoleon was exiled to St. Helena, an island in the South Atlantic off the coast of West Africa controlled by the British, where he died in 1821.

NAPOLEON'S LEGACY IN EUROPE

Napoleon's legacy in France and Europe is tied to the ideas of the French Revolution and the years during which he became Europe's most influential ruler. During his rule, Napoleon advanced the ideas of the French Revolution. In the areas of Europe under Napoleon's control, many changes and reforms took place. He supported the writing of constitutions and reforms based on the ideas of the Napoleonic Code. This led to the recognition of the basic principles of equality before the law and freedom of religion in many European countries. Also, wherever Napoleon's influence reached, the last traces of feudalism were destroyed.

Napoleon was an excellent administrator who modernized the French government. The emperor's administrative reforms spread to other nations in

Europe under France's control. The end of absolutism in western Europe can be tied to the long-term effects of Napoleon's rule. Moreover, the spirit of nationalism that Napoleon awakened could never be completely destroyed. The revolutionary ideas of social justice that spread during the time of the Napoleonic Empire continued to grow and ultimately triumphed in Europe later in the nineteenth century.

NAPOLEON'S LEGACY IN THE AMERICAS

The United States

During this period, the United States, despite its claim of neutrality, could not avoid involvement with Napoleonic France and its military rival Great Britain. In 1803, Napoleon needed funds to finance his military campaigns. He was also aware that he could not defend the French Louisiana territory against the British. France decided to sell the territory to a surprised American government during the presidency of Thomas Jefferson. The purchase of the Louisiana territory almost doubled the land area of the United States.

Napoleon was also responsible in large measure for the United States' problems with the British. Napoleon's Continental System led to increased American conflict with

Thomas Jefferson was the U.S. president when France sold its territory to the American government.

Great Britain on the high seas. By 1812, the United States went to war with Great Britain over trade issues and the *impressing*, or the forced service, of American sailors into the British navy. The outbreak of war between the United States and Great Britain was a violation of America's stated policy of neutrality. The young American nation reluctantly became involved in the military and economic conflicts in Europe during the Napoleonic Era.

Haiti

Haiti was an important French colonial possession because of its valuable sugar cane production. The production of sugar depended on the exploitation of black slave labor. The movement for Haitian independence can be directly tied to the events of the French Revolution of the 1790s. News of the revolution spread to Haiti, particularly the ideas written in the Declaration of the Rights of Man and the Citizen of liberty, fraternity, and equality. The French white planter class refused to consider that their black slaves were deserving of these rights.

The production of sugar in Haiti depended on the exploitation of black slave labor.

Resentment grew among the free mulattos and black slaves.

During the 1790s, a revolution broke out in Haiti against French rule. **Toussaint L'Ouverture**, became the leader of the violent uprising of slaves against the French sugar plantation owners. The revolutionaries massacred the French colonists and took control of Haiti. Toussaint's leadership of the bloody revolution led to the destruction of the French-owned plantation system and resulted in Haitian independence.

After he became emperor, Napoleon tried to reestablish French rule in Haiti. He sent a French army under the command of **General LeClerc** to restore French rule. Although the French army tried, it was never able to militarily defeat the Haitians. Haiti, the second independent nation in the Western Hemisphere, was able to maintain its freedom. Despite Napoleon's attempts to restore French authority and the capture of L'Ouverture, the Haitians now led by Jean-Jacques Dessalines drove out the French and secured Haitian independence.

Toussaint L'Ouverture became the leader of the violent uprising of slaves against the sugar plantation owners.

The Haitians, led by Jean-Jacques Dessalines, drove out the French and secured Haitian independence.

The Spanish Colonial Empire in the Americas

Nationalism in Latin America Leads to Independence

After becoming emperor of France, Napoleon gradually reduced Spain to a helpless satellite. Popular resentment against French influence and troops stationed in Spain caused the weak King Charles IV to abdicate in favor of his son, Ferdinand. Napoleon took advantage of the unstable political situation in Spain. He used his military forces to remove the Spanish royal family from power and put his brother Joseph on the Spanish throne. Neither the Spanish people in Spain nor the Creoles in the Spanish American colonies accepted Napoleon's choice as their new monarch.

Napoleon's total domination of Spain led to the rise of revolutionary movements throughout Latin America. Spanish officials and the wealthy Creoles in Latin America refused to accept Joseph as their new king. Revolutions occurred throughout the region from 1808 to 1826. Here again, a legacy of the Napoleonic Era influenced events in the Americas. The events of the French Revolution and the Napoleonic Era were closely followed by the Creole class and led to the growth of nationalism in Latin America. The spirit of nationalism could not be crushed in Latin America. Nationalism is the belief that a group of people who share a common culture, language, and historical tradition should have their own specific area of land to control. This nationalistic goal called for political unification of a people who considered themselves a separate national group. Their goal was the creation of a nation-state that could then make its own laws and have autonomy. Nationalism increasingly became the most important issue in Latin America as the nineteenth century progressed.

By the early 1800s, revolutionary movements in the future Latin America began to overcome earlier obstacles to independence. The leaders of these Latin American revolutions were mostly members of the Creole class. The Creoles were primarily the wealthy white land owners and merchants who made up the upper class of colonial society. They had been born in the Americas and became the leaders of the independence movements in the Spanish vice royalties.

The Creoles resented the privileges that were granted to the Spaniards. Spanish merchants dominated the colonial trade, which angered local merchants and land owners engaged in commercial agricultural production such as sugar and tobacco. The Creoles disliked the Spanish officials who ruled the colonies, including the Catholic Church hierarchy appointed from among the natives of Spain. These government and Church officials looked down on the Creole class. They exploited their political and religious power to enrich themselves before being called back to Spain.

The Creole class read works written by Enlightenment authors. For example, Francisco Miranda, an early independence supporter, was well aware of happenings in other parts of the world. News of European events was easily obtained when ships arrived with newspapers and journals. Nevertheless, despite feelings of anger against the Spaniards, the Creoles were for the most part unwilling to turn their resentment against the monarchy during the 1700s into revolutionary activities. They recognized that the Spanish Empire had weakened and that Spain's military power and economic situation continued to decline. However, they worried about the consequences of revolutionary changes. The Creoles feared that a violent revolution would unleash the hatred and fury of the other classes of the colonial population: the mestizos, mulattos, Native Americans, and other categories of mixed-blood people.

The exile of the Spanish royal family to France and the placement of Joseph Bonaparte on the Spanish throne broke the bond that tied the Spanish American vice royalties to Spain. The movement that began as a rejection of French rule ended in a series of wars of independence against Spain. The Creole class was finally forced to act to save their own political, economic, and social situations. Moreover, they increasingly interpreted the political events taking place in Europe as an opportunity to rid themselves of the Spanish overlords and gain complete economic control and political power in the lands that they controlled.

The Independence of Mexico and Central America

Mexico was the heart of the viceroyalty of New Spain. News of the Napoleonic takeover of the Spanish throne reached Mexico. By 1810, an uprising broke out. The leader of the first movement against Spanish rule was Miguel Hidalgo, a Creole priest. He was joined by other discontented Creoles in a plan to end Spanish rule. This group issued the famous "Grito de Dolores." This was the symbolic cry of revolution against what the revolutionaries called the illegitimate Spanish government in New Spain. The first phase of the revolution ended with the royalists defeating Hidalgo's rebel army composed mainly of mestizos and Native Americans. The execution of Hidalgo and many other leaders of the bloody uprising ended the first phase of the decade long struggle for independence.

The leader of the first movement against Spanish rule in Mexico was Miguel Hidalgo, a Creole priest.

Despite this setback, one of Hidalgo's lieutenants, Jose Morelos, called together a congress, which wrote a constitution and declared independence. In 1815, Morelos was captured and executed. The movement for independence continued to develop even though most of the Creole class still refused to support the cause of independence. The Creoles were still frightened by the violence against land owners that took place earlier during the Hidalgo rebellion. However by 1821, Mexican independence was secured. Agustin de Iturbide, a Creole military officer, turned against the Spanish government. He negotiated an agreement, known as the Plan of Iguala, with the new leader of the rebellion, Vincente Guerrero. The plan called for Mexico's independence and the nation to be ruled by a monarch. The declaration of independence led to the final defeat of the Spanish forces and their withdrawal.

Mexico was liberated, and Iturbide declared himself as the new Emperor. Within a decade, revolutions against Mexican rule broke out in the southern part of the country. These revolutions resulted in the creation of new nations in what became Central America in the 1830s. Within Central America, political disputes among competing Creole regional leaders led to further revolutions and the creation of the nations of Guatemala, Nicaragua, Honduras, and El Salvador.

The Revolutions in the Vice Royalty of Rio de La Plata: South America

The Independence of Argentina, Paraguay, Uruguay, and Chile

In 1810, a revolutionary group composed of Creoles in Buenos Aires declared the independence of the vice royalty of the Rio de La Plata. Here, too, the Creole class refused to accept the idea of Napoleon's takeover of the Spanish throne and saw the new political situation in Spain as an opportunity to take over the government of the vice royalty. Jose de San Martin was the real architect of independence, and he helped liberate Argentina by 1816. The Creole leaders based in Buenos Aires soon faced problems with other Creole leaders in the interior of the former vice royalty. Revolutions against Argentine rule broke out in Paraguay and Bolivia, which fought for and became independent nations. In addition, a war broke out with Brazil over who should control the northern side of the Rio de la Plata. This war ended when both countries agreed to the creation of the nation of Uruguay after the British intervened and forced both nations to come to negotiate.

A statue of Jose de San Martin.

San Martin, who was increasingly frustrated with the political turmoil, went on to participate in the independence movements that freed Chile and Peru from Spanish rule. In Argentina, political discord resulted from the attempts by the Buenos Aires Creole class to control all the regions of the former Rio de la Plata. These regions wanted political autonomy and left the Argentine Confederation.

The Revolutions of the Vice Royalties of New Granada and Peru: South America

The Independence of Venezuela, Colombia, Ecuador, Bolivia, and Peru

Simon Bolivar was the architect of independence in the Andean nations of South America. Bolivar is known as the liberator because his leadership in the **Wars of Independence** brought an end to Spanish rule. He is sometimes called the George Washington of Latin American independence. Bolivar was, like so many of the leaders of revolutions in Latin America, a wealthy Creole landowner. He also wanted to remove the Spanish officials who ruled in the name of the illegitimate king placed on the throne by Napoleon.

Between 1810 and 1821, Bolivar and his lieutenants Antonio Sucre and Francisco Santander waged war against the Spanish forces and their royalist allies. After a series of wars, they eventually freed the future nations of Venezuela, Colombia, Ecuador, and Peru. They also participated in the struggle that resulted in the independence of Bolivia. Peru was the last nation freed by Bolivar's armies. By 1826, the last Spanish royalist forces withdrew, thereby ending the wars for Latin American independence.

Simon Bolivar is known as the liberator of the Andean nations of South America.

The Portuguese Colonial Empire in the Americas

The Independence of Brazil: South America

Napoleon's invasion of Portugal resulted in the royal family leaving for Brazil with the help of the British navy. Joao VI became the king of Portugal, Brazil, and the Algarve in 1816. Joao helped the British commercial interests by opening the Brazilian ports to trade with friendly nations. This measure also resulted in promoting Brazil's economic independence. In 1821, political events in Portugal caused Joao to return to Portugal. He left behind his son Pedro I as regent of Brazil.

In 1822, Pedro, who was summoned back to Portugal by the Portuguese government, issued his famous "Eu fico" or I am staying proclamation. In 1822, Brazilian independence was declared, and Pedro I became the Emperor of Brazil. Brazil benefited from the stabilizing influence of the monarchy. Nevertheless, in the 1830s, Brazil experienced its own rebellions in the northern and southern areas of the nation. However, by the 1840s, the coronation of the new emperor Pedro II led to a long period of political stability and kept the largest nation in Latin America a united country. This was a contrast to the political problems encountered by the newly created Spanish-speaking republics, which faced continuing wars, rebellions, and social turmoil in the 1800s.

THE AGE OF METTERNICH: THE CONGRESS OF VIENNA

After Napoleon's defeat, five major European powers—England, Russia, Prussia, Austria, and France—met in Vienna, Austria, in 1814 and 1815. They wanted to fashion a lasting peace and settle a number of important territorial questions by redrawing the map of Europe. Kings, princes, and diplomats gathered for a peace conference known as the **Congress of Vienna**. The delegates to the conference had two major goals. They wanted to *restore*, or bring back, the legitimate or rightful rulers to their thrones and reestablish the political balance in Europe. The delegates wanted to return to the pre-revolutionary period in Europe and recreate old boundaries. Their intention was to turn back the clock and make Europe what it was prior to 1789. They also sought a way to ensure that future disputes would be settled in a way that would avoid the terrible wars of the past twenty years. The French Revolution and Napoleonic Empire had led to these wars. A key idea the delegates agreed upon was the need to make agreements that would return Europe to the time of strong absolute monarchies. The overall goal was to maintain peace and stability. The rulers of Europe were willing to join together and create alliances to accomplish these goals.

The delegates to this conference were mostly reactionaries. A **reactionary** is a person who wants to return to the ideas and traditions of the past and who will resist new ideas that lead to change and reforms. The delegates who were reactionaries wanted to crush the rise of nationalism throughout Europe. In addition, they hoped to prevent the spread of liberalism. In the 1800s, European **liberalism** was a political philosophy that was influenced by the ideas of the Enlightenment. In this time period, liberal politicians supported reforms in

Kings, princes, and diplomats gathered for a peace conference known as the Congress of Vienna.

Charles Maurice de Talleyrand had been a politician of the Old Regime and was known for his ability as a diplomatic negotiator.

Main Idea:
Metternich worked to create a political system in which no one nation could threaten the peace, as had happened during France's previous 20 years of revolution and empire.

favor of democracy and the concepts of freedom of speech, press, and religion.

There were many important figures representing their nations at this historic gathering. Lord Castlereagh (Great Britain), Czar Alexander I (Russia), King Frederick William III (Prussia), and **Prince Klemens von Metternich** (Austria) were the leaders of the conference. **Charles Maurice de Talleyrand** who represented Louis XVIII of France had been a politician of the Old Regime and was known for his ability as a diplomatic negotiator. Among all of these powerful people, Prince Metternich stood out as the most influential leader during the meetings of the Congress of Vienna. Prince Metternich presided over the Congress and served as its host. He strongly opposed the French Revolution's ideas of *liberty*, or freedom, and equality. Metternich championed the arguments for the return of what had been the *status quo*, or the existing situation, in Europe prior to the French Revolution.

Metternich was guided by three principles: legitimacy, compensation, and the balance of power. His goal was to establish a situation of long-term political stability in Europe. Metternich worked to create a political system in which no one nation could threaten the peace, as had happened during France's previous twenty years of revolution and empire. Therefore, he sought to bring the rightful hereditary rulers back to their thrones. Metternich also believed that the losing nation, France, had to pay compensation for the damages caused by the wars.

The victorious European powers redrew the map of Europe. France was the big loser in terms of giving up territory. It also had to make a large payment for damages caused by the war. France lost most of its remaining islands in the Caribbean to Great Britain. Austria gained the future Italian provinces of Lombardy and Venetia on the eastern coast of the Adriatic Sea. Not all of the victorious powers got what they wanted at the Congress of Vienna. Russia and Prussia failed to gain former French lands because of opposition by Great Britain and Austria. These nations were against the expansion of Russian and Prussian political power because they believed it would upset the balance of power in central Europe. Nevertheless, a compromise was reached: Russia received territory in Poland, and Prussia gained much of the Kingdom of Saxony and land along the Rhine River.

The leading powers of Europe supported the idea of divine right monarchy as necessary to restore political order and stabilize Europe. The Congress reestablished the royal dynasties of France, Spain, Naples, Portugal, Sicily, and Sardinia. Louis

Prince Metternich presided over the Congress and served as its host.

XVIII, the Bourbon heir, once again was brought back to the throne of France. The political stability that was hoped for after the monarchs of Spain and Portugal were restored to their thrones proved impossible to accomplish. Revolutionary movements in Latin America had advanced too far to be stopped.

In addition, the Congress agreed to territorial changes to make sure France would not threaten the peace of Europe. The French frontiers were reduced to their previous pre-1789 limits. *Buffer states*, or neutral lands, were also created along the French borders. To France's north, the Netherlands was united under a Dutch ruler. The German Confederation of thirty-nine states was placed under Austrian control to the northeast of France. Switzerland was given back its status of neutrality, and the Kingdom of Piedmont was united with Sardinia.

The leaders of Europe were aware of the demands for independence that existed in many areas of Europe. They were against the idea that all peoples had the right to create their own country. European monarchs were opposed to fulfilling the nationalistic aspirations of the people who lived in the lands they ruled. This is called the right of national self-determination. They also opposed democratic reforms, fearing they would lead to revolution and threaten their rule.

In order to prevent future problems, Europe's rulers further agreed to form new alliances. Austria, Russia, Prussia, and Great Britain joined in the Quadruple Alliance to protect the agreements made in Vienna. Several years later, France was admitted into this alliance. In succeeding years, representatives of the alliance met regularly to safeguard order and stability and put down revolutionary movements.

In addition, Czar Alexander I of Russia, seeking to preserve international order based on the principles of "justice, Christian charity, and peace," formed a **Holy Alliance**. This alliance united the Christian monarchs of Russia, Prussia, and Austria. Great Britain refused to join in this new alliance mainly because it had international ambitions that conflicted with the purposes of the Holy Alliance.

During the Age of Metternich (1815–1848), there were challenges to the status quo or political situation created by the Congress. Nevertheless, in the decades that followed, most attempts by European peoples to achieve national independence failed. The reactionary policies of the Congress of Vienna were for the most part supported by those nations who had united to defeat Napoleon. However, revolutions in some areas of Europe and Latin America that were inspired by a nationalistic spirit and liberal sentiments had succeeded.

LINK TO TODAY

Today in many parts of the world, people are still strongly motivated by the spirit of nationalism and revolution. Many groups of people would be willing to participate in a revolution if it would mean that the end result would give them freedom and independence. Numerous groups of people live in countries where people from another ethnic group, culture, and religion rule the land in which they live. These peoples are motivated by ideas of nationalism, religious beliefs, the desire for political unification, and cultural ties, and are seeking to gain control of areas of land that are ruled as part of an existing nation and create their own country.

This is no different from the time of the Napoleonic Empire and Congress of Vienna when groups of people in Europe and Latin America, motivated by ideas of nationalism, religious freedom, and self-determination, rose up against those who controlled the political power in what they considered to be their country.

Not all peoples who believe they are entitled to be a nation will ultimately be able to gain control of what they believe to be their land and create a state. There are too many nations in the world today that have multiethnic populations for this to happen. Therefore, it is no surprise that the history of revolution that we read about in Chapter 21 and this chapter is repeating itself throughout the world today. It is also logical to assume that in the future we will continue to read and hear about revolutions taking place in different parts of the world. Nationalism, self-determination, and religious ideas continue to motivate people to seek independence at whatever the cost to themselves and others.

CHAPTER SUMMARY

The French Revolution and the Napoleonic Period began a time of increased revolution, rising nationalism, political reaction, and nation creation. The period of history beginning in 1789 and continuing throughout the nineteenth century often was a time of revolution, violent movements demanding independence and nationhood, harsh reaction, and political change. In this time period, important historical events and changes continued to take place with increasing frequency throughout the world. Some of these nationalist struggles for independence were successful, whereas others failed. Many of the same ideas that were unleashed by the French Revolution and Napoleonic Empire Era continued to develop even after the death of the one of the century's most important personalities, Napoleon Bonaparte.

IMPORTANT
PEOPLE,
PLACES,
AND TERMS

KEY TERMS

Directory	Quadruple Alliance	Holy Alliance
Napoleonic Code	Wars of Independence	Grand Army
Concordat of 1801	Congress of Vienna	Hundred Days
Continental System	reactionary	
nationalism	liberalism	

PEOPLE

Napoleon Bonaparte	Czar Alexander I	Simon Bolivar
Lord Nelson	Louis XVIII	Talleyrand
Joseph Bonaparte	Duke of Wellington	Prince Klemens von
King Frederick	Toussaint L'Ouverture	Metternich
William III	General LeClerc	

PLACES

Waterloo	Moscow	Prussia
Corsica	Haiti	Czarist Russia

EXERCISES FOR CHAPTER 22

MULTIPLE CHOICE

Select the letter of the correct answer.

1. Napoleon's Continental System and the British sea blockade were similar in that they

   a. sought to provide their enemies with military aide during wartime.
   b. sought to stop the Ottoman Empire from trading with Europe.
   c. were intended to destroy their enemies economies and trading relationships.
   d. were not intended to interfere with the enemies economic relationships.

2. Which three principles best describe the goals of the Congress of Vienna

   a. Liberty, equality, and fraternity
   b. Democracy, representation, and nationalism
   c. Liberalism, self-determination, and alliances
   d. Legitimacy, restoration, and balance of power

3. Prince Metternich wanted to restore Europe to the time of the

   a. French Revolution.
   b. Napoleonic Empire.
   c. pre-French Revolution.
   d. Directory in 1795.

4. The nations of the Second Coalition that fought against France were

   a. Czarist Russia, Great Britain, and Austria.
   b. Spain, Great Britain, and Prussia.
   c. Austria, Italy, and Portugal.
   d. Great Britain, Sweden, and the Netherlands.

5. Which title would best complete this partial outline? Select the letter.

   I. _____

   1. Napoleon becomes First Consul
   2. Napoleon crowns himself Emperor
   3. Napoleon puts his brother on the Spanish throne
   4. Napoleon invades Czarist Russia

   a. Napoleon Bonaparte spreads ideas of democracy in Europe.
   b. Napoleon Bonaparte limits his personal ambitions.
   c. Napoleon Bonaparte seeks to dominate European affairs.
   d. Napoleon Bonaparte develops ideas of the French Revolution.

6. The French people supported Napoleon Bonaparte because they hoped that he would

   a. adopt the ideas of the Protestant Reformation.
   b. restore Louis XVI to power.
   c. provide stability for the nation.
   d. end British control of France.

7. In which region of the world did the French Revolution and Napoleonic Era have the greatest influence in the early decades of the 1800s?

   a. Southeast Asia
   b. Latin America
   c. South Asia
   d. Sub-Saharan Africa

8. Simon Bolivar, Toussaint l'Ouverture, and Jose San Martin are important in Latin American history because they were

   a. important Spanish royalists.
   b. leaders of liberation movements.
   c. participants in the Congress of Vienna.
   d. generals in the Napoleonic wars.

9. A major goal of the Congress of Vienna was to

   a. establish democratic governments in all European nations.
   b. maintain a balance of power in Europe.
   c. return Napoleon Bonaparte to power.
   d. create independent governments in Latin America.

10. Which is the correct chronological order that traces Napoleon's rise and fall from power?

   a. The Directory > First Consul > Emperor > Waterloo
   b. Austerlitz > the Directory > First Consul > Treaty of Amiens
   c. Waterloo > Emperor > Invasion of Russia > First Consul
   d. Emperor > Concordat > the Directory > Waterloo

11. Napoleon Bonaparte was not able to advance early in his career because

   a. his training as a military officer was as an artillery officer.
   b. he was handicapped by his Corsican birth and lack of connections.
   c. of his involvement in anti-French Revolutionary activities.
   d. his first military assignments resulted in defeats for his troops.

12. In 1799, Napoleon returned to France and

   a. took part in the overthrow of the Directory.
   b. resigned as a military officer to begin a political career.
   c. became an admiral during a military revolt.
   d. assumed the title of emperor of the French.

13. During the period 1799 to 1804, Napoleon achieved the following goal:

   a. establishment of the Bank of England.
   b. privatization of France's educational system.
   c. unification of French law under the Napoleonic Code.
   d. strengthening of the legal rights for women and children.

14. Napoleon's putting his brother Joseph on the throne of Spain led to

   a. revolutions in Spain's American colonies.
   b. a revolution and the independence of Haiti.
   c. an uprising in Spain in support of Joseph.
   d. a Portuguese military campaign to remove Joseph.

15. Great Britain was able to hold off Napoleon's armies because it

   a. developed an effective artillery weapon.
   b. maintained its naval supremacy.
   c. had the nation of Spain as an ally.
   d. had an army equal to that of Napoleon.

16. After the destruction of the French fleet by Lord Nelson in 1805, Napoleon decided to

a. invade Great Britain.
b. make peace with Great Britain.
c. boycott British goods.
d. sell Louisiana to the United States.

17. The Continental System resulted in

a. a sharp rise in France's maritime trade.
b. an decrease of smuggling in Europe.
c. a successful French sea blockade of British trade.
d. growing resentment among neutral nations.

18. Napoleon's military success in Europe eventually led to

a. rising nationalist sentiment.
b. a decline in patriotic sentiments.
c. increased support by people of other nations.
d. growing support for the French Empire.

19. Napoleon's defeat in the Russian campaign in 1812 was mostly due to

a. Russia's strategic alliance with Great Britain.
b. an extremely cold Russian winter.
c. Russia's decision to stand and fight the Grand Army.
d. Napoleon's failure to use seasoned troops of the Grand Army.

20. Napoleon's defeat by the European alliance led to the

a. restoration of legitimate monarchies.
b. creation of a democratically elected government in France.
c. re-establishment of feudalism in Europe.
d. victory of nationalist movements throughout the Americas.

ESSAYS FOR CHAPTER 22

1. Explain how Napoleon was able to rise and become the emperor of the French Empire.
2. Explain the reasons why Napoleon's Continental System did not work out the way he intended it to.
3. Explain the reasons why Napoleon's Russian campaign of 1812 led to his downfall.
4. It is 1806, and you are Napoleon Bonaparte. You have decided to punish the British by starting the Continental System. Write an essay to the rulers of the nations of Europe explaining how the Continental System will work. Also in your essay indicate what will happen if any nation does not agree to take part in the Continental System.
5. It is 1814. You are Prince Metternich. Write an essay to the monarchs and representatives of European nations attending the Congress of Vienna explaining the goals that you have outlined for the meeting. In your essay, also discuss how you want France to be treated.

DOCUMENT-BASED QUESTIONS

This task is based on the accompanying documents. Some of these documents have been edited for the purposes of this task. This task is designed to test your ability to work with historical documents. As you analyze the documents, take into account both the source of the document and the author's point of view.

Directions: Read the following documents and answer the questions after each document. Use the information in the reading and this chapter in writing your answers.

Document #1   Soldiers of France! Hear my call. . . . All of you are consumed with a desire to extend the glory of the French people; all of you long to humiliate those arrogant kings who dare to contemplate [think about] placing us in chains; all of you desire to dictate a glorious peace, one which will repay the Patrie [French Nation] for the immense sacrifices it has made. You must sacrifice yourselves for the good of France so that your children will benefit from the liberty and freedoms so hard fought for by your brethren [fellow citizens].

From *The Corsican: A Diary of Napoleon Bonaparte's Life* by Napoleon Bonaparte

Questions   1. What nationalist ideas is Napoleon expressing to his soldiers?
2. Why is Napoleon trying to stir up the spirit of nationalism in his soldiers?

Document #2   We are not Europeans; we are not Indians; we are a mixed species of aborigines and Spaniards. Americans by birth and Europeans by law, we find ourselves engaged in a dual conflict: we are disputing with the natives for titles of ownership, and at the same time we are struggling to maintain ourselves in the country that gave us birth against the opposition of foreigners . . . for we, having been placed in a state lower than slavery, have been robbed not only of our freedom, but also of our rights.

From the *Address to the Congress of Angostura* by Simon Bolivar (1819)

Questions   1. How is Bolivar seeking to stir up a sense of nationalism?
2. What similarities do you see in Napoleon Bonaparte's and Simon Bolivar's speeches?

Document #3   Admiration for the American revolution was tremendous during the early years of the republic. But the great ideological inspiration came from the French philosophers of the Enlightenment, whose grand ideas filled a deeply felt, if at times unconscious need of Spanish Americans who were capable of reading and understanding these works, the lawyers, bureaucrats, parish priests, teachers, scientists and students. They all wanted and needed a non-religious alternative to the airtight explanations of the universe offered by Catholic scholasticism in the past.

From *The Buried Mirror* by Carlos Fuentes

Questions   1. Why did the Creole class in Latin America have great respect for the French philosophers?
2. What type of alternative were the educated Latin Americans seeking?

Document #4   It was a result of the French Revolution that a personality such as Napoleon Bonaparte was able to rise to power. His success was proof that a brilliant military career that led to the top was open to all people. His rise to power was part of the grand revolutionary tide. He always saw himself as representing liberalism, progress, and new ideas in spite of the political despotism that he justified by war and the challenge of reactionary Europe. But even while waging war, he was capable of drafting laws. The French civil code, the modern tax system, the penal code and the modern administrative and educational systems were Napoleon's great accomplishments.

From *The Buried Mirror* by Carlos Fuentes

Questions
1. How did the French Revolution help Napoleon's military career?
2. How did Napoleon's laws change France?

Document #5   Napoleon's attempt to alter the balance of power was characteristically bold and risky. He took advantage of Britain's weak position militarily and launched his Continental System. Economic factors intermeshed with military strategy. He sought to ruin the English economically since he was not capable of crossing the Channel and invading England. There is no doubt that Britain's unusually large dependence upon foreign commerce made it vulnerable to the trading ban imposed by Napoleon. Nevertheless the British navy proved in the end to be a force that Napoleon did not completely take into account when he started his Continental System.

From *The Rise and Fall of the Great Powers* by Paul Kennedy

Questions
1. Why did Napoleon choose to attack England economically?
2. Why did the Continental System ultimately fail?

Indexes

GENERAL INDEX

A

Aachen, 177
Abbasid Caliphate, 208, 216, 318, 444
Abbey of Saint Denis, 195
Abelard, Peter, 197
Abraham, 8–9, 209
absolutism, 362, 374, 399
acrophobia, 83
acropolis, 71
Act of Settlement, 384, 397
Act of Supremacy, 276, 359
Address to the Nobility of the
        German Nation, 279
administrative bureaucracy, 339
Adolphus, Gustavus, 366
Adriatic Sea, 78, 92
Aegean World, dark age, 69–70
Aeneas, 93
Aeneid, 106
Aeschylus, 73
affirmative action, 32
Africa, 265
        ancient, 2–27
        civilizations, 428–441
Age of reason, 463–465
aghora, 71
agoraphobia, 83
Agra, 449
ahimsa, 40, 56
Ahmose I, 14
Akbar, 448–450
        reign of, 442
        successors to, 449–450
al-Rashid, Harun, 218
Alcibiades, 78
Alcuin, 177
Alexander I, 511–512, 521–522
Alexander III, 79, 84
Alexander the Great, 7, 10, 12, 15, 40,
        83
        conquests, 84–85
Alexandria, 15, 84, 87
Alexiad, 164
Alexius I, 159, 184
Alfonso Henriques, 190
Alfonso VII of Castile, 190
Algarve, 190
algebra, 219
Ali, 214
        Sunni, 431
al-Idrisi, 219
Allah, 209
Almoravids, 430

almsgiving, 213
Alps, 93
al-Razi, 219
Amazon basin, 135
Ambedkar, Bhimrao Ramji, 33
Amenhotep III, 14
Amenhotep IV, 14
America:
        ancient, 130–151
                classic period, 138
American Revolution, 462
        ancient:
                agricultural developments,
                132–133
                development of cultures,
                133–138
                first peoples, 132
Americas, 236–252
        discovery of, 410–412
        empires, 334–354
        English colonization, 418–419
        French colonization, 418
        Spanish colonization, 516–517
Amiens, cathedral, 195
Amish, 281, 290
Amorites, 4
Anabaptists, 281
Analects, The, 45
Anatomical Exercise on the Motion of
        the Heart and Blood in
        Animals, An, 476
Andean Region, 244–247, 343
Angelico, Fra, 261–262
Angevin Empire, 182–183
Angkor Empire, 49–51
Anglican Church, 284–285, 359, 361,
        388, 390–391
Anglo-Saxon tribes, 175
animism, 55, 430
Anjou, 182
Annals, 108
annulment, 182, 284
Anselm of Canterbury, 197
Antigonid dynasty, 86
Antigonus, 86
Antilles, 245
Antioch, 10, 87, 185
Antoinette, Marie, 488
Antonius, 104
Antony, Mark, 101
apathy, 89
Apennine mountains, 93
Aphrodite of Melos, 88
Apollo Belvedere, 115
Apostles, 109
Apulia, 92

Aquinas, Thomas, 197
arab, 209
        invasions, 152, 157
Arabia, 3, 7
Arabian Nights, The, 219–220
arachnophobia, 83
Aragon, 190–191
Arawak, 243–244
arch, 105
Archaic Period, 13, 64, 70–74
Archbishop of Canterbury, 183, 284
Archimedes, 90
architecture:
        classical, 79
        Mayan, 142
        Roman, 105–106
archons, 76
areopagus, 71
Argentina, independence, 518
Aristarchus, 89
aristocracy, 71
Aristophanes, 73
Aristotelian humanism, 267
Aristotle, 81–82, 474
Armagnacs, 189
Armenia, annexation of, 158
Arouet, Francois Marie, 467
Art of Love, The, 107
Arthashastra, 40
Arthur, King, 196
artisan, 340
Aryabhata, 41
Aryan, 29–30
        culture, 30–33
        invasion of India, 28
As You Like It, 266
ascetics, 110, 281
Ashikaga Shogunate, 325
Asia, 226–235
        ancient, 28–63
        central, Mongol rule, 318
        global interactions, 316–333,
                442–460
        minor, 5
        southeast, ancient, 49–50
        southern, 227–228
Asoka, 38, 40, 62
Assassination of Phillip II, 84
Assembly of tribes, 95
Assyrian civilization, 2, 5–6, 9, 15
astrolabe, 409
astronomical clock, 229
astronomy, 472–475
        theories, 319
Atacama Desert, 245
Atahualpa, 416

Athena, 79
Athenian:
    Acropolis, 79
    democracy, 64
    Golden Age, 64
    imperialism, 75–76
Atlantic trade routes, 311
Atlantis, 67
atomic theory, 73
Attica, 74–75, 77
Augustinian Canons, 194
Augustulus, Romulus, 110–111
Augustus, 103, 108
    reign of, 102–103
Aurangzeb, 450
Aurelius, Marcus, 104, 108
auto, 83
autobiography, 83
autocracy, 5
    establishment, 102
autocrat, 362
auto-da-fe, 371
automobile, 83
autonomy, 83
Avignon, 257
Axhumite Kingdom, 18
Axum, 18
    kingdom of, 433
Azores, exploration, 410
Aztecs, 238, 241
    arrival in Mexico, 334
    clothing, 340–341
    culture, 340–341
    education, 341
    diet, 341
    empire, 335
        conquering, 415
    political system, 337–338
    religion, 338–339
    rise of, 336–337
    treasures, 302
    social organization, 339–340

B

Babar, 442
*Babylonian Captivity of the Church,
    On the*, 279
Babylonians, 4–5
    captivity, 6, 257–258, 280
    civilization, 2, 4–5
    Law, tradition of, 19
Bach, Johann Sebastian, 470
Bacon, Francis, 464, 477
Bacon, Roger, 197
Bactria, 85
Baghdad, 216
    Mongol invasion, 316, 318
Bahamas, 418–419
Bakr, Abu, 212, 214
bakufu, 325

Balearic Islands, 190
Bang, Liu, 48
Bantus, 432
Baptists, 281, 290
Barana, 433
Barbados, 419
barbarian, 87
barbaroi, 66
barons, 182
Barrack Emperors, 109
Basho, Matsuo, 327
Basil I, 158
Basil II, 158
basilicas, 106
bas-relief, 106
Bastille, 490
Battle of:
    Aljubarotta, 191
    Bouvines, 182
    the Boyne, 397
    Chaeronea, 79
    Crecy, 189
    Guagamela, 84–85
    Hastings, 182
    Las Navas de Tolosa, 191
    Marathon, 75
    Orleans, 189
    Poitiers, 189
    Talas, 229
    Tours, 215
    Vienna, 374
    Zama, 97
Bavaria, 180
bazaars, 452
Becket, Thomas, 183
Beijing, 451–452
Belisarius, 154
Bellini, Giovanni, 262
Benares, 34–35, 37
Benedictine Rule, 193
Benin, Kingdom of, 428, 432
Beowulf, 195
Berbers, 430
    Army, 191
Bering Strait, 131
Bernard of Clairvaux, 193
Bhagavad Gita, 36
Bharata, 31
Bible, King James Version, 388
Biblical stories, 8
Birth of Venus, The, 261
black death, 174, 191–192, 258
    in Europe, 192, 202
Black Sea, 3
blasphemy, 109
Boccaccio, Giovanni, 265
Bodhisattva, 39
Boleyn, Anne, 284, 360
Bolivar, Simon, 471, 518–519
Bolivia, independence, 518–519
Bonaparte, Joseph, 510, 517

Bonaparte, Napoleon, 496, 505
Book of Common Prayer, The, 284–285
Book of the Courtier, 256, 274–275
Book of the Dead, 25–26
Borobodur, 49–50
Bosch, Hieronymus, 263, 265
Botticelli, Sandro, 261
Bourbon family, 364, 522
bourgeoisie, 485
Bourges, cathedral, 195
boy tribute, 446–447
Boyle, Robert, 476
Brahe, Tycho, 472–473
Brahma, 33
Brahmins, 31
Bramante, Donato, 260–261
Brasidas, 78
Brazil, 413
    independence, 519
    mineral riches, 302
British East India Company, 301
Brittany, 182
bronze, 6
Bruegel, Pieter, the elder, 263
Brunelleschi, Filippo, 260
Bruni, Leonardo, 266, 272–273
Brutus, Marcus, 101
bubonic plague, 191–192
Buddhism, 36–40, 50
    Japan, 321–322
    spread in Asia, 38–39
buffer states, 522
Bulgaria, conquest of, 158
bullion, 305
Buonarroti, Michelangelo, 260, 262,
    264
bureaucracy, 305
burgesses, 387
Burgundians, 189
    tribes, 175
Burma, 36
bushido, 324
business methods, changes, 299–300
Byzantine, 15, 110, 153
    commonwealth, 152, 158
    coronation ceremony of Manuel II,
        172
    empire, 152–173
        early, 152, 154–157
        high, 152, 157–159
        late, 152, 160
        renaissance, 254
        society, 161–164
            architecture, 162–163
            church, 161
            literature, 163–164
            painting, 163
            sculpture, 163
            writing, 164

C

Cabot, John, 418
Cabral, Pedro, 413
cacao beans, 340
Caesar:
    dictatorship of, 101
    Gaius Julius, 100–102
    Julius, 108
    Octavian, 101
Calabria, 92
Calakmul, 141
calculus, 474
Caligula, 103
caliphate, 214
calligraphy, 324
Calvin, John, 276, 282–283, 290
Calvinism, 282–283
Cambodia, 36
Cambyses, 7
camel caravans, 407
Campania, 92
Canaan, 9
Canary Islands, 412
Candide, 467
Cano, Juan Sebastian del, 414
canon law, 110
Canterbury Tales, 196
Canzoni, 265
Cape of Good Hope, 410
Cape of Storms, 414
Cape Verde islands, exploration, 410
Capet, Hugh, 181
Capetians, 188
    dynasty, 181–182
capital, 300
    punishment, 19
capitalism, beginning of, 303–304
Capuchins, 288
caravel ships, 409
Cardinal Richelieu, 356
Carib, 244, 413
Caribbean:
    ancient, 130–151
    and Antilles, 246
    basin, 244–247
    region, 134
    topographical areas, 150
Carolingians, 158
    empire, 174–176
    renaissance, 177
Carthage, 12, 94, 96
Carthusian Order, 193
Cartier, Jacques, 406, 418
cartography, 409
Caspian Sea, 3
Cassius, Gaius, 101
caste system, 31, 37–38
Castiglione, Baldassarre, 256, 274–275
Castile, 190
Castlereagh, Lord, 521

Catalonia, 190
Cathedral:
    Church of Worms, 194
    of Florence, 260
    of Saint Sophia, 155
    of Santiago, 194
    schools, 197
Catherine of Aragon, 284–285, 359
Catullus, 107
causeways, 340
cavaliers, 391
cave paintings, 228
Cavendish, Henry, 476
Cecil, Robert, 360
Cellini, Benvenuto, 255
Central America, 238
    independence, 517–518
Central:
    high middle ages, 179–187
    middle ages, 174
Centuries, 94
Cervantes, Miguel de, 266, 374
Chagatai, Khanate of, 318, 320
Chaldeans, 4–5, 9
    civilization, 2, 5–6
Champlain, Samuel de, 418
Chancellor, 183
Chancery, 183
Chang'an, 228, 322
chanson de geste, 195–196
charisma, 83
charity, 213
Charlemagne, 176
    empire of, 177
Charles I, 371, 384, 393, 399
    rule of, 389–391
Charles II, 384, 393–395, 477
Charles IV, 516
Charles the Bald, 181
Charles V, 189, 278, 281, 372
Charles VI, 189, 375
Charles VII, 189
charter, 299, 301
Chartres, cathedral, 195
Chaucer, Geoffrey, 196
Chavin culture, 142–143
chiaroscuro, 260
Chibcha chiefdom, 135–136
Chichen Itza, 243–244
chiefdom, 135
Chile, independence, 518
Chimu Kingdom, 236
Chin dynasty, 46–47
China, 228–230, 452
    ancient, 42–48
    Ming dynasty, 451–452
    Mongol rule, 318
chinampas, 336
Chinatown, 57
Chinese Heritage, The, 61
Chosen dynasty, 328
Choson, 55

Christian:
    church, rise of, 110
    humanism, 254, 256
Christian IV, 366
Christianity, 108–109, 209
    rise of , 91
Christians, 39
    persecution of, 104
Christmas tree, origins, 198
Chronicles of Japan, 53
chronicles, 164
Chronicles, 197
Chronographia, 164
Chrysoloras, Manuel, 266–267
Church schism, 162
Cicero, 100, 107
Circuit Court System, 183
circumnavigation, 414
Cistercian, 193
cities, planned, 29
citizens, 77
citizenship, 70–71
city-states, 66
    development of, 70
civic humanism, 254, 256
Civil War, Roman, 100–101
civitas, 256
Classical:
    Greece, 74–77
        development, 74
    ideal, 79
    period, 64
Claudius, 103
claustrophobia, 83
Cleisthenes, 77
Cleon, 78
Cleopatra VII, 15, 101–102
clergy, 279
Clermont, 184
clients, 94
Clovis, 176
Cluniac, 193
Code of Hammurabi, 23–24
Code of Manu, 31
Codex Justinianus, 155
codices, 142
Colbert, Jean Baptiste, 306, 369
Cologne, cathedral, 195
Colombia, independence, 518–519
colonies, importance of, 305–307
Coliseum, 106
Columbian Exchange, 408, 410, 419
Columbus, Christopher, 371, 407–412, 414
comedy, 73, 88
Commercial revolution, 296–315
    economic effects, 308–309
    political effects, 309
    social effects, 309
Committee of Public Safety, 494
common law, 387
Common Sense, 471

commoners, 135
commonwealth, 392–393
commune, 258
Comnena, Anna, 164
compass, 229, 409
competition, law of, 468
Concordat of Worms, 181
Concordat, 507
Confucian ideals, 452
Confucianism, 44–45
Confucius, birth of, 28
Congress of Vienna, 504–505,
    520–522
conquistador, 415
conspiracy, 506
Constantine V, 157
Constantine VII Porphyroghenitos,
    164
Constantine XI Paleologus, 160
Constantine, reign of, 110
Constantinople, 110, 153, 155, 158,
    186, 444
    fall of, 152, 160
        Ottoman conquest of, 442
        patriarch of, 162
constitution, 71
    Athenian, 117
    Roman, 95
constitutional monarchy, 397
Constitutions of Claredon, 183
contemplative life, 256
continental system, 510–512
Copan, 141
Copernicus, Nicolaus, 462, 464, 472
copper, 302
Coptic, 19
    writing, 17
Copts, 15
corbelled, Mayan, 142
Corcyra, 78
Cordova, 191
Corfu, 78
Corinth, 78
Corinthian columns, 79
Corneille, Pierre, 470
Coronado, Francisco, 416
Corpus Juris Civilis, 155
Corsica, 96, 505
Cortes, Hernando, 335, 370
Cortez, Hernando, 406, 415–416
Council of:
    Constance, 258
    Counter reformations, Catholic
        church, 287–288
    500, 77
    Florence, 160
    Nicaea, 110
    Trent, 276, 287
coup d'etat, 496, 506
covenant, 9
Cranmer, Thomas, 284

Crassus, Marcus Licinius, 100
Creation of Adam, 262–263
Creoles, 516
Crete, 67
Cromwell, Oliver, 384, 391–393, 405
Crusades, 158–159, 174, 184–187, 444
    early, 186, 206
    first, 185, 205
    fourth, 152, 186, 197
    second, 185–186
    third, 186
Crusades, 208
cultural diffusion, 7, 66, 83, 151
cuneiform, 6, 8, 11
Curia Regis, 182
Curiae, 94
currency, 300
Cushite Kingdom, 18
Cushitic civilization, 2, 18–19
Cuzco, 335, 344–346
Cynics, 89
Cyril, 158
Cyrus, 7

D

da al-Islam, 217
da Gama, Vasco, 406–407, 410
da Gama, Vasco, explorations, 296,
    298
da Vinci, Leonardo, 256, 262
daimyos, 323
Damascus, 216
Dante Aligheri, 264
Danton, Georges, 493–495
Daoism, 45–46
Darius I, 7–8, 74
Dark Age, 64
Daud, Askia, 431
David, 9
David, Jacques-Louis, 470
David, 263–264
de Balboa, Vasco Nunez, 414
de Beauharnais, Josephine, 506
de Leon, Ponce, 414
de Montaigne, Michel, 266
de Soto, Hernando, 416
de Talleyrand, Charles Maurice de,
    521
de Vega, Lope, 374
Death of Arthur, The, 196
Decameron, 265
decentralization, period of, 257–259
decimal system, 41
Declaration of the Rights of Man, The,
    484, 491, 514
deforestation, 140
Delhi, 449
Delian League, 76, 78
Delphi, 80
democracy:

Athenian, development of, 76
development of, 70
growth in England, 384–405
Demosthenes, 79
Dengel, Lebna, 433
Deocritus, 73
deposing, 396
Descartes, Rene, 464, 477
despots, 258
Dessalines, Jean-Jacques, 515
dharma, 33
dhimmis, 447
dialectic, 197
*Dialogue Concerning the Two Chief
    Systems of the World*,
    462, 474
Dialogues on Motion, 474
diamonds, 302
Dias, Bartholomeu, 406, 410
Diaspora, 10
Diderot, Denis, 462, 465–466
Digenes Akritos, 164
digging stick, 133
Diocletian, 109
Dionysius, 72
Diplomatic Revolution, 375
direct democracy, 71
Directory, 506
Discourse on Method, 462, 477
Disputa, 262, 264
Divine Comedy, 264
divine right, 367, 388, 485
Djenne, 431
Doctor Faustus, 266
Dofu, 228
dome, 105
Domesday Book, The, 183
domestic system, 304, 309
Dominicans, 194
Domitian, 104, 108
Don Quixote de la Mancha, 266
Donatello, 263
Donation of Constantine, 259–260
Doomsday Book, 357
Dorians, 69
Doric columns, 79
Draco, 76
Drake, Francis, 418
Dravidians, 30
dualism, 34
Duoro River, 190
Durer, Albrecht, 263
Durga, 34
Dutch:
    colonies, 417–418
    East India Company, 301,
        417–418
    New Amsterdam, 417
    West India Company, 417
duties, 305
dynastic cycle, 42

E

Early middle ages, 174–179
East African civilizations, 432–433
Eastern:
    Europe, Ottoman rule, 443–447
    European Nations, rise of,
        152–173
    Roman Empire, 153
Ecuador, independence, 518–519
Edessa, 185
Edict of:
    Expulsion, 371
    Milan, 110
    Nantes, 276, 283, 364–365, 369
Edo, 326–327
Education of a Christian Prince, The,
    267
Edward I, 184, 387
Edward II, 266
Edward III, 188
Edward VI, 284
egalitarian, 134
Egypt, 3
    ancient, 13–17
    civilization, ancient, 2
    culture, 16–17
Eightfold Path of Conduct, 37
Einhard, 196
Einstein, Albert, 478
El Greco, 374
El Salvador, 518
Elba, 92
electors, 187
elites, 135
Elizabeth I, 266, 285, 307, 356,
    360–363, 387, 418
Elizabethan Era, 266
empiricism, 81–82, 464
Empress Theodora, 156
encomienda, 416
Encyclopedia, 462, 465
endogamy, 32
England:
    commercial expansion, 307
    growth of democracy, 384–405
    late middle ages, 188–190
English:
    Bill of Rights, 384, 396–397, 405
    Channel, 369
    Civil War, 384, 391, 401
    Joint Stock Company, 296
    colonization of Americas, 418
enlightened despots, 376
enlightenment, 37, 462–483
    cultural ideas, 470
    economic ideas, 468–469
    France, 465–466
    impact on Americas, 470–471
    political ideas, 466–467
entrepreneur, rise of, 303
Epic of Gilgamesh, The, 6, 24–25

epic poems, 73, 88, 195
Epicureans, 89
Episcopalians, 286
Epitome of Copernican Astronomy, 462
equality, 385
equites, 98
Erasmus, Desiderius, 267, 280
Eratosthenes, 89
Erectheum, 79
Escorial, 372
Estates-general, 364–365, 488–490
ethical monotheism, 9
ethics, 89
Ethiopian:
    civilization, 18–19
        ancient, 2
    empire, 19, 428, 433
    Orthodox Church, 19
ethnos, 66
Etruria, 92
Etruscans, 93, 95
Euclid, 90
Euphrates River, 3
Euripides, 73
Europe:
    development of mercantilism,
        305
    economic revival, 297–299
    late middle ages, 188
    trade routes, 272
    western, 18th century, 463
evolution, 132
Ewuare the great, 432
Exchequer, 183
excommunication, 278
Exploration:
    age of, 406–427
        results, 419–420
    techonology permitting, 408–409
Ezena, King, 19

F

factorias, 410
Faerie Queen, The, 266
faith, proclamation of, 213
fasting, 213
Fatima, 216
Ferdinand I, 372
Ferdinand II, 191, 366
Ferdinand, 302, 370–371, 410–411
Fertile Crescent, 3
feudalism, 43–44, 174, 178, 184
    decline, 303
    Japan, 323–325
Ficino, Marsilio, 267
fiefs, 178
filial piety, 45
First:
    Estate, 485-487
    Intermediate Period, 14
    Punic War, 96–97

five pillars of Islam, 212–213
Flavian dynasty, 104
Flemish school, 262–263
Florence, 258–259
flying buttress, 195
Forbidden City, 451, 453
Four Noble Truths, 37
Fourth Crusade, 159
France, 490
    late middle ages, 188–190
    mercantilism, 306
Francesca, Pierro della, 262
Francis of Assisi, 194
Franciscans, 194, 288
Franconia, 180
Frankish tribes, 175
Franklin, Benjamin, 470
Frederick II, 376–377
Frederick the Great, 356, 376
Frederick the Wise of Saxony, 278
free enterprise, 303
Freedom of a Christian Man, The, 279
Freidrich II, 181
French Revolution, 462, 484–-503
    lasting impact, 496
    third stage, 496
French, and the Americas, 418
frescoes, 163
Friedrich I Barbarossa, 181, 186
Friedrich II, 186, 257
Froissart, Jean, 197
Fronde, 367
Fuggers, 300
Fujiwara family, 323
Funan, 49–50
    empire temple, 49

G

Gaius Gracchus, 99
Gaius, 103
Galen, 90, 108, 475–476
Galilei, Galileo, 462, 464, 472–474
Gallic Wars, 100
Gandhi, Mahatma, 32, 40, 56
Ganges River, 34, 37
Gao, 431
Garden of Delights, 265
Gargantua and Pantagruel, 266
Gates of Paradise, The, 263
Gauls, 95, 100
Gautama, Siddhartha, 37, 50
    birth of, 28
Gaya, 37
Ge'ez, 19
Gedi, 433
geocentric theory, 472
Geoffin, Marie Therese, 465
Geoffrey of Monmouth, 196
geometric designs, 70
George I, 384
Georgics, 107

Gerald of Wales, 197
Germania, 108
Germanic:
   invasions, fifth century, 175
   kingdoms, 174
Ghana, 428–430
Ghibblines, 181
Ghiberti, Lorenzo, 263
Giaconda, La, 262
Giotto, 260
Girgione, 262
Girondists, 492
glaciers, retreat of, 130, 132
global economy, 421–422
Glorious Revolution, 384, 395–398
glyphs, 142
gold, 302, 305
Golden Age, 14, 259
   of Athens, 79
Golden Bull, 187
Golden Horder, Khanate of, 318, 320
Gothic style, 195
governors, 97
Grand:
   Army, 511
   Canal, 228
   Remonstrance, 390
   vizier, 444
gravitation, law of, 475
Great:
   Council, 259, 386–387
   Khan, Khanate of, 318
   Schism, 258, 280
   Wall of China, 43, 47–48, 57, 228
Greater:
   Antilles, 245
   Vehicle, 39
Greco-Roman:
   Civilization, 85
   World, 64–129
Greece, ancient, 65–83
   geography, 65–66
   unification under Macedonia,
      78–79
Greek:
   alphabet, 70
   architecture, 72
   art, 72
   civilization, characteristics,
      65–67
   culture, 7
   fire, 157
   league, 74
   miracle, 64, 70
   nation, 66–67
   world, 65
Gregorian chant, 193
Gregory I the great, 193
Gregory of Tours, 196
Grenada, 191
   conquest of, 410
griots, 434

Guatemala, 518
Guelf, 181
   -Ghibelline struggles, 258
Guianas, 244
Guicciardini, Francesco, 266
guilds, 303–304
guillotine, 493, 495
gunpowder, 226, 228
Gupta Empire, 28, 40–42
Gutenberg, Johannes, 304

H

Habeas Corpus Act, 384, 394
Habsburg rulers, 366
Hadrian, 104
haigiography, 163, 196
haj, 219
Hamlet, 266
Hammurabi, 3, 5, 19
   Law Code, 5
Han dynasty, 28, 48, 228
Hanging Gardens of Babylon, 5
Hangul, 328
Hangzhou, 229
haniwa, 52
Hannibal, 97
Hanoverian Dynasty, 384
Hanuman, 36
harem, 447
harijans, 32
hari-kari, 324
Harold, 357
Harrapa, 29
Harun al Rashid as Caliphate, 108
Harvey, William, 476
Hausa city-states, 428, 431
Hawkins, John, 418
Haydn, Joseph, 470
Hebrew:
   civilization, ancient, 8–10
   culture, 10
Heian period, 316, 322–323
Heinrich II, 180
Heinrich III, 180
Heinrich IV, 181
Heinrich V, 181
heliocentric theory, 89, 472
Hellenic:
   culture, 7
   league, 79
Hellenism, 83
Hellenistic Kingdoms, 86–87
   conquest of, 97–98
   world, 83–90
helots, 77
Henri of Burgundy, 190
Henrique the Navigator, 191
Henry I, 183
Henry II, 182–183, 386
Henry III, 183
Henry IV, 180, 189, 364–365, 388

Henry V, 189
Henry V, 266
Henry VI, 189
Henry VII, 190, 356, 358, 360
Henry VIII, 283-285, 359, 361–363,
   387
Henry, the navigator, 409–410
Heraclitus, 74, 156
Herodotus, 80
Hesiod, 73
hidalgo, 415
Hidalgo, Miguel, 517
Hideyoshi, Toyotomi, 326
hieroglyphics, 17
hieroglyphs, 142
High:
   gate, 447
   Middle Ages, Europe, 179
   renaissance, 254, 256
Hijra, 208, 210
Hinayana, 39
Hindi, 448
Hindu Kush mountains, 85
Hinduism, 30–36, 50
   gods, 33–35
   holy literature, 35–36
Hindus, 39, 450
Hipparchus, 89
Hippocrates, 82
Hippocratic Oath, 82
Hippodrome, 155
Historia, 80
Histories, 108
History and Topography of Ireland, 197
History of Italy, 266
History of Modern India, A, 62
History of Rome, 107
*History of the English Church and
      People*, 196
History of the Florentine People, 266
History of the Franks, 196
Hittites, 11–12
   civilization, 2, 11–12
   empire, 11
Hobbes, Thomas, 398–399, 466
Hohenzollern family, 376
Holbein, Hans, 263
Holy
   Alliance, 522
   Roman Emperor, 177–178, 180
Homer, 69
hominocentrism, 65
Honduras, 518
Hongwu, 451
Honshu, 326
Hooke, Robert, 476
Horace, 107
Horus, 13
House of:
   Commons, 387
   Lords, 387
Hsun-tzu, 46

Huang He River, 42, 228
Huari Empire, 236
Huguenots, 283, 361, 364–366
humanism, 164, 254–255, 264–265
Hundred Schools, 43
Hundred years' war, 174, 188–190, 358
Husayn, 214
Huss, John, 280, 290
Hykos, 14

I

ice age, 131
iconoclasm, 157
Iconoclast Controversy, 162
Ides of March, 101
Ieyasu, Tokugawa, 326
Ife, 432
Iliad, 69, 73
Ilkhanate, 318, 320
Imperial Diet, 188
imperium, 94
Inca, Pachucati, 342–343
Incas, 341–348
    agriculture, 346
    arts, 345–346
    conquering of, 416
    economics, 346–348
    education, 345–346
    empire, 335
    imperial rule, 343–345
    Index of Prohibited Books, 287, 472
    nobility, 344
    origins, 342–343
    religion, 345–346
    rule, 334
    treasures, 302
India, 7, 449
    ancient, 29–42
    muslims in, 447–450
    religions, 38–40
    trade, development of, 41–42
Indian Constitution, 32–33
Indiginous civilizations of Africa, 436
Indochina, 49
Indo-Europeans, 7
Indonesia, 36, 50
indulgence, 277
Indus River, 28–29, 85
infinity, 41
inflation, 302–303, 373
Innocent III, 181
Inquisition, 191, 288
Institutes of the Christian Religion, The, 282–283
Interregnum, 384, 392–393
Inti, 345
Ionic columns, 79
Iran, 317
Irene, 162

Iron age, 70
Isabella I, 191, 302, 370–371, 410–411
Isaurian dynasty, 157
Isis, 13
Islam, 15, 157
    decline, 219
    rise and spread, 208–225
    spread of, 214–218, 225
    law, 431, 445
isolationists, 77
Israel, 9
Israelites, 9
Isthmus of Kra, 50
Italo-Byzantine art, 260
Italy, 500 B.C., 92
    conquest of, 95
Izanagi, 54
Izanami, 54

J

Jacob, 9
Jacobins, 493
Jacquerie, 189
Jahan, Nur, 449
Jahan, Shah, 449–450
    Shah, reign of, 442
Jainism, 39–40
Jains, 39
Jamaica, 418–419
James I, 384, 388–389
James II, 384, 395–396
James VI, 387
Jamestown, 301, 419
Janissaries, 443, 446–447
Japan, 321–327
    ancient, 51–55
    feudal organizations, 333
    Mongol attacks, 316
    unification of, 326
Jatakas, 38
Java, 50
Jean II, 189
Jeanne of Arc, 189
Jefferson, Thomas, 399, 471, 514
Jerusalem, 9, 185, 211, 216
Jesuits, 288, 290
    founding of, 276
    missionairies, 418
Jesus of Nazareth, 108–109, 209
Jew of Malta, The, 266
Jewish Kingdoms, ancient, 8
Jews, expulsion from Spain, 302
jihad, 217
Jimmu, 54
Jin empire, 229
Joao I, 191
Joao VI, 519
John, 386
John II, 410, 412
John, King, 183
Joint-Stock Company, 301

Joliet, Louis, 418
Jomon period, 51–52
Joseph II, 376
Journey Through Wales, 197
Juan Carlos, 371
Judah, 6, 9
Judaism, 209
Judas Maccabaeus, 10
judicial power, 387
Julio-Claudian dynasty, 103–104
Julius Caesar, 266
Jurchen, 229
jury system, 183, 386
Justinian Code, The, 170–171
Justinian:
    building program, 155
    legal code, 155
    reign of, 154–156
Juvenal, 107

K

Ka'ba, 211
Kabuki, 327
Kaifeng, 229
Kali, 34
Kalidasa, 41
Kamakura period, 316, 324–325
kami, 54–55
kamikaze, 325
Kano, 431
Kapaleeswarar, 34
Karanga, 434
Karl IV, 187
karma, 33
Kashta, 18
Kassites, 5
Katnaga, kingdom of, 433–434
Katsina, 431
Kautilya, 40
Kenya, 433
Kepler, Johannes, 472–473
Khan:
    Genghis, 316–318
    Kublai, 319, 325
khanates, 318
Khmer empire, 49–51
Kievan Russia, 154, 171
Kija, 55
Kilwa, 433
King Lear, 266
King of Kings, 8
King, Jr., Martin Luther, 56
kinship, 136
Knights Hospitaler, 185
Knights Templar, 185
knights, 178, 387
Knox, John, 286
koans, 322
Kofun, Tomb period, 51–53
Koguryo, 55
Koine, 88, 163

Kojiki, 53
Konrad II, 180
Konrad III, 185
Koran, 430
Korea, 327–328
    ancient, 55–56
    mongol rule, 327
    taxation, 328
Koryo dynasty, 327
kouros, 72
Krishna, 34–36
Kshatriyas, 31
Kukulkan, 243
Kush, 433
kut, 56
Kyoto, 322, 326

L

La Venta, 139
Lagash, 4
laissez-faire, 468
Lake Texcoco, 139, 241, 335
Lakshman, 36
Lancaster, house of, 190
Langland, William, 196
Langton, Stephen, 183
Last Supper, The, 262
Late middle ages, 174
Latin America:
    climate zones, 149
    revolutions, 504
    topographical areas, 150
Latin league, 95
Latins, 93
Latium, 93–95
Lavoisier, Antoine, 476
Laws, The, 81, 107
lay investiture, 180
Lebanon, 12
LeClerc, General, 515
Legalism, 46
legislative power, 387
Leo III, Emperor, 157
Leo IX, 180
Leon, 190
Leonidas, 74–75
Lepanto, 445
    battle of, 373
Lepidus, 101–102
Lesser Antilles, 245
Letters Concerning the English, 467
Leviathan, 398
Li Boi, 228
liberalism, European, 520
libraries, 88, 90
Libyans, 15
Life of Charlemagne, 196
light, composition of, law of, 475
Limpopo River, 434
Lincoln, cathedral, 195
linear perspective, 260

Lisbon, 190
Literary renaissance, 254
literature:
    development of, 73
    Roman, 106–107
Little Vehicle, 39
liturgies, 193
Lives of the Artists, The, 266
Livy, 103, 107
Locke, John, 398-399, 462, 466–467, 472, 487
Lombard League, 181
Long parliament, 384, 390, 393
lords, 178, 203
Lorraine, 180
lotus position, 38
Louis IX, 182, 186
Louis the Pious, 177
Louis VII, 182, 185
Louis XI, 189, 363
Louis XIII, 365
Louis XIV, 306, 356, 477, 484
    rule of, 367–370
Louis XV, 370, 465–466, 484, 486
Louis XVI, 370, 484, 491–492, 493
Louis XVIII, 521
Loyola, Ignatius, 288
Lucretius, 107–108
lunar calendar, 6
Luther, Martin, 276–279
    and Jews, 282
    supporters, 281
    teaching of, 279
Lutheranism, 281
Lyceum, 82
Lycurgus, 77
lyric poetry, 73, 88
Lysander, 78

M

Macbeth, 266
Maccabean Revolt, 86
Macedonia, 67, 74
    unification of Greece, 78–79
Macedonian:
    dynasty, 157–158
    Greece, 64
Machiavelli, Niccolo, 267, 273–274
Madeira islands, exploration, 410
Madras, 34
Magadha kingdom, 40
Magellan, Ferdinand, 406, 414
Magna Carta, 183, 206, 386
Magna Graecia, 94–95
Magyars, 179–180
Mahabharata, The, 35–36, 62
Mahal, Mumtaz, 449
Mahavira, 40
Mahayana, 39
Mahmud of Ghazni, 226
    empire of, 227

Maimonides, 219
Maine, 182
maize, 133
Makkah, see: Mecca
Malay peninsula, 50
Mali, empire of, 428, 430–431
Malindi, 433
Mallory, Thomas, 196
Malpighi, Marcello, 476
Manchuria, 452
Manchus, 319, 452
Mandate of Heaven, 45, 61
Mande people, 430
mandela, 33
manorialism, 179
mansa, 430
Manuel II, 172
manuscript illumination, 195
Manzikert, 158
Marat, Jean-Paul, 493, 495
Marathon, 74
Maria Theresa, 375
Marius, 99
marketplace, 71
Marlowe, Christopher, 266
Marquette, Jacques, 418
Marranos, 373
Mars, 93
Martel, Charles, 176
martial law, 393
Mary I, 359–360
Mary II, 395–396
Mary, Queen of Scots, 361, 387
Masaccio, 260
Materialists, 73
Mathematical Principles of Natural Philosphy, The, 462
mathematics, 90
    Mayan, 142
    origins in India, 41
Matope, 434
Maurya
    Chandragupta, 40–41
    empire, 28, 40–41
Mayan:
    ceremonial centers, 236, 238–239
    civilization, 136, 140–142
    decline, 241–244
Mayapan, 244
    rise of, 236
Mazarin, Cardinal, 367
Mecca, 209
mechanics, 474
medicant, 194
Medici family, 258–259, 300
    Lorenzo de, il Magnifico, 259
    Marie de, 365
medicine, 475–476
medieval:
    Europe, 174–207
    manor, 204
    society, 192–198

Medina, 210–211
Meditations, 108
Mediterranean Sea, 3
megalomania, 85
Mehmet II, 442, 444
Melinik I, 19
Mencius, 45
Menes, 13
Mennonites, 281, 290
mercantilism:
    development in Europe, 305
    France, 296
Mercator projection, 409
mercenaries, 238
mercenary troops, 184
Merchant of Venice, The, 266
Mesoamerica, 237–244
Mesopotamia, 85
    civilization, 3–4
messiah, 109
mestizo, 413
metal working, 12
metallurgy, 138, 143
metals, precious, 305
metalwork production, 321
Metamorphoses, 107
Methodius, 158
methodology, 471–472
Metternich, Klemens von, 504,
    521–522
Mexico, 238
    independence, 517–518
Michael VIII, 160
Middle:
    ages, late, 186–192
    east:
        ancient, 2–27
        globalization, 142–160
        Ottoman rule, 443–447
    kingdom, 14
middle way, the, 37
Midsummer Night's Dream, A, 266
Migrations to Americas, 130
Milan, 258, 262
millet system, 444
Miltiades, 74
Minamoto family, 324
Ming Dynasty, 451–452
Minoan civilization, 64, 67–68
Minos, 67
Miranda, Francisco, 471, 516
Mirandola, Count of, 267
missionaries, 288, 326
Mississippi Valley, exploration, 418
mita, 416
Mochica:
    civilization, 136
    culture, 142–143
Moctezuma II, 337
model parliament, 387
Mogadishu, 433
Mohenjo-Daro, 29

moksha, 33
molasses, 419
Moliere, Jean Baptiste, 470
Mombasa, 433
Mona Lisa, 262
Monastery of St. Catherine, 163
monastics, 110, 164
money supply, increase, 302–303
Monfort, Simon de, 183
Mongols, 317–318, 443, 451
    rule, 318
        decline, 320
monks, 110
Monophysite controversy, 156–157
Montaigne, Michel de, 135
Montesquieu, Baron de, 462, 467,
    472, 487
Montezuma II, 415–416
Moor, Marston, 391
Moors, 176
More, Sir Thomas, 265, 266, 284–285
Morelos, Jose, 517
Moriscos, 373
mosaics, 106
Moses, 9, 209, 264
    at Mount Sinai, 26–27
mosques, 431
Mozambique, 433
Mozart, Wolfgang Amadeus, 470
mudras, 38
Mugahl:
    dynasty, 448–449
    empire, 442, 447–449
        decline, 442
Muhammad:
    life of, 208
    significance, 209
Muhammed, Askia, 101
Muisca chiefdom, 135–136
mulatto, 413
mummification, 14, 16
Munster, 281
Musa, mansa, 431
museums, 88
Muslims, 39, 209–211
    basic beliefs, 212–213
    expulsion from Spain, 302
    South Asia, 226
Mutapa Empire, 434
Mutota, 434
Mwanamutapa, 434
My Big Fat Greek Wedding, 82
Myanmar, 36
Mycale, 75
Mycenean civilization, 64, 67–69

N

Nahuatl, 139
Najaf, 220
Napata, 18
Naples, 257

Napoleon:
    age of, 504–528
    downfall, 511–512
    early life, 505–506
    emperor, 508–509
    European domination, 509–510
    exile, 513
    legacy:
        Americas, 514–515
        Europe, 513—514
        Haiti, 514–515
        United States, 514
    military career, 505–506
Napoleonic:
    Code, 507
    Empire, rise of, 508
    Era, 471
Nara period, 316, 321–322
Narayanan, Kocheri R., 33
Narses, 154
Nation States, rise of, 356–383
    Austria, 374–376
    England, 357–363
    France, 363–370
    Spain, 370–374
National:
    Assembly, 489, 491–492
    Convention, 493
nationalism, 505
    Prussia, 511
nationality, 357
naturalism, 260
nautical inventions, 229
Navarre, 190
navigation:
    act, 296, 307
    school of, 406
Nazca culture, 142–143
Nebuchadnezzar, 5
Necker, Suzanne, 465
Negras, 141
Nelson, Lord, 506, 508–509
nepotism, 277
Nero, 103–104, 109
Nerva, 104
New:
    Amsterdam, 419
    kingdom, 14
    world, 131
    York, 419
Newton, Isaac, 462, 474–475, 478
Nicaea, 159, 186
Nicaragua, 518
Nike, 79
Nile River, 13
900 Theses, 267
95 Theses, 276–278, 290
Nineveh, 5
nirvana, 37, 39
Noah, 6
Nobilis, 96
Nobunaga, Oda, 326

nomads, 317
Norman-Angevin dynasty, 183
Normandy, 182
Norse Sagas, 195
Northern School, 39
Notre Dame Cathedral, 195
Notre Dame la Grande, 194–195
Nouvelle Heloise, La, 469
Novum Organum, 477
Nubia, 18, 433
Nubians, 15
Nuclear America, 136
nunneries, 193

O

O'Neill, Hugh, 361
Oba, 432
obelisks, 17
Octavian, 102
Odoacer, 110–111
Odyssey, 73
Old Kingdom, 13–14
Old Regime, 485
Old Testament, 6, 8, 89
Oligarchy, 99
    development of, 70
Olmec civilization, 136, 138–139
Olympics:
    development of, 72
    first, 64
On the Buildings, 164
On the Ceremonies, 164
On the Civil War, 108
On the Gallic War, 108
On the Imperial Administration, 164
On the Nature of the Universe, 107
On the Structure of the Human Body,
    476
On the Wars, 164
opportunist, 366
Optimates, 98
oracle bones, 43
"Oration on the Dignity of Man",
    267
Osirus, 13
Osman of Bithynia, 444
Ostrogothic tribes, 175
Othello, 266
Othman I, 444
Otto I, 180
Ottoman:
    empire, 298–299, 407–408
        decline of, 445–446
        expansion of, 443
        rise of, 444–445
    Imperial Court, 445
    rule:
        eastern Europe, 443–447
        middle east, 443–447
        society, 446–447
    state, formation, 442

Turks, 160, 372–373
outcast, 31, 56
Ovid, 107
Oyo, 432

P

Paekche, 55–56
pagoda, 38
Paine, Thomas, 471
Palace of Versailles, 368–370
Palenque, 141
Paleologian dynasty, 160
Palestine, 9–10, 14
Palladio, Andrea, 260
panchayat, 41
pancration, 72
panegyrics, 164
pantheism, 464
Pantheon, 105–106
papacy, 181, 192–193
papal:
    bull, 278
    states, 176, 257
    supremacy, 192–193
paper money, 229
papyri, 17
Paracelsus, 476
Paraguay, independence, 518
Parallel Lives, 107
Paris Commune, 493
Paris, 465
parliament, 183, 359, 386
Parthenon, 79
Parthia, 85
pashas, 444
pastoralists, 317
Patagonia, 132
Pate, 433
Patriarchate system, 162
Patricians, 94
patrons, 94
Pax:
    Mongolia, 318–319
    Ottomanica, 447
    Romana, 103
Peace of Augsberg, 276, 281
peasant's, 508
    rebellion, 282
    revolt, 189
Pedro I, 519
Pedro II, 519
Peking Man, 42
Peloponnese, 76
Peloponnesian:
    League, 78
    War, 64, 77–78, 80
People's Court, 76
Pepin the short, 176
Pergamum, 87
Pericles, 79
Period of the Second Temple, 10

perioeci, 77
Persepolis, 8, 85
Persia, 3, 5
    mongol rule, 318
    civilization, 2, 7–8
    empire, 7
    gulf, 3, 432
Persian War, 64, 74–75, 156
Persians, 7, 15, 448
Peru, independence, 518–519
Peten, 140, 241
    rain forest, 242
Peter, 109
Petition of Right, 384, 389
Petrarca, Francesco, 264
Petrarch, 264
Petrine Theory, 192
phalanx, 72
pharaohs, 14
Phenician civilization, 12
Phidias, 79
philanthropy, 83, 161
philharmonic, 83
philia, 83
Philip II, 78–79, 83, 302, 306, 360,
    372–374
Philip, 356
Philippe II Augustus, 182–183, 188
Philippe IV the Fair, 182
Philippe of Valois, 188
Philippe VI, 188
Philistines, 9
Phillip II, 362
philology, 259
Philosophers, 464–465
philosophy, 80, 83
    development of, 73–74
    Roman, 108
phobia, 83
Phoenicia, 12
Phoenicians, 96
    city states, 12
    civilization, 2
Physics, 472–475
Physiocrats, 468
pi, 41, 90
Piankhy, 18
piazzas, 260
Pico, Giovanni, 267
Piedras, 141
Piers the Ploughman, 196
Pieta, 264
pilgrimage, 213
pilgrims, 185, 419
Pillow Book, The, 323
Pindar, 73
Pisano, Nicola, 263
Pisistratus, 76
Pizarro, Francisco, 341, 348, 406, 416
Platea, 75
Plateau of Assure, 5
Plato, 81

Platonic Academy of Florence, 267
plebians, 94
plebiscite, 508
Pliny the elder, 108
plow, 18
Plutarch, 107
Po valley, 92
Podromos, Theodore, 164
Poet Laureate, 265
polis, 256
    development of, 70
Politician, The, 81
Polo, Marco, 319
Polybius, 105, 107
Polyclitus, 79
polytheistic, 239
Pompadour, Madame de, 465
Pompey, Cneius, 100–101
Pope, 158–159
    Alexander, 412, 470
    Boniface VIII, 182
    Clement V, 257
    Clement VII, 181, 284
    Gregory XI, 258
    Innocent III, 183, 186
    Julius II, 258
    Leo X, 276–278
    Paul III, 287
    Pius VII, 509
    Urban II, 184
popular sovereignty, 385
populares, 98
porcelain, 228, 319
Portugal:
    colonial rivalry with Spain,
        412–414
    late middle ages, 190–192
    wealth, 302
Portuguese empire, 413
Poynings's Law, 361
Praetorian Guard, 103
Pragmatic Sanction, 375
Praise of Folly, 267
Praxiteles, 79
prayer, 213
    Islam, 219
precipitation, 131
predestination, 283
Predynastic Period, 13
Presbyterians, 286, 390–391
Pride's Purge, 392
Priestly, Joseph, 476
primogeniture, 415
Prince, The, 267, 273–274
princeps, 102
printing press, 287, 304
*Proclamation of the second council of
    Nicaea*, 172
Procopius, 164
procurators, 97
proletariat, 98
Protagorus, 80

protectorate, 10, 392
Protestant Reformation, *see*:
        Reformation
Protestantism:
    in England, 283–285
    growth, 281–287
    Proto-Greeks, 67–70
Prussia, 376–377
Psellus, Michael, 164
Ptolemaic:
    Egypt, 15
    kingdom, 86
Ptolemaios, 86
Ptolemy, 90, 108, 472, 474
Punic Wars, 91, 96–97
Punjab, 227
Puritans, 388, 419
pyramid age, 16
Pythagoras, 74

Q

Qin dynasty, 28, 46–47
Quakers, 281, 290
Quebec, founding, 4118
Quetzalcoatyl, 240–241, 243, 339, 415
quipu, 343
Quran, 212–213

R

Rabelais, Francois, 266
raised fields, 141
Rama, 34–36
Ramadan, 219
Ramayana, The, 34–36
Ramses II, 9, 15
Raphael, 262
rationalism, 464
raw materials, 305
reactionary, 520
Reconquista, 190
Records of Ancient Matters, 53
refectory, 262
reformation, 256, 276–295
    factors leading to, 279–280
    results of, 289
regicide, 392
Reign of Terror, 484, 494–495
religious authority, 279
Remus, 93
Renaissance, 255–275
Republic, of Rome, 94
    collapse of, 98–102
Republic, The, 81, 107
republican government, 256
revenues, 389
*Revolutions of the Heavenly Bodies, On
    the*, 469, 472
Revolutions, age of, 461–528
Rhea Silvia, 93
Rheims, cathedral, 195

rhetoric, 80
Rhodesian plateau, 434
Ricci, Matteo, 451
Richard I the Lion Hearted, 183, 186
Richard II, 189
Richard III, 190
Richelieu, Cardinal, impact of,
        365–366
rifles, 409
Rise of the Roman Republic, The, 105
Rivera, Diego, 336
Robespierre, Maximilian, 493, 495,
        506
Roman:
    civil war, 91
    conquest, 84
        Hellenic Kingdoms, 91
        Hellenistic Kingdoms, 84
    empire, 98
        division of, 91, 109–111
        fall of, 91
        western, fall of, 110–111
    mythological origins, 93
    republic, collapse, 91
    senate, 100
    society, 105–109
Romance of the Rose, 196
romance poetry, 196
Romanesque style, 194
Romanization, 95
Romanus the Melodist, 163–164
Rome:
    ancient, 91–112
    early, 91
    foundation, 94
    geography, 92–93
    republic, establishment, 94
Romeo and Juliet, 266
Romulus, 93
roundheads, 391
Rousseau, Jean Jacques, 462,
        467–469, 472, 487
Roxanne, 85
Royal:
    Capitularies, 176
    Law Courts, 183
    power, limitations, 386
royalist sympathizers, 492
Rubicon, 100
Rudolf of Habsburg, 181, 187
rum, 307, 419
Rump parliament, 392
Russia, 3
    mongol rule, 318

S

sacraments, 279
sacrifice, 339
Safavid dynasty, 442, 444
Sailendra dynasty, 50
Saint George, 263–264

Saint Jerome Vulgate, 259
Saint Peter's Basilica, 260–261, 273
Saint-Sernin, 194
Saladin, 186
Salamis, 75
Salian dynasty, 180
Salisbury, cathedral, 195
salons, 465
salvation, 182–283, 279
samsara, 33
Samudra, 41
samurai, 324
    legacy, 328
San Martin, Jose de, 471
sangha, 38
sankin kotai, 327
Sanskrit, 40
sanskritization, 32
Sant'Ambrogio, 194
Santander, Francisco, 519
Sappho, 73
    poems of, 116
Saragossa, 190
Sardinia, 96
Sargon I, 4
Sargon II, 5
satori, 322
satrapies, 7
Saudi Arabia, 209, 310
Saul, 9
Saul of Tarsus, 109
Saxony, 180
schism, 158
Schleimann, Heinrich, 68
Scholastics, 197
School of Athens, The, 262, 264
School of Hellas, 79
science:
    classical period, 82
    development of, 73–74
scientific:
    method, 471–472
    revolution, 462–483
Scipio, Cornelius, 97
Scotism, 198
Scotus, John Duns, 198
scribes, 136
sculpture, classical, 79
sea peoples, 15
seafaring, 298
Second:
    estate, 485–487
    intermediate period, 14
    Punic War, 97
    Vatican Council, 287
Secret History, The, 164
secular, 8, 163–164
Sejong, King, 328
Sekigahara, 326
Seleucid Empire, 10, 86–87
Seleucus, 40, 86
self-interest, law of, 468

Selim!, 442, 444
Seljuks, 444
    Turks, 158–159, 184
Semites, 4
Senate, 94
Seneca, 108
Sengoku, 325
Sennacherib, 5
Seoul, 328
Septuagint, 89
serf, 179
Seven Years' War, 309
Seville, 191
Sforza, Ludovico, the Moor, 258
Sha'ana, 434
Sha'aria, 431, 445
Shakespeare, William, 266
Shakuntala, 41
shamanism, 56
Shang dynasty, 43, 28
Sheba, Queen of, 19
Sherif of Mecca, 444
sheriffs, 182
Shi Huangdi, 46–47
Shi'ite muslims, 213–214
Shi'ites, 444
Shikibu, Lady Murasaki, 323
Shinto Creation Myth, 53
Shintoism, 53–55
shire, 387
Shiva, 33–35
Shogun, 325
shogunate, 325
Shona, 434
Shonagon, Sei, 323
Shotoku, Prince, 322
Shudras, 31, 38
Sic et non, 197
Sicilian Expedition, 78
Sicily, 92, 96, 257
Sidon, 12
Siena, 258
Sieyes, Abbe de, 488
Sikhism, 39–40
Sikhs, 39, 450
Silesia, 375
silk:
    production, 321
    road, 39, 48, 63, 228–229, 233,
        318, 407
Silla, 55–56
silver, 302, 305
simony, 277
Sistine Chapel, 262
Sita, 36
Skeptics, 89
slash and burn, 133
slavery, 410
slaves, 307, 339–340
slavic peoples, conversion of, 152,
    158
Slavonic language, 158

Smith, Adam, 462, 468–469
Social Contract, The, 462, 467
social stratification, 134
Social War, 99–100
socialist empire, 341
Society of Jesus, 288
socii, 95, 98
    revolt, 99
Socrates, 81
Sofala, 433
Solomon, 9, 19
Solon, 76
Somalia, 432
Song dynasty, 226, 228–229
Song of Roland, 195
Song of the Cid, 196
Song, Taizu, 229
Song-gye, Yi, 328
Songhai empire, 428, 431
Songs, 265
Soninke people, 429
sophists, 80–81
Sophocles, 73
sophomore, 83
South African Civilization, 433
South America:
    Andean region, 244–247
    cultures, 351
    natural setting, 148
Southern Africa, 433–434
Southern School, 39
Spain:
    art, 374
    colonial:
        rivalry with Portugal,
            412–414
        trade, 306
    conquers Americas, 413–414
    expulsion of Jews and Muslims,
        302
    late middle ages, 190–192
    wealth, 302
Spanish:
    Armada, 306, 356, 362–363
    conquests, Americas, 296
    Inquisition, 371
    Succession, War of, 369–370
Sparta, 74
Spartacus, 100
Spartan system, 77
Spenser, Edmund, 266
sphere of influence, 78
Spinoza, Baruch, 469–470
Spinoza, Benedict de, 464
Spirit of the Laws, The, 462, 467
Spiritual Exercises, 288
Spring, 261
Srivijaya empire, 49–50
St. Bartholomew's Day Massacre,
    276
St. Moses, Prayer to, 27
stained glass windows, 195

Star Chamber court, 390
states, 135–136
status quo, 521
Statute of Drogheda, 361
stelae, 142
steppes, 317
Stoics, 89
Strabo, 90
Strait of:
    Magellan, 414
    Malacca, 50–51
Strasbourg, cathedral, 195
Struggle of the Orders, 95
Stuart:
    absolutism, 387–388
    dynasty, 384
    Magna Carta, 389
    restoration, 393–394
    Mary, 395
stupas, 38
Su, Li, 47
Suarez, Francisco, 374
Sublime Porte, 447
subsistence farming, 69
subvassals, 182
Sucre, Antonio, 519
Sudan, 18
sugar plantations, 419
Suleiman I, 442
Suleiman II, 444–445
Sulla, dictatorship of, 99
Sully, Duke of, 364–365
sultan, 444
Sumer, 29
Sumerian, 11
    civilization, 2–4
Summa Theologica, 197
sun calendar, 347
Sundiate, 430–431
Sunni muslims, 213–214
Sunni, 444
Sun-shin, Yi, 328
Suppiluliumas, 11
supply and demand, law of, 468
Susa, 85
sutras, 38
Swabia, 180
Swahili:
    city-states, 428
    civilization, 432–433
symmetry, 72
Syracuse, 78
Syria, 4, 11, 14

T

taboo, 32, 56
Tacitus, 107
Taj Mahal, 447, 450
    completed, 442
    war, 453
Tale of Genji, The, 323

Talmud, 10
Tamburlaine the Great, 266
Tan'gun, 55
Tanach, 8, 89
Tang:
    dynasty, 226, 228–229
    empire, 232
    Taizong, 228
Tanzania, 433
Taoism, 45–46
taxes, 305
tea, 321
    ceremony, 324
telos, 82
Temple of:
    Solomon, 9–10
    the tooth, 38
Tennis Court Oath, 489
Tenochtitlan, 335–337, 340, 415
Teotihuacan:
    civilization, 136, 139–140
    decline and fall, 236, 238–239
Test Act, 394
Tetzel, Johann, 277–278
Teutonic Knights, 185
Thailand, 36
theater, development of, 72–73
Thebes, 14, 78
Themistocles, 74
theocracy, 283
Theodora, 162
Theodosius I, 110
Theravada, 39
third:
    estate, 485–487
    France, 365
    Punic War, 97
Thirty Years' War, 289, 356, 366
Thrifty, The, 78
Thucydides, 80
Thutmose III, 14
Tiahuanaco Empire, 236
Tiber River, 93–94
Tiberius, 99, 103
Tierra del fuego, 131
Tigris River, 3
Tigris-Euphrates valley, 4
Tikal, 141
Timbuktu, 431
Tintoretto, 262
tithe, 177, 486
Titian, 262
Titus, 104
Tlaxcala, 337
Tokugawa shogunate, 316, 325–327
Tokyo, 326
Toledo, 190
Toleration Act, 384
Toltecs, 236, 238–241
tools, 12
Topiltzin, 240, 243
tories, 394

Torquemada, Tomas de, 191
Toulouse, 364
Touraine, 182
Toussaint L'Ouverture, 515
Tower of London, 389
trade, balance of, 305, 308
trading route, all water, 407
tragedy, 73, 88
Trajan, 104
Treasury, 183
Treaty of:
    Amiens, 508
    Bretigny, 189
    Hubertusburg, 375
    Paris, 375
    Tordesillas, 412
    Troyes, 189
    Utrecht, 356, 370
    Verdun, 178
trial by jury, 71, 76
triangular trade, 307, 419
Tribonian, 155
Tribunes, 95
tribute, 338
tricolor, 491
Triennial Act, 384, 390
Tripoli, 185
Tristan and Isolde, 196
Triumvirate:
    first, 91, 100
    second, 91, 101–102
Trojans, 93
troubadours, 195
Troy, 69
Ttipitaka, 38
Tudor:
    dynasty, 190, 356, 358
    Henry, 190
    Margaret, 387
    Mary, 285
Tuileries, 491
Tula 236, 240–241, 244
Tupi, 413
Turgot, Robert, 488
Turks, 443
Tuscany, 264
Twelve Caesars, The, 108
Twelve Tables, 96
Two Treatises of Government, 399, 404,
    462, 466
tyrant, 76
Tyre, 12
Tyrrhenian Sea, 92
Tzu, Lao, 45

U

Ukiyo-e, 327
Umayyad Caliphate, 208, 214–216
umma, 210
universal manhood suffrage, 493
Untouchables, 31, 38

Upanishads, 35
Ur, 4
Urban II, 205
Urdu, 448
Ursuline order, 288
Uruguay, independence, 518
Utopia, 266
Uzmal, 243

V

Vaishya, 31
Valencia, 190
Valla, Lorenzo, 259
Valley of Mexico, 335, 337
van der Weyden, Rogier, 263
van Eyck, Jan, 263
van Leeuwenhoek, Anton, 476
Vandal tribes, 175
varnas, 31
Vasari, Giorgio, 266
vassals, 178, 203
Vatican, 260, 262
Vedas, 28, 30, 35
Velazquez, Diego, 374
Venetian merchants, 298
Venezuela, independence, 518–519
Venice, 262
    republic of, 259
Ventris, Michael, 69
Venus de Milo, 88
Vergil, 103, 106–107
Verrazano, Giovanni, 418
Vesalius, Andreas, 476
Vespasian, 104
Vespucci, Amerigo, 408
viceroy, 161
Vikings, 179
villas, 260
Virgin and Child with Saint Anne, 262
Virginia Company, 301, 419
Vishnu, 33–36
Visigothic tribes, 175
Voltaire, 467
von Strasbourg, Gottfried, 196

W

War of the Roses, 190, 358
Warens, Louise de, 465
Wars of Independence, 518–519
Waterloo, Napoleon's defeat, 513
Wealth of Nations, The, 462, 468
weaponry, 409
weapons, 12
West African civilizations, 429–432
Western Europe, religious divisions, 289, 293
Westminster, 183
Whigs, 394
Whitehead, Alfred, 472

William I, 182, 357–358
William III, 395–396
William of Ockham, 198
William the Conqueror, 357
William the Silent, 374
Williams, Roger, 286
Women, status, improved, 172
Works and Days, 73
Worms, edict of, 276, 278
writing:
    historical, development, 80
    system, 321
Wyatt, Sir Thomas, 266
Wycliffe, John, 280, 290

X

X'ian, 228–229
xenophobia, 433
Xeres, 74–75
Xerxes, 7–8
Xi'an, 47, 322

Y

Yahweh, 9
Yamato period, 51–52, 54
yang, 43
Yayoi period, 51–52
Yellow River, 42, 228
Yemen, 19
Yi dynasty, 316, 328
yin, 43
yoga position, 38
Yonglo, 451
Yoritomo family, 324
York:
    cathedral, 195
    house of, 190
Yoruba kingdoms, 428, 432
Yuan dynasty, 316, 319–320, 451
Yuanzhang, Zhu, 320
Yumednono Pavilion Hall, 321

Z

Zambezi River, 434
Zanzibar, 433
Zapotes, 139
Zarathustra, 8
Zaria, 431
Zazzau, 431
zealots, 10
Zen, 322
Zeno, 89
zero, 41
Zheng He, 451
    ocean voyages, 442
Zhou, 61
    dyanasty, 43–44
ziggurat, 4

Zimbabwe, 428
    great, 434
Zoe, 162
Zoroaster, 8
Zoroastrianism, 8
Zwingli, Ulrich, 282

EVENT INDEX

A

Abbasid Caliphate, 208
Act of:
    settlement, 384
    supremacy, 276
Akbar, reign of, 442
Alexander the Great, conquests, 84–85
American Revolution, 462
Angkor empire, 49–51
Arab invasions, 152, 157
Archaic period, 13, 64, 70–74
Aryan invasion of India, 28
Assyrian civilization, 2, 5
Athenian:
    democracy, 64
    Golden Age, 64
Aztecs, arrival in Mexico, 334

B

Babylonian captivity, 257–258, 280
Baghdad, Mongol invasion, 316, 318
Battle of:
    Aljubarotta, 191
    Boyne, 397
    Crecy, 189
    Guagamela, 84–85
    Las Navas de Tolosa, 191
    Orleans, 189
    Poitiers, 189
    Talas, 229
    Vienna, 374
black death, 174
Byzantine Empire:
    early, 152, 154–157
    high, 152, 157–159
    late, 152, 160
Byzantine Renaissance, 254

C

Carolingian Empire, 174–176
Central:
    high middle ages, 179–187
    middle ages, 174
Chaldean civilization, 2, 5–6
Chimu Kingdom, 236
Chin dynasty, 46–47

Christianity, rise of, 91
Civil War, Roman, 100–101
Classical Greece, 74–77
    development, 74
Classical Period, 64
Congress of Vienna, 504–505
Constantinople, 153
    fall of, 152
    Ottoman conquest of, 442
Council of Trent, 276, 287
crusades, 152, 158–159, 174, 208
Cushitic civilization, 2, 18–19

D

Da Gama, Vasco, explorations, 296, 298
Dark Age, 64
decentralization, period of, 257–259

E

Early middle ages, 174–179
Edict of Nantes, 276, 283
Egyptian civilization, ancient, 2
English:
    Bill of Rights, 384
    Civil War, 384
    Joint Stock Company, 296
Ethiopian civilization, 18–19
    ancient, 2

F

feudalism, 174
first:
    intermediate period, 14
    Punic War, 96–97
fourth crusade, 159
French Revolution, 462
Fronde, 367
Funan empire temple, 49

G

Germanic Kingdoms, 174
glaciers, retreat of, 130, 132
Glorious Revolution, 384, 395–398
Golden Age, 14, 259
Grand Remonstrance, 390
Great Schism, 280
Greek Miracle, 64
Guelf-Ghibelline struggles, 258
Gupta Empire, 28, 40–42

H

Habeas Corpus Act, 384, 394
Han Dynasty, 28, 48
Hebrew civilization, ancient, 8–10
Heian period, 316, 322–323

High Renaissance, 254
Hijra, 208
Hittite Civilization, 2, 11–12
Huari Empire, 236
Hundred years' war, 174, 188–190, 358

I

ice age, 131
Iconoclast Controversy, 162
Inca rule, 334
Indus River Valley Civilization, 28
Inquisition, 191
Interregnum, 384, 392–393
Iron age, 70
Isaurian dynasty, 157

J

Japan, mongol attacks, 316
Jesuits, founding of, 276
Jomon period, 51–52
Julio-Claudian dynasty, 103–104
Justinian I, reign of, 154–156

K

Kamakura period, 316
Khan, Genghis, reign, 316
Khmer empire, 49–51
Kofun, Tomb period, 51–53
Koguryo, 55

L

Late middle ages, 174
Latin American revolutions, 504
Literary Renaissance, 254

M

Macedonian:
    dynasty, 157–158
    Greece, 64
Maurya empire, 28, 40–41
Mayapan, rise of, 236
Mercantilism, France, 296
Middle ages, late, 186–192
Migrations to Americas, 130
Minoan civilization, 64
Mughal empire, decline, 442
Mycenean civilization, 64

N

Napoleonic Era, 471
Nara period, 316, 321–322
Navigation Act, 296
New Kingdom, 14
95 Theses, 276–278, 290

O

Old Kingdom, 13–14
Olympics, first, 64
Ottoman state, formation, 442

P

Paekche, 55–56
Paleologian dynasty, 160
Pax:
    Mongolia, 318–319
    Romana, 103
Peace of Augsberg, 276, 281
Peasant's Rebellion, 282
Peloponnesian War, 64, 77–78
Persian War, 64, 156
Petition of Right, 384, 389
Polo, Marco, 319
Predynastic Period, 13
Punic Wars, 91, 96–97
Pyramid Age, 16

Q

Qin dynasty, 28, 46–47

R

Reformation, 276–295
    factors leading to, 279–280
Reign of Terror, 484
Roman:
    civil war, 91
    conquest, 84, 84, 91
    empire:
        division, 91
        fall of, 91
        western, fall of, 110–111
    republic, collapse, 91

S

Safavid dynasty, 442
second:
    intermediate period, 14
    Punic War, 97
Shang dynasty, 28, 43
Sicilian expedition, 78
slavic peoples, conversion of, 152
Social War, 99–100
Socii Revolt, 99
Song dynasty, 226, 228–229
Spanish:
    Armada, 306, 356
    conquests, Americas, 296
Srivijaya empire, 49
St. Bartholomew's Day Massacre, 276
Stuart dynasty, 384
Sumerian civilization, 2–4

T

Taj Mahal completed, 442
Tang dynasty, 226, 228–229
Teotihuacan, decline and fall, 236, 238–239
Test Act, 394
Third Punic War, 97
Thirty Years' War, 289, 356
Tiahuanaco Empire, 236
Tokugawa shogunate, 316
Toleration Act, 384
Toltec Empire, 236
Treaty of Utrecht, 356
Triennial Act, 384, 390
Triumvirate, 91, 100–102
Tudor dynasty, 356

U

Umayyad Caliphate, 208

V

Varanasi, 34–35

W

Worms, edict of, 276, 278

Y

Yamato period, 51–52, 54
Yayoi period, 51–52
Yi dynasty, 316
Yuan dynasty, 316

Z

Zheng He, ocean voyages, 442
Zhou dynasty, 43–44

MAPS INDEX

A

Andes Mountain Region, 245
Arabia, 3, 7
Atacama Desert, 245
Atlantic trade routes, 311

B

Battle of Marathon, 75
Beijing, 452
Bering Strait, 131
Black Death in Europe, 192, 202
Black Sea, 3
Byzantine Empire, 154, 171

C

Caribbean region, 134, 246
    and Antilles, 246
        topographical areas, 150
Caspian Sea, 3
Central America, 238
Charlemagne, empire of, 177
China, 452
Crusades, 185, 186, 206
Cushite Kingdom, 18

D

Dutch New Amsterdam, 417

E

Egypt, 3
    ancient, 13
English Civil War, 391, 401
Ethiopian empire, 19
Euphrates River, 3
Europe:
    late middle ages, 188
    westeren, 18th century, 463
European Trade Routes, 272

F

Fertile Crescent, 3
France, 490

G

Germanic Invasions, fifth century, 175
Greco-Roman Civilization, 85
Greek world, 65

H

High Middle Ages, Europe, 179
Hittite Empire, 11

I

India, 449
Indigenous civilizations of Africa, 436
Indochina, 49
Islam, spread of, 225
Italy, 500 B.C., 92

J

Jerusalem, 216
Jewish Kingdoms, Ancient, 8
K
Kievan Russia, 154, 171

L

Latin America:
    climate zones, 149
    topographical areas, 150

M

Mahmud of Ghazni, empire of, 227
Manchuria, 452
Mediterranean Sea, 3
Mesoamerica, 238
Mexico, 238
Middle East, ancient, 3

N

New World, 131

O

Ottoman Empire, 299
    expansion of, 443

P

Paris, 465
Persia, 3
    empire, 7
    gulf, 3
Peten rain forest, 242
Phoenicia, 12
Punjab, 227

R

Roman Empire, 98
Russia, 3

S

Silk Roads, 39, 63, 233
South African Civilization, 433
South America:
    natural setting, 148
    cultures, 351
Saudi Arabia, 310

T

Tang empire, 232
Teotihuacan civilization, 139
Tigris River, 3

W

West African Civilizations, 429
Western Europe, Religious Divisions, 289, 293

NAMES INDEX

A

Abelard, Peter, 197
Abraham, 8–9, 209
Aeneas, 93
Ahmose I, 14
Akbar, 448–450
    successors to, 449–450
al-Rashid, Harun, 218
Alcibiades, 78
Alexander I, 521–522
Alexander III, 79, 84
Alexander the Great, 7, 10, 12, 15, 40, 83
Alexius I, 159, 184
Alfonso Henriques, 190
Alfonso VII of Castile, 190
Ali, 214
    Sunni, 431
Ambedkar, Bhimrao Ramji, 33
Amenhotep III, 14
Amenhotep IV, 14
Angelico, Fra, 261–262
Anglo-Saxon tribes, 175
Anselm of Canterbury, 197
Antoinette, Marie, 488
Antonius, 104
Antony, Mark, 101
Apollo Belvedere, 115
Archbishop of Canterbury, 284
Archimedes, 90
Aristarchus, 89
Aristotle, 81–82, 474
Arouet, Francois Marie, 467
Arthur, King, 196
Aryabhata, 41
Asoka, 38, 40, 62
Assyrians, 5–6, 9
Atahualpa, 416
Athena, 79
Augustulus, Romulus, 110–111
Augustus, 103, 108
    reign of, 102–103
Aurangzeb, 450
Aurelius, Marcus, 104, 108

B

Babylonians, 4–5
Bach, Johann Sebastian, 470
Bacon, Francis, 464, 477
Bacon, Roger, 197
Bang, Liu, 48
Basho, Matsuo, 327
Basil I, 158
Basil II, 158
Belisarius, 154
Bellini, Giovanni, 262
Bernard of Clairvaux, 193

Boccaccio, Giovanni, 265
Boleyn, Anne, 284, 360
Bolivar, Simon, 471, 518–519
Bonaparte, Joseph, 510, 517
Bonaparte, Napoleon, 496, 505
Bosch, Hieronymus, 263, 265
Bourbon family, 364
Boyle, Robert, 476
Brahe, Tycho, 472–473
Brahma, 33
Bramante, Donato, 260–261
Brasidas, 78
Bruegel, Pieter, the elder, 263
Brunelleschi, Filippo, 260
Bruni, Leonardo, 266, 272–273
Brutus, Marcus, 101
Buonarroti, Michelangelo, 260, 262, 264

C

Cabot, John, 418
Cabral, Pedro, 413
Caesar, Julius, 100–102, 108
    dictatorship of, 101
Caligula, 103
Calvin, John, 276, 282–283, 290
Cambyses, 7
Capet, Hugh, 181
Carolingians, 158
Cartier, Jacques, 406, 418
Cassius, Gaius, 101
Castiglione, Baldassarre, 274–275
Catherine of Aragon, 284–285, 359
Catullus, 107
Cavendish, Henry, 476
Cecil, Robert, 360
Cellini, Benvenuto, 255
Cervantes, Miguel de, 266
Champlain, Samuel de, 418
Charlemagne, 176
Charles I, 384, 393, 399
    rule of, 389–391
Charles II, 384, 393–395, 477
Charles IV, 516
Charles the Bald, 181
Charles V, 189, 278, 281
Charles VI, 189, 375
Charles VII, 189
Chrysoloras, Manuel, 266–267
Cicero, 100, 107
Claudius, 103
Cleisthenes, 77
Cleon, 78
Cleopatra VII, 15, 101–102
Clovis, 176
Colbert, Jean, 369
Columbus, Christopher, 371, 407–409
Comnena, Anna, 164
Confucius, birth of, 28
Constantine V, 157

Constantine VII Porphyroghenitos, 164
Constantine XI Paleologus, 160
Constantine, reign of, 110
Constantinople, 158
    fall of, 160
    Patriarch of, 162
Copernicus, Nicolaus, 462, 464, 472
Corneille, Pierre, 470
Coronado, Francisco, 416
Cortes, Hernando, 335
Cortez, 406
Cranmer, Thomas, 284
Crassus, Marcus Licinius, 100
Cromwell, Oliver, 384, 391–393, 405
Cyril, 158
Cyrus, 7

D

da Gama, Vasco, 406–407
da Vinci, Leonardo, 256, 262
Dante Aligheri, 264
Danton, Georges, 493–495
Darius I, 7–8, 74
Daud, Askia, 431
David, Jacques-Louis, 470
de Beauharnais, Josephine, 506
de Montaigne, Michel, 266
de Soto, Hernando, 416
de Talleyrand, Charles Maurice de, 521
Demosthenes, 79
Dengel, Lebna, 433
Deocritus, 73
Descartes, Rene, 464, 477
Dessalines, Jean-Jacques, 515
Dias, Bartholomeu, 406, 410
Diderot, Denis, 462, 465–466
Diocletian, 109
Dofu, 228
Domitian, 104, 108
Donatello, 263
Draco, 76
Drake, Francis, 418
Dravidians, 30
Durer, Albrecht, 263
Durga, 34

E

Edward I, 184
Edward III, 188
Edward VI, 284
Einhard, 196
Einstein, Albert, 478
Elizabeth I, 266, 285, 307, 360–363, 387, 418
Empress Theodora, 156
Erasmus, Desiderius, 267, 280
Eratosthenes, 89

Euclid, 90
Ewuare the great, 432
Ezena, King, 19

F

Ferdinand, 302, 370–371, 410–411
Ficino, Marsilio, 267
Francesca, Pierro della, 262
Francis of Assisi, 194
Franklin, Benjamin, 470
Frederick the Wise of Saxony, 278
Friedrich I Barbarossa, 181, 186
Friedrich II, 181, 186, 257
Froissart, Jean, 197

G

Gaius Gracchus, 99
Gaius, 103
Galen, 90, 108, 475–476
Galilei, Galileo, 464, 472–474
Gandhi, Mahatma, 32, 40
Gauls, 95
Gautama, Siddhartha, 28, 37, 50
Geoffin, Marie Therese, 465
Geoffrey of Monmouth, 196
George I, 384
Gerald of Wales, 197
Ghibblines, 181
Ghiberti, Lorenzo, 263
Giotto, 260
Girgione, 262
Gregory I the great, 193
Gregory of Tours, 196
Guicciardini, Francesco, 266
Gutenberg, Johannes, 304

H

Hadrian, 104
Hammurabi, 3, 5, 19
Hannibal, 97
Hanuman, 36
Harold, 357
Harvey, William, 476
Hawkins, John, 418
Haydn, Joseph, 470
Heinrich II, 180
Heinrich III, 180
Heinrich IV, 181
Heinrich V, 181
Henri of Burgundy, 190
Henrique the Navigator, 191
Henry I, 183
Henry II, 182–183, 386
Henry III, 183
Henry IV, 180, 189, 364–365, 388
Henry V, 189
Henry VI, 189
Henry VII, 190, 358, 360

Henry VIII, 283–285, 387
Henry, the navigator, 409–410
Heraclitus, 74, 156
Herodotus, 80
Hesiod, 73
Hidalgo, Miguel, 517
Hideyoshi, Toyotomi, 326
Hipparchus, 89
Hippocrates, 82
Hobbes, Thomas, 398–399, 466
Holbein, Hans, 263
Homer, 69
Hongwu, 451
Hooke, Robert, 476
Horace, 107
Horus, 13
Huguenots, 283, 361, 365–366
Husayn, 214
Huss, John , 280, 290
Hykos, 14

I

Ieyasu, Tokugawa, 326
Inca, Pachucati, 342–343
Indo-Europeans, 7
Innocent III, 181
Inti, 345
Irene, 162
Isabella, 302, 410–411
Isis, 13
Israelites, 9
Izanagi, 54
Izanami, 54

J

Jacob, 9
Jacobins, 493
Jahan, Nur, 449
Jahan, Shah, 449–450
    reign of, 442
James I, 384, 388–389
James II, 384, 394–396
James VI, 387
Jean II, 189
Jeanne of Arc, 189
Jefferson, Thomas, 399, 471, 514
Jesus of Nazareth, 108–109, 209
Jimmu, 54
Joao I, 191
Joao VI, 519
John II, 410
John, King, 183
Joliet, Louis, 418
Juan Carlos, 371
Judah, 6
Judas Maccabaeus, 10
Jurchen, 229
Juvenal, 107

K

Kali, 34
Kalidasa, 41
Karl IV, 187
Kashta, 18
Kassites, 5
Kautilya, 40
Kepler, Johannes, 472–473
Khan, Kublai, 325
Kija, 55
Knights Hospitaler, 185
Knights Templar, 185
Konrad II, 180
Konrad III, 185
Krishna, 34–36
Kshatriyas, 31

L

Lakshman, 36
Langland, William, 196
Lavoisier, Antoine, 476
LeClerc, General, 515
Leo III, Emperor, 157
Leo IX, 180
Leon, 190
Leonidas, 74–75
Lepidus, 101–102
Li Boi, 228
Livy, 103, 107
Locke, John, 398–399, 462, 466–467,
    472, 487
Louis IX, 182, 186
Louis the Pious, 177
Louis VII, 182, 185
Louis XI, 189, 363
Louis XIII, 365
Louis XIV, 306, 477, 484
Louis XV, 465–466, 484, 486
Louis XVI, 484, 493
Louis XVIII, 521
Loyola, Ignatius, 288
Lucretius, 107–108
Luther, Martin, 276–279
    and Jews, 282
    supporters, 281
    teaching of, 279
Lycurgus, 77
Lysander, 78

M

Machiavelli, Niccolo, 267, 273–274
Magellan, Ferdinand, 406, 414
Magyars, 179–180
Mahal, Mumtaz, 449
Mahavira, 40
Mahmud of Ghazni, 226
Mallory, Thomas, 196
Malpighi, Marcello, 476

Manchus, 319
Manuel II, 172
Marat, Jean-Paul, 493, 495
Maria Theresa, 375
Marquette, Jacques, 418
Mars, 93
Martel, Charles, 176
Martial, 107
Mary I, 359–360
Mary II, 395–396
Mary, Queen of Scots, 361, 387
Masaccio, 260
Matope, 434
Maurya, Chandragupta, 40–41
Mazarin, Cardinal, 367
Medici family, 300
    Lorenzo de, il Magnifico, 259
    Marie de, 365
Mehmet II, 444
Melinik I, 19
Mencius, 45
Menes, 13
Methodius, 158
Metternich, Klemens von, 504,
    521–522
Michael VIII, 160
Miltiades, 74
Minamoto family, 324
Minos, 67
Miranda, Francisco, 471, 516
Mirandola, Count of, 267
Moliere, Jean Baptiste, 470
Montaigne, Michel de, 135
Montesquieu, Baron de, 462, 467,
    472, 487
Montezuma II, 415–416
Moor, Marston, 391
More, Sir Thomas, 265–266, 284–285
Morelos, Jose, 517
Moses, 9, 209
    at Mount Sinai, 26–27
Mozart, Wolfgang Amadeus, 470
Muhammad, significance, 209
Muhammed, Askia, 431
Muslims, 209–211

N

Narayanan, Kocheri R., 33
Narses, 154
Nebuchadnezzar, 5
Necker, Suzanne, 465
Nelson, Lord, 506, 508–509
Nero, 103–104, 109
Nerva, 104
Newton, Isaac, 462, 474–475, 478
Noah, 6
Nobunaga, Oda, 326

O

O'Neill, Hugh, 361
Octavian, 102
Odoacer, 110–111
Osman of Bithynia, 444
Ostrogothic tribes, 175
Othman I, 444
Otto I, 180
Ottoman Turks, 160
Ovid, 107

P

Paine, Thomas, 471
Palladio, Andrea, 260
Paracelsus, 476
Pedro I, 519
Pedro II, 519
Peking Man, 42
Pepin the short, 176
Pericles, 79
Peter, 109
Petrarca, Francesco, 264
Petrarch, 264
Phidias, 79
Philip II, 78–79, 83, 302, 306, 360
Philippe II Augustus, 182–183, 188
Philippe IV the Fair, 182
Philippe of Valois, 188
Philippe VI, 188
Phillip II, 362
Piankhy, 18
Pico, Giovanni, 267
Pisano, Nicola, 263
Pisistratus, 76
Pizarro, Francisco, 341, 348, 406
Plato, 81
Pliny the elder, 108
Plutarch, 107
Podromos, Theodore, 164
Polybius, 105, 107
Polyclitus, 79
Pompadour, Madame de, 465
Pompey, Cneius, 100–101
Pope, 158–159
    Alexander, 470
    Boniface VIII, 182
    Clement V, 257
    Clement VII, 284
    Gregory VII, 181
    Gregory XI, 258
    Innocent III, 183, 186
    Julius II, 258
    Leo X, 276–278
    Paul III, 287
    Urban II, 184
Priestly, Joseph, 476
Procopius, 164
Protagorus, 80

Psellus, Michael, 164
Ptolemy, 90, 108, 472, 474
Pythagoras, 74

Q

Quetzalcoatyl, 240–241, 243, 415

R

Rabelais, Francois, 266
Rama, 34–36
Ramses II, 9, 15
Raphael, 262
Remus, 93
Rhea Silvia, 93
Ricci, Matteo, 451
Richard I the Lion Hearted, 183, 186
Richard II, 189
Richard III, 190
Rivera, Diego, 336
Robespierre, Maximilian, 493, 495,
    506
Romanus the Melodist, 163–164
Romulus, 93
Rousseau, Jean Jacques, 462,
    467–469, 472, 487
Roxanne, 85
Rudolf of Habsburg, 181, 187

S

Saladin, 186
Samudra, 41
San Martin, Jose de, 471
Santander, Francisco, 519
Sargon II, 5
Saul, 9
Saul of Tarsus, 109
Scipio, Cornelius, 97
Scotus, John Duns, 198
Sejong, King, 328
Sekigahara, 326
Seleucus I, 40
Selim I, 442, 444
Seljuk Turks, 158–159, 184
Seneca, 108
Sennacherib, 5
Shakespeare, William, 266
Sheba, Queen of, 19
Shi Huangdi, 46–47
Shiva, 33–35
Shonagon, Sei, 323
Shotoku, Prince, 322
Shudras, 31, 38
Sieyes, Abbe de, 488
Sita, 36
Smith, Adam, 462, 468–469
Socrates, 81
Solomon, 9, 19
Solon, 76

Song-gye, Yi, 328
Spartacus, 100
Spenser, Edmund, 266
Spinoza, Baruch, 469–470
Spinoza, Benedict de, 464
Strabo, 90
Stuart, Mary, 395
Sucre, Antonio, 519
Suleiman I, 442
Sulla, dictatorship of, 99
Sully, Duke of, 364–365
Sundiate, 430–431
Sun-shin, Yi, 328
Suppiluliumas, 11

T

Tacitus, 107
Tan'gun, 55
Tang, Taizong, 228
Tetzel, Johann, 277–278
Teutonic Knights, 185
Themistocles, 74
Theodora, 162
Theodosius I, 110
Thucydides, 80
Thutmose III, 14
Tiberius, 99, 103
Tintoretto, 262
Titian, 262
Titus, 104
Topiltzin, 240, 243
Torquemada, Tomas de, 191
Toussaint L'Ouverture, 515
Trajan, 104
Tribonian, 155
Trojans, 93
Tudor, Henry, 190
Tudor, Margaret, 387
Tudor, Mary, 285
Turgot, Robert, 488
Tzu, Lao, 45

V

Vaishya, 31
Valla, Lorenzo, 259
van der Weyden, Rogier, 263
van Eyck, Jan, 263
van Leeuwenhoek, Anton, 476
Vasari, Giorgio, 266
Ventris, Michael, 69
Vergil, 103, 106–107
Verrazano, Giovanni, 418
Vesalius, Andreas, 476
Vespasian, 104
Vespucci, Amerigo, 408
Villehardouin, Geoffroy de, 197
Vishnu, 33–36
Voltaire, 467
von Strasbourg, Gottfried, 196

W

Warens, Louise de, 465
Whitehead, Alfred, 472
William I the Conqueror, 182, 357–358
William III, 395–396
William of Ockham, 198
William the Conqueror, 357
Wyatt, Sir Thomas, 266
Wycliffe, John, 280, 290

X

Xeres, 74–75
Xerxes, 7–8

Y

Yahweh, 9
Yonglo, 451

Z

Zarathustra, 8
Zeno, 89
Zheng He, 451
Zhou, 61
Zoe, 162
Zoroaster, 8
Zwingli, Ulrich, 282

ERA I INDEX

A

Abraham, 8–9
acrophobia, 83
acropolis, 71
Adriatic Sea, 78, 92
Aegean world, 69–70
Aeneas, 93
Aeneid, 106
Aeschylus, 73
affirmative action, 32
Africa, ancient, 2–27
aghora, 71
agoraphobia, 83
ahimsa, 40, 56
Ahmose I, 14
Alcibiades, 78
Alexander III, 79, 84
Alexander the Great, 7, 10, 12, 15, 40, 83
    conquests, 84–85
Alexandria, 15, 84, 87
Alps, 93
Amazon basin, 135
Ambedkar, Bhimrao Ramji, 33

Amenhotep III, 14
Amenhotep IV, 14
America, ancient, 130–151
    agricultural developments, 132–133
    classic period, 138
    development of cultures, 133–138
    first peoples, 132
Amorites, 4
Analects, The, 45
Angkor empire, 49–51
animism, 55
Annals, 108
Antigonid dynasty, 86
Antigonus, 86
Antioch, 10, 87
Antonius, 104
Antony, Mark, 101
apathy, 89
Apennine mountains, 93
Aphrodite of Melos, 88
Apollo Belvedere, 115
Apostles, 109
Apulia, 92
Arabia, 3, 7
arachnophobia, 83
arch, 105
Archaic Period, 13, 64, 70–74
Archimedes, 90
architecture:
    classical, 79
    Mayan, 142
    Roman, 105–106
archons, 76
areopagus, 71
Aristarchus, 89
aristocracy, 71
Aristophanes, 73
Aristotle, 81–82
Art of Love, The, 107
Arthashastra, 40
Aryabhata, 41
Aryans, 29–30
    culture, 30–33
    invasion of India, 28
ascetics, 110
Asia:
    ancient, 28–63
    minor, 5
    southeast, ancient, 49–50
Asoka, 38, 40, 62
Assassination of Phillip II, 84
Assembly of tribes, 95
Assyrian, 5–6, 9, 15
    civilization, 2, 5
Athena, 79
Athenian:
    acropolis, 79
    democracy, 64
    Golden Age, 64
    imperialism, 75–76

Atlantis, 67
atomic theory, 73
Attica, 74–75, 77
Augustulus, Romulus, 110–111
Augustus, 103, 108
    reign of, 102–103
Aurelius, Marcus, 104, 108
auto, 83
autobiography, 83
autocracy, 5
    establishment, 102
automatic, 83
automobile, 83
autonomy, 83
Axhumite Kingdom, 18
Axum, 18

B

Babylonians, 4–5
    captivity, 6
    civilization, 2, 4–5
    Law, tradition of, 19
Bactria, 85
Bang, Liu, 48
barbarian, 87
barbaroi, 66
Barrack Emperors, 109
basilicas, 106
bas-relief, 106
Battle of:
    Chaeronea, 79
    Guagamela, 84–85
    Marathon, 75
    Zama, 97
Benares, 34–35, 37
Bering Strait, 131
Bhagavad Gita, 36
Bharata, 31
Biblical stories, 8
Black Sea, 3
blasphemy, 109
Bodhisattva, 39
Book of the Dead, 25–26
Borobodur, 49–50
Brahma, 33
Brahmins, 31
Brasidas, 78
bronze, 6
Brutus, Marcus, 101
Buddhism, 36–40, 50
    spread in Asia, 38–39
Burma, 36
Byzantine, 15
Byzantium, 110

C

Caesar:
    dictatorship of, 101
    Julius, 100–102, 108
    Octavian, 101

Calabria, 92
Calakmul, 141
Caligula, 103
Cambodia, 36
Cambyses, 7
Campania, 92
Canaan, 9
canon law, 110
capital punishment, 19
Caribbean:
    region, 134
    ancient, 130–151
    topographical areas, 150
Carthage, 12, 96
Carthaginians, 94, 96
Caspian Sea, 3
Cassius, Gaius, 101
caste system, 31, 37–38
Catullus, 107
Centuries, 94
Chaldeans, 4–5, 9
    civilization, 2, 5–6
charisma, 83
Chavin culture, 142–143
Chibcha chiefdom, 135–136
chiefdom, 135
Chin dynasty, 46–47
China, ancient, 42–48
Chinatown, 57
Chinese Heritage, The, 61
Choson, 55
Christian church, rise of, 110
Christianity, 39, 108–109
    rise of, 91
Christians, persecution of, 104
Chronicles of Japan, 53
Cicero, 100, 107
cities, planned, 29
citizens, 77
citizenship, 70–71
city-states, 66
    development of, 70
Civil War, Roman, 100–101
Classical:
    Greece, 74–77
    development, 74
    ideal, 79
    period, 64
Claudius, 103
claustrophobia, 83
Cleisthenes, 77
Cleon, 78
Cleopatra VII, 15, 101–102
clients, 94
Code of:
    Hammurabi, 23–24
    Manu, 31
codices, 142
Colosseum, 106
comedy, 73, 88
commoners, 135
Confucianism, 44–45

Confucius, birth of, 28
Constantine, reign of, 110
Constantinople, 110
constitution, 71
    Athenian, 117
    Roman, 95
Copan, 141
Coptic, 19
    writing, 17
Copts, 15
Corcyra, 78
Corfu, 78
Corinth, 78
Corinthian columns, 79
Corsica, 96
Council of 500, 77
Council of Nicaea, 110
covenant, 9
Crassus, Marcus Licinius, 100
Crete, 67
cultural diffusion, 7, 66, 83
cuneiform, 6, 8, 11
Curiae, 94
Cushite Kingdom, 18
Cushitic civilization, 2, 18–19
Cynics, 89
Cyrus, 7

D

Daoism, 45–46
Darius I, 7-8, 74
Dark Age, 64
David, 9
decimal system, 41
deforestation, 140
Delian League, 76, 78
Delphi, 80
democracy, development of, 70, 76
Demosthenes, 79
Deocritus, 73
dharma, 33
Diaspora, 10
digging stick, 133
Diocletian, 109
Dionysius, 72
direct democracy, 71
dome, 105
Domitian, 104, 108
Dorians, 69
doric columns, 79
Draco, 76
Dravidians, 30
dualism, 34
Durga, 34
dynastic cycle, 42

E

Edict of Milan, 110
egalitarian, 134
Egypt, 3

ancient, 13–17
civilization, 2
culture, 16–17
Eightfold Path of Conduct, 37
Elba, 92
elites, 135
empiricism, 81–82
endogamy, 32
enlightenment, 37
Epic of Gilgamesh, The, 6, 24–25
epic poems, 73, 88
Eratosthenes, 89
Erectheum, 79
ethical monotheism, 9
ethics, 89
Ethiopian civilization, 18–19
ancient, 2
empire, 19
Orthodox Church, 19
ethnos, 66
Etruria, 92
Etruscans, 93, 95
Euclid, 90
Euphrates River, 3
Euripides, 73
evolution, 132
Ezena, King, 19

F

Fertile Crescent, 3
feudalism, 43–44
filial piety, 45
First:
Intermediate Period, 14
Punic War, 96–97
Flavian dynasty, 104
Four Noble Truths, 37
Funan, 49–50
empire temple, 49

G

Gaius Gracchus, 99
Gaius, 103
Galen, 90, 108
Gallic Wars, 100
Gandhi, 56
Mahatma, 32, 40
Ganges River, 34
Ganges, 37
Gauls, 95, 100
Gautama, Siddhartha, 37, 50
birth of, 28
Gaya, 37
Ge'ez, 19
geometric designs, 70
Georgics, 107
Germania, 108
glaciers, retreat of, 130, 132
glyphs, 142
Golden Age, 14

of Athens, 79
governors, 97
Great Wall of China, 43, 47–48, 57
Greater Vehicle, 39
Greco-Roman:
Civilization, 85
World, 64–129
Greece:
ancient, 65–83
geography, 65–66
unification under Macedonia,
78–79
Greek:
alphabet, 70
architecture, 72
art, 72
civilization, characteristics,
65–67
culture, 7
league, 74
miracle, 64, 70
nation, 66–67
world, 65
Gupta Empire, 28, 40–42

H

Hadrian, 104
Hammurabi, 3, 5, 19
Law Code, 5
Han Dynasty, 28, 48
Hanging Gardens of Babylon, 5
haniwa, 52
Hannibal, 97
Hanuman, 36
harijans, 32
Harrapa, 29
Hebrew:
civilization, ancient, 8–10
culture, 10
heliocentric theory, 89
Hellenic:
culture, 7
League, 79
Hellenism, 83
Hellenistic:
kingdoms, 86–87
conquest of, 97–98
world, 83–90
helots, 77
Heraclitus, 74
Herodotus, 80
Hesiod, 73
hieroglyphics, 17, 142
Hinayana, 39
Hindu Kush mountains, 85
Hinduism, 30–36, 50
gods, 33–35
holy literature, 35–36
Hindus, 39
Hipparchus, 89
Hippocrates, 82

Hippocratic Oath, 82
Historia, 80
Histories, 108
History of Modern India, A, 62
History of Rome, 107
Hittites, 11–12
civilization, 2, 11–12
empire, 11
Homer, 69
hominocentrism, 65
Horace, 107
Horus, 13
Hsun-tzu, 46
Huang He River, 42
Hundred Schools, 43
Hykos, 14

I

ice age, 131
Ides of March, 101
Iliad, 69, 73
imperium, 94
India, 7
ancient, 29–42
religions, 38–40
trade, development of, 41–42
Indian Constitution, 32–33
Indochina, 49
Indo-Europeans, 7
Indonesia, 36, 50
Indus River Valley, 29, 85
civilization, 28
infinity, 41
ionic columns, 79
iron age, 70
Isis, 13
Islam, 15
isolationists, 77
Israelites, 9
Isthmus of Kra, 50
Italy, conquest of, 95
Izanagi, 54
Izanami, 54

J

Jacob, 9
Jainism, 39–40
Jains, 39
Japan, ancient, 51–55
Jatakas, 38
Java, 50
Jerusalem, 9
Jesus of Nazareth, 108–109
Jewish Kingdoms, ancient, 8
Jimmu, 54
Jomon period, 51–52
Judah, 6, 9
Judas Maccabaeus, 10
Julio-Claudian dynasty, 103–104
Juvenal, 107

K

Kali, 34
Kalidasa, 41
kami, 54–55
Kapaleeswarar, 34
karma, 33
Kashta, 18
Kassites, 5
Kautilya, 40
Khmer empire, 49–51
Kija, 55
King of Kings, 8
King, Jr., Martin Luther, 56
kinship, 136
Kofun, Tomb period, 51–53
Koguryo, 55
Koine, 88
Kojiki, 53
Korea, ancient, 55–56
kouros, 72
Krishna, 34–36
Kshatriyas, 31
kut, 56

L

La Venta, 139
Lagash, 4
Lake Texcoco, 139
Lakshman, 36
Latin America:
    climate zones, 149
    topographical areas, 150
Latins, 93
Latium, 93–95
Laws, The, 81, 107
Lebanon, 12
Legalism, 46
Leonidas, 74–75
Lepidus, 101–102
libraries, 88,90
Libyans, 15
literature:
    development of, 73
    Roman, 106–107
Little Vehicle, 39
Livy, 103, 107
lotus position, 38
Lucretius, 107–108
lunar calendar, 6
Lyceum, 82
Lycurgus, 77
lyric poetry, 73, 88
Lysander, 78

M

Maccabean Revolt, 86
Macedonia, 67, 74
Madras, 34

Magadha kingdom, 40
Magna Graecia, 94–95
Mahabharata, The, 35–36, 62
Mahavira, 40
Mahayana, 39
maize, 133
Malay peninsula, 50
Mandate of Heaven, 45, 61
mandela, 33
Marathon, 74
Marius, 99
marketplace, 71
Mars, 93
Martial, 107
Materialists, 73
mathematics, 90
    Mayan, 142
    origins in India, 41
Maurya Empire, 28, 40–41
Maurya, Chandragupta, 40–41
Maya civilization, 136, 140–142
Meditations, 108
Mediterranean Sea, 3
megalomania, 85
Melinik I, 19
Mencius, 45
Menes, 13
Mesopotamia, 85
    civilization, 3–4
messiah, 109
metal working, 12
metallurgy, 138, 143
Metamorphoses, 107
Middle east, ancient, 2–27
Middle Kingdom, 14
middle way, the, 37
Migrations to Americas, 130
Miltiades, 74
Minoan civilization, 64, 67–68
Minos, 67
Mochica:
    civilization, 136
    culture, 142–143
Mohenjo-Daro, 29
moksha, 33
monastics, 110
monks, 110
Montaigne, Michel de, 135
mosaics, 106
Moses, 9
    at Mount Sinai, 26–27
mudras, 38
Muisca chiefdom, 135–136
mummies, 14
mummification, 16
museums, 88
Muslims, 39
My Big Fat Greek Wedding, 82
Myanmar, 36
Mycale, 75
Mycenean civilization, 64, 67–69

N

Nahuatl, 139
Napata, 18
Narayanan, Kocheri R., 33
Nazca culture, 142–143
Nebuchadnezzar, 5
Negras, 141
Nero, 103–104, 109
Nerva, 104
New:
    kingdom, 14
    world, 131
Nike, 79
Nile River, 13
Nineveh, 5
nirvana, 37, 39
Noah, 6
Nobilis, 96
Northern School, 39
Nubians, 15, 18
Nuclear America, 136

O

obelisks, 17
Octavian, 102
Odoacer, 110–111
Odyssey, 73
Old Kingdom, 13–14
Old Testament, 6, 8, 89
Oligarchy, 99
    development of, 70
Olmec civilization, 136, 138–139
Olympics:
    development of, 72
    first, 64
On the Civil War, 108
On the Gallic War, 108
On the Nature of the Universe, 107
Optimates, 98
oracle bones, 43
Osirus, 13
outcast, 31, 56
Ovid, 107

P

Paekche, 55–56
pagoda, 38
Palenque, 141
Palestine, 9–10, 14
panchayat, 41
pancration, 72
Pantheon, 105–106
papyri, 17
Parallel Lives, 107
Parthenon, 79
Parthia, 85
Patagonia, 132
Patricians, 94

patrons, 94
Pax Romana, 103
Peking Man, 42
Peloponnese, 76
Peloponnesian:
    League, 78
    War, 64, 77–78
Peloponnesian War, The, 80
People's Court, 76
Pergamum, 87
Pericles, 79
Period of the Second Temple, 10
perioeci, 77
Persepolis, 8, 85
Persia, 3, 5
    civilization, 2, 7–8
    empire, 7
    gulf, 3
    war, 64, 74–75
Persians, 7, 15
Peten, 140
Peter, 109
phalanx, 72
pharaohs, 14
Phenician civilization, 12
Phidias, 79
philanthropy, 83
philharmonic, 83
philia, 83
Philip II, 78–79, 83
Philistines, 9
philosophy, 80, 83
    development of, 73–74
    Roman, 108
phobia, 83
Phoenicia, 12
Phoenicians, 12, 96
    city-states, 12
    civilization, 2
pi, 41, 90
Piankhy, 18
Piedras, 141
Pindar, 73
Pisistratus, 76
Platea, 75
Plateau of Assure, 5
Plato, 81
Plebians, 94
Pliny the elder, 108
plow, 18
Plutarch, 107
Po valley, 92
polis, development of, 70
Politician, The, 81
Polybius, 105, 107
Polyclitus, 79
Pompey, Cneius, 100–101
Populares, 98
Praetorian Guard, 103
Praxiteles, 79
precipitation, 131

Predynastic Period, 13
princeps, 102
procurators, 97
proletariat, 98
Protagorus, 80
protectorate, 10
Proto-Greeks, 67–70
Ptolemaic:
    Egypt, 15
    Kingdom, 86
Ptolemaios, 86
Ptolemy, 90, 108
Punic Wars, 91, 96–97
pyramids, 16
Pythagoras, 74

Q

Qin Dynasty, 28, 46–47

R

raised fields, 141
Rama, 34–36
Ramayana, The, 34–36
Ramses II, 9, 15
Records of Ancient Matters, 53
Remus, 93
Republic:
    of Rome, 94
        collapse of, 98–102
Republic, The, 81, 107
Rhea Silvia, 93
rhetoric, 80
Rise of the Roman Republic, The, 105
Roman:
    civil war, 91
    conquest, 84
        of Hellenic Kingdoms, 91
        of Hellenistic Kingdoms, 84
    empire, 98
        division of, 91, 109–111
        fall of, 91
        western, fall of, 110–111
    republic, collapse, 91
    senate, 100
    society, 105–109
Romanization, 95
Romans, mythological origins, 93
Rome:
    ancient, 91–112
    early, 91
    foundation, 94
    geography, 92–93
    republic, establishment, 94
Romulus, 93
Roxanne, 85
Rubicon, 100
Russia, 3

S

Sailendra dynasty, 50
Salamis, 75
samsara, 33
Samudra, 41
sangha, 38
Sanskrit, 32, 40
Sappho, 73
    poems of, 116
Sardinia, 96
Sargon I, 4
Sargon II, 5
satrapies, 7
Saul, 9
Saul of Tarsus, 109
Schleimann, Heinrich, 68
science:
    classical period, 82
    development of, 73–74
Scipio, Cornelius, 97
scribes, 136
sculpture, classical, 79
sea peoples, 15
Second Punic War, 97
secular culture, 8
Seleucid Empire, 10, 86–87
Seleucus, 40, 86
Semites, 4
Senate, 94
Seneca, 108
Sennacherib, 5
Septuagint, 89
Shakuntala 41
shamanism, 56
Shang Dynasty, 28, 43
Sheba, Queen of, 19
Shi Huangdi, 46–47
Shinto Creation Myth, 53
Shintoism, 53–55
Shiva, 33–35
Shudras, 31, 38
Sicilian Expedition, 78
Sicily, 92, 96
Sidon, 12
Sikhs, 39–40
Silk Roads, 39, 48, 63
Silla, 55–56
Sita, 36
Skeptics, 89
slash and burn, 133
social:
    stratification, 134
    war, 99–100
socii, 95, 98
Socrates, 81
Solomon, 9, 19
Solon, 76
sophists, 80–81
Sophocles, 73
sophomore, 83

South America, natural setting, 148
Southern School, 39
Sparta, 74
Spartacus, 100
Spartan system, 77
sphere of influence, 78
Srivijaya empire, 49
Srivijaya, 50
St. Moses, Prayer to, 27
states, 135–136
stelae, 142
Stoics, 89
Strabo, 90
Strait of Malacca, 50–51
Struggle of the Orders, 95
stupas, 38
Su, Li, 47
subsistence farming, 69
Sudan, 18
Sulla, dictatorship of, 99
Sumer, 29
Sumerians, 11
    civilization, 2–4
Suppiluliumas, 11
Susa, 85
sutras, 38
symmetry, 72
Syracuse, 78
Syria, 4, 11, 14

T

taboos, 32, 56
Tacitus, 107
Talmud, 10
Tan'gun, 55
Tanach, 8, 89
Taoism, 45–46
telos, 82
Temple of:
    Solomon, 9–10
    the tooth, 38
Teotihuacan civilization, 136,
    139–140
Thailand, 36
theater, development of, 72–73
Thebes, 14, 78
Themistocles, 74
Theodosius I, 110
Theravada, 39
Thermopolaye, 74–75
Third Punic War, 97
Thrifty, The, 78
Thucydides, 80
Thutmose III, 14
Tiber River, 93–94
Tiberius, 99, 103
Tierra del fuego, 131
Tigris River, 3
Tigris-Euphrates valley, 4
Tikal, 141

Titus, 104
tools, 12
tragedy, 73, 88
Trajan, 104
trial by jury, 71, 76
Tribunes, 95
Triumvirate:
    first, 91, 100
    second, 91, 101–102
Trojans, 93
Troy, 69
Ttipitaka, 38
Twelve Caesars, The, 108
Twelve Tables, 96
tyrant, 76
Tyre, 12
Tyrrhenian Sea, 92
Tzu, Lao, 45

U

Untouchables, 31, 38
Upanishads, 35
Ur, 4

V

Vaishya, 31
Varanasi, 34–35
varnas, 31
Vedas, 28, 30, 35
Ventris, Michael, 69
Venus de Milo, 88
Vergil, 103, 106–107
Vespasian, 104
Vishnu, 33–36

W

weapons, 12
Works and Days, 73
Writing, historical, development, 80

X

Xeres, 74–75
Xerxes, 7–8
Xi'an, 47

Y

Yahweh, 9
Yamato period, 51–52, 54
yang, 43
Yayoi period, 51–52
Yellow River, 42
Yemen, 19
yin, 43
yoga position, 38

Z

Zapotes, 139
Zarathustra, 8
zealots, 10
Zeno, 89
zero, 41
Zhou, 61
    dyanasty, 43–44
ziggurat, 4
Zoroaster, 8
Zoroastrianism, 8

ERA II INDEX

A

Aachen, 177
Abbey of Saint Denis, 195
Abelard, Peter, 197
Abraham, 209
al-Rashid, Harun, 218
Alcuin, 177
Alexiad, 164
Alexius I, 159, 184
Alfonso Henriques, 190
Alfonso VII of Castile, 190
Algarve, 190
algebra, 219
Ali, 214
al-Idrisi, 219
Allah, 209
almsgiving, 213
al-Razi, 219
Americas, 236–252
Amiens, cathedral, 195
Andean Region, 244–247
Angevin Empire, 182–183
Anglo-Saxon tribes, 175
Anjou, 182
annulment, 182
Anselm of Canterbury, 197
Antilles, 245
Antioch, 185
Aquinas, Thomas, 197
arab invasions, 152, 157
Arabian Nights, The, 219–220
Aragon, 190–191
Arawak, 243–244
Archbishop of Canterbury, 183
Armagnacs, 189
Armenia, annexation of, 158
Arthur, King, 196
Asia, 226–235
    southern, 227–228
Atacama Desert, 245
astronomical clock, 229
Augustinian Canons, 194
Aztecs, 238, 241

B

Bacon, Roger, 197
Baghdad, 216
Bakr, Abu, 212, 214
Balearic Islands, 190
barons, 182
Basil I, 158
Basil II, 158
Battle of:
    Aljubarotta, 191
    Bouvines, 182
    Crecy, 189
    Hastings, 182
    Las Navas de Tolosa, 191
    Orleans, 189
    Poitiers, 189
    Talas, 229
    Tours, 215
Bavaria, 180
Becket, Thomas, 183
Belisarius, 154
Benedictine Rule, 193
Beowulf, 195
Berber Army, 191
Bernard of Clairvaux, 193
black death, 174, 191–192
    in Europe, 192, 202
Bourges, cathedral, 195
Brittany, 182
bubonic plague, 191–192
Bulgaria, conquest of, 158
Burgundians, 189
    tribes, 175
Byzantine:
    commonwealth, 152, 158
    Coronation ceremony of Manuel II,
        172
    empire, 152–173
        early, 152, 154–157
        high, 152, 157–159
        late, 152, 160
    society, 161–164
        architecture, 162–163
        church, 161
        literature, 163–164
        painting, 163
        sculpture, 163
        writing, 164
Byzantium, 153

C

caliphate, 214
Canterbury Tales, 196
Capet, Hugh, 181
Capetians, 188
    dynasty, 181–182
Carib, 244
Caribbean:
    and Antilles, 246
    basin, 244–247

Carolingians, 158
    empire, 174–176
    renaissance, 177
Carthusian Order, 193
Castile, 190
Catalonia, 190
Cathedral:
    Church of Worms, 194
    of Saint Sophia, 155
    of Santiago, 194
    schools, 197
cave paintings, 228
Central America, 238
Central:
    high middle ages, 179–187
    middle ages, 174
Chancellor, 183
Chancery, 183
Chang'an, 228
chanson de geste, 195–196
charity, 213
Charlemagne, 176
    empire of, 177
Charles the Bald, 181
Charles V, 189
Charles VI, 189
Charles VII, 189
Chartres, cathedral, 195
Chaucer, Geoffrey, 196
Chichen Itza, 243–244
Chimu Kingdom, 236
China, 228–230
Christianity, 209
Christmas Tree, origins, 198
chronicles, 164, 197
Chronographia, 164
Church schism, 162
Circuit Court System, 183
Cistercian, 193
Clermont, 184
Clovis, 176
Cluniac, 193
Codex Justinianus, 155
Cologne, cathedral, 195
Comnena, Anna, 164
compass, 229
Concordat of Worms, 181
Constantine V, 157
Constantine VII Porphyroghenitos,
    164
Constantine XI Paleologus, 160
Constantinople, 153, 155, 158, 186
    fall of, 152, 160
    patriarch of, 162
Constitutions of Claredon, 183
Cordova, 191
Corpus Juris Civilis, 155
Council of Florence, 160
crusades, 158–159, 174, 184–187
    early, 186, 206
    first, 185, 205
    fourth, 152, 186, 197

    second, 185–186
    third, 186
Crusades, 208
cultural diffusion, 151
Curia Regis, 182
Cyril, 158

D

da al-Islam, 217
Damascus, 216
Death of Arthur, The, 196
dialectic, 197
Digenes Akritos, 164
Dofu, 228
Domesday Book, The, 183
Dominicans, 194
Duoro River, 190

E

Early middle ages, 17–179
Eastern:
    European Nations, rise of,
        152–173
    Roman Empire, 153
Edessa, 185
Edward I, 184
Edward III, 188
Einhard, 196
electors, 187
Empress Theodora, 156
England, late middle ages, 188–190
epic poem, 195
Europe, late middle ages, 188
Exchequer, 183

F

faith, proclamation of, 213
fasting, 213
Fatima, 216
Ferdinand II, 191
feudalism, 174, 178, 184
fiefs, 178
five pillars of Islam, 212–213
flying buttress, 195
France, late middle ages, 188–190
Franciscans, 194
Franconia, 180
Frankish tribes, 175
Freidrich II, 181
frescoes, 163
Friedrich I Barbarossa, 181, 186
Friedrich II, 186
Froissart, Jean, 197

G

Geoffrey of Monmouth, 196
Gerald of Wales, 197

Germanic:
    invasions, 175
    kingdoms, 174
Ghibblines, 181
Golden Bull, 187
Gothic style, 195
Grand Canal, 228
Great Wall, 228
Greater Antilles, 245
Greek fire, 157
Gregorian chant, 193
Gregory I the great, 193
Gregory of Tours, 196
Grenada, 191
Guelfs, 181
Guianas, 244
gunpowder, 226, 228

H

haigiography, 163, 196
haj, 219
Han dynasty, 228
Hangzhou, 229
Harun al Rashid as Caliphate, 108
Heinrich II, 180
Heinrich III, 180
Heinrich IV, 181
Heinrich V, 181
Henri of Burgundy, 190
Henrique the Navigator, 191
Henry I, 183
Henry II, 182–183
Henry III, 183
Henry IV, 180, 189
Henry V, 189
Henry VI, 189
Henry VII, 190
Heraclius, 156
High Middle Ages, Europe, 179
Hijra, 208, 210
Hippodrome, 155
History and Topography of Ireland, 197
History of the English Church and
    People, 196
History of the Franks, 196
Holy Roman Emperor, 177–178, 180
Huang He River, 228
Huari Empire, 236
humanistic, 164
Hundred years' war, 174, 188–190
Husayn, 214

I

iconoclasm, 157
Iconoclast Controversy, 162
Imperial Diet, 188
Innocent III, 181
Inquisition, 191
Irene, 162

Isabella I, 191
Isaurian dynasty, 157
Islam, 157
    decline, 219
    rise and spread, 208–225
    spread of, 214–218, 225

J

Jacquerie, 189
Jean II, 189
Jeanne of Arc, 189
Jerusalem, 185, 211, 216
Jesus, 209
jihad, 217
Jin empire, 229
Joao I, 191
John, King, 183
Journey Through Wales, 197
Judaism, 209
Jurchen, 229
jury system, 183
Justinian Code, The, 170–171
Justinian I, reign of, 154–156
Justinian Legal Code, 155
Justinian's Building Program, 155

K

Ka'ba, 211
Kaifeng, 229
Karl IV, 187
Kievan Russia, 154, 171
knights, 178
    Hospitaler, 185
    Templar, 185
Koine, 163
Konrad II, 180
Konrad III, 185
Kukulkan, 243

L

Lake Texococo, 241
Lancaster, house of, 190
Langland, William, 196
Langton, Stephen, 183
Late middle ages, 174
lay investiture, 180
Leo III, Emperor, 157
Leo IX, 180
Leon, 190
Lesser Antilles, 245
Li Boi, 228
Life of Charlemagne, 196
Lincoln, cathedral, 195
Lisbon, 190
liturgies, 193
Lombard League, 181
lords, 178, 203
Lorraine, 180

Louis IX, 182, 186
Louis the Pious, 177
Louis VII, 182, 185
Louis XI, 189

M

Macedonian dynasty, 157–158
Magna Carta, 183, 206
Magyars, 179–180
Mahmud of Ghazni, 226
    empire of, 227
Maimonides, 219
Maine, 182
Makkah, *see*: Mecca
Mallory, Thomas, 196
manorialism, 179
Manuel II, 172
manuscript illumination, 195
Manzikert, 158
Martel, Charles, 176
Mayan:
    ceremonial centers, 236, 238–239
    decline, 241–244
Mayapan, 244
    rise of, 236
Mecca, 209
medicant, 194
Medieval:
    europe, 174–207
    manor, 204
    society, 192–198
Medina, 210–211
mercenaries, 184, 238
Mesoamerica, 237–244
Methodius, 158
Mexico, 238
Michael VIII, 160
Middle ages, late, 186–192
Monastery of St. Catherine, 163
monastic, 164
Monfort, Simon de, 183
Monophysite controversy, 156–157
Moors, 176
Moses, 209
Muhammad:
    life of, 208
    significance, 209
Muslims, 209–211
    basic beliefs, 212–213
    South Asia, 226

N

Najaf, 220
Narses, 154
nautical inventions, 229
Navarre, 190
Nicaea, 159, 186
Norman-Angevin dynasty, 183
Normandy, 182

Norse Sagas, 195
Notre Dame Cathedral, 195
Notre Dame la Grande, 194–195
nunneries, 193

O

On the Buildings, 164
On the Ceremonies, 164
On the Imperial Administration, 164
On the Wars, 164
Ostrogothic tribes, 175
Otto I, 180
Ottoman Turks, 160

P

Paleologian dynasty, 160
panegyrics, 164
Papacy, 181, 192–193
papal:
    states, 176
    supremacy, 192–193
paper money, 229
parliament, 183
Patriarchate system, 162
Peasant's Revolt, 189
Pepin the short, 176
Persian War, 156
Peten, 241
    rain forest, 242
Petrine Theory, 192
philanthropic work, 161
Philippe II Augustus, 182–183, 188
Philippe IV the Fair, 182
Philippe of Valois, 188
Philippe VI, 188
Piers the Ploughman, 196
pilgrimage, 213
pilgrims, 185
Podromos, Theodore, 164
polytheistic, 239
Pope, 158-159
    Boniface VIII, 182
    Gregory VII, 181
    Innocent III, 183, 186
    Urban II, 184
porcelain, 228
Portugal, late middle ages, 190–192
prayer, 213
    Islam, 219
Proclamation of the second council of Nicaea, 172
Procopius, 164
Psellus, Michael, 164
Punjab, 227

Q

Quetzalcoatyl, 240–241, 243
Quran, 212–213

R

Ramadan, 219
Reconquista, 190
Rheims, cathedral, 195
Richard I the Lion Hearted, 183, 186
Richard II, 189
Richard III, 190
Romance of the Rose, 196
romance poetry, 196
Romanesque style, 194
Romanus the Melodist, 163–164
Royal:
    capitularies, 176
    law courts, 183
Rudolf of Habsburg, 181, 187

S

Saint-Sernin, 194
Saladin, 186
Salian dynasty, 180
Salisbury, cathedral, 195
Sant'Ambrogio, 194
Saragossa, 190
Saudi Arabia, 209
Saxony, 180
schism, 158
Scholastics, 197
Scotism, 198
Scotus, John Duns, 198
Secret History, The, 164
secular, 163–164
Seljuk Turks, 158–159, 184
serf, 179
Seville, 191
sheriffs, 182
Shi'ite muslims, 213–214
Sic et non, 197
Silk Road, 228–229, 233
slavic peoples, conversion of, 152, 158
Slavonic language, 158
Song:
    of the Cid, 196
    dynasty, 226, 228–229
    of Roland, 195
    Taizu, 229
Spain, late middle ages, 190–192
stained glass windows, 195
Strasbourg, cathedral, 195
subvassals, 182
Summa Theologica, 197
Sunni muslims, 213–214
Swabia, 180

T

Tang:
    dynasty, 226, 228–229
    empire, 232
    Taizong, 228

Teotihuacan, decline and fall, 236, 238–239
Teutonic Knights, 185
Theodora, 162
Tiahuanaco Empire, 236
tithe, 177
Toledo, 190
Toltecs, 238–241
Topiltzin, 240, 243
Torquemada, Tomas de, 191
Touraine, 182
Treasury, 183
Treaty of:
    Bretigny, 189
    Troyes, 189
    Verdun, 178
Tribonian, 155
Tripoli, 185
Tristan and Isolde, 196
troubadours, 195
Tudor:
    dynasty, 190
    Henry, 190
Tula, 236, 240–241, 244

U

Umayyad Caliphate, 208, 214–216
umma, 210
Urban II, 205
Uzmal, 243

V

Valencia, 190
Vandal tribes, 175
vassals, 178, 203
viceroy, 161
Vikings, 179
Villehardouin, Geoffroy de, 197
Visigothic tribes, 175
von Strasbourg, Gottfried, 196

W

War of the Roses, 190
Westminster, 183
William I the Conqueror, 182
William of Ockham, 198
Women, status, improved, 172

X

X'ian, 228–229

Y

Yellow River, 228
York:
    cathedral, 195
    house of, 190

Z

Zoe, 162

ERA III INDEX

A

Abbasid Caliphate, 318
Act of Supremacy, 276
Address to the Nobility of the German Nation, 279
administrative bureaucracy, 339
Africa, 265
Americas, empires, 334–354
Amish, 281, 290
Anabaptists, 281
Andes, 343
Angelico, Fra, 261–262
Anglicans, 284–285
annulment, 284
Archbishop of Canterbury, 284
Aristotelian humanism, 267
artisan, 340
As You Like It, 266
ascetism, 281
Ashikaga Shogunate, 325
Asia:
  central, Mongol rule, 318
  global interactions, 316–333
astronomy theories, 319
Atlantic trade routes, 311
Avignon, 257
Aztec:
  arrival in Mexico, 334
  clothing, 340–341
  culture, 340–341
  diet, 341
  education, 341
  empires, 335
  political system, 337–338
  religion, 338–339
  rise of, 336–337
  social organization, 339–340
  treasures, 302

B

Babylonian Captivity of the Church, On the, 279
Babylonian captivity, 257–258, 280
Baghdad, Mongol invasion, 316, 318
bakufu, 325
Baptists, 281, 290
Basho, Matsuo, 327
Bellini, Giovanni, 262
Birth of Venus, The, 261
black death, 258
Boccaccio, Giovanni, 265
Boleyn, Anne, 284
Book of Common Prayer, The, 284–285
Book of the Courtier, 256, 274–275
Bosch, Hieronymus, 263, 265
Botticelli, Sandro, 261

Bramante, Donato, 260–261
Brazil, mineral riches, 302
British East India Company, 301
Bruegel, Pieter, the elder, 263
Brunelleschi, Filippo, 260
Bruni, Leonardo, 266, 272–273
Buddhism, Japan, 321–322
bullion, 305
Buonarroti, Michelangelo, 260, 262, 264
bureaucracy, 305
bushido, 324
business methods, changes, 299–300
Byzantine Renaissance, 254

C

cacao beans, 340
calligraphy, 324
Calvin, John, 276, 282–283, 290
Calvinism, 282–283
Canzoni, 265
capital, 300
capitalism, beginning of, 303–304
Capuchins, 288
Castiglione, Baldassarre, 256, 274–275
Cathedral of Florence, 260
Catherine of Aragon, 284–285
causeways, 340
Cellini, Benvenuto, 255
Cervantes, Miguel de, 266
Chagatai, Khanate of, 318, 320
Chang'an, 322
Charles V, 278, 281
charter, 299, 301
chiaroscuro, 260
China, Mongol rule, 318
chinampas, 336
Chosen dynasty, 328
Christian humanism, 254, 256
Chrysoloras, Manuel, 266–267
Civic humanism, 254, 256
civitas, 256
clergy, 279
Colbert, Jean Baptiste, 306
colonies, importance of, 305–307
Commercial revolution, 296–315
  economic effects, 308–309
    political effects, 309
    social effects, 309
commune, 258
contemplative life, 256
copper, 302
Cortes, Hernando, 335
Council of:
  Constance, 258
  Trent, 276, 287
Counter reformations, Catholic church, 287–288
Cranmer, Thomas, 284

Creation of Adam, 262–263
currency, 300
Cuzco, 335, 344–346

D

Da Gama, Vasco, explorations, 296, 298
da Vinci, Leonardo, 256, 262
daimyos, 323
Dante Aligheri, 264
David, 263–264
de Montaigne, Michel, 266
Decameron, 265
decentralization, period of, 257–259
despots, 258
diamonds, 302
Disputa, 262, 264
Divine Comedy, 264
Doctor Faustus, 266
domestic system, 304, 309
Don Quixote de la Mancha, 266
Donatello, 263
Donation of Constantine, 259–260
Durer, Albrecht, 263
Dutch East India Company, 301
duties, 305

E

Edict of Nantes, 276, 283
Edo, 326–327
Education of a Christian Prince, The, 267
Edward II, 266
Edward VI, 284
Elizabeth I, 266, 285, 307
Elizabethan Era, 266
England, commercial expansion, 307
English Joint Stock Company, 296
entrepreneur, rise of, 303
Episcopalians, 286
Erasmus, Desiderius, 267, 280
Europe:
  development of mercantilism, 305
  economic revival, 297–299
European Trade Routes, 272
excommunication, 278

F

Faerie Queen, The, 266
Ferdinand, 302
feudalism:
  decline, 303
  Japan, 323–325
Ficino, Marsilio, 267
Flemish school, 262–263
Florence, 258–259
France, mercantilism, 306

Francesca, Pierro della, 262
Franciscans, 288
Frederick the Wise of Saxony, 278
free enterprise, 303
Freedom of a Christian Man, The, 279
Friedrich II, 257
Fuggers, 300
Fujiwara family, 323

G

Garden of Delights, 265
Gargantua and Pantagruel, 266
Gates of Paradise, The, 263
Ghiberti, Lorenzo, 263
Giaconda, La, 262
Giotto, 260
Girgione, 262
gold, 302, 305
Golden:
    Age, 259
    Horder, Khanate of, 318, 320
Great:
    Council, 259
    Khan, Khanate of, 318
    Schism, 258, 280
Guelf-Ghibelline struggles, 258
Guicciardini, Francesco, 266
guilds, 303–304
Gutenberg, Johannes, 304

H

Hamlet, 266
Hangul, 328
hari-kari, 324
Heian period, 316, 322–323
Henry V, 266
Henry VIII, 283–285
Hideyoshi, Toyotomi, 326
High renaissance, 254, 256
History of Italy, 266
History of the Florentine People, 266
Holbein, Hans, 263
Honshu, 326
Huguenots, 283
Humanism, 254–255, 264–265
Huss, John , 280, 290

I

Ieyasu, Tokugawa, 326
Ilkhanate, 318, 320
Incas, 341–348
    agriculture, 346
    arts, 345–346
    economics, 346–348
    education, 345–346
    empire, 335
    imperial rule, 343–345
    nobility, 344

    origins, 342–343
    Pachucati, 342–343
    religion, 345–346
    rule, 334
    treasures, 302
Index, fom Catholic Church, 287
indulgence, 277
inflation, 302–303
Inquisition, 288
Institutes of the Christian Religion, The,
    282–283
Inti, 345
Iran, 317
Isabella, 302
Italo-Byantine art, 260

J

Jamestown, 301
Japan, 321–327
    feudal organizations, 333
    Mongol attacks, 316
    unification of, 326
Jesuits, 288, 290
    founding of, 276
Jew of Malta, The, 266
Jews, expulsion from Spain, 302
Joint-Stock Company, 301
Julius Caesar, 266

K

Kabuki, 327
Kamakura period, 316, 324–325
kamikaze, 325
Khan, Genghis, 317–318
    reign, 316
    Kublai, 319, 325
khanates, 318
King Lear, 266
Knox, John, 286
koans, 322
Korea, 327–328
    Mongol rule, 327
    taxation, 328
Koryo dynasty, 327
Kyoto, 322, 326

L

Lake Texcoco, 335
Last Supper, The, 262
linear perspective, 260
Literary Renaissance, 254
Lives of the Artists, The, 266
Louis XIV, 306
Loyola, Ignatius, 288
Luther, Martin, 276–279
    and Jews, 282

    supporters, 281
    teaching of, 279
Lutheranism, 281

M

Macbeth, 266
Machiavelli, Niccolo, 267, 273–274
Manchus, 319
Marlowe, Christopher, 266
Masaccio, 260
Medici family, 258–259, 300
    Lorenzo de, il Magnifico, 259
Mennonites, 281, 290
mercantilism:
    development in Europe, 305
    France, 296
Merchant of Venice, The, 266
metals, precious, 305
metalwork production, 321
Midsummer Night's Dream, A, 266
Milan, 258, 262
Minamoto family, 324
Mirandola, Count of, 267
missionaries, 288, 326
Moctezuma II, 337
Mona Lisa, 262
money supply, increase, 302–303
Mongols, 317–318
    rule, 318
        decline, 320
More, Sir Thomas, 265–266, 284–285
Moses, 264
Munster, 281
Muslims, expulsion from Spain, 302

N

Naples, 257
Nara period, 316, 321–322
Nara, 322
naturalism, 260
Navigation Act, 296, 307
nepotism, 277
900 Theses, 267
95 Theses, 276–278, 290
Nobunaga, Oda, 326
nomads, 317

O

"Oration on the Dignity of Man",
    267
Othello, 266
Ottoman Empire, 298–299

P

Palladio, Andrea, 260
Papal:
    Bull, 278
    states, 257

pastoralists, 317
Pax Mongolia, 318–319
Peace of Augsberg, 276, 281
Peasant's Rebellion, 282
Persia, Mongol rule, 318
Petrarca, Francesco, 264
Petrarch, 264
Philip II, 302, 306
philology, 259
piazzas, 260
Pico, Giovanni, 267
Pieta, 264
Pillow Book, The, 323
Pisano, Nicola, 263
Pizarro, Francisco, 341, 348
Platonic Academy of Florence, 267
Poet Laureate, 265
polis, 256
Polo, Marco, 319
Pope:
    Clement V, 257
    Clement VII, 284
    Gregory XI, 258
    Julius II, 258
    Leo X, 276–278
    Paul III, 287
porcelain, 319
Portugal, wealth, 302
Praise of Folly, 267
predestination, 283
Presbyterianism, 286
Primavera, 261
Prince, The, 267, 273–274
printing press, 287, 304
Protestant Reformation, *see:*
    Reformation
Protestantism:
    in England, 283–285
    growth, 281–287

Q

Quakers, 281, 290
Quetzalcoatl, 339
quipu, 343

R

Rabelais, Francois, 266
Raphael, 262
raw materials, 305
refectory, 262
reformation movement, 256
reformation, 276–295
    factors leading to, 279–280
    results of, 289
religious authority, 279
Renaissance, 255–275
    society, 259–267
republican government, 256

Rivera, Diego, 336
Romeo and Juliet, 266
Rum, 307
Russia, Mongol rule, 318

S

sacraments, 279
sacrifice, 339
Saint George, 263–264
Saint Jerome Vulgate, 259
Saint Peter's Basilica, 260–261, 273
salvation, 182–283, 279
samurai, 324
    legacy, 328
sankin kotai, 327
satori, 322
School of Athens, The, 262, 264
seafaring, 298
Second Vatican Council, 287
Sejong, King, 328
Sekigahara, 326
Sengoku, 325
Seoul, 328
Seven Years' War, 309
Sforza, Ludovico, the Moor, 258
Shakespeare, William, 266
Shikibu, Lady Murasaki, 323
Shogun, 325
shogunate, 325
Shonagon, Sei, 323
Shotoku, Prince, 322
Sicily, 257
Siena, 258
silk:
    production, 321
    road, 318
silver, 302, 305
simony, 277
Sistine Chapel, 262
slaves, 307, 339–340
socialist empire, 341
Society of Jesus, 288
Song-gye, Yi, 328
Songs, 265
South American cultures, 351
Spain:
    colonial trade, 306
    expulsion of Jews and Muslims,
      302
    wealth, 302
Spanish:
    Armada, 306
    conquests, Americas, 296
Spenser, Edmund, 266
Spiritual Exercises, 288
Spring, 261
St. Bartholomew's Day Massacre,
    276
steppes, 317
sun calendar, 347
Sun-shin, Yi, 328

T

Tale of Genji, The, 323
Tamburlaine the Great, 266
taxes, 305
tea, 321
    ceremony, 324
Tenochtitlan, 335–337, 340
Tetzel, Johann, 277–278
theocracy, 283
Thirty Years' Wars, 289
Tintoretto, 262
Titian, 262
Tlaxcala, 337
Tokugawa shogunate, 316, 325–327
Tokyo, 326
trade, balance of, 305, 308
triangular trade, 307
tribute, 338
Tudor, Mary, 285
Tuscany, 264

U

Ukiyo-e, 327
Ursuline order, 288
Utopia, 266

V

Valla, Lorenzo, 259
Valley of Mexico, 335, 337
van der Weyden, Rogier, 263
van Eyck, Jan, 263
Vasari, Giorgio, 266
Vatican, 260, 262
Venetian merchants, 298
Venice, 262
    republic of, 259
villas, 260
Virgin and Child with Saint Anne, 262
Virginia Company of London, 301

W

Western Europe, Religious Divisions,
    289, 293
Williams, Roger, 286
Worms, edict of, 276, 278
writing system, 321
Wyatt, Sir Thomas, 266
Wycliffe, John, 280, 290

X

Xian, 322

Y

Yi dynasty, 316, 328

Yoritomo family, 324
Yuan dynasty, 316, 319–320
Yuanzhang, Zhu, 320
Yumednono Pavilion Hall, 321

Z

Zen, 322
Zwingli, Ulrich, 282

ERA IV INDEX

A

Abbasid Caliphs of Baghdad, 444
absolutism, 362, 374, 399
Act of:
    Settlement, 384, 397
    Supremacy, 359
Adolphus, Gustavus, 366
Africa, civilizations, 428–441
Agra, 449
Akbar, 448–450
    reign of, 442
    successors to, 449–450
Ali, Sunni, 431
Almoravids, 430
Americas:
    discovery of, 410–412
    English colonization, 418–419
    French colonies, 418
Anglican Church, 359, 361, 388,
        390–391
animism, 430
Asia, globalization, 442–460
astrolabe, 409
Atahualpa, 416
Aurangzeb, 450
autocrat, 362
auto-da-fe, 371
Axum, kingdom of, 433
Azores, exploration, 410
Aztec empire, conquering, 415

B

Babar, 442
Bahamas, 418–419
Bantus, 432
Barana, 433
Barbados, 419
Battle of:
    the Boyne, 397
    Vienna, 374
bazaars, 452
Beijing, 451–452
Benin, kingdom of, 428, 432
Berbers, 430
Bible, King James Version, 388

Boleyn, Anne, 360
Bourbon family, 364
boy tribute, 446–447
Brazil, 413
burgesses, 387

C

Cabot, John, 418
Cabral, Pedro, 413
camel caravans, 407
Canary Islands, 412
Cano, Juan Sebastian del, 414
Cape of:
    Good Hope, 410
    Storms, 414
Cape Verde islands, exploration, 410
caravel ships, 409
Cardinal Richelieu, 356
Carib, 413
Cartier, Jacques, 406, 418
cartography, 409
Catherine of Aragon, 359
cavaliers, 391
Cecil, Robert, 360
Cervantes, Miguel, 374
champlain, Samuel de, 418
Charles I, 371, 384, 393, 399
    rule of, 389–391
Charles II, 384, 393–395
Charles V, 372
Charles VI, 375
China, 452
    Ming dynasty, 451–452
Christian IV, 366
circumnavigation, 414
Colbert, Jean, 369
Columbian exchange, 407–408, 410,
        419
Columbus, Christopher, 371,
        409–412, 414
common law, 387
commonwealth, 392–393
compass, 409
Confucian ideals, 452
conquistador, 415
Constantinople, 444
    Ottoman conquest of, 442
constitutional monarchy, 397
Coronado, Francisco, 416
Cortes, 370
Cortez, Hernando, 406, 415–416
Cromwell, Oliver, 384, 391–393, 405
Crusade, 444

D

Daud, Askia, 431
de Balboa, Vasco Nunez, 414
de Gama, Vasco, 406–407, 410
de Leon, Ponce, 414

de Soto, Hernando, 416
de Vega, Lope, 374
Delhi, 449
democracy, growth in England,
        384–405
Dengel, Lebna, 433
deposing, 396
dhimmis, 447
Dias, Bartholomeu, 406, 410
Diplomatic Revolution, 375
divine right, 367, 388
Djenne, 431
Doomsday Book, 357
Drake, Francis, 418
Dutch:
    colonies, 417–418
    East India Company, 417–418
    New Amsterdam, 417
    West India Company, 417

E

East African civilizations, 432–433
Eastern Europe, Ottoman rule,
        443–447
Edict of:
    Expulsion, 371
    Nantes, 364–365, 369
Edward I, 387
El Greco, 374
Elizabeth I, 356, 360–363, 387, 418
encomienda, 416
England, growth of democracy,
        384–405
English:
    Bill of Rights, 384, 396–397, 405
    Channel, 369
    Civil War, 384, 391, 401
    colonization of Americas, 418
enlightened despots, 376
equality, 385
Escorial, 372
Estates-general, 364–365
Ethiopian empire, 428, 433
Ewuare the great, 432
Exploration, age of, 406–427
    age of, results, 419–420
    techonology permitting, 408–409

F

factorias, 410
Ferdinand, 370–371, 410–411
Ferdinand I, 372
Ferdinand II, 366
Forbidden City, 451, 453
Frederick II, 376–377
Frederick the Great, 356, 376
French, and the Americas, 418
Fronde, 367

G

Gao, 431
Gedi, 433
George I, 384
Ghana, 428–430
global economy, 421–422
Glorious Revolution, 384, 395–398
Grand Remonstrance, 390
grand vizier, 444
Great Council, 386–387
Grenada, conquest of, 410
griots, 434

H

Habeas Corpus Act, 384, 394
Habsburg rulers, 366
Hanoverian Dynasty, 384
harem, 447
Harold, 357
Hausa city-states, 428, 431
Hawkins, John, 418
Henry II, 386
Henry IV, 364–365, 388
Henry VII, 356, 358, 360
Henry VIII, 359, 361–363, 387
Henry, the navigator, 409–410
hidalgo, 415
High gate, 447
Hindi, 448
Hindus, 450
Hobbes, Thomas, 398–399
Hohenzollern family, 376
Hongwu, 451
House of:
    Commons, 387
    Lords, 387
Huguenots, 361, 364–366
Hundred Years' War, 358

I

Ife, 432
Incas, conquering of, 416
India, 449
    muslims in, 447–450
Indiginous civilizations of Africa, 436
inflation, 373
Interregnum, 384, 392–393
Isabella, 370–371, 410–411
Islamic law, 431, 445

J

Jahan:
    Nur, 449
    Shah, 449–450
        reign of, 442

Jamaica, 418–419
James I, 384, 388–389
James II, 384, 394–396
James VI, 387
Jamestown, 419
Janissaries, 443, 446–447
Jefferson, Thomas, 399
Jesuit missionairies, 418
John II, 410, 412
Joliet, Louis, 418
Joseph II, 376
Juan Carlos, 371
judicial power, 387
jury systems, 386

K

Kano, 431
Karanga, 434
Katnaga, kingdom of, 433–434
Katsina, 431
Kenya, 433
Kilwa, 433
knights, 387
Koran, 430
Kush, 433

L

legislative power, 387
Lepanto, 445
    Battle of, 373
Leviathan, 398
Limpopo River, 434
Locke, John, 398–399
Long parliament, 384, 390, 393
Louis XI, 363
Louis XIII, 365
Louis XIV, 356
    rule of, 367–370
Louis XV, 370
Louis XVI, 370

M

Madeira islands, exploration, 410
Magellan, Ferdinand, 406, 414
Magna Carta, 386
Mahal, Mumtaz, 449
Mali, empire of, 428, 430–431
Malindi, 433
Manchuria, 452
Manchus, 452
Mande people, 430
mansa, 430
Maria Theresa, 375
Marquette, Jacques, 418
Marranos, 373
martial law, 393
Mary I, 359–360
Mary II, 395–396

Mary, Queen of Scots, 361, 387
Matope, 434
Mazarin, Cardinal, 367
Medici, Marie de, 365
Mehmet II, 442, 444
Mercator projection, 409
mestizo, 413
Middle East:
    globalization, 442–460
    Ottoman rule, 443–447
millet system, 444
Ming Dynasty, 451–452
Mississippi Valley, exploration, 418
mita, 416
model parliament, 387
Mogadishu, 433
molasses, 419
Mombasa, 433
Mongols, 443, 451
Montezuma II, 415–416
Moor, Marston, 391
Moriscos, 373
mosques, 431
Mozambique, 433
Mughal:
    dynasty, 448–449
    empire, 442, 447–449
        decline, 442
Muhammed, Askia, 431
mulatto, 413
Musa, mansa, 431
Mutapa Empire, 434
Mutota, 434
Mwanamutapa, 434

N

Nation States, rise of, 356–383
    Austria, 374–376
    England, 357–363
    France, 363–370
    Spain, 370–374
nationality, 357
navigation, school of, 406
New:
    Amsterdam, 419
    York, 419
Nubia, 433

O

O'Neill, Hugh, 361
Oba, 432
opportunist, 366
Osman of Bithynia, 444
Othman I, 444
Ottoman:
    empire, 407–408
        decline of, 445–446
        expansion of, 443
        rise of, 444–445

Imperial Court, 445
rule:
    eastern Europe, 443–447
    middle east, 443–447
society, 446–447
state, formation, 442
Turks, 372–373
Oyo, 432

P

Palace of Versailles, 368–370
Parliament, 359, 386
pashas, 444
Pate, 433
Pax Ottomanica, 447
Persian Gulf, 432
Petition of Right, 384, 389
Philip II, 360, 362, 372–374
Pilgrims, 419
Pizarro, Francisco, 406, 416
Pope Alexander VI, 412
popular sovereignty, 385
Portugal, colonial rivalry with Spain,
    412–414
Portuguese empire, 413
Poynings's Law, 361
Pragmatic Sanction, 375
Presbyterians, 390–391
Pride's Purge, 392
primogeniture, 415
protectorate, 392
Prussia, 376–377
Puritans, 388, 419

Q

Quebec, founding, 418
Quetzalcoatyl, 415

R

regicide, 392
revenues, 389
Rhodesian plateau, 434
Ricci, Matteo, 451
Richelieu, Cardinal, impact of,
    365–366
rifles, 409
roundheads, 391
royal power, limitations, 386
rum, 419
Rump parliament, 392

S

Safavid dynasty, 442, 444
Selim I, 442, 444
Seljuks, 444
Sha'ana, 434

Sha'aria, 431, 445
Sherif of Mecca, 444
Shi'ites, 444
shire, 387
Shona, 434
Sikhs, 450
Silesia, 375
Silk Road, 407
slavery, 410
Sofala, 433
Somalia, 432
Songhai empire, 431, 428
Soninke people, 429
South African Civilization, 433
Southern Africa, 433–434
Spain:
    art, 374
    colonial rivalry with Portugal,
        412–414
    conquers Americas, 413–414
Spanish:
    Armada, 356, 362–363
    Inquisition, 371
    Succession, War of, 369–370
Star Chamber court, 390
Statute of Drogheda, 361
Strait of Magellan, 414
Stuart:
    absolutism, 387–388
    dynasty, 384
    Magna Carta, 389
    restoration, 393–394
    Mary, 395
Suarez, Francisco, 374
Sublime Porte, 447
sugar plantations, 419
Suleiman I, 442
Suleiman II, 444–445
Sully, Duke of, 364–365
sultan, 444
Sundiate, 430–431
Sunni, 444
Swahili:
    city-states, 428
    civilization, 432–433

T

Taj Mahal, 442, 447, 450
    war, 453
Tanzania, 433
Tenochtitlan, 415
Test Act, 394
Third Estate, France, 365
Thirty Years' War, 356, 366
Timbuktu, 431
Toleration Act, 384
Tories, 394
Toulouse, 364
Tower of London, 389

trading route, all water, 407
Treaty of:
    Hubertusburg, 375
    Paris, 375
    Tordesillas, 412
    Utrecht, 356, 370
triangular trade, 419
Triennial Act, 384, 390
Tudor dynasty, 356, 358
Tudor, Margaret, 387
Tupi, 413
Turks, 443
Two Treatises of Government, 399, 404

U

Urdu, 448

V

Velazquez, Diego, 374
Verrazano, Giovanni, 418
Vespucci, Amerigo, 408
Virginia Company, 419

W

War of the Roses, 358
weaponry, 409
West African civilizations, 429–432
Whigs, 394
William I, 357–358
William III, 395–396
William the Conqueror, 357
William the Silent, 374

X

xenophobia, 433

Y

Yonglo, 451
Yoruba kingdoms, 428, 432
Yuan dynasty, 451

Z

Zambezi River, 434
Zanzibar, 433
Zaria, 431
Zazzau, 431
Zheng He, 451
    ocean voyages, 442
Zimbabwe, 428
    great, 434

ERA V INDEX

A

Age of reason, 463–465
Alexander I, 511–512, 521–522
American Revolution, 462
Americas, Spanish Colonialism, 516–517
Anatomical Exercise on the Motion of the Heart and Blood in Animals, An, 476
Antoinette, Marie, 488
Argentina, independence, 518
Aristotle, 474
Arouet, Francois Marie, 467
Astronomy, 472–475

B

Bach, Johann Sebastian, 470
Bacon, Francis, 464, 477
Bastille, 490
Bolivar, Simon, 471, 518–519
Bolivia, independence, 518–519
Bonaparte:
    Joseph, 510, 517
    Napoleon, 496, 505
Bourbon heir, 522
bourgeoisie, 485
Boyle, Robert, 476
Brahe, Tycho, 472–473
Brazil, independence, 519
buffer states, 522

C

calculus, 474
Candide, 467
Castlereagh, Lord, 521
Cavendish, Henry, 476
Central America, independence, 517–518
Charles II, 477
Charles IV, 516
Chile, independence, 518
Colombia, independence, 518–519
Committee of Public Safety, 494
Common Sense, 471
competition, law of, 468
Concordat, 507
Congress of Vienna, 504–505, 520–522
conspiracy, 506
Continental System, 510–512
Copernicus, Nicolaus, 462, 464, 472
Corneille, Pierre, 470
Corsica, 505
coup d'etat, 496, 506
Creoles, 516

D

Danton, Georges, 493–495
David, Jacques-Louis, 470
de Beauharnais, Josephine, 506
de Talleyrand, Charles Maurice de, 521
Declaration of the Rights of Man, The, 484, 491, 514
Descartes, Rene, 464, 477
Dessalines, Jean-Jacques, 515
Dialogue Concerning the Two Chief Systems of the World, 462, 474
Dialogues on Motion, 474
Diderot, Denis, 462, 465–466
Directory, 506
Discourse on Method, 462, 477
divine right, 485

E

Ecuador, independence, 518–519
Einstein, Albert, 478
El Salvador, 518
empiricism, 464
Encyclopedia, 462, 465
Enlightenment, 462–483
    cultural ideas, 470
    economic ideas, 468–469
    France, 465–466
    impact on Americas, 470–471
    political ideas, 466–467
Epitome of Copernican Astronomy, 462
Estates-General, 488–490
Europe, western, 18th century, 463

F

First Estate, 485–487
France, 490
Franklin, Benjamin, 470
French Revolution, 462, 484–503
    lasting impact, 496
    third stage, 496

G

Galen, 475–476
Galilei, Galileo, 462, 464, 472–474
geocentric theory, 472
Geoffin, Marie Therese, 465
Girondists, 492
Grand Army, 511
gravitation, law of, 475
Guatemala, 518
guillotine, 493, 495

H

Harvey, William, 476
Haydn, Joseph, 470

heliocentric theory, 472
Hidalgo, Miguel, 517
Hobbes, Thomas, 466
Holy Alliance, 522
Honduras, 518
Hooke, Robert, 476

I

Index of Prohibited Books, 472

J

Jacobins, 493
Jefferson, Thomas, 471, 514
Joao VI, 519

K

Kepler, Johannes, 472–473

L

laissez-faire, 468
Latin American revolutions, 504
Lavoiser, Antoine, 476
LeClerc, General, 515
Letters Concerning the English, 467
liberalism, European, 520
light, composition of, law of, 475
Locke, John, 462, 466–467, 472, 487
Louis XIV, 477, 484
Louis XV, 465–466, 484, 486
Louis XVI, 484, 491–493
Louis XVIII, 521
Louis, XVI, 491

M

Malpighi, Marcello, 476
Marat, Jean-Paul, 493, 495
Mathematical Principles of Natural Philosphy, The, 462
mechanics, 474
medicine, 475–476
methodology, 471–472
Metternich, Klemens von, 504, 521–522
Mexico, independence, 517–518
Miranda, Francisco, 471, 516
Moliere, Jean Baptiste, 470
Montesquieu, Baron de, 462, 467, 472, 487
Morelos, Jose, 517
Mozart, Wolfgang Amadeus, 470

N

Napoleon:
    age of, 504–528

downfall, 511–512
early life, 505–506
emperor, 508–509
European domination, 509–510
exile, 513
legacy:
    Americas, 514–515
    Europe, 513–514
    Haiti, 514–515
    United States, 514
military career, 505–506
Napoleonic:
    Code, 507
    Empire, rise of, 508
    Era, 471
National:
    Assembly, 489, 491–492
    Convention, 493
nationalism, 505
    Prussia, 511
Necker, Suzanne, 465
Nelson, Lord, 506, 508–509
Newton, Isaac, 462, 474–475, 478
Nicaragua, 518
Nouvelle Heloise, La, 469
Novum Organum, 477

O

Old Regime, 485
On the Structure of the Human Body, 476

P

Paine, Thomas, 471
pantheism, 464
Paracelsus, 476
Paraguay, independence, 518
Paris, 465
    Commune, 493
peasants, 508

Pedro I, 519
Pedro II, 519
Peru, independence, 518–519
Philosophers, 464–465
Physics, 472–475
Physiocrats, 468
Plan of Iguala, 517
plebiscite, 508
Pompadour, Madame de, 465
Pope:
    Alexander, 470
    Pius VII, 509
Priestly, Joseph, 476
Ptolemy, 472, 474

R

rationalism, 464
reactionary, 520
Reign of Terror, 484, 494–495
Revolutions of the Heavenly Bodies, On the, 462, 472
Revolutions, age of, 461–528
Robespierre, Maximilian, 493, 495, 506
Rousseau, Jean Jacques, 462, 467–469, 472, 487
royalist sympathizers, 492

S

salons, 465
San Martin, Jose de, 471
Santander, Francisco, 519
Scientific:
    Method, 471–472
    revolution, 462–483
Second Estate, 485–487
self-interest, law of, 468
Sieyes, Abbe de, 488
Smith, Adam, 462, 468–469
Social Contract, The, 462, 467

Spinoza:
    Baruch, 469–470
    Benedict de, 464
Spirit of the Laws, The, 462, 467
status quo, 521
Sucre, Antonio, 519
supply and demand, law of, 468

T

Tennis Court Oath, 489
Third Estate, 485–487
tithe, 486
Toussaint L'Ouverture, 515
Treaty of Amiens, 508
tricolor, 491
Tuileries, 491
Turgot, Robert, 488
Two Treatises on Civil Government, 466
Two Treatises on Government, 462

U

universal manhood suffrage, 493
Uruguay, independence, 518

V

van Leeuwenhoek, Anton, 476
Venezuela, independence, 518–519
Vesalius, Andreas, 476
Voltaire, 467

W

Warens, Louise de, 465
Wars of Independence, 518–519
Waterloo, Napoleon's defeat, 513
Wealth of Nations, The, 462, 468
Whitehead, Alfred, 472